XML WEB SERVICES

SERVICES

Professional Projects

XML WEB SERVICES
Professional Projects

Geetanjali Arora

Sai Kishore

with NIIT

Premier
Press

Acknowledgments

We owe many thanks to our families and friends for being patient with us while we authored this book. They also motivated and inspired us at all times to bring out our best in the book. Thank you all for this!

We also want to thank Anita Sastry and Sripriya at NIIT for showing complete trust in us. Their valuable input while reviewing the book and constant guidance helped us a lot in successfully completing the book. A very special thanks to both of you!

We were given constant help on the technical aspects of the book by Vineet Arora, who not only provided us with technical help while writing the chapters, but also validated the accuracy of the chapters after they were written. We also cannot forget the help provided by our peer, Shadab Siddique, in some of the chapters of the book.

We are thankful to Stacy Hiquet for entrusting NIIT on this valuable project. We also extend our sincere thanks to Karen Gill for editing the chapters so well. Without her help, the book would not be in its present form.

About NIIT

NIIT is a Global IT Solutions Corporation with a presence in 38 countries. With its unique business model and technology creation capabilities, NIIT delivers software and learning solutions to more than 1,000 clients across the world.

The success of NIIT's training solutions lies in its unique approach to education. NIIT's Knowledge Solutions Business conceives, researches, and develops all the course material. A rigorous instructional design methodology is followed to create engaging and compelling course content. NIIT has one of the largest learning material development facilities in the world.

NIIT trains more than 200,000 executives and students each year in Information Technology areas using stand-up training, video-aided instruction, computer-based training (CBT), and Internet-based training (IBT). NIIT has been featured in the *Guinness Book of World Records* for the largest number of students trained in one year!

NIIT has developed more than 10,000 hours of instructor-led training (ILT) and more than 3,000 hours of Internet-based training and computer-based training. IDC ranked NIIT among the top 15 IT training providers globally for the year 2000. Through the innovative use of training methods and its commitment to research and development, NIIT has been in the forefront of computer education and training for the past 20 years.

Quality has been the prime focus at NIIT. Most of the processes are ISO-9001 certified. NIIT was the 12th company in the world to be assessed at Level 5 of SEI-CMM. NIIT's Content (Learning Material) Development facility is the first in the world to be assessed at this high maturity level. NIIT has strategic partnerships with companies such as Computer Associates, IBM, Microsoft, Oracle, and Sun Microsystems.

About the Authors

Geetanjali Arora is an instructional designer who has worked with NIIT for more than two years. She has done several projects with NIIT that include ILTs, CBTs, and WBTs on subjects such as Microsoft FrontPage 2000, SQL Server 200, Active Directory, Visual C#, and Visual Basic .NET.

Geetanjali has experience in writing for both technical and non-technical subjects, and she is also familiar with various technical languages and software. Her responsibilities at the workplace include scripting, constructing, reviewing, planning, and scheduling. She has trained her peers on NexGen and Dreamweaver. Geetanjali recently authored *C# Professional Projects*, published by Premier Press.

Sai Kishore is currently working as a programmer. He has six years of experience in programming, teaching programming, and writing about programming.

Sai currently works at the Knowledge Solutions Business of NIIT as a consultant and develops e-learning applications for various platforms. Previously, he worked as a programmer and technical trainer. As a trainer, Sai conducted training on C, C++, Unix systems programming, PowerBuilder, DB-Library, Pro C (Oracle), Windows programming using C, Visual C++, and Visual Basic. His competencies include technologies such as COM+, J2EE, .NET, and XML and programming languages/tools such as Visual C++, Visual Basic, and Dreamweaver. Recently, Sai wrote *Visual C++ .NET Professional Projects*, published by Premier Press.

Contents

Introduction

This book, which provides a comprehensive approach to XML Web services, is aimed at readers who are already familiar with XML, the .NET technologies, VC++, and Java. This book contains detailed explanatory concepts and professional projects to implement the concepts.

The initial Parts of this book provide you with an overview of XML, XML Web services, and the XML Web services technologies, such as SOAP, UDDI, and WSDL. Parts I, II, and III introduce you to some basic Web services concepts, which are then covered in detail in the later Parts.

Part IV onward includes several professional projects that include creating, testing, and deploying XML Web services. These projects use the concepts discussed in the initial Parts (I, II, and III) of the book to build projects that can be used in everyday scenarios. You can enhance these projects to create real-life business solutions.

The professional projects in this book are built using several technologies and toolkits that various vendors have provided. These toolkits include the SOAP toolkit, the Java Web Services Developers Pack, and the IBM toolkit. In addition, the projects include XML Web services that are created using JDeveloper IDE and the .NET languages, such as Visual Basic .NET, Visual C#, and VC++ .NET.

This book also discusses how to consume a Web service from several client applications, including Visual Basic Windows applications and mobile Web applications. After you develop the projects in the Parts IV–XII, you will be able to appreciate the ease of creating and consuming Web services by using the available toolkits. You will also appreciate the advantages of using Web services in real-life scenarios.

Part XIII uses another upcoming scripting language called Perl to create a Web service. This Part includes another chapter that discusses the ease of integrating the Web services that are available with existing SQL Server 2000 and Office XP applications.

Apart from the overview chapters and the professional projects, this book also includes another section, Part XIV, which is composed of five Appendixes. This Part provides an overview of the .NET languages that have been used to create Web services in the Professional Projects section. In addition, this Part includes an Appendix on Microsoft .NET My Services, which is a collection of XML Web services. The book wraps up with an Appendix on the future of Web services as seen by the programmers who have been working extensively on XML Web services.

This Appendix introduces some of the latest concepts that will soon be used with the Web services to increase their performance.

How to Use This Book

This book has been organized to facilitate a better grasp of the content covered in the book. The various conventions used in the book include the following:

♦ **Tips.** Tips have been used to provide special advice or unusual shortcuts with the product.

♦ **Notes.** Notes offer additional information that might be of interest to the reader, but that is not essential to performing the task at hand.

♦ **Sidebars.** Sidebars give additional information that is not part of the main text.

♦ **Cautions.** Cautions are used to warn users of possible disastrous results if they perform a task incorrectly.

♦ **New term definitions.** All new terms have been italicized and then defined as part of the text.

PART I

Introduction to XML

Chapter 1

Extensible Markup Language (XML) is a new markup language that is used to store data in a structured format. A markup language provides you with a set of tags that you can use to describe and format the text in a document. Consider a situation in which you need to create a Web page, which involves deciding the structure of the page and the content to be included in the page. You can do all of this easily by using the tags of a markup language.

For example, markup languages such as HTML have a set of predetermined tags that you can use to format the text in a document. However, sometimes you will not need the elements that exist in a markup language. In such cases, you need to create your own tags. This can be achieved using XML. Therefore, XML is called a *metamarkup language*.

This chapter introduces the Standard Generalized Markup Language (SGML) and the markup languages derived from it, such as XML and Hypertext Markup Language (HTML). This enables you to compare the different markup languages that are available and identify the benefits that XML provides. In addition, this chapter focuses on the various components of an XML document. These components include type definitions, tags, attributes, and comments. Using this knowledge, you will further learn to create a sample XML document. Finally, this chapter discusses namespaces and XML schemas used with XML documents.

Origin of Markup Languages

Markup Languages (MLs), such as SGML, HTML, and Extensible Hypertext Markup Language (XHTML), are used to format text. In ancient times, the set of instructions given to printers to print a page in a specified format was called *markup*, and the collection of such instructions was called a *Markup Language*. This is how the concept of MLs originated. These instructions were written in a format that was different from the main text so that they were easily differentiated from the main text. This format was later transformed in the form of tags that are currently used with the markup languages.

For example, to convert the main text written in a document to bold, HTML uses the `<B>` tag at the beginning of the text. Similarly, the `</B>` tag is used to mark the end of the text that needs to be bold, as shown in the following example:

```
<B>HTML</B>
```

The following sections discuss SGML, HTML, and XML in detail.

SGML

Introduced in 1969, Generalized Markup Language (GML) was the first markup language. GML used tags to format the text in a document. However, different documents created using GML required different compilers to compile them. In addition, standards were not available for compiling the documents written in GML. This led to the evolution of SGML.

SGML, introduced in 1986, is the markup language used to define another markup language. Therefore, SGML is considered a meta language. It is the first international standard used to describe the structure of a document. Due to this, the International Organization for Standardization (ISO) recognized SGML as the standard markup language. SGML allows you to define and create documents that are platform independent and can be used to exchange data over a network.

Despite the advantages that SGML offered, developers felt a need for another markup language because the authoring software (software used to create SGML documents) was complex and expensive. In addition, with the increasing popularity of the Internet, it was necessary to create a markup language that could be used to develop Web pages easily and efficiently. As a result, HTML was developed in 1997.

HTML

HTML is the markup language that was evolved from SGML. However, unlike SGML, HTML does not require expensive software for creating documents. Instead, you can create an HTML using text editing software, such as Notepad.

HTML is used to describe and format data so that the data can be viewed using a Web page browser. Similar to SGML and any other markup language, an HTML document also contains tags. For example, to provide a title to the document, you use the <TITLE> tag. Similarly, to include headings in your document, you can use heading tags, such as <H1>, <H2>, and so on. Using these and several other tags, you can create a Web page as shown in the following example:

```
<title>Home Page</title>
<img src="APB.bmp" width="330" height="40" align="right">
<h1>Home Page</h1>
<h2>About the Company</h2>
<p>
<b><i>APB Publications Inc.,</i></b>
APB Publications Inc. is a group of publishers based in New York. It has been
 publishing technical books for the past 10 years and is now moving into
 publishing books on fiction.
</p>
<h2>Employees</h2>
<p>
<b><i>APB Publications Inc.,</i></b>
It has over 10,000 employees working in different branches of the organization.
</p>
<h2>Departments</h3>
<p>
<b><i>APB Publications Inc.,</i></b> has the following departments:
</p>
<ul>
        <li>Human Resource</li>
        <li>Authoring</li>
        <li>Publishing</li>
        <li>Finance</li>
        <li>Marketing</li>
</ul>
```

After writing the preceding code, you need to save the file with an extension of .htm or .html. You can now open the file in the browser, such as Internet Explorer, to view the output of the code. The output of the preceding code will look like Figure 1-1.

As you can see, creating documents using HTML is easy. However, HTML does not allow you to create custom tags. This implies that you are limited to using only the tags that are predefined by HTML to define the formatting of the text in the page. To create your own tags with generic names, you need XML, which is another markup language. In addition, HTML does not allow you to present information in different browsers.

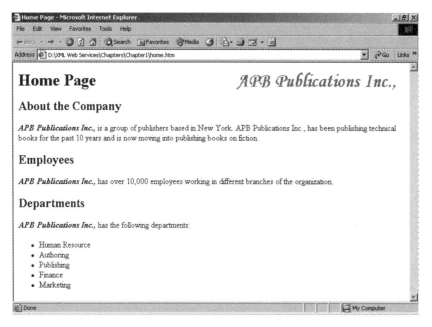

FIGURE 1-1 *A sample HTML document.*

XML

Having discussed markup languages, such as SGML and HTML, we will now look at XML and present the advantages offered by XML over these languages.

XML, a subset of SGML, is a text-based markup language used to describe data. However, you cannot format data using XML. To do so, you need to use style sheets. You will learn about style sheets later in this section.

You can create an XML document by using authoring tools that are simple and readily available. Similar to HTML documents, you can create an XML document in a text editor, such as Notepad. To store a text file as an XML document, you need to save it with the .xml extension. You will learn to create an XML document later in this section.

Another significant advantage of XML is its ability to create tags with names that users can identify easily. This implies that XML allows you to create elements, attributes, and containers with meaningful names, as and when the user requires.

Now we will consider another example of an HTML file:

```
<img src="APB.bmp" width="330" height="40" align="right">
<title>Home Page</title>
<h1>Employee Details</h1>
<h2>Employee Name</h2>
<h3>John Roger</h3>
```

```
<h2>Employee Name</h2>
<h3>George Smith</h3>
<h2>Employee Name</h2>
<h3>Bob Murray</h3>
<h2>Employee Name</h2>
<h3>Daniel Clark</h3>
```

The output of the preceding code is shown in Figure 1-2.

As you can see, the tags that HTML uses are difficult to interpret. For example, it would be easier for a user to interpret a tag with the name `Employee_Name` than a tag with the name `<h2>`. Therefore, the preceding document can include custom tags by using XML as shown:

```
<Home_Page>
<Employee_Details>
<Employee_Name>John Roger</Employee_Name>
<Employee_Name>George Smith</Employee_Name>
<Employee_Name>Bob Murray</Employee_Name>
<Employee_Name>Daniel Clark</Employee_Name>
</Employee_Details>
</Home_Page>
```

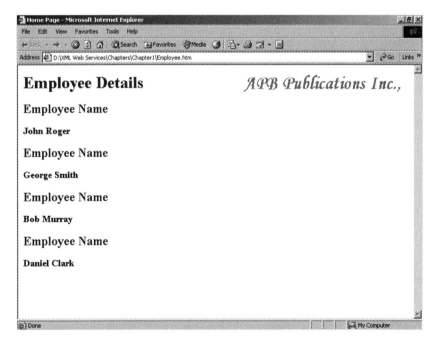

FIGURE 1-2 *Another HTML document.*

You can view the output of the preceding code by saving the Notepad file with a name `Employee.xml` and opening the file in Internet Explorer. The XML document will appear as shown in Figure 1-3.

The ability to create custom and meaningful tags in XML makes it a hardware and software-independent markup language. This implies that an XML document can be interpreted easily by any computer that is running on any operating system. Therefore, XML is widely used as a markup language that transfers structured data over a network. In addition, XML is used to transfer structured data in high-level Business-to-Business (B2B) transactions.

The following list summarizes the advantages of XML as a markup language:

◆ In recent times, XML has been used as a standard markup language for the exchange of data over a network. This is because XML allows you to describe content in a text-based format that the two applications can understand easily. Due to its extensibility and universal format, XML is being widely used for data exchange between applications.

◆ XML can make searching for information easy on the Internet. At present, the popular search engines on the Internet return huge amounts of data because search engines either search for the entire text in an HTML page or the search terms in the keyword called *metadata*. However, using metadata to search for text is not an accurate method because a search based on keywords can be misleading. The search engines need to do a full-page search, which is time-consuming. In addition, because the HTML tags only describe the format of the page and not the content that is stored in the page, the results returned by searching the HTML tags are not satisfactory.

For example, by your specifying the keywords *Linux programming* if you need to search for sites on Linux programming, the search engine returns all pages that contain these two words. The search result might also include the Web pages on Windows programming with passing information on Linux. The search engine cannot judge the context in which the words *Linux* and *programming* are used in the Web page.

However, consider a situation in which XML is used to create Web pages, which include tags as shown in the following example:

```
<subject>programming</subject>
<category>Linux</category>
```

If a search engine parses the document containing the tags and retrieves the data from the `<subject>` and `<category>` tags, then the result returned by the search engine is accurate. This helps to omit several thousand Web pages that contain these keywords in a different context. However, this scenario is not plausible because Web will not become XML based in the near future.

◆ XML allows you to create custom tags. The tags that you create using XML can be based on the requirements of a document; therefore, they can be used as a vocabulary for all related documents. For example, you can create a vocabulary of tags for describing the details of an employee. After creating the tags, the tags can be used as a template to describe the information about all the employees of the organization.

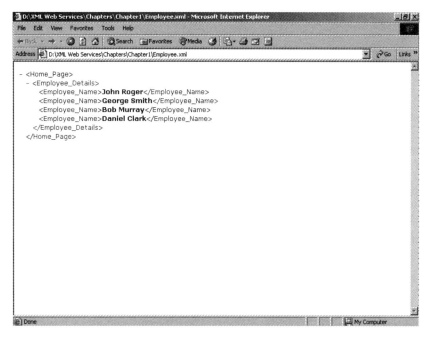

FIGURE 1-3 *A sample XML document.*

An example of such a template is shown in the following code:

```
<Employees>
        <Name>John Smith</Name>
        <Age>30</Age>
        <Designation>HR Executive</Designation>
        <Department>Human Resources</Department>
</Employees>
```

XML is used to describe data. However, you cannot use XML to format data for display in a Web page. A markup language, such as HTML, is used to describe data, and it includes information about the presentation of data in a Web page. Therefore, to present the same data in different formats by using HTML, you need to create separate Web pages.

To format the data in an XML document, you can use style sheets, such as Extensible Style Sheet Language (XSL) or Cascading Style Sheet (CSS). These style sheets contain information about how to present the data in the document. As a result, using XML, you can present the same data in different formats.

Overview of DTD

XML allows you to create custom tags. However, when you create your own structured document, you need to convey the structure to the users who use the XML document. You can provide this information to the users in the form of Document Type Definitions (DTDs).

A DTD is a vocabulary that defines the structure and elements in an XML document. XML documents that you created in the previous examples were syntactically correct, but they do not conform to vocabulary rules. Such XML documents are called *well-formed XML documents*. However, an XML document that has a DTD attached to it is called a *valid XML document*. This implies that a valid XML document is both syntactically correct and conforms to the rules of vocabulary as described in a DTD. The following bulleted list discusses some of the rules that you need to follow while creating a valid XML document:

- An XML document should start with an XML declaration statement.
- Every starting tag should have a corresponding ending tag.
- Empty tags should end with /.
- Names of elements and attributes are case sensitive.
- An XML document can have only one root element, which in turn contains all the elements that you need to include in the document.
- Attribute values should be enclosed in quotes.

CSS AND XSL

- **CSS.** CSS is used to format the text in an HTML document. You can use CSS to set the formatting properties, such as color, font, font size, text spacing, and so on for elements in an HTML document.

- **XSL.** XSL, a language based on XML, is used to format the data in an XML document. In addition, XSL is used to transform an XML document into a document that different media or browsers can understand. For example, you can transform an XML document into another XML document or an HTML document. To do this, you can use Extensible Style Sheet Language Transformation (XSLT), which is an extension of XSL.

Consider the Employee.xml file that you created in the previous example. To make this document, you need to include a DTD with the document. In this case, a DTD would contain information such as the elements in the Employee.xml file and the relationship between these elements. In addition, a DTD contains the vocabulary rules that are used as standards to exchange data in an XML document. However, it is not essential to have a DTD associated with every XML document.

Advantages of Using DTDs

A DTD is used to validate the content in an XML document. When the data in an XML document is exchanged over a network, the receiving application can validate the structure of the XML document based on the rules defined in a DTD. However, to do so, the receiving application requires a parser.

In addition to validating a document after it is created, you can also use DTDs with the authoring tools to ensure that the document you create conforms to the rules defined in a DTD. In other words, when you create an XML document by using an authoring tool that has a DTD associated with it, the authoring tool ensures that you can use only the elements and attributes that are defined in a DTD in your document.

To use a DTD with an XML document, you first need to associate the XML document with a DTD. To do this, the DOCTYPE declaration statement is included in the beginning of the XML document.

The DOCTYPE Declaration Statement

The DOCTYPE declaration statement includes the keyword DOCTYPE. In addition, the DOCTYPE declaration statement might include the markup declaration statement as a subset. The markup declaration statements, which are included as a subset of the DOCTYPE declaration statement, are called *internal DTD subset*. The syntax of the DOCTYPE declaration statement is as shown:

XML PARSERS

An XML parser is used to parse or validate an XML document. This involves checking the XML document for errors. For example, while creating an XML document, if you omit a bracket, the parser can trace the error in the document.

Two types of parsers are used with XML documents: non-validating and validating.

◆ **Non-validating parsers.** Non-validating parsers are used with well-formed XML documents that do not have a DTD associated with them. As a result, a non-validating parser only ensures that an XML document is well formed.

◆ **Validating parsers.** Validating parsers validate the structure of an XML document against the rules defined in a DTD; therefore, validating parsers can be used only with valid XML documents. After checking for the structure and content of an XML document, the parser raises an error if the document is not valid. However, if the document conforms to the rules in a DTD, the document is transferred to the receiving application.

```
<!DOCTYPE name [markup statements]>
```

In the preceding syntax, name is the root element in the XML document. Consider the Employee.xml file that you created. The root element in this case is Employees; therefore, the DOCTYPE declaration statement in this case would be as shown:

```
<!DOCTYPE Employees [markup statements]>
```

Similarly, you can include an external DTD in the XML document. To do this, include the source and path of the external DTD in the DOCTYPE declaration statement. The path of a DTD is the URL of the .dtd file.

The DOCTYPE declaration statement also includes a keyword, which can be either SYSTEM or PUBLIC.

◆ The SYSTEM keyword denotes that the markup declaration statements are directly included in the .dtd file present at the specified URL.

◆ The PUBLIC keyword denotes that the DTD to be included is a well-known vocabulary in the form of a local copy of the .dtd or .dtd file placed in a database server. If you use the PUBLIC keyword, then the application that is associated with the .dtd file needs to locate the file on its own. The syntax for associating an external DTD in the XML document is as shown:

```
<!DOCTYPE name keyword URL>
```

As discussed earlier, name is the root element in the XML document, and the keyword is either SYSTEM or PUBLIC.

Having looked at the DOCTYPE declaration statement, we will next discuss the other components of an XML document.

Components of an XML Document

An XML document consists of several components, such as declaration statements, elements, tags, and attributes. The following sections discuss these components in detail.

Markup Syntax

Components, such as declaration statements or markup tags, define the syntax for creating an XML document. The syntax used to create an XML document is called *markup syntax*. The markup syntax is used to define the structure of the data in the document. The markup syntax includes all tags, DOCTYPE declaration statements, comments, DTDs, and character references.

XML Entities

In addition to the markup syntax, an XML document consists of the content or data to be displayed. Consider the following example:

```
<Employees>
    <Name>John Smith</Name>
    <Age>30</Age>
    <Designation>HR Executive</Designation>
    <Department>Human Resources</Department>
</Employees>
```

In this case, the tags <Employees>, <Name>, <Age>, <Designation>, and <Department> are the markup syntax for the Employees.xml file. However, the content of the XML file is the data enclosed within tags, such as John Smith, 30, HR Executive, and Human Resources.

UNICODE CHARACTER SET

An XML document supports 16-bit ASCII characters and the Unicode 2.1 character set. The ASCII character set includes the characters and symbols present in the English language. The Unicode character set includes English as well as other Western European alphabets and alphabets from scripts, such as Greek, Hebrew, Arabic, Cyrillic, Chinese, Japanese, Devanagri, and Korean.

The data stored in an XML document is in the form of text, and it is commonly called an *XML entity* or a *text entity*. The text entity is used to store the text in the form of character values as defined in the Unicode Character Set. The following example shows the text data in an XML document:

```
<Employee_Name>John Smith</Employee_Name>
```

XML Declaration Statement

The XML declaration statement is included in the beginning of an XML document. It is used to indicate that the specified document is an XML document. The XML declaration statement includes a keyword, xml, preceded by a question mark (?). This statement includes the XML specification to which the XML document adheres. For example, if the XML document that you create is based on XML Specification 1.0, then the XML declaration statement would be as shown here:

```
<?xml version="1.0" ?>
```

In addition to the information about the XML version being used, you might provide information such as whether external markup declaration statements are included in the XML document. To do this, you can use the standalone keyword. Consider the following declaration statement:

```
<?xml version="1.0"  standalone="yes">
```

The attribute value of yes in the preceding code indicates that no external markup declarations are used in the XML document. You can include external markup declaration statements in the XML document by changing the attribute value to no.

Comments

Another important component of an XML document is comment entries. Comments allow you to include instructions or notes in an XML document. These comments help you to provide any metadata about the document to the users of the document. Any data that is not part of the main content or the markup syntax can be included in comment entries.

 TIP

The XML processor ignores any text that you include in comment entries. This implies that the XML processor does not execute the text in the comment entries. Therefore, you need to be careful while writing comments.

The syntax for writing a comment in an XML document is the same as that of writing a comment in an HTML document. The syntax is as shown:

```
<!--comment-->
```

The exclamation (!) sign in the preceding code indicates that the text within the tags is a comment entry. Consider the following example:

```
<?xml version="1.0" ?>
<Employees>
<!--This XML document contains information about the employees of the organization.-->
    <Name>John Smith</Name>
    <Age>30</Age>
    <Designation>HR Executive</Designation>
    <Department>Human Resources</Department>
  </Employees>
```

The use of comments in a document provides users with additional information about the document. However, while writing comments, you need to follow the listed guidelines:

◆ You cannot include the comment entries in the beginning of an XML document. The first line in the XML document is essentially the XML declaration statement. Therefore, the following code snippet results in an error:

```
<!--This XML document contains information about the employees of the
organization.-->
<?xml version="1.0" ?>
```

◆ You cannot include hyphens (––) within the comment text. For instance, the following code statement produces an error:

```
<!--This XML document contains information about the --employees-- of the
organization.-->
```

◆ You cannot include comments within tags. For example, the following code statement produces an error:

```
<Employees <!--This XML document contains information about the employees of the
organization.--> >
```

◆ You cannot have nested comment entries. For example, the following code statement produces an error:

```
<!--This XML document contains information about the employees <!--John Smith-->
of the organization.-->
```

Elements

The building blocks of any XML document are its elements. Elements are containers that contain XML data, such as text, text references, entities, and so on. You can also include elements within another element. This implies that you can have nested elements. The content within an element is called the *element content*. It is essential that you enclose all XML data within elements.

While creating an element, you need to include the starting tags and the ending tags, both of which contain the name of the element. As discussed earlier, you can give any user-defined name to an element.

TIP

You cannot include white spaces in an element name, but you can begin the name of an element with an underscore (_) symbol or a letter.

Consider the following example:

```
<?xml version="1.0" ?>
<Employees>
        <!--This XML document contains information about the employees of the
organization.-->
        <Name>John Smith</Name>
</Employees>
```

In the preceding code, the `Employees` element has `<Employees>` as the starting tag and as the ending tag.

TIP

It is essential to have corresponding ending tags for all starting tags.

Also, remember that the names given to elements are case sensitive. Therefore, `<Employees>` and `<employees>` are interpreted as different tags.

Empty Elements

You have seen that all elements include starting and ending tags. However, if you have to create elements with no content, you can create empty elements. Empty elements can be written in an abbreviated form. For example, if the `<Employees>` element in the previous example contains no text, you can write the element as shown:

```
<Employees />
```

However, if you include both starting and ending tags as shown in the following code, an error is not generated:

```
<Employees></Employees>
```

It is essential for HTML users to understand the concept of empty elements because not all the tags in HTML require ending tags. As a result, the following code in HTML would not produce an error:

```
<img src="APB.gif">
```

However, the preceding code will generate an error in XML. To avoid an error, you need to include the ending tags as shown:

```
<img src="APB.gif"/>
```

Nested Elements

As discussed earlier, you can include nested elements in an XML document. Consider the following example:

```
<?xml version="1.0" ?>
<Books>
<!—This XML document contains information about the books published by an
  organization.—>
        <Technical>
                <Software/>
                <Operating_Systems/>
                <Programming_Languages/>
        </Technical>
        <Non_Technical>
                <Literature/>
                <Fiction/>
                <Autobiographies/>
        </Non_Technical>
        </Books>
```

The output of the preceding code is shown in Figure 1-4.

Attributes

Attributes are used to specify properties of an element. An attribute has a value associated with it. Consider the following statement:

```
<img src="APB.gif"/>
```

```
<?xml version="1.0" ?>
- <Books>
    <!-- This XML document contains information about the books published by an
      organization. -->
  - <Technical>
      <Software />
      <Operating_Systems />
      <Programming_Languages />
    </Technical>
  - <Non_Technical>
      <Literature />
      <Fiction />
      <Autobiographies />
    </Non_Technical>
  </Books>
```

FIGURE 1-4 *Nested elements.*

In the preceding code, the keyword `src` is an attribute of the element `img`, and the value assigned to the `src` attribute is `APB.gif`. Attributes allow you to provide additional information in an XML document. For example, the `src` attribute of the `img` element specifies the name of the image file to be included in the XML document. The value of an attribute is assigned to it by using the equal sign (=), and it is enclosed within double quotes (") as shown.

Similar to an element, you can assign meaningful names to attributes. An attribute name can begin only with a letter or an underscore (_) symbol and cannot include white spaces. However, an attribute value can include white spaces and can even begin with a numeral.

All the attributes that you declare for an element are included in a DTD. A DTD contains the `ATTLIST` tag that includes the attribute declaration statement for each attribute.

TIP

You can include multiple attribute definitions in one `ATTLIST` tag. However, to avoid confusion, it is advisable that you include a different `AATLIST` tag for each attribute.

The syntax for the ATTLIST tag is as shown:

```
<!ATTLIST element_name attribute_name value>
```

Consider that you need to create an element with the name Books. In this case, you can create an attribute with the name type and assign a value, Technical, to it. To do so, add the following statement:

```
<Books type="Technical" />
```

After an attribute is declared and a value is assigned to it, you need to include its declaration in a DTD as shown:

```
<!ATTLIST Books type CDATA>
```

In the preceding code, CDATA implies that the value of the attribute is stored in a character string.

We have discussed all important components of an XML document. You can use these components to create a simple XML document as discussed in the following section.

Creating a Simple XML Document

In this section, you will learn to create a simple XML document that contains the details of students studying in Form 5. The information about the students is stored in the form of elements, attributes, and the values assigned to the attributes. In addition, the XML document contains the XML declaration statement and the DOCTYPE declaration statement as shown:

 NOTE

The following code uses a hypothetical URL, http://students/Student.dtd, to provide a location for the Student.dtd file.

```
<?xml version="1.0"?>
<!DOCTYPE Student_Details SYSTEM "http://students/Student.DTD">
<!--This XML document contains information about the students studying in Form 5.-->
<Student_Details>
    <Student ID="S001" Form="5">
        <Name>
              Harry Brown
        </Name>
        <Address>
```

```
        10932 Bigge Rd.
    </Address>
    <City>
      Menlo Park
    </City>
    <State>
      CA
    </State>
    <Zip>
      94025
    </Zip>
</Student>
<Student ID="S002" Form="5">
    <Name>
      Livia Carson
    </Name>
    <Address>
      54 Upland Hts.
    </Address>
    <City>
      Oakland
    </City>
    <State>
      CA
    </State>
    <Zip>
      94612
    </Zip>
</Student>
<Student ID="S003" Form="5">
    <Name>
      Albert Green
    </Name>
    <Address>
      31 Putnam
    </Address>
    <City>
      Vacaville
```

```
            </City>
            <State>
                CA
            </State>
            <Zip>
                95688
            </Zip>
        </Student>
        <Student ID="S004" Form="5">
            <Name>
                Dean White
            </Name>
            <Address>
                79 Darwin Ln.
            </Address>
            <City>
                Berkeley
            </City>
            <State>
                CA
            </State>
            <Zip>
                94705
            </Zip>
        </Student>
        <Student ID="S005" Form="5">
            <Name>
                Dirk Smith
            </Name>
            <Address>
                48 Silver Ct.
            </Address>
            <City>
                Walnut Creek
            </City>
            <State>
                CA
            </State>
```

```
    <Zip>
       94595
    </Zip>
  </Student>
</Student_Details>
```

You can save the file as `Student.xml` and open it in Internet Explorer to view the output of the code. The output of the preceding code is shown in Figure 1-5.

XML Namespaces

The biggest advantage of using XML is the ability to create custom tags. You can create a vocabulary of tags that can be applied to an application or similar applications. Consider the Student.xml file that you created in the previous section. The file contains tags, such as `Student`, `Name`, `Address`, `State`, and `Zip`, which are used to describe the information about the students who are studying in Form 5.

Because XML allows you to declare user-defined tags, it is likely that another user will create a tag with the same name and use it in a different context. Consider a situation in which you create a tag with the name `<Average>` to store the average scores of students who are studying

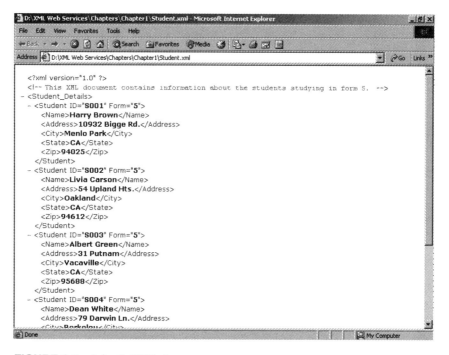

FIGURE 1-5 *A simple XML document.*

in Form 5. However, another user can create a tag <Average> to store the average number of students who enroll for a course in a month. The following examples show use of the <Average> tag in different contexts:

```
<?xml version="1.0"?>
<!DOCTYPE Student_Details SYSTEM "http://students/Student.DTD">
<!--This XML document contains information about the average scores of students
studying in form 5.-->
<Student_Details>
   <Student ID="S001" Form="5">
      <Name>
         Harry Brown
      </Name>
      <Average>
         89
      </Average>
   </Student>
<Student_Details>
```

Now, consider the following code that uses the <Average> tag in a different context:

```
<?xml version="1.0"?>
<!DOCTYPE Student_Details SYSTEM "http://students/Student.DTD">
<!--This XML document contains information about the average number of students
who enroll in a course in a month.-->
<Course_Details>
   <Course>
      1
   </Course>
      <Average>
         9
      </Average>
<Course_Details>
```

As you can see, use of the tag is different. This situation can lead to a problem if you try to integrate data from these two documents.

The World Wide Web Consortium (W3C), the group that issues XML specifications, found a solution to this problem in the form of namespaces. An *XML namespace* is a collection of names of elements or attributes. This collection of names can be referred by a Uniform Resource Identifier (URI). Therefore, you can include a namespace in an XML document to uniquely identify the elements and attributes in the XML document.

Element and attribute names are stored in a structured format in a namespace. A DTD can be considered an example of a namespace that is referred to by its URL.

Before using a namespace, you need to declare it. The following section discusses declaring namespaces.

Declaring XML Namespaces

You declare XML namespaces by using the xmlns keyword. A namespace is referred to by its URI. Therefore, while you are declaring a namespace, you also

> **URI**
>
> A URI is any unique set of characters, such as a name or address that can be used to access a resource on the Internet. A URI contains more information than just the location of a resource on the Internet; therefore, it can be used to locate a resource on the Web without specifying the exact location of the resource. For example, a URL is a kind of URI.

need to mention the URI that you use to access the namespace. The syntax for declaring a namespace is as follows:

```
xmlns=<URI>
```

As you can see, xmlns is an attribute that takes a value as the URI of the namespace. After you have created a namespace, you can create elements with the same name in different namespaces. For example, you can declare two namespaces and have the <Average> tag in both these namespaces. Consider the following code:

```
xmlns="http://www.student.com/studentdetails/student.dtd"
xmlns="http://www.student.com/coursedetails/course.dtd"
```

To uniquely identify an element, you need to prefix it with the name of the namespace. However, you can not prefix an element with the URI of the namespace, therefore, while declaring a namespace, you can assign an alias name to the namespace. This alias name is called a *namespace prefix*, or simply *prefix*. You then need to prefix the alias name with an element name to uniquely identify it. The syntax for declaring a namespace with a prefix is as shown:

```
xmlns:prefix=<URI>
```

You can provide an alias name as follows:

```
xmlns:student="http://www.student.com/studentdetails/student.dtd"
xmlns:course="http://www.student.com/coursedetails/course.dtd"
```

The syntax to access an element in a namespace is this:

```
namespace:element
```

Now, the <Average> tag in the student namespace can be accessed as follows:

```
<student:Average/>
```

Using XML Namespaces

After declaring a namespace, you can use it in an XML document. The following code declares a namespace and uses it in the previous example:

```
<?xml version="1.0" xmlns:students="http://www.student.com/studentdetails/
student.dtd" ?> <!--This XML document contains information about the average scores
of students who are studying in Form 5.-->
<students:Student_Details>
  <students:Student ID="S001" Form="5">
    <students:Name>
      Harry Brown
    </students:Name>
    <students:Average>
      89
    </students:Average>
  </students:Student>
<students:Student_Details>
```

 NOTE

In the preceding example, we have used a hypothetical namespace, `student.dtd`. The URL of the site is given as http://www.student.com/studentdetails/student.dtd, and a namespace prefix, `students`, is given to the namespace.

XML Schemas

XML schemas are used to define the structure of an XML document. In this context, schemas are similar to DTDs that we discussed earlier. Because XML documents are platform independent, they are used extensively to transfer data over a network. This implies that an XML document should adhere to a standard structure. This standard structure is referred to as the XML schema.

When an XML document is transferred over a network, the receiving application might need to process the data to produce a result. However, first the application needs to validate the data in the XML document. Validating the data ensures that no errors are generated while processing the data. In addition, validating the data ensures that the application does not produce erroneous results after processing the data. To validate the data, the receiving application verifies that the data adheres to the XML schema. If the structure of the XML document is not validated, an error is produced.

Defining XML Schemas

An XML schema is a document written in XML syntax that defines the structure of other XML documents. An XML schema consists of elements, attributes, and data types that are allowed to be included in an XML document. In addition, XML schemas define the rules that you need to follow while designing the structure of an XML document. An XML document that adheres to an XML schema is called the *document instance* of the schema and is an example of a valid document.

As discussed earlier, XML schemas provide a standard against which an XML document is validated. The following section discusses how to validate XML documents in detail.

Validating XML Documents

When an XML document is created and needs to be transferred over a network, both the sending and receiving applications need to mutually agree on a set of elements, attributes, data types, and the structure of the XML document. All this information is included in the XML schema on which the XML document is based.

However, doing this limits the user to use only the components that are included in the XML schema. Therefore, the XML schema constrains the user, as described in the following list:

◆ **Data type constraint.** A data type constraint defines the permissible data types that you can include in an XML document.

◆ **Content type constraint.** As discussed, an XML schema defines the structure of XML data. Therefore, the content type constraint defines the structure and sequence of the data in an XML document.

When an XML document is transferred, the parsers of the receiving application validate the data based on the data type and content type constraints. The parsers then verify the validity of the document.

An example of an XML schema is a DTD. A DTD also defines the structure of a document; therefore, a DTD is used to validate an XML document. However, DTDs have some limitations because of which W3C had to look for an alternative in the form of XML schemas. The following section compares traditional DTDs with XML schemas.

Comparing DTDs with XML Schemas

Before comparing XML schemas with DTDs, we will list the problems that users face while working with DTDs. This will help you analyze the advantages of XML schemas over DTDs.

Limitations of Using DTDs

Following are some of the limitations of using DTD:

◆ DTDs are not written using XML syntax. However, to write a DTD, you use another syntax called Extended Backus Naur Form (EBNF). The EBNF syntax is different from XML and might be difficult for some users to write or understand.

◆ DTDs define limited data types that you can use in an XML document. As discussed, DTDs define only the structure, elements, and attributes that you can use in an XML document and support only a few data types—primarily text. Therefore, all non-textual data needs to be transferred to a data type that is defined in a DTD so that a user can work with non-textual data.

◆ DTDs cannot be inherited from an existing DTD. This implies that you need to create DTDs again and cannot reuse an existing DTD.

◆ DTDs do not support namespaces. Therefore, to validate an XML document that is based on a namespace, you first need to explicitly declare all the elements and attributes of the namespace in a DTD.

The following section discusses how schema can be a solution to the preceding problems.

XML Schema as a Solution to the Limitations of DTDs

The following list describes the advantages of XML schemas over DTDs:

◆ XML schemas are written using XML syntax, which makes it easier for users to create and understand an XML schema. In addition, they are extensible because you can use your own tags.

◆ XML schemas support a rich set of data types. The data types that XML schemas support include integers, Boolean, date, time, and so on. In addition, XML schemas support user-defined data types.

◆ XML schemas can be inherited from an existing schema. Therefore, you can reuse an existing schema to customize it, as required.

◆ XML schemas support namespaces. You can include a namespace in an XML schema so that you can validate an XML document against the elements or attributed defined in the namespace. You do not need to explicitly include all elements declared in an XML namespace in a schema.

Summary

This chapter introduced you to the basics of XML. XML is a new markup language that is used to store data in a structured format. In addition to XML, you learned about other markup languages, such as SGML and HTML. SGML is the meta language used to define other languages, such as markup languages. It is the first international standard used to describe the structure of a document. HTML is a markup language that is evolved from SGML. HTML is used to describe and format data.

Then, you looked at the advantages that XML offers over SGML and HTML, and were introduced to DTDs. A DTD is a vocabulary that defines the structure and elements in an XML document.

Next, you looked at the components of an XML document, including XML declaration statements, comments, elements, and attributes. Using these components, you learned to create a simple XML document.

After that, you learned about namespaces and the schemas in an XML document. An XML namespace is a collection of names of elements or attributes, referred to as a URI. An XML schema is a document written in XML syntax that defines the structure of other XML documents. In addition, XML schemas define the rules that you need to follow while designing the structure of an XML document. Finally, you learned to validate an XML document based on an XML schema.

PART II

Introduction to Web Services

Chapter 2

In today's business scenario, people need scalable and reliable multi-user applications. This need has led to a shift from traditional desktop applications to distributed applications.

A traditional desktop application is a monolithic entity. All the functionality is built into a single application. Therefore, when you make a change in the application, you need to recompile and redistribute the entire application. This results in an increase in the overall cost of deploying the application. In addition, desktop applications have a limited access to another's processes and data. Therefore, upgrading these applications so that they can cope with the increasing requirements is difficult. Consequently, distributed applications were developed.

A distributed application is a scalable application. The functionality of the distributed applications is spread across various modules or tiers as listed:

◆ Presentation tier

◆ Business logic, or middle, tier

◆ Data tier

For example, consider a distributed application that consists of a database forming the data tier. You can access the data in the database from a client application, which forms the presentation tier. You access the data by using an intermediate application. This intermediate application provides the business logic and forms the middle tier. Traditionally, in distributed applications, the middle tier is developed using technologies, such as COM and CORBA.

With distributed applications, you do not need to maintain the database, the client application, and the intermediate application on the same computer. In most cases, the client application and the database are present on separate remote computers.

Distributed applications, which are highly efficient, are created using architectures, such as DCOM, CORBA, RMI, and so on. The distributed applications that use these architectures depend on protocols that are specific to respective technologies and architectures, which reduces the usability of these models for developing cross-platform applications. As a result, Web services are being considered as an alternative that allows you to create distributed applications that are interoperable. This implies that Web services make data available to applications that run on multiple platforms and are developed using multiple technologies.

For example, when you create a Web service, you can access it from applications created using various languages such as Visual Basic, Java, Delphi, and so on. In addition, you can access the Web service from applications that run on various operating systems, such as Windows, Linux, or Solaris.

This chapter gives you an overview of Web services. It also discusses the architecture of Web services, the components, and the technologies involved in the creation of a Web service. In subsequent chapters, you will learn how to create these services by using various programming languages.

You can create Web services by using several programming languages, such as Visual C#, Visual Basic .NET, and Java. Because Web services use XML for transferring data, Web services are also referred to as *XML Web services*.

Overview of Web Services

In a distributed environment, applications might be created on different platforms by using different programming languages. Consider a scenario in which you need to access the functionality of an application that was created using Visual Basic .NET from a client application that is present on a computer running in the Unix environment.

In this case, you can create a Web service containing Web methods that allow you to access the functionality of the Visual Basic .NET application from an application running on a Unix-based system. This allows you to integrate applications that were created and deployed on heterogeneous platforms.

Defining Web Services

A Web service is a new technology that you can use to create platform-independent applications. You can develop a Web service by using languages and platforms that adhere to a standard set of technologies. Therefore, using Web services, it is possible to access the functionality of an application that was created using Visual Basic .NET from a computer running on Unix, as we discussed in the previous example.

A Web service is an application that exposes functionality coded in an application to several applications. To do this, you need to invoke a Web service from an application called the *Web service client application*. In addition, the application that hosts the Web service is called the *Web service provider application*.

Accessing Web Services

To access the functionality that a Web service provides, a Web service client application needs to invoke the Web service by using its URL.

 NOTE

A Web service can invoke another Web service as well. In this case, the Web service that sends a request for another Web service is the Web service client application.

Suppose you created a Web service to validate the details of the credit card as entered by a user. This Web service accepts the details, such as the name of the credit card holder and the credit card number. Based on this information, the details of the user, such as the credit card number, the expiration date of the credit card, and the credit amount available for the specified credit card, are validated. You can name this Web service Credit_Details. You can now invoke this Web service by using the URL http://www.exampleurl.com/Credit_Details.

 NOTE

In the preceding example, we used a hypothetical site, http://www.exampleurl.com, which hosts the Credit_Details Web service.

After introducing you to the basics of a Web service, we will discuss the architecture of a Web service. Understanding the architecture of a Web service will enable you to understand how a Web service works.

Web Service Architecture

As discussed earlier, you can create a Web service by using any programming language or tool. However, certain components in the architecture of a Web service are common to all Web services. The following list discusses these components:

◆ All Web services require a standard format for transfer of data. In most cases, this standard format is XML.

◆ Web services transfer data across a network by using a standard protocol called *Simple Object Access Protocol* (SOAP).

◆ All Web services have a detailed description available with it in the form of an XML document called a *Web Services Description Language* (WSDL) document.

◆ When you create a Web service, you can register it in a directory by using Universal Description, Discovery, and Integration (UDDI).

You will learn about these components in the later section "Components of a Web Service." Using these components, the internal structure of a Web service is divided into two layers: the listener layer and the business layer. The following section discusses these layers in detail.

Layers of a Web Service

The layers in the architecture of a Web service are as follows:

◆ Listener layer
◆ Business layer

The two layers in the internal structure of a Web service work in cooperation to allow applications to interoperate. These layers are shown in Figure 2-1.

The following sections discuss the layers of a Web service in detail.

The Listener Layer

As shown in Figure 2-1, the listener layer is the topmost layer in a Web service and is closest to the Web service client application. Therefore, when a client application needs to communicate with the Web service provider application, the client application sends a request to the listener layer of a Web service.

The listener layer interprets the request that the client application sends so that the Web service provider application understands the request. The request is then forwarded to the next layer in the Web service architecture. Similarly, when the request for the data is processed and

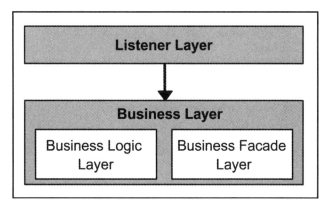

FIGURE 2-1 *Layers in a Web service.*

the result is returned to the listener layer, the layer again converts the data to a form that the client application can decipher easily. The data is then sent to the client application in the form of an XML message.

The Business Layer

When you create a Web service, you need to write the business logic for the Web service. The business layer implements this business logic so that the Web service is made accessible to the Web service client application. The business logic is divided into two layers: the business logic and the business facade layer. The functionality or the service provided by a Web service is made accessible to the client application by the business logic layer and the business facade layer provides the interface for the service.

The working of a Web service depends on the architecture of the Web service. The following section discusses the working of a Web service.

Working of a Web Service

To understand the working of a Web service, consider the example of a Web service, Credit_ Details, which validates the credit card details of a customer. Any Web service that you create consists of one or more Web methods. These Web methods expose the functionality of a Web service to the client application. Therefore, to access these Web methods, the client application sends a request for the Web methods by using the URL of the Web service.

In the example, the request that is sent to the listener layer consists of the URL of the Web service. In addition, the request contains the information, such as the name and the credit card number of the user. You need to pass this data as a parameter to the Web service call statement.

The listener layer receives the request for the Web service. After listening to the request of the client application, this layer interprets the request in the form of an XML message that is passed on to the business layer.

When the request reaches the business layer, the request needs to be processed according to the business logic of the Web service. The result of processing the request is sent back to the listener layer. This data is in the form of a SOAP package and is, therefore, converted by the listener layer in a form that the client application can understand. Finally, the data is transferred to the client application.

With the Credit_Details Web service, processing of the request involves validating the information that the user entered against the data in the data source. The data source includes the required information about the credit details of the user, such as the credit card number, the expiration date, and the credit limit. If the data is valid, then the result in the form of an XML message is transferred back to the client application and the user is allowed to shop on the Internet. Alternatively, if the data is not valid, an error message is returned. The working of a Web service is displayed in Figure 2-2.

The architecture and the working of a Web service are defined in the Web services model, as discussed in the following section.

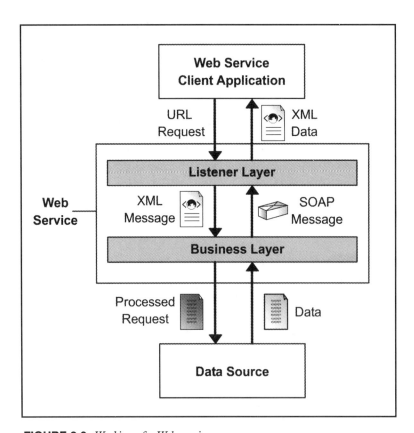

FIGURE 2-2 *Working of a Web service.*

The Web Services Model

The Web services model has the following features:

- ◆ Three applications perform the roles of requesting the data, providing the application with the data, and registering the services.
- ◆ These applications need to exchange data or interact with one another. The interactions involved in the Web services model are publishing, finding, and binding.
- ◆ The preceding interactions are performed on the objects of the Web services model. These objects include the service and the description of the service.

The following sections discuss these features in detail.

Applications in the Web Services Model

Table 2-1 discusses the roles that the three applications in the Web services model perform.

Table 2-1 Roles That Applications in a Web Service Perform

Application	Role
Service requestor	This client application requests data or functionality. To request the data, the requestor application needs to invoke the Web service.
Service provider	This application hosts the Web service that any application can use.
Service registry	When you create a Web service, the Web service provider application must publish it. Publishing a Web service involves registering the description of the Web service with the service registry. Therefore, a *service registry* is a registry that contains the description of all Web services that a user creates. When a request for a Web service is made, the service registry searches for the required Web service and sends the result of the search to the service requestor application.

Interactions in the Web Services Model

To access a Web service, the three applications discussed in the preceding section need to interact with one another. Table 2-2 discusses the interactions that are involved in the Web services model.

Table 2-2 Interactions in the Web Services Model

Interaction	Description
Publishing	When you create a Web service, you need to publish the Web service with the service registry. This enables the service requestor application to find the Web service when required.

(continues...)

Table 2-2 (continued) Interactions in the Web Services Model

Interaction	Description
Finding	When the service requestor application requests for a Web service, the description of the Web service is searched in the service registry. After finding a similar Web service, the service registry returns its description to the Web service requestor application.
Bind	When the details of the Web service are returned to the Web service requestor application, the application can invoke the Web service, if required. The description of a Web service includes the binding information about the Web service. The information helps the requestor application bind to the Web service.

Objects in the Web Services Model

The Web services model contains the objects or artifacts that are described in Table 2-3.

Table 2-3 Objects in the Web Services Model

Object	Description
Service description	When you publish a Web service, you need to provide a description. This description is called the *service description*. The service description includes the details of a Web service, such as binding details and the information about the implementation of the Web service. In addition, the service description includes the location of the Web service and the details of the functionality that the Web service provides. This implies that the service description provides the metadata or the information for the Web service.
Service	A service is an implementation of the Web service. It contains the code to implement the Web service. When the service requestor application invokes the Web service, the code in the service is executed.

The Web services model is shown in Figure 2-3.

In addition to describing the architecture of a Web service, the Web services model defines the development life cycle (DLC) of the Web service.

DLC of a Web Service

The DLC of a Web service involves designing, developing, deploying, invoking, and managing the Web service. As discussed in the preceding section, the Web services model consists of three parts: service requestor, service provider, and service registry. All three parts of the Web

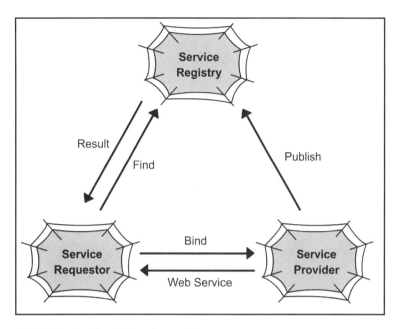

FIGURE 2-3 *The Web services model.*

services need to go through the phases of DLC. The following list discusses the phases in the DLC of a Web service in detail:

◆ **Design phase.** The design phase of a Web service includes deciding the functionality and components of a Web service. Based on the design, the Web service is created in the development phase.

◆ **Development phase.** The development phase includes writing and testing the code for the Web service. In addition, the service description of the Web service is written in the development phase.

◆ **Deployment phase.** The deployment phase includes registering the Web service with the service registry. In addition, to make the Web service accessible to service requestor applications, you need to deploy the executable files in a Web service on a server.

◆ **Implementation phase.** The implementation phase involves invoking the Web service. The service requestor application can find the required Web service and use the functionality provided.

◆ **Maintenance phase.** The maintenance phase involves managing and administering a Web service after it is created and deployed. Maintenance of a Web service is essential to ensure that the Web service is available to requestor applications when required. In addition, the security and performance features of the Web service are monitored during this phase.

The different phases of the DLC are shown in Figure 2-4.

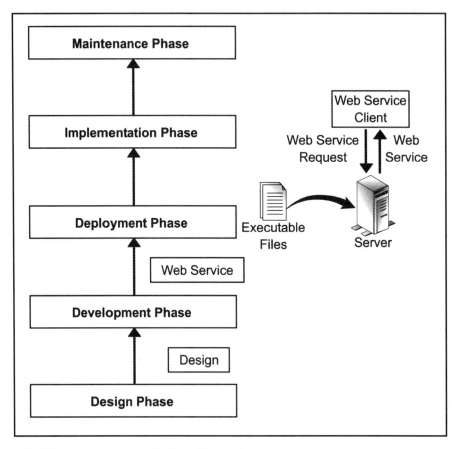

FIGURE 2-4 *Phases in the DLC of a Web service.*

Components of a Web Service

The Web services architecture is based on the following basic components:

◆ XML
◆ XSD
◆ SOAP
◆ WSDL
◆ UDDI

The following sections discuss these components in detail.

XML

XML is the markup language used to describe data in a document. Because XML is a text-based and platform-independent language, it is used as the standard format for transferring data over a network by using Web services.

XSD

You learned about XML schemas in Chapter 1, "Basics of XML." An XML schema document consists of elements, attributes, and data types that can be included in an XML document.

To allow you to create XML schemas, the World Wide Web Consortium (W3C) published the XML schema recommendation in 2001. This XML schema recommendation was called *W3C XML schema*. To implement XML schema recommendations, Microsoft developed a new language known as *XML Schema Definition* (XSD). XSD forms a part of the XML schema recommendation.

XSD is a schema language that defines the structure of an XML document. In addition, XSD uses the XML syntax to define the data in the XML document. To do this, XSD provides you with a set of predefined tags. We will discuss these tags and other components of an XSD document in the following sections.

Components of an XSD Document

An XSD document consists of the declaration statement and the elements that define the data in an XSD document. These components of an XSD document are discussed in detail in the following sections.

The Declaration Statement

In the beginning of the XSD document, you need to include the XML declaration statement as in any other XML document. The following code shows the XML declaration statement:

```
<?xml version = "1.0" ?>
```

The schema Element

Similar to an XML document, the content of the XSD document is stored in the form of elements. An XSD document consists of the schema element, which further comprises elements containing the data. This data includes the data types and the elements that define the data in the XML document. In addition, the schema element contains information about the namespace that is associated with the XML document. To define the namespace, the schema element uses the xmlns keyword.

NOTE

The latest version of the XSD specification that you need to use in the XSD document is available at http://www.w3.org/2001/XMLSchema.

The syntax of the XSD document is as shown:

```
<?xml version = "1.0" ?>
<xsd:schema xmlns:xsd="http://www.w3.org/2001/XMLSchema">
        <elements>
</xsd:schema>
```

The element Element

element is used to define the structure of the XML document and has two attributes: name and type. The name attribute specifies the name of the element, and the type attribute specifies the data type of the element. The syntax for element is as follows:

```
<xsd:element name=<name> type=<data type>>
        <data>
</xsd:element>
```

Having discussed the components of an XSD document, you will learn to create a sample XSD document in the following section.

Creating a Sample XSD Document

An XSD document needs to be associated with an XML document. You will be using the XML document that you created in Chapter 1. The code for the XML document is as shown:

```
<?xml version="1.0"?>
<!DOCTYPE Student_Details SYSTEM "http://students/Student.DTD">
<!--This XML document contains information about the students studying in form 5.-->
<Student_Details>
  <Student ID="S001" Form="5">
    <Name>
          Harry Brown
    </Name>
    <Address>
        10932 Bigge Rd.
    </Address>
```

```
    <City>
        Menlo Park
    </City>
    <State>
        CA
    </State>
    <Zip>
        94025
    </Zip>
</Student >
<Student ID="S002" Form="5">
    <Name>
        Livia Carson
    </Name>
    <Address>
        54 Upland Hts.
    </Address>
    <City>
        Oakland
    </City>
    <State>
        CA
    </State>
    <Zip>
        94612
    </Zip>
</Student>
<Student ID="S003" Form="5">
    <Name>
        Albert Green
    </Name>
    <Address>
        31 Putnam
    </Address>
    <City>
        Vacaville
    </City>
    <State>
        CA
    </State>
```

```
        <Zip>
          95688
        </Zip>
    </Student>
    <Student ID="S004" Form="5">
        <Name>
          Dean White
        </Name>
        <Address>
          79 Darwin Ln.
        </Address>
        <City>
          Berkeley
        </City>
        <State>
          CA
        </State>
        <Zip>
          94705
        </Zip>
    </Student>
    <Student ID="S005" Form="5">
        <Name>
          Dirk Smith
        </Name>
        <Address>
          48 Silver Ct.
        </Address>
        <City>
          Walnut Creek
        </City>
        <State>
          CA
        </State>
        <Zip>
          94595
        </Zip>
    </Student>
  </Student_Details>
```

Adding Code to the XSD Document

Now you can create an XSD document for the preceding XML document. To create an XSD document, you can use the available tools. These tools help you to create XSD documents for existing XML documents. The XSD document for the preceding XML document is as follows:

```
<?xml version ="1.0" ?>
<xsd:schema xmlns:xsd="http://www.w3.org/2001/XMLSchema">
    <xsd:element name="Student_Details" type="studdata" />
        <xsd:complexType name="studdata">
            <xsd:sequence>
                <xsd:element name="Student" type="Stud" maxOccurs="unbounded"/>
            </xsd:sequence>
        </xsd:complexType>
    <xsd:complexType name="Stud">
        <xsd:sequence>
            <xsd:element name="Name" type="xsd:string" />
            <xsd:element name="Address" type="xsd:string" />
            <xsd:element name="State" type="xsd:string" />
            <xsd:element name="City" type="xsd:string" />
            <xsd:element name="Zip" type="xsd:float" />
        </xsd:sequence>
            <xsd:attribute name="ID" type="xsd:string" use="required" />
            <xsd:attribute name="Form" type="xsd:float" default="5"
use="required" />
        </xsd:complexType>
    </xsd:schema>
```

Save the preceding file with the name StudData.xsd.

The preceding code is an XSD document for the corresponding XML file. The following section discusses the structure of that XSD document.

Structure of the Sample XSD Document

As discussed earlier, an XSD document consists of a declaration statement followed by the schema element that specifies the schema recommendation to be included in the document. Then an element with the name Student_Details is declared with a user-defined data type: studdata. studdata is a complex data type. You can create simple or complex data types to define the type of data that an element can store. The simple or complex data types are discussed in the following list:

◆ **Simple data type.** You declare a simple data type for elements that do not contain other elements or attributes.

◆ **Complex data type.** You declare a complex data type for elements that contain other elements or attributes.

Therefore, to declare the `studdata` data type as complex, you use the `complexType` attribute. Next, the `sequence` element is used to define the sequence of child elements within the `Student_Details` element. Inside the `sequence` element, another element with the name `Student` is declared with a user-defined data type of `Stud`. Because this data type has a user-defined name, it is called a *named data type*.

TIP

You can create data types without specifying a name for them. For example, the previous code can also be written as follows:

```
<xsd:element name="Student">
<xsd:complexType>
    <xsd:sequence>
        <xsd:element name="Name" type="xsd:string" />
        <xsd:element name="Address" type="xsd:string" />
        <xsd:element name="State" type="xsd:string" />
        <xsd:element name="City" type="xsd:string" />
        <xsd:element name="Zip" type="xsd:float" />
    </xsd:sequence>
        <xsd:attribute name="ID" type="xsd:string" use="required" />
        <xsd:attribute name="Form" type="xsd:float" default="5"
use="required" />
    </xsd:complexType>
```

As you can see in the preceding code, the `Student` element has a `maxOccurs` attribute assigned to it. This attribute specifies the maximum number of times that the associated element can occur in the document. Because the Student.xml document can contain any number of entries for students, we have assigned the value for the `maxOccurs` attribute as `unbounded`.

Then, within the `Stud` data type, the child elements for the `Student` element are defined. These child elements include `Name`, `Address`, `City`, `State`, and `Zip`. In addition, you can specify the data type for these child elements in the `Stud` data type.

The `Student` element in the XML document has two attributes: `ID` and `Form`. Therefore, you need to declare these attributes in the XSD document. You can declare attributes by using the `attribute` element. This element specifies the name and data type of the attribute. In addition, you can assign a default value to the attribute by using the `default` attribute.

NOTE

The standard data types that you can include in an XML document are `string`, `float`, `decimal`, `date`, and so on.

NOTE

If you need to assign a fixed value to an attribute, you can use the `fixed` attribute. A *fixed value* is a value that you cannot change in the XML document.

As you can see in the XSD document, the attribute declaration statement also includes the `use` attribute. The value that is assigned to this attribute is `required`. This implies that you cannot leave the associated attribute blank. If no value is assigned to this attribute, an error is generated when the XML document is validated.

Finally, you need to provide closing tags for the elements `sequence`, `complexType`, and `schema`.

Role of XSD in XML Web Services

Consider a scenario in which two organizations decide to exchange their data by using Web services. As discussed earlier, the standard used to exchange data over the network is XML. Therefore, the two organizations need to mutually decide on the standards and structure of the XML documents that are transferred. This enables the two organizations to easily create and interpret the XML documents. The standards, elements, attributes, values, data types, and structure of the XML documents are defined in the XSD document. This implies that the two organizations mutually agree on the XSD document to enable transfer of data across organizations.

SOAP

Another important component of Web services is SOAP, which is used to define a standard way of packaging a message for interpretability. The reason for choosing SOAP as the standard protocol is that it is both a simple and a light mechanism for transferring data. SOAP uses XML to transfer data; therefore, it is a light protocol. In addition, the sending and receiving applications can easily interpret the data.

To transfer messages by using SOAP, the message in any form is packaged as a SOAP package, which is a well-formed XML document. The SOAP package is then transferred over protocols, such as FTP or HTTP.

The SOAP specification defines the standards or rules used to transfer SOAP messages over the network by using any of the standard network transfer protocols. However, SOAP is not a network or a transfer protocol. In addition, the syntax for creating the XML document is defined in the specification. You will learn about SOAP packages in detail in Chapter 3, "Introduction to SOAP."

WSDL

As discussed earlier, you need to register the Web service with the service registry. The description language used to define a Web service and its interface is called WSDL. WSDL is an XML-based language that defines a Web service. It is used to provide information about a Web service to the requesting applications. This information includes a description of the Web service, a location of the Web service, binding information, a method for accessing a Web service, and a way to exchange data by using a Web service.

Consider a scenario in which a Web service client application requests a Web service to validate the user and password information that a user enters. The Web service includes one or more Web methods that the Web service client application needs to access. The information about the mechanism to access the Web service is described using WSDL.

In addition, when a request for the Web service is made, the user needs to pass the name and password as parameters to the Web service call statement. The information about these parameters is also specified using WSDL in a WSDL document.

You will learn about WSDL in detail in Chapter 5, "Introduction to WSDL."

UDDI

A Web service is registered with a group of Web-based registries called *UDDI Business Registries*. UDDI registries are an industry standard in which organizations, such as Microsoft and IBM, register their Web services. The mechanism used to register a Web service is called *UDDI*. You will learn in detail about UDDI in Chapter 4, "Introduction to UDDI."

A UDDI directory is a Web site that provides a listing and references for all Web services. Therefore, a UDDI directory is like yellow pages for Web services. To provide information about a Web service, UDDI creates a pointer to all Web services. This pointer points to the WSDL document for the respective Web services. When a user searches for information about a Web service, UDDI returns the information stored in the WSDL document. The requesting application can then use the Web service if required.

The following list discusses the benefits of registering a Web service with the UDDI directory:

- ◆ It provides a mechanism for Web service provider applications to register a Web service with the UDDI directory.
- ◆ It provides a mechanism to search for a required Web service in a UDDI directory. The client applications can then use the created Web service.
- ◆ It provides a mechanism for developers who create Web services to search for similar existing Web services. The developers then can create their own Web services based on the ideas from existing Web services. Alternatively, the developers can customize the existing Web services according to their needs.

Summary

In this chapter, you learned about distributed applications. A distributed application is a scalable application in which data is shared across various applications or databases. The applications that are created and deployed in a distributed environment are integrated using Web services. Web services are a new technology that you can use to create platform-independent distributed applications.

Next, you looked at the architecture and working of Web services. The internal architecture of a Web service is divided into two layers: the listener layer and the business layer.

Then you learned about the architecture of Web services as defined in the Web services model. The Web services model defines the components and the DLC of a Web service.

Finally, you looked at the technologies used with Web services. These technologies include XML, XSD, SOAP, WSDL, and UDDI.

XML is a text-based markup language that describes data in a document. XSD is a schema language that you can use to define the structure of an XML document. SOAP is used to define a standard way of packaging a message for interpretability.

WSDL is an XML-based language that is used to provide information about a Web service to requesting applications. UDDI is a mechanism used to discover a Web service. UDDI provides the information stored in the WSDL documents to Web services client applications.

PART III

Protocols for Web Services

Chapter 3

Introduction to SOAP

Consider a scenario in which you need to access an application that is on a remote computer. The remote computer might be running in a different environment. To enable you to access an application on a remote computer, you need a simple, light, descriptive, and flexible protocol that can make the applications in a distributed environment interoperable with each other. The standard protocol used to exchange data between applications in a distributed environment is known as *Simple Object Access Protocol* (SOAP).

This book introduced you to SOAP in Chapter 2, "Basics of Web Services." In this chapter, you will learn about SOAP in detail. In addition, you will learn about the need to use SOAP with Web services. Next, you will learn about the SOAP architecture and the SOAP messages. Finally, you will learn about processing a SOAP message.

Defining SOAP

In today's business scenario, the need for exchanging data over a network has increased significantly. A simple business solution involves huge amounts of data to be transferred. Consider the Web site http://www.someURL.com of the bookstore SomeBookStore, Inc. The http://www.someURL.com Web site picks up data from the Web sites of each of its publishers. As a result, the data of the books published is stored in the data source of each publisher. This implies that data can be present in any format on computers running in different environments.

SomeBookStore, Inc. plans to integrate the data from each of its publishers. When a user searches for a book on the Web site of SomeBookStore, Inc., the site will match the search conditions with the data present on http://www.someURL.com. However, integrating data that is present on remote computers is not an easy task. It requires you to create huge data sources on the servers of SomeBookStore, Inc., which, in turn, will prove to be expensive.

The situation could be worse if a publisher's Web site had firewalls for security purposes. As a result, it would be better if SomeBookStore, Inc. extracted data from the site of publishers instead of integrating data on their servers. This discovery led to a need for.a standard protocol that could be used to extract data from an application present on a remote computer. As a result, SOAP was developed.

As discussed earlier, SOAP is the protocol that applications use to communicate in a distributed environment. This implies that SOAP can be used to request information on a network. Because SOAP uses XML, a request can be made from one computer to another computer running on a different operating system. The response of the request is sent back to the requesting application in the form of a SOAP message. Therefore, SOAP is considered a protocol based on the request-response format, as shown in Figure 3-1. You will learn about the SOAP package in the later section "Architecture of SOAP."

The following list discusses the advantages of SOAP:

◆ All big vendors, including Microsoft and Sun Microsystems, support the Web services model that uses SOAP. In addition, SOAP is a widely accepted protocol for transferring data between distributed applications that are created using all recent programming languages. These languages include Visual C#, Visual Basic .NET, Perl, Java, Python, and so on.

◆ The Web services model is based on the Web infrastructure; therefore, you do not need to re-create the infrastructure.

◆ SOAP supports XML, which makes the interacting applications interoperable because XML transfers data in text format. The data is self-describing; therefore, the receiving applications can interpret it easily. This implies that SOAP can be used to exchange data between applications created using any programming language and deployed on a computer running on different platforms.

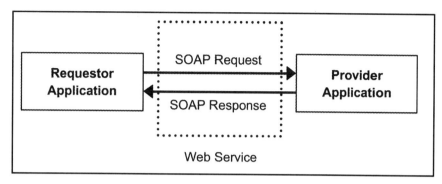

FIGURE 3-1 *The SOAP protocol.*

◆ SOAP messages can overcome firewalls. SOAP messages can use HTTP to exchange information. HTTP messages can pass through firewalls, allowing easy transfer of data.

◆ SOAP uses XML that enables you to transfer heavy and complicated data easily by encoding the data.

◆ Data that is transferred using SOAP is secure. SOAP extends support to several protocols, such as FTP and HTTP. Therefore, data that is transferred using SOAP can be encrypted using HTTP standards and transmitted using HTTP security methods.

In addition to the advantages of using SOAP, SOAP has certain limitations. The following list discusses the limitations of using SOAP with Web services.

◆ As discussed earlier, you can transfer only packaged data by using SOAP. Therefore, while sending data across the network with SOAP, you first need to package the data in the form of a SOAP package. This package includes the SOAP request and the message that needs to be transferred.

When the request reaches the provider application, the application sends an acknowledgement to the requesting application. In addition, the data in the form of an XML message is passed to the requesting application. Therefore, the requesting application needs to parse the XML message by using XML parsers and then extract the required information from the data that is transferred. All this requires extensive coding at the developer's end. The process of transferring data by using SOAP is shown in Figure 3-2. You will learn about the processing of SOAP messages in the later section "Processing of SOAP Messages."

◆ XML documents along with DTDs and schema documents require huge memory and CPU requirements. This is mainly because developing and parsing XML documents require huge memory allocation and are time-consuming. In addition, when data is transferred as a SOAP package, the actual XML data forms just a small part of the package. Therefore, in network transactions that are sensitive to performance issues, transferring data by using SOAP can be an overhead.

◆ SOAP does not allow you to check for errors at the time of compiling the document. You can only test for errors at run time.

◆ Organizations communicating by using Web services need to mutually agree on the standard issues that are defined in the XML schemas. For example, consider a situation where you choose a format for depicting the monthly sales figures of your organization. In this case, your customer can choose the same format of the sales report to depict the yearly sales of their organization. To avoid such a situation, you and your customer need to mutually agree on the definition of sales report. However, in most real-life situations, it is unlikely for all business organizations to agree on a single schema definition.

Despite the previously mentioned limitations, SOAP is a commonly used protocol for transferring data across applications.

Architecture of SOAP

The internal architecture of SOAP can be divided into three components, as shown in the following list:

◆ The SOAP message

◆ The SOAP remote procedure calls (RPCs)

◆ The SOAP encoding rules

The following section discusses these components in detail.

The SOAP Message

A SOAP message is a one-way communication from a sending application to a receiving application. The message might contain the request for data from the receiving application. When the request is processed, the result of the request is retuned as another SOAP message. Therefore, several SOAP messages are combined to allow communication between applications that are present on remote computers. This implies that SOAP messages follow the request-response format as depicted in Figure 3-2.

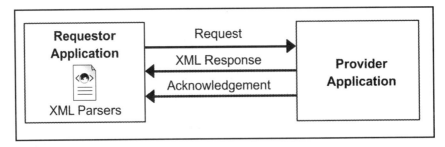

FIGURE 3-2 *Process of transferring data using SOAP.*

The SOAP message is an XML document that contains the data to be transferred. This data is transferred using several network protocols, such as FTP and HTTP. The data to be transferred is internally stored within the components of the SOAP message. These components are as listed:

♦ Envelope
♦ Header
♦ Body

The components of a SOAP message are shown in Figure 3-3.

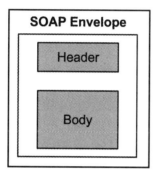

FIGURE 3-3 *Components of a SOAP message.*

As you can see in Figure 3-3, Envelope forms the root element of the SOAP message. The Header and the Body components are child elements of the Envelope element. The following sections discuss the components of the SOAP message in detail.

Envelope

As the name suggests, the SOAP envelope is a framework of the SOAP message. It contains the essential information about the messages that are sent using SOAP. The SOAP envelope is, therefore, a mandatory component of the SOAP message. This information might include the content or data stored in the message. In addition, the SOAP envelope contains information about the sending application and the receiving application. This information is included in the Envelope element shown in the following syntax:

```
<SOAP-ENV:Envelope xmlns:SOAP-ENV="http://schemas.xmlsoap.org/soap/envelope/">

    --------

</SOAP-ENV:Envelope>
```

To understand the data stored in the SOAP envelope, consider the following code, which is an example of a simple SOAP message that demonstrates a function call by passing parameters to it:

```
<SOAP-ENV:Envelope xmlns:SOAP-ENV="http://schemas.xmlsoap.org/soap/envelope/">
    <soap:Body xmlns:taxCalc="urn:http://www.someurl.com/taxcalc">
```

```
      <taxCalc:getTax>
      <fGross xsi:type="float">35000</fGross>
      <iGrade xsi:type="int">1</iGrade>
      </taxCalc:getTax>
    </soap:Body>
</SOAP-ENV:Envelope>
```

The response of the preceding code sample is as shown:

```
<SOAP-ENV:Envelope xmlns:SOAP-ENV="http://schemas.xmlsoap.org/soap/envelope/">
    <soap:Body xmlns:taxCalc="urn:http://www.someurl.com/taxcalc">
        <taxCalc:getTaxResponse>
        <return>234.0</return>
        </taxCalc:getTaxResponse>
    </soap:Body>
</SOAP-ENV:Envelope>
```

As shown in the preceding code, the SOAP message includes a namespace, envelope, as shown: xmlns:SOAP-ENV="http://schemas.xmlsoap.org/soap/envelope/"

The envelope namespace is included to define the structure of the Envelope, Body, and Header elements of the SOAP message. Figure 3-4 shows the envelope namespace, represented by the alias SOAP-ENV.

In addition, the SOAP message might include another namespace as shown:

```
SOAP-ENV:encodingStyle="http://schemas.xmlsoap.org/soap/encoding/"
```

Including the encoding namespace in your SOAP message indicates that the text in the body of the SOAP message follows the encoding rules. These rules are defined in the SOAP package. The encoding namespace is shown in Figure 3-5.

 NOTE

It's essential to include the envelope namespace in all SOAP messages. However, including the encoding namespace is optional.

These namespaces point to XML schemas; therefore, they are included in a SOAP message to validate it. The SOAP messages are validated according to the rules that are defined in the XML schemas.

To include a namespace in a SOAP message, you first need to create an element, Envelope. You can include additional attributes in the SOAP envelope. You can also include other namespaces and subelements in the SOAP message by declaring them in the Envelope element.

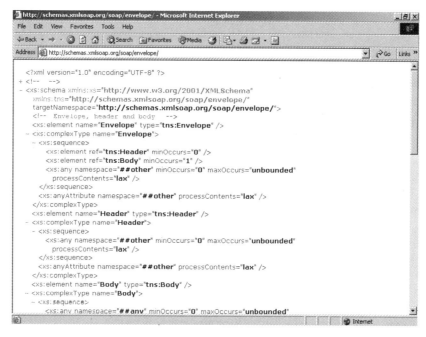

FIGURE 3-4 *The* envelope *NAMESPACE.*

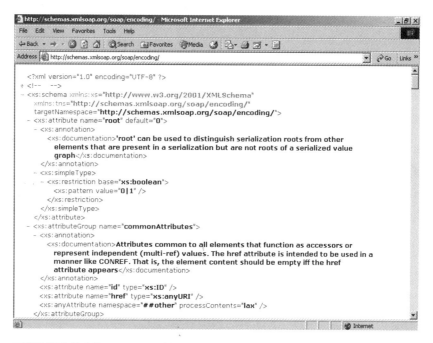

FIGURE 3-5 *The* encoding *NAMESPACE.*

In addition to namespace declaration statements, a SOAP message includes the serialization rules that are used to define the SOAP message. The serialization rules are defined in the encodingStyle attribute. The value of this attribute is the URI address of the namespace that defines the serialization rules. An example of such a namespace is the encoding namespace discussed earlier.

Header

In addition to the Envelope element, a SOAP message includes the Header element. Header is an optional element that is used as a generic location to provide information in a SOAP message. The information that is included in the Header element is provided in a decentralized manner and is represented by the Header element. The syntax for the Header element is shown in the following code sample:

```
<SOAP-ENV:Header>

        ---------.

</SOAP-ENV:Header>
```

 NOTE

The Header element is optional. In a SOAP message, you can include as many Header elements as required. However, the Header element should be an immediate child of the Envelope element. Therefore, the structure of the Header element should be as follows:

```
<SOAP-ENV:Envelope xmlns:SOAP-ENV="http://schemas.xmlsoap.org/soap/envelope/">
    <SOAP-ENV:Header>

        ---------.

    </SOAP-ENV:Header>
    <SOAP-ENV:Header>

        ---------.

    </SOAP-ENV:Header>

    ---------

</SOAP-ENV:Envelope>
```

The Header element includes information about how the receiving application should process the SOAP message. This information is represented in the form of elements of the Header element. These elements must be fully qualified and include a namespace, which is identified by a URI and a local name.

An example of the `Header` element is shown in the following code sample:

```
<soap:Header>
        <m:l xmlns:m="http://www.someUrl/locale/">
                <m:currency>dollars</m:currency>
</soap:Header>
```

The `Header` element might include several subelements. However, the `Header` attribute applies to only its immediate subelement. Consider a situation in which a SOAP message includes a `Header` attribute with two subelements, as shown in the following code:

```
<soap:Header>
        <m:l xmlns:m="http://www.someUrl/locale/">
                <m:currency>dollars</m:currency>
                <m:country>US</m:country>
        </m:l>
</soap:Header>
```

In this case, the first `Header` element applies only to the `currency` subelement and not to the `country` subelement, which is not the immediate subelement of the `Header` element.

A SOAP `Header` element can include several attributes to define the information in the `Header` element. These attributes are explained in the following list:

- ◆ `mustUnderstand` **attribute.** The `mustUnderstand` attribute of the `Header` element specifies whether it is mandatory for the receiving application to process the `Header` element. This attribute takes a `Boolean` value. A value of `0` indicates that it is not essential that the receiving application process the `Header` element. However, if the `mustUnderstand` attribute takes the value of `1`, it is essential for the receiving application to process the `Header` element. The `Header` element is processed according to the encoding rules defined in the namespace that you include in the `Header` element.

- ◆ `actor` **attribute.** When a SOAP message is passed from a sending application to a receiving application, the message might pass through one or more intermediary applications. Therefore, to indicate whether the application that receives the SOAP message is the final application or an intermediate application, you can include the `actor` attribute in the `Header` element. An example of the `actor` attribute is shown in the following code:

```
<SOAP-ENV:Header http://schemas.xmlsoap.org/soap/actor/next>

        ---------

</SOAP-ENV:Header>
```

  As you can see, the preceding code includes a URI of http://schemas.xmlsoap.org/soap/actor/next. This URI indicates that the receiving application is the intermediate application that needs to forward the SOAP message to another application.

◆ **encodingStyle attribute.** The encodingStyle attribute specifies the serialization rules that you can use to encode the Header attribute. These rules that are defined in the encodingStyle attribute apply to the Header attribute and all its subelements. The value of the encodingStyle attribute is the URI of the namespace that defines the serialization rules.

Body

A SOAP message includes a mandatory Body element that contains the main text of the message. All data that needs to be transferred in the SOAP message forms a part of the Body element. The body element is denoted by the Body element, which is the child element of the Envelope element. The syntax of the Body element is as shown:

```
<SOAP-ENV:Envelope xmlns:SOAP-ENV="http://schemas.xmlsoap.org/soap/envelope/">
        <SOAP-ENV:Header>

            --------- .

        </SOAP-ENV:Header>
        <SOAP-ENV:Body>

            --------- .

        </SOAP-ENV:Body>
        </SOAP-ENV:Envelope>
```

To define the text in the Body element, you can include subelements. The text is encoded in the Body element by using the encodingStyle attribute. In addition, the Body element might include a Fault element. This element is used to send the status information or any error message with the SOAP message.

An example of the Body element is as shown:

```
<soap:Body xmlns:taxCalc="urn:http://www.someurl.com/taxcalc">
        <taxCalc:getTax>
        <fGross xsi:type="float">35000</fGross>
        <iGrade xsi:type="int">1</iGrade>
        </taxCalc:getTax>
</soap:Body>
```

SOAP Serialization

When a SOAP message is transferred over the network, you must ensure that the message is in the format that the receiving application can easily understand and interpret. This implies that you need to serialize the content of the Header and Body elements of the SOAP message in the format that the receiving application understands. To do this, you can use the System.XML. Serialization namespace, which serializes data to an XML document. Most applications can understand an XML document that is being text based. You can include this XML document in the Body element of a SOAP message to be transferred over the network.

Formats for Serializing SOAP Messages

The SOAP specification supports two formats of serializing SOAP messages, as discussed in the following list:

◆ **Literal format.** In this type of serialization, data is serialized based on the XML schema or XSD. Therefore, the interacting applications deal with the data in the form of XML documents instead of objects and structures. However, in literal format, no special rules of serializing data are followed.

◆ **Encoded format.** In this type of serialization, data is serialized according to some special encoding rules that are defined in the SOAP specifications. These rules define how specific objects, structures, arrays, and so on should be serialized. Unlike literal format, in the encoded format, the interacting applications deal with structures and objects.

Styles of SOAP Messages

The SOAP specification defines two styles in which you can format a SOAP message. These formats are discussed in the following list:

◆ **Document style.** In this style, the SOAP Body element contains one or more child elements called *parts*. However, the specification does not specify rules for including the child elements in the Body element. It can include any data that the sending application needs to send to the receiving application.

◆ **RPC style.** In this style, the Body element includes the methods or remote procedures that you need to call. In addition, the Body element includes the parameters that the remote procedures accept.

 NOTE

For more information on the RPC style of SOAP messages, refer to Section 7 of the SOAP specification.

The Microsoft SOAP Toolkit uses RPC/encoded SOAP messages by default. When you're using .NET, you can expose Web services in two ways: Remoting and .NET Web services. Remoting uses RPC/encoded SOAP, whereas .NET Web services, designed for document exchange via messaging, use the document/literal SOAP by default.

The SOAP RPC

Consider a situation in which you need to call a procedure that is located on a remote computer. While calling the procedure, you need to pass parameters to the procedure `call` statement. The process of calling a procedure from a remote computer is called RPC.

The request for the procedure can be made using SOAP in the form of a SOAP message. This message includes the request or the response of the request. To define the manner in which the messages are exchanged, a specification called the *RPC convention* is developed. The RPC convention defines a set of rules that you can use to serialize the procedure calls in the form of a SOAP message.

As discussed earlier, SOAP is based on a request-response format. Therefore, when you need to call a remote procedure, you send in a request. The statement used to request the remote procedure is called a `call` statement. When the request is processed and the response is returned, this response is called the *result* of the `call` statement. Figure 3-6 explains the RPC procedure in detail.

The following sections discuss the `call` and `result` statements.

The *call Statement*

To call a remote procedure by using SOAP, you need to create a SOAP message that includes the `call` statement. The `call` statement is an XML statement that includes a struct that makes a serialized call to the required procedure. The parameters of the required procedure are sent as child elements of the struct.

After a `call` statement is written, it is serialized in the form of an XML message, whose elements define the procedure and its parameters. Therefore, the name of the elements should correspond to the name of the procedure and its parameters. Consider the following example of a procedure that is used to change the case of a string. The string is passed as a parameter to the procedure:

```
void ChangeCase([in] string str, [out] string str1);
```

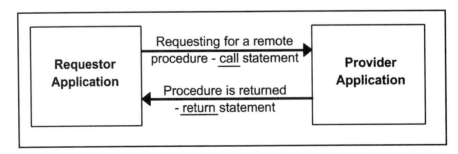

FIGURE 3-6 *The RPC procedure.*

To call the `ChangeCase` procedure, you need to use the following `call` statement:

```
<x:ChangeCase xmlns:x="http://www.someURL.com/">
     <str xsi:type="xsd:string">SOAP</str>
</x:ChangeCase>
```

The preceding code calls the `ChangeCase` procedure and passes a `string` type parameter to the method `call` statement.

NOTE

The preceding code uses a namespace that is represented by the hypothetical URL http://www.someURL.com.

The `result` *Statement*

The `result` statement includes the processed result of the `call` statement. Similar to the `call` statement, the `result` statement also includes a struct and the value that the procedure returns. However, unlike the struct in the procedure `call` statement, the struct in the `result` statement can be assigned any name.

TIP

As a convention, the name of the struct in the `result` statement is followed by the word Response. For example, the struct in the `result` statement for the `ChangeCase` procedure can be called `ChangeCaseResponse`.

The following code shows the response to the `call` statement for the `ChangeCase` procedure:

```
<x:ChangeCaseResponse xmlns:x="http://www.someURL.com/">
     <x:str1 xsi:type="xsd:string">soap</x:str1>
</x:ChangeCase>
```

The preceding code sends a response to the `call` statement after processing the request. The `string` type value, `soap`, that the `ChangeCase` procedure returns is an output parameter and is defined by the same name: `str1`.

The SOAP Encoding Rules

When you create a SOAP message, you need to adhere to a set of rules to encode the SOAP message. This set of rules is defined in the SOAP specification and is called *SOAP encoding*. The SOAP encoding rules are similar to XML schemas and define the types and constructs that you can use to create the SOAP message. These rules are present in the encoding namespace. The URL of the encoding namespace refers to the XML schema that defines the encoding rules for a SOAP message. The URL of the encoding namespace is http://schemas.xmlsoap.org/soap/encoding/.

Types of Data Types

The encoding rules specify the types that you can include in a SOAP message. These data types can be either simple or compound. The following section discusses the simple and compound data types.

The Simple Data Type

The data types that are specified in the XML Schema Specification are called *simple types*. Therefore, a simple type either is defined in the XML Schema Specification or derived from the data type that is defined in the XML Schema Specification. The simple data types that you can use in a SOAP message are integer, float, negativeInteger, string, date, and so on. These built-in data types are defined in the namespace XMLSchema, which is present at http://www.w3.org/1999/XMLSchema.

The Compound Data Type

Compound data types are created using one or more simple data types. Compound data types contain child elements that define the elements or the fields of the data type. SOAP encoding supports two types of compound data types: structs and arrays. The following list discusses these data types in detail:

◆ **Struct.** A struct is a collection of variables with the same or different data types. However, the name of the variables that are defined in a struct cannot be the same. Consider the following example of a construct, Student.

```
struct Student
{
    string ID;
    string FirstName;
    string LastName;
    string Address;
    int Age;
};
```

To invoke this struct, you need to create an instance as shown:

```
Student std = {"S001", "Daniel", "Smith", "10932 Bigge Rd.", 15};
```

Now you can serialize the struct `Student` by using the SOAP encoding rules, as shown in the following code:

```
<std xsi:type="n:Student">
    <ID xsi:type="xsd:string">S001</ID>
    <FirstName xsi:type="xsd:string">Daniel</FirstName>
    <LastName xsi:type="xsd:string">Smith</LastName>
    <Address xsi:type="xsd:string">10932 Bigge Rd.</Address>
    <Age xsi:type="xsd:integer">15</Age>
</std>
```

In the preceding code, a struct called `Student` is declared. In addition, a namespace, n, is declared with a `Student` data type. The n namespace points to the schema that defines the `Student` struct.

◆ **Array.** An array is a compound data type that contains values with the same data type. These values are referred to by their index value. To declare a data type of the `type` array, you need to use the `xsi:type` attribute. The value of this attribute is `SOAP-ENC:Array`. Consider the following example of an array, `scores`:

```
<scores xsi:type="SOAP-ENC:Array" SOAP-ENC:arrayType="xsd:integer[5]">
    <item>96</item>
    <item>92</item>
    <item>87</item>
    <item>56</item>
    <item>70</item>
</scores>
```

The preceding code creates an array called `scores`. The data type of the array is `integer`, which is specified by the `arrayType` attribute. The values are assigned to the `scores` array by using the `item` attribute.

Having looked at the types of data types, you will now learn about the rules for encoding data types in a SOAP message.

Rules for Serializing Data Types

The rules for serializing data types are discussed in the following list:

◆ You can define values in a SOAP message by using elements.

◆ You can define simple values as character data without subelements.

◆ You can define compound values as a sequence of elements.

◆ You can define arrays as single-reference or multi-reference values.

◆ You can declare arrays as compound values by using the `SOAP-ENC:Array` attribute.

◆ You can define the data type of an array by using the `SOAP-ENC:arrayType` attribute.

◆ You can define `string` and `byte` arrays as multi-reference simple types.

◆ You can encode several references to a value. However, you should not alter the meaning of the XML instance.

Until now, we have discussed the architecture of SOAP. Now we will discuss the processing of SOAP messages.

Processing of SOAP Messages

SOAP is used to transfer data across applications on the network. These applications are called *SOAP nodes*. A SOAP message is sent from an application, called the *sender application* in the form of a SOAP request, to a receiving application called the *receiver application*. The data is then processed, and the receiver application returns the response to the sender application. The response is also in the form of a SOAP message. The SOAP Message Exchange Model defines the mechanism in which the messages are transferred using SOAP.

The SOAP Message Exchange Model

The SOAP Message Exchange Model defines the manner in which a SOAP message is transferred from a sender node to a receiver node. When a sender node sends a SOAP request, the request might need to pass through one or more intermediate applications called the *intermediate nodes*. The path that a SOAP message follows to reach the final node is called the *message path*. Therefore, when a SOAP message reaches a node that is following the message path, the receiver application processes the SOAP request. The procedure for processing the SOAP request is described in the following list:

1. The receiver node first identifies the components of a SOAP message. These components include envelope, header, and body. You have learned about the components of a SOAP message in the preceding sections.

2. After identifying the SOAP components, the receiver application verifies that all components of the SOAP message are supported by the application and then processes the request if the components are verified. However, if the components are not verified, the receiving application discards the request.

3. If the receiving application is an intermediate application and not the final application (called the *ultimate SOAP receiver*), the optional components are removed and the final SOAP message is forwarded to the next application, as defined in the message path.

As you can see, an application can act as a sending node, an intermediate node, or a receiver node. The role of the application is specified in the SOAP `Header` element. The processing of a SOAP message is explained in Figure 3-7.

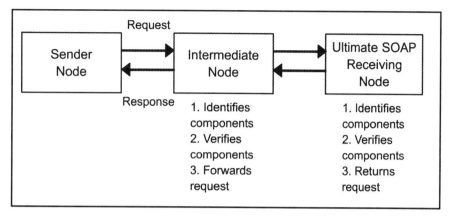

FIGURE 3-7 *SOAP Message Exchange Model.*

Summary

In this chapter, you learned about the basics of SOAP, which is a protocol that applications use to communicate in a distributed environment. Next, you learned about the advantages and disadvantages of SOAP.

In addition, you learned about the architecture of SOAP. The internal architecture of a SOAP package is divided into three components: the SOAP message, the SOAP RPC, and the SOAP encoding rules. A SOAP message is divided into an `Envelope`, a `Header`, and a `Body` element.

Next, you learned about RPC convention and the SOAP encoding rules. RPC convention is a set of rules that you can use to serialize the procedure calls in the form of a SOAP message. The SOAP encoding rules are defined in the SOAP specification. You need to adhere to these rules while you create a SOAP message. The encoding rules also define the data types that you can include in the SOAP message. These data types can be simple or compound. Finally, you learned about the SOAP Message Exchange Model.

Chapter 4

You learned about Web services in Chapter 2, "Basics of Web Services." A Web service is a reusable piece of code. Consider a scenario in which your company needs to develop an application that allows a customer to post queries on your company's products through e-mail. Whenever a new client query is received, the query is then allocated to a particular customer support executive. Then an SMS is sent to the mobile phone of the allocated executive.

Consider that the application is ready except for the SMS feature. Providing support for the SMS feature involves a lot of programming effort because the developers need to understand and bind telephone technology with computer protocols. Because a Web service is available that offers the SMS service, the best solution is to make use of that service in the application. However, before using the Web service, you must locate it. You use the Universal Description, Discovery, and Integration (UDDI) directory to search for such a Web service. The search can be based on various parameters, such as the business type, service type, and keywords.

On the other hand, the company that created the SMS Web service needs to let customers know about its Web service. To do this, the company has to register the Web service with a UDDI registry. Therefore, both the providers and the consumers of Web services find the UDDI registry a convenient tool to use.

Chapter 2 introduced you to UDDI. This chapter provides more detail about UDDI. It teaches you about how UDDI works and what its specifications are. Next, it introduces the UDDI data model. Finally, it presents some of the common scenarios in which you use the UDDI directory.

Defining UDDI

UDDI, initiated by Ariba, IBM, and Microsoft, is an industry standard for registering, publishing, and discovering Web services in a central registry called the *UDDI directory*. Since the time that the UDDI initiative started, UDDI has grown to more than 300 organizations that work in coordination to develop the UDDI specifications. UDDI is an attempt to encourage interoperability and adoption of Web services.

A UDDI directory is a platform-independent framework that allows you to publish information about a Web service. This information includes the description of the Web service, Web methods that are included in the Web service, the procedure that a client application needs to follow to communicate with the Web service, and a programmer's interface that allows users to interact with the UDDI directory.

For example, perhaps you want to create a B2B solution for an online departmental store. This involves creating the components, such as a database and an interface, in the form of Web pages that are used to interact with users. In addition, you need to provide the users with a catalog of goods sold at the departmental store. The catalog picks up the data from the database.

The Web site also includes a user authentication page that validates the username and the password. The information is validated based on the user's data in the database. When a user places an order for an item on the Web site, the credit card details need to be validated. This common scenario is applicable to almost all Web sites.

As you know, using Web services allows service providers to expose functionality on the Web that application developers can use on any platform. However, when you need functionality, you must search for a service provider. Searching for Web services in the UDDI directory is similar to searching for information in any search engine, such as Google or Yahoo. You simply need to perform a search based on keywords, and the matching results are returned to you.

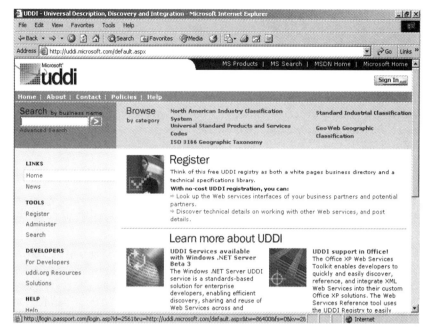

FIGURE 4-1 *Home page of http://uddi.microsoft.com.*

The information in the UDDI directory is exposed to the users through a Web site. This Web site consists of a group of Web-based registries called the *UDDI business registries*. Several operator sites execute and manage the UDDI business registries. Anyone who needs to access the information about Web services or other business entities can log on to these registries. In addition, you can make information about your Web service available to other users in the UDDI business registries. An example of such a Web-based registry is http://uddi.microsoft.com. It is an official UDDI Web site by Microsoft that allows you to search for business entities based on several search criteria. These search criteria includes business name, business location, business identifiers, discovery URLs, and so on. Figure 4-1 shows the home page of http://uddi.microsoft.com.

 NOTE

The http://uddi.microsoft.com Web site provides the basic services, such as accessing and providing information about business entities, free of cost.

Working with the UDDI Business Directories

Working with a UDDI business directory involves registering the Web service with the directory. After a Web service is registered, any user can use it. However, you first need to find the required Web service in the UDDI directory. The following sections discuss the procedure for registering and finding information in the UDDI directory.

Registering a Web Service with the UDDI Business Directories

To register a Web service with a UDDI business directory, you need to perform the following steps:

1. The business organizations or the developers who create Web services provide a description of various Web services they support. This information is in the form of Technical Models, commonly called *tModels*, of the Web service. We will discuss tModels in detail in the later section titled "The UDDI Data Structures Document."

2. UDDI assigns a unique identification number to each tModel that is registered in the UDDI business directory. This identification number is called *Unique Universal Identifier* (UUID), and it is stored in the registry. UUID is then used to find information about a Web service in the UDDI directory.

Finding Information in the UDDI Business Directories

As discussed earlier, the UDDI business directories allow you to search for information about Web services. We will now discuss the procedure for finding information about a Web service in the UDDI business directories:

1. Find simple information, such as the name and contact numbers of the organization that hosts the Web service. In addition, you can find the business identification number of the organization. This information will help you query about Web services based on the business organization that hosts them. You can find this information in the White Pages of the UDDI directory.

2. Retrieve data about the classification of Web services. Web services are classified based on the type of the business organization that hosts the Web service. For example, you can find a Web service for the software export business or the garments export business. To do this, you need to find the information about the industry codes of the organization and the Web services that the organization provides. You can find this information in the Yellow Pages of the UDDI directory.

3. Register the Web service.

4. Find information about the features and working of the Web service. The features of a Web service include the Web methods that the Web service exposes and the working of the Web service. The information about how the Web service works is provided in the form of tModels.

To register or find information in the UDDI business registry, you need to interact with the registry. The UDDI Software Development Kit (SDK) allows your applications to interact with the UDDI registries.

The UDDI SDK

As discussed earlier, the UDDI SDK allows you to develop applications that can interact with the UDDI registries. You can use the UDDI SDK tools to develop programs that can interact with the registry. To use the UDDI SDK, it is not essential for you to have basic knowledge of the technologies, such as XML, SOAP, or UDDI. You can use the SDK to add registration features of a Web service to development tools, installation programs, or any other software that needs to locate and bind to the remote Web services. An example of such an SDK is Microsoft.UDDI.SDK.

To interact with the UDDI registries, the UDDI SDK provides you with three basic components. These components are discussed in the following list:

◆ **UDDI document object.** This creates a request, which is then sent to the UDDI request manager.

◆ **UDDI request manager.** This processes the request that it receives. This processed request is then sent to the UDDI business registry.

◆ **UDDI business registry.** This is located on a remote server and receives a request in the form of a SOAP message that is sent using HTTP. This SOAP message is called the *SOAP RPC request object*. The UDDI business registry then locates a Web service based on the request that it receives. The result of the request is then sent back to the UDDI request manager. The result is also in the form of a SOAP message, called the *SOAP RPC response object*. Finally, the result is forwarded to the UDDI document object.

The working of the UDDI registries is shown in Figure 4-2.

UDDI Specifications

To implement the UDDI initiative, UDDI specifications are developed. UDDI specifications consist of a set of XSD documents. You learned about XSD in Chapter 2.

XSD documents in the UDDI specifications define the format of the data in the UDDI specifications. Since its evolution, several versions of the UDDI specifications have been issued, with version 2.0 being the latest. These versions of the UDDI specifications are available as freely downloadable files on the official UDDI Web site (http://www.uddi.org). Figure 4-3 shows the home page of the http://www.uddi.org site.

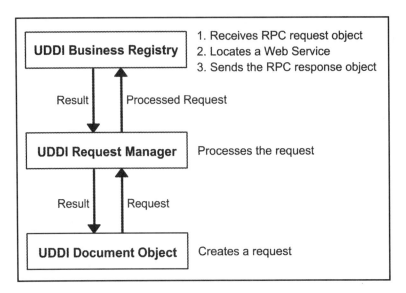

FIGURE 4-2 *Working of the UDDI registries.*

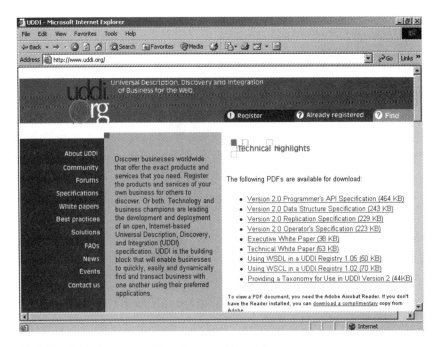

FIGURE 4-3 *Home page of http://www.uddi.org site.*

As you can see in Figure 4-3, the UDDI specifications include several documents, such as these:

◆ UDDI replication

◆ UDDI operators

◆ UDDI programmer's APIs

◆ UDDI data structures

We will discuss these documents in detail.

The UDDI Replication Document

When UDDI data is transferred across a network, the data is replicated from one operator site to another. The process of replication of data is defined in the UDDI replication document. In addition, to allow replication of data, the UDDI registry must adhere to the interfaces as specified in the UDDI replication document.

To understand the data that is stored in the UDDI replication document, you first need to understand the replication process. Consider a situation in which a business organization exposes a Web service. The information about this Web service will then be available in the UDDI directory. Several operator sites, called *nodes*, manage this directory. Therefore, if the organization makes some changes to the Web service, these changes need to be reflected in the UDDI directory. In addition, the changes need to be replicated across all operator sites.

Now, consider that the changes need to be replicated from operator node A to operator node B. In this case, operator node A specifies a unique number to the changes made to the UDDI data. This unique number is called *Update Sequence Number* (USN), and the operator site maintains it in a register called the *USN register*.

In addition, operator node A creates a record specifying the changes made to the UDDI data. This record is called a *change record*. This record contains information such as the UUID of operator node A, the USN of the changes made at node A, and the semantics of the changes.

After creating the change record, the operator node A transfers the change record to operator node B. When node B receives the change record, it assigns a local USN to the change record. Node B then replicates changes that are specified in the change record based on the ascending order of the local USN. The next time that node B receives a change record from node A, the change record will be assigned a USN number greater than the previously assigned USN. This process of replication is explained in Figure 4-4.

The UDDI Operators Document

To implement a Web service, you need to register it. The UDDI node operators provide the information about registering a Web service. The behavioral and operational information about these node operators is available in the UDDI operators document. The following list discusses the operations that an operator node performs:

◆ **Storing information.** An operator node allows a business organization or a user who registers a Web service with the UDDI registry to update or delete the UDDI data.

When you store information about a Web service in the UDDI registry, the operator node assigns and maintains an e-mail address of the business organization that hosts the Web service. The operator node also secures this e-mail address so that the address is not accessible outside the operator node.

◆ **Maintaining the integrity of data.** The information about a Web service is stored at multiple locations in the registry. Therefore, when you make changes to this information, the operator nodes must replicate the changes to all locations to maintain the integrity of data.

◆ **Making backups of the UDDI data.** The main function of an operator node is to make backups of the data that is stored in the UDDI registry.

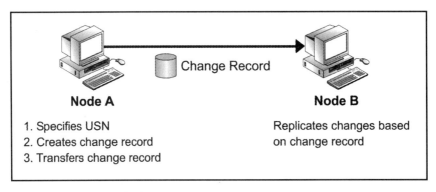

Node A

1. Specifies USN
2. Creates change record
3. Transfers change record

Node B

Replicates changes based on change record

FIGURE 4-4 *The replication process.*

The UDDI Programmer's API Document

As discussed earlier, you can register a Web service or find information about a Web service in a UDDI directory. The UDDI programmer's API document specifies the functions that UDDI supports to allow you to publish or find information about a Web service. These functions are categorized as inquiry API functions and publish API functions. The following list discusses these functions in detail:

◆ **Inquiry API functions.** These include the messages that inquire about operator nodes. These messages are synchronous in nature and are exposed using HTTP-POST statements.

◆ **Publish API functions.** These include messages that are used to publish or update information in a UDDI directory. These messages are also synchronous in nature and are posted using HTTP-POST statements.

In addition to providing the inquiry and publish API functions, the UDDI programmer's API document forms the programming interface of a UDDI registry by specifying a set of SOAP messages. The UDDI registry receives and responds to a request in the form of SOAP messages.

NOTE

The UDDI programmer's API document contains nearly 40 inquiry and publish API functions.

The UDDI Data Structures Document

The SOAP messages that are defined in the UDDI programmer's API consist of XML structures. The UDDI data structures document contains information about these XML structures. Based on the type of information, these data structures are divided into five types. You will learn about the data structures later in this section.

The data structures, defined in the UDDI data structures document, consist of the UDDI data model, which in turn consists of five data structures. These data structures contain elements called *data fields*. The data fields provide information about the Web service that is registered with the UDDI registry. Each data structure in the UDDI data model is assigned a UUID.

In this section, we will discuss the type of information that is stored in the data structures.

The businessEntity Data Structure

The businessEntity data structure contains information about the business organization that publishes a Web service with the UDDI registry. This information includes the UUID, name, address, and other contact numbers of the business organization. In addition, the businessEntity data structure might contain the business descriptions and references to the businessService data structure. The businessEntity data structure allows a business organization to establish a business relationship with partner organizations.

For example, two organizations whose details are present in the businessEntity data structure can establish a partnership. The details of this partnership are maintained in the businessEntity data structure as well.

When a business organization exposes a service with the UDDI registry, the operator node assigns a discovery URL to the business organization. This discovery URL is unique for operator sites, and it enables users to access the content that is stored in the businessEntity data structure.

The businessService Data Structure

A businessEntity data structure contains references to one or more businessService data structures. These data structures store the UUID of the businessEntity structure that contains a reference to these structures. In addition, the businessService data structure contains descriptive information about the services that the business organization provides. Each businessService is assigned a unique serviceKey, which is a UUID number. The businessService data structure might also contain a reference to the bindingTemplate data structures. You will learn about the bindingTemplate data structures in the following section.

A businessService data structure is a reusable component. This implies that one businessService data structure can be used by one or more businessEntity data structures. For example, a business organization can develop a Web service to expose the inventory database. The information about this Web service is contained in the businessService data structure. Now, several divisions of the organization, such as production, sales, and marketing, can use this data structure.

The tModel Data Structure

Consider a situation in which an organization needs to share its sales data with its customers. To allow sharing or exchanging of data between two organizations, the organizations need to agree on the design goals and the technical specifications. The tModel data structure contains descriptive information about these specifications. You can use the tModel data structure to retrieve information about the technical concepts and the interfaces that the design of the service uses. However, the tModel data structure does not contain these specifications directly. Instead, the data structure contains pointers or references to URLs of the specifications.

The tModel data structure provides you with the information about how you can interact with a Web service. For example, a business organization plans to develop a service that allows its customers or partner organizations to place online orders for their goods. The technical specifications and the information about the manner in which the customers can use the service are available in the tModel data structure. Each tModel data structure is assigned a unique key, called the *tModelKey*, which is a UUID number.

The bindingTemplate Data Structure

After a tModel data structure is created, you need to associate it with the service. The mechanism for associating a tModel with the service is defined in the bindingTemplate data structure. To define the mechanism, the bindingTemplate data structure contains pointers to the technical descriptions and not the service itself. In addition, the bindingTemplate data structure includes a text description of the Web service, its URL, and references to the tModel data structures.

The unique key that is assigned to the bindingTemplate data structure is called *bindingKey*. This key is contained in the bindingTemplate data structure in addition to the serviceKey of the service.

The publisherAssertion Data Structure

The publisherAssertion data structure contains information about the relationships between two businessEntity data structures. However, to make this information public, the business organizations need to assert the information. This assertion is included in different publisherAssertion data structures, one for each businessEntity data structure.

Figure 4-5 shows the UDDI data model.

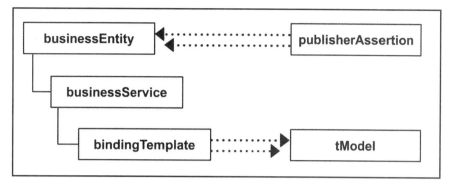

FIGURE 4-5 *The UDDI data model.*

Having looked at UDDI in detail, you will now look at the scenarios in which you can use the UDDI registry.

UDDI Scenarios

UDDI is used extensively in various business scenarios. These scenarios are divided into two categories: finding information about the registered services and maintaining and updating the UDDI data. The following list discusses some of these scenarios in detail:

◆ **Publish Web service.** When you plan to publish a Web service with the UDDI directory, you first need to select an operator site that will manage the information about the Web service. After selecting the operator site, you need to sign up on the registry Web site. When you sign up on the Web site, a username and password are assigned to you. These form your publishing credentials. You can use these publishing credentials to log on to the publishing server.

◆ **Register organizations.** Before registering a Web service with the UDDI, you need to register your business organization by providing the general details of the organization, such as the name, description, and contact information.

◆ **Register software that uses Web service.** In addition to providing information about a Web service, you might want to provide technical information about the service, such as installing and configuring information. You can provide this information in the UDDI directory.

◆ **Inquiry Web services.** You can inquire for existing or potential Web services on the UDDI registry.

◆ **Locate partner services.** You can find existing services for simple operations, such as mathematic calculations or user validations. Several business organizations expose such common services. Therefore, you can find an appropriate service in the UDDI directory and then, invoke the service.

Summary

In this chapter, you learned about UDDI, which is an industry standard for registering, publishing, and discovering Web services in a central registry called the UDDI directory. A UDDI directory is a platform-independent framework that allows you to publish information about a Web service. Next, you learned about how to work with the UDDI business directories. Working with a UDDI business directory involves registering the Web service with the directory.

Next, you learned about the UDDI specifications that are developed to implement the UDDI initiative. The UDDI specifications consist of a set of XSD documents that define the format of the data in the UDDI specifications. Finally, you learned about the common business scenarios where you can use UDDI.

Chapter 5

A Web service allows users to reuse the functionality that a vendor provides. To enable users to use a Web service, you need to expose the service in the UDDI directory. You learned about UDDI in Chapter 4, "Introduction to UDDI."

After exposing a Web service, you need to provide the user with the information about the Web service. This information includes the location of the Web service, the Web methods that the Web service exposes, and so on. In addition, you need to provide this information in a standard format so that users can easily interpret and understand them. As a result, a standard language was developed to describe a Web service. This standard description language is called *Web Services Description Language* (WSDL).

This chapter introduces you to WSDL. You will look at a sample WSDL document and use it to learn about the components of a WSDL document.

Overview of WSDL

Consider a scenario in which you need to use a Web service that performs complicated scientific calculations. You can search for this type of Web service in the UDDI directory. The directory provides you with a list of Web services that matches your search criteria. You can then register for the Web service that contains several Web methods to perform scientific calculations. However, to use the Web methods, you need to have information about them, such as the description of the Web methods, the parameters that are passed to the Web methods, and so on. You also need to know the manner in which you can interact with the Web service. This information is provided in an XML format in a document called the *WSDL document.*

As stated earlier, the language that describes the Web service in a WSDL document is called *WSDL*. WSDL, a specification that the W3C developed, aims to provide a standard that can describe services. WSDL is based on XML; therefore, it provides an easy and a simple way to describe services in a text format. WSDL uses XML messages to allow structured communication between a set of endpoints. For example, an XML message can transfer between the client application and the service provider application. In this case, the client application and the service provider application are called *endpoints.*

The XML messages contain either procedure-oriented information or document-oriented information, which is bound to a network protocol, such as SOAP, and transferred between the endpoints. WSDL can also be extended to provide information about the endpoints and the XML messages that are exchanged between them.

WSDL provides an interface for a Web service. Therefore, when you create a Web service, you need to create a corresponding WSDL file. A WSDL file has an extension of .wsdl.

We will now create a sample WSDL document for a credit card validation Web service. You can use this document as an interface for consuming the Web service.

A Sample WSDL Document

As discussed earlier, a WSDL document contains the description of a Web service, the Web methods, the way in which a client application can interact with the Web service, and so on. In addition, a client application can use WSDL to frame a request for the Web service. This information is contained in various components of a WSDL document. These components are mentioned in the following list:

- ◆ Definitions
- ◆ Types
- ◆ Messages
- ◆ Operations
- ◆ Port Types
- ◆ Bindings
- ◆ Ports
- ◆ Services

So that you can understand the preceding components, we will create a sample WSDL document for a Web service that validates the credit card details of a customer. When you create a Web service by using Visual Studio .NET, the description of the Web service is created automatically. The description of the Web service has the same name as that of the Web service: CCValidate.wsdl.

 NOTE

In this chapter, we have created a WSDL document in Visual Studio .NET. However, you can create a WSDL document in other ways as well. You will learn about the ways to create a WSDL document in the next projects of this book.

When you open the CCValidate.wsdl document, the file contains the following code:

```
<?xml version="1.0" encoding="utf-8"?>
<definitions xmlns:http="http://schemas.xmlsoap.org/wsdl/http/"
xmlns:soap="http://schemas.xmlsoap.org/wsdl/soap/"
xmlns:s="http://www.w3.org/2001/XMLSchema"
xmlns:s0="http://cardvalidationservices.org/"
xmlns:soapenc="http://schemas.xmlsoap.org/soap/encoding/"
xmlns:tm="http://microsoft.com/wsdl/mime/textMatching/"
xmlns:mime="http://schemas.xmlsoap.org/wsdl/mime/"
targetNamespace="http://cardvalidationservices.org/"
xmlns="http://schemas.xmlsoap.org/wsdl/">
  <types>
    <s:schema elementFormDefault="qualified"
targetNamespace="http://cardvalidationservices.org/">
      <s:element name="validateCC">
        <s:complexType>
          <s:sequence>
            <s:element minOccurs="0" maxOccurs="1" name="CardType"
type="s:string" />
            <s:element minOccurs="0" maxOccurs="1" name="CardNumber"
type="s:string" />
          </s:sequence>
        </s:complexType>
      </s:element>
      <s:element name="validateCCResponse">
        <s:complexType>
```

```
            <s:sequence>
            <s:element minOccurs="1" maxOccurs="1" name="validateCCResult"
   type="s:boolean" />
            </s:sequence>
          </s:complexType>
        </s:element>
        <s:element name="boolean" type="s:boolean" />
      </s:schema>
    </types>
    <message name="validateCCSoapIn">
      <part name="parameters" element="s0:validateCC" />
    </message>
    <message name="validateCCSoapOut">
      <part name="parameters" element="s0:validateCCResponse" />
    </message>
    <message name="validateCCHttpGetIn">
      <part name="CardType" type="s:string" />
      <part name="CardNumber" type="s:string" />
    </message>
    <message name="validateCCHttpGetOut">
      <part name="Body" element="s0:boolean" />
    </message>
    <message name="validateCCHttpPostIn">
      <part name="CardType" type="s:string" />
      <part name="CardNumber" type="s:string" />
    </message>
    <message name="validateCCHttpPostOut">
      <part name="Body" element="s0:boolean" />
    </message>
    <portType name="CCValidatorSoap">
      <operation name="validateCC">
        <input message="s0:validateCCSoapIn" />
        <output message="s0:validateCCSoapOut" />
      </operation>
    </portType>
    <portType name="CCValidatorHttpGet">
      <operation name="validateCC">
        <input message="s0:validateCCHttpGetIn" />
```

```
        <output message="s0:validateCCHttpGetOut" />
      </operation>
  </portType>
  <portType name="CCValidatorHttpPost">
    <operation name="validateCC">
      <input message="s0:validateCCHttpPostIn" />
      <output message="s0:validateCCHttpPostOut" />
    </operation>
  </portType>
  <binding name="CCValidatorSoap" type="s0:CCValidatorSoap">
    <soap:binding transport="http://schemas.xmlsoap.org/soap/http"
style="document" />
    <operation name="validateCC">
    <soap:operation
soapAction="http://cardvalidationservices.org/validateCC" style="document"
/>
      <input>
        <soap:body use="literal" />
      </input>
      <output>
        <soap:body use="literal" />
      </output>
    </operation>
  </binding>
  <binding name="CCValidatorHttpGet" type="s0:CCValidatorHttpGet">
    <http:binding verb="GET" />
    <operation name="validateCC">
      <http:operation location="/validateCC" />
      <input>
        <http:urlEncoded />
      </input>
      <output>
        <mime:mimeXml part="Body" />
      </output>
    </operation>
  </binding>
  <binding name="CCValidatorHttpPost" type="s0:CCValidatorHttpPost">
    <http:binding verb="POST" />
```

```
    <operation name="validateCC">
      <http:operation location="/validateCC" />
      <input>
        <mime:content type="application/x-www-form-urlencoded" />
      </input>
      <output>
        <mime:mimeXml part="Body" />
      </output>
    </operation>
  </binding>
  <service name="CCValidator">
    <port name="CCValidatorSoap" binding="s0:CCValidatorSoap">
      <soap:address
location="http://cardvalidationservices/CCValidate/CCValidate.asmx" />
    </port>
    <port name="CCValidatorHttpGet" binding="s0:CCValidatorHttpGet">
      <http:address
location="http://cardvalidationservices/CCValidate/CCValidate.asmx" />
    </port>
    <port name="CCValidatorHttpPost" binding="s0:CCValidatorHttpPost">
      <http:address
location-"http://cardvalidationservices/CCValidate/CCValidate.asmx" />
    </port>
  </service>
</definitions>
```

Now we will discuss the components of a WSDL file with reference to the preceding code.

The definitions Element

Because WSDL is an XML document, it begins with the definition for the XML version that is used in the document. In addition, you need to include the definitions for all namespaces in the document. To include the definitions for the namespaces, you use the definitions element. The definitions element is the root element for all elements in the WSDL document. The syntax for the definitions element is shown in the following code snippet:

```
<?xml version="1.0" encoding="utf-8"?>
<definitions xmlns:http=http://schemas.xmlsoap.org/wsdl/http/
xmlns:soap=http://schemas.xmlsoap.org/wsdl/soap/
xmlns:s="http://www.w3.org/2001/XMLSchema"
```

```
xmlns:s0=http://cardvalidationservices.org/

xmlns:soapenc=http://schemas.xmlsoap.org/soap/encoding/

xmlns:tm=http://microsoft.com/wsdl/mime/textMatching/

xmlns:mime=http://schemas.xmlsoap.org/wsdl/mime/

targetNamespace=http://cardvalidationservices.org/

xmlns="http://schemas.xmlsoap.org/wsdl/">
```

The previous code includes the definitions element that contains the declarations for including the namespaces in the WSDL document. You can provide a name to the definitions by using the name attribute of the definitions element. For example, you can name the definitions in the previous code as CreditCard by adding the following code:

```
<definitions name="CreditCard"--------

</definitions>
```

Next, the URLs of the namespaces that you need to include in the WSDL document are added using the xmlns keyword. You can also provide a prefix to the namespace, as shown:

```
xmlns:soap=http://schemas.xmlsoap.org/wsdl/soap/
```

In the preceding code, soap is the prefix that is assigned to the http://schemas.xmlsoap.org/wsdl/soap/ namespace.

In addition to adding namespaces to the WSDL document, you can specify a target namespace by using the targetNamespace element. A target namespace uniquely identifies a WSDL document. Therefore, the same target namespace cannot be present in any other WSDL document. In addition, you can specify only one target namespace for a WSDL document. The targetNamespace element takes the name of the Web service as its value. In this case, the URL http://cardvalidationservices.org represents the target namespace.

The types *Element*

After including the namespaces in the WSDL document, you need to include schemas or references to schemas. You can do this by using the types element. The syntax for the types element is as shown:

```
<definitions -------- >

    <types>

        --------

    </types>

</definitions>
```

As you can see in the preceding syntax, the types element is included within the definitions element of the WSDL document.

A WSDL document contains abstract data type definitions that are required for exchanging messages between endpoints. These data type definitions are included in the **types** element.

 NOTE

The abstract data type definitions that you define in the **types** element can be included in multiple WSDL documents.

To include the data type definitions, WSDL uses XSD because XSD is used extensively as a data type definition mechanism for SOAP. In addition, XSD supports a large set of data types, which you can include in the WSDL document. You learned about the data types that XSD supports in Chapter 2, "Basics of Web Services."

The **types** element is optional. In addition, you can include only one **types** element in a WSDL document. However, the **types** element can, in turn, contain several schemas, as shown in the following code:

```
<types>
    <s:schema elementFormDefault="qualified"
targetNamespace="http://cardvalidationservices.org/">
        <s:element name="validateCC">
          <s:complexType>
            <s:sequence>
              <s:element minOccurs="0" maxOccurs="1" name="CardType" type="s:string" />
              <s:element minOccurs="0" maxOccurs="1" name="CardNumber" type="s:string" />
            </s:sequence>
          </s:complexType>
        </s:element>
        <s:element name="validateCCResponse">
          <s:complexType>
            <s:sequence>
            <s:element minOccurs="1" maxOccurs="1" name="validateCCResult" type="s:boolean" />
            </s:sequence>
          </s:complexType>
        </s:element>
        <s:element name="boolean" type="s:boolean" />
      </s:schema>
    </types>
```

THE EXTENSIBILITY ELEMENT

WSDL supports the XSD grammar for defining the type systems. However, if required, you can include other type systems in the WSDL document by using the extensibility element. The extensibility element allows you to extend the range of type systems that you can include in a WSDL document. The extensibility element is a container element that specifies the type definitions to be included. The extensibility element is contained within the types element. The syntax for the extensibility element is as shown:

```
<definitions ---------- >
  <types>
     <-- type-system extensibility element -->
  </types>
</definitions>
```

The preceding code contains definitions for abstract data types that can be serialized as a network protocol. For example, the data types that map to the messages can be serialized in the form of a SOAP message or an HTTP request.

Now we will discuss the statements in the preceding code. The preceding code uses the schema element that contains the targetNamespace attribute to specify the target namespace for the WSDL document.

Next, the code uses element to declare an element with a name validateCC. When you define an element, you need to specify its data type. The validateCC element is a complex data type. You can specify an element as a complex data type by using the complexType element.

The sequence element defines the sequence of the child elements that are declared as complex data types. In this case, two string type child elements with the names CardType and CardNumber are declared. These elements represent the input values that the user needs to provide to validate the credit details.

As you can see, the child element takes two attributes, minOccurs and maxOccurs. The minOccurs attribute specifies the minimum number of times that the element can appear in the containing element validateCC. To make this element optional, you can specify a value of 0. Similarly, the maxOccurs attribute specifies the maximum number of times that the element can appear in the containing element validateCC. Because the CardType and CardNumber elements can accept only one value, the maxOccurs attribute is set to 1.

Next, the code includes another complex type element with the name validateCCResponse. This element contains a Boolean type child element with the name validateCCResult. This element represents the value that the Web service returns and can be present only once in the containing element.

In addition to the validateCC and validateCCResponse elements, the types element declares a Boolean type element with the name boolean.

The message *Element*

As you know, the information is exchanged in the form of messages between two endpoints. Therefore, after declaring the data types of the messages in the types element, you need to define the structure of the message. Messages are defined using the message element. The syntax of the message element is as follows:

```
<definitions ---------- >
    <message>
        ----------
    </message>
</definitions>
```

Messages represent an abstract definition of the data that you need to transfer between two endpoints. In addition, the message element defines the structure of the messages. To do this, the message element consists of a number of parts. Parts are logical units containing information that you need to communicate, and they are associated with the type systems that you define in the types element. In addition to associating a part with the type system that is defined in the types element, you can associate a part with the type system that is defined in other XML schema files or XML data types schema. To associate a part with a type system, you use the message-typing attribute.

You can use the part element to define a part in a message. A message that contains a part element is shown here:

```
<message name="validateCCSoapIn">
    <part name="parameters" element="s0:validateCC" />
  </message>
  <message name="validateCCSoapOut">
    <part name="parameters" element="s0:validateCCResponse" />
</message>
<message name="validateCCHttpGetIn">
    <part name="CardType" type="s:string" />
    <part name="CardNumber" type="s:string" />
</message>
<message name="validateCCHttpGetOut">
    <part name="Body" element="s0:boolean" />
  </message>
<message name="validateCCHttpPostIn">
    <part name="CardType" type="s:string" />
    <part name="CardNumber" type="s:string" />
</message>
<message name="validateCCHttpPostOut">
```

```
        <part name="Body" element="s0:boolean" />
</message>
```

The preceding code uses the `message` element to define the message `validateCCSoapIn`. The WSDL document contains a message definition for the messages that are transferred using SOAP, HTTP GET, and HTTP POST. In addition, each `In` message that is defined for a protocol has a corresponding `Out` message. Therefore, the previous code contains six message declaration statements—two for each protocol.

The `validateCCSoapIn` message contains a part called `parameters`. The `validateCC` element that is defined in the `types` element is passed as a parameter to the `parameters` part. The `parameters` part is associated with the complex type that is defined in the `types` element.

The `validateCCSoapIn` message has a corresponding `validateCCSoapOut` message that contains the `parameters` part. The `validateCCResponse` element that represents the value that is returned by the Web service is passed as a parameter to the `validateCCSoapOut` message.

> **NOTE**
>
> As you can see, the part declaration statement contains the prefix s0, which indicates that the WSDL document is created using Visual Studio .NET.

Similarly, the `validateCCHttpGetIn` and `validateCCHttpGetOut` messages are defined for the HTTP GET protocol. The `validateCCHttpGetIn` message contains two `string` type parts: `CardType` and `CardNumber`. In addition, the `validateCCHttpGetOut` message contains a `Boolean` type part, `Body`, which represents the value that the Web service returns.

Similarly, Visual Studio .NET creates a code for the HTTP POST protocol, as shown in the preceding code.

The `operation` *Element*

As you already know, a Web service contains Web methods that you can use to perform a specific operation. A client application can request these operations and then execute them. Therefore, after you define messages, you need to associate them with the corresponding operation. To do this, you use the `operation` element, which, in turn, is included in the `portType` element. You will learn about the `portType` element in the later section titled "The `portType` Element."

The syntax of the `operation` element is as shown:

```
<portType ------->
    <operation -------->
        ----------
    </operation>
</portType>
```

Similar to the message element, you need to have operations for all network protocols, such as SOAP, HTTP GET, and HTTP POST. The operation element has the input and output elements. The input element takes the input message as the value, and the output element takes the output message as the value.

For example, an operation with the name validateCC is created. The operation has an input element. The value assigned to the input element is validateCCSoapIn message. In addition, the operation element contains an output element. The value assigned to the output element is validateCCSoapOut message. The code for the operation element is as shown:

```
<portType name="CCValidatorSoap">
  <operation name="validateCC">
    <input message="s0:validateCCSoapIn" />
    <output message="s0:validateCCSoapOut" />
  </operation>
</portType>
<portType name="CCValidatorHttpGet">
  <operation name="validateCC">
    <input message="s0:validateCCHttpGetIn" />
    <output message="s0:validateCCHttpGetOut" />
  </operation>
</portType>
<portType name="CCValidatorHttpPost">
  <operation name="validateCC">
    <input message="s0:validateCCHttpPostIn" />
    <output message="s0:validateCCHttpPostOut" />
  </operation>
</portType>
```

A WSDL document supports four types of operations. These operations are discussed in the following list:

◆ **One-way operation.** As the name suggests, in a one-way operation, one endpoint sends a message to another endpoint. However, the first endpoint, which is the client application, does not receive a response from the second endpoint, which is the provider application.

For example, an operation element that contains only the input element is a one-way operation. The following code snippet shows an example of a one-way operation.

```
<portType name="InputValueSoap">
  <operation name="InputValue">
    <input message="s0:InputValueSoapIn" />
  </operation>
</portType>
```

◆ **Notification operation.** A notification operation is similar to a one-way operation. However, in a notification operation, the service provider application sends a message to the client application. For example, the operation that contains only the `output` element is a notification operation. Consider the following code snippet:

```
<portType name="OutputNotificationSoap">
    <operation name="OutputNotification">
        <input message="s0:OutputNotificvationSoapOut" />
    </operation>
</portType>
```

◆ **Request-Response operation.** As the name suggests, in a request-response operation, the client application sends a request to the provider application that processes the request and sends the response back to the client application. The request-response operation contains both the `input` and `output` elements. It is the most common operation used in Web services. The `validateCC` operation that you created in the previous code is an example of a request-response operation.

◆ **Solicit-Response operation.** The solicit-response operation is similar to the request-response operation. However, in the solicit-response operation, the provider application sends a message to the client application. The solicit-response operation contains the `input` and `output` elements.

This operation is not commonly used in the Web services scenario. The example of this type of operation is shown in the following code:

```
<portType name="CallResultSoap">
    <operation name="CallResult">
        <output message="s0:CallResultSoapOut" />
        <input message="s0:CallResultSoapIn" />
    </operation>
</portType>
```

The `portType` *Element*

You can combine the operations in a WSDL document to form a set of operations called a *port type*. You can declare port types by using the `portType` element. In addition, you can specify a name for the port type by using the `name` attribute of the `portType` element. For example, you can combine the `input` and `output` elements of the `validateCC` operation in a port type, `CCValidatorSoap`. The code for the `CCValidatorSoap` port type is as shown:

```
<portType name="CCValidatorSoap">
    <operation name="validateCC">
        <input message="s0:validateCCSoapIn" />
        <output message="s0:validateCCSoapOut" />
```

```
    </operation>
</portType>
```

The preceding code declares a port type with the name CCValidatorSoap, which contains the validateCC operation. The CCValidatorSoap port type is used to bind the operation to a protocol, such as SOAP, HTTP GET, and HTTP POST.

The binding *Element*

After creating a port type, it needs to be associated with a protocol, such as SOAP. This is called *binding*. To bind a port type with a protocol, you use the binding element. In addition, you can bind a port type to any number of protocols. For example, you can bind the same port type to the SOAP, HTTP GET, and HTTP POST protocols. These protocols, in turn, transfer the message from one endpoint to another.

Consider the following code snippet for the binding element:

```
<binding name="CCValidatorSoap" type="s0:CCValidatorSoap">
    <soap:binding transport="http://schemas.xmlsoap.org/soap/http"
style="document" />
    <operation name="validateCC">
      <soap:operation
soapAction="http://cardvalidationservices.org/validateCC" style="document"
/>
        <input>
          <soap:body use="literal" />
        </input>
        <output>
          <soap:body use="literal" />
        </output>
    </operation>
  </binding>
  <binding name="CCValidatorHttpGet" type="s0:CCValidatorHttpGet">
    <http:binding verb="GET" />
    <operation name="validateCC">
      <http:operation location="/validateCC" />
      <input>
        <http:urlEncoded />
      </input>
      <output>
        <mime:mimeXml part="Body" />
```

```
        </output>
      </operation>
    </binding>
    <binding name="CCValidatorHttpPost" type="s0:CCValidatorHttpPost">
      <http:binding verb="POST" />
      <operation name="validateCC">
        <http:operation location="/validateCC" />
        <input>
          <mime:content type="application/x-www-form-urlencoded" />
        </input>
        <output>
          <mime:mimeXml part="Body" />
        </output>
      </operation>
</binding>
```

The preceding code creates a binding with the name CCValidatorSoap. The name attribute specifies a unique name for the binding. In addition, you need to specify the port type for the binding element. You can do this by using the type attribute.

As you can see, the binding element contains many extensibility elements. These extensibility elements specify additional information about the service that the WSDL document defines. The transport element that is used in the preceding code is an example of an extensibility element. The transport element specifies the transport protocol.

In addition, the binding element includes a style element that specifies the style that is used to serialize a message to SOAP. The style can be either RPC based or document based. In the preceding code, the document-based serialization is used. In the document-based serialization, messages are serialized by using a standard schema.

The binding element also includes the operation element, which specifies additional information about the operations. This information includes the style of the messages within the operation. You can specify the style by using the style attribute, which takes the value rpc or document. In addition, you can specify the soapAction header field in the soap:operation element. The soapAction header field provides information about the way in which a SOAP request is processed.

When you create a message, it needs to be associated with a protocol. This means that a message is serialized in the form of either a SOAP request or a response. Therefore, you need to specify the encoding form used for the input and output elements of a message. You can do this by using the soap:body element.

soap:body is another extensibility element that is used inside the binding element. Each input and output element in a message has a different soap:body element that is defined.

For example, you need to include the soap:body element for the input and output elements of the validateCC operation as follows:

```
<operation name="validateCC">
    <soap:operation
soapAction="http://cardvalidationservices.org/validateCC" style="document" />
    <input>
        <soap:body use="literal" />
    </input>
    <output>
        <soap:body use="literal" />
    </output>
</operation>
```

The soap:body element contains a use attribute that specifies the encoding form for a message. The use attribute can take two values: literal or encoded. The following list discusses the encoding forms in detail:

- ◆ **Literal form.** In the literal encoding form, the message part is encoded as per the DTD that is specified in the schema. This means that when a part is serialized, the schema validates the part. To specify the value of the use attribute as literal, you use the literal keyword, as shown in the previous code.
- ◆ **Encoded form.** The encoded form defines a specific or a user-defined way to serialize a message. To do this, the encodingStyle attribute is used.

The port *Element*

A binding is located at an individual endpoint. The port element, which is contained within the service element, specifies the address of a binding. We will explain the service element in the next section, "The service Element."

While defining a port, you need to specify a unique name. To do so, you use the name attribute of the port element. In addition, the port element contains an extensibility element: soap:address. This element binds the port to an address of an endpoint, which is a URI of an endpoint. The users can connect to the service by using the URI. Following is an example of a port element:

```
<service name="CCValidator">
    <port name="CCValidatorSoap" binding="s0:CCValidatorSoap">
      <soap:address location="http://cardvalidationservices/CCValidate/CCValidate.asmx" />
    </port>
    <port name="CCValidatorHttpGet" binding="s0:CCValidatorHttpGet">
      <http:address location="http://cardvalidationservices/CCValidate/CCValidate.asmx" />
    </port>
    <port name="CCValidatorHttpPost" binding="s0:CCValidatorHttpPost">
```

```
        <http:address location="http://cardvalidationservices/CCValidate/CCValidate.asmx" />
    </port>
</service>
```

The preceding code creates a port for each binding that corresponds to the SOAP, HTTP POST, and HTTP GET protocols. Next, the `soap:address` element binds the port to the corresponding URIs.

The `service` Element

As you can see in the previous code, a single WSDL document might contain several ports. Therefore, you need to combine these ports. You can define a service to combine the ports in a WSDL document. In addition, you can specify a unique name for this set of ports.

A service is defined using the `service` element. The syntax of the `service` element is as shown:

```
<service --------->
        <port --------->
                --------------
        </port>
</service>
```

The `service` element contains ports that correspond to each of the protocols. However, you should ensure that all ports expose the same functionality.

The elements that are used in a WSDL document are summarized in Table 5-1.

Table 5-1 The Elements That Are Used in a WSDL Document

Element	Description
definitions	This element includes the definitions for the XML version that is used in a WSDL document. In addition, the definitions for all the namespaces that you need to include in the WSDL document are present in the `definitions` element.
types	This element includes schemas or references to schemas that are used in a WSDL document.
message	This element defines the structure of the message in a WSDL document.
operation	This element associates a message with the corresponding operation.
portType	This element declares port types.
binding	This element binds a port type with a protocol.
port	This element specifies the address of a binding.
service	This element defines a service.

As stated earlier, we created the Web service that corresponds to the CCValidate.wsdl document in Visual Studio .NET. To see the document in Visual Studio .NET, refer to Figure 5-1.

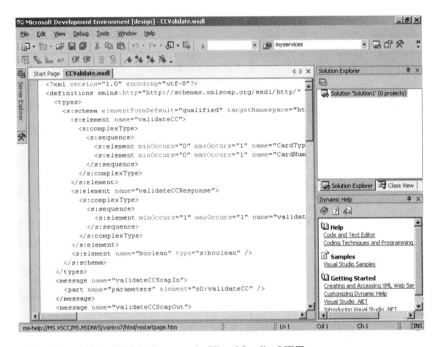

FIGURE 5-1 *The WSDL document in Visual Studio .NET.*

Summary

In this chapter, you learned about WSDL, which is a standard description language that describes a Web service. The information about the Web service is presented in the XML format in the WSDL document.

In addition, you examined a sample WSDL document that was created in Visual Studio .NET. A WSDL document contains several elements that define a Web service. These components include definitions, types, messages, operations, port types, bindings, ports, and services.

In the forthcoming chapters, you will use the concepts that I have discussed so far to create Web services. You can then enhance these Web services to use in real-life scenarios.

PART IV

Professional Project 1

Project 1

Creating the Product Details Web Service

Project 1 Overview

Until now, you have been learning the basics of XML Web services. In addition, you have studied the technologies—such as XML, SOAP, UDDI, and WSDL—that are part of the Web services architecture. Beginning in this chapter, you will apply the knowledge you have gained so far to create and deploy Web services by using several tools. You also will be able to apply this knowledge in real-life projects.

In this project, you will create your first Web service by using Visual Basic 6.0, ASP, and the Microsoft Soap Toolkit. You also will learn how to secure your Web services and create client applications that can access these secure Web services.

The Web service that you will create in this project allows CompareNShop users to compare and shop for products on its site. To enable users to buy products online, CompareNShop shares its data with its trading partners.

Chapter 6

Y ou have learned about XML Web services and some of its components in the preceding chapters. From this chapter onward, you will use that knowledge to create projects that you can use in real-life situations.

In this chapter, you will create a Web service from an existing COM component by using the SOAP Toolkit 2.0. In addition, you will learn to secure the Web service that you create.

Before developing the application, we will discuss the scenario in which you can use the Web service. The following section discusses the scenario for the Product Details Web service.

Product Details Web Service

CompareNShop (CNS) is a U.S.-based organization that provides data for shoppers all over North America. This data includes the prices, features, and descriptions of a wide range of products. In June 1996, the company went online (http://www.CompareNShop.net). The Web site allows users to query information about products of the organization. In addition, the users can compare the features and prices of similar products from different vendors.

An important feature of CNS's business model is to syndicate data to other online content providers. Most of CNS's clients are horizontal portals that make use of CNS's database to provide information to their visitors. Currently, CNS makes its data available to its clients by replicating the database and distributing it every month. The clients then integrate the database with their own sites. This involves a lot of effort because not only must the database be replicated, but the clients also must update their sites with new data every month. In addition, the integrity of the data is affected; even though the database at CNS is updated daily, the clients receive the updated data only once a month.

To overcome the preceding problems and to make the data-sharing process more flexible, CNS has decided to expose the functionality of its systems through XML Web services. After the Web service is developed, the client sites will be able to access the updated data and display it at all times.

In addition, Web services offer another advantage: All the clients of CNS will be able to access the updated data regardless of the technology and platforms they use. This also will enable CNS to make new clients because the clients will find it easy to access and integrate the content from the CNS database.

CNS plans to bring in more flexibility to their business model by allowing clients to access data on a per-search basis. In addition, CNS will be able to expand their clients' base because the clients will not be required to maintain the infrastructure to store and update the CNS database.

The current infrastructure at CompareNShop.net, the portal of CNS, is based on Windows Distributed interNet Applications Architecture (DNA). The business logic of the portal is encapsulated in COM components, and the user-interface facade is done using ASP. To save effort and time, CNS plans to create a Web service by reusing the existing COM components.

Having looked at the scenario in which you can use the Products Details Web service, we will now discuss the life cycle of the project.

Project Life Cycle

The development life cycle of a project involves the following three phases:

- ◆ Project initiation
- ◆ Project execution
- ◆ Project deployment

In the project-initiation phase, the project plan is prepared and the development team for the project is identified. The development team further prepares a comprehensive list of tasks involved in the execution and the deployment phases of the project's life cycle.

In the project execution phase, the development team develops the application. However, before developing the application, the design of the application is created. You will learn to create the design of the CNS Web service in the following section.

The final stage in the project life cycle is the project deployment phase. In this stage, the application is deployed at the client location and support is provided to the client for a specified period. In addition, any bugs that are identified in the application are debugged.

The Project Execution Phase

As discussed in the previous section, you create the design of the application in the project execution phase. After creating the design, the application is developed. The project execution phase consists of the following stages:

- Requirements analysis
- Design
- Construction
- Testing
- Project deployment

The subsequent sections detail the tasks that the team performs in each of these stages.

Requirements Analysis

During the requirements analysis phase, the development team at CNS analyzes the need to create a Web service. The following two points are required:

- The Web service should expose the functionality of existing COM components.
- The solution implemented should be compatible with the existing ASP, IIS, and COM-based Windows 2000 infrastructure.

Design

During the design phase of the application, the development team determines the functionality to be implemented and the technology to be used. The current infrastructure at CNS has ASP pages with embedded COM components. These COM components are used to access data from an SQL Server database. Because the requirement of CNS is to reuse existing components, the development team decided to create the Web service by using the Soap Toolkit 2.0. You will learn about the Soap Toolkit 2.0 in the section "Microsoft SOAP Toolkit 2.0."

Construction

During this phase, the CNS team constructs the application. The following are the primary tasks that the team needs to cater to:

◆ Create a Web service from an existing COM component.

◆ Secure the Web service.

◆ Test the Web service from different client applications.

Testing

In the testing phase, the development team in cooperation with the testing team performs various tests and validations on various modules and checks their functionality. In this chapter, clients who are using Visual Basic and ASP will test the Web service that is created.

Microsoft SOAP Toolkit 2.0

You learned about SOAP in Chapter 3, "Introduction to SOAP." SOAP is a protocol used to create distributed applications. To enable you to create distributed applications by using SOAP, several SOAP toolkits are available from different vendors. These toolkits include Microsoft's SOAP Toolkit, Apache SOAP Toolkit, Paul Kulchenko's SOAP::Lite, and so on.

Microsoft's SOAP toolkit is an easy-to-use toolkit especially for a developer who uses traditional Microsoft technologies and programming languages, such as COM, Visual Basic, and Visual C++. The first version of the toolkit had certain limitations. One of the main problems with Microsoft SOAP Toolkit Version 1.0 was that it did not implement all required sections of the SOAP specification. In addition, the earlier version of the SOAP Toolkit was an MSDN demo and not a product. However, with Version 2.0 of the toolkit, Microsoft fixed the major bugs and also changed the architecture to make it simpler and intuitive. Also, the new version of the toolkit is a Microsoft product instead of just a demo.

The Microsoft SOAP Toolkit 2.0 allows you to create Web services that expose the functionality of existing COM components. It also allows you to create Web service clients using tools like Visual Basic 6.0. The Microsoft SOAP Toolkit 2.0 includes the following:

◆ A client-side component that allows a client application to invoke methods of a Web service based on the description of the Web service from a WSDL document.

◆ A server-side component that is used to create a WSDL document, a WSML file, and an ASP or ISAPI endpoint for a Web service from an existing COM component. All these put together can be used to expose the functionality of an existing component as a Web service. The WSDL document describes a Web service, the ASP or ISAPI endpoint provides a port where client applications can call the Web service, and the WSML document maps the Web service operations to the methods of the component.

Microsoft SOAP Toolkit Version 2.0 provides high-level and low-level interaction APIs. To access the high-level interface, you can use a SOAP toolkit object called SoapClient. This object contains several methods and properties, some of which are included in the follow ing list:

- ◆ **mssoapinit() method.** This method initializes the SoapClient object by using the WSDL file as an input.
- ◆ **Client property.** This property sets and gets various properties of the SoapClient object.
- ◆ **ConnectorProperty property.** This property initializes and retrieves the transport protocol-specific parameters.
- ◆ **detail property.** This is a read-only property that retrieves the value of the `<detail>` element of the `<Fault>` node in a SOAP message.
- ◆ **faultactor property.** This is a read-only property that retrieves the URI of the generated fault.
- ◆ **faultcode property.** This is a read-only property that provides the value of the `<faultcode>` element of the `<Fault>` node in a SOAP message.
- ◆ **faultstring property.** This is a read-only property that provides the value of the `<faultstring>` element of the `<Fault>` node in a SOAP message.

To understand the methods and properties associated with the SoapClient object, consider the following example. You can use the code to connect to a Web service, which adds two numbers, from a Visual Basic client.

```
Set oClient = CreateObject("MSSOAP.SoapClient")
oSOAPClient.mssoapinit("Adder.wsdl", "", "", "")
MsgBox oClient.Add(10,10)
```

As you see in the preceding code, you can call a Web service method as if it were a member of the SoapClient object. This simplifies the development of the client applications.

The SOAP toolkit retrieves information about how to interpret and use a Web service from the WSDL document of the Web service. In addition, the toolkit provides a tool, called the WSDL generator, to SOAP-enable existing COM components. The WSDL generator accepts the path for a COM component as input, analyzes its type library, and creates a Web service consisting of a WSDL file, a WSML file, and an ASP file.

 NOTE

You learned about WSDL files in Chapter 5, "Introduction to WSDL." The WSML file is not a standard file. It is a Web Services Meta Language file that is specific to the Microsoft toolkit. WSML is an XML file that maps SOAP messages to the original COM interfaces.

When a COM component method is called and the method returns a value, the value is serialized into SOAP format and passed on to the SoapClient object, which further deserializes the SOAP response and returns the appropriate COM data type. This serialization and deserialization happens automatically when the value passed is compatible to one of the XSD types. When the value is a custom data type or an object, such as an ADODB recordset, then the SOAP toolkit allows the creation of custom type mappers. You will learn to create a custom type mapper in the section "Handling Recordsets and Other Custom Data Types in SOAP Messages."

The SOAP toolkit allows you to create both ASP-based and ISAPI-based Web services. Having discussed the SOAP toolkit in general, we will now move on to creating the Web service from an existing COM component by using the Microsoft SOAP toolkit.

Creating a Web Service by Using the Soap Toolkit 2.0

In this section, you will learn to create a Web service from a COM component. You can refer to Appendix A, "Creating COM Components By Using Visual Basic 6.0," for the code for the COM component and the database design.

Before creating the application, it is important to discuss the working of the Web service. As discussed in Appendix A, the existing COM component contains methods that allow applications to query a database and returns data as an ADODB recordset. The Web service needs to convert this data into SOAP format because the ADODB recordset is not an XSD-defined data type. The requesting application then processes the SOAP message to retrieve and display the data.

The first step in the creation of a Web service is to reuse the existing COM component. The COM component is called GetData.dll. The DLL file for the COM component has several classes. You can use these classes to query the CNS database. This chapter will concentrate on the ExecSP class. The ExecSP class has two methods: getAll() and getByCategory(). The signature of these methods is as follows:

```
Function ExecSP.getAll() As ADODB.Recordset
Function ExecSP.getByCategory(category As String) As ADODB.Recordset
```

 NOTE

To get the implementation details of these methods, you can refer to Appendix A.

As you see, the ExecSP.getAll() method does not accept a parameter, but it returns an ADODB Recordset object that contains information on the products in the CNS database. The second method accepts the name of a category as a parameter and returns data of all products in this category.

We will now create the Web service that reuses the preceding component. To create a Web service that reuses any COM component, you need to use the Microsoft SOAP Toolkit 2.0.

 NOTE

If you do not have the Soap toolkit installed on your computer, you can download it from http://msdn.microsoft.com/downloads/default.asp?URL=/downloads/sample.asp?url=/MSDN-FILES/027/001/580/msdncompositedoc.xml.

To create a Web service by using the Microsoft SOAP Toolkit 2.0, follow these steps:

1. Start the WSDL Generator of the Soap Toolkit 2.0.

   Figure 6-1 shows the Start page of the Soap Toolkit 2.0 WSDL Generator Wizard.

FIGURE 6-1 *Soap Toolkit 2.0 WSDL Generator Wizard.*

2. Click on the Next button. This will display the Soap Toolkit 2.0 Wizard dialog box.
3. In the dialog box, enter the name of the Web service as `ProductSummary`. The wizard creates the WSDL and WSML files with this name.
4. Click on the Select COM object button and browse for the path for the GetData.dll file (see Figure 6-2).
5. Click on the Next button.

   Figure 6-3 shows a tree view of the classes and methods that are contained in the COM component.

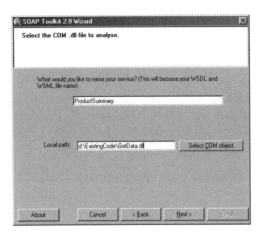

FIGURE 6-2 *Naming the Web service.*

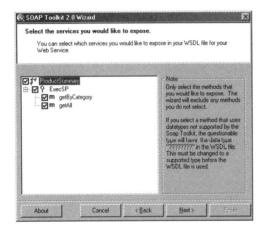

FIGURE 6-3 *The component classes and methods.*

6. Select the classes and methods that you need to include in your Web service.

   With the GetData.dll component, select the `getByCategory()` and `getAll()` methods.

 NOTE

When you select the `getByCategory()` and `getAll()` methods, a note displays on the screen. The note states that if any method that you select returns a value of a data type that the Soap Toolkit does not recognize, the data type will be written as ??????? in the WSDL file that is generated.

7. Click on the Next button.

    The Soap Listener Information screen is displayed.

    In the first text box of the Soap Listener Information screen, type the URL where you want to host the Web service. In this case, you can host the Web service at the http://ServerName/ProductSummary URL.

8. To create an ASP-based Web service, select the listener type as ASP and the XSD type as 2001 (see Figure 6-4).

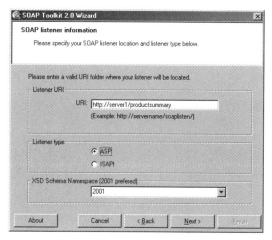

FIGURE 6-4 *The SOAP Listener Information screen.*

9. Click on the Next button. The wizard displays the screen shown in Figure 6-5.

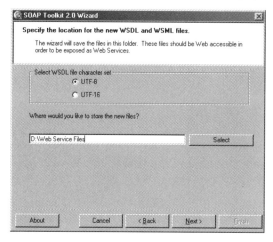

FIGURE 6-5 *Specifying the folder for the WSDL and WSML files.*

As you can see, UTF-8 is selected by default. You also need to specify the folder where the files that the wizard generates will be saved.

10. After specifying the path, click on the Next button.

Clicking on the Next button starts the file generation process. After the files are generated, you will get a warning message, as shown in Figure 6-6. The message indicates that some of the methods had data types that the Soap toolkit didn't understand; therefore, the data types are replaced by ?????? in the WSDL file.

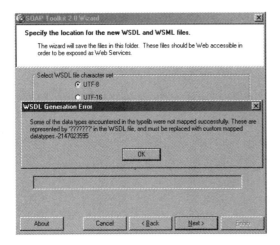

FIGURE 6-6 *The data type error message.*

11. Click on the OK button.

12. Click on the Finish button. The wizard creates the following files:

- ProductSummary.wsdl
- ProductSummary.wsml
- ProductSummary.asp

The ProductSummary.wsdl File

The ProductSummary.wsdl file is the Web service description file that contains information about the Web service and the operations that it supports. The operations supported by a Web service are contained in the <message> element of the WSDL file. We will now discuss the content of the WSDL file in detail.

The WSDL file contains the declarations for the SOAP messages that interact with the getAll() method of the component. The syntax of the SOAP messages as generated by the wizard is as follows:

```
<message name='ExecSP.getAll'>
  </message>
  <message name='ExecSP.getAllResponse'>
    <part name='Result' type='xsd:???????' />
  </message>
```

As discussed earlier, the getByCategory() method accepts a string as a parameter and returns a recordset. Therefore, to interact with the getByCategory() method, you need to declare a pair of SOAP messages as shown here:

```
<message name='ExecSP.getByCategory'>
  <part name='category' type='xsd:string'/>
</message>
<message name='ExecSP.getByCategoryResponse'>
  <part name='Result' type='xsd:???????' />
  <part name='category' type='xsd:string'/>
</message>
```

As you can see, the preceding code snippet contains the type='xsd:???????' /> declarations. This is because the return type of the methods in the COM component is ADODB.Recordset, which is not a data type that the SOAP toolkit recognizes.

After declaring the pair of SOAP messages, you need to bind the operations (getAll and getByCategory) to the corresponding messages. You can accomplish this by using <portType> declarations. For example, the operation getAll has an input message, getAll, and an output message, getAllResponse. The following code snippet shows the <portType> declarations:

```
<portType name='ExecSPSoapPort'>
    <operation name='getAll' parameterOrder=''>
      <input message='wsdlns:ExecSP.getAll' />
      <output message='wsdlns:ExecSP.getAllResponse' />
    </operation>
    <operation name='getByCategory' parameterOrder='category'>
      <input message='wsdlns:ExecSP.getByCategory' />
      <output message='wsdlns:ExecSP.getByCategoryResponse' />
    </operation>
  </portType>
```

After binding the operations to corresponding messages, you need to bind the operations to corresponding ports. To do this, you use the <bindings> section as shown in the following code snippet:

```
<binding name='ExecSPSoapBinding' type='wsdlns:ExecSPSoapPort' >
    <stk:binding preferredEncoding='UTF-8'/>
    <soap:binding style='rpc' transport='http://schemas.xmlsoap.org/soap/http' />
```

```
<operation name='getAll' >
  <soap:operation soapAction='http://tempuri.org/action/ExecSP.getAll' />
  <input>
    <soap:body use='encoded' namespace='http://tempuri.org/message/'
        encodingStyle='http://schemas.xmlsoap.org/soap/encoding/' />
  </input>
  <output>
    <soap:body use='encoded' namespace='http://tempuri.org/message/'
        encodingStyle='http://schemas.xmlsoap.org/soap/encoding/' />
  </output>
</operation>
<operation name='getByCategory' >
  <soap:operation soapAction='http://tempuri.org/action/ExecSP.getByCategory' />
  <input>
    <soap:body use='encoded' namespace='http://tempuri.org/message/'
        encodingStyle='http://schemas.xmlsoap.org/soap/encoding/' />
  </input>
  <output>
    <soap:body use='encoded' namespace='http://tempuri.org/message/'
        encodingStyle='http://schemas.xmlsoap.org/soap/encoding/' />
  </output>
</operation>
</binding>
```

Next, the WSDL file contains the `<service>` section that identifies the name of the Web service and its location. The `<service>` section is shown in the following code:

```
<service name='ProductSummary' >
    <port name='ExecSPSoapPort' binding='wsdlns:ExecSPSoapBinding' >
      <soap:address location='http://server1/ProductSummary/ProductSummary.ASP' />
    </port>
</service>
```

The ProductSummary.wsml File

Next, consider the WSML file that the wizard creates. This file is used to map the Web service and its operation to the COM component and its methods. The WSML file is an XML document as shown:

```
<?xml version='1.0' encoding='UTF-8' ?>
<!-- Generated 05/06/02 by Microsoft SOAP Toolkit WSDL File Generator, Version
1.02.813.0 -->
```

```
<servicemapping name='ProductSummary'>
  <service name='ProductSummary'>
    <using PROGID='GetData.ExecSP' cachable='0' ID='ExecSPObject' />
    <port name='ExecSPSoapPort'>
      <operation name='getAll'>
        <execute uses='ExecSPObject' method='getAll' dispID='1610809344'>
          <parameter callIndex='-1' name='retval' elementName='Result' />
        </execute>
      </operation>
      <operation name='getByCategory'>
        <execute uses='ExecSPObject' method='getByCategory' dispID='1610809345'>
          <parameter callIndex='1' name='category' elementName='category' />
          <parameter callIndex='-1' name='retval' elementName='Result' />
        </execute>
      </operation>
    </port>
  </service>
</servicemapping>
```

The ProductSummary.asp File

The ASP file provides an interface for external applications to communicate with the Web service. The content of the ASP file is as shown:

```
<%@ LANGUAGE=VBScript %>
<%
Option Explicit
On Error Resume Next
Response.ContentType = "text/xml"
Dim SoapServer
If Not Application("ProductSummaryInitialized") Then
  Application.Lock
  If Not Application("ProductSummaryInitialized") Then
    Dim WSDLFilePath
    Dim WSMLFilePath
    WSDLFilePath = Server.MapPath("ProductSummary.wsdl")
    WSMLFilePath = Server.MapPath("ProductSummary.wsml")
    Set SoapServer = Server.CreateObject("MSSOAP.SoapServer")
    If Err Then SendFault "Cannot create SoapServer object. " & Err.Description
```

```
      SoapServer.Init WSDLFilePath, WSMLFilePath
      If Err Then SendFault "SoapServer.Init failed. " & Err.Description
      Set Application("ProductSummaryServer") = SoapServer
      Application("ProductSummaryInitialized") = True
    End If
    Application.UnLock
  End If
  Set SoapServer = Application("ProductSummaryServer")
  SoapServer.SoapInvoke Request, Response, ""
  If Err Then SendFault "SoapServer.SoapInvoke failed. " & Err.Description
  Sub SendFault(ByVal LogMessage)
    Dim Serializer
    On Error Resume Next
    ' "URI Query" logging must be enabled for AppendToLog to work
    Response.AppendToLog " SOAP ERROR: " & LogMessage
    Set Serializer = Server.CreateObject("MSSOAP.SoapSerializer")
    If Err Then
      Response.AppendToLog "Could not create SoapSerializer object. " & Err.Description
      Response.Status = "500 Internal Server Error"
    Else
      Serializer.Init Response
      If Err Then
        Response.AppendToLog "SoapSerializer.Init failed. " & Err.Description
        Response.Status = "500 Internal Server Error"
      Else
        Serializer.startEnvelope
        Serializer.startBody
        Serializer.startFault "Server", "The request could not be processed due
to a problem in the server. Please contact the system admistrator. " & LogMessage
        Serializer.endFault
        Serializer.endBody
        Serializer.endEnvelope
        If Err Then
          Response.AppendToLog "SoapSerializer failed. " & Err.Description
          Response.Status = "500 Internal Server Error"
        End If
      End If
    End If
```

```
    Response.End
End Sub
%>
```

The wizard has created a basic Web service for you. However, you will not be able to use this Web service because the WSDL file still has the ?????? declarations for the values returned by two of the SOAP messages. You will fix this in the next section.

Handling Recordsets and Other Custom Data Types in SOAP Messages

To handle custom data types that the SOAP toolkit does not support, you need to modify the declarations in the WSDL file. Follow these steps to modify the declarations:

1. Modify the WSDL file that the wizard created.
2. Create a handler for the data type.

Open the WSDL file in a text editor. Consider the <types> node in the WSDL file.

```
<definitions name ='ProductSummary'    targetNamespace =
'http://tempuri.org/wsdl/'
        xmlns:wsdlns='http://tempuri.org/wsdl/'
        xmlns:typens='http://tempuri.org/type'
        xmlns:soap='http://schemas.xmlsoap.org/wsdl/soap/'
        xmlns:xsd='http://www.w3.org/2001/XMLSchema'
        xmlns:stk='http://schemas.microsoft.com/soap-toolkit/wsdl-extension'
        xmlns='http://schemas.xmlsoap.org/wsdl/'>
    <types>
      <schema targetNamespace='http://tempuri.org/type'
        xmlns='http://www.w3.org/2001/XMLSchema'
        xmlns:SOAP-ENC='http://schemas.xmlsoap.org/soap/encoding/'
        xmlns:wsdl='http://schemas.xmlsoap.org/wsdl/'
        elementFormDefault='qualified'>
      </schema>
    </types>
```

To declare the custom data type, add the code highlighted in bold:

```
<types>
    <schema targetNamespace='http://tempuri.org/type'
      xmlns='http://www.w3.org/2001/XMLSchema'
      xmlns:SOAP-ENC='http://schemas.xmlsoap.org/soap/encoding/'
```

```
        xmlns:wsdl='http://schemas.xmlsoap.org/wsdl/'
        elementFormDefault='qualified'>
        <complexType name="RecordsetXML">
                    <sequence>
                            <any/>
                    </sequence>
            </complexType>
        </schema>
    </types>
```

The `ComplexType` declaration in the preceding code depends on the data type for which you need to create a custom mapper. For example, consider a method that returns an object of the type `Distributor`. The `Distributor` class encapsulates details of a distributor in the `CompareNSave` database in Appendix A. The following code is the declaration for the `Distributor` class:

```
Option Explicit
Private mDistributorID as String
Private mDistributorName as String
Private mAddress as String
Private mCity as String
Private mZip as String


Public Property Let DistributorID(ByVal Value As String)
    MDistributorID-value
End Property


Public Property Get DistributorID()
    DistributorID=mDistributorID
End Property
```

You can create a `<complexType>` declaration for the `Distributor` class as follows:

```
<complexType name="Distributor">
    <sequence>
        <element name='DistributorID' type='xsd:string'/>
        <element name='DistributorName' type='xsd:string'/>
        <element name='Address' type='xsd:string'/>
        <element name='City' type='xsd:string'/>
        <element name='Zip' type='xsd:string'/>
    </sequence>
</complexType>
```

After declaring the complex type for the recordset, you need to replace the ??????? in the data type declarations of the WSDL file with the complex type that you created:

```
<message name='ExecSP.getAll'>
  </message>
  <message name='ExecSP.getAllResponse'>
    <part name='Result' type='typens:RecordsetXML'/>
  </message>
  <message name='ExecSP.getByCategory'>
    <part name='category' type='xsd:string'/>
  </message>
  <message name='ExecSP.getByCategoryResponse'>
    <part name='Result' type='typens:RecordsetXML'/>
    <part name='category' type='xsd:string'/>
  </message>
```

Now, the WSDL file is created. The next step is to create a component that will do the custom type mapping. To do so, perform the following steps:

1. Start Visual Basic 6.0 from the Programs menu.
2. Create a new COM component.
3. Rename the project as `CustomMapp`.
4. In the Project, References menu, add a reference for the following:
   - ◆ Microsoft ActiveX Data Objects 2.5 library
   - ◆ Microsoft XML type library
   - ◆ Microsoft SOAP type library

The project contains a default class `Class1`. This class handles the type mapping; therefore, this class should implement the `SoapTypeMapper` interface. To do this, you need to add the following code to the class:

```
Implements MSSOAPLib.ISoapTypeMapper
```

In addition to the `SoapTypeMapper` interface, the class should implement the methods of the interface. Therefore, you need to add the following code to the class:

```
Private Sub ISoapTypeMapper_Init(ByVal pFactory As
MSSOAPLib.ISoapTypeMapperFactory, ByVal pSchema As MSXML2.IXMLDOMNode, ByVal
xsdType As MSSOAPLib.enXSDType)


End Sub
```

```
Private Function ISoapTypeMapper_varType() As Long
    ISoapTypeMapper_varType = vbObject
End Function


Private Function ISoapTypeMapper_read(ByVal pNode As MSXML2.IXMLDOMNode, ByVal
bstrEncoding As String, ByVal encodingMode As MSSOAPLib.enEncodingStyle, ByVal
lFlags As Long) As Variant
End Function


Private Sub ISoapTypeMapper_write(ByVal pSoapSerializer As
MSSOAPLib.ISoapSerializer, ByVal bstrEncoding As String, ByVal encodingMode As
MSSOAPLib.enEncodingStyle, ByVal lFlags As Long, pvar As Variant)
    On Error GoTo err
    Dim RS As ADODB.Recordset
    Dim DS As ADODB.Stream
    Set RS = pvar
    Set DS= New ADODB.Stream

    ' write the recordset object as XML into the stream
    RS.Save DS, adPersistXML
    ' pass the XML string to the SoapSerialized object
    pSoapSerializer.writeXML DS.ReadText
    Exit Sub
    err:
    App.LogEvent err.Description & "CustomMapp"
End Sub
```

The preceding code contains the `ISoapTypeMApper_Write()` function, which is used to perform the actual type mapping. Therefore, the contents of the recordset are converted into a data stream object, and the string containing the XML data is passed to the SoapSerialized object.

After writing the code, you need to compile it into a DLL file. This creates a custom type mapper DLL that you need to bind to the Web service. To bind the mapper DLL to the Web service, perform the following steps:

1. Open the WSML file.

   The file currently contains a reference to the GetData.dll COM component, as shown here:

   ```
   servicemapping name='ProductSummary'>
     <service name='ProductSummary'>
   ```

```
    <using PROGID='GetData.ExecSP' cachable='0' ID='ExecSPObject' />
  <port name='ExecSPSoapPort'>
```

2. Add a reference to the CustomMapp.dll file, as shown in the following code:

    ```
    <servicemapping name='ProductSummary'>
    <service name='ProductSummary'>
    <using PROGID='GetData.ExecSP' cachable='0' ID='ExecSPObject' />
    <using PROGID='CustomMapp.Class1' cachable='0' ID='RecordsetMapper' />
    <port name='ExecSPSoapPort'>
    ```

3. Link CustomMapp.Class1 to the RecordSetXML complex type that you have declared in the WSDL file by adding the following <types> declaration in the WSML file:

    ```
    <servicemapping name='ProductSummary'>
      <service name='ProductSummary'>
      <using PROGID='GetData.ExecSP' cachable='0' ID='ExecSPObject' />
      <using PROGID='CustomMapp.Class1' cachable='0' ID='RecordsetMapper' />
    <types>
    <type name='RecordsetXML' targetNamespace='http://tempuri.org/type'
    uses='RecordsetMapper'/>
    </types>
    <port name='ExecSPSoapPort'>
    ```

4. Save the file.

The Web service for CNS is now created. After creating the Web service, you need to test it before deploying it at the client site.

Testing the Web Service

To access the Web service, you need to create a proxy component that consumes the Web service. The clients, in turn, will use this component to access the Web service. To create a proxy component, perform the following steps:

1. Start Visual Basic 6.0 from the Programs menu. Name the project ClientProxy.
2. Create a new project of the type ActiveX DLL.
3. In the Project, Reference menu, add a reference to the Microsoft SOAP type library and the Microsoft XML type library.

    The project contains a default class: Class1.

4. Add the following code to Class1:

    ```
    Function getAll() As String
     Dim soapclient As New soapclient
    ```

```
soapclient.mssoapinit "http://server1/ProductSummary/ProductSummary.wsdl"
Dim s As IXMLDOMNodeList
Set s = soapclient.getAll()
str1 = s.Item(0).xml
getAll = str1
End Function


   Function getByCategory(sCategory As String) as string
       Dim soapclient As New soapclient
       Dim s As IXMLDOMNodeList
soapclient.mssoapinit "http://localhost/ProductSummary/ProductSummary.wsdl"
       Set s = soapclient.getByCategory(sCategory)
       str1 = s.Item(0).xml
       Set getByCategory = str1
   End Function
```

As you can see, both `getAll()` and `getByCategory()` function in a similar way. Both initialize the SoapClient object by calling the `mssoapinit()` method. Then the code calls the Web service method, `getAll()`, which returns the XML data that is converted to a `string` value.

Compile the project and create the DLL file.

Next, you will create a client application in Visual Basic 6.0. This application connects to the Web service, calls one of its methods, and displays the data that the service returns. The client application can connect to the Web service through the client proxy that you have created. As discussed earlier, the proxy component returns a `string` value, which contains the XML form of the recordset object, returned by the original COM component. Therefore, the client application needs to convert this data back to a recordset object and display it in a DataGrid (OLEDB) control. To convert the XML data to a recordset object, perform the following steps:

1. Start Visual Basic 6.0 from the Programs menu.
2. Create a new project of the type Standard EXE.
3. In the Project, References menu, add a reference to the ClientProxy.DLL file and the Microsoft XML type library.
4. Select Components from the Project menu.

 NOTE

We will refer to the application that we created in the previous steps as the test application.

5. In the resulting dialog box, select ADODC and DataGrid (OLEDB) controls.

6. Add the Data control and the DataGrid control to the form along with a Button control. After adding these controls, the form should look like Figure 6-7.

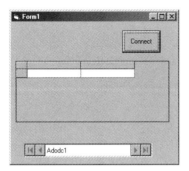

FIGURE 6-7 *The test application.*

7. In the `Click` event handler for the button control, add the following code:

```
Private Sub Command1_Click()
    Dim xDoc As New MSXML2.DOMDocument
    Dim rs As New ADODB.Recordset
    Dim ds As New ADODB.Stream
    Dim clntPrxy As New ClientProxy.Class1
    xDoc.loadXML (clntPrxy.getAll())
    ds.Open
    ds.WriteText xDoc.xml
    ds.Position = 0
    rs.Open ds
    Set Adodc1.Recordset = rs
    DataGrid1.DataSource = Adodc1
End Sub
```

The preceding code retrieves a string containing the XML data. Next, the code writes the string into an ADODB.Stream object and then inserts the string into a recordset object. As you will notice, the whole process is the reverse of what you did to serialize the data in recordset in the custom type mapper application. Finally, the code sets the data source property of the DataGrid control to `Adodc1`, where `Adodc1` is the instance of the ADODC control on the form.

Setting Up the Web Service

Web service files and the test client application are ready. Now, you need to set up the Web service. To do this, perform the following steps:

1. In the Control Panel, Administrative Tools, run the Internet Services Manager (ISM). The ISM is shown in Figure 6-8.

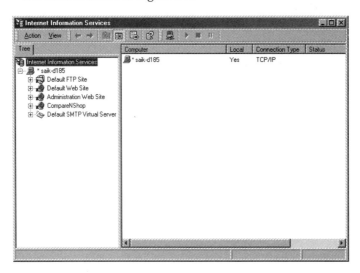

FIGURE 6-8 *Internet Services Manager.*

2. Right-click on Default Web Site.

3. In the resulting menu, select New and Virtual Directory. Doing so launches the Virtual Directory Creation Wizard.

4. Click on the Next button.

   In the Virtual Directory Creation Wizard, you need to specify the name or alias for the virtual directory.

5. Enter the name as ProductSummary in the screen that appears (see Figure 6-9).

6. Click on the Next button.

   In the resultant screen, you need to specify the path for the Web site content directory. The resultant screen is shown in Figure 6-10.

7. Select the folder that contains your Web service files.

8. Click on the Next button. The Access Permissions screen appears, as shown in Figure 6-11.

9. Click on the Next button.

10. In the resulting screen, click on the Finish button to complete the creation of the virtual directory.

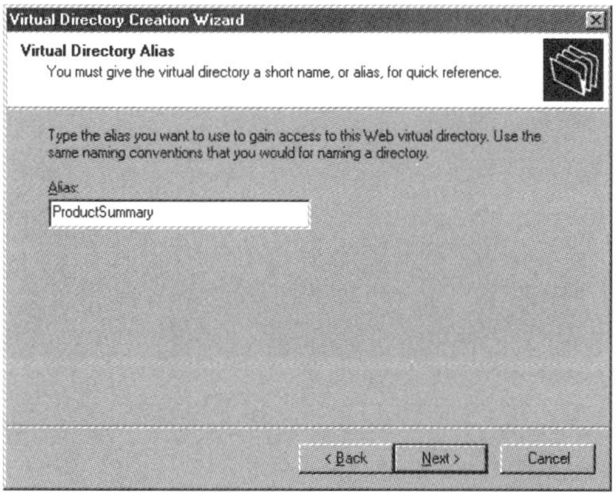

FIGURE 6-9 *The Virtual Directory Creation Wizard.*

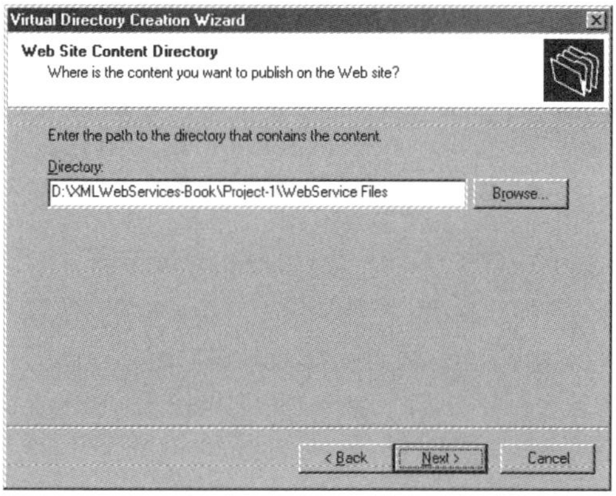

FIGURE 6-10 *The Web Site Content Directory screen.*

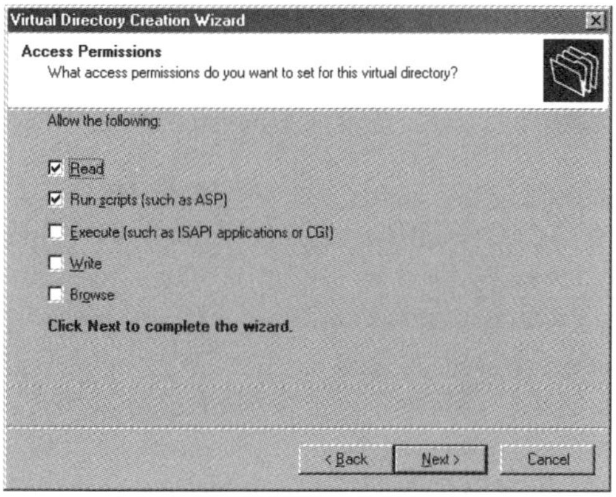

FIGURE 6-11 *The Access Permissions screen.*

After setting up the Web service, you can now run the test application and verify the data that is displayed in the DataGrid control.

Securing the Web Service

After creating and testing the Web service, the next step is to secure the Web service. SOAP currently does not implement security; instead, it delegates security to the Transport layer. In this case, the Transport layer is HTTP. A Web service that you have created is an example of a Web application running on the IIS/Windows 2000 platform. Therefore, all methods of securing Web applications also apply to the Web service.

Securing a Web service includes preventing unauthorized access to it. You can accomplish this by authenticating the users who connect to the Web service. Several methods allow you to authenticate users. However, if you do not use an authentication method, the Anonymous Access mode is enabled by default.

We will now discuss the authentication methods in the following list:

◆ **Basic authentication method.** This method is a basic and insecure method. In this method, to connect to a Web service, the client needs to supply a username and password. This username and password are sent over the wire with base-64 encoding and no encryption. Therefore, the username and password can be trapped and used to access other resources.

 NOTE

Base-64 encoding/decoding is a convention for converting binary data to a string of printable, alphanumeric characters. This technique is taken from RFC 1521.

◆ **Digest authentication method.** This method is a new method that was introduced in Windows 2000 and is part of the HTTP 1.1 standard protocol. However, it is not widely supported on other Web servers and platforms. The main limitation of the digest authentication method is the lack of support from other Web client and server implementations. The digest authentication method is more secure than the basic authentication method.

◆ **Kerberos authentication method.** This method is used on the Windows 2000 operating system. Even though it is a secure authentication method, its main drawback is that it is used for the Windows 2000 operating system only. This authentication mode is better suited for an intranet environment.

◆ **Windows integrated authentication method.** This method is the native Windows authentication scheme, although it is implemented differently on different versions of Windows. The main drawback of Windows integrated authentication is that it is used only for Windows. Also, it does not work through proxies. It is the best scheme for an intranet consisting of Windows-based machines.

◆ **SSL and client certificates authentication method.** This method involves the use of digital certificates for authentication. A server verifies its own identity through a server side digital certificate, and a client application can provide proof of its identity through a client side digital certificate. A Certification Authority (CA), such as VeriSign, issues the digital certificate. Using SSL with basic authentication ensures that the usernames and passwords are encrypted when they're sent over the wire. As a result, this is a secure and popular form of authentication.

Having looked at various ways in which you can secure your Web service, you will now secure your Web service by using the basic authentication method. To do this, perform the following steps:

1. From the Start menu, select Programs, Administrative Tools, Internet Services Manager.

2. In the Internet Services Manager, select the Web server or the virtual directory that you had previously set up for the ProductSummary Web service.

3. Right-click the virtual directory, and in the resulting menu, select Properties. The Properties dialog box is displayed.

4. In the Properties dialog box, select the Directory Security tab. The Directory Security dialog box is shown in Figure 6-12.

5. In the Anonymous Access and Authentication Control section, click on the Edit button.

6. In the resulting Authentication Methods dialog box, clear the Anonymous Access check box, if it's checked. You have now disabled anonymous access.

7. Select the Basic Authentication check box. A dialog box is displayed that warns you of the perils of using basic authentication. Ignore it for now and click on the Yes button.

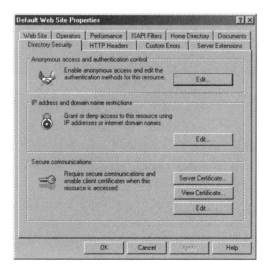

FIGURE 6-12 *The Directory Security dialog box.*

Now, try to connect to the Web service from the test client application that you created. You will get an `Access Denied` error message.

For the client to authenticate itself to the Web service, make the following changes to the ClientProxy DLL:

```
Function getAll() As String
    Dim soapclient As New soapclient
    soapclient.mssoapinit "http://server1/ProductSummary/ProductSummary.wsdl"
    soapclient.ConnectorProperty("AuthUser") = "username"
    soapclient.ConnectorProperty("AuthPassword") = "password"
    Dim ss As DOMDocument
    Dim s As IXMLDOMNodeList
    Set s = soapclient.getAll()
    str1 = s.Item(0).xml
    getAll = str1
End Function
```

You can use the `ConnectorProperty()` method of the `SoapClient` class to pass the username and password to the Web service. If the virtual directory where the Web service is located requires authentication, you can pass it as shown:

```
Function getAll() As String
    Dim soapclient As New soapclient
    soapclient.mssoapinit
"https://username:password@server1/ProductSummary/ProductSummary.wsdl"
    soapclient.ConnectorProperty("AuthUser") = "username"
    soapclient.ConnectorProperty("AuthPassword") = "password"
```

Compile and generate the ClientProxy.dll file again with the previous changes. Run the test application and verify the connectivity to the Web service.

The basic authentication is now enabled for the Web service. The next step is to make the authentication more secure by adding an SSL Certificate. To do this, you can use the SSL trial feature at VeriSign.com.

However, before you request for a trial certificate, you need to prepare a certificate request. To prepare a certificate request, perform the following steps:

1. In the control under Administrative Tools, open the Internet Services Manager.
2. Open the Properties dialog box for the Web site that hosts your Web service.
3. Right-click on the Web site name in the tree view and select Properties in the resulting dialog box. This opens the Web Site Properties dialog box shown in Figure 6-13.
4. Click on the Directory Security tab.

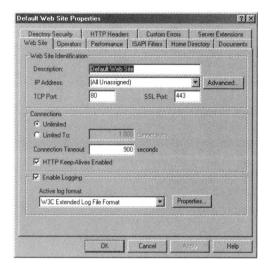

FIGURE 6-13 *The Web Site Properties dialog box.*

5. In the Directory Security tab, click on the Server Certificate button in the Secure Communications section. The IIS Certificate Wizard is invoked, as shown in Figure 6-14. Click on the Next button.

FIGURE 6-14 *The IIS Certificate Wizard.*

6. Select the Create a New Certificate option.

7. Click on the Next button, and in the resulting dialog box, select Prepare the Request Now, But Send It Later option, as shown in Figure 6-15.

8. Click on the Next button. The resultant dialog box is shown in Figure 6-16.

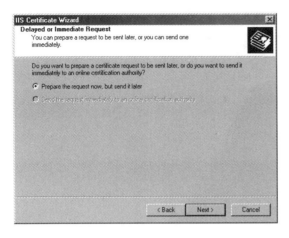

FIGURE 6-15 *Creating the certificate request.*

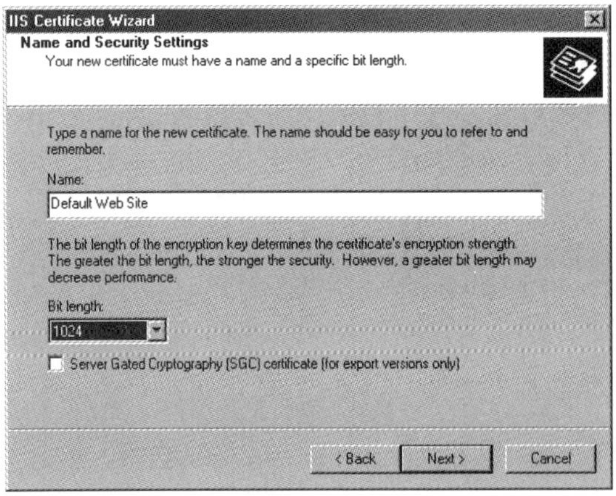

FIGURE 6-16 *The Name and Security Settings screen.*

In the screen shown in Figure 6-16, decide the encryption strengths for the keys that the certificate generates. The bit length of the encryption key depends on your need for security and speed. A higher bit length makes your application more secure, but if you are running a processor- and memory-intensive application over SSL, then a larger key might slow down your application.

9. The Internet Services Manager creates a public/private key pair. The private key is stored locally on your machine, and the public part can be sent to a CA as part of a Certificate Signing Request (CSR).

10. Create the CSR by entering your company's details. When you create a certificate for commercial use, you need to enter the data in the registration documents of the company.

11. In the next few dialog boxes, enter the details about your company and contact information of the technical contact for the Web site.

12. Specify the path and file name to store the CSR, as shown in Figure 6-17.

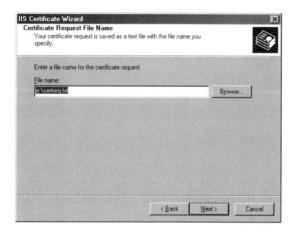

FIGURE 6-17 *Saving the file with the CSR.*

13. When you specify the path, the wizard displays a confirmation screen with the data that you have entered. Click on the Finish button to generate the request file.

After the file is created, you can open it. The content of the file is displayed as shown:

```
-- ---BEGIN NEW CERTIFICATE REQUEST-- ---
MIICcjCCAhwCAQAwYjESMBAGA1UEAxMJc2Fpay1kMTg1MQwwCgYDVQQLEwNrc2Ix
DTALBgNVBAoTBG5paXQxEjAQBgNVBAcTCU5ldyBEZWxoaTEOMAwGA1UECBMFRGVs
aGkxCzAJBgNVBAYTAklOMFwwDQYJKoZIhvcNAQEBBQADSwAwSAJBAMyQ8v9Ij1fx
Q4aq9cma6Hcwru00KPPE1zbfqIFxHwExQftJGv0zZIEHi+dGH2WoEYxhLsKEArzH
2XAdgUCkOAcCAwEAAaCCAVMwGgYKKwYBBAGCNw0CAzEMFgo1LjAuMjE5NS4yMDUG
CisGAQQBgjcCAQ4xJzAlMA4GA1UdDwEB/wQEAwIE8DATBgNVHSUEDDAKBggrBgEF
BQcDATCB/QYKKwYBBAGCNw0CAjGB7jCB6wIBAR5aAE0AaQBjAHIAbwBzAG8AZgB0
ACAAUgBTAEEAIABTAEMAaABhAG4AbgBlAGwAIABDAHIAeQBwAHQAbwBnAHIAYQBw
AGgAaQBjACAAUAByAG8AdgBpAGQAZQByA4GJAI7mD82T6Wy4AlmJ16DXl9oEup7i
OKLK1h5UECnEuu1SXJYRC5Z094QW/QZa+yNAbCf5YLmb2RU2ZwtWzHjVC0YNe24R
MU4Pp1KL8z3CYTLxuxtw0dez6ye1fnoBwLEFeHUAtoThhoTp7/PCYT/T8KbKN7dr
aiUTmuWTUUUiUpMPAAAAAAAAAAwDQYJKoZIhvcNAQEFBQADQQDBcK0geQaK/QMs
txpOQv2UOgsYBhyz+9VLsNiQIZf6gi8+BTC3ozSwcY0sKt6E49Gez8ogWFAqF93K
lK7jACIN
-- ---END NEW CERTIFICATE REQUEST-- ---
```

The content is encrypted, so it is not intelligible.

The next step is to approach a CA for an SSL certificate. VeriSign offers a 14-day trial SSL ID, which you can become familiar with while you're setting up the SSL on your Web server. To do this, perform the following steps:

1. Access the site http://www.VeriSign.com and click on the link Free Guides and Trials.
2. In the Web page that appears, scroll down to the Free Trials section and click on the Free Trial SSL ID link.
3. Follow the instructions as displayed. After you have finished registering for the free trial, your certificate will be e-mailed to you at the e-mail address you specified while registering.

 NOTE

This page at http://www.VeriSign.com contains links to many informative guides and tutorials related to Web site security. You can download them after registering.

The certificate will be in a format similar to the request. A sample certificate response sent through e-mail is as shown:

```
-- ---BEGIN CERTIFICATE-- ---
MIIDATCCAqugAwIBAgIQNUDTln0qYiqaOt89VfXD4zANBgkqhkiG9w0BAQUFADCB
qTEWMBQGA1UEChMNVmVyaVNp724sIEluYzFHMEUGA1UECxM+d3d3LnZlcmlzaWdu
LmNvbS9yZXBvc2l0b3J5L1Rlc3RDRUFMgSW5jb3JwLiBCeSBSZWYuIExpYWIuIExU
RC4xRjBEBgNVBAsTPUZvciBWZXJpU2lnbiBhdXRob3JpemVkIHRlc3Rpbmcgb25s
eS4gTm8gYXNzdXJhbmNlyAoQylWUzE5OTcwHhcNMDIwNTA2MDAwMDAwWhcNMDIw
NTIwMjM1OTU5WjBiMQswCQYDVQQGEwJJTjEOMAwGA1UECBMFRGVsaGkxEjAQBgNV
BAcUCU5ldyBEZWxoaTENMAsGA1UEChQEbmlppdDEMMAoGA1UECxQDa3NiMRIwEAYD
VQQDFAlzYW1rLWQxODUwXDANBgkqhkiG9w0BAQEFAANLADBIAkEAzJDy/0iPV/FD
hqr1yZrodzCu7TQo88TXNt+ogXEfATFB+0ka/TNkgQeL50YfZagRjGEuwoQCvMfZ
cB2BQKQ4BwIDAQABo4H0MIHxMAkGA1UdEwQCMAAwCwYDVR0PBAQDAgWgMDwGA1Ud
HwQ1MDMwMaAvoC2GK2h0dHA6Ly9jcmwudmVyaXNpZ24uY29tL1JTQVNlY3VyZVNl
cnZlci5jcmwwRAYDVR0gBD0wOzA5BgtghkgBhvhFAQcXAzAqMCgGCCsGAQUFBwIB
FhxodHRwczovL3d3dy52ZXJpc2lnbi5jb20vcnBhMB0GA1UdJQQWMBQGCCsGAQUF
BwMBBggrBgEFBQcDAjA0BggrBgEFBQcBAQQoMCYwJAYIKwYBBQUHMAGGGGh0dHA6
Ly9vY3NwLnZlcmlzaWduLmNvbTANBgkqhkiG9w0BAQUFAANBAFeqzxSAspegv7ny
omrOtfoQWtxaetQE/vQVZc4cTGb/3tXYbaLNm5JI+iyNuiSPZwvbKXWo9Zg1azkD
uFk+rOM=
-- ---END CERTIFICATE-- ---
```

To install the certificate, perform the following steps:

1. Add the previous content to a text file.
2. Run the Internet Services Manager.
3. Open the Properties dialog box of the Web site for which you will install the certificate.
4. Click the Directory Security tab.
5. Under the Secure Communications section, click on the Server Certificate button.
6. In the Web Site Certificate Wizard, click on the Next button. The dialog box should now look like Figure 6-18.

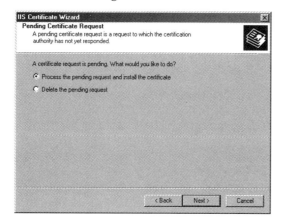

FIGURE 6-18 *The Pending Certificate Request page.*

7. Click on the Process the Pending Request and Install the Certificate option.
8. Click on the Next button. Browse and locate the certificate response file that you save with the .cer extension.
9. Click on the Next button.
10. In the Summary screen, verify that you are installing the correct certificate; then finish the certificate installation.

You now have a server certificate installed. To securely connect to the Web service, you now have to use https instead of http.

To connect to the newly secured Web service from the Visual Basic client, perform the following steps:

1. Change the code in the ClientProxy DLL project as shown:

```
Function getAll() As String
    Dim soapclient As New soapclient
    soapclient.mssoapinit
 "https://username:password@server1/ProductSummary/ProductSummary.wsdl"
```

```
    soapclient.ConnectorProperty("AuthUser") = "username"
    soapclient.ConnectorProperty("AuthPassword") = "password"
    Dim ss As DOMDocument
    Dim s As IXMLDOMNodeList
    Set s = soapclient.getAll()
    str1 = s.Item(0).xml
    getAll = str1
  End Function
```

2. Re-create the client proxy DLL file and run the test application.

3. Verify the connectivity with the Web service.

You have created a secure and functional Web service. You can now test the functioning of the service from an ASP page. The ASP page also uses the client proxy that you have created. The code for the ASP page is given next:

```
<% set obj=Server.CreateObject("ClientProxy.Class1")
   set xmlObj=Server.CreateObject("MSXML2.DOMDocument")
   set rs =Server.CreateObject("ADODB.Recordset")
   set ds=Server.CreateObject("ADODB.Stream")
   xmlObj.loadXML(obj.getAll())
   ds.open
   ds.writeText xmlobj.xml
   ds.position=0
   rs.open ds
   Response.write(rs.fields(0))
   Response.write(rs.fields(1))
   Response.write(rs.fields(2))
%>
```

The code for the ASP page is similar to the test Visual Basic application you created previously. Here, a string that contains the XML data is received from the Web service and an ADODB recordset is populated from the data. The first three fields of the first record in the recordset are then displayed. Create a virtual directory for this ASP page and verify the functioning of the Web service.

Summary

In this chapter, you created a Web service using the Microsoft Soap Toolkit 2.0. You also learned how to secure the Web service. Finally, you created clients using Visual Basic and ASP to verify the functioning of the Web site.

PART V

Professional Project 2

Project 2

Creating the News Web Service Using Visual Studio .NET

Project 2 Overview

Visual Studio .NET enables you to create Web services by using several languages that are part of the .NET Framework. In this project, you will create a Web service by using Visual Studio .NET and Visual Basic .NET. You also will look at the files and support features that Visual Studio .NET creates to make it easy for you to start creating Web services.

The Web service that you will create will be used by a company named NewsShop Pvt. Ltd., which provides information to its users in XML format on a wide range of topics.

Chapter 7

In the previous project, you learned to create a Web service that provides you with data on a wide range of commercial products. This Web service for http://www.CompareNShop.net was created using the Microsoft SOAP toolkit. You can create an XML Web service in several other ways. For example, you can create an XML Web service by using ASP.NET or Java. In this project, you will learn to create a Web service by using the ASP.NET technology.

Before going into creating a Web service by using ASP.NET, this chapter introduces you to ASP.NET. In addition, it refreshes your knowledge about static and dynamic Web pages. Next, it teaches you how to create a sample ASP.NET application in Visual Studio .NET. Creating a sample ASP.NET application can help you understand the components of the application, such as the server controls, that you can include in it.

This chapter also discusses the ADO.NET technology and its architecture. Finally, it teaches you how to create a sample ASP.NET application in Visual Studio.NET that connects to a database by using the ADO.NET technology.

Introduction to ASP.NET

Active Server Pages .NET (ASP.NET) is a new technology that is used to create dynamic Web pages. You can combine these Web pages to form a data-driven Web site that accesses data from a data source. You will learn about dynamic Web pages in detail in the later section titled "Dynamic Web Pages."

ASP.NET is evolved from the Active Server Pages (ASP) 3.0 technology, which has been used over the years to create Web pages. ASP allows you to create dynamic Web pages easily and quickly. Therefore, ASP.NET allows you to create scalable, dynamic, and interactive Web pages by using any of the .NET languages, such as Visual Basic .NET (VB.NET), Visual C#, and so on.

Features of the ASP.NET Technology

As stated earlier, the ASP.NET technology extends full support to the .NET initiative. As a result, the Web services that you create using ASP.NET benefit from the .NET technology. We will now discuss some of the features of the ASP.NET technology:

◆ **Create Web pages using any of the .NET languages.** The .NET platform includes several programming and scripting languages, such as Visual Basic .NET, Visual C#, Visual FoxPro, and JScript .NET. Therefore, you can create Web pages by using any of these languages or a combination of one or more languages. Although it's not possible to use more than one language on the same page, a Web site can contain Web pages written in different languages.

For example, the programmers who develop applications in Visual Basic can use Visual Basic .NET to develop Web pages. Similarly, the programmers who work in C++ or VC++ can use Visual C# or managed extensions in Visual C++ .NET to develop Web pages. Various .NET languages that you can use to create ASP.NET applications are shown in Figure 7-1.

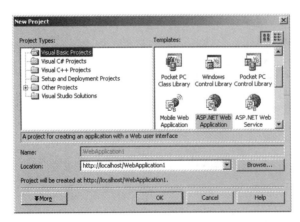

FIGURE 7-1 *.NET languages used to create ASP.NET applications.*

◆ **Compile the ASP.NET code easily.** Code that is written using any of the .NET languages is compiled as managed code by using the Common Language Runtime (CLR). The CLR ensures safe and efficient execution of code.

◆ **Support .NET base classes.** ASP.NET is a component of the .NET Framework. Therefore, you can use the classes contained in the .NET base class library to perform versatile operations in ASP.NET Web pages. For example, the .NET class library contains a Thread class that you can use to include threads in a Web application. Similarly, the Exception class of the .NET class library can be included to raise exceptions in the application.

◆ **Provide server controls.** ASP.NET Web applications are created in Visual Studio .NET, which provides you with a wide range of server controls. You can use these controls to create your own Web pages. The server controls that ASP.NET Web applications support are shown in Figure 7-2. You will learn about these controls in detail in the later section titled "Web Form Controls."

CLR

The CLR is a common runtime environment for applications that are developed using any of the .NET languages, such as Visual Basic .NET, Visual C#, and so on. The CLR compiles the code as managed code. Managed code contains information (metadata) about itself, such as the classes, methods, namespaces, and variables that are used in the application. Because the code contains information about itself, it makes the application interoperable across multiple languages.

The following list details the functions that the CLR performs:

◆ Executing code efficiently and safely

◆ Managing memory

◆ Executing threads

◆ Handling exceptions

◆ Achieving interoperability across languages

◆ **Allow customization of Web pages.** You can also customize Web pages according to user's preference. For example, ASP.NET allows you to change the appearance of a page, such as the layout of the page, the controls in the page, and so on, according to users' preferences. In addition, you can store information in a database or an XML file about the users who access the Web page.

◆ **Separate the code from the programming logic.** The Web applications that you create using ASP.NET contain an .aspx file. This file contains the HTML code for the application. In addition, the application includes an .aspx.vb or .aspx.cs file that contains the programming logic of the application. This implies that the HTML code and the programming logic of the application are stored in separate files.

FIGURE 7-2 *Server controls that ASP.NET Web applications support.*

 NOTE

The .aspx.vb file is formed if you create a Web application by using Visual Basic .NET. Similarly, if you use Visual C#, a file with the extension .aspx.cs is created.

◆ **Customize the Web page according to the browser used.** You can view ASP.NET pages on several browsers. However, while you're designing a Web page, you don't need to worry about the browser used. ASP.NET customizes the Web page according to the browser settings.

◆ **Allow the creation of Web services.** The ASP.NET technology allows you to create Web services, which is an important feature of the .NET Framework.

◆ **Support Visual Studio .NET debugging tools.** Visual Studio .NET contains a debugger that you can use to debug ASP.NET applications efficiently and quickly. In addition, the .NET base class library contains several classes, such as Debug and Trace, for debugging applications.

THE WEB.CONFIG FILE

The Web.config file is an XML file that stores the configuration settings for a Web application or a Web service. Configuring an ASP.NET application by using the Web.config file allows you to specify different configuration settings for different directories and subdirectories of the application. For example, you can configure a Web page so that only authorized users can view it.

THE .NET BASE CLASS LIBRARY

The .NET Framework provides you with a wide range of base classes that contain methods you can use to perform several operations. The base classes are included in the .NET base class library, which is an Application Programming Interface (API) similar to Microsoft Foundation Classes (MFC) that you use with Visual C++ 6.0.

You can use the base classes that are included in the .NET base class library in all .NET languages. For example, you can use the Thread class, which we discussed earlier, in both Visual Basic .NET and Visual C# applications. This implies that you can create interoperable applications by using the classes that are available in the class library. In addition, these classes can be used to create various applications, such as Windows applications and Web applications.

In addition to classes, the .NET base class library contains interfaces, data types, value types, enumerations, and so on.

♦ **Configure applications by using IIS.** You can configure ASP.NET applications by using Internet Information Server (IIS). In addition, you can configure the applications by using the Web.config file.

Architecture of ASP.NET Applications

When you create ASP.NET applications in Visual Studio .NET, it creates several default files. These files have different file names and extensions. For example, Visual Studio .NET creates a user interface, a file that contains the code for the user interface, reference files, a file containing the programming logic of the application, and so on. You will learn about these files in detail in the section "Default Files in a Web Application."

In addition to the files containing the code, an ASP.NET application consists of the directives and the layout of the application. The following list discusses the components of an ASP.NET application:

♦ **Code.** The code of an application is written to implement the business logic of the application. A code for an application includes namespaces, classes, methods, and so on. After writing the code for an application, you can reuse the code in other applications.

♦ **Layout.** The layout forms a template of the application, as it would appear on the browser.

♦ **Directives.** Directives are used to provide additional information about the Web page, such as the language used and the resources required in a transaction. In addition, you can use directives to insert messages for the compiler and the browser.

As you know, the ASP.NET technology creates dynamic Web pages. We will now briefly discuss the types of Web pages.

Types of Web Pages

Web pages are of two types:

◆ Static Web pages
◆ Dynamic Web pages

You can use the ASP.NET technology to create both types of Web pages. The following sections discuss static and dynamic Web pages in detail.

Static Web Pages

A static Web page is an .html file that consists of the HTML code. The data that you need to display in the Web page is contained in the HTML code. You cannot change the content of a static page after it is created. As a result, it is essential for the developer to be sure of the content before creating the Web page.

In addition, the content of a static Web page does not change depending on the user preference. This implies that in a static Web page, there is no mechanism by which you can tailor the Web page according to the user preference.

Creating a Sample Static Web Page

We will now create a sample static Web page by using HTML. Doing this will help you understand the concept of static Web pages.

To create a static Web page, perform the following steps:

1. Open a Notepad file.
2. Add the following code to the Notepad file:

```
<img src="Welcome.bmp" width="370" height="71" align="right">
<title>Home Page</title>
<h1>Welcome to the Home Page of SomeOrganization, Inc.</h2>
<h2>About SomeOrganization, Inc.</h1>
<p><b><i>SomeOrganization, Inc.</i></b> is a group of exporters based in Los
Angeles. SomeOrganization, Inc. has been in the garments export business for
the past 15 years. Since then, the organization has evolved to form a leading
export house in the U.S.</p>
<h2>Employees of SomeOrganization, Inc.</h2>
<p><b><i>SomeOrganization, Inc.</i></b> has more than 50,000 employees
```

```
working in different branches of the organization. The branches of the
organization are spread across the major cities of the world.</p>
<h2>Departments of SomeOrganization, Inc.</h3>
<p><b><i>SomeOrganization, Inc.</i></b> has the following departments:</p>
<ul>
            <li>Human Resource</li>
            <li>Manufacturing</li>
            <li>Finance</li>
            <li>Marketing</li>
</ul>
```

3. Save the file as Sample.htm. Saving the file as an .htm file converts the Notepad file into an HTML file.

4. Open the file in a browser.

The previous code creates a sample Web page for a hypothetical organization, SomeOrganization, Inc. After saving the file as Sample.htm, you can open it in any browser, such as Internet Explorer or Netscape Navigator.

The Sample.htm file should look like Figure 7-3.

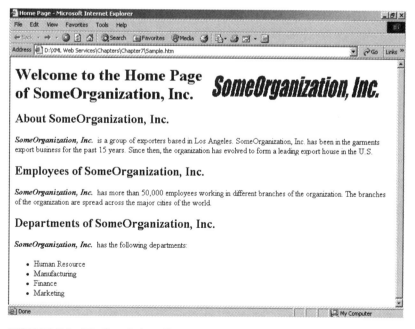

FIGURE 7-3 *The Sample.htm file.*

Accessing Static Web Pages

After you have created a Web page, you need to save it on a Web server. For example, the Web page that you created in the previous section, Sample.htm, is accessible only to a local user. To make it accessible to all users, you need to host the Web page on a Web server. After you have hosted a Web page on a Web server, a URL address is assigned to it. Any user can then access the Web page by using its URL.

To access a Web page, the user needs to send in a request from a browser for the Web page. The request is then forwarded to the Web server, which converts the request to an HTML stream. The Web server then processes the HTML stream and sends the result back to the browser. The result is also in the form of an HTML stream. Finally, the browser processes the HTML stream and displays the result in the form of a Web page. This process is illustrated in Figure 7-4.

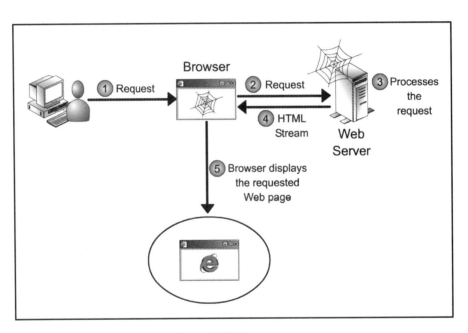

FIGURE 7-4 *The process of accessing static Web pages.*

Limitations of Using Static Web Pages

As you can see, creating static Web pages is easy because it involves simple HTML coding. However, HTML has some limitations. For example, you cannot customize the Web page according to a user's preference. All users who access a static Web page see the same page. In addition, you can use HTML to display only static content.

Consider a situation in which you need to display a welcome thought in the Web page. You can do this by using HTML. However, if you want to update the welcome thought daily, you cannot do this using HTML alone. Consider another situation in which you want to display a welcome message to the user who accesses your Web page. In addition, you want to display the time when the user logs on to your page, as shown in Figure 7-5.

HTML does not allow you to display such dynamic features in a Web page. Another limitation of a static Web page is that the code behind the Web page is accessible to all users. This implies that any user can reuse your code to create their Web pages. To overcome these limitations, dynamic Web pages are used in a Web application. The following section discusses dynamic Web pages in detail.

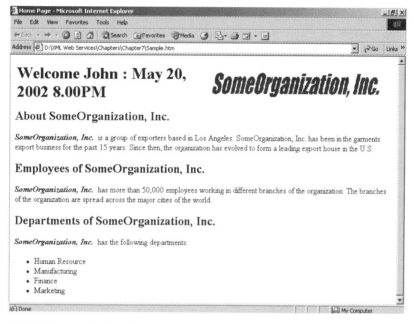

FIGURE 7-5 *The Sample.htm page.*

Dynamic Web Pages

As the name suggests, dynamic Web pages allow you to display dynamic content. In contrast to static Web pages, in a dynamic Web page, the HTML code is generated after a user requests a Web page. This implies that you can customize the Web page to be displayed according to the preference of the user who makes a request for the page.

You can use two models to develop dynamic Web pages:

- ◆ Server-side coding model
- ◆ Client-side coding model

We will now discuss the two models of creating dynamic Web pages in detail.

Server-Side Coding Model

In the server-side coding model, when a user requests a Web page, the user needs to send a set of instructions to the browser. The browser then forwards the request and the set of instructions to the Web server. The Web server finds the file that contains these instructions and then creates an HTML stream based on the set of instructions. This enables the Web server to dynamically generate an HTML stream.

The HTML stream is passed on to the browser, which then processes it to display the Web page. The process of the server-side coding model is depicted in Figure 7-6.

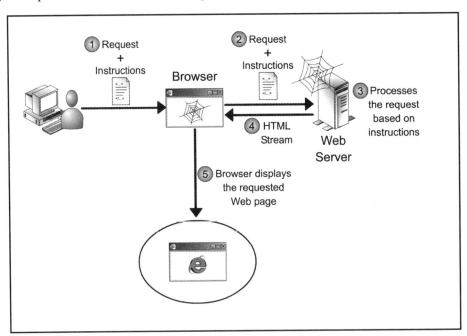

FIGURE 7-6 *The server-side coding model.*

Client-Side Coding Model

The client-side coding model is similar to the server-side coding model. However, in the client-side coding model, the set of instructions in the form of an HTML file is processed at the client side. For example, the user might need to customize the appearance of the Web page. To do this, the user preference needs to be included as a set of instructions that the client processes.

When a user requests a Web page, the request is passed to the Web server. The Web server locates the HTML page and creates an HTML stream. The HTML stream along with the set of instructions is sent back to the browser. The browser contains modules that process the HTML stream according to the instructions. The HTML page that is returned is then displayed in the browser. The process of the client-side coding model is displayed in Figure 7-7.

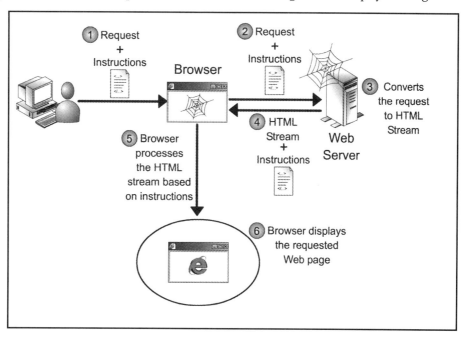

FIGURE 7-7 *The client-side coding model.*

The client-side coding model has some limitations, as discussed in the following list:

◆ Because the processing of a request takes place at the client side, different browsers might process the request differently, which could result in undesirable results.

◆ The Web pages that are using the client-side model require a lot of time to download. This is because the files that contain the instructions are downloaded at the client side in addition to the Web page.

◆ In the client-side coding model, the code behind a Web page is easily accessible to users who can use the code to create their Web pages.

As a result of the previously mentioned limitations, ASP.NET applications use server-side coding. These applications include ASP.NET Web applications and ASP.NET Web services. In this chapter, we will discuss how to create a simple ASP.NET Web application. You can use this knowledge to create a client application that requests a Web service. You will learn to create an ASP.NET Web service in Chapter 8, "Creating an ASP.NET Web Service."

Creating ASP.NET Applications in Visual Studio .NET

ASP.NET applications require only a text editor, such as Notepad. However, creating an ASP.NET application in a text editor involves a lot of HTML and ASP.NET coding. To create ASP.NET applications easily and efficiently, you can use a tool developed by Microsoft called Visual Studio .NET.

Visual Studio .NET provides you with several features and utilities that help you create ASP.NET applications. For example, Visual Studio .NET provides you with different templates that you can use to create ASP.NET Web applications and ASP.NET Web services. In addition, you can create ASP.NET applications in any of the .NET languages, such as Visual C# and Visual Basic .NET.

NOTE

In this chapter, you will create an ASP.NET Web application in Visual Basic .NET.

When you use the template that Visual Studio .NET provides to create an ASP.NET application, Visual Studio .NET creates the default classes for the application. In addition, it automatically includes the required namespaces in your application. This implies that Visual Studio .NET creates a framework for the application. You can then add the code of the application to this framework.

Visual Studio .NET provides you with the color schemes for keywords and values, making them easier to read and understand. In addition, Visual Studio .NET includes an auto complete feature that completes the entries as you type the code. Visual Studio .NET also includes an auto help feature that provides instant help on any of the keywords, such as the class, event, and method names. You will learn about these and many more features of Visual Studio .NET throughout this project.

Creating a Sample ASP.NET Application

To create an ASP.NET Web application in Visual Studio .NET, perform the following steps:

1. Launch Visual Studio .NET from the Programs menu.

   When you launch Visual Studio .NET for the first time, the interface for Visual Studio .NET looks like Figure 7-8.

2. To create a new project, click on the File menu.

3. In the list that is displayed, point to the New menu.

4. In the displayed list, select the Project option.

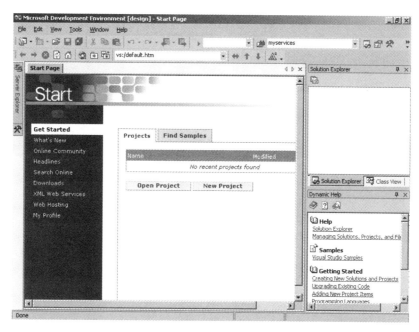

FIGURE 7-8 *The interface for Visual Studio .NET.*

5. The New Project dialog box is displayed, as shown in Figure 7-9.

   As you can see, the New Project dialog box offers you various templates to create different applications.

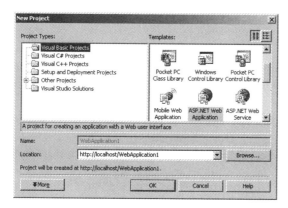

FIGURE 7-9 *The New Project dialog box.*

6. In the Project Types pane, select the Visual Basic Projects option.

7. In the Templates pane, select the ASP.NET Web Application option.

8. In the Location text box, type the address of the Web server on which you will develop the Web application.

 NOTE

In our case, the development server is the local computer, so the address of the development server will appear as http://localhost/.

You can also specify the name of the Web application in the Location text box.

9. Type the name of the application as `WebApplication1`.

10. Click on the OK button to create the Web application.

The Web application connects to the Web server, as shown in Figure 7-10.

FIGURE 7-10 *The Web application connecting to a Web server.*

The Web application opens in the Design view. The Design view of the Web application is shown in Figure 7-11.

Web Form

When a Web application is created, Visual Studio .NET creates a blank Web form with the name WebForm1.aspx, as shown in Figure 7-12. You can also include several Web forms in a Web application.

A Web form is a user interface for a Web application and is used to create programmable and interactive Web pages. A Web form consists of two parts: an interface that accepts user input or presents information to the user, and the code behind the interface that implements the business logic of the application. To accept input from a user, you need to include Web form controls in the Web form. The Web form controls are explained in the following section.

Web Form Controls

Visual Studio .NET provides you with several Web form controls that you can add by dragging them to the form. Web form controls contain a variety of controls that are designed to work within the ASP.NET page framework. These Web form controls are shown in Figure 7-2.

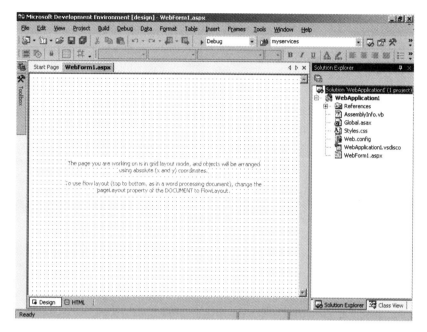

FIGURE 7-11 *The Design view of the Web application.*

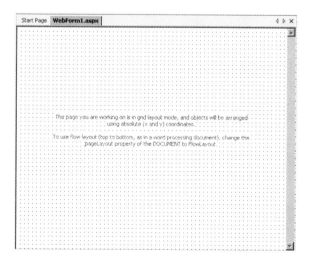

FIGURE 7-12 *The Web form that Visual Studio .NET created.*

ASP.NET supports different types of Web form controls or server controls. Table 7-1 discusses the types of Web form controls in detail.

Table 7-1 Types of Web Form Controls

Web Form Control	Description
User controls	These create controls that are reusable across multiple Web pages, such as menu items, toolbars, and so on.
Validation controls	These validate the data that a user enters against the rules that the programmer defines. To validate a control, you associate it with another control that accepts data from a user. For example, you can use a RequiredFieldValidator control to check whether the user has specified a value for the control or left it blank.
Web server controls	These create Web pages with controls, such as Label, TextBox, Button, DataGrid, or Table.
HTML server controls	These expose an object to a server to make it accessible to programmers. After a control is exposed, you can program these controls within an ASP.NET file.

Default Files in a Web Application

In addition to a Web form, Visual Studio .NET creates default files for a Web application. These default files are included in a solution.

 NOTE

A solution is a collection of projects or related projects. For example, you can include a project and its deployment projects in the same solution.

A solution for WebApplication1 is shown in Figure 7-13.

Table 7-2 discusses in detail the default files that Visual Studio .NET created.

Table 7-2 The Default Files in a Web Application

Default File	Description
References	The References folder contains the Web references for the application. These Web references include the System, System.Data, System.Drawing, System.Web, and System.XML namespaces.
bin	The bin folder contains the .dll file for the application.

Default File	Description
AssemblyInfo.vb	A Web application contains an assembly, which includes the namespaces, classes, interfaces, and so on that you need to include in the Web application. The information about the assembly, such as the name and version number, is stored in the AssemblyInfo.vb file.
Global.asax	The Global.asax folder contains the Global.asax.vb file. This file handles the events that the application generates. For example, when a user clicks on a button, the `Click` event of the Button control is generated. The Global.asax.vb file handles this event.
Styles.css	The Styles.css file contains a style sheet for the Web application.
Web.config	The Web.config file contains the configuration settings for the Web application.
WebApplication1.vsdisco	The WebApplication1.vsdisco file contains a description of the Web application, such as a description of the classes and methods included in the application.
WebForm1.aspx	The WebForm1.aspx folder contains the WebForm1.aspx.vb file. This file contains the code for the Web form.

FIGURE 7-13 *The default files that Visual Studio .NET created.*

Creating an Interface for WebApplication1

To create an interface for the sample Web application, you need to include an Image control, six Label controls, one Button control, five TextBox controls, and one ListBox control in the Web form. To add these controls, you need to drag them from the Web Forms toolbox and place them on the form. Next, you need to change the properties of the controls, as listed in Table 7-3.

Table 7-3 Controls in the Web Form

Control Type	Control ID	Properties Changed
Image	Image1	ImageURl: `Welcome.bmp`
Label	Label1	Text: `Name` ForeColor: `MidnightBlue`
Label	Label2	Text: `Employee ID` ForeColor: `MidnightBlue`
Label	Label3	Text: `Designation` ForeColor: `MidnightBlue`
Label	Label4	Text: `Department` ForeColor: `MidnightBlue`
Label	Label5	Text: `Address` ForeColor: `MidnightBlue`
Label	Label6	Text: `City` ForeColor: `MidnightBluc`
TextBox	TextBox1	None
TextBox	TextBox2	None
TextBox	TextBox3	None
TextBox	TextBox4	None
TextBox	TextBox5	None
Button	Button1	Text: `Submit`

Adding Items to the ListBox Control

As you can see, we have added a list box to the form. You can now add items to the ListBox control by performing the following steps:

1. Click on the ListBox control to display its properties.

2. Click on the Items property of the control to add items to the control.
    The ListItem Collection Editor dialog box is displayed.

3. Click on the Add button to add an item to the list.

4. In the Marketing Properties pane, change the following properties of the list item:
    Selected: `True`
    Text: `Marketing`
    Value: `Marketing`

5. Similarly, add the `Human Resources`, `Sales`, `Finance`, and `Manufacturing` items to the list box.

6. Click on the OK button to close the ListItem Collection Editor dialog box.

After you have added the controls and changed their properties, the Web form should look like Figure 7-14.

However, the button in the Web form is not functional. To make the button functional, you need to add code to it.

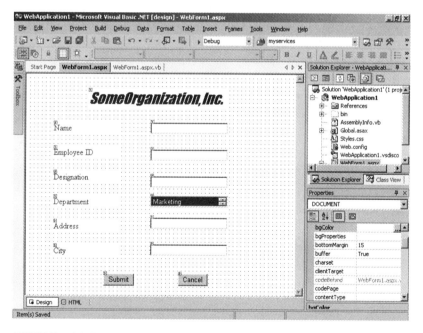

FIGURE 7-14 *The Web form in the Design view.*

Adding Code to the Submit Button

When a user enters values in the text boxes and clicks on the Submit button, the text boxes should become blank. To do this, add the following code to the `Click` event of the Button control:

```
Private Sub Button1_Click(ByVal sender As System.Object, ByVal e As
System.EventArgs) Handles Button1.Click
        TextBox1.Text = ""
        TextBox2.Text = ""
        TextBox3.Text = ""
        TextBox4.Text = ""
        TextBox5.Text = ""
    End Sub
```

After you have added the code to the Button control, the entire code for the application is as follows:

```
Public Class WebForm1
    Inherits System.Web.UI.Page
    Protected WithEvents Image1 As System.Web.UI.WebControls.Image
    Protected WithEvents Label1 As System.Web.UI.WebControls.Label
    Protected WithEvents Label2 As System.Web.UI.WebControls.Label
    Protected WithEvents Label3 As System.Web.UI.WebControls.Label
    Protected WithEvents Label4 As System.Web.UI.WebControls.Label
    Protected WithEvents Label5 As System.Web.UI.WebControls.Label
    Protected WithEvents Label6 As System.Web.UI.WebControls.Label
    Protected WithEvents Button1 As System.Web.UI.WebControls.Button
    Protected WithEvents TextBox1 As System.Web.UI.WebControls.TextBox
    Protected WithEvents TextBox2 As System.Web.UI.WebControls.TextBox
    Protected WithEvents TextBox3 As System.Web.UI.WebControls.TextBox
    Protected WithEvents TextBox4 As System.Web.UI.WebControls.TextBox
    Protected WithEvents TextBox5 As System.Web.UI.WebControls.TextBox
    Protected WithEvents ListBox1 As System.Web.UI.WebControls.ListBox


Private Sub Page_Load(ByVal sender As System.Object, ByVal e As
System.EventArgs) Handles MyBase.Load
        'Put user code to initialize the page here
    End Sub


    Private Sub Button1_Click(ByVal sender As System.Object, ByVal e As
System.EventArgs) Handles Button1.Click
        TextBox1.Text = ""
        TextBox2.Text = ""
        TextBox3.Text = ""
        TextBox4.Text = ""
```

```
        TextBox5.Text = ""
    End Sub
End Class
```

The code contains the declarations for all controls that you added to the Web application. In addition, the code for the `Click` event of the Button control is included.

Testing the Application

You can now run the application to test it. To test the application, press the F5 key. Alternatively, you can select the Start option on the Debug menu. Figure 7-15 shows the Web form at runtime.

Until now, you learned to create a simple ASP.NET application. However, in most common business scenarios, the ASP.NET application needs to interact with a database. This can be achieved using the ADO.NET technology in an ASP.NET application.

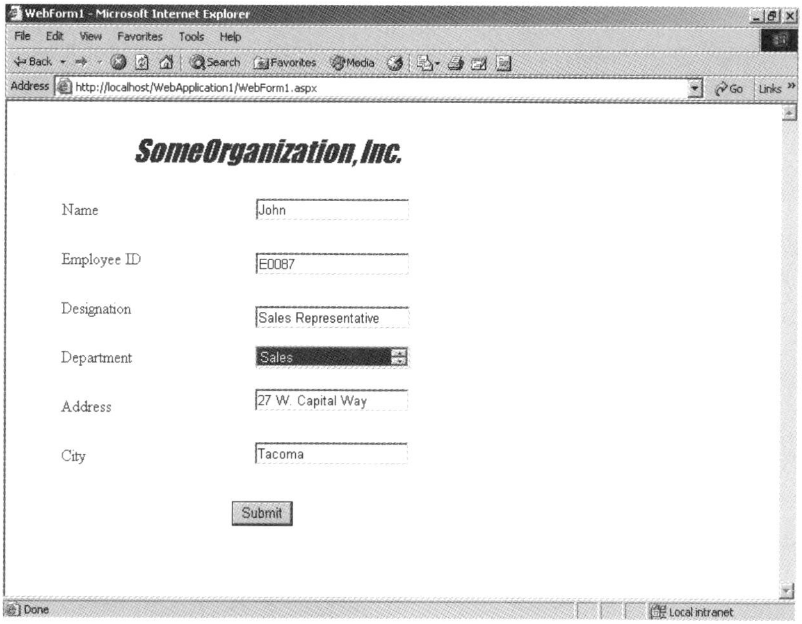

FIGURE 7-15 *The Web form at runtime.*

Introduction to ADO.NET

Programmers worldwide have been creating applications that access data from a database. One of the technologies that an application uses to interact with a database is ActiveX Data Object (ADO). ADO is an easy-to-use data access method that is based on COM. Microsoft combined the features of ADO with the .NET Framework to develop a technology called ADO.NET.

ADO.NET is a data access model that distributed applications use to communicate with data sources such as Microsoft SQL Server and Oracle. Using ADO.NET, you can develop high-performance scalable applications that can interact with a database. In addition, the applications that use ADO.NET are based on the .NET Framework; therefore, they are interoperable across platforms.

ADO.NET allows you to access or modify the data in a database. To do this, the application first needs to connect to a database. After a connection is established, you can make changes to the data in the database. Because ADO.NET is based on the .NET Framework, you can use the classes provided in the .NET base class library. These classes include `OleDbConnection`, `SqlDbConnection`, and so on.

Advantages of ADO.NET

As discussed earlier, ADO.NET offers you an easy and efficient way to create applications that access data from a data source. The following list discusses the advantages of the ADO.NET technology:

◆ **Allows the creation of high-performance applications.** ADO.NET uses XML to transfer data between a data source and an ASP.NET application. This implies that the receiving application can easily interpret and understand the data that is transferred. In addition, when data is transferred using XML, the receiving application does not need to convert data types, as in the case of transferring data by using ADO. This improves the performance of the applications that use ADO.NET.

◆ **Allows the creation of applications with easy programming.** .NET provides you with several components, classes, and commands that allow easy and quick programming. This significantly reduces the effort required to develop applications. In addition, by using the debugging tools of .NET, you can reduce the number of errors in the application.

◆ **Allows the creation of scalable applications.** ADO.NET uses a disconnected architecture to allow multiple users to access the same application. In the disconnected architecture, the locks on the database are not retained very long. As soon as a user finishes working on a

DISCONNECTED ARCHITECTURE

In the disconnected architecture, an application can connect to a data source only for the time that the application accesses data from the data source. For example, when a Web application connects to a data source to modify data, the connection is made only for the time that the data is being updated. This improves the performance of the application.

The disconnected architecture is in contrast to the traditional connected architecture in which the connection is retained for the time the application is running. As a result, multiple users are not able to connect to the same data source simultaneously.

database, the lock on the database is released. This enables multiple users to access a
database simultaneously.

◆ **Allows the creation of interoperable applications.** ADO.NET uses XML to transfer data.
Therefore, any application that can understand XML can read the data that is transferred
using XML. This enables you to create interoperable applications by using ADO.NET. In
addition, ADO.NET applications can be created in any of the .NET languages.

Architecture of ADO.NET

ADO.NET applications consist of at least two components:

◆ Datasets
◆ Data providers

The architecture of the ADO.NET applications is shown in Figure 7-16.

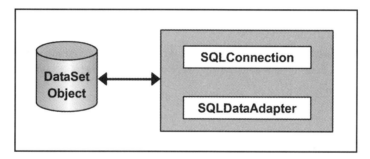

FIGURE 7-16 *The architecture of the ADO.NET applications.*

We will now discuss these components in detail.

Datasets

A *dataset* is a memory cache object that provides a relational view of the data from a data
source, such as a database. To create a dataset, you can use the `DataSet` class, which in turn
uses the `DataTable` class to store the tables within the dataset. The data in a dataset is stored
in XML format.

A dataset is a virtual database that is used in disconnected data architecture. When an application accesses or modifies data in a database, the data is first stored in the dataset. This is
because in disconnected architecture, the application cannot access the data after modifying
each row. Therefore, the data needs to be stored in a temporary memory cache, which is a
dataset. The application can then access the data from the dataset.

Components of a Dataset

You can use a DataSet object to store data from one or more tables in a database, the relationships between the tables, and the constraints and keys defined for the tables in the database.

These form the components of the DataSet object, as discussed in the following list:

◆ **DataTableCollection.** The DataTableCollection object represents the set of Data Table objects that contains one or more tables from a data source. The DataTable Collection object is represented by the `DataTableCollection` class. This class contains several methods that you can use to work with DataTableCollection objects. For example, you can add or remove a specific DataTable object from the `DataTable Collection` class by using the `Add()` and `Remove()` methods, respectively.

◆ **DataRowCollection.** A table consists of rows and columns. All rows in the Data Table object, represented by the DataRow object, constitute the DataRowCollection object.

◆ **DataColumnCollection.** The columns in a DataTable object, represented by a DataColumn object, are contained in the DataColumnCollection object.

◆ **DataRelationCollection.** A DataTable object might contain one or more tables. The DataRelation object represents the relationship between the columns of the tables in the DataTable object. The DataRelationCollection object is a collection of DataRelation objects in a dataset.

◆ **ConstraintCollection.** You can create a constraint, such as a unique key or a foreign key, for a data table. These constraints are stored in the ConstraintCollection object.

The components of a DataSet object are shown in Figure 7-17.

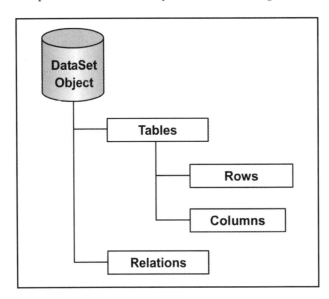

FIGURE 7-17 _The components of the DataSet object._

Types of Datasets

Having discussed the components of the dataset, we'll next discuss the types of DataSet objects.

◆ **Typed datasets.** You can inherit classes from the DataSet class. These classes are called typed datasets and are created using the information stored in XML schema. A typed dataset class inherits all the methods, events, and properties of the dataset class from which it is derived. Using typed datasets in an application reduces the time taken to access a column or a table. In addition, the typed dataset classes allow you to create applications with minimum errors and are used to perform data manipulation and data binding.

◆ **Untyped datasets.** The datasets that are not created with reference to the information in the XML schema are called untyped datasets. Unlike typed datasets, untyped datasets are not classes, but they do provide you with the functionality of a dataset. To create an untyped dataset, you need to create an instance of the DataSet class in a form or a component.

Data Providers

Data providers are used to provide access to data in a database. To do this, data providers allow you to establish a connection with the data source, execute commands, and retrieve results.

Data providers contain several methods that allow you to connect to a database, retrieve data from the database, and update changes to the database. ADO.NET supports several data providers, such as Microsoft Jet OLE DB Provider, Microsoft OLE DB Provider for Oracle, Microsoft OLE DB Provider for SQL Server, and so on.

A data provider has four components, as discussed in the following list:

◆ **The Connection object.** To access data from a database, you first need to connect to the database. To do this, ADO.NET provides you with the Connection object that establishes and manages a connection with the database.

◆ **The DataReader object.** To read data in a sequential manner from a database, you need to use the DataReader object. The data from the database is read in the form of a data stream. The DataReader object allows only one row to be stored in the memory at any point of time. This results in more efficient performance of the application and reduction in the system overheads.

◆ **The DataAdapter object.** This object is used to transfer data between a data source and a dataset. When you need to update the data in a database, the changes are first stored in the dataset and are then replicated to the database. Therefore, the DataAdapter object is used to communicate between the data source and the dataset.

◆ **The Command object.** After establishing a connection with the database, you can use the Command object to perform operations such as modifying the records in the database. This object is used when there is a connection with the database.

Having discussed the components of an ADO.NET application, we will now create a simple application that uses these components.

Creating a Sample ADO.NET Application

To create an ADO.NET application in Visual Studio .NET, perform the following steps:

1. Launch Visual Studio .NET from the Programs menu.
2. Click on the File menu. In the list that is displayed, point to the New menu and then select the Project option. The New Project dialog box is displayed.
3. In the Project Types pane, select the Visual Basic Projects option.
4. In the Templates pane, select the ASP.NET Web Application option.
5. In the Location text box, type the address of the Web server on which you will develop the Web application.
6. Type the name of the application as `SampleWebApplication`.
7. Click on the OK button to create the Web application. Visual Studio .NET creates a blank form for you.
8. From the Web Forms Toolbox, add a DataGrid control and a Button control to the form.

TIP

If the Toolbox is invisible, click on the Toolbox option on the View menu.

The previous steps create the interface for SampleWebApplication. To make the application functional, you need to add the programming logic to the DataGrid and Button controls.

Adding the Programming Logic to the DataGrid Control

A DataGrid control displays or modifies the data in a dataset. The data from the dataset is displayed in the form of rows and columns. However, before displaying the data, you need to connect to a database by using ADO.NET. Visual Studio .NET provides you with several data adapters that you can use to connect to a database.

As discussed earlier, the data from a database is first stored in the dataset. A data adapter acts as an interface between a database and its corresponding dataset. You can use a data adapter to transfer data between a database and a dataset.

A data adapter is a control in the Data toolbox that is used to connect to a database. Visual Studio .NET provides you with data adapters, such as OleDbDataAdapter and SqlDataAdapter. You can use SqlDataAdapter to connect to an SQL database. However, to connect to a database other than SQL, you need to use OleDbDataAdapter.

NOTE

In this chapter, we will use SqlDataAdapter to connect to the SQL database, Employees.

To create a connection to a database, perform the following steps:

1. Drag SqlDataAdapter from the Data toolbox.

    The Data Adapter Configuration Wizard is displayed.

2. Click on the Next button to start the wizard.

3. In the Choose Your Data Connection page, click on the New Connection button to create a new connection to an SQL database.

    The Connection page of the Data Link Properties window is displayed.

NOTE

If you are using a database other than SQL, you need to select the appropriate data adapter in the OLE DB Provider(s) list in the Provider tab of the Data Link Properties window. By default, the Microsoft OLE DB Provider for SQL Server option is selected.

4. From the Select or Enter a Server Name combo box, select the server to which you want to connect.

5. In the Enter Information to Log On to the Server group box, select the authentication mode to connect to an SQL server.

NOTE

Visual Studio .NET provides you with two options. To connect to an SQL server by using the Windows authentication mode, select the Use Windows NT Integrated Security option. However, if you select the Use a Specific Name and Password option, you need to specify the username and the password in the Username and Password text boxes, respectively. To leave the password blank, check the Blank Password check box.

6. Select the Select the Database on the Server option to choose the database to which you want to connect.

7. Select the name of the database from the drop-down list as Employees.

8. Click on the Test Connection button to test the connection to the Employees database. If the connection is successful, a message box showing the text Test connection succeeded is displayed.

9. Click on the OK button to close the message box.

10. Click on the OK button to close the Data Link Properties window.

   The Choose Your Data Connection page is displayed. The name of the Employees database is displayed in the Which Data Connection Should the Data Adapter Use list box.

   Click on the Next button to continue with the wizard.

   The Choose a Query Type page is displayed. This page provides you with several options to access the database.

11. Select the Use SQL Statements option.

   This option allows you to create an SQL statement that enables the data adapter to access the database.

12. Click on the Next button.

   The Generate the SQL Statements page is displayed. You can type the query in the What Data Should the Data Adapter Load into the Dataset text box.

13. Type the following SQL statement into the text box:

```
SELECT *
FROM Employee
```

   Here, `Employee` is the name of the table in the Employees database. The preceding SQL statement allows you to select all fields from the Employee table. You can also click on the Query Builder button to graphically create the query.

   The Data Adapter Configuration Wizard uses the SQL query to create the Insert, Update, and Delete statements to insert, update, and delete records from the table.

14. Click on the Next button.

   The View Wizard Results page is displayed. This page displays a list of the tasks that the wizard has performed. The Data Adapter Configuration Wizard creates the `SELECT`, `INSERT`, `UPDATE`, and `DELETE` statements.

15. Click on the Finish button to create the data adapter.

The Data Adapter Configuration Wizard creates a data adapter named `sqlDataAdapter1`, which contains information about the Employee table. In addition, Data Adapter Configuration Wizard creates a connection, `sqlConnection1`, which contains information about how to access the Employees database.

After you create a connection by using the Data Adapter Configuration Wizard, you need to create a DataSet object. To generate a DataSet object, perform the following steps:

1. Click anywhere in the form to activate it.

2. On the Data menu, select the Generate Dataset option.

   The Generate Dataset window is displayed.

3. From the Choose a Dataset group box, select the New option button. In the text box that is adjacent to the New option button, type the name of the DataSet object as `EmpDataSet`.

TIP

Make sure that the Employee table is selected in the Choose Which Table(s) to Add to the Dataset text box.

4. Check the Add This Dataset to the Designer check box.

   This adds the dataset to the component tray of the form.

5. Click on the OK button to close the Generate Dataset window.

Visual Studio .NET creates a dataset with the name `EmpDataSet1`, which contains the data from the Employee table. In addition, an EmpDataSet1.xsd file is created that contains information about the `EmpDataSet1` dataset.

The data from the table is still not visible in the DataGrid control. To display the records from the dataset, you need to bind the DataGrid control to the dataset. To do so, perform the following steps:

1. In the Design view, click on the DataGrid control to display its properties.

TIP

If the Properties window is not displayed, select the Properties Window option from the View menu or press the F4 key.

2. In the Properties window, select the `DataSource` property.

3. Click on the down arrow to select the `EmpDataSet1` dataset.

4. Click on the down arrow of the `DataMember` property and select the Employee table.

A DataGrid control showing the column headings is displayed, as shown in Figure 7-18.

After you perform the preceding steps, the DataGrid control contains only the column headings. To load the records from the table to the DataGrid control, you need to write the code for the Button control.

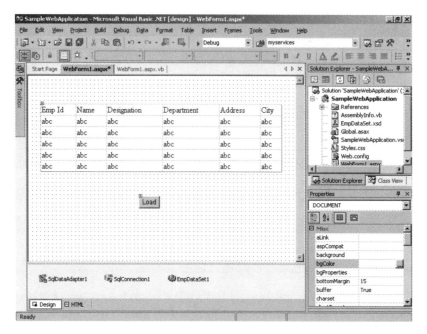

FIGURE 7-18 *The Web form in Design view.*

Adding the Programming Logic to the Button Control

Before you add code to the Button control, change the Name property of the control to Load. Now, double-click on the control to display the code window. Alternatively, you can choose the Code option on the View menu or press the F7 key. In the Click event of the Button control, add the following code:

```
Private Sub Button1_Click(ByVal sender As System.Object, ByVal e As
System.EventArgs) Handles Button1.Click
        EmpDataSet1.Clear()
        SqlDataAdapter1.Fill(EmpDataSet1)
        DataGrid1.DataBind()
End Sub
```

In the previous code, the Click event of the Button control takes two parameters, sender and e, of the Object type. Inside the Click event, the Clear() method of the DataSet class is called. This method clears all records in the EmpDataSet1 dataset.

Next, the Fill() method of the DataSet class adds or refreshes the data in the dataset to match the data to the records in the database. The Fill() method takes the name of the dataset as the parameter. Finally, the DataBind() method is called to bind the DataGrid control to the database that the DataSource property of the control specifies: EmpDataSet1.

Testing the Application

After adding the code, you have created the application. You can now test it. To test the application, select the Start option on the Debug menu. Alternatively, you can press the F5 key. The application opens a Web form in the browser. The Web form contains a Load button. Click on the button to display the records from the Employee table. Figure 7-19 shows the Web form at runtime.

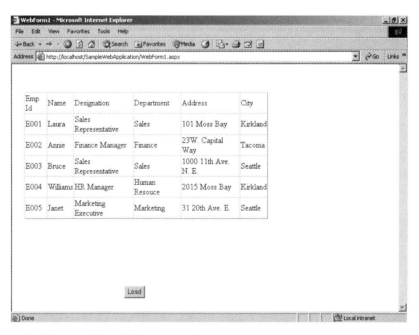

FIGURE 7-19 *The Web form at runtime.*

Summary

This chapter introduced you to the ASP.NET technology. ASP.NET is a new technology that creates dynamic Web pages. Next, you learned about the features and the architecture of ASP.NET applications. ASP.NET can be used to create two types of Web pages: static and dynamic.

You also learned to create a sample ASP.NET application and were introduced to ADO.NET. ADO.NET is a data access model that distributed applications use to communicate with data sources such as Microsoft SQL Server and Oracle. Finally, you created a sample application that accesses data from a database by using ADO.NET.

Chapter 8

In the previous project, you learned how to create a Web service by using the SOAP
Toolkit 2.0. You use the SOAP toolkit to create Web services when you need to use the
existing COM-based code in the Web services architecture. In addition, you use the SOAP
toolkit to create Web services for a COM-based platform. Although the SOAP toolkit
helps you create Web services easily and efficiently, you can develop complex Web services
for the Windows 2000 platform in another way: by using Visual Studio .NET.

This chapter teaches you how to create an ASP.NET Web service by using Visual Studio
.NET. It also shows you how to create a client application that can test the Web service.

Case Study for NewsShop Web Service

NewsShop Pvt. Ltd. provides real-time information management solutions to various organizations that use these solutions to deliver essential online information to their customers. Essentially, NewsShop provides news feed in XML format on a wide range of topics. Clients, such as business organizations and Internet portals, can use these news feeds to provide current news to their own employees and customers.

NewsShop has a database that has information and URLs to online resources on various topics. NewsShop updates the database every 15 minutes. Clients of NewsShop can make use of this data to provide information, such as current news, lifestyle, fashion, fitness, and so on, to their own clients. NewsShop provides information on some categories of the news feed free of cost, whereas other categories require a fee.

The format of all news feed at NewsShop is XML because XML allows easy integration with the client's intranets and Web sites. In the future, NewsShop expects to provide news feeds in multiple formats, such as Resource Description Framework (RDF), Channel Definition Format (CDF), and Information and Content Exchange (ICE) format.

Having discussed the scenario in which the organization will use the NewsShop Web service, we will now discuss the life cycle of the NewsShop project.

Project Life Cycle

The Development Life Cycle (DLC) of a project involves the following three phases:

- ◆ Project initiation
- ◆ Project execution
- ◆ Project deployment

We discussed these phases in Chapter 6, "Creating a Web Service Using the Microsoft SOAP Toolkit." Now we will discuss only the project execution phase that includes creating the project.

The Project Execution Phase

You create the design of an application and the actual application in the project execution phase. After creating the design, you need to develop the application. The project execution phase consists of the following stages:

- ◆ Requirements analysis
- ◆ Design
- ◆ Construction
- ◆ Testing

The following sections discuss in detail the stages in the project execution phase for the NewsShop project.

Requirements Analysis

During the requirements analysis phase, the development team at NewsShop analyzes the need for creating a Web service. NewsShop needs to provide the news feeds to various client applications running on different platforms. For example, the clients of NewsShop might be using applications that are built on various platforms, such as Linux, Unix, or Windows. In addition, some of the clients might want to integrate the information that NewsShop provides to their existing intranet or Internet sites. However, other clients might want to access the information from desktop applications. Therefore, in such a varied scenario, developing Web services is the easiest solution.

The Web service that the development team at NewsShop creates must have the following features:

◆ The Web service should provide a list of URLs for resources on a particular topic or category.

◆ The list should be in XML format.

◆ The Web service should allow a client to query a list of categories.

◆ Some of the categories should be available to only registered customers.

Design

During the design phase of the application, the development team decides the functionality to be implemented and the technology to be used. The team at NewsShop has decided to host the site and the services on Windows 2000.

Currently, the Web site of NewsShop is developed using ASP.NET. The Web site displays data from a SQL database. Therefore, the team has decided to create the Web service by using Visual Studio .NET, which allows easy and efficient creation of ASP.NET applications.

Construction

During the construction phase, the NewsShop team constructs the application. The primary tasks that the team performs in the construction phase are these:

◆ Create the database required to store the data

◆ Create the Web service

◆ Test the Web service from different client applications

Testing

In the testing phase, the development team and the testing team test the functionality of the application that is created. You will learn about testing the application in detail in the section titled "Testing the Web Service from a Client Application."

You will now learn to create a sample ASP.NET Web service. This will help you to create the Web service for NewsShop Pvt. Ltd.

Creating a Sample ASP.NET Web Service

You learned how to create a sample ASP.NET Web application in Chapter 7, "Building Web Applications on the .NET Platform." Creating Web services with the ASP.NET Framework is as simple as creating Web applications. Similar to creating Web applications, you need a text editor and the ASP.NET runtime to create Web services.

An ASP.NET Web service consists of an .asmx file that contains the code for the Web service. Let's look at a sample .asmx file for a Web service that returns the day of the week. The .asmx file contains a Web processing directive that specifies a class name for a Web service and the language used to create the Web service. You can create the .asmx file in a text editor, such as Notepad. To do so, add the following code to a Notepad file:

```vb
<%@ WebService Language="vb" Class="SampleService" %>
Imports System.Web.Services


Public Class SampleService
    <WebMethod()>
        Public Function QuoteForTheDay() as string
        Return "This is the quote for today"
    End Function
End Class
```

After you add the code to a Notepad file, save the file with the extension .asmx.

The preceding code creates a class, `SampleService`, in Visual Basic .NET. In addition, the code imports the `System.Web.Services` namespace to your application. Next, a Web method, `QuoteForTheDay()`, is declared inside the `SampleService` class. The Web method returns a string to the requesting application.

As you can see, the .asmx file contains the code for the Web service. Therefore, each time an application sends a request for the Web service, the code in the .asmx file is compiled. (Here, we are not taking into account the fact that pages are being cached.) To prevent this, you can shift the code that provides the functionality into a separate Visual Basic .NET or Visual C# file. You then can compile the code for the Web service and store it in an assembly. The client application can access the assembly through the .asmx file. However, to be able to access the assembly from a client application, you first need to create a reference to the file that contains the code for the Web service. To do this, you use the `Codebehind` attribute of the Web service directive, as shown in the following code snippet:

```vb
<%@ WebService Language="vb" Codebehind="Service1.asmx.vb" Class="NewsShop.Service1"
%>
```

The previous code contains the `Codebehind` attribute that has a reference to the Service1.asmx.vb file. Service1.asmx.vb is a Visual Basic .NET file that contains the code to provide the functionality for the Web service. You can use the previous code to implement a

Web service in Visual Studio .NET by using .NET languages, such as Visual C# and Visual Basic .NET.

Creating a Web Service Using Visual Studio .NET

Similar to ASP.NET Web applications, Visual Studio .NET also provides you with a template to create an ASP.NET Web service. The steps for creating an ASP.NET Web service are similar to those for creating an ASP.NET Web application. To create an ASP.NET Web service, perform the following actions:

1. Launch Visual Studio .NET from the Programs menu.
2. To create a new project, choose File, New, Project. The New Project dialog box is displayed.
3. In the Project Types pane, select the Visual Basic Projects option.
4. In the Templates pane, select the ASP.NET Web Service option.
5. In the Location text box, type the address of the Web server on which you will develop the Web application. For a local server, type the address `http://localhost/` followed by the name of the Web service.

TIP

You cannot specify a name for the Web service in the Name text box. To specify a name for the Web service, type the name in the Location text box.

After specifying the values in the New Project dialog box, the dialog box should look like Figure 8-1.

6. Click on the OK button to create a simple Web service project.

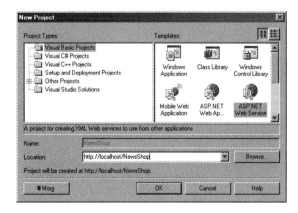

FIGURE 8-1 *The New Projects dialog box.*

When you create a Web service by using the ASP.NET Web services template, Visual Studio .NET creates a simple Web service project that you can see in the Solution Explorer window. The design view for a Web service looks like Figure 8-2.

As you can see in the Solution Explorer window, Visual Studio .NET creates some default files for the Web service. Table 8-1 explains the default files that Visual Studio .NET creates.

Table 8-1 Default Files for a Web Service

File	Description
AssemblyInfo.vb	This file contains information about the assembly of a Web service. This information includes the description, the build, and the version number of the assembly.
Global.asax	This file contains a `Codebehind` directive that redirects you to the Global.asax.vb file.
Global.asax.vb	This file contains the code for handling the events that the ASP.NET application raises.
Service1.asmx	This file is a source file for the Web service. Similar to Global.asax, Service1.asmx contains a `Codebehind` directive that redirects you to the Wservice1.asax.vb file.
Service1.asmx.vb	This file is a Visual Basic .NET module that implements the functionality of the Web service.
Web.Config	This file is a configuration file for an ASP.NET Web application that allows you to configure session-state settings, customize error messages, and so on.
Service1.vbproj	This file is a Visual Studio .NET project file.
Service1.vbproj.webinfo	This file is used to edit and compile projects remotely.
Service1.vsdisco	This file is used by Visual Studio .NET to locate the local Web services.
Service1.sln	This file is a solution file for the Web service.
Service1.suo	This file is a solution option file. You cannot edit the contents of this file.

Look at the code in the .asmx file that Visual Studio .NET creates for a Web service:

```
<%@ WebService Language="vb" Codebehind="Service1.asmx.vb"
Class="NewsShop.Service1" %>
```

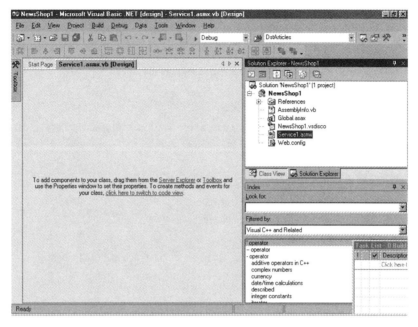

FIGURE 8-2 *The IDE for a Web service.*

As you can see, the Web service directive contains a `Codebehind` attribute that has a reference to the Service1.asmx.vb file. The code for the Web service is present in this file. In addition, a class directive is included that defines a class, `Service1`, for the Web service. Visual Studio .NET allows you to view the code present in the Service1.asmx.vb file. To do this, perform the following steps:

1. In the Solution Explorer window, click on the Service1.asmx file to view the file in the Design view.

2. Click on the link titled Click Here to Switch to Code View to see the code for the Web service.

The code for the Web service is as shown:

```
Imports System.Web.Services


<WebService(Namespace := "http://tempuri.org/")>
        Public Class Service1
        Inherits System.Web.Services.WebService


#Region " Web Services Designer Generated Code "
```

```
Public Sub New()
    MyBase.New()

    'This call is required by the Web Services Designer.
    InitializeComponent()

    'Add your own initialization code after the InitializeComponent() call

End Sub

'Required by the Web Services Designer
Private components As System.ComponentModel.IContainer

'NOTE: The following procedure is required by the Web Services Designer
'It can be modified using the Web Services Designer.
'Do not modify it using the code editor.
<System.Diagnostics.DebuggerStepThrough()> Private Sub InitializeComponent()
    components = New System.ComponentModel.Container()
End Sub

Protected Overloads Overrides Sub Dispose(ByVal disposing As Boolean)
    'CODEGEN: This procedure is required by the Web Services Designer
    'Do not modify it using the code editor.
    If disposing Then
        If Not (components Is Nothing) Then
            components.Dispose()
        End If
    End If
    MyBase.Dispose(disposing)
End Sub

#End Region

' WEB SERVICE EXAMPLE
' The HelloWorld() example service returns the string Hello World.
' To build, uncomment the following lines; then save and build the project.
' To test this Web service, ensure that the .asmx file is the start page
' and press F5.
```

```
'<WebMethod()> Public Function HelloWorld() As String
        'HelloWorld = "Hello World"
' End Function
End Class
```

The preceding code contains the `WebService` attribute that declares http://tempuri.org as the default namespace for the Web service, as shown in the following code snippet:

```
<WebService(Namespace := "http://tempuri.org/")>
```

By default, `http://tempuri.org` is declared as the default namespace. To specify another default namespace, you can change the value of the `Namespace` property of the `WebService` attribute. You can also change the `Name` and `Description` properties of the `WebService` attribute to specify a name and provide a description for the Web service, respectively. The code for the `WebService` attribute is as shown:

```
<WebService(Description := "This simple Web service provides links to online resources
on various categories."
Namespace := "http://www.NewsShop.com")>
```

The code contains the declaration for a `public` class, `Service1`. This class is inherited from the `System.Web.Services.WebService` class. Then, the code contains the `# Region` preprocessor directive, which contains the boilerplate code for the Web service. Visual Studio .NET generates this code and provides the same functionality for all ASP.NET Web services. The developers rarely need to change this code.

 NOTE

The `#Region` preprocessor directives are used to mark a region of the code that you need to have executed as a block. To end the region marked with the `#Region` preprocessor directive, you use the `#End Region` preprocessor directive.

After the `#Region-#End Region` preprocessor directives is the code for the Web method, `HelloWorld()`, which is marked with comment entries. A Web service contains one or more Web methods that provide you with the functionality of the Web service. A Web method is similar to any other function but is preceded by the `WebMethod` attribute. The use of this attribute differentiates a Web method from all other methods and makes the Web method accessible to Web applications. The following list discusses some of the properties of the `WebMethod` attribute:

◆ **BufferResponse.** This property specifies whether the response is buffered. The response of the Web service is buffered until it is complete and is then sent back to the client. When the response of the Web service includes large amounts of data, it is preferable that the data not be buffered, but transferred as it is generated.

◆ **CacheDuration.** This property specifies the duration for which a response should be retained in the cache. The use of this property can increase the performance of the application because the responses in which the data is unchanged over a period of time can be cached safely for a longer duration.

◆ **Description.** This property provides a description of the Web method.

◆ **EnableSession.** This property enables session-based state management. You rarely will use session-based state management. It degrades the performance, and the client requesting the service might not support the http cookies that are required for this feature.

◆ **MessageName.** This property can be used to provide an alias for a Web method.

◆ **TransactionOption.** This property allows the method to participate in a transaction and make use of the COM+ services.

When you create the Web service in Visual Studio .NET, it creates a sample Web method, `HelloWorld()`, and marks the Web method as a comment. To implement the Web method, remove the comment entries and run the Web service. When you run the Web service, the `HelloWorld()` Web method returns a string, `HelloWorld`, as shown in Figure 8-3.

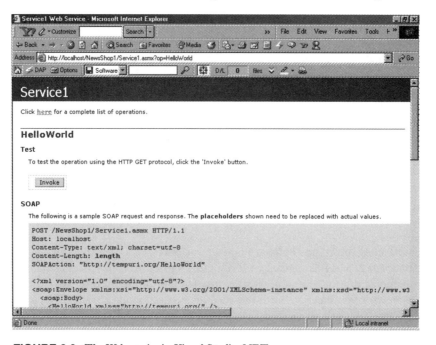

FIGURE 8-3 *The Web service in Visual Studio .NET.*

When you run the Web service, the Service1.asmx page is opened on the http://localhost/ NewsShop/Service1.asmx URL. The Service1.asmx page provides you with the links for the functionality that the Web service exposes. Because the sample Web service contains only the

`HelloWorld()` Web method, you will see only one link for the HelloWorld operation. In addition, the Service1.asmx page contains a link, Service Description. When you click on this link, the WSDL document for the Web service is displayed, as shown in Figure 8-4.

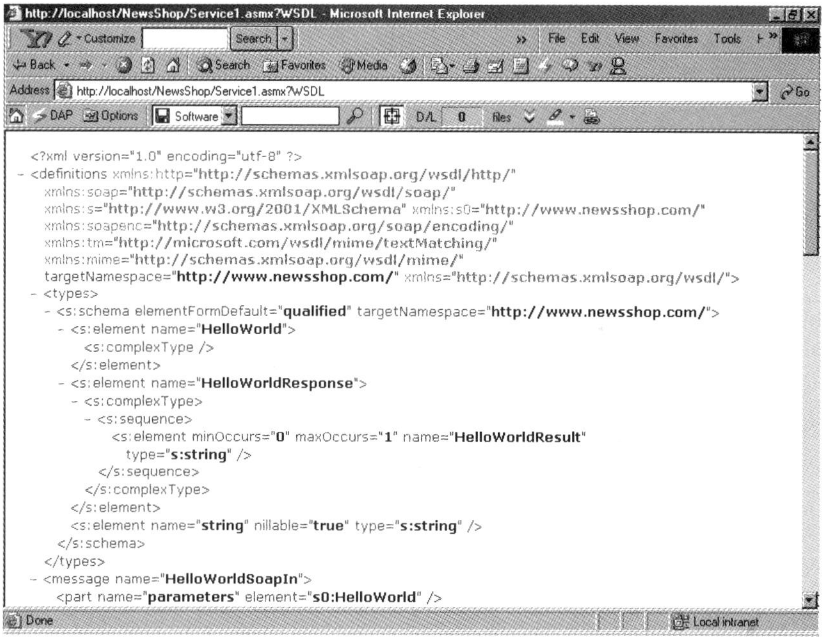

FIGURE 8-4 *The WSDL document for the Web service.*

The Service1.asmx page also recommends that you change the default namespace. The Web service that Visual Studio .NET creates uses http://tempuri.org as the default namespace. You saw how to change the default namespace for a Web service in the previous section.

When you click on the HelloWorld link, the Service1.asmx page for the HelloWorld operation opens. This page contains an Invoke button that you can use to invoke the HelloWorld Web service. In addition to the Invoke button, the page specifies the syntax for invoking the operation. As you know, you can call a Web service by sending a request in the form of a SOAP message. The Service1.asmx page shows the request for and the response of a Web service in the form of SOAP messages, HTTP GET, and HTTP POST protocols, as shown in Figure 8-5.

Now we will discuss the request and response messages for the SOAP protocol. The following is the code for the request message:

```
<?xml version="1.0" encoding="utf-8"?>

<soap:Envelope xmlns:xsi="http://www.w3.org/2001/XMLSchema-instance"

xmlns:xsd="http://www.w3.org/2001/XMLSchema"

xmlns:soap="http://schemas.xmlsoap.org/soap/envelope/">
```

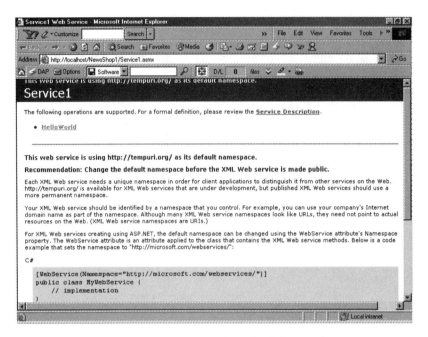

FIGURE 8-5 *The Service1.asmx page for the HelloWorld operation.*

```
    <soap:Body>
        <HelloWorld xmlns="http://tempuri.org/"/>
    </soap:Body>
</soap:Envelope>
```

The code contains the XML declaration statement followed by the `soap:Envelope` element that includes the namespaces to be used in the SOAP message. Then, the `soap:Body` element that contains a request for the HelloWorld operation is included. Similarly, the syntax of the response message is as shown:

```
<?xml version="1.0" encoding="utf-8"?>
<soap:Envelope xmlns:xsi="http://www.w3.org/2001/XMLSchema-instance"
xmlns:xsd="http://www.w3.org/2001/XMLSchema"
xmlns:soap="http://schemas.xmlsoap.org/soap/envelope/">
    <soap:Body>
        <HelloWorldResponse xmlns="http://tempuri.org/">
        <HelloWorldResult>string</HelloWorldResult>
        </HelloWorldResponse>
    </soap:Body>
</soap:Envelope>
```

The soap:Envelope element is the same for the request and response messages. However, the soap:Body element is different. The soap:Body element in the response message returns a string to the requesting application.

When you click on the Invoke button, the response of the Web service is sent in the form of an HTTP-GET message, as shown in the following code:

```
<?xml version="1.0" encoding="utf-8"?>
<string xmlns="http://tempuri.org/">Hello World</string>
```

The response of the Web service is shown in Figure 8-6.

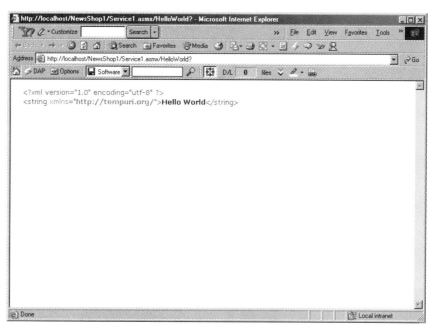

FIGURE 8-6 *The response of the Web service.*

Now, change the WebMethod attribute for the HelloWorld Web method as shown:

```
<WebMethod(CacheDuration:=60, Description:="This is the famous Hello World method.)>
```

After making the changes as in the previous code snippet, run the Web service again. As you can see, the recommendation for changing the namespace is no longer present in the Service1.asmx page. In addition, the Web service now has a description. The Service1.asmx page is shown in Figure 8-7.

After you learn to create a sample Web service, you need to create a database for NewsShop that will store the data to be returned by the Web service.

TIP

You should provide a description for a Web service and the Web methods by using the Description property. Doing this helps other users who want to use the Web service.

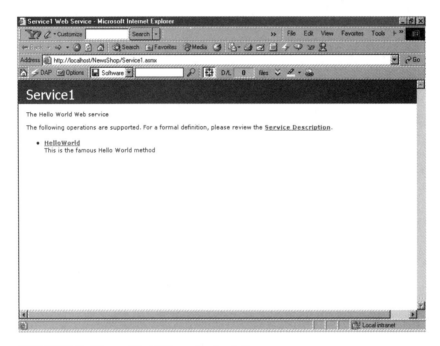

FIGURE 8-7 *The modified Web service description.*

The NewsShop Database

The online resources on which NewsShop provides information are divided into various channels. These channels define a broad range of related resources that are further categorized into different categories. These categories are stored in tables, as discussed in the following list:

◆ **User.** NewsShop provides a few categories free of cost to all users. However, to access other categories that are paid, a user needs to register at the Web site of NewsShop. The user can then log on to the site by specifying a username and a password. The information about the usernames and passwords of registered users is stored in the User table.

◆ **Channel.** The Channel table contains the channels, such as Business, Education, and so on.

◆ **Category.** The Category table contains the valid categories for which NewsShop provides information. This table contains a CategoryType field that specifies whether a category is free or paid.

◆ **Article.** The Article table contains information about the online resources and their descriptions.

The database design of the NewsShop database is shown in Figure 8-8.

You can create the tables for the NewsShop database, shown in Figure 8-8, on SQL Server.

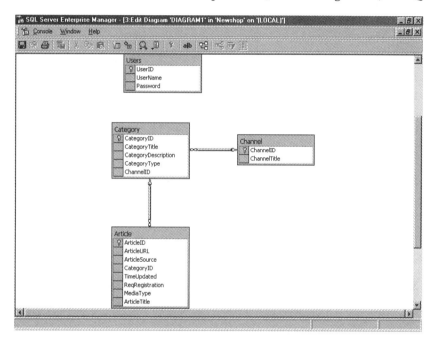

FIGURE 8-8 *The NewsShop database.*

When a user requests the data in the NewsShop database by using a Web service, the Web service might need to display data from more than one table. Therefore, you can create a view in SQL that contains data from the Category and Article tables. To create such a view, use the following SQL statement:

```
CREATE VIEW dbo.ArticleList
AS
SELECT dbo.Article.ArticleTitle, dbo.Article.ArticleURL, dbo.Article.ArticleSource,
dbo.Category.CategoryTitle, dbo.Article.TimeUpdated,
dbo.Article.ReqRegistration, dbo.Category.CategoryType FROM dbo.Article
INNER JOIN
dbo.Category ON dbo.Article.CategoryID = dbo.Category.CategoryID
```

In addition, you will create a stored procedure, `ValidateLogin`, which validates the username and the password of the users who try to log on to the Web service of NewsShop, as shown:

```
CREATE PROCEDURE dbo.ValidateLogin(@username varchar(50),

@password varchar(200))

As

Select UserID from Users where UserName=@UserName and Password=@Password
```

After creating the database, you can create a Web service for NewsShop. We will discuss how to create a Web service in the following section.

Creating a Web Service for NewsShop

You can create a Web service for NewsShop by using the ASP.NET Web services template that Visual Studio .NET provides. Creating a Web service involves adding Web methods to the Web service. To do so, add the following Web methods to the Service1.asmx file:

- ◆ `GetCategoryList()`
- ◆ `GetArticleList()`

The `GetCategoryList()` Web method returns a list of categories, and the `GetArticle List()` Web method returns a list of articles from the NewsShop database. To create the Web methods, add the following code to the `Service1` class:

```
<WebMethod()> Public Function getCategoryList() As String

End Function
```

The `GetCategoryList()` method accepts no parameters and returns a list of all categories for which resources are available. Next, add the code for the `GetArticleList()` Web method to the `Service1` class, as follows:

```
<WebMethod()> Public Function GetArticleList(ByVal Category As String, ByVal UserName

As String, ByVal Password As String) As String

End Function
```

As you can see, the `GetArticleList()` Web method accepts three parameters: the category for which the articles will be returned, the username, and password for a registered user. If the username or the password that a user enters is not valid, the Web method returns an exception. You will learn about the exception that is generated in the section, "Customizing SOAP Faults."

 TIP

Because the username and password are passed as text to the Web method, it is advisable that you secure the server using SSL. We discussed how to secure IIS by using SSL in Chapter 6.

After adding the code for the Web method, you need to implement the code. You can implement the `GetCategoryList()` method by using the following code:

```
<WebMethod()> Public Function getCategoryList() As String
        Dim Conn As SqlConnection
        Dim CategoryDataset As DataSet
        Dim CategoryAdapter As SqlDataAdapter
        Conn = New SqlConnection("Data Source=Server1;Initial Catalog=NewsShop;
Integrated Security=SSPI")
        Conn.Open()
        CategoryDataset = New DataSet()
        CategoryAdapter = New SqlDataAdapter("Select CategoryTitle from
ArticleList", Conn)
        CategoryAdapter.Fill(CategoryDataset)
        getCategoryList = CategoryDataset.GetXml()
End Function
```

The previous code contains the declaration for the SqlConnection, DataSet, and SqlDataAdapter objects. Next, an instance of the SqlConnection object, `Conn`, is created. `Conn` is used to connect to the NewsShop database.

After a connection to the database is made, an instance of the SqlDataAdapter object is created to query the Category table. The value that the Category table returns is stored in the DataSet object, which is then converted to XML and returned to the requesting application. This conversion is done so that the data can be returned to a client as a string containing XML, which the client can then parse and use.

Similarly, the implementation of the `GetArticleList()` Web method is as shown:

```
<WebMethod()> Public Function getArticleList(ByVal Category As String, ByVal UserName
As String, ByVal Password As String) As String

        Dim ArticleDataset As DataSet
        Dim Conn As SqlConnection
        Dim ArticleAdapter As SqlDataAdapter
        Dim ArticleReader As SqlDataReader
        Dim CmdArticle As SqlCommand
        Dim CmdUser As SqlCommand
        Dim CategoryType As Integer
        Dim ValidUser As SqlDataReader
        Dim PassHash As String
        Dim strCommand As String
```

```
        Conn = New SqlConnection("Data Source=saik-d185;Initial Catalog=
NewShop;Integrated Security=SSPI")
        Conn.Open()

        strCommand = "Select CategoryType from Category where
CategoryTitle='" & Category & "'"
        CmdArticle = New SqlCommand(strCommand, Conn)
        ArticleReader = CmdArticle.ExecuteReader()
        ArticleReader.Read()
        CategoryType = ArticleReader("CategoryType")
        ArticleReader.Close()

        If (CategoryType = 1) Then

            CmdUser = New SqlCommand("ValidateLogin", Conn)
            CmdUser.CommandType = CommandType.StoredProcedure
            CmdUser.Parameters.Add("@UserName", UserName)
            CmdUser.Parameters.Add("@Password", Password)

            Dim strTemp As String
            strTemp = CmdUser.ExecuteScalar()
            If (strTemp = 0) Then
                Throw New SoapException("This is a paid category. Please login
with your user name and password", SoapException.ClientFaultCode)
            End If
        End If
        'ValidUser.Close()
        ArticleDataset = New DataSet()
        ArticleAdapter = New SqlDataAdapter("Select * from ArticleList", Conn)
        ArticleAdapter.Fill(ArticleDataset)
        getArticleList = ArticleDataset.GetXml()
End Function
```

The code contains the declaration of the objects that are used in the code, such as DataSets, SqlConnection, and SqlDataAdapters. The method then connects to SQL Server and queries for the CategoryType field to identify whether the specified category is free or paid.

If the category is free, the method queries the ArticleList view and returns the required rows for the specified category. Alternatively, if the category is paid, the method verifies the username and the password that are passed with the request. To validate the username and the password, the method uses the ValidateLogin stored procedure.

If the username and the password are valid, the method retrieves the list of articles from the ArticleList view for the required category. Finally, the returned result is stored in a dataset, which is then converted into XML and returned to the calling application.

Customizing SOAP Faults

When you send a request for a Web service, an error might be generated. To handle application-level errors and return a customized error message to a client, you use the `SoapException` class.

For example, consider the following code that validates a username and a password. To do this, the code calls the stored procedure, which returns a user ID if the username and the password are validated. However, if the username and the password are not validated, the code throws the exception, `SoapException`, as shown:

```
If (CategoryType = 1) Then
            CmdUser = New SqlCommand("ValidateLogin", Conn)
            CmdUser.CommandType = CommandType.StoredProcedure
            CmdUser.Parameters.Add("@UserName", UserName)
            CmdUser.Parameters.Add("@Password", Password)

            Dim strTemp As String
            strTemp = CmdUser.ExecuteScalar()
            If (strTemp = 0) Then
                Throw New SoapException, SoapException.ClientFaultCode)
            End If
End If
```

If the username and password are not validated, then the error message `This is a paid category. Please login with your user name and password` is displayed, as shown in Figure 8-9.

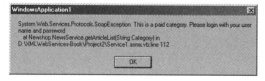

FIGURE 8-9 *The error message displayed when the username and password are not validated.*

As you know, you can send a request for a Web service in the form of a SOAP request. Therefore, the parameters to the Web methods, such as the username and the password, are sent as part of the body of the SOAP request. Sometimes, it is convenient to use the header of a SOAP message to pass some values to and from the Web service. The following section discusses using the `Header` element of the SOAP message to pass data to the Web service.

SOAP Header

SOAP headers provide a convenient way to store data (such as usernames and passwords), encryption information (such as keys), and other information related to the Web service.

Visual Studio .NET provides attributes and classes that help in the processing of SOAP headers. These classes include `SoapHeaderAttribute` and `SoapHeader`. In addition, the `SoapHeader` class allows you to access the contents of the SOAP header. An example of a SOAP header is shown here:

```
<WebMethod(Description := "This Web method has a Soap Header"),_
SoapHeader("myHeader", Direction := SoapHeaderDirection.InOut, Required := True)>
```

The preceding code contains the `SoapHeader` attribute that contains the `Direction` property. This property specifies whether the client application or the Web service will process the SOAP header. In addition, the `SoapHeader` attribute has the `Required` property, which specifies whether it is mandatory for the client application or the Web service to process the SOAP header. This property takes a Boolean value. If the value of this property is `True`, the application needs to process the SOAP header element, and if the value is `False`, it is not mandatory for the application to process the `Header` element.

You will now create the `GetArticleList()` method that uses SOAP headers to pass the username and password. To do so, open the Service1.asmx.vb file and add the following class declaration:

```
Public Class Header1
    Inherits SoapHeader
    Public username As String
    Public password As String
End Class
```

To pass the parameters to a Web method as part of a SOAP message, you need to create a class, `Header1`, and declare two `public string` variables, `username` and `password`, in it. However, to implement this class in the `Service1` class, create an instance of the `Header1` class in `Service1`, as shown in the following code:

```
Public InHeader As Header1
```

Now, make the highlighted changes to the `GetArticleList()` method in the `Service1` class:

```
<WebMethod(MessageName:="getArticleList1"), SoapHeaderAttribute("InHeader", _
            Direction:=SoapHeaderDirection.In, _
            Required:=False)> Public Function getArticleList(ByVal Category
As String) As String

        Dim ArticleDataset As DataSet
        Dim Conn As SqlConnection
```

```
Dim ArticleAdapter As SqlDataAdapter
Dim ArticleReader As SqlDataReader
Dim CmdArticle As SqlCommand
Dim CmdUser As SqlCommand
Dim CategoryType As Integer
Dim ValidUser As SqlDataReader
Dim Password As String
Dim strCommand As String

Dim username As String
Dim password As String
Dim strTemp As String

username = InHeader.username
password = InHeader.password

Conn = New SqlConnection("Data Source=Server1;Initial
Catalog=NewShop;Integrated Security=SSPI")
Conn.Open()

strCommand = "Select CategoryType from Category where
CategoryTitle='" & Category & "'"
CmdArticle = New SqlCommand(strCommand, Conn)
ArticleReader = CmdArticle.ExecuteReader()
ArticleReader.Read()
CategoryType = ArticleReader("CategoryType")
ArticleReader.Close()

If (CategoryType = 1) Then

    CmdUser - New SqlCommand("ValidateLogin", Conn)
    CmdUser.CommandType = CommandType.StoredProcedure
    CmdUser.Parameters.Add("@UserName", username)
    CmdUser.Parameters.Add("@Password", Password)


    strTemp = CmdUser.ExecuteScalar()
    If (strTemp = 0) Then
```

```
                    Throw New SoapException("This is a paid category. Please
login with your user name and password", SoapException.ClientFaultCode)
            End If
        End If
        'ValidUser.Close()
        ArticleDataset = New DataSet()
        ArticleAdapter = New SqlDataAdapter("Select * from ArticleList", Conn)
        ArticleAdapter.Fill(ArticleDataset)
        getArticleList = ArticleDataset.GetXml()
End Function
```

The preceding code uses the `MessageName` property of the `WebMethod` attribute to provide an alias to the method. Next, the code assigns a value `SoapHeaderDirection.In` to the `Direction` property of the `SoapHeader` attribute. Doing this enables the Web method to process the SOAP header that contains the data. In addition, the `Required` property is set to `False` because the Web service is not required to process the SOAP header with free categories.

Finally, the Web service accesses the SOAP header element to retrieve the data, as shown in the following code snippet:

```
username = InHeader.username
password = InHeader.password
```

After you create the Web service, you need to create client applications that access the Web service. We will now create a client application by using Visual Studio .NET.

Accessing Web Services from Client Applications

Visual Studio .NET makes it easy to call a Web service from any kind of application. Using Visual Studio .NET, we will create a client application that you can use to test the Web service. To do so, perform the following steps:

1. Open the project for NewsShop.
2. Create a Visual Basic Windows Application project.
3. In the Name text box, assign a name to the Windows application, and in the Location text box, type or browse for the location where you want to save the application. Select the Add to Solution option button to ensure the new project is added to the same solution.

TIP

It's best to save the Windows application in the same folder as the NewsShop Web service.

4. Click on the OK button. The Windows application is added to the same solution, as shown in Figure 8-10.

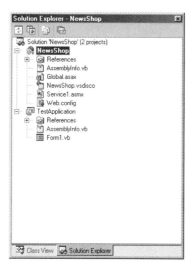

FIGURE 8-10 *The NewsShop project solution.*

Now, you need to add a Web reference for the Web service to the Windows application. To do so, perform the following steps:

1. Right-click on the Windows application project in the Solution Explorer window.
2. In the displayed list, select the Add Web Reference option. The Add Web Reference dialog box is displayed, as shown in Figure 8-11.
3. In the Address text box, enter the path for the WSDL of the Web service you created earlier as http://localhost/NewsShop/service1.asmx?wsdl and press Enter. The WSDL document will be displayed.
4. Click on the Add Reference button.

Visual Studio .NET creates a proxy class. The following section discusses proxy classes in detail.

Proxy Class

A proxy class is similar to a Web service class. When you add a Web reference to a client application, Visual Studio .NET creates a proxy class and adds it to the project. The proxy class is created in the Web References folder.

To view the structure of the proxy class, click on the Class View option in the Solution Explorer window and expand the tree structure. The tree structure contains proxy classes for each of the classes in the original Web service. The tree structure of the proxy class is shown in Figure 8-12.

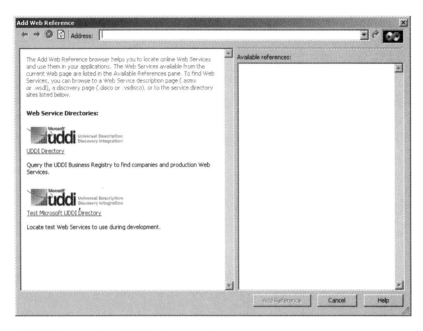

FIGURE 8-11 *The Add Web Reference dialog box.*

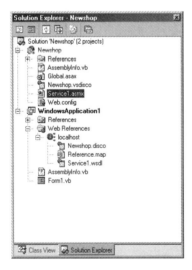

FIGURE 8-12 *The tree structure of the proxy class.*

NOTE

The Web References folder contains several folders that have references to Web services. The names of these folders depend on the location where the Web service is hosted. If the Web service is hosted on the local server, the name of the folder is Local-Host. This folder contains a Disco file, a WSDL file, and a proxy class file, Service1.vb.

The code for the proxy class is as shown:

```vb
'---------------------------------------------------------------------------
' <autogenerated>
'     This code was generated by a tool.
'     Runtime Version: 1.0.3328.4
'
'     Changes to this file may cause incorrect behavior and will be lost if
'     the code is regenerated.
' </autogenerated>
'---------------------------------------------------------------------------


Option Strict Off
Option Explicit On

Imports System
Imports System.ComponentModel
Imports System.Diagnostics
Imports System.Web.Services
Imports System.Web.Services.Protocols
Imports System.Xml.Serialization

'

'This source code was auto-generated by Microsoft.VSDesigner, Version 1.0.3328.4.
'

Namespace localhost

    '<remarks/>
    <System.Diagnostics.DebuggerStepThroughAttribute(), _
     System.ComponentModel.DesignerCategoryAttribute("code"), _
```

```vb
    System.Web.Services.WebServiceBindingAttribute(Name:="NewsServiceSoap",
[Namespace]:="http://www.NewShop.org/")> _
    Public Class Service1
        Inherits System.Web.Services.Protocols.SoapHttpClientProtocol

        Public Header1Value As Header1

        '<remarks/>
        Public Sub New()
            MyBase.New
            Me.Url = "http://localhost/Newshop/Service1.asmx"
        End Sub
        '<remarks/>
        <System.Web.Services.Protocols.SoapDocumentMethodAttribute
("http://www.NewShop.org/getCategoryList", RequestNamespace:=
"http://www.NewShop.org/", ResponseNamespace:=
"http://www.NewShop.org/", Use:=System.Web.Services.Description.
SoapBindingUse.Literal, ParameterStyle:=
System.Web.Services.Protocols.SoapParameterStyle.Wrapped)> _
      Public Function getCategoryList() As String
      Dim results() As Object = Me.Invoke("getCategoryList", New Object(-1) {})
      Return CType(results(0),String)
    End Function


        '<remarks/>
        Public Function BegingetCategoryList(ByVal callback As System.AsyncCallback,
ByVal asyncState As Object) As System.IAsyncResult
            Return Me.BeginInvoke("GetCategoryList", New Object(-1) {}, callback,
asyncState)
        End Function


        '<remarks/>
        Public Function EndGetCategoryList(ByVal asyncResult As System.IAsyncResult)
As String
            Dim results() As Object = Me.EndInvoke(asyncResult)
            Return CType(results(0),String)
        End Function
```

```
      '<remarks/>
      <System.Web.Services.Protocols.SoapHeaderAttribute("Header1Value"),  _
       System.Web.Services.Protocols.SoapDocumentMethodAttribute
("http://www.NewShop.org/getArticleList1", RequestElementName:="getArticleList1",
RequestNamespace:="http://www.NewShop.org/",
ResponseElementName:="getArticleList1Response",
ResponseNamespace:="http://www.NewsShop.org/", Use:=
System.Web.Services.Description.SoapBindingUse.Literal,
ParameterStyle:=System.Web.Services.Protocols.SoapParameterStyle.Wrapped)>  _
      Public Overloads Function getArticleList(ByVal Category As String) As
<System.Xml.Serialization.XmlElementAttribute("getArticleList1Result")> String
          Dim results() As Object = Me.Invoke("getArticleList", New Object()
{Category})
          Return CType(results(0),String)
      End Function


      '<remarks/>
      Public Function BegingetArticleList(ByVal Category As String, ByVal callback
As System.AsyncCallback, ByVal asyncState As Object) As System.IAsyncResult
          Return Me.BeginInvoke("getArticleList", New Object() {Category},
callback, asyncState)
      End Function


      '<remarks/>
      Public Function EndgetArticleList(ByVal asyncResult As System.IAsyncResult) As
 String
          Dim results() As Object = Me.EndInvoke(asyncResult)
          Return CType(results(0),String)
      End Function


      '<remarks/>
      <System.Web.Services.WebMethodAttribute(MessageName:="getArticleList1"),  _
       System.Web.Services.Protocols.SoapDocumentMethodAttribute
("http://www.NewShop.org/getArticleList2",
RequestElementName:="getArticleList2",
RequestNamespace:="http://www.NewShop.org/",
ResponseElementName:="getArticleList2Response",
ResponseNamespace:="http://www.NewShop.org/",
```

```vb
Use:=System.Web.Services.Description.SoapBindingUse.Literal,
ParameterStyle:=System.Web.Services.Protocols.SoapParameterStyle.Wrapped)> _
        Public Overloads Function getArticleList(ByVal Category As String, ByVal
username As String,
ByVal password As String) As <System.Xml.Serialization.XmlElementAttribute
("getArticleList2Result")> String
            Dim results() As Object = Me.Invoke("getArticleList1",
New Object() {Category, username, password})
            Return CType(results(0),String)
        End Function


        '<remarks/>
        Public Function BegingetArticleList1(ByVal Category As String, ByVal username
As String, ByVal password As String, ByVal callback As System.AsyncCallback, ByVal
asyncState As Object) As System.IAsyncResult
            Return Me.BeginInvoke("getArticleList1", New Object()
 {Category, username, password}, callback, asyncState)
        End Function
        '<remarks/>
        Public Function EndgetArticleList1(ByVal asyncResult As System.IAsyncResult)
As String
            Dim results() As Object = Me.EndInvoke(asyncResult)
            Return CType(results(0),String)
        End Function
    End Class


    '<remarks/>
    <System.Xml.Serialization.XmlTypeAttribute([Namespace]:=
"http://www.NewsShop.org/"), _
    System.Xml.Serialization.XmlRootAttribute([Namespace]:=
"http://www.NewsShop.org/", IsNullable:=false)> _
    Public Class Header1
        Inherits SoapHeader

        '<remarks/>
        Public username As String

        '<remarks/>
```

```
        Public password As String
    End Class
End Namespace
```

The preceding code contains declarations for the Service1 class and the Header1 class. In addition, the code contains declarations to call each of the methods in two ways: synchronously and asynchronously. The code to call the GetArticleList() method synchronously is shown here:

```
Dim ws1 As NewsService
Dim header1 As New Header1()
Dim DSData As DataSet
Dim strTemp As String


        DSData = New DataSet()
        ws1 = New NewsService()
        ws1.Header1Value = header1
        header1.username = "user1"
        header1.password = "pass1"
    Try
        MsgBox(ws1.getArticleList("E news"))
    Catch
        MsgBox(Err.GetException.Message)
    End Try
```

The previous code creates an instance, ws1, of the NewsService class and calls the GetArticle List() method by using ws1.

Testing the Web Service from a Client Application

After you have added a proxy for the Web service class to the project, you can instantiate the proxy class and call the Web methods in the Web service. To do this, add a Button control to the blank form in the Windows application. Now, add the following code to the Click event of the Button control:

```
Dim ws1 As Service1
    ws1 = New Service1()
Try
        MsgBox(ws1.GetArticleList("ECommerce","user1","password"))
    Catch
        MsgBox(Err.GetException.Message)
End Try
```

After you add a button to the Windows form, run the application, and click on the button to test the Web service.

Summary

In this chapter, you learned how to create a Web service using Visual Studio .NET. You also learned how to create a client application in Visual Studio .NET and then access the Web service by using a client application.

PART VI

**Professional
Project 3**

Project 3

Creating the Exchange Rate Web Service

Project 3 Overview

As you know, Visual Studio .NET makes it easy for you to create, test, and deploy ASP.NET Web services. However, using Visual Studio .NET is not the only way to create ASP.NET Web services. You also can create ASP.NET Web services by using the tools that are part of the .NET platform SDK and are freely downloadable from Microsoft's Web site.

In this project, you will learn how to define an interface of a Web service by using WSDL. In addition, you will explore the structure of a WSDL document and how you can create Web services and client applications from the WSDL document.

Chapter 9

In the previous projects, you learned to create a Web service for the .NET platform by using Visual Studio .NET. As you know, Visual Studio .NET contains several tools that simplify the process of creating a Web service. In addition to creating a Web service by using Visual Studio .NET, you can use the .NET Framework SDK to create a Web service. In this project, you will consider a scenario for which you can create a Web service for the .NET platform by using the .NET Framework SDK.

When you create a Web service by using Visual Studio .NET, you normally define various methods that will be exposed by the Web service first; then when the Web service is built and deployed, Visual Studio .NET automatically creates the WSDL document for the Web service. However, when you create a Web service by using the .NET Framework SDK, you need to start by creating an interface for a Web service. You will then create a Web service based on the WSDL document that defines this interface for the Web service.

Building software components, such as a Web service after defining the interface allows you to standardize the way in which a software component interacts with another system. In addition, it helps to separate the interface from its implementation. As a result, you can define several implementations for the same service.

In times to come, various organizations that define the standards for different industries might also define the standards for Web services. They can define these standards in the form of a WSDL document, which can be made publicly available. Doing this allows various service providers to implement services differently. However, all services can expose the same interface.

When you have different implementations for a same service, the client application can be programmed so that it can dynamically select an implementation based on factors such as the availability of service, the connection speed, and the service cost.

In this chapter, you will learn how to create an ASP.NET Web service starting from a WSDL document and using the tools provided with the .NET Framework SDK. Before you start with the actual creation of the Web service, consider the scenario in which you can use the Web service.

The ABCFinances Web Service

ABCFinances is a New York-based financial services organization. The internal business processes of the organization are fully automated. However, the process of automation was not performed on a company-wide scale. Instead, automation was done differently for different departments. This has resulted in a heterogeneous system. For example, some of the departments of ABCFinances are on mainframes, some are on Java-based systems, and the rest are on Microsoft technologies. As a result, the organization is facing problems with integration and interoperability of the systems. In addition, the company is not able to maintain the integrity of the data because there is a lot of duplication of data.

As a solution to the organization's problem, the MIS head plans to shift the entire business logic to some system that is interoperable with various types of clients that use these systems. Currently, the organization has several client applications that are developed on various platforms and by using different software technologies. To develop a system that is interoperable across platforms, Web services would be an ideal solution. However, converting the entire system to a Web service architecture base would require a huge amount of resources and effort. Therefore, the MIS head has decided to start a pilot project on one system. If the results of the pilot project are satisfactory, the development team will use the Web services architecture to integrate all applications as much as possible.

One of the most frequently used data on most of the systems at ABCFinances is the exchange rate for various countries compared to the US Dollar. This data is stored in databases of ABCFinances and is accessed by various middle tier components, which supply the business logic for various functions. This data is updated on a daily basis. After updating, this data needs to be replicated on various databases so that the data is accessible from a wide range of applications.

Because the problem faced by ABCFinances is to replicate the data across various databases, Web services can be an ideal solution. As a result, the development team at ABCFinances decides to create a Web service that makes the data accessible to applications created on diverse platforms. This would enable the organization to verify the interoperability and robustness of a Web service-based solution.

Project Life Cycle

The development life cycle (DLC) of a project involves the following three phases:

◆ Project initiation
◆ Project execution
◆ Project deployment

You learned about these phases in the earlier projects. We will discuss only the project execution phase, which is different from the earlier projects.

In the project execution phase, the development team creates the design of an application. After creating the design, the team develops the actual application. The project execution phase consists of the following stages:

◆ Analyzing the requirements
◆ Creating the design of the application
◆ Constructing the application

Analyzing the Requirements

During the requirements analysis phase, the development team at ABCFinances analyzed the need for creating a Web service and came up with the following requirements:

◆ The Web service should contain a method that accepts the name of a country and returns the current exchange rate for that country.
◆ The Web service should contain a method that accepts the name of a country and returns the current exchange rate and the denomination of the country.
◆ The Web service should allow retrieval of the exchange rate by passing the denomination.
◆ The Web service should contain some support methods, such as a method that returns a list of countries and denominations from the database to simplify populating controls in the client tools.

Creating the Design of the Application

During the design phase of the application, the development team decides the functionality to be implemented and the technology to be used. The team at ABCFinances has decided to develop the pilot Web service by using ASP.NET and verify its functionality and use. The first Web service will be developed using the .NET Framework SDK. However, if the company moves ahead with its plans to shift the entire business systems to Web services, the development team will use Visual Studio .NET as the primary development tool.

Constructing the Application

During the construction phase, the development team constructs the application. The primary tasks that the team performs in the construction phase are as follows:

◆ Create the Web service

◆ Test the Web service from different client applications

Having leaned about the DLC of the ABCFinances Web service project, you will now learn to create an ASP.NET Web service without using Visual Studio .NET.

Creating the WSDL Document by Using .NET SDK

In this section, we will discuss the components of WSDL specifications. Then, you will create the WSDL document that contains these components.

The Components of the WSDL Specification

The components of the WSDL specification are discussed in the following list:

◆ **definitions.** This is the root element in any WSDL document. It contains the name of the Web service, a description of all the service elements, and the namespace declaration statements.

◆ **types.** This element contains the definitions of all types used in the Web service. The types that can be included in a WSDL document are a part of the W3C XML schema specification.

◆ **message.** This element describes the messages that are exchanged between the Web service and the client application. The message element also contains various part elements that refer to the parameters and the return types of the Web service operations.

◆ **portType.** This element is a combination of similar message elements. A portType element can be used to combine messages for operations that can be grouped as one category.

◆ **binding.** This element defines how the service will be transported. It binds the various ports to specific wire protocols.

◆ **service.** This element defines the location from which you can invoke a Web service.

NOTE

For a more detailed description of the components of the WSDL specification, refer to Chapter 5, "Introduction to WSDL."

Creating the `definitions` Element

You will now create the WSDL document. The first step is to create the `definitions` element, as shown in the following code snippet:

```
<definitions name ="ExchangeRateService"    targetNamespace =
"http://abcFinance.com/wsdl/"
        xmlns:wsdlns="http abcFinance.com /wsdl/"
        xmlns:typens="http:// abcFinance.com /type"
        xmlns:soap="http://schemas.xmlsoap.org/wsdl/soap/"
        xmlns:xsd="http://www.w3.org/2001/XMLSchema"
        xmlns="http://schemas.xmlsoap.org/wsdl/"
        xmlns:s0="http://abcFinance.com/services">
```

As discussed earlier, the `definitions` element defines the name of the Web service. It also contains the namespace declarations that will help you refer to multiple types defined in external specifications. In addition, the `definitions` element defines the `targetNamespace`, which is an XML schema declaration that allows a document to refer to it.

The `definitions` element also defines a default namespace, as shown in the following statement:

```
xmlns=http://schemas.xmlsoap.org/wsdl/
```

All elements in the WSDL document that do not have a namespace prefix are assumed to belong to this namespace. It is recommended that you include this namespace because you will be using types and elements, defined in the SOAP schema, in the WSDL document.

NOTE

In all preceding namespace declaration statements, it is not necessary to use the URIs that exist. The URIs that are included in a WSDL document should be unique.

Creating the types and message Elements

The data exchanged between a Web service and a client application is passed in the form of messages. Therefore, the process of creating WSDL documents includes creating the types and messages that are exchanged.

Although the WSDL specification can support any type, the specification uses the types that are declared in the XML schema as its native types. In addition, the types element in the WSDL document includes any data of a type that is not a part of the Schema declaration.

For every operation in a Web service that involves calling a method exposed by the Web service and retrieving data from the data source, you need to declare two messages. Each message will contain part elements that define the type and the name of parameters that are passed to the methods and the values that those methods return. You will create the messages for the GetRateByCurrency operation that returns exchange rate for the currency that is passed as a parameter to the method. The message element for the GetRateByCurrency operation is as follows:

```
<message name='GetRateByCurrency'>
        <part name='strCurrency' type='xsd:string'/>
</message>
<message name='GetRateByCurrencyResponse'>
        <part name='Result' type='xsd:float'/>
</message>
```

As you can see, the float and string types are preceded with the prefix xsd. The xsd prefix indicates that the float and string types are part of the XMLSchema namespace, as defined by the following declaration in the definitions element:

```
xmlns:xsd="http://www.w3.org/2001/XMLSchema"
```

Each of the messages in the GetRateByCurrency operation contains one part element. The part element for the request message stores the parameter that is passed to the message, and the part element for the response message stores the value that the method returns.

Consider a situation in which you create a Visual Basic class that contains a method from these declarations.

 NOTE

You will learn to create a Visual Basic class and the GetRateByCurrency() function in the later section titled "Using the wsdl.exe Tool."

The method in this case will have the following signature:

```
Function GetRateByCurrency(ByVal strCurrency As String) as Single
```

The preceding statement declares a function, `GetRateByCurrency()`, which accepts a `string` parameter, `strCurrency`. This parameter is passed as a value parameter.

NOTE

The preceding method passes the parameter as a value parameter (`ByVal`). To pass the parameter as a reference parameter (`ByRef`), you need to include an additional `part` element in the `message` element, as shown in the following example:

```
<message name="GetRateByCountryResponse">
    <part name="Result" type="xsd:float"/>
    <part name="strCountry" type="xsd:string"/>
</message>
```

The `GetRateByCurrency()` function processes the value passed as a parameter and returns a `Single` type value.

TIP

`Single` is the equivalent of `float` in Visual Basic .NET.

Another operation that a Web service can perform is to return an exchange rate depending on the currency and denomination that the user passes. The messages for this operation are declared as shown in the following code:

```
<message name='GetRateByCountry'>
    <part name='strCountry' type='xsd:string'/>
</message>
<message name='GetRateByCountryResponse'>
    <part name='Result' type='xsd:float'/>
</message>
```

In addition to the preceding operations, you can define the `GetCountryData` operation. This operation accepts the name of a country as a parameter and returns the currency or the denomination and exchange rate. Because the operation in this case returns two values, you cannot directly use any of the types that are available in the XML schema. Therefore, you need to create a custom type in the **types** element, as shown in the following code:

```
<types>
      <schema targetNamespace='http://ABCFinances.com/type'
          xmlns='http://www.w3.org/2001/XMLSchema'
          xmlns:SOAP-ENC='http://schemas.xmlsoap.org/soap/encoding/'
          xmlns:wsdl='http://schemas.xmlsoap.org/wsdl/'
          elementFormDefault='qualified'>
          <complexType name="CountryData">
              <sequence>
                  <element minOccurs="1" maxOccurs="1" name="Rate"
type="xsd:float" />
                  <element minOccurs="0" maxOccurs="1" name="Currency"
type="xsd:string" />
              </sequence>
          </complexType>
      </schema>
</types>
```

The preceding code uses the **complexType** element to define a new type **CountryData**. You can use this type to specify the return type of an operation, as shown in the following code:

```
<message name='GetCountryData'>
      <part name='strCountry' type='xsd:string'/>
</message>
<message name='GetCountryDataResponse'>
      <part name='Result' type='xsd:CountryData'/>
</message>
```

Consider another situation in which you need to pass or return a type that is not user defined, as explained in the previous example. Further, consider that the user-defined type is an array of **string** or **float** values. Therefore, you need to declare the type in the **types** element as shown:

```
<complexType  name ='ArrayOfstring'>
      <complexContent>
          <restriction base='SOAP-ENC:Array'>
              <attribute ref='SOAP-ENC:arrayType' wsdl:arrayType='string[]'/>
          </restriction>
      </complexContent>
</complexType>
```

After declaring the type, you can use it in the message, as shown in the following example:

```
<message name='GetCountriesList'>
</message>
<message name='GetCountriesListResponse'>
        <part name='Result' type='typens:ArrayOfstring'/>
</message>
```

As you can see, the `GetCountriesList` operation is simple enough. It does not accept parameters, but it returns an array of strings.

Creating the `portTypes` Element

Next, you need to group all related operations supported by the Web service together. The Web service in this case does not have various kinds of operations. All operations that the Web service exposes can be put into a single category, and therefore, a single `portType`. Each `portType` section has at least one `operation` element. This element links the names of the operations that the Web service supports and the messages that are related to the operation. The `portType` section for the Web service is shown in the following code:

```
<portType name='ExchangeRateSoapPort'>
        <operation name='GetRateByCountry' parameterOrder='strCountry'>
           <input message='wsdlns:GetRateByCountry' />
           <output message='wsdlns:GetRateByCountryResponse' />
        </operation>
        <operation name='GetRateByCurrency' parameterOrder='strCurrency'>
           <input message='wsdlns:GetRateByCurrency' />
           <output message='wsdlns:GetRateByCurrencyResponse' />
        </operation>
        <operation name='GetCountryData' parameterOrder='strCountry'>
           <input message='wsdlns:GetCountryData' />
          <output message='wsdlns:GetCountryDataResponse' />
        </operation>
</portType>
```

The preceding code defines a `portType` element with a name `ExchangeRateSoapPort` and groups various operations in it. Each operation can have an input message that transfers some data from a client to the Web service and an output message that transfers the data back to the client application. Various types of operations that can be grouped into a WSDL document are explained in the following list:

◆ A one-way operation that contains only an `input` element and an `input` message. In a one-way operation, the client calls the Web service by passing some data as a parameter; however, the Web service does not return a value.

◆ A one-way operation in which the Web service sends a message to the client application, which does not accept a parameter. This operation contains only an `output` message element.

◆ A request-response operation in which the client calls the Web service by passing some data as a parameter and the Web service in turn processes the data and returns the output. A request-response operation has both the `input` and the `output` messages.

◆ A request-response operation in which the Web service sends a message to the client and accepts a reply from the client. This operation will have an `output` message followed by an `input` message.

Creating the `binding` Element

Now that you have specified the operations that the Web service will support and the messages that will be used to support the operations, and you have categorized the operations into various `portTypes` in the WSDL document, the next step is to add details about the protocols that will be used in the Web service. The `binding` section specifies this information in the WSDL document. The binding section for the Web service is as shown here:

```
<binding name='ExchangeRateSoapBinding' type='wsdlns:ExchangeRateSoapPort' >
        <soap:binding style='rpc' transport='http://schemas.xmlsoap.org/soap/http' />
            <operation name='GetRateByCountry' >
            <soap:operation
soapAction='http://ABCFinances.com/action/GetRateByCountry' />
            <input>
                <soap:body use='encoded' namespace='http://ABCFinances.com/message/'
                    encodingStyle='http://schemas.xmlsoap.org/soap/encoding/' />
            </input>
            <output>
                <soap:body use='encoded' namespace='http://ABCFinances.com/message/'
                    encodingStyle='http://schemas.xmlsoap.org/soap/encoding/' />
            </output>
            </operation>
    </binding>
```

Creating the `service` Element

The final section in a WSDL document is the `service` element. This element specifies the location from which you can access the Web service. Because the Web service that you have created is an ASP.NET Web service, the URL will point to an .asmx file.

Add the following `service` element to the WSDL file:

```
<service name='ExchangeRateService' >
    <port name='ExchangeRateSoapPort' binding='wsdlns:ExchangeRateSoapBinding' >
        <soap:address location='abcFinances.com/ExchangeRateService.asmx' />
    </port>
</service>
```

After specifying the individual elements in a WSDL document, the entire WSDL document is as follows:

```
<?xml version='1.0' encoding='UTF-8' ?>
    <definitions name ='ExchangeRateService'   targetNamespace =
'http://ABCFinances.com/wsdl/'
        xmlns:wsdlns='http://ABCFinances.com/wsdl/'
        xmlns:typens='http://ABCFinances.com/type'
        xmlns:soap='http://schemas.xmlsoap.org/wsdl/soap/'
        xmlns:xsd='http://www.w3.org/2001/XMLSchema'
        xmlns='http://schemas.xmlsoap.org/wsdl/'>
            <types>
                <schema targetNamespace='http://ABCFinances.com/type'
                    xmlns='http://www.w3.org/2001/XMLSchema'
                    xmlns:SOAP-ENC='http://schemas.xmlsoap.org/soap/encoding/'
                    xmlns:wsdl='http://schemas.xmlsoap.org/wsdl/'
                    elementFormDefault='qualified'>
                    <complexType name ='ArrayOfstring'>
                        <complexContent>
                            <restriction base='SOAP-ENC:Array'>
                                <attribute ref='SOAP-ENC:arrayType'
wsdl:arrayType='string[]'/>
                            </restriction>
                        </complexContent>
                    </complexType>
                    <complexType name="CountryData">
                        <sequence>
                            <element minOccurs="1" maxOccurs="1" name="Rate"
type="xsd:float" />
                            <element minOccurs="0" maxOccurs="1" name="Currency"
type="xsd:string" />
                        </sequence>
```

```xml
                    </complexType>
                </schema>
            </types>
    <message name='GetRateByCountry'>
        <part name='strCountry' type='xsd:string'/>
    </message>
    <message name='GetRateByCountryResponse'>
        <part name='Result' type='xsd:float'/>
    </message>
    <message name='GetRateByCurrency'>
        <part name='strCurrency' type='xsd:string'/>
    </message>
    <message name='GetRateByCurrencyResponse'>
        <part name='Result' type='xsd:float'/>
    </message>
    <message name='GetCountryData'>
        <part name='strCountry' type='xsd:string'/>
    </message>
    <message name='GetCountryDataResponse'>
        <part name='Result' type='xsd:CountryData'/>
    </message>
    <message name='GetCountriesList'>
    </message>
    <message name='GetCountriesListResponse'>
        <part name='Result' type='typens:ArrayOfstring'/>
    </message>
    <message name='GetCurrencyList'>
    </message>
    <message name='GetCurrencyListResponse'>
        <part name='Result' type='typens:ArrayOfstring'/>
    </message>
        <portType name='ExchangeRateSoapPort'>
    <operation name='GetRateByCountry' parameterOrder='strCountry'>
        <input message='wsdlns:GetRateByCountry' />
        <output message='wsdlns:GetRateByCountryResponse' />
    </operation>
    <operation name='GetRateByCurrency' parameterOrder='strCurrency'>
        <input message='wsdlns:GetRateByCurrency' />
```

```
        <output message='wsdlns:GetRateByCurrencyResponse' />
    </operation>
    <operation name='GetCountryData' parameterOrder='strCountry'>
        <input message='wsdlns:GetCountryData' />
        <output message='wsdlns:GetCountryDataResponse' />
    </operation>
    <operation name='GetCountriesList' parameterOrder=''>
        <input message='wsdlns:GetCountriesList' />
        <output message='wsdlns:GetCountriesListResponse' />
    </operation>
    <operation name='GetCurrencyList' parameterOrder=''>
        <input message='wsdlns:GetCurrencyList' />
        <output message='wsdlns:GetCurrencyListResponse' />
    </operation>
    </portType>
        <binding name='ExchangeRateSoapBinding'
type='wsdlns:ExchangeRateSoapPort' >
            <soap:binding style='rpc'
transport='http://schemas.xmlsoap.org/soap/http' />
    <operation name='GetRateByCountry' >
        <soap:operation
soapAction='http://ABCFinances.com/action/GetRateByCountry' />
        <input>
            <soap:body use='encoded' namespace='http://ABCFinances.com/message/'
                encodingStyle='http://schemas.xmlsoap.org/soap/encoding/' />
        </input>
        <output>
            <soap:body use='encoded' namespace='http://ABCFinances.com/message/'
                encodingStyle='http://schemas.xmlsoap.org/soap/encoding/' />
        </output>
    </operation>
    <operation name='GetRateByCurrency' >
        <soap:operation
soapAction='http://ABCFinances.com/action/GetRateByCurrency' />
        <input>
            <soap:body use='encoded' namespace='http://ABCFinances.com/message/'
                encodingStyle='http://schemas.xmlsoap.org/soap/encoding/' />
        </input>
```

```
            <output>
                <soap:body use='encoded' namespace='http://ABCFinances.com/message/'
                    encodingStyle='http://schemas.xmlsoap.org/soap/encoding/' />
            </output>
        </operation>
    </operation>
        <operation name='GetCountryData'>
            <soap:operation soapAction='http://ABCFinances.com/action/GetCountryData' />
                <input>
                    <soap:body use='encoded'
namespace='http://ABCFinances.com/message/'
                        encodingStyle='http://schemas.xmlsoap.org/soap/encoding/' />
                </input>
                <output>
                    <soap:body use='encoded'
namespace='http://ABCFinances.com/message/'
                        encodingStyle='http://schemas.xmlsoap.org/soap/encoding/' />
                </output>
        </operation>
        <operation name='GetCountriesList' >
            <soap:operation
soapAction='http://ABCFinances.com/action/GetCountriesList' />
            <input>
                <soap:body use='encoded' namespace='http://ABCFinances.com/message/'
                    encodingStyle='http://schemas.xmlsoap.org/soap/encoding/' />
            </input>
            <output>
                <soap:body use='encoded' namespace='http://ABCFinances.com/message/'
                    encodingStyle='http://schemas.xmlsoap.org/soap/encoding/' />
            </output>
        </operation>
        <operation name='GetCurrencyList' >
                <soap:operation
soapAction='http://ABCFinances.com/action/GetCurrencyList' />
                <input>
                    <soap:body use='encoded'
namespace='http://ABCFinances.com/message/'
                        encodingStyle='http://schemas.xmlsoap.org/soap/encoding/' />
                </input>
```

```
                    <output>
                        <soap:body use='encoded'
namespace='http://ABCFinances.com/message/'
                        encodingStyle='http://schemas.xmlsoap.org/soap/encoding/' />
                    </output>
        </operation>
        </binding>
        <service name='ExchangeRateService' >
            <port name='ExchangeRateSoapPort' binding='wsdlns:ExchangeRateSoapBinding' >
                <soap:address location='http://abcFinances.com/ExchangeRateService/
Webservice1.asmx' />
            </port>
        </service>
</definitions>
```

Creating the Web Service from the WSDL Document

You have created the WSDL document, which defines the interface for the Web service. You can now create the Web service from the document. To create a Web service, you need to create a Visual Basic .NET file, which contains class definitions for the Web service that is created from this WSDL document.

To create a Web service form the WSDL document, create a virtual directory on your local IIS installation and copy the WSDL document to it. Name the virtual directory ExchangeService. You can create the .vb file for the WSDL document by executing the wsdl.exe tool.

The wsdl.exe Tool

wsdl.exe is a command-line utility that is a part of the .NET Framework SDK and will be installed under the <Drive>:\Program Files\Microsoft Visual Studio .NET\FrameworkSDK\ Bin folder. The wsdl.exe tool contains various command-line options. The following list discusses some of the most commonly used command-line options:

- ◆ **/language: or /l:.** This command-line option allows you to select the .NET language to be used to create the Server class or the proxy class. The value for the /language: or /l: command-line option can be VB (for Visual Basic .NET), CS (for C#), or JS (for JScript). The default value for the /language: command-line option is C#.
- ◆ **/Server:.** This command-line option specifies that the class is a Server class for a Web service. However, by default, a client proxy is created.
- ◆ **/protocol:.** This command-line option selects the protocol that you can use to transfer the Web service messages. These protocols include SOAP, HttpGet, and HttpPost.

◆ **/username: or /u:.** This command-line option specifies the username to use when the WSDL document is present on a Web server that requires authentication.

◆ **/password: or /p:.** This command-line option specifies the password, if any, for accessing a Web server that requires authentication.

◆ **/domain: or /d:.** This command-line option specifies the domain in which the Web server is present.

◆ **/proxy:.** This command-line option specifies the URL of a proxy server, if any. The default value of the /proxy: command-line option is to use the Internet Explorer settings.

◆ **/proxyusername: or /pu:.** This command-line option specifies the username to access the proxy server as specified by the /proxy: command-line option.

◆ **/proxypassword: or /pp:.** This command-line option specifies the password to access the proxy server as specified by the /proxy: command-line option.

Using the wsdl.exe Tool

To execute the wsdl.exe tool to generate the Web service class, use the following command:

```
Wsdl /out:ExRate.vb /language:VB /Server
http://localhost/ExchangeService/ExchangeService.wsdl
```

The preceding code uses the out parameter to specify the name of the .vb file. This file contains the classes for the Web service. The language parameter specifies the .NET language in which the classes are created.

The .vb file that is created by executing the wsdl.exe tool contains a class declaration for each portType declared in the WSDL document. The .vb file also contains the method declarations for each of the operations that is defined in the WSDL document. The code for the file created by wsdl.exe is shown here:

```
'-----------------------------------------------------------------
'<autogenerated>
'     This code was generated by a tool.
'     Runtime Version: 1.0.3328.4
'     Changes to this file may cause incorrect behavior and will be lost if
'     the code is regenerated.
' </autogenerated>
'-----------------------------------------------------------------


Option Strict Off
Option Explicit On
```

```
Imports System

Imports System.ComponentModel

Imports System.Diagnostics

Imports System.Web.Services

Imports System.Web.Services.Protocols

Imports System.Xml.Serialization


'This source code was auto-generated by wsdl, Version=1.0.3328.4.


'<remarks/>

<System.Web.Services.WebServiceBindingAttribute(Name:="ExchangeRateSoapBinding",

[Namespace]:="http://ABCFinances.com/wsdl/")>  _

Public MustInherit Class ExchangeRateService

    Inherits System.Web.Services.WebService


'<remarks/>

    <System.Web.Services.WebMethodAttribute(),  _

System.Web.Services.Protocols.SoapRpcMethodAttribute("http://ABCFinances.com/action/

GetRateByCountry", RequestNamespace:="http://ABCFinances.com/message/",

ResponseNamespace:="http://ABCFinances.com/message/")>  _

    Public MustOverride Function GetRateByCountry(ByVal strCountry As String) As

<System.Xml.Serialization.SoapElementAttribute("Result")> Single


'<remarks/>

    <System.Web.Services.WebMethodAttribute(),  _

    System.Web.Services.Protocols.SoapRpcMethodAttribute("http://ABCFinances.com/

action/

GetRateByCurrency", RequestNamespace:="http://ABCFinances.com/message/",

ResponseNamespace:="http://ABCFinances.com/message/")>  _

    Public MustOverride Function GetRateByCurrency(ByVal strCurrency As String)

As <System.Xml.Serialization.SoapElementAttribute("Result")> Single


'<remarks/>

    <System.Web.Services.WebMethodAttribute(),  _

     System.Web.Services.Protocols.SoapRpcMethodAttribute("http://ABCFinances.com/

action/GetCountryData", RequestNamespace:="http://ABCFinances.com/message/",

ResponseNamespace:="http://ABCFinances.com/message/")>  _

    Public MustOverride Function GetCountryData(ByVal strCountry As String) As
```

```
<System.Xml.Serialization.SoapElementAttribute("Result")> CountryData

'<remarks/>
    <System.Web.Services.WebMethodAttribute(), _
    System.Web.Services.Protocols.SoapRpcMethodAttribute("http://ABCFinances.com/
action/
GetCountriesList", RequestNamespace:="http://ABCFinances.com/message/",
ResponseNamespace:="http://ABCFinances.com/message/")> _
    Public MustOverride Function GetCountriesList() As
<System.Xml.Serialization.SoapElementAttribute("Result")> String()

'<remarks/>
    <System.Web.Services.WebMethodAttribute(), _
    System.Web.Services.Protocols.SoapRpcMethodAttribute("http://ABCFinances.com/
action/
GetCurrencyList", RequestNamespace:="http://ABCFinances.com/message/",
ResponseNamespace:="http://ABCFinances.com/message/")> _
    Public MustOverride Function GetCurrencyList() As
<System.Xml.Serialization.SoapElementAttribute("Result")> String()
End Class
```

The preceding code contains a class containing a `MustInherit` declaration. Also, some of the methods in the class have the `MustOverride` declaration. This class is an abstract class. You cannot create objects out of a class declared as `MustInherit`. You need to create another class that inherits from this class and overrides all methods in the base class declared as `MustOverride`.

TIP

You cannot create an instance of an abstract class. To implement the methods of an abstract class, you need to derive a new class from the abstract class.

While you've been working with the wsdl.exe tool, you must have noticed that the tool has problems identifying and converting user-defined types. For example, the wsdl.exe tool is unable to understand the `CountryData` type that you declared in the `types` element of the WSDL document. Therefore, the tool converts the complex type to a `string` type, as shown in the following example:

```
Public MustOverride Function GetCountryData(ByVal strCountry As String) As
<System.Xml.Serialization.SoapElementAttribute("Result")> String
```

Now you need to explicitly add a declaration for the `CountryData` class and change the return type of the method declaration, as shown in the following code snippet:

```
    Public MustOverride Function GetCountryData(ByVal strCountry As String) As
<System.Xml.Serialization.SoapElementAttribute("Result")> CountryData
```

The declaration of the `public` class `CountryData` is shown here:

```
Public class CountryData
Public Rate as single
Public Denomination as string
End Class
```

After you add the declaration for the `CountryData` class, you can use the `Server` class. Because the `Server` class is abstract, you will use it as a base class. To implement the methods of the `Server` class, derive a new class that a Web service can use to provide the required functionality.

Next, you need to create an .asmx file and its corresponding codebehind.asmx.vb file. The .asmx.vb file contains the class, which is derived from the `ExchangeRateService` class that you created in the preceding example. The derived class will contain the implementation for all methods in the base class. The directive for the .asmx.vb file is shown here:

```
<%@ WebService Language="vb" Codebehind="Webservice1.asmx.vb"
Class="Webservice1" %>
```

The preceding code specifies that the code that implements the logic for the .asmx file is stored in the Webservice.asmx.vb file. In addition, the class that implements the Web service is called `Webservice1`. To implement the functionality in the Webservice.asmx.vb file, you need to compile the .vb file as a DLL file and copy the DLL file to the bin folder.

 TIP

Remember: The bin folder should be in the folder that contains the .asmx file.

The next step in the implementation of a Web service is to create the Webservice1.asmx.vb file. To create this file, perform the following steps:

1. Use any text editor, such as Notepad, to create a new file named Webservice1.asmx.vb.
2. Copy the contents of the ExRate.vb file to the Webservice1.asmx.vb file.

NOTE

The ExRate.vb file was created using the wsdl.exe tool.

3. Write the code to create a new class, Webservice1, which is derived from the ExchangeRateService class.

4. Set the WebserviceBinding attribute for the Webservice1 class.

TIP

Although the WebserviceBinding attribute is set for the ExchangeRateService class, you need to explicitly set the attribute for the Webservice1 class that is derived from the ExchangeRateService class.

The code for the Webservice1 class is shown in the following example:

```
<WebServiceBinding( Namespace:="http://localhost/Webservice1"), _
        WebServiceBindingAttribute(Name:="Service1", _
        Namespace:="http://localhost/Webservice1", _
        Location:="http://localhost/ExchangeService/Webservice1.wsdl")> _
        Public Class Webservice1
        Inherits ExchangeRateService
```

5. Override all methods of the ExchangeRateService class by using the MustOverride attribute. For example, to override the GetRateByCountry() method, use the following code:

```
        <System.Web.Services.WebMethodAttribute(), _
        System.Web.Services.Protocols.SoapRpcMethodAttribute("http://
ABCFinances.com/
action/
GetRateByCountry", RequestNamespace:="http://ABCFinances.com/message/",
ResponseNamespace:="http://ABCFinances.com/message/")> _
        Public Overrides Function GetRateByCountry(ByVal strCountry As String) As
<System.Xml.Serialization.SoapElementAttribute("Result")> Single

        'Functionality still to be implemented....
        End Function
```

NOTE

Overriding the methods does not implement the functionality for retrieving the data from the database and returning the data to the client application. You will learn to implement the functionality later in this chapter.

Similar to the `GetRateByCountry()` method, you can override the rest of the methods of the abstract class, `ExchangeRateService`. The code for overriding the `GetCountryData()` method is shown in the following example:

```
<WebServiceBinding( Namespace:="http://localhost/Webservice1"), _
        WebServiceBindingAttribute(Name:="Service1", _
        Namespace:="http://localhost/Webservice1", _
        Location:="http://localhost/ExchangeService/Webservice1.wsdl")> _
        Public Class Webservice1
        Inherits ExchangeRateService

        <System.Web.Services.WebMethodAttribute(),  _
        System.Web.Services.Protocols.SoapRpcMethodAttribute("http://
ABCFinances.com/action/
GetCountryData", RequestNamespace:="http://ABCFinances.com/message/",
ResponseNamespace:="http://ABCFinances.com/message/")>  _
        Public overrides Function GetCountryData(ByVal strCountry As String)
As <System.Xml.Serialization.SoapElementAttribute("Result")> CountryData
        Dim data As new CountryData

        GetCountryData = data
        End Function

        <System.Web.Services.WebMethodAttribute(),  _
        System.Web.Services.Protocols.SoapRpcMethodAttribute("http://ABCFinances.
com/action/
GetRateByCountry", RequestNamespace:="http://ABCFinances.com/message/",
ResponseNamespace:="http://ABCFinances.com/message/")>  _
        Public Overrides Function GetRateByCountry(ByVal strCountry As String)
As <System.Xml.Serialization.SoapElementAttribute("Result")> Single
        End Function
```

```
        <System.Web.Services.WebMethodAttribute(), _
        System.Web.Services.Protocols.SoapRpcMethodAttribute("http://localhost/
Webservice1/
GetRateByCurrency",
RequestNamespace:="http://www.abcfinances.com/GetRateByCurrency",
ResponseNamespace:="http://www.abcfinances.com/GetRateByCurrency")> _
Public Overrides Function GetRateByCurrency(ByVal Currency As String) As _
Single
        End Function


        <System.Web.Services.WebMethodAttribute(), _
        System.Web.Services.Protocols.SoapRpcMethodAttribute("http://
ABCFinances.com/action/
GetCountriesList", RequestNamespace:="http://ABCFinances.com/message/",
ResponseNamespace:="http://ABCFinances.com/message/")> _
Public Overrides Function GetCountriesList() As
<System.Xml.Serialization.SoapElementAttribute("Result")> String()
        End Function


        <System.Web.Services.WebMethodAttribute(), _
        System.Web.Services.Protocols.SoapRpcMethodAttribute("http://
ABCFinances.com/action/
GetCurrencyList", RequestNamespace:="http://ABCFinances.com/message/",
ResponseNamespace:="http://ABCFinances.com/message/")> _
Public Overrides Function GetCurrencyList() As
<System.Xml.Serialization.SoapElementAttribute("Result")> String()
        End Function


End Class
```

Compiling the Webservice1.asmx.vb File

The final step in the creation of the Web service is to compile the Webservice1.asmx.vb file. To compile the file, use the Visual Basic .NET command-line compiler, vbc.exe, which is available as part of the .NET Framework SDK at a path similar to <Drive>:\winnt\ microsoft.net\ framework\v1.0.3705.

To execute the vbc.exe compiler, use the following command-line command:

```
vbc /out:Webservice1.dll /target:library
```

```
/libpath:<Drive>:\winnt\microsoft.net\framework\v1.0.3705
/reference:system.dll,system.web.dll,system.web.services.dll,system.xml.dll
Webservice1.asmx.vb
```

As you can see, the preceding code uses the `reference` attribute to add references to all assemblies that contain the methods that you use in the Web service. In addition, the `/target` option specifies the type of the assembly. In this case, you need to use the `library` type assembly. However, the default value of the `/target` option is a console application. Next, the `libpath` option specifies the path of the Framework assemblies that are specified by the `reference` option.

Executing the preceding command-line command creates the Webservice1.dll file in the current folder. Copy this file to the bin folder.

Now your Web service is ready for access. You can access the Web service by using the address http://localhost/ExchangeService/Webservice1.asmx. Figure 9-1 shows the list of operations that support the Web service.

To test the `GetRateByCountry()` Web method, click on the `GetRateByCountry` link. You can see the page from which you can actually invoke the Web operation in Figure 9-2.

When you invoke the `GetRateByCountry()` Web method, an empty page is displayed. This is because you have not completed the implementation of the Web service. To complete the

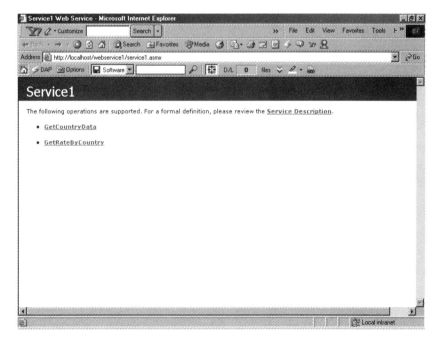

FIGURE 9-1 *The list of operations that the Web service supports.*

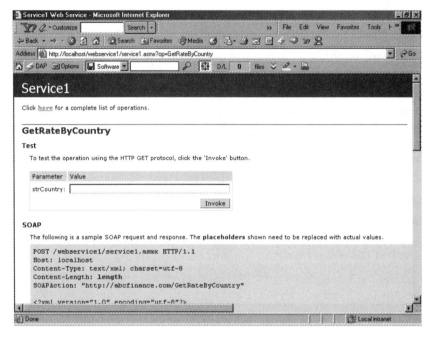

FIGURE 9-2 *Invoking the* `GetRateByCountry` *LINK.*

implementation of the Web service, you need to connect your Web service to a database. The following section discusses how to connect the Web service to a database.

Accessing Data from a Database

A Web service needs to access the exchange rate of currencies against the U.S. dollar for a specified country. This data is stored in the Rates table, as shown in Figure 9-3.

Column Name	Data Type	Length	Allow Nulls
Country	varchar	25	
Denomination	varchar	50	
ExRate	varchar	10	✓

FIGURE 9-3 *The Rates table.*

 NOTE

You can retrieve the current exchange rates from http://www.imf.org/external/np/tre/sdr/drates/8101.htm. This URL is the site of the International Monetary Fund (IMF).

After creating the Rates table, you can connect your Web service to this table, as discussed in the following section.

Accessing Data by Using the SQL Server .NET Data Provider

To connect to a database, Visual Studio .NET provides you with data providers, such as the SQL Server .NET data providers and OLEDB .NET data providers. In addition to connecting to a database, you can use these data providers to execute commands on a database. These commands include accessing data from a database, adding data to a database, deleting data from a database, and modifying data in a database.

When you try to access data from a database by using a data provider, the data is first stored in a DataSet object, which acts as an interface between the Web service and the database. Similarly, when you need to modify the data in the database, the changed data is first stored in the DataSet object, and the changes are then reflected to the underlying database. You learned about the data providers and the DataSet object in Chapter 7, "Building Web Applications on the .NET Platform."

SQL Server .NET Data Providers

The SQL Server .NET data provider is a lightweight data provider that connects to an SQL database. To connect to an SQL database, you should use the SQL Server .NET data provider. While connecting to an SQL database, the SQL Server .NET data provider does not use the ODBC or OLE-DB calls layer; therefore, the connection is direct and fast.

Connecting to a Database

To connect a Web service to a database, perform the following steps:

1. Add the following declarations to the beginning of your Visual Basic file, Webservice1.asmx.vb:

   ```
   Imports System.Data
   Imports System.Data.SqlClient
   ```

   The preceding statement includes the `System.Data` and `System.Data.SqlClient` namespaces in your application.

 NOTE

The `System.Data` namespace is included in the .NET base class library that constitutes the classes that are used by the ADO.NET technology. This technology connects a .NET application to a database, such as an SQL database.

2. Create an object of the `SqlClient.SqlConnection` class.

3. To the constructor of the class, pass the name and details of your SQL Server connection.

   For example, to connect to the ABCFinance database that is present at SQL Server, Server1, when the mode of authentication is Windows Security, use the following command:

   ```
   Dim conn As New SqlClient.SqlConnection("Data Source=server1;Initial
   Catalog=ABCFinance;Integrated Security=SSPI")
   conn.Open()
   ```

4. Pass the name of the connection object as a parameter to the constructor of the `SqlClient.SqlConnection` class. The code to pass the connection object as a parameter is shown here:

   ```
   Dim cmdTxt As String
   cmdTxt = "select ExRate,denomination  from  rates where country='" &_
   strCountry & "'"
   Dim cmd As New SqlClient.SqlCommand(cmdTxt, conn)
   ```

5. Declare a SqlDataReader object as shown in the following code statement:

   ```
   Dim reader As SqlClient.SqlDataReader
   ```

6. Execute the command to read the data from a database table. The command is shown here:

   ```
   reader = cmd.ExecuteReader()
   ```

   The preceding statement calls the `ExecuteReader()` method that returns the rows from the database table in the form of an SqlReader object.

7. Move to the first record of the dataset to the SqlReader object and extract the required data by using the column name in the table.

   For example, in the following code, `Denomination` and `ExRate` are columns in the Rates table in the ABCFinance database. The `Read()` method reads the data in the Rates table.

   ```
   reader.Read()
   Data.Rate = reader.Item("ExRate")
   Data.Denomination = reader.Item("Denomination")
   ```

8. Close the reader and the connection objects.

   ```
   conn.Close()
   reader.close
   ```

The following is the entire code listing for the implementation of the `GetCountryData()` method:

```
<WebServiceBinding( Namespace:="http://localhost/Webservice1"), _
```

```
WebServiceBindingAttribute(Name:="Service1", _
Namespace:="http://localhost/Webservice1", _
Location:="http://localhost/ExchangeService/Webservice1.wsdl")> _
    Public Class Webservice1
    Inherits ExchangeRateService

        <System.Web.Services.WebMethodAttribute(),_
        System.Web.Services.Protocols.SoapRpcMethodAttribute("http://
ABCFinances.com/action/
GetCountryData", RequestNamespace:="http://ABCFinances.com/message/",
ResponseNamespace:="http://ABCFinances.com/message/")>  _
        Public overrides Function GetCountryData(ByVal strCountry As
String) As <System.Xml.Serialization.SoapElementAttribute("Result")> CountryData

        Dim data As new CountryData
        Dim conn As New SqlClient.SqlConnection("Data Source=saik-
d185;Initial Catalog=ArtFinance;Integrated Security=SSPI")
        conn.Open()
        Dim cmdTxt As String
        cmdTxt = "select ExRate,denomination  from  rates where
country='" & strCountry & "'"

        Dim cmd As New SqlClient.SqlCommand(cmdTxt, conn)
        Dim reader As SqlClient.SqlDataReader

        Try
            reader = cmd.ExecuteReader()
        Catch
            Throw New Exception("Invalid Country")
        End Try

        reader.Read()
        Data.Rate = reader.Item("ExRate")
        Data.Denomination = reader.Item("Denomination")
        reader.Close()
        GetCountryData = data
        End Function
```

Similarly, you can add code for the GetRateByCountry() method. The entire code for the GetRateByCountry() method is as follows:

```
<System.Web.Services.WebMethodAttribute(),  _
       System.Web.Services.Protocols.SoapRpcMethodAttribute("http://
ABCFinances.com/action/
GetRateByCountry", RequestNamespace:="http://ABCFinances.com
/message/", ResponseNamespace:="http://ABCFinances.com/message/")>  _
       Public Overrides Function GetRateByCountry(ByVal strCountry As String) As
<System.Xml.Serialization.SoapElementAttribute("Result")> Single

        Dim strDenom As String
        Dim conn As New SqlClient.SqlConnection("Data Source=saik-d185;Initial
Catalog=ArtFinance;Integrated Security=SSPI")
        conn.Open()
        Dim cmdTxt As String
        cmdTxt = "select exrate  from  rates where country='" & strCountry &
"'"

        Dim cmd As New SqlClient.SqlCommand(cmdTxt, conn)
        Dim reader As SqlClient.SqlDataReader

        Try
            reader = cmd.ExecuteReader()
        Catch
            Throw New Exception("Invalid Country")
        End Try

        reader.Read()
        strDenom = reader.Item("ExRate")
        reader.Close()
        GetRateByCountry = strDenom
        End Function
```

After you add the code for the GetCountryData() and GetRateByCountry() methods, you need to recompile the Webservice1.asmx.vb file. Because you are using the classes and methods in the data access assemblies of the .NET Framework, the command line for compiling the DLL file changes is as follows:

```
vbc /out:Webservice1.dll /target:library
```

```
/libpath:e:\winnt\microsoft.net\framework\v1.0.3328

/reference:system.dll,system.web.dll,system.web.services.dll,system.xml.dll,

system.data.dll Webservice1.asmx.vb
```

After you compile the DLL file, copy the file to the bin folder. This creates the Web service, which you can now test. Testing the Web service is discussed in the following section.

Testing the Web Service

To test a Web service, you first need to create a client application. In this case, you will create a small Console application in Visual Basic .NET. To create a client application, you can use the .NET Framework SDK.

You have already used the WSDL.exe utility to create a server component that was used to create a Web service. Now you will use the same tool to create a client side proxy application that encapsulates the Web service operations.

To create the proxy class, execute the WSDL.exe tool from the command line by using the following syntax:

```
Wsdl /out:proxy.vb /language:vb

http://localhost/ExchangeService/webservice1.asmx?wsdl
```

The preceding command creates a file with the name proxy.vb, which contains the proxy definitions for the client application. The options in the command specify the name of the output file, the language used to generate the proxy class definitions, and the location of the WSDL document for the Web service.

The proxy class contains declarations for all Web methods that the Web service supports.

 NOTE

The proxy class contains two sets of declarations for each Web method. The set of declarations includes synchronous and asynchronous calls for the methods in the Web service.

The definitions in the proxy class are shown in the following code snippet. These declarations refer to the original Web service.

```
<System.Diagnostics.DebuggerStepThroughAttribute(),  _

     System.ComponentModel.DesignerCategoryAttribute("code"),  _

     System.Web.Services.WebServiceBindingAttribute(Name:="Webservice1Soap",

[Namespace]:="http://ABCFinances.com/")>  _
```

```
Public Class Webservice1
Inherits System.Web.Services.Protocols.SoapHttpClientProtocol

'<remarks/>
    Public Sub New()
        MyBase.New
        Me.Url = "http://localhost/ExchangeService/webservice1.asmx"
    End Sub
```

Next, consider the method exposed by the Web service. This method contains the following declarations that allow the Web method to be called synchronously.

```
<System.Web.Services.Protocols.SoapRpcMethodAttribute("http://ABCFinances.com/
action/GetRateByCountry", RequestNamespace:="http://ABCFinances.com/message/",
ResponseNamespace:="http://ABCFinances.com/message/")> _
    Public Function GetRateByCountry(ByVal strCountry As String) As
<System.Xml.Serialization.SoapElementAttribute("Result")> Single
' Code removed
    End Function
```

The following set of the declarations allows the `GetRateByCountry()` Web method to be called asynchronously:

```
Public Function BeginGetRateByCountry(ByVal strCountry As String, ByVal callback
As System.AsyncCallback, ByVal asyncState As Object) As System.IAsyncResult
End Function
    Public Function EndGetRateByCountry(ByVal asyncResult As
System.IAsyncResult) As Single
    End Function
```

After you look at the code for the `GetRateByCountry()` Web method, you will look at the entire code for the proxy class that the WSDL.exe utility creates, as shown here:

```
'----------------------------------------------------------------------------
' <autogenerated>
'       This code was generated by a tool.
'       Runtime Version: 1.0.3328.4
'
'       Changes to this file may cause incorrect behavior and will be lost if
'       the code is regenerated.
' </autogenerated>
'----------------------------------------------------------------------------
```

```vb
Option Strict Off
Option Explicit On

Imports System
Imports System.ComponentModel
Imports System.Diagnostics
Imports System.Web.Services
Imports System.Web.Services.Protocols
Imports System.Xml.Serialization

'
'This source code was auto-generated by wsdl, Version=1.0.3328.4.
'

'<remarks/>
    <System.Diagnostics.DebuggerStepThroughAttribute(), _
    System.ComponentModel.DesignerCategoryAttribute("code"), _
    System.Web.Services.WebServiceBindingAttribute(Name:="Webservice1Soap", _
[Namespace]:="http://ABCFinances.com/")> _
     Public Class Webservice1
     Inherits System.Web.Services.Protocols.SoapHttpClientProtocol

  '<remarks/>
      Public Sub New()
          MyBase.New
          Me.Url = "http://localhost/ExchangeService/webservice1.asmx"
      End Sub

  '<remarks/>
      <System.Web.Services.Protocols.SoapRpcMethodAttribute("http://ABCFinances.com/
action/GetCountryData", RequestNamespace:-"http://ABCFinances.com/message/",
ResponseNamespace:="http://ABCFinances.com/message/")> _
     Public Function GetCountryData(ByVal strCountry As String) As CountryData
          Dim results() As Object = Me.Invoke("GetCountryData", New Object()
{strCountry})
          Return CType(results(0),CountryData)
      End Function
```

```
        '<remarks/>
        Public Function BeginGetCountryData(ByVal strCountry As String, ByVal
callback As System.AsyncCallback, ByVal asyncState As Object) As
System.IAsyncResult
            Return Me.BeginInvoke("GetCountryData", New Object() {strCountry},
callback, asyncState)
        End Function


        '<remarks/>
        Public Function EndGetCountryData(ByVal asyncResult As
System.IAsyncResult) As CountryData
            Dim results() As Object = Me.EndInvoke(asyncResult)
            Return CType(results(0),CountryData)
        End Function


        '<remarks/>
        <System.Web.Services.Protocols.SoapRpcMethodAttribute("http://ABCFinances.com/
action/GetRateByCountry", RequestNamespace:="http://ABCFinances.com/message/",
ResponseNamespace:="http://ABCFinances.com/message/")> _
        Public Function GetRateByCountry(ByVal strCountry As String) As
<System.Xml.Serialization.SoapElementAttribute("Result")> Single
            Dim results() As Object = Me.Invoke("GetRateByCountry", New Object()
{strCountry})
            Return CType(results(0),Single)
        End Function


        '<remarks/>
        Public Function BeginGetRateByCountry(ByVal strCountry As String, ByVal
callback As System.AsyncCallback, ByVal asyncState As Object) As
System.IAsyncResult
            Return Me.BeginInvoke("GetRateByCountry", New Object() {strCountry},
callback, asyncState)
        End Function


        '<remarks/>
        Public Function EndGetRateByCountry(ByVal asyncResult As
System.IAsyncResult) As Single
            Dim results() As Object = Me.EndInvoke(asyncResult)
```

```
        Return CType(results(0),Single)
    End Function
End Class


    '<remarks/>
    <System.Xml.Serialization.SoapTypeAttribute("CountryData",
"http://ABCFinances.com/encodedTypes")>  _
    Public Class CountryData

    '<remarks/>
    Public Rate As Single

    '<remarks/>
    Public Denomination As String
    End Class
```

Now create a file, WS1Client.vb, by using a text editor, such as Notepad, and add the following code to it:

```
Module Module1
    Sub Main()
    End Sub
End Module
```

You will now create a simple application that contains the `Main()` method. Copy the entire code from the proxy.vb file to the WS1Client.vb file.

TIP

Ensure that the `Import` declaration statements should be included before the `Module1` declaration.

To the WS1Client.vb file, you need to add the code to call the `GetCountryData()` Web method synchronously. To do this, add the following code to the `Main()` method of the application:

```
Sub Main()
    Dim strCountry
    Dim data As New CountryData()
    Dim ws As New Webservice1()
    Console.Write("Enter the name of the Country:")
    strCountry = Console.ReadLine()
```

```
        Try
                data = ws.GetCountryData(strCountry)
         Catch
                Console.WriteLine(Err.Description)
                Console.ReadLine()
                Exit Sub
         End Try
         Console.WriteLine("The Exchange rate of " & data.Denomination & " used
in " & strCountry & " is " & data.Rate)
         Console.ReadLine()
End Sub
```

You can also access `GetCountryData()` asynchronously by using the `Begin()` and `End()` methods in the proxy class, as shown in the following code:

```
Module Module1
      Sub Main()
              Dim ar As IasyncResult
              Dim ws As New Webservice1()
              Dim sync As AsyncCallback
              Console.WriteLine("Enter the name of a country:")
              ar = ws.BeginGetRateByCountry(Console.ReadLine(), Nothing, Nothing)
              ar.AsyncWaitHandle.WaitOne()
              Dim results As Single
              results = ws.EndGetRateByCountry(ar)
              Console.WriteLine(results)
              Console.ReadLine()
      End Sub
End Module
```

This version of the client application uses the `BeginGetRateByCountry()` and `EndGetRateByCountry()` methods to call the `GetRateByCountry()` operation of the Web service asynchronously. Next, the `WaitOne()` method delays the execution of the `EndGetRateByCountry()` method until the Web service call is returned.

 NOTE

Although this is similar to the previous example functionally, in this case, the client application is free to process something else until the Web service call returns.

Compile the synchronous and asynchronous client applications by using the `vbc.exe` command line or Visual Basic .NET compiler, and verify the functioning of the Web service.

Testing Web Services by Using the Web Service Behavior

Visual Studio .NET makes the task of creating clients that consume Web services fairly simple. However, without Visual Studio .NET, creating clients can be slightly difficult and requires knowledge of handling SOAP messages. To make it easier for a Web developer to consume a Web service, Microsoft provides the Web service behavior Webservice.htc.

You can use the Web service behavior to test a Web service. To use the Web service behavior to access a Web service, perform the following steps:

1. Attach the Web service behavior to any element in a Web page.
2. Specify the URL of the Web page by using the `useService()` method of the Web service behavior.
3. Invoke a Web method by using the `callService()` method of the Web service behavior.

You first need to attach the Web service behavior to an element in an HTML page. You can attach the Web service behavior to a `<div>` element by using the following syntax:

```
<div id="Service1"
style="behavior:url(webservice.htc)"></div>
```

Next, you need to initialize the Web service behavior by using the `useService()` method. The `useService()` method has the following syntax:

```
sElementID.useService(sWebServiceURL, sFriendlyName [, oUseOptions])
```

The parameters that are used in the `useService()` method of the Web service behavior are explained in the following list:

- ◆ **sElementID.** This is a required parameter that specifies the ID of the element to which you attach the Web service behavior.
- ◆ **sWebServiceURL.** This is a required parameter that specifies the URL of the Web service. You can specify the URL of the Web service in four ways, as shown in Table 9-1.
- ◆ **sFriendlyName.** This is a string parameter that represents a friendly name for the Web service URL. It is a required parameter.
- ◆ **oUseOptions.** This is an instance of the `useOptions` object. It contains a single property, `reuseConnection`, which specifies the connection information required by a Web service that uses Secure Sockets Layer (SSL) authentication.

Table 9-1 Different Methods of Specifying the URL of a Web Service

Method	Description
Web service file	This is an .asmx file that specifies a short form of the URL of the Web service. It is essential that the Web service be located in the same folder as the Web page that the Web Service behavior uses. In this case, the Web service behavior assumes the ?WSDL query string.
WSDL file name	This is a WSDL file name with an extension of .wsdl.
Full file path	This is an .asmx or .wsdl file that specifies the full path of a Web service or the WSDL file that includes the ?WSDL query string. You can use the full path file to specify either a local file path or a URL.
Relative path	This is an .asmx or .wsdl file that specifies the relative path of a Web service or the WSDL file. Similar to a full path file, the relative path file also includes the ?WSDL query string.

For your Web service, you can use the following syntax for the useService() method:

```
Service1.useService(http://localhost/ExchangeService/Webservice1.asmx?wsdl,"WebService1")
```

The useService() method takes the URL of the Web service and creates a friendly name, WebService1, which you will use to refer to the Web service. After this, you need to invoke the Web service by using the callService() method. The callService() method initiates the engagement of the Web service behavior with the Web service. The syntax for the callService() method is as shown:

```
iCallID = sElementID.sFriendlyName.callService(  [oCallHandler], funcOrObj, oParam)
```

The parameters that are used in the callService() method are explained in the following list:

◆ **iCallID.** This is the return ID of the service call.

◆ **sElementID.** This is the ID of the element in the Web page that is attached to the Web services behavior.

 TIP

With asynchronous calls, it is essential to match the iCallID parameter with the ID that is returned as a property of the result object. The result object cannot be associated with the service call until the two IDs match.

- ◆ **sFriendlyName.** This is the friendly name, as specified in the `useService()` method, that is associated with a Web service.
- ◆ **oCallHandler.** This is an optional parameter used as a callback handler function for processing the result object.
- ◆ **funcOrObj.** This is a required parameter that specifies either the Web method that you want to call or the call options object. You can set this object with the `createCallOptions()` method.

 TIP

The `createCallOptions()` method contains nine properties. You don't need to set all nine properties, but you do need to set the `funcName` property to specify the name of the Web method that you want to call. If this property is not set, the Web service will not know the Web method that you want to call.

- ◆ **oParam.** This is a list of required parameters that the Web method expects. The parameters are separated by commas.

The syntax for calling a Web method from Webservice1 that you created is shown here:

```
nId = Service1.Webservice1.callService("GetRateByCountry","India")
```

Apart from the `useService()` and `callService()` Web methods, the Web service behavior also supports the `createUseOptions()` and `createCallOptions()` methods, as discussed in the following sections.

The `createUseOptions()` Method

The `createUseOptions()` method creates a `useOptions` object that is used to set the authentication persistence property. This property decides whether authentication is required for each method invocation. The syntax for the `createUseOptions()` method is as follows:

```
ObjOptions=Service1.CreateUseOptions(true/false)
```

The preceding code creates an `ObjReuseAuthentication` object of the type `useOptions` and has a property `reUseConnection`. This property is useful when the Web site that hosts the service uses SSL. In addition, by using this property, you can specify whether the Web service client needs to log in for each method invocation. The code for the `createUseOptions()` method for WebService1 is as follows:

```
Dim ObjOptions
    ObjOptions=service1.CreateUseOptions()
```

```
        ObjOptions.reUseConnection=true;
        Service1.useService(http://localhost/ExchangeService/Webservice1.asmx?wsdl,
"WebService1", ObjOptions)
```

The `createCallOptions()` *Method*

The `createCallOptions()` method creates an object of the type `options` for the Web service behavior. The syntax for the method is shown here:

```
objCallOptions.createCallOptions();
```

This method can initialize `callObject`, which can be passed as a parameter to the `callService()` method. The following is a sample snippet of the `callService()` method:

```
Var obj;
        obj = service.createCallOptions();
        obj.async = true;
        obj.params = new Array();
        obj.params.Country = "SomeCountry";
        obj.params.Denomination="denomination" ;
        obj.funcName = "GetRateByCountryAndCurrency";
```

As you can see, the `createCallOptions()` method returns a call options object.

The Result Object

The Web service behavior uses the result object to return a value from the Web service. The result object uses the `onresult` and `onServiceAvailable` event handlers, as discussed in the following sections.

The `onresult` Event Handler

You can use the `onresult` event handler to access this data. The `onresult` event handler is accessible only to the HTML element that is attached to the Web service behavior.

```
<DIV ID="service" STYLE="behavior:url(webservice.htc)"
onresult="ProcessResult()">
```

In the preceding syntax, you specified that the `ProcessResult()` method will be called when the `onresult` event is fired. You can then use the `ProcessResult()` method to retrieve the value returned by the Web service, if any, or to collect the information about an error that might have generated. The code for the `ProcessResult()` method is shown here:

```
function ProcesResult()
{
```

```
        if((event.result.error)
        {
                event.result.errorDetail.code
                document.write("Error:"+event.result.errorDetail.string);
        }
        else
        {
                document.write(Value from the service: "+event.result.value);
        }
}
```

The onServiceAvailable Event Handler

The onServiceAvailable() event handler is fired after the behavior has successfully obtained the WSDL from a Web service. This event has the following properties:

- **ServiceAvailable.** This is a Boolean property that indicates whether the behavior was successful in retrieving the WSDL from the Web service.

- **ServiceURL.** This is a string value that contains the URL of the Web service, which is connected to the behavior.

- **username.** This property contains the string that you passed as the friendly name to the useService() method.

- **WSDL.** This property contains the WSDL for the Web service, which is connected to the behavior.

The Web service behavior makes it easy to access Web services from Web pages. However, the behavior has certain limitations, as discussed in the following list:

- You can use the behavior to access only those Web services that are in the same domain as the Web page that contains it.

- Although the behavior supports all .NET data types, it does not support the complex types, such as datasets, recordsets, and other user-defined types.

Now that you have briefly learned about the Web service behavior, you will learn to create an HTML page that you can use to connect to Webservice1 and retrieve data from it.

```
<html>
<head>
<SCRIPT language="JavaScript">
var iCallID = 0;
function init()
{
        service1.useService("http://localhost/ExchangeService/webservice1.asmx?wsdl",
```

```
"Webservice1");
}
function ProcessResult()
{
        if((event.result.error))
        {
                document.writeln("ERROR. Method call failed!");
                document.write(event.result.errorDetail.string);
        }
        else
        {
                document.write(event.result.value);
        }
}


function callWS()
{
        iCallID = service1.Webservice1.callService("GetRateByCountry","india");
}

</SCRIPT>
</head>
<body onload="init()">
        <div id="service1" style="behavior:url(webservice.htc)"
onresult="ProcessResult()">
        </div>
        <input type="button" onClick="callWS()">
</body>
</html>
```

The preceding code creates an HTML page that contains a Button control.

The Web service behavior is bound to the <div> element with an ID of service1. The body element has an onLoad event handler that calls the useService() method to initialize the location of the Web service with which the behavior will interact.

When the button is clicked, the callWS() method is called, which in turn calls a Web service method using the callService() method. Then the method calls the getRateByCountry() method with the name of a country passed as a parameter.

After the method call returns, the control is passed to the `ProcessMessage()` method, which handles the `onResult` event. The method returns a returned value or an error message, whichever applies.

You can save and open the HTML file in Internet Explorer 5.0 or later to test the working of the Web service.

Summary

In this chapter, you learned how to create a Web service and client by using the tools that are provided with the .NET Framework SDK. You also learned how the Web service behavior allows you to access Web services from Web pages in a simple way.

PART VII

Professional
Project 4

Project 4

Creating a Web Service for Gizmo Wrap Using the ATL Server Library

Project 4 Overview

Similar to creating Web services by using Visual Basic 6.0, Visual Basic .NET, and the .NET platform SDK, you can use Visual C++ to create XML Web services.

Visual C++ has undergone some changes in Visual Studio .NET. One of the noteworthy changes is the introduction of the ATL Server Library, which is based on the ATL library that is available with earlier versions of Visual C++. This library provides all the tools and templates required to build efficient Web sites. It also allows you to build Web services.

In this project, you will use the ATL Server library to build and test a Web service for Gizmo Wrap. This Web service will be used to expose the products of Gizmo Wrap on other popular sites to increase the visibility of their products. This will help them gain new customers and increase their profits.

Chapter 10

In previous projects, you learned to create Web services by using the SOAP toolkit and ASP.NET. However, you have several other options for creating Web services, such as using the ATL Server library.

Before you create a Web service by using the ATL Server, you need to learn about the ATL Server library. This chapter provides a brief introduction of the ATL Server library. In addition, you will create a simple Web application by using the ATL Server.

Evolution of the ATL Server

In the early days of the Web, Web pages were static in nature. This implies that the content displayed in a static Web page couldn't change. In addition, static Web pages that used HTML alone were not interactive; therefore, they could not retain users' attention for a long time. As a result, dynamic Web pages that could present data from an external source, such as a database, were developed. The content in such a Web page is dynamic; therefore, when the data in the underlying data source is changed, the modified data can be reflected in the dynamic Web page.

You can create dynamic Web pages in several ways. You learned to create dynamic Web pages by using Visual Studio .NET in Chapter 7, "Building Web Applications on the .NET Platform." You can also create dynamic Web pages by using Common Gateway Interface (CGI) scripts and applications.

CGI applications are compiled applications that are developed by using languages, such as C or C++. The CGI technology is used to create high-performance applications that are deployed on servers based on operating systems, such as Unix.

Deploying CGI applications on servers using the Windows platform is an overhead. This is because CGI applications are executable files created using various programming languages. Whenever a CGI application is deployed on a Windows environment, the operating system assigns a process to the file. Processes require a large number of resources; therefore, they increase the overall cost of deploying the application. In addition, the process overhead associated with each CGI call makes CGI applications non scalable. Therefore, to create high-performance multithreaded Web applications for the Windows platform, Microsoft came up with the Internet Services Application Programming Interface (ISAPI) technology. ISAPI is an API that extends the functionality of the Web server, such as IIS.

Although ISAPI applications are high-performance applications, they are not widely used because Visual C++ 6.0 offers limited support for creating ISAPI applications. As a solution to this problem, Microsoft created an MFC-based wizard for ISAPI extensions. However, the wizard did not include support for standard Web features, such as session management and cookies. In addition, the wizard did not provide a built-in support for accessing database from the application. To provide a solution in the form of a simpler COM component development environment, Microsoft developed the ATL Server. The following section provides an overview of the ATL Server.

Overview of the ATL Server

The ATL Server is a library of C++ classes that you can also use to develop Web applications and Web services through compiled code. The ATL library was originally developed to provide classes to create lightweight and fast COM components. Microsoft has based the ATL Server on the ATL library.

Advantages of the ATL Server

As discussed earlier, ATL Servers can be used to create high-performance Web applications and Web services. In addition, ATL Servers provide other advantages, as discussed in the following list:

◆ **Allows reusability of code.** The ATL Server allows you to create applications by reusing the existing code. This is because the source code of the ATL Server applications is easily available to all users. Therefore, you can create a Web service or Web application by customizing the existing code according to your needs.

◆ **Allows creation of applications in Visual Studio .NET.** Microsoft has based the ATL Server on the .NET platform. Therefore, while you're creating ATL Server applications, you can benefit from the features of the .NET platform, such as CLR, managed code, debugging tools, and so on. In addition, Visual Studio .NET provides you with a template for creating ATL Server applications, as shown in Figure 10-1.

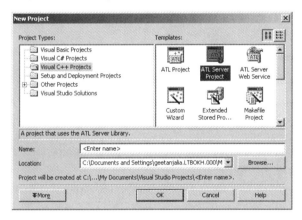

FIGURE 10-1 *The template for ATL Server applications.*

◆ **Allows use of conditional constructs.** While you're creating applications by using the ATL Server, you can use constructs, such as `if-else` or `while` to perform conditional execution of code. Doing this helps a block of code be executed based on the value returned by a condition. The syntax for the `if-else` and `while` loops is as follows:

```
{{if  condition}}
    <!     HTML statements    >
{{else}}
    <!     HTML statements    >
{endif}}


{{while}}
    <!     HTML statements    >
{{endwhile}}
```

◆ **Allows monitoring performance of applications.** You can monitor the performance of ATL Server applications by accessing Windows 2000 Performance Monitor. In addition, the ATL Server library contains classes and attributes that allow you to add performance counters to ATL Server applications. You can then use these counters to monitor the performance of the application.

◆ **Allows access of the Crypto API library.** The Crypto API library is a collection of classes that enables Visual C++ and Visual Basic programmers to include cryptography functionality in their applications. ATL Server applications can access the Crypto API library.

◆ **Allows data access by using OLE-DB.** ATL Server applications can use OLE-DB to access data from a data source. OLE-DB is a specification that allows you to access data by using several data providers. The Visual Studio .NET IDE provides wizards that allow simple access to various data sources.

◆ **Allows support for storing and retrieving of session state data.** ATL Server applications can store cookie values and session state data in a database that ATL provides.

Features of ATL Server Applications

The features of ATL Server applications are discussed in the following list:

◆ ATL Servers are used to create dynamic Web pages, which in turn contain the business logic used to display the output to the user in the form of an HTML page. Coding these dynamic pages includes creating the programming logic and the HTML code. In an ATL Server application, the programming logic and the HTML code are stored in different files.

◆ ATL Servers are capable of handling multiple client requests simultaneously. To do this, ATL Servers implement internal thread-pools. This implies that when an ATL Server receives a request from a client, it allocates a thread to handle the client request. Therefore, when a client sends in a request, a thread processes the request. The client application is not required to wait until the server is finished processing another request.

◆ ATL Server applications can process a client request. Therefore, when a client sends a request to a Web server, the server forwards the request to the ATL Server. The ATL Server then allocates threads and resources to process the request.

Architecture of ATL Server Applications

An ATL Server application consists of the following components:

◆ ISAPI extension DLL

◆ Web application DLL

◆ Server Response File (SRF)

In addition to the previous list, the architecture includes a Web server (which is not a component of the ATL Server application) that receives the request sent by a client application. We will discuss these components in detail now.

Web Server

In ATL Server applications' architecture, the Web server forwards the request that a client application sends to an ATL Server. The ATL Server processes the request. The Web server that can be used in ATL Server applications' architecture is IIS.

ISAPI Extension DLL

The ISAPI extension DLLs contain the desired functionality of a Web service. The ISAPI extension DLLs are of two types:

- **ISAPI filters.** When a Web server forwards a request that a client sends to an ATL Server, the ISAPI filters process the request. However, a client application can never explicitly invoke an ISAPI filter.
- **ISAPI applications.** ISAPI applications are similar to CGI applications because you can invoke an ISAPI application by using a URL. In addition, ISAPI applications provide the same functionality as CGI applications. However, ISAPI applications provide better performance than CGI applications.

Web Application DLL

When the ATL Server processes a request, the SRF needs to call the Web methods. These Web methods are contained in the classes within the Web application DLLs. In addition, to process a request, the ISAPI application DLL interacts with the Web application DLL. You will learn about SRFs in the following section.

SRFs

As you know, the ATL Servers create dynamic Web pages. However, the Web pages that you create might also contain some static text. The code for the static text is stored in the Simple Text Files (STFs). In addition, these files contain tags to invoke the request-handling methods from the Web application DLLs. You will learn about the request-handling methods in the section "Default Class."

To understand the content of an SRF, refer to the following sample code:

```
<html>
        {{handler application.dll/Default}}
           <head>
           </head>
           <body>
```

```
                    This is a test {{Hello}} <br>
        </body>
</html>
```

As you can see, the SRF is an HTML file; therefore, it begins with the `<html>` tag. Next, the code specifies the name of the Web application DLL, which the SRF calls. In this case, the Web application DLL is `application.dll`. The name of the Web application DLL is included in the `handler` tag, which defines the class that contains the request-handling methods that the SRF invokes. Using the `Default` keyword indicates that the request-handling methods are contained in the class marked with the `default` attribute.

The previous SRF calls request-handling methods from just one Web application DLL. However, you can modify the code to call request-handling methods from multiple Web application DLLs, as shown here:

```
{{handler application.dll/Default}}
{{id=CalculatorObj handler Calculator.dll/Math}}
```

In the preceding code, `CalculatorObj` calls the request-handling methods of the `Math` class in Calculator.dll. To do so, the `id` property is assigned a value `CalculatorObj`.

Next, the file contains the `head` and `body` elements. Inside the `body` element, you need to specify the request-handling method that the SRF invokes. The name of the request-handling method is enclosed in the `{{Hello}}` placeholder. Therefore, the output of the request-handling method replaces the placeholder at runtime. The ATL Server keeps track of the placeholders and their corresponding request-handling methods. This information is stored within a file called the ATL Server map.

The architecture of ATL Server applications is depicted in Figure 10-2.

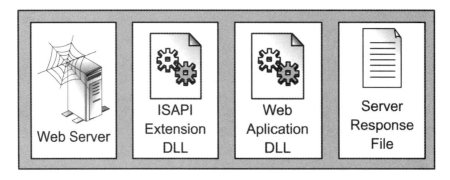

FIGURE 10-2 *The architecture of ATL Server applications.*

Default Class

As discussed earlier, to process a request, the SRFs call the request-handling methods that are contained in the classes of a Web application DLL. These classes are derived from a base class, CrequestHandlerT. Data in the ATL Server application architecture is exchanged by using the HTTP protocol. The CrequestHandlerT class contains methods to access the request and response messages that are transferred using HTTP.

A class in a Web application DLL might contain one or more request-handling methods. In addition, each Web application DLL contains a default class. If you do not explicitly relate a request-handling method to an SRF, the file invokes the request-handling methods of the default class. A default class is marked with the Default keyword, as shown in the following code snippet:

```
[ request_handler("Default") ]
class ExampleClass
{
        ---------
}
```

After a class is declared as default, the entry for the class is created in the ATL Server map. However, to do this, you first need to create an ATL Server map. You can create an ATL Server map by using the MFC-style macros, as shown in the following code:

```
BEGIN_REPLACEMENT_METHOD_MAP(ExampleClass)
REPLACEMENT_METHOD_ENTRY("Hello",OnHello)
END_REPLACEMENT_METHOD_MAP()
```

Alternatively, you can create ATL Server maps by using the attributes provided by the ATL Server Project Wizard. The following code creates an ATL Server map by using the attributes provided by the ATL Server Project Wizard:

```
[ tag_name(name="Hello") ]
HTTP_CODE OnHello(void)
{
        m_HttpResponse << "Hello World!";
        return HTTP_SUCCESS;
}
```

The default class in any Web application DLL contains two methods. These methods are discussed in the following list:

◆ **OnHello() method.** At runtime, the placeholder {{Hello}} is replaced by a request handler method in the Web application DLL. To replace this placeholder, the application calls the OnHello() method. You can add user-defined placeholders to an SRF.

Therefore, you need to create methods similar to the `OnHello()` method that are used to replace these placeholders with the corresponding request-handler methods.

◆ **`ValidateAndExchange()` method.** When a client application sends a request, ATL Server processes the request and returns the result to the calling application. However, before the result is displayed, the `ValidateAndExchange()` method is called implicitly to declare the state variables.

Processing of the ATL Server Applications

You have looked at the architecture of the ATL Server applications. Now you will learn about the processing of these applications based on their architecture. The processing of the ATL Server applications primarily involves the interaction between a client application and an ATL Server application. These interactions are explained in the following list:

1. The interactions between the client application and the ATL Server application start when a client application sends a request to the Web server.

2. The request that the client application sends can be for an SRF. If this is the case, the Web server forwards the request to the ISAPI extension DLLs. When the request is forwarded to the ISAPI extension DLLs, the Web server is free to receive other client requests.

3. The ISAPI extension DLLs assign a thread from their thread pool to the client request.

4. The thread processes the client application by loading the Web application DLL mentioned in the SRF.

 NOTE

An ISAPI extension DLL maintains a cache for the SRFs and Web application DLLs. Therefore, when the SRF is processed, the ISAPI extension DLL looks for the required Web application DLL in the DLL cache. If the required DLL is not present, the DLL is loaded from its actual location.

5. The request-handling methods, as specified in the SRF, are called from the Web application DLL.

6. The values that the methods return then replace the placeholders in the SRFs.

7. The processed result is sent back to the requesting application.

The processing of the ATL Server applications is shown in Figure 10-3.

Until now, you have learned about the ATL Server. You will now create a sample ATL Server application by using the knowledge you have gained in the previous sections.

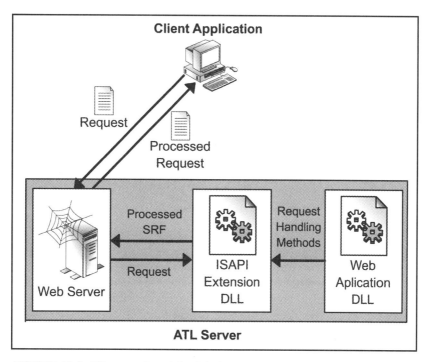

FIGURE 10-3 *The processing of the ATL Server applications.*

Creating a Sample ATL Server Application

Visual Studio .NET provides you with two templates: ATL Server Projects and ATL Server Web Service. You can use these templates to create ATL Server Web applications and ATL Server Web services, respectively. In this section, you will learn to create an ATL Server application in Visual Studio .NET. To do this, perform the following steps:

1. Launch Visual Studio .NET from the Programs menu.
2. To create a new project, choose File, New, Project. The New Project dialog box is displayed.
3. In the Project Types pane, select the Visual C++ Projects option.
4. In the Templates pane, select the ATL Server Project option.
5. In the Name text box, specify the name of the project as `SampleATLApplication`.
6. In the Location text box, browse for the location where you want to store the ATL Server project. The New Project dialog box for the ATL Server application is shown in Figure 10-4.
7. Click on the OK button.

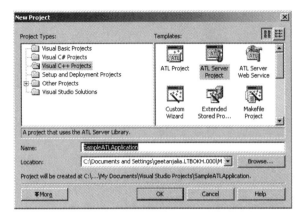

FIGURE 10-4 *The New Project dialog box for the ATL Server application.*

When you click on the OK button, Visual Studio .NET launches the ATL Server Project Wizard (see Figure 10-5). This wizard provides an easy and efficient method for creating Web applications or XML Web Service projects that use the ATL Server.

As you can see, the first screen in the ATL Server Project Wizard is the Overview screen. This screen provides an overview of the current settings of the ATL Server project. Visual Studio .NET allows you to exit the wizard if you do not want to make changes to the current project settings. However, if required, you can change the current settings by using the other screens of the ATL Server Project Wizard. You will learn about these screens in the following sections.

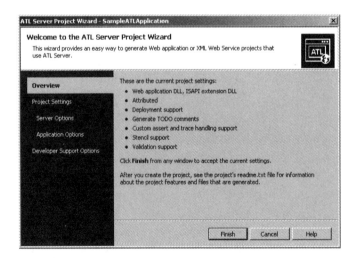

FIGURE 10-5 *The ATL Server Project Wizard.*

When you click on the Finish button to complete the wizard, Visual Studio .NET by default creates an ATL Server application project, SampleATLApplication, and an ISAPI extension DLL, SampleATLApplicationIsapi. These projects are added to the Solution Explorer window, as shown in Figure 10-6.

FIGURE 10-6 *The Solution Explorer Window.*

As you can see, these projects include several files. Some of these files are discussed in Tables 10-1 and 10-2.

Table 10-1   Files in the ATL Server Project

File	Description
SampleATLApplication.cpp	This file contains the functionality and the default request-handling methods for your project.
SampleATLApplication.h	This file, similar to SampleATLApplication.h file, contains the functionality of the project.
SampleATLApplication.srf	This file is the SRF for the project.

Similar to the ATL Server project, the ISAPI extension DLLs also contain several files, as explained in Table 10-2.

Table 10-2 Files in the ISAPI Extension DLL

File	Description
SampleATLApplicationIsapi.cpp	This file contains the code that is compiled to create an ISAPI extension DLL.
SampleATLApplicationIsapi.def	This file contains default methods, `HttpExtensionProc()`, `GetExtensionVersion()`, and `TerminateExtension()`, for the ISAPI extension DLL. The `HttpExtensionProc()` method is the entry point for the project. The `GetExtensionVersion()` method maintains the version information for the DLL, and the `TerminateExtension()` method downloads the ISAPI extension DLL from IIS.

After you have created the ATL Server project and the ISAPI extension DLL by using the ATL Server Project Wizard, you can add code to the SampleATLApplication.h and SampleATLApplication.srf files to implement the functionality that the application provides. You will learn to add code to the project files in Chapter 11, "Creating a Web Service Using the ATL Server Library."

We will now discuss the screens of the ATL Server Project Wizard.

Project Settings

The Project Settings screen allows you to select the types of projects that you need to include in your ATL Server project. To select a type of project to be included, you need to select the corresponding check box. By default, the Web application and ISAPI extension DLLs are included in the project, as shown in Figure 10-7.

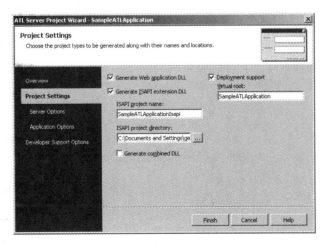

FIGURE 10-7 *The Project Settings screen.*

In addition to specifying the project types, you can specify a name and location for the project types. Finally, you can specify the virtual directory where you want to host the ATL Server project.

Server Options

The Server Options screen allows you to specify the additional server options that the ISAPI extension DLL supports. You can use these options to implement caching for the ATL Server project. The options in the Server Options screen are displayed in Figure 10-8.

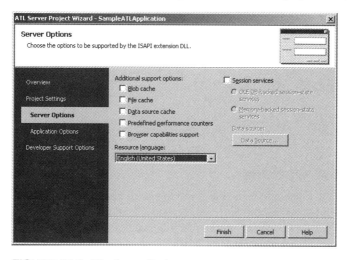

FIGURE 10-8 *The Server Options screen.*

As discussed earlier, you can access the Windows 2000 Performance Monitor and store session state information for an ATL Server application. To do this, you need to select the respective options in the Server Options screen.

Application Options

The Application Options screen allows you to select the options that the Web Application DLL supports. By default, the Validation Support and Stencil Processing Support options are selected. The Validation Support option enables the application to perform validations in application forms. The Stencil Processing Support option creates simple tags for your application. These options are displayed in Figure 10-9.

As you can see in Figure 10-9, the Application Options screen allows you to create the ATL Server project as a Web service.

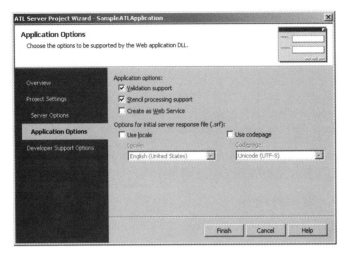

FIGURE 10-9 *The Application Options screen.*

Developer Support Options

The Developer Support Options screen allows you to specify the options that will help you in working with the ATL Server project. For example, you can add ToDo comments in the code. These comments help you by marking all the pending activities in your code. The Developer Support Options screen is shown in Figure 10-10.

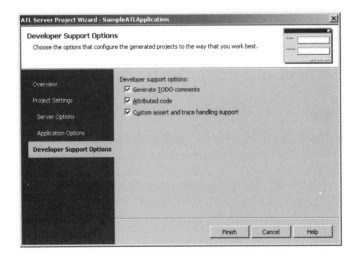

FIGURE 10-10 *The Developer Support Options screen.*

Deploying ATL Server Applications

After an application is created, you need to deploy it on a Web server. However, before you deploy the application, you need to build it. To deploy a project in Visual Studio .NET, perform the following steps:

1. Select the Build, Build Solution option.
2. In the Solution Explorer window, select the SampleATLApplication option.
3. Select the Build, Deploy option.
4. Select the Debug, Start option to run the application.

The result of the ATL Server project is shown in Figure 10-11.

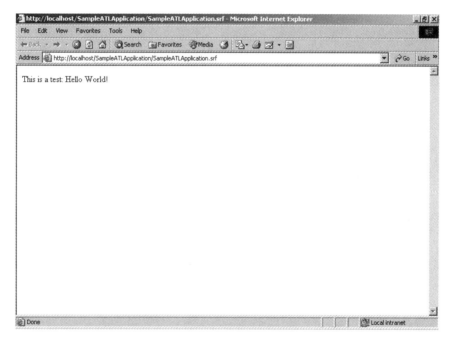

FIGURE 10-11 *The result of the ATL Server project.*

Summary

This chapter introduced you to the ATL Server. The ATL Server is a library of C++ classes that you can use to develop Web applications and Web services through compiled code. Next, you learned about the advantages, features, and architecture of the ATL Server applications. Based on this knowledge, you learned to create a sample ATL Server project in Visual Studio .NET.

Chapter 11

In this project, you will learn to create a Web service by using the ATL Server library in Visual Studio .NET. Before creating the Web service, you will take a look at the case study on which the project is based. Finally, you will create a Web service based on the design of the project.

Case Study

Gizmo Wrap (GW) is a small retail store based in New York. GW specializes in selling expensive electronic devices, such as digital cameras, surveillance equipment, and robot kits. The organization has a small clientele for its brick and mortar business. GW wants to expand its horizons by increasing its clientele, and therefore, its revenues. To do this, the organization has gone online and will now sell its range of products on the Internet.

GW has set up an online store at http://www.gizmowrap.com. Although the site was hosted a few months back, the developers are still working on the site to enhance it. The developers created the site by using ASP for the Windows 2000 platform. In addition to ASP, the developers used the ATL Server library to construct parts of the site where performance was a critical issue. You learned in Chapter 10, "Introduction to the ATL Server," about how the ATL Server can be used to create performance intensive applications.

The GW site maintains a log of the visitors to the site. After analyzing the data in the log, GW senior management realized that most of the visitors were their existing customers or sometimes, the people who were recommended by their existing customers. This is because GW is a small store in a niche market with little visibility.

The senior management at GW realized that one way to increase the visibility and the revenue of the organization was to advertise heavily on the Internet. Until now, the publicity of GW was limited to a few advertisements in the local print media. The management of GW was aware of the high cost that most retail shops spent on advertising, but they never thought of doing the same. However, after putting up the Web site, GW thought of increasing the sale of their products by advertising on the popular sites.

In addition, the management thought of using another strategy to increase its sales. They decided to sell their product range on other popular sites, including horizontal portals, news sites, and so on. The reason for doing this was to make their products visible among the high number of visitors to these sites. They also realized the importance of having an associate program that could promote their products on a site with high visibility. To do this, GW created an associate program that involved selling their products by positioning them on other sites.

According to the program, when a sale was made on another site, the owner of the site would earn a commission from GW. GW realized that having a program like this would involve sharing of information about their products with other sites and also enabling a customer to place an order for the product from the associate's site. To do this, they needed to integrate their data with the associate site.

They could share the data by replicating their products database and distributing it to the associate sites. However, replicating the data for various databases that the associate sites used could be tedious and costly. In addition, whenever GW would make a change to its databases, the changes would need to be replicated across the databases of all associate sites. However, replication of the changes could happen only at regular time intervals, which would affect the integrity of the data because the data in the GW database and their associate sites would be different at some point in time.

As a solution to the previously discussed problems, the development team at GW decided to expose their data as a Web service. In addition, the team decided to create a Web service that could accept orders from the visitors of the associate sites.

The management at GW realized the advantages of using Web services and suggested that the development team incorporate Web services with their Web site.

The GW development team has competency primarily in C++; therefore, it plans to create the Web service by using the ATL Server.

Having discussed the scenario for which the development team will create the Web service, we will next discuss the project life cycle that the team followed to create the GW Web service.

Project Life Cycle

The development life cycle of a project, as discussed in Chapter 8, "Creating an ASP.NET Web Service," involves three phases:

- Project initiation
- Project execution
- Project deployment

You are already familiar with these phases; therefore, we will discuss only the project execution phase, which involves creating the design and the project.

The Project Execution Phase

The project execution phase involves designing, creating, and testing of the project. In addition, the team decides on the features of the application, which are as listed:

- The application needs to be installed on the Web site of GW.
- The Web site of GW runs on a Windows 2000 server.
- The Web site does not use the .NET Framework.
- The application should allow an associate member to display the product details on their site.
- The application allows customers to place an order on an associate Web site.
- The data for the site is currently being stored in an SQL database.

You will now look at the tasks that the development team performs in the project execution phase:

- Requirements analysis
- Design
- Construction
- Testing

In the subsequent sections, we will detail the tasks that the team performs in each of these stages.

Requirements Analysis

During the requirements analysis phase, the development team at GW identified the need for the Web services application. The details of the requirements are gathered from the input that senior management at GW provides and the problem statement as listed by James Shatner, the CEO of the organization. The problem statement is as follows:

GW needs to provide its associate sites with their product data so that the associates can host the data on their sites. This would make the products of GW popular among the visitors of the associate sites. Therefore, the visitors can place orders for desirable products on the associate sites.

Then, the development team performed a detailed analysis of the requirements of GW and came up with the following results:

◆ The Web service should run on a Windows platform other than .NET.

◆ The Web service should expose methods that allow a client application or Web site to access the product details and then place an order.

◆ Depending on the associate site, the Web service should expose product IDs of selective products to the associate site.

◆ Depending on the product IDs, the Web service should provide the details of the respective product to the associate sites.

On further discussions with the GW management, the development team realized that GW did not want to expose its entire catalog. Instead, the team planned to share the details of a few of their products with their associates. GW currently promotes a feature product each month and offers discounts on it. GW wants the associates to be able to access this product's data and promote it on their site.

Design

During this phase, the development team decides the functionality that the Web service will implement and the technology to be used. The design specifications of the product are as listed:

◆ The data to be exposed to the associate sites should be stored in an SQL 2000 database. The data for the original GW Web site is also stored in an SQL database.

◆ Because the team has competence in Visual C++, it was decided that the Web service would be developed using Visual C++ .NET and the ATL Server library.

◆ The associate site can access the data through stored procedures created in SQL.

◆ The entire business solution will contain three Web services: to return the details of the featured product of the month, to return the details of products whose ID is exposed to the associate site, and to enable a client application to place an order for a product.

Construction

During this phase, the development team constructs the application. The primary tasks that the team needs to perform in this phase are as follows:

- ◆ Design and create the database.
- ◆ Design and create the stored procedures.
- ◆ Create a Web Service application by using the ATL Server library in Visual C++. NET.

Testing

You can test a Web service by calling it from a client application. The development team plans to create a client application in Visual Basic .NET and then, request the Web service from the client application.

Advantages of Creating a Web Service by Using the ATL Server Library

As you know, a Web service is a way for a Web site to expose programmatic functionality. Web services accept input in the form of messages and respond through messages. You can send and receive these messages by using HTTP-POST, HTTP-GET, or SOAP.

Creating a Web service by using the ATL Server is not as simple and easy as doing it in any of the .NET languages, such as Visual Basic .NET or Visual C#. However, there are some reasons why a developer might use the ATL Server library to create Web services (see Chapter 10). The following list shows some of the reasons so that you can appreciate the effort required to create Web services by using the ATL Server library:

- ◆ **Create high-performance Web services.** The most important reason for using the ATL Server library to create Web services is that ATL Server Web services offer high performance.
- ◆ **Use classes in the ATL Server library.** To create ATL Server Web services, you can use the classes that the ATL-based libraries provide. These classes make the work easier for developers.

Creating a Web Service for GW by Using the ATL Server Library

Creating a Web service for GW involves creating the database and the stored procedures in SQL. After you create the database and stored procedures, you will create the Web service.

Creating the Database for GW

In your local installation of SQL Server, create a database and the following tables:

◆ **Products table.** The Products table contains the fields shown in the Figure 11-1. The CategoryID field has a foreign key relationship with the CategoryID field of the Category table. The ManufID field has a foreign key relationship with the ManufID field of the Manufacturer table, and the SupplierID field has a foreign key relationship with the SupplierID field of the Supplier table.

Column Name	Data Type	Length	Allow Nulls
⚷ ProdID	int	4	
Name	varchar	50	
Description	varchar	200	✓
CategoryID	int	4	
ManufID	int	4	✓
SupplierID	int	4	✓
Cost	money	8	
ImageURL	varchar	50	✓
▶ FeaturedProduct	int	4	✓

FIGURE 11-1　*The Products table.*

◆ **Category table.** The Category table contains the fields shown in Figure 11-2. This table stores data on various categories of products that are available at the store. In addition, the table contains the descriptions of the respective categories.

Column Name	Data Type	Length	Allow Nulls
⚷ CategoryID	int	4	
▶ CategoryTitle	varchar	25	✓
Description	varchar	50	✓

FIGURE 11-2　*The Category table.*

◆ **Manufacturer table.** The Manufacturer table stores the information about the manufacturers of the products, as shown in Figure 11-3.

Column Name	Data Type	Length	Allow Nulls
▶⚷ ManufID	int	4	
ManufName	varchar	50	✓
ManufDesc	varchar	50	✓

FIGURE 11-3　*The Manufacturer table.*

◆ **Supplier table.** The Supplier table contains the details of the suppliers of various products, as shown in Figure 11-4.

Column Name	Data Type	Length	Allow Nulls	
SupplierID	int	4		
SupplierName	varchar	25		
SalesContact	varchar	50	✓	
URL	varchar	25	✓	

FIGURE 11-4 *The Supplier table.*

◆ **Orders table.** The orders that are placed on the Web site and through the Web services are stored in this table. The table has foreign key relationships with the Products table and the Customer table. The Orders table is shown in Figure 11-5.

Column Name	Data Type	Length	Allow Nulls	
OrderID	int	4		
ProdID	int	4		
CustomerID	int	4		
Qty	int	4		

FIGURE 11-5 *The Orders table.*

◆ **Customer table.** The Customer table contains the details of the customers who are registered with the site. In addition, the table contains details about the members of the associate program. The table has an integer field, associate, which is set to 1 for storing the details of an associate program member. The details of the Customer table are shown in Figure 11-6.

Column Name	Data Type	Length	Allow Nulls	
CustomerID	int	4		
CustomerName	varchar	50	✓	
CustomerPass	varchar	50	✓	
CustomerAddress	varchar	200	✓	
Associate	int	4	✓	

FIGURE 11-6 *The Customer table.*

The relationship between these tables is shown in Figure 11-7.

After you create the database with the previously discussed tables, you will create the stored procedures as discussed in the following section.

Creating the Stored Procedures for GW

As discussed earlier, the business solution for GW will contain three Web services, and the stored procedures will provide the data that the Web services require. You will now create these stored procedures.

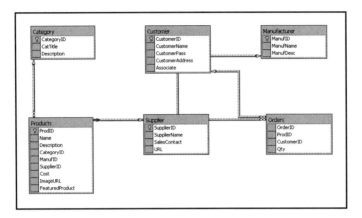

FIGURE 11-7 *The relationship between the tables of the GW database.*

The `GetFeaturedProduct` Stored Procedure

The `GetFeaturedProduct` stored procedure returns the details of the featured product of the month. The code of the stored procedure is as shown:

```
CREATE PROCEDURE dbo.GetFeaturedProduct
AS
Select Name,Products.Description,CategoryTitle,Cost,ImageURL from
Products,Category
where Products.FeaturedProduct=1 and Products.CategoryID=
Category.CategoryID
```

The `GetProductDetail` Stored Procedure

The `GetProductDetail` stored procedure accepts a product ID from the Web service and returns the corresponding product details from the Products table. The code of the stored procedure is as follows:

```
CREATE PROCEDURE DBO.GetProductDetail (@ProdID integer)
AS
Select Name, Products.Description, CategoryTitle,Cost,ImageURL
from Products,Category
where Products.CategoryId=Category.CategoryID and ProdID=@ProdID
```

The PlaceOrder Stored Procedure

The PlaceOrder stored procedure accepts the data for an order that a customer places and then inserts a record for the order into the Orders table. The code for the PlaceOrder stored procedure is as follows:

```
CREATE PROCEDURE DBO.PlaceOrder(@ProdName varchar(50),
@Qty integer, @CustName varchar(50), @CustPass Varchar(20))
AS
declare @CustID integer
declare @ProdID integer
select @CustID=CustomerID from Customer where
CustomerName=@CustName and CustomerPass=@CustPass

if @CustID is null
        return "Invalid User Name or Password"
        select @ProdID=ProdID from Products where
        Name=@ProdName

if @ProdID is null
        return "Invalid Product Name"

insert into orders(ProdID,CustomerID,Qty) values(@ProdID, @CustID,@Qty)

return "Order Entered"
```

Creating the ATL Server Web Service

After you create the database and the stored procedures, you will create the Web service. To create a Web service by using the ATL Server library, perform the following steps:

1. Start Visual Studio .NET and create a new Visual C++ project.
2. Select ATL Server Web Service as the project type and specify the project name as GizmoWS.
3. Click on the OK button. Figure 11-8 shows the New Project dialog box.

When you click on the OK button, Visual Studio .NET launches the ATL Server Project Wizard. We discussed the screens of the ATL Server Project Wizard in detail in Chapter 10. The ATL Server Project Wizard appears as shown in Figure 11-9.

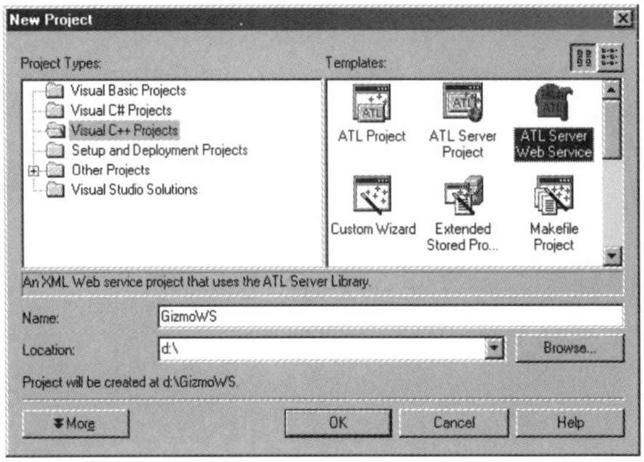

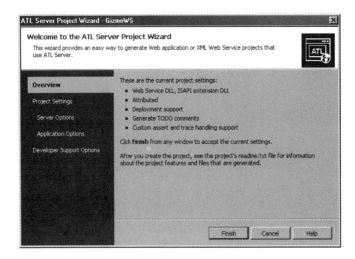

FIGURE 11-8 *The New Project dialog box.*

FIGURE 11-9 *The Overview page.*

After you click on the Finish button in the ATL Server Project Wizard, Visual Studio .NET creates a HelloWorld Web service and opens it in the design view. In addition, Visual Studio .NET creates several files for the project and adds them to the Solution Explorer window. Figure 11-10 shows the Solution Explorer window for a Web service.

As you can see, Visual Studio .NET creates two projects as listed:

◆ **GizmoWS.** GizmoWS is the Web service that the ATL Server Project Wizard creates.

◆ **GizmoWSIsapi.** GizmoWSIsapi is the ISAPI extension DLL for the ATL Server project.

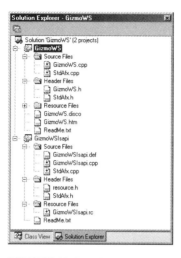

FIGURE 11-10 *The Solution Explorer window.*

You are not required to make any modifications to the ISAPI Extension DLL project. Therefore, I will discuss only the GizmoWS project in detail. Table 11-1 discusses the files that the ATL Server Project Wizard creates for the GizmoWS project.

Table 11-1 Default Files for the GizmoWS Project

Default File	Description
GizmoWS.cpp	This file contains the method declarations, such as DllMain(), which the DLL requires.
GizmoWS.h	This file contains the functionality that the Web service provides. We will discuss this file in detail later in this section.
GizmoWS.Disco	This file contains the data required for the dynamic discovery of the Web service.
GizmoWS.htm	This file contains the path to the WSDL file for the Web service. In addition, the GizmoWS.htm file contains a description of the default operation, HelloWorld, which the Web service provides.

 NOTE

As discussed, the GizmoWS.htm file contains the hard-coded description of the Hello World Web service. The information about this Web service does not change when you add more operations to the Web service or delete the HelloWorld Web service. Therefore, when you deploy the Web service, you will find a description of the Hello World Web service, even if it is not functional.

At this point, we will discuss the contents of the GizmoWS.h file, which contains the functionality of the Web service. The code of the Web service is as follows:

```
// ExRateWS.h : Defines the ATL Server request handler class
//
#pragma once

namespace GizmoService
    {
            // all struct, enum, and typedefs for your Web service
            //should go inside the namespace

            // IGizmoService - web service interface declaration

            [
                    uuid("AE109AEE-3C52-4CD4-906B-53EF750DD621"),
                    object
            ]
        __interface IGizmoService
        {
            //HelloWorld is a sample ATL Server Web service method. It shows how to
            //declare a Web service method and its in-parameters and out-parameters
                [id(1)] HRESULT HelloWorld([in] BSTR bstrInput,
[out, retval] BSTR *bstrOutput);
                // TODO: Add additional Web service methods here
        };

// GizmoService - Web service implementation
[
        request_handler(name="Default", sdl="GenGizmoWSDL"),
        soap_handler(
                name="GizmoService",
                namespace="urn:GizmoService",
                protocol="soap")
]
class CGizmoService :
        public IGizmoService
        {
```

```
        public:
        // This is a sample Web service method that shows how to use the
        // SOAP_method attribute to expose a method as a Web method
    [ soap_method ]
        HRESULT HelloWorld(/*[in]*/ BSTR bstrInput, /*[out, retval]*/
BSTR *bstrOutput)
        {
                CComBSTR bstrOut(L"Hello ");
                bstrOut += bstrInput;
                bstrOut += L"!";
                *bstrOutput = bstrOut.Detach();
                return S_OK;
        }
        // TODO: Add additional web service methods here
    }; // class CGizmoService
} // namespace GizmoService This interface for the component declares
just one method, HelloWorld. The method is defined as
[ soap_method ]
    HRESULT HelloWorld(/*[in]*/ BSTR bstrInput, /*[out, retval]*/ BSTR *bstrOutput)
    {
        //code edited out
        return S_OK;
    }
```

In the preceding code, the [soap_method] attribute indicates to the compiler that the method is for an operation that a Web service exposes. In addition, the parameters that are sent to the Web service or are returned by the Web service are encoded in the form of a SOAP message.

The preceding code is the default code for the Web service. To create your own Web service, you need to add Web methods to the Web service. The Web methods to be added are discussed in the following list:

- **GetFeaturedProduct().** The GetFeaturedProduct() method returns the details of the Featured product of the month.
- **GetProductDetail().** The GetProductDetail() method accepts a product ID from an associate member and returns the corresponding product details.
- **PlaceOrder().** The PlaceOrder() method stores an order that a customer places for a product.

Before you add the code for the Web methods, you need to make interface declarations for these methods. The interface declarations for the methods are shown in the following code snippet:

```
__interface IGizmoService
{
        [id(1)] HRESULT GetFeaturedProduct([out] BSTR
*bstrName,[out] BSTR *bstrDesc,[out] BSTR *bstrCategory,[out]
BSTR *bstrCost,[out] BSTR *bstrImageURL);
        [id(2)] HRESULT GetProductDetail([in] LONG ProdID,[out]
BSTR *bstrName,[out] BSTR *bstrDesc,[out] BSTR *bstrCategory,[out]
BSTR *bstrCost,[out] BSTR *bstrImageURL);
        [id(3)] HRESULT PlaceOrder([in]BSTR ProductName,[in]
LONG Qty,[in] BSTR  bstrUserName,[in] BSTR bstrPass);
};
```

After you add the interface declarations for the methods, add the code for the Web methods in the GizmoWS.h file:

```
[ soap_method ]
        HRESULT GetFeaturedProduct(/*[out]*/ BSTR *bstrName, BSTR
*bstrDesc,BSTR *bstrCategory, BSTR *bstrCost,BSTR *bstrImageURL )
        {
                return S_OK;
        }


        [ soap_method ]
        HRESULT GetProductDetail(/*[in]*/ LONG lProdID,/*[out]*/
BSTR *bstrName, BSTR *bstrDesc,BSTR *bstrCategory, BSTR *bstrCost,BSTR *bstrImageURL )
        {
                return S_OK;
        }


[ soap_method ]
        HRESULT PlaceOrder(/*[in]*/BSTR bstrProductName, /*[in]*/
 LONG Qty, /*[in]*/ BSTR  bstrUserName, /*[in]*/ BSTR bstrPass)
        {
                return S_OK;
        }
```

The preceding methods need to interact with the database. For example, when a user places an order, the PlaceOrder() Web method stores the details of the order in the Orders table. Consider another situation in which an associate member requests the product details; the GetProductDetail() Web method needs to retrieve the details of the requested product from the Products table and expose it to the Web service.

To allow your application to interact with a database, you can use the ATL OLE DB Consumer Wizard. Using this wizard greatly simplifies the ability to access databases from Visual C++ applications. To run the ATL OLE DB Consumer Wizard, perform the following steps:

1. Right-click on the Web service project name in the Solution Explorer window.
2. Select Add, Add Class from the resulting menus. The Add Class dialog box appears as shown in Figure 11-11.

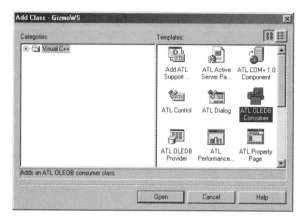

FIGURE 11-11 *The Add Class dialog box.*

3. In the dialog box, select the ATL OLE DB Consumer option.
4. Click on the Open button. This launches the ATL OLE DB Consumer Wizard. The first page of the wizard is shown in Figure 11-12.

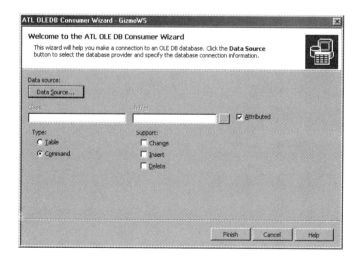

FIGURE 11-12 *The ATL OLE DB Consumer Wizard.*

5. Click on the Data Source button. The Data Link Properties dialog box is displayed, as shown in Figure 11-13.

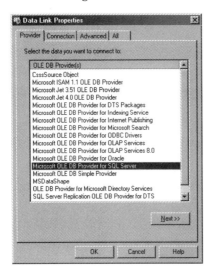

FIGURE 11-13 *The Data Link Properties dialog box.*

6. In the displayed list, select the Microsoft OLE DB Provider for SQL Server option.

7. Click on the Next button. In the Connection dialog box, enter the details for connecting to the SQL Server. The Connection dialog box is shown in Figure 11-14.

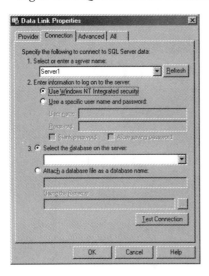

FIGURE 11-14 *The Connection page of the Data Link Properties dialog box.*

8. Select the name of your SQL server and the authentication type as appropriate to your local SQL server installation. Also, select the name of the database you created. To validate the connection string, click on the Test Connection button. A message confirming the successful connection of the database is displayed.

9. Click on the OK button. The Select Database Object dialog box appears, as displayed in Figure 11-15.

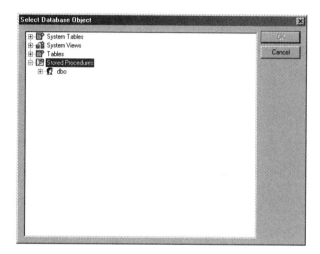

FIGURE 11-15 *The Select Database Object dialog box.*

10. Expand the tree for the stored procedures and select the `GetFeatureProduct` stored procedure.

11. Click on the OK button. This will bring you back to the ATL OLE DB Consumer Wizard dialog box. This dialog box now has the names for the files added to it. If required, you can change the names of the files and the classes. The ATL OLE DB Consumer Wizard dialog box is shown in Figure 11-16.

12. Click on the Finish button. The wizard adds a header file, GetFeaturedProduct.h, to the project.

To view the contents of the GetFeaturedProduct.h file, open the file. The file contains the following code:

```
// GetFeaturedProduct.h : Declaration of the CGetFeaturedProduct


#pragma once


// code generated on Friday, January 25, 2002, 12:51 PM
```

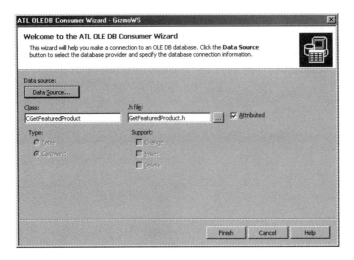

FIGURE 11-16 *The ATL OLE DB Consumer Wizard dialog box.*

```
[
        db_source(L"Provider=SQLOLEDB.1;Integrated Security=SSPI;Persist Security
Info=False;Initial Catalog=Gizmo;Data Source=SAIK-D185;Use Procedure for
Prepare=1;Auto Translate=True;Packet Size=4096;Workstation
ID=Server1-D185;Use Encryption for Data=False;Tag with column
collation when possible=False"),
        db_command(L"{ ? = CALL dbo.GetFeaturedProduct }")
]

class CGetFeaturedProduct
{
        public:

        // To fix several issues with some providers, the code below may bind
        // columns in a different order than reported by the provider

            [ db_column(1, status=m_dwNameStatus, length=m_dwNameLength)
] TCHAR m_Name[51];
            [ db_column(2, status=m_dwDescriptionStatus,
length=m_dwDescriptionLength) ] TCHAR m_Description[201];
            [ db_column(3, status=m_dwCatTitleStatus,
length=m_dwCatTitleLength) ] TCHAR m_CatTitle[26];
```

```
        [ db_column(4, status=m_dwCostStatus,
length=m_dwCostLength) ] CURRENCY m_Cost;
        [ db_column(5, status=m_dwImageURLStatus,
length=m_dwImageURLLength) ] TCHAR m_ImageURL[51];


    // The following wizard-generated data members contain status
    // values for the corresponding fields. You
    // can use these values to hold NULL values that the database
    // returns or to hold error information when the compiler returns
    // errors. See Field Status Data Members in Wizard-Generated
    // Accessors in the Visual C++ documentation for more information
    // on using these fields.
    // NOTE: You must initialize these fields before setting/inserting data!

    DBSTATUS m_dwNameStatus;
    DBSTATUS m_dwDescriptionStatus;
    DBSTATUS m_dwCatTitleStatus;
    DBSTATUS m_dwCostStatus;
    DBSTATUS m_dwImageURLStatus;


    // The following wizard-generated data members contain length
    // values for the corresponding fields.
    // NOTE: For variable-length columns, you must initialize these
    //       fields before setting/inserting data!

    DBLENGTH m_dwNameLength;
    DBLENGTH m_dwDescriptionLength;
    DBLENGTH m_dwCatTitleLength;
    DBLENGTH m_dwCostLength;
    DBLENGTH m_dwImageURLLength;

    [ db_param(1, DBPARAMIO_OUTPUT) ] LONG m_RETURN_VALUE;


    void GetRowsetProperties(CDBPropSet* pPropSet)
    {
        pPropSet->AddProperty(DBPROP_CANFETCHBACKWARDS,
true, DBPROPOPTIONS_OPTIONAL);
        pPropSet->AddProperty(DBPROP_CANSCROLLBACKWARDS,
```

```
true, DBPROPOPTIONS_OPTIONAL);
        }
};
```

As you can see, the CGetFeaturedProduct class encapsulates the GetFeaturedProduct stored procedure. To do this, the CGetFeaturedProduct class contains variable declarations for each of the values that the stored procedure returns. For example, for the Name field in the Products table, the class has the following code:

```
[ db_column(1, status=m_dwNameStatus, length=m_dwNameLength) ] TCHAR m_Name[51];
```

Similarly, the ATL OLE DB Consumer Wizard creates a class for encapsulating the GetProductDetail stored procedures. This class is contained in the GetProductDetail.h file as shown:

```
// GetProductDetail.h : Declaration of the CGetProductDetail


#pragma once


// code generated on Friday, January 25, 2002, 2:30 PM


[
        db_source(L"Provider=SQLOLEDB.1;Integrated Security=SSPI;Persist Security
Info=False;Initial Catalog=Gizmo;Data Source=SAIK-D185;Use Procedure for
Prepare=1;Auto Translate=True;Packet Size=4096;Workstation
ID=SAIK-D185;Use Encryption for Data=False;Tag with column collation when
possible=False"),
        db_command(L"{ ? = CALL dbo.GetProductDetail(?) }")
]
class CGetProductDetail
{
        public:

                // To fix several issues with some providers, the code below may bind
                // columns in a different order than reported by the provider

                [ db_column(1, status=m_dwNameStatus,
        length=m_dwNameLength) ] TCHAR m_Name[51];
                [ db_column(2, status=m_dwDescriptionStatus,
        length=m_dwDescriptionLength) ] TCHAR m_Description[201];
                [ db_column(3, status=m_dwCatTitleStatus,
```

```
length=m_dwCatTitleLength) ] TCHAR m_CatTitle[26];
        [ db_column(4, status=m_dwCostStatus,
length=m_dwCostLength) ] CURRENCY m_Cost;
        [ db_column(5, status=m_dwImageURLStatus,
length=m_dwImageURLLength) ] TCHAR m_ImageURL[51];


    // The following wizard-generated data members contain status
    // values for the corresponding fields. You
    // can use these values to hold NULL values that the database
    // returns or to hold error information when the compiler returns
    // errors. See Field Status Data Members in Wizard-Generated
    // Accessors in the Visual C++ documentation for more information
    // on using these fields.
    // NOTE: You must initialize these fields before setting/inserting data!

    DBSTATUS m_dwNameStatus;
    DBSTATUS m_dwDescriptionStatus;
    DBSTATUS m_dwCatTitleStatus;
    DBSTATUS m_dwCostStatus;
    DBSTATUS m_dwImageURLStatus;


    // The following wizard-generated data members contain length
    // values for the corresponding fields.
    // NOTE: For variable-length columns, you must initialize these
    //       fields before setting/inserting data!

    DBLENGTH m_dwNameLength;
    DBLENGTH m_dwDescriptionLength;
    DBLENGTH m_dwCatTitleLength;
    DBLENGTH m_dwCostLength;
    DBLENGTH m_dwImageURLLength;

    [ db_param(1, DBPARAMIO_OUTPUT) ] LONG m_RETURN_VALUE;
    [ db_param(2, DBPARAMIO_INPUT) ] LONG m_ProdID;

    void GetRowsetProperties(CDBPropSet* pPropSet)
    {
            pPropSet->AddProperty(DBPROP_CANFETCHBACKWARDS, true,
```

```
DBPROPOPTIONS_OPTIONAL);
                pPropSet->AddProperty(DBPROP_CANSCROLLBACKWARDS, true,
DBPROPOPTIONS_OPTIONAL);
        }
};
```

The `CGetFeaturedProduct` and `CGetProductDetail` classes are contained in the GetFeaturedProduct.h and GetProductDetail.h files, respectively. To use these files in your Web service, you need to include them in the Gizmo.h file, as shown in the following code snippet:

```
#include "GetFeaturedProduct.h"
#include "GetProductDetail.h"
```

The next step in the creation of the Web service is to modify the `GetFeaturedProduct()` and `GetProductDetail()` methods. These methods are similar, but the `GetProductDetail()` method accepts the ID of the product whose details are to be retrieved. To use this method in your Web service, you need to create an instance of the `CGetFeaturedProduct` class, which encapsulates the stored procedure. The code for creating an instance, p, of the `GetFeaturedProduct` class is as shown:

```
CGetFeaturedProduct *p;
p=new CGetFeaturedProduct();
```

Next, you need to call the `OpenAll()` method to invoke the stored procedure. After you call the `OpenAll()` method, call the `MoveFirst()` method to store the data in the variables of the `GetFeaturedProduct` class. For example, the m_Name variable contains the data from the Name field. This data needs to be stored in the variable of the `GetFeaturedProduct` class. To do this, call the following methods by using the instance, p, of the `GetFeaturedProduct` class:

```
p->OpenAll();
p->MoveFirst();
```

When the data becomes accessible, copy the values from the variables of the encapsulating class to the variables of the `GetFeaturedProduct()` method as shown:

```
CComBSTR tempBstr=p->m_Name;
tempBstr.CopyTo(bstrName);
```

TIP

Remember that the data in the `CgetFeaturedProduct` class is an array of TCHARs, whereas the return variables are of the BSTR type.

Now the variables of the `GetFeaturedProduct()` method contain the values from the encapsulating class. The complete code for the `GetFeaturedProduct()` method is as shown:

```
[ soap_method ]
        HRESULT GetFeaturedProduct(/*[out]*/ BSTR *bstrName, BSTR
*bstrDesc,BSTR *bstrCategory, BSTR *bstrCost,BSTR *bstrImageURL )
        {
                CGetFeaturedProduct *p;
                p=new CGetFeaturedProduct();
                p->OpenAll();
                p->MoveFirst();
                CComBSTR tempBstr=p->m_Name;
                tempBstr.CopyTo(bstrName);
                tempBstr=p->m_Description;
                tempBstr.CopyTo(bstrDesc);
                tempBstr=p->m_CatTitle;
                tempBstr.CopyTo(bstrCategory);
                VarBstrFromCy(p->m_Cost,0,LOCALE_NOUSEROVERRIDE,bstrCost);
                tempBstr=p->m_ImageURL;
                tempBstr.CopyTo(bstrImageURL);
                return S_OK;
        }
```

The code for the corresponding `GetProductDetail()` method is similar and is as shown:

```
[ soap_method ]
        HRESULT GetProductDetail(/*[in]*/ LONG lProdID,/*[out]*/ BSTR
*bstrName, BSTR *bstrDesc,BSTR *bstrCategory, BSTR *bstrCost,BSTR *bstrImageURL )
        {
                CGetProductDetail *p;
                p=new CGetProductDetail();
                p->m_ProdID=lProdID;
                p->OpenAll();
                p->MoveFirst();
                CComBSTR tempBstr=p->m_Name;
                tempBstr.CopyTo(bstrName);
                tempBstr=p->m_Description;
                tempBstr.CopyTo(bstrDesc);
                tempBstr=p->m_CatTitle;
                tempBstr.CopyTo(bstrCategory);
```

```
                    VarBstrFromCy(p->m_Cost,0,LOCALE_NOUSEROVERRIDE,bstrCost);
                    tempBstr=p->m_ImageURL;
                    tempBstr.CopyTo(bstrImageURL);
                    return S_OK;
        }
```

After you add the preceding methods to the Web service, you will create another Web method that allows a customer of the Web service to place an order with GW. To add this method, you need to follow the same procedure as adding the `GetFeaturedProduct()` and `GetProductDetail()` methods. Add the interface declaration statement for the `PlaceOrder()` method as shown:

```
[id(3)] HRESULT PlaceOrder([in]BSTR ProductName,[in] LONG Qty,[in]
BSTR bstrUserName,[in] BSTR bstrPass);
```

The `PlaceOrder()` method accepts the product name, the quantity of items to be purchased, the username, and the password of the customer. Now use the ATL OLE DB Consumer Wizard to create one more class that encapsulates the `PlaceOrder` stored procedure. The code for the class is shown here:

```
// PlaceOrder.h : Declaration of the CPlaceOrder
#pragma once
// code generated on Friday, January 25, 2002, 3:53 PM
[
        db_source(L"Provider=SQLOLEDB.1;Integrated Security=SSPI;
Persist Security Info=False;Initial Catalog=Gizmo;Data
Source=SAIK-D185;Use Procedure for Prepare=1;Auto
Translate=True;Packet Size=4096;Workstation ID=SAIK-D185;Use
Encryption for Data=False;Tag with column collation
when possible=False"),
        db_command(L"{ ? = CALL dbo.PlaceOrder(?,?,?,?) }")
]
class CPlaceOrder
{
        public:
          [ db_param(1, DBPARAMIO_OUTPUT) ] LONG m_RETURN_VALUE;
          [ db_param(2, DBPARAMIO_INPUT) ] TCHAR m_ProdName[51];
          [ db_param(3, DBPARAMIO_INPUT) ] LONG m_Qty;
          [ db_param(4, DBPARAMIO_INPUT) ] TCHAR m_CustName[51];
          [ db_param(5, DBPARAMIO_INPUT) ] TCHAR m_CustPass[21];
        void GetRowsetProperties(CDBPropSet* pPropSet)
        {
```

```
                          pPropSet->AddProperty(DBPROP_CANFETCHBACKWARDS,
true, DBPROPOPTIONS_OPTIONAL);
                          pPropSet->AddProperty(DBPROP_CANSCROLLBACKWARDS,
true, DBPROPOPTIONS_OPTIONAL);
        }
};
```

Now add a `PlaceOrder()` method to the Web service. Following is the code for the Web method:

```
[ soap_method ]
        HRESULT PlaceOrder(/*[in]*/BSTR bstrProductName, /*[in]*/ LONG
Qty, /*[in]*/ BSTR  bstrUserName, /*[in]*/ BSTR bstrPass)
        {
                CPlaceOrder *p;
                p=new CPlaceOrder();
                Convert(bstrProductName,p->m_ProdName,51);
                p->m_Qty=Qty;
                Convert(bstrUserName,p->m_CustName,51);
                Convert(bstrPass,p->m_CustPass,21);
                p->OpenAll();
                return S_OK;
        }
```

The `PlaceOrder()` method accepts the required parameters and initializes the members of the class, `CPlaceOrder`, with the corresponding values. The strings that are in the `BSTR` format need to be converted into `TCHAR[]`. To do this, add a helper method, `Convert()`, as shown:

```
LPTSTR Convert(BSTR pStr, LPTSTR szStr, INT nSize)
{
        DWORD dwRet=WideCharToMultiByte(CP_ACP,0,(LPCWSTR)pStr,-
1,szStr,nSize,NULL,NULL);
        return szStr;
}
```

After adding the three Web methods, you're ready to deploy the Web service. To deploy a Web service, perform the following steps:

1. Select the Build, Build Solution option.
2. In the Solution Explorer window, select the GizmoWS project.
3. Select the Build, Deploy option.

Testing the Application

A client application tests a Web service. To create a client application, perform the following steps:

1. Select File, Add Project, New Project.
2. Create a new Windows application project in Visual Basic .NET. Visual Studio .NET adds one more project to the same solution.
3. In the Windows Application form, add a Button control from the Windows Forms toolbox.
4. Right-click on the name of the Visual Basic .NET project in the Solution Explorer window and select the Add Web Reference option. The Add Web Reference dialog box is displayed, as shown in Figure 11-17. In the Address text box, enter the URL of the Web service WSDL as `http://localhost/Gizmo/Gizmo.dll?Handler=GenGizmoWSDL`.

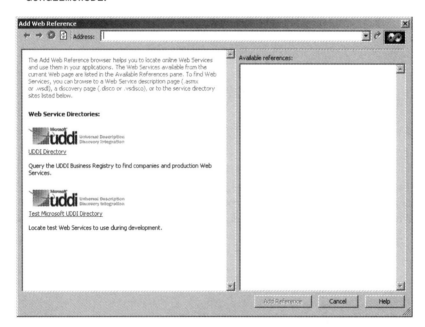

FIGURE 11-17 *The Add Web Reference dialog box.*

5. Click on the Add Reference button.

Visual Studio .NET adds a proxy class to the Web service. In addition, some default files are added to the project. You can find these files under the `Local` host node in the Solution Explorer window. One such file is the Reference.map file, which is a simple XML file that contains the links to the .disco and .WSDL files of the Web service. The contents of the Reference.map file are as shown:

```
<?xml version="1.0" encoding="utf-8"?>
<DiscoveryClientResultsFile xmlns:xsd="http://www.w3.org/2001/
XMLSchema" xmlns:xsi="http://www.w3.org/2001/XMLSchema-instance">
        <Results>
                <DiscoveryClientResult
referenceType="System.Web.Services.Discovery.ContractReference"
url="http://localhost/Gizmo/Gizmo.dll?Handler=GenGizmoWSDL"
filename="Gizmo.wsdl" />
        </Results>
</DiscoveryClientResultsFile>
```

Visual Studio .NET adds a proxy class for the Web service to the Web References folder. In addition to the proxy class, Visual Studio .NET creates a local copy of the WSDL file for the Web service.

 NOTE

Because the WSDL file is a local copy, it is not updated if you make a change to the Web service. For example, consider a situation in which you need to add another method to the Web service class. The information about this method will not be automatically updated in the WSDL file. To update the information in the WSDL file, you need to update the Web reference.

After you add a Web reference to your project, add a namespace declaration statement, as shown in the following code:

```
Imports WindowsApplication1.localhost
```

Next, add the following code to the Click event of the Button control to invoke the Web service from the control:

```
private void button1_Click(object sender, System.EventArgs e)
Private Sub Button1_Click(ByVal sender As System.Object, ByVal e As
System.EventArgs) Handles Button1.Click
        Dim ws As New GizmoService()
        ws.PlaceOrder("Product100", 1, "user10", "password")
```

Run the application by selecting the Start option on the Debug menu and check the functioning of the Web service.

Summary

In this chapter, you learned about the case study and design of the Gizmo WS project. Based on the case study and design, you created a Web service using the ATL Server library and tested it from a Visual Basic .NET application.

PART VIII

Professional Project 5

Project 5

Creating a Knowledge Share Web Service

Project 5 Overview

In this project, you will create a simple Web service by using Visual Studio .NET and C# for Flex Automobiles, Inc. The organization's employees will use this Web service to share and enhance their knowledge. You will learn about some of the advanced features of Web services that include enabling transactions in your Web services, creating SOAP extensions, and securing ASP.NET Web services.

Chapter 12

In the previous projects, you learned how to create ASP.NET Web services by using Visual Studio .NET. This chapter introduces you to a few advanced features and concepts related to building Web services by using Visual Studio .NET. These concepts include securing Web services by using Windows authentication and SOAP extensions, managing transactions and session states, and caching strategies.

This chapter begins with a case study and design of a Web service that you will create by using the ASP.NET technology.

The Knowledge Share Web Service

Flex Automobiles, Inc. is a leading car manufacturing company in the U.S. Since 1933, when the company was established, it has grown into a multi-billion dollar company. The company manufactures 12 different models of cars, ranging from economy cars to luxury cars. The company has a Web portal, http://www.flexautomobiles.com, which provides information about the organization, various models of cars, finance schemes available to the customers, and so on. In addition, the portal allows customers to book a car and avail the facilities for servicing their car.

Flex Automobiles, Inc. has a huge clientele, and more than 50,000 employees working in different branches spread across the U.S. The employees of the company work for different departments, such as finance, sales, production, human resources, customer services, and so on.

Flex Automobiles, Inc. provides several benefits and services to its customers. As a result, the company has a multitude of satisfied customers. Because of its services, the organization has gained many new customers and increased its revenue. The organization wants to concentrate on its employees as well. It has already taken a number of steps in this direction, such as providing yearly bonuses and other allowances for leave, travel, conveyance, and medical care. The company also wants to increase its employees' knowledge and skills.

The employees of Flex Automobiles, Inc. have competencies in several areas. Some employees have expertise in client communication, whereas others are good at handling accounts. The organization now wants all its employees to increase their skill set by gaining knowledge of the fields other than in which they are working. For example, employees who are working in the production department of the organization should also be able to communicate with the client. In addition, the employees should be able to increase their interpersonal skills by interacting with employees in the sales and marketing department of the organization.

To achieve these goals, Flex Automobiles, Inc. posted several presentations and tutorials that the employees, who are experts in an area, created on the intranet site. The organization now wants to set up a forum on its intranet site that allows its employees to post a query on any subject, including finance, management, interpersonal skills, investing, and so on. This forum will enable experts in specific areas to answer queries of employees, thereby enabling them to increase knowledge on various subjects. It is an excellent initiative taken by the organization that aims to increase communication and sharing among its employees.

To help you understand the advantages of this knowledge-sharing initiative, we will first discuss how Flex Automobiles, Inc. plans to work it out. The following list discusses the working of the knowledge-sharing initiative:

1. An employee who is working on any platform and on any application can post a query on the site. At present, different departments of the organization work on different platforms. Therefore, employees can send a query from applications created on various platforms. In addition, they can send a query from Web-based or desktop applications.

2. When an employee posts a query, the query is assigned a unique ID and stored in a database.

3. The queries in the database are divided into categories. This query is then forwarded to the expert of the category. The experts are selected based on their knowledge and experience in their specific fields.

4. The expert returns a reply to the query.

5. The employee who posts a query receives a response and, if need be, can seek further information. In addition, the employee can rate the answer, view a list of queries that other employees posted, view all queries based on categories, search for a query by its query ID, and so on.

All this reads like a common Web services scenario in which a client sends a query from an application called the client application. The receiving application using Web services to access data from a database that stores queries answers the query. As a result, the organization decides to create a Web service for this scenario. The decision to create a Web service is based on the fact that employees of the organization send queries from different client applications running on different platforms.

To create the Web service, Allen Lee, a senior project manager at Flex Automobile, Inc. has appointed a team of two developers, Ed Young and Ronald Billing. Ed Young will create the Web service, and Ronald Billing will create a sample application to test the Web service. The team has named this project Kshare.

Project Life Cycle

The Development Life Cycle (DLC) of a project involves the following three phases:

◆ Project initiation

◆ Project execution

◆ Project deployment

You learned about these phases in earlier projects. We will now discuss only the project execution phase, which is different from the earlier projects.

The Project Execution Phase

In the project execution phase, the development team creates the design of an application. After creating the design, they develop the application. The project execution phase consists of the following stages:

◆ Analyzing the requirements

◆ Creating the design of the application

◆ Constructing the application

Analyzing the Requirements

During the requirements analysis phase, the development team at Flex Automobiles, Inc. analyzes the need for creating a Web service with the following features:

◆ The Web service should access the data on queries from the database of Flex Automobiles, Inc.

◆ The Web service should contain Web methods that allow a user to post a query, view queries based on categories, and so on.

◆ The Web service should process the query and send the response back to the user who posted the query.

◆ The Web service should allow the user to query for further information or rate the response sent by the expert on the subject.

The requirements of the organization, as discussed in the previous list, are based on a problem statement from Mike Womack, the human resources manager of Flex Automobiles, Inc. Womack states, "We want to enhance the skill set of our employees by enabling them to interact with the experts on various subjects. These experts are employees who are proficient in a particular area or subject."

Creating the Design of the Application

During the design phase of the application, the development team decides upon the functionality to be implemented and the technology to be used.

As discussed earlier, the solution to the organization's requirements is a Web service. The developers decide to use ASP.NET technology and the Visual Studio .NET tools to create the intranet site of Flex Automobiles, Inc. because of their experience with them. The development team decided to test the Web service by using a client application that is also developed by using the Visual Studio .NET tools.

Construction

During the construction phase, the development team constructs the application. The primary tasks that the team performs in the construction phase are as follows:

◆ Creates the Web service

◆ Secures the Web service

◆ Deploys the Web service on a different computer

◆ Tests the Web service

Having discussed the DLC of the Kshare Web service project, we will now look at the database design that the organization uses.

The Database Design for the Kshare Application

The Kshare database consists of tables that store data in a structured format. In addition, the database consists of stored procedures that are used to access data from the tables in the Kshare database.

Tables in the Kshare Database

The tables in the Kshare database and their structures are described in the following list:

♦ **Queries table.** This table stores the queries posted by various users of Kshare. The structure of the Queries table is shown in Figure 12-1.

Column Name	Data Type	Length	Allow Nulls
QID	int	4	
UID	char	10	
Category	char	10	
RefQID	int	4	✓
Query	varchar	200	
TimesAccessed	int	4	
Status	char	1	

FIGURE 12-1 *The Queries table.*

As discussed earlier, whenever a user posts a query, a unique query ID is assigned to the query. This query ID along with the query is stored in the Queries table. To learn more about the data stored in the fields of the Queries table, refer to Table 12-1.

Table 12-1 Fields in the Queries Table

Field	Data
QID	Stores the ID of a query that a user posts. It is the primary key field for the table.
Query	Stores the query that a user posts.
UID	Stores the login name of the user who has posted the query.
Category	Stores the category of the query.
RefQID	Stores the query ID of a previous query, in case the new query is a response of the previous query.
TimesAccessed	Stores the number of times a user has viewed the response to a query. It is useful to track the query that is viewed the most often.
Status	Stores the status of the query. This field either stores a value U or A. U is the status of the queries that are pending. A refers to queries that are answered.

◆ **Category table.** This table stores a list of permissible categories on which a user can post a query. In addition, the Category table stores the descriptions of various categories, as discussed in Table 12-2. The structure of the Category table is shown in Figure 12-2.

Column Name	Data Type	Length	Allow Nulls
Category	char	10	
Description	varchar	100	

FIGURE 12-2 *The Category table.*

Table 12-2 Fields in the Category Table

Field	Data
Category	Stores the name of the category for which a user can post a query. It is the primary key field for the table.
Description	Stores a description of the category.

◆ **Answers table.** This table stores the response of the experts to the queries that the users post. The fields in the Answers table are shown in Table 12-3, and the structure of the Answers table is shown in Figure 12-3.

Column Name	Data Type	Length	Allow Nulls
AID	int	4	
EID	char	10	
QID	int	4	
Answer	varchar	200	

FIGURE 12-3 *The Answers table.*

Table 12-3 Fields in the Answers Table

Field	Data
AID	Stores a unique ID for each response that an expert sends. It is a field of type identity, and it is declared as the primary key for this table.
EID	Stores the login name of the expert who has answered the query.
QID	Stores the ID of the query in the Queries table for which this is a response.
Answer	Stores the response for the query.

◆ **Experts table.** This table stores a list of people, as discussed in Table 12-4, who are nominated as experts for different topics or categories. The structure of the Experts table is shown in Figure 12-4.

Column Name	Data Type	Length	Allow Nulls
EID	char	10	
UID	char	10	
Category	char	10	

FIGURE 12-4 *The Experts table.*

Table 12-4 Fields in the Experts Table

Field	Data
EID	Stores an expert for a particular category. The EID field usually contains a login name (UID) of the expert. However, it can be different from the UID. This field is the primary key for the Experts table.
UID	Stores the login or the user name of the expert.
Category	Stores the category of the query for which an expert sends a response.

Figure 12-5 shows the relationship between the tables in the Kshare database.

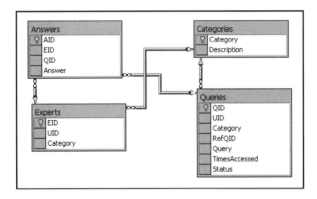

FIGURE 12-5 *The relationship between the tables in the Kshare database.*

As discussed, the database at Flex Automobiles, Inc. also contains stored procedures to access data from the tables in the database. The following section discusses the stored procedures in the Kshare database.

Stored Procedures in the Kshare Database

For the Kshare Web services project, the team has decided to provide the database interactivity through stored procedures because they offer performance advantages.

The stored procedures used in the Kshare Web services project are discussed in the following list:

◆ **AddQuery.** This stored procedure accepts a query, the category, a reference ID for a previous query, and a user's name as parameters; then it adds a new record to the Queries table.

◆ **PostAnswer.** This stored procedure accepts a response for a query, the ID of the query for which this is an answer, and the expert's login name.

◆ **GetAllQueries.** This stored procedure returns a complete list of all queries in the Queries table.

◆ **GetQueriesbyCategory.** This stored procedure accepts a category name as a parameter and returns a list of all queries for that category.

◆ **GetMyQueries.** This stored procedure returns a list of the queries posted by a particular user.

◆ **AddExpert.** This stored procedure adds an expert in the Experts table.

Now, to create the stored procedures, as discussed in the previous list, add the following code to the Enterprise Manager of Microsoft SQL Server:

```
CREATE PROCEDURE dbo.GetQueriesByCategory(@Category char(10))

As

Select Query from queries where category=@category

GO


CREATE Procedure dbo.GetQueriesByUID(@UID varchar(50))

As

Select Query from queries where UID=@UID

GO


Create Procedure dbo.AddAnswer(@EID char(10),@QID int ,@Answer varchar(200))

As

Insert into Answers(EID,QID,Answer) values(@EID,@QID,@Answer)


CREATE Procedure dbo.AddExpert(@EID char(10),@Category char(10),@UID char(10))

As

Insert into Experts(EID,Category,UID) values(@EID,@Category,@UID)

GO


CREATE Procedure dbo.AddQuery(@UID char(10),@Category char(10),@RefQID
```

```
int,@Query varchar(200))

As

Insert into queries(UID,Category,RefQID,Query,TimesAccessed,Status)

values(@UID,@Category,@RefQID,@Query,0,'U')

GO


Create Procedure dbo.GetAnswer(@QID int) as

Select Answer from answers where QID=@QID

Update Queries set TimesAccessed=TimesAccessed+1

Where Queries.QID=@QID

GO


Create Procedure dbo.GetExperts(@Category char(10)) as

Select EID from experts where category=@category

GO
```

Advanced Features of ASP.NET Web Services

After you create the database, you need to create the ASP.NET Web service. However, before you create the Web service, you need to know some of the advanced features of ASP.NET Web services that you can add to your Web service.

Accessing and Modifying the SOAP Messages by Using SOAP Extensions

SOAP extensions allow you to create functionality in an encapsulated form that you can reuse in your Web service. To do this, SOAP extensions allow you to intercept SOAP messages exchanged between the client and the Web service. You can apply a SOAP extension to either the server or the client.

A SOAP extension contains a class derived from the `SoapExtension` class. This class contains information about how you can modify an erroneous SOAP message. You can then define an attribute derived from the `SoapExtensionAttribute` class. This attribute associates a SOAP extension with a specified Web method or class.

SOAP EXTENSION ATTRIBUTES

You use the SOAP extension attribute to indicate that a specific SOAP extension should be called by the ASP.NET runtime for a particular Web method. You can also use the SOAP extension attribute to collect information that the SOAP extension uses.

The SoapExtension *Class*

As discussed, the SoapExtension class implements the SOAP extensions. To do this, the SoapExtension class contains several methods that the ASP.NET runtime uses to process the SOAP request. The SOAP extensions can override the methods in the SoapExtension class to provide custom implementation. The most common methods of the SoapExtension class are discussed in the following list:

◆ **GetInitializer() method.** This method initializes variables in a Web method. You can either use the GetInitializer() method to initialize variables separately for a method or overload the method to initialize variables for all methods of a type.

◆ **Initialize() method.** This method receives data that the GetInitializer() method returns.

◆ **ProcessMessage() method.** This method allows SOAP extensions to verify and modify the SOAP messages while they are being processed.

◆ **ChainStream() method.** This method accesses the memory buffer that contains the SOAP request or response messages.

The SOAP Extension Framework

The SOAP extension framework provides you with two ways to access the contents of a SOAP message. These methods are discussed in the following list:

◆ Use the stream object received by the ChainStream() method. This object contains the raw content of the method.

◆ Use the properties and methods exposed by an instance of the SoapMessage class.

In addition, the SOAP extension framework provides a two-step initialization process that helps to reduce the cost of initializing the SOAP extension. To do this, the SOAP extension framework uses the GetInitializer() and Initialize() methods.

You can also associate a Web method to multiple SOAP extensions. In such a case, every SOAP extension is called on the basis of its priority. The extension with the priority 1 is called first, and then all extensions are called in the ascending order of their priority. An exception to this is the ProcessMessage() method that is invoked during the BeforeSerialize and AfterSerialize stages. In this case, the extensions are called in the descending order of their priorities.

Creating SOAP Extensions

You have seen what SOAP extensions are. We will now discuss the steps that you need to follow to create SOAP extensions:

1. Derive a class from the SoapExtension class.
2. Save a reference to the stream representing future SOAP messages.
3. Initialize the data that is specific to SOAP extensions.

4. Process the SOAP messages during the related SOAP message stage or stages.

5. Configure the SOAP extension to run with specific XML Web service methods.

To modify a SOAP message, you must override the `ChainStream()` method. This is the only method by which you can receive a reference to the stream that is used to obtain the contents of future SOAP messages.

However, the stream that is passed to the `ChainStream()` method is not the stream that a SOAP extension modifies. Therefore, a SOAP extension creates a new instance of a stream, saves the instance in a `private` variable, and then returns the instance to the `ChainStream()` method.

Because the SOAP extension executes and modifies a SOAP message during each `SoapMessage Stage`, a SOAP extension should read from the stream passed to the `ChainStream()` method. In addition, the SOAP extension writes the value returned for the `ChainStream()` method. As a result, it becomes essential to save both stream references within the `ChainStream()` method.

Implementation of the `ChainStream()` method is shown in the following code sample:

```
public override Stream ChainStream( Stream stream )
{
        // Save the passed in stream in a member variable.
        oldStream = stream;

        // Create a new instance of a stream and save that in a member
        // variable.
        newStream = new MemoryStream();
        return newStream;
}
```

A SOAP extension can also initialize internal data on the basis of the Web service method that it is applied to. For example, a SOAP extension that logs the SOAP message might initialize the name of a file to save the login information in the file.

```
public override object GetInitializer(LogicalMethodInfo
methodInfo,SoapExtensionAttribute attribute)
{
   return ((MyExtensionAttribute) attribute).Filename;
}
public override object GetInitializer(Type WebServiceType)
{
   return WebServiceType.GetType().ToString() + ".txt";
}
```

The class that is derived from the SoapExtension class implements the SoapExtension. ProcessMessage() method, which is called at every stage of the SoapMessageStage enumeration. When the SoapExtension.ProcessMessage() method is called, a SoapMessage class or its derived class is passed at each stage. This class contains information about the SOAP message for the particular stage.

The following code shows an example of the ProcessStage() method of a SOAP extension:

```
public override void ProcessMessage(SoapMessage message)
{
    switch (message.Stage)
    {
        case SoapMessageStage.BeforeSerialize:
            break;
        case SoapMessageStage.AfterSerialize:
            // Write the SOAP message out to a file.
            OutputMessage( message );
            break;
        case SoapMessageStage.BeforeDeserialize:
            // Write the SOAP message out to a file.
            InputMessage( message );
            break;
        case SoapMessageStage.AfterDeserialize:
            break;
        default:
            throw new Exception("Invalid or unknown error");
    }
}
```

The preceding code traces a call to a Web service. The code uses a switch case to find the stage of the SOAP extension. If the stage is SoapMessageStage, the parameters are serialized into XML, and the XML code is written to a file.

Invoking SOAP Extensions

The following list discusses the steps to invoke a SOAP extension at the client side.

1. The client application invokes a proxy class method.

2. The client application creates a new instance of the SOAP extension.

3. The GetInitializer() method of the SOAP extension that is running on the client application is invoked.

NOTE

In this section, it is assumed that the SOAP extension is running at both the client and server sides.

TIP

Remember that the `GetInitializer()` method is called only if the SOAP extension is being executed for the first time for the corresponding Web method on a particular client.

4. The client application invokes the `Initialize()` method.
5. The `ChainStream()` method is invoked.
6. The `ProcessMessage()` method is invoked and `SoapMessageStage` is set to `Before Serialize`.
7. The ASP.NET client application serializes the arguments of the Web method into XML.
8. The `ProcessMessage()` method is invoked and `SoapMessageStage` is set to `AfterSerialize`.
9. ASP.NET sends the SOAP message over the network to the Web server that hosts the Web service.

The SOAP extension is also invoked at the server side. The steps to do so are shown in the following list:

1. The ASP.NET application on the Web server receives the SOAP message.
2. A new instance of the SOAP extension is created on the Web server.
3. The `GetInitializer()` method is called on the SOAP extension that is running on the server.

TIP

Remember that the `GetInitializer()` method is called only if the SOAP extension that is corresponding to a Web service is being executed for the first time on the Web server.

4. The `Initialize()` method is invoked.
5. The `ChainStream()` method is invoked.

6. The `ProcessMessage()` method is invoked and `SoapMessageStage` is set to `BeforeDeserialize`.

7. ASP.NET deserializes the arguments within XML.

8. The `ProcessMessage()` method is invoked and the `SoapMessageStage` is set to `AfterDeserialize`.

 NOTE

The new instance of the class that is created resides on the same computer on which the Web server is present.

9. ASP.NET creates a new instance of the class that implements the Web service and invokes the Web service method by passing the deserialized arguments.

10. The Web service method executes its code and sets the return value and output parameters, if required.

11. The `ProcessMessage()` method is invoked and `SoapMessageStage` is set to `BeforeSerialize`.

12. ASP.NET serializes the return value and the output parameters to XML.

13. The `ProcessMessage()` method is invoked and the `SoapMessageStage` is set to `AfterSerialize`.

14. ASP.NET sends the SOAP response message to the XML Web service client over the network.

When the client receives the request, certain steps are followed at the client side. These steps are discussed in the following list:

1. ASP.NET on the client computer receives the SOAP message.

2. The `ProcessMessage()` method is invoked, and `SoapMessageStage` is set to `BeforeDeserialize`.

3. ASP.NET deserializes the XML into the return value and the output parameters.

4. The `ProcessMessage()` method is invoked and `SoapMessageStage` is set to `AfterDeserialize`.

5. ASP.NET passes the return value and the output parameters to the object of the proxy class.

6. The client receives the return value and the output parameters.

After the SOAP extension class is created, you need to create a corresponding attribute class that allows you to use and bind the SOAP extension to Web methods. The code for a simple attribute class is as shown:

```
[AttributeUsage(AttributeTargets.Method)]
```

```
public class MyExtensionAttribute : SoapExtensionAttribute
{
    private string filename = "c:\\Trace.txt";
    private int priority;

    public override Type ExtensionType
    {
        get { return typeof(MyExtension); }
    }

    public override int Priority
    {

        .......................
    }

    public string Filename
    {
        get
        {
            return filename;
        }
        set
        {
            filename = value;
        }
    }
}
```

After the attribute class is created, you can bind the extension to a Web method by using the syntax as shown:

```
[MyExtensionAttribute]
    public string HelloWorld()
    {

        .......................
    }
```

Managing Transactions in Web Services

The transaction support available to ASP.NET applications is based on the model that was used in MTS and COM+ services. In .NET, the classes that are in the EnterpriseServices namespace extend the functionality that allows you to provide transactional support to your ASP.NET applications.

As in COM+, you follow a declarative approach in which you specify whether an object takes part in a transaction by specifying an attribute for it. To enable a method of a Web service to be in a transaction, you need to use the `TransactionOption` property of the `WebMethod` attribute. If the `TransactionOption` property is set appropriately and an exception occurs while the method is executing, all previous commands will be rolled back. The syntax for the `WebMethod` attribute is shown in the following example:

```
[WebMethod (TransactionOption=TransactionOption.RequiresNew)]
```

Now consider an example of a Web method that uses transactions to maintain the database integrity. This Web method allows a user to delete a record from the Queries table and then delete the corresponding responses to the query from the Answers table. In this case, consider that an exception is raised on the second action. Because the two actions are part of a single transaction, the first command, although executed correctly, will be rolled back.

```
[WebMethod(TransactionOption=TransactionOption.RequiresNew)]
public void DeleteQuery(int nQID)

        {
                SqlConnection conn=new SqlConnection("data source=Server;initial
catalog=KShare;UID=sa;PWD=;");
                conn.Open();
                SqlCommand cmd=new SqlCommand("",conn);
                SqlCommand cmd2=new SqlCommand("",conn);
                cmd.CommandText = "delete from queries where QID=" + nQID ;
                cmd.ExecuteNonQuery();
                cmd2.CommandText= delete from answers where QID=" + nQID;
                cmd.ExecuteNonQuery();
        }
```

Exception Handling

You need to handle exceptions, which are runtime errors, when you encounter them in a program. The process of handling exceptions is called *exception handling*. Exceptions are raised in Web services through SOAP faults.

Whenever a Web service method throws an exception, it is sent back to the client as a SOAP fault. However, the client application does not need to parse the SOAP message to access the message in the `fault` element. The regular `try` and `catch` statements and the `SoapException` class handle this. You learned about SOAP faults in Chapter 3, "Introduction to SOAP."

When an error is generated during the execution of a Web service, the error is returned to the client by using any of the following methods:

- ◆ The Web service throws an object of the `SoapException` class.
- ◆ The Web service throws an object of the `SoapHeaderException` class.
- ◆ The Web service throws an exception that specifically points out the problem.
- ◆ The Web service lets ASP.NET handle the problem.

The `SoapException` *Class*

As already discussed, the `SoapException` class handles the exceptions that are raised in the SOAP `fault` element. The SOAP `fault` element has the following structure:

```
<soap:Body>
  <soap:Fault>
    <faultactor>Server</faultactor>
        <faultcode>soap:Server</faultcode>
        <faultstring>Service Error</faultstring>
  </soap:Fault>
</soap:Body>
```

The `SoapException` class includes the following properties that correspond to the subelements of the `fault` element:

- ◆ **Actor.** This property provides information about the source of the fault and corresponds to the `faultactor` element.
- ◆ **Code.** This property corresponds to the `faultcode` element and contains the predefined code for the error.
- ◆ **Detail.** This property stores the details of the fault and corresponds to the `fault-detail` element.
- ◆ **Message.** This property corresponds to the `faultstring` element and contains the error message to be sent to the client.

The constructor for the `SoapException` class has the following syntax:

```
public SoapException(string message, XmlQualifiedName code, string actor,
XmlNode detail, Exception innerException);
```

As discussed, a Web service might throw an exception using the `SoapException` class. To do this, the `SoapException` class uses the following syntax:

```
throw new SoapException("My Error", SoapException.ClientFaultCode);
```

In the preceding example, the message parameter and the code parameter are used. Some of the other optional parameters include the actor parameter, which is a string that indicates the origin or the source of the exception.

You can also use the detail parameter, which is of type XmlNode, to provide a detailed description of the error that might have occurred. The detail parameter is shown in the following code sample:

```
System.Xml.XmlDocument doc = new System.Xml.XmlDocument();
System.Xml.XmlNode node = doc.CreateNode(XmlNodeType.Element,
SoapException.DetailElementName.Name,
SoapException.DetailElementName.Namespace);

system.Xml.XmlNode details = doc.CreateNode(XmlNodeType.Element, "MoreDetails",
"http://tempuri.org/");

node.AppendChild(details);
SoapException SoapObject = new SoapException("Error!",
SoapException.ClientFaultCode,Context.Request.Url.AbsoluteUri,node);
throw SoapObject;
```

Managing States in Web Services

HTTP is a stateless protocol. Although the facility to maintain a connection across calls was introduced in HTTP 1.1, not all requests from a client are sent over a single connection. Therefore, to maintain states in your Web application on a user's behalf, you need to develop custom solutions.

Programmers have been using the ASP state management services that the ASP development platform provides for maintaining both session and application states. You can use the ASP.NET state management services to implement states for Web forms as well as Web services.

Session State

To maintain session states on behalf of a user, you need to associate several HTTP requests with one user session. To do this, ASP.NET uses a unique identifier called a *session ID*. This session ID is saved in the form of a cookie or is embedded within the URL of the Web application. This identifier recognizes a session that a client application passes. In the case of Web services, the unique identifier is saved in the form of a cookie. However, for Web applications, ASP.NET can use either cookies or URLs.

In the case of Web services, if the proxy class that the client application uses supports cookies, ASP.NET automatically sends the corresponding session ID with every request. Because cookies are HTTP specific, the session state mechanisms are bound to the HTTP protocol. Therefore, you can pass the session ID by embedding it into the header of the SOAP message.

However, ASP.NET does not support this. As a result, you need to create custom state management system for your Web service.

 NOTE

Avoid maintaining states for requests in real-life applications. As a result, the session state management service will be disabled by default. You need to explicitly enable the service to maintain states for an application.

 NOTE

By default, cookies are maintained only for the time that the proxy class used to access the Web service is alive.

After identifying a session, you need to store and access the session states. To do this, you can use any of the following methods:

◆ **In Process.** In the In Process method, the calls for the read or write session states are handled in process. As a result, this method is the fastest for accessing session states. At the same time, however, this method is not a very robust method because, if an ASP.NET worker process terminates, all session states maintained for an application are lost. You can use this method for Web services that are hosted on a single computer and need the fastest way to access states.

◆ **Out of Process.** In this method, a different process maintains session states, which can run on a different computer or on multiple Web servers. Therefore, this process is more robust than the In Process method because if the ASP.NET worker process terminates, the session states for the application will not be lost.

With the Out of Process method, the session states are maintained in the memory of a system. Therefore, even this method has limitations because if the session state server terminates, all session states are lost. This method is an ideal configuration for Web services that are hosted in a Web farm; in this case, the security of session states is not a critical issue.

◆ **SQL Server.** This is the most robust and scalable method of accessing session states. In this case, a session state is maintained within the tables of a SQL Server database. The tables contain the session state information that is serialized in a binary form. This scenario is ideal for Web services hosted in a Web farm that uses SQL Server as a backend. In addition, you can use this scenario if the security of the session state information is critical.

NOTE

The .NET Framework only supports the In Process method of accessing session states.

Application State

A state that is global to the application should be stored within the application object. Such a state is called an *application state*. Application states are always accessed by the In Process method.

Classes that derive from the WebService class expose the Application property. This property retrieves an instance of the HttpApplicationState object, which is derived from the NameObjectCollectionBase class. The object of the HttpApplicationState class contains application states. When the NameObjectCollectionBase class is implemented, the object of the class creates a hash table; therefore, retrieving a particular value from the application object is efficient.

Using Caching to Improve Performance

Caching is one way to improve performance. If output caching is enabled, the results of a Web service method call are stored in the cache for a specified period. If the same or another client calls the same method, the result can be retrieved from the cache. This reduces the amount of processing required by the server that hosts the Web service.

Caching can be enabled on both the client as well as the server. The following code ensures that the client picks up ASP.NET pages from the cache. The pages are stored in the cache for 60 seconds.

```
<% Page Language="C#" %>
<% Import Namespace="System.Net" %>
<% OutputCache Duration="60" %>
```

The preceding statements ensure that the client will not use the Web service to access data that it retrieved recently.

TIP

Because Web service clients can be implemented on various platforms and languages that do not support the caching feature, it is advisable that you enable server-side caching for Web service methods that do not return frequently changing data.

In your Web service, it is unlikely that users will send queries frequently; therefore, you can cache the GetAllQueries() Web method that you will create for the Kshare Web services by using the following code sample.

 NOTE

You will learn to create the Web service and the Web methods in the following section.

```
[WebMethod(CacheDuration=60)]
        public string[] GetAllQueries()
                {
                        int NoOfRecs;
                        int i=0;
                        SqlDataReader reader;
                        SqlConnection conn=new SqlConnection("data
source=Server1;initial catalog=KShare;UID=sa;PWD=pass1;");
                        conn.Open();
                        SqlCommand cmd=new SqlCommand("",conn);
                        cmd.CommandText="Select count(*) from queries";
                        NoOfRecs=(int) cmd.ExecuteScalar();
                        string [] strArray=new string[NoOfRecs];
                        cmd.CommandText = "GetAllQueries"; reader=cmd.ExecuteReader();
                        while(reader.Read())
                        {
                                strArray[i]=reader.GetString(0);
                        }

                        return strArray;
        }
```

Creating the Kshare Web Service

We have talked about the various advanced features that you can include in the Kshare Web service. We will now discuss how to create the Web service.

The Kshare Web service exposes several Web methods that client applications can use. These Web methods are discussed in the following list:

♦ **AddQuery() method.** This method adds a query to the Queries table. The parameters for the AddQuery() Web method are the query text, the username, and the category.

♦ **AddAnswer() method.** This method adds an expert's answer to the Answers table. The parameters for the AddAnswer() method are the ID of the query, the answer text, and the user ID of the expert.

♦ **GetAllQueries() method.** This method returns a list of all queries in the Queries table in the form of an array of strings.

♦ **GetMyQueries() method.** This method returns a list of all queries that a specific user has posted.

♦ **GetAnswer() method.** This method accepts the ID of a query and returns all corresponding answers.

♦ **DeleteQuery() method.** This method deletes a query from the Queries table. In addition, all answers for the particular query are deleted.

The code for the Kshare Web service is as shown:

```
using System;
using System.Collections;
using System.ComponentModel;
using System.Data;
using System.Data.SqlClient ;
using System.Diagnostics;
using System.Web;
using System.Web.Services;
using System.Web.Services.Protocols;
using System.EnterpriseServices;


public class Service1 : System.Web.Services.WebService
{
    public Header1 Service1Header;
    public Service1()
    {
        //CODEGEN: This call is required by the ASP.NET Web Services Designer
        InitializeComponent();
        Service1Header=new Header1();
    }

#region Component Designer generated code
//Required by the Web Services Designer
    private IContainer components = null;
```

```csharp
/// <summary>
// Required method for Designer support - do not modify
/// the contents of this method with the code editor.
/// </summary>
    private void InitializeComponent()
    {
    }
/// <summary>
/// Clean up any resources being used.
/// </summary>
    protected override void Dispose( bool disposing )
    {
        if(disposing && components != null)
        {
            components.Dispose();
        }
        base.Dispose(disposing);
    }
#endregion

// WEB SERVICE
    [WebMethod]
    public void AddQuery(string strCategory,int nRefQID,string strQuery)
    {
        SqlConnection conn=new SqlConnection("data source=SERVER1;initial
catalog=KShare;UID=sa;PWD=pass;persist security info=True;workstation
id=SERVER1;packet size=4096");
        conn.Open();
        SqlCommand cmd=new SqlCommand("",conn);
        cmd.CommandText = "AddQuery";
        cmd.CommandType = CommandType.StoredProcedure;
        cmd.Parameters.Add("@Category", strCategory);
        cmd.Parameters.Add("@UID",User.Identity.Name);
        cmd.Parameters.Add("@RefQID", nRefQID);
        cmd.Parameters.Add("@Query",strQuery);
        cmd.ExecuteNonQuery();
    }
```

```
[WebMethod]
public void AddAnswer(string strEID,int nQID,string strAnswer)
{
        SqlConnection conn=new SqlConnection("data source=SERVER1;initial
catalog=KShare;UID=sa;PWD=pass;persist security info=True;packet size=4096");
        conn.Open();
        SqlCommand cmd=new SqlCommand("",conn);
        cmd.CommandText = "AddAnswer";
        cmd.CommandType = CommandType.StoredProcedure;
        cmd.Parameters.Add("@EID",User.Identity.Name);
        cmd.Parameters.Add("@QID",nQID);
        cmd.Parameters.Add("@Answer", strAnswer);
        try
        {
            cmd.ExecuteNonQuery();
        }
        catch(Exception e)
        {

        }
    }


    [WebMethod]
public string[] GetAllQueries()
    {
        int NoOfRecs;
        int i=0;
        SqlDataReader reader;
        SqlConnection conn=new SqlConnection("data source=SERVER1;initial
catalog=KShare;UID=sa;PWD=pass;persist security info=True;workstation
id=SERVER1;packet size=4096");
        conn.Open();
        SqlCommand cmd=new SqlCommand("",conn);
        cmd.CommandText="Select count(*) from queries";
        NoOfRecs=(int)cmd.ExecuteScalar();
        string [] strArray=new string[NoOfRecs];
        cmd.CommandText = "GetAllQueries";
        reader=cmd.ExecuteReader();
```

```
            while(reader.Read())
                  strArray[i]=reader.GetString(0);


            return strArray;
      }


       [WebMethod]
      public string[] GetMyQueries()
      {
            int NoOfRecs;
            int i=0;
            SqlDataReader reader;
            SqlConnection conn=new SqlConnection("data source=SERVER1;initial
catalog=KShare;UID=sa;PWD=pass;persist security info=True;workstation
id=SERVER1;packet size=4096");
            conn.Open();
            SqlCommand cmd=new SqlCommand("",conn);
            cmd.CommandText="Select count(*) from queries";
            NoOfRecs=(int)cmd.ExecuteScalar();
            string [] strArray=new string[NoOfRecs];
            cmd.CommandText = "GetQueriesByUID";
            cmd.Parameters.Add("@UID",User.Identity.Name);
            reader=cmd.ExecuteReader();
            while(reader.Read())
            {
                  strArray[i]=reader.GetString(0);
            }
            return strArray;
      }


       [WebMethod(TransactionOption=TransactionOption.RequiresNew)]
      public void DeleteQuery(int nQID)
      {
            SqlConnection conn=new SqlConnection("data source=SERVER1;initial
catalog=KShare;UID=sa;PWD=pass;persist security info=True;workstation
id=SERVER1;packet size=4096");
            conn.Open();
            SqlCommand cmd=new SqlCommand("",conn);
```

```
SqlCommand cmd2=new SqlCommand("",conn);
cmd.CommandText = "delete from queries where QID=" + nQID ;
cmd.ExecuteNonQuery();
cmd2.CommandText="delete from answers where QID=" + nQID ;
cmd2.ExecuteNonQuery();
    }
}
```

NOTE

To access the classes in the `EnterpriseServices` namespace, you need to add a reference to the System.EnterpriseServices.dll file.

Securing ASP.NET Web Services

In this section, we introduce you to securing ASP.NET Web services. You explore securing a Web service by using Windows authentication and by creating a custom security option.

Securing a Web Service by Using Windows Authentication

The process of securing a Web service involves authenticating a user and validating his authorization. In simple terms, the username and password of the user who tries to access the Web service are verified; if the username and password are valid, the user's rights are verified. If the user is authorized, he can access the Web service in two ways for an ASP.NET Web service, as discussed in the following list:

◆ Using the authentication and authorization check facilities that Windows provides

◆ Using a custom solution

Securing Web Services by Using Windows Authentication Methods

If you decide to use the first method of using the authentication and authorization check facilities, Windows provides you with several authentication methods, as detailed in the following list:

◆ **Basic.** You can use this authentication method to identify users who log on. However, the Basic authentication method is not a very secure method because the username and password of the client are sent as base64-encoded strings in the text format, which can be easily decoded.

◆ **Basic with SSL.** This authentication method is similar to the Basic authentication method, but it is more secure method because it uses SSL encryption to send the username and password. However, the security of this method is at the cost of the performance.

◆ **Digest.** This authentication method encrypts the login data by hashing it and then transmits it. The digest authentication method is not supported by non-Windows platforms.

◆ **Integrated.** This is the default Windows scheme that uses NTLM or Kerberos. It is an ideal authentication method for an intranet scenario, in which all users are working on the Windows platform and use Internet Explorer.

◆ **Client Certificates.** You can obtain this authentication method from a Certificate Authority (CA), such as VeriSign, and map it to user accounts. IIS uses the Client Certificates method to verify a user's access.

NOTE

For securing the Kshare Web service, you will use the Basic authentication method. However, if required, you can make the Web service more secure by using SSL.

To secure your Web service by configuring basic authentication, perform the following steps:

1. Run Internet Services Manager from Administrative Tools, and expand the tree structure to view a list of all virtual directories in the default server.

NOTE

You will learn to create a virtual directory in the section "Deploying the Kshare Web Service."

2. Right-click on the virtual directory for your Web service, and select the Properties option. The <virtual directory> Properties dialog box is displayed, as shown in Figure 12-6.

3. Click on the Directory Security tab, as shown in Figure 12-7.

4. In the Anonymous Access and Authentication Control section, click on the Edit button, which opens the Authentication Methods dialog box shown in Figure 12-8.

5. If the Anonymous access check box is selected, deselect it. This deactivates anonymous access, which enables any user on the network to access the Web application.

FIGURE 12-6 *The <virtual directory> Properties dialog box.*

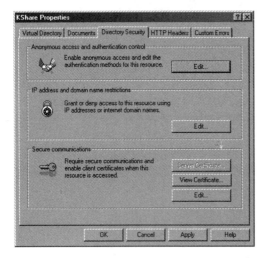

FIGURE 12-7 *The Directory Security tab in the Properties dialog box.*

6. In the Authenticated Access section of the Authentication Methods dialog box, select the Basic Authentication (Password Is Sent in Clear Text) check box.

7. Deselect the Integrated Windows Authentication check box, if it's selected. Windows displays a warning about the Basic authentication method being insecure. The warning is displayed in Figure 12-9.

FIGURE 12-8 *The Authentication Methods dialog box.*

FIGURE 12-9 *Warning raised by Windows.*

8. Click on the Yes button to close the warning.

9. Click on the OK buttons to close all dialog boxes.

Modifying the Web.Config File

The next step in securing Web services is to modify the Web.Config file and set the `mode` attribute of the `authentication` element to `Windows`. The following code shows the Web.Config file and the changes made to the file:

```
<?xml version="1.0" encoding="utf-8" ?>
<configuration>
     <system.web>
   <compilation
       defaultLanguage="c#"
       debug="true"
   />
```

```
        <customErrors
        mode="RemoteOnly"
        />


        <!--   AUTHENTICATION
               This section sets the authentication policies of the application.
Possible modes are "Windows," "Forms,"
               "Passport," and "None"
        -->
        <authentication mode="Windows" />
        <trace
            enabled="false"
            requestLimit="10"
            pageOutput="false"
            traceMode="SortByTime"
                  localOnly="true"
        />
        <sessionState
              mode="InProc"
              stateConnectionString="tcpip=127.0.0.1:42424"
              sqlConnectionString="data source=127.0.0.1;user id=sa;password="
              cookieless="false"
              timeout="20"
        />
        <globalization
              requestEncoding="utf-8"
              responseEncoding="utf-8"
        />
    </system.web>
</configuration>
```

 TIP

Remember that you need to store the Web.Config file, which contains the authentication information, only in the root of the application or in the virtual directory. However, you cannot place this file in any of the subdirectories of the virtual directory.

You can use the Web.Config file to further set up the authorization levels for the application. We will not use authorization levels in this Web service. Using Web.Config for configuring authorization levels in a Web application is both simple and useful.

Consider a situation in which you want only authenticated users who belong to the category of group managers to be able to access a particular directory. In this case, you can use the configuration file, as shown in the following code:

```
<?xml version="1.0" encoding="utf-8" ?>
<configuration>
    <system.web>
      <authorization>
        <allow roles="Domain\Managers" />
        <deny users="*"/>
      </authorization>
    </system.web>
</configuration>
```

As you can see, you can use two wild cards * and ? in the configuration file. * represents all users, whereas ? represents all unauthenticated users.

Now consider a situation in which you need to deny permission on a directory to all unauthenticated users. In this case, you use the following configuration file:

```
<?xml version="1.0" encoding="utf-8" ?>
<configuration>
    <system.web>
      <authorization>
        <deny users="?"/>
      </authorization>
    </system.web>
</configuration>
```

Passing Logon Credentials of the Clients

The next step in configuring the basic authentication method is to pass the logon credentials of the clients who access a Web service. To connect to the Web service, perform the following steps:

1. Create an instance of the Web service proxy class.
2. Create an instance of the `NetworkCredential` class and set its `Username`, `Password`, and `Domain` properties.
3. Create an instance of the `CredentialCache` class and add the `NetWorkCredential` class object to the `CredentialCache` class by using its `Add()` method.

The `CredentialCache` class stores authentication credentials for multiple Internet resources. Applications that need to access multiple resources can store the credentials for those resources in an object of this class and then provide the credentials when the Internet resource requests them. To do this, the `CredentialCache` class contains the following methods:

◆ **Add() method.** This method adds an object of the type `NeworkCredential` class to the `CredentialCache` class. The syntax of the `Add()` method is as shown:

```
public void Add(Uri uriPrefix,string authType,NetworkCredential credo);
```

The following code shows an example of the `Add()` method:

```
CredentialCache credo = new CredentialCache();
credo.Add(new Uri("http://www.MyServer.com/"),"Basic",new
NetworkCredential("User1","Pass1"));
```

◆ **GetCredential() method.** This method returns the first matching credential. The syntax of the `GetCredential()` method is as shown:

```
public NetworkCredential GetCredential
  (
    Uri uriPrefix,
    string authType
  );
```

◆ **Remove() method.** This method deletes a credential from the cache. The syntax of the `Remove()` method is as shown:

```
public void Remove(Uri uriPrefix, string authType);
```

In the preceding discussion, the credential of the client is stored in an object of the `Network-Credential` class. This class stores authentication credentials for Windows authentication schemes, such as Basic, Digest, and NTLM. The following code shows an example of the `NetworkCredential` class:

```
NetworkCredential Credo = new NetworkCredential("user1","pass1","Domain");

CredentialCache LoginCache = new CredentialCache();

LoginCache.Add(new Uri("http://www.MyServer.com"),""), "Basic", Credo);
LoginCache.Add(new Uri("http://www.MyServer.com"),""), "Basic", Credo);
WebRequest wr = WebRequest.Create("http://www.MyServer.com"),"");
wr.Credentials = myCache;
```

Next, you need to assign the instance of the `CredentialCache` class to the `Credentials` property of the proxy class, as shown in the following code sample:

```
Dim ws As New WindowsApplication1.localhost.Service1()
```

```
        Dim CCach As CredentialCache = New CredentialCache()
        Dim credo As NetworkCredential = New NetworkCredential("User1",
"password", "DOMAIN2")
        CCach.Add(New Uri(ws.Url), "Basic", credo)
        ws.Credentials = CCach
```

After you perform these steps, your Web service is secured. A user can now call any of the Web methods that the Web service exposes.

Securing Web Services by Using a Custom Solution

As discussed, you can create a custom solution to secure a Web service. In this section, we will discuss a simple way to implement a custom authentication solution for a Web service.

In this method of authentication, you will create a Login Web service. This Web service is different from the Kshare Web service. The methods of this Web service can authenticate a client. To do this, the Web service contains a method `LoginCheck()` that accepts a username and password to authenticate a client. Then the method is added to a new Web service and isolated from the rest of the Web services; this enables a user to connect to this Web service through SSL.

As you know, SSL provides encryption and security, but it has performance problems. In a Web service, security is the main issue. Therefore, you will create a separate Web service to which a user can connect through SSL. The other Web services in the application will simply connect through HTTP.

For the Login Web service, you need a Users table and a Sessions table. The Users table contains a user's username and password. Whenever a user calls the `LoginCheck()` method, his username and password are validated. If the user's credentials are found to be valid, the `LoginCheck()` method generates a session ID for the user and returns it. Each session ID that is created is valid for an hour and stored in the Sessions table. In addition, the Sessions table states the date and time when the corresponding session was created.

Now when a Web method is called, the Session ID is passed as part of the SOAP header message, and a check is made to see if the particular session ID exists in the Sessions table. In addition, it is confirmed that the session is not more than an hour old and is valid.

The structures of the Users and Sessions table are shown in Figures 12-10 and 12-11:

Column Name	Data Type	Length	Allow Nulls
UserID	int	4	
EmpID	int	4	
Password	varchar	100	✓
Email	varchar	25	
UserName	varchar	20	

FIGURE 12-10 *The Users table.*

Column Name	Data Type	Length	Allow Nulls
Sessionkey	varchar	200	
SessionExpiry	datetime	8	✓
SessionUID	int	4	✓

FIGURE 12-11 *The Sessions table.*

Similar to the Kshare Web service, you will use stored procedures to access data from the database for the Login Web service. To validate the user's credential, create a stored procedure called Login. If the user credentials are validated, the stored procedure creates a new session ID by using the NewID() function, which is contained within the stored procedure. Then a new record for the session ID is added to the Sessions table. This record stores information such as the session ID and the user ID. In addition, when the record is added to the Sessions table, the last field in the table is updated with the current date and time. The code for the Login stored procedure is shown in the following code:

```
CREATE PROCEDURE dbo.Login(@name char(10), @pass char(10), @SessionIDuniqueidentifier
output)
As
        if exists( select * from users where UserID=@name and password=@pass)
                Begin
                Set @SessionID=NewID()
                insert into sessions(SessionKey,SessionUID) values(@SessionID,@Name)
        end
        else
          return 0
```

After you create the stored procedure, you need to implement the Login Web service. To do this, perform the following steps:

1. Add a new Web service, Login, to your Web service project. This adds a Web service to the Kshare project and includes the standard Web service files to the project.

2. Open the file Login.asmx.vb. This file provides functionality to the Web service. Add a new Web method called LoginCheck() to the Web service, as shown in the following code:

```
public string LoginCheck(string name, string pass)
{
        SqlConnection conn=new SqlConnection("data source=server1;initial
catalog=KShare;UID=sa;PWD=;persist security info=True;workstation
id=SAIK;packet size=4096");
        SqlCommand cmd=new SqlCommand("Login",conn);
```

```
            SqlParameter p;
            cmd.CommandType=CommandType.StoredProcedure;
            p=cmd.Parameters.Add(new SqlParameter("@Name",name));
            p=cmd.Parameters.Add(new SqlParameter("@pass",pass));
            p=cmd.Parameters.Add(new
    SqlParameter("@SessionID",SqlDbType.UniqueIdentifier));
            p.Direction=ParameterDirection.Output;
            conn.Open();
            cmd.ExecuteNonQuery();
            string sessionkey;
            sessionkey=cmd.Parameters["@SessionID"].Value.ToString();
            return sessionkey;
        }
```

 NOTE

Because the preceding code uses ADO.NET, you need to add the following statement along with the rest of the `using` statements:

```
using System.Data.SqlClient
```

As you see, the `LoginCheck()` method accepts a user's login name and password and calls the `Login` stored procedure. Then the method retrieves the session ID from the parameter's collection and returns the session ID.

SOAP Headers

SOAP headers are a useful place to store data that is related to the SOAP message. The message is contained in the `Body` element of the SOAP message. For the Login Web service, you will create a SOAP header that is used to send the session ID created by the `LoginCheck()` method.

Sending session IDs in a SOAP message is preferred over sending usernames and passwords. The advantages to using session IDs are discussed in the following list:

◆ The usernames and passwords are sent over the wire by using a Web service that is accessible through SSL, and is, therefore, secure. You learned about the advantages of SSL in Chapter 6, "Creating a Web Service Using the Microsoft SOAP Toolkit."

◆ Because only the Login Web service is on SSL, the performance of the Kshare Web service is not affected. To access other methods of the Kshare Web service, you can use the session ID that the `LoginCheck()` method returns. Because these methods do not use SSL, performance is not affected.

◆ Even if a user gains access to the session ID, it will not be of much use because the session ID expires in an hour.

As you saw in Chapter 3, "Introduction to SOAP," a SOAP message contains a `Body` element and an optional `Header` element within an `Envelope`. You can use the `Header` element to send and receive data that is not related to the message contained within the body of the message.

To create a SOAP header, you need to declare a class that derives from the `SoapHeader` class, as shown in the following code:

```
public class Header1 : System.Web.Services.Protocols.SoapHeader
{
        ....................

}
```

We will now discuss the `SoapHeader` class in detail. The `SoapHeader` class has the following properties:

◆ **Actor.** This property specifies the recipient of the header.

◆ **DidUnderstand.** This property specifies whether the recipient received and under- stood the header, if the `MustUnderstand` property is set to `True`.

◆ **EncodedMustUnderstand.** This property specifies whether the recipient must understand and process a header, whose `MustUnderstand` property is `true` and whose value is encoded.

◆ **MustUnderstand.** This property specifies whether the recipient must understand and process the header.

To send data in a SOAP header, you need to add a `public` variable to the class. The following code shows how to add a `public string` type variable to store the session ID:

```
public class Header1:System.Web.Services.Protocols.SoapHeader
{
        public string SessionID;
}
```

After you declare the class, you need to add an instance of it to the Web service class, as shown in the following code:

```
public class Service1 : System.Web.Services.WebService
{
        public Header1 Service1Header;
        public Service1()
        {
                //CODEGEN: This call is required by the ASP.NET Web Services Designer
                InitializeComponent();
```

```
        Service1Header=new Header1();
    }
```

Next, you need to add the `SoapHeader` attribute to all methods of the Web service that need to access these SOAP headers. For example, to ensure that the `GetAllQueries()` Web method has access to the session ID of the user, add the following code:

```
[WebMethod]
[SoapHeader("Service1Header",Direction=SoapHeaderDirection.In, Required=true)]
    public string GetAllQueries()
    {
        int Result;
        Result=ValidateSession (this.Service1Header.SessionID);
        if(Result==-1)
        {
            throw new SoapHeaderException("Wrong user name or
password",SoapException.ClientFaultCode);
        }
    }
```

The preceding method retrieves the session ID from the SOAP header object, `Service1Header`, and passes it to the `validateSession()` method. The code for the `validateSession()` method is as shown:

```
public int ValidateSession(String SessionID)
    {
        SqlDataReader reader;
        SqlConnection conn=new SqlConnection("data source=SAIK;initial
catalog=KShare;UID=sa;PWD=shangrila;persist security info=True;workstation
id=SAIK;packet size=4096");
        conn.Open();
        SqlCommand cmd=new SqlCommand(" ",conn);
        cmd.CommandText="Select SessionID from  Sessions";
        reader-cmd.ExecuteReader();
        int Result=-1;
        while(reader.Read())
        {
            if(reader[0].ToString().CompareTo(SessionID)==0)
            Result=1;
        }
        return Result;
    }
```

Following are the properties of the `SoapHeader` attribute:

◆ **Direction property.** This property specifies whether the header is received from the client, sent to the client, or both. When the Web service receives the SOAP message, the Web service sends a `Receipt` header to the client application, which, in turn, sends a `Payment` header to the Web service. To do this, you need to set the `Direction` property to `SoapHeaderDirection.In` and `SoapHeaderDirection.Out`, respectively. However, in cases in which the SOAP header is received from the client and returned to the client, the value of the `Direction` property is set to `SoapHeaderDirection.InOut`.

◆ **Required property.** This property specifies whether you must include the `Header` element within the SOAP message so that the Web service considers the SOAP message valid. The `Required` property takes a `Boolean` value, either `true` or `false`. The `true` value, which is the default value of the `Required` property, indicates that it is essential to include the SOAP header. If the `Required` property is set to `true` and the required headers are not included in the SOAP message, a `SoapException` is thrown. If the `Required` property is set to `false`, ASP.NET cannot support the HTTP GET/POST bindings.

◆ **MustUnderstand property.** This property specifies whether the Web service must understand and process the `Header` element of the SOAP message.

Therefore, as you can see, to declare and access a SOAP header in a Web service, you need to perform the following steps:

1. Declare a class that derives from the `SoapHeader` class.
2. Create an instance of the `SoapHeader` class in your Web service class.
3. Add the `SoapHeader` attribute to the methods of the Web service that need to access the SOAP header.

Deploying the Kshare Web Service

When you build an application, Visual Studio .NET deploys the ASP.NET Web service. However, in some cases, you need to deploy a Web service explicitly. For example, consider a situation in which you need to transfer the Web service from your development computer to an online server. In this case, you first need to create a virtual directory on the online server. To do this, perform the following steps:

1. Run the Internet Services Manager from the Administrative Tools and expand the tree of the enabled services.
2. Right click on the Default Web Site node and select the New, Virtual Directory option, as shown in Figure 12-12.

   Clicking on the Virtual Directory option starts the Virtual Directory Creation Wizard, as shown in Figure 12-13.

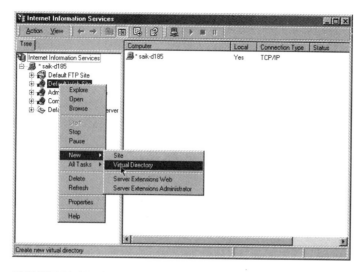

FIGURE 12-12 *Creating a virtual directory.*

FIGURE 12-13 *The Virtual Directory Creation Wizard.*

3. Click on the Next button to start the wizard. The Virtual Directory Alias page is displayed, as shown in Figure 12-14.

4. Enter an alias for your Web service and click on the Next button. The Web Site Content Directory page is displayed, as shown in Figure 12-15.

5. Browse for the directory that contains the Web service files. This directory will be mapped to the virtual directory that you create; therefore, it should be marked as IIS Web application.

6. Click on the Next button to display the Access Permissions page. In this page, do not change the default settings. The Access Permissions page is shown in Figure 12-16.

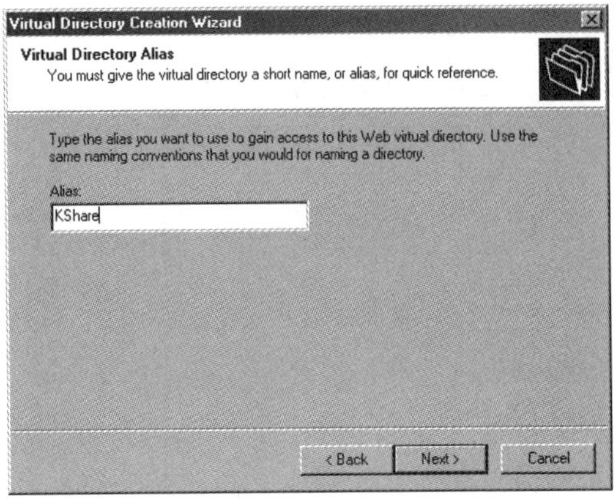

FIGURE 12-14 *The Virtual Directory Alias page.*

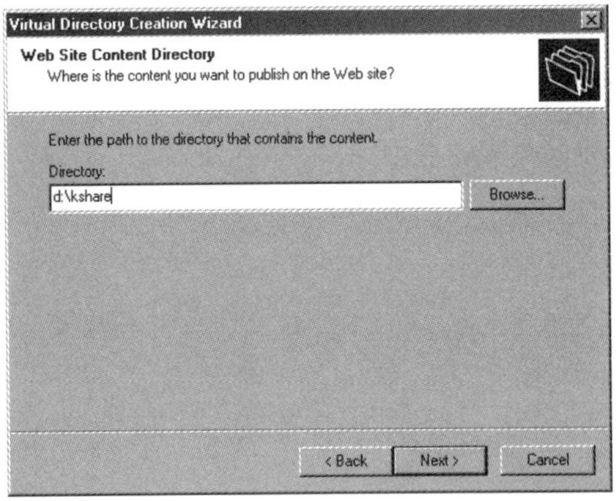

FIGURE 12-15 *The Web Site Content Directory page.*

7. Click on the Next button, and in the resulting screen, click on the Finish button to close the Virtual Directory Creation Wizard.

After you create the virtual directory, you need to copy the required files of the Web service to the directory that is mapped to the virtual directory. In addition, you need to create a subdirectory with the name Bin under the main directory. The Bin folder will contain the assemblies required for the Web service. The files that you need to copy to the main directory are discussed in the following list:

◆ **.asmx files.** You need to copy these files to the directory that is mapped to a virtual directory. The .asmx files act as the base URLs for clients that call the Web services.

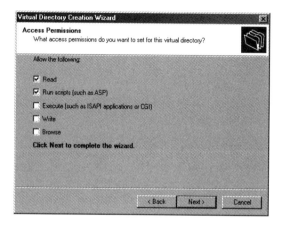

FIGURE 12-16 *The Access Permissions page.*

◆ **Web.config.** This is an optional file that allows you to override and alter the default configuration settings for a Web application.

◆ **.disco file.** This is another optional file that allows client applications to discover a Web service. Visual Studio does not generate the .disco file automatically; you need to create it.

◆ **Assemblies.** When you compile and build your Web service, Visual Studio .NET creates the assemblies. However, these assemblies are different from the assemblies that are part of the .NET Framework. You need to copy the assemblies to the Bin folder.

Testing the Kshare Web Service

Next, you will create a Visual Basic .NET Windows application that accesses the Kshare and Login Web services. You will use this application to test the Kshare and Login Web services.

Create an Application That Accesses the Kshare and Login Web Services

To create a Visual Basic .NET Windows application that accesses the Kshare Web service, which is secured using the Windows security options, perform the following steps:

1. To the existing solution, add a Visual Basic .NET Windows application.

2. Using the Add Web reference dialog box, add a reference to the Kshare Web service.

3. Add a button to the default form, and in the `Click` event of the button, add the following code:

```
Dim ws As New WindowsApplication1.localhost.Service1()
Dim CCach As CredentialCache = New CredentialCache()
Dim credo As NetworkCredential = New NetworkCredential("User1", "password",
"DOMAIN2")
        CCach.Add(New Uri(ws.Url), "Basic", credo)
        ws.Credentials = CCach
```

We have already discussed how to supply login credentials from the client in the section titled "Securing Web Services by Using Windows Authentication Methods." Next, you will look at creating a client for a Web service that implements the custom authentication discussed in the section "Securing Web Services by Using a Custom Solution."

To create a Visual Basic .NET Windows application that accesses the Kshare Web service, which uses the Login Web service, perform the following steps:

1. Launch Visual Studio .NET and create a Visual Basic .NET Windows application.

2. In the Add Web Reference dialog box, add a Web reference to the Kshare Web service and the Login Web service. The .NET Framework creates a proxy class as usual. A portion of the declaration for the proxy class is shown in the following code:

```
Public Class Header1
        Inherits SoapHeader
        '<remarks/>
        Public SessionID As String
End Class
```

3. Add a Button control to the form of the client application. Then add the code to call the `LoginCheck()` method of the Login Web service. The `LoginCheck()` method allows you to log in to the Web service.

4. Add the code to store the returned session ID in a `string` variable. Next, use the session ID to call a Web method in the Service1 Web service. The code to do this is as follows:

```
Private Sub Button1_Click(ByVal sender As System.Object, ByVal e As
System.EventArgs) Handles Button1.Click
        Dim ws2 As New WindowsApplication1.localhost1.login()
        This is the login web service
        Dim sID As String
        ID = ws2.LoginCheck("user1", "pass1")

        Dim ws As New WindowsApplication1.localhost.Service1()
        'This is the web service we are securing
```

5. Declare and initialize an object of the `Header1` type. Store the session ID and assign it to the `Header1` variable that is declared in the Web service. In the code for the proxy, rename the variable to `Header1Value`.

```
Dim header1 As New WindowsApplication1.localhost.Header1()
header1.SessionID = sID
ws.Header1Value = header1
'call a Web service method .
MsgBox(ws.GetAnswerQueries(QID))
'Rest of the code
End Sub
```

Adding Code to the Button Control

Now add a Button control to the Visual Basic .NET Windows application that you created in the previous section. In the `Click` event handler for the Button control, add the following code:

```
Dim ws As New WindowsApplication1.localhost.Service1()
Dim CCach As CredentialCache = New CredentialCache()
Dim credo As NetworkCredential = New NetworkCredential("User1", "pass1", "Domain1")
    CCach.Add(New Uri(ws.Url), "Basic", credo)
    ws.Credentials = CCach
    ws.AddQuery("Personal Finance",0,"Some query ?")
```

Because your Web service is secured using Windows Basic authentication, you need to provide the login credentials, as shown in the previous code sample.

Summary

In this chapter, you learned about the case study and design of the Kshare Web service. Next, you looked at the design and structure of the tables and stored procedures contained in the Kshare database.

You also learned about the advanced features of the ASP.NET Web services. These features include securing Web services using Windows authentication, accessing and modifying the SOAP messages by using SOAP extensions, managing transactions in a Web service, handling exceptions in Web services, managing states in Web services, and using caching to improve performance of Web services. Finally, you learned to create, deploy, and test the Kshare Web service.

PART IX

**Professional
Project 6**

Project 6

Creating a Web Service Using Java Technologies

Project 6 Overview

In this project, you'll learn to create a Web service for currency conversion. This Web service will convert American dollars to the British pounds. You can use this Web service with various client applications, such as bank applications.

Similar to Microsoft, Inc., Sun Microsystems, Inc. also provides you with tools to create, test, and deploy Web services. The Web service in this project will be created by using Sun ONE Studio that Sun Microsystems, Inc. provides. Sun ONE Studio provides you with an ease of creating and deploying Web services that you can access by using several client applications that are running on different platforms. You will use the test browser that Sun ONE Studio will launch to test the functionality of the currency conversion Web service.

Chapter 13

Introduction to Java XML Technologies

The use of XML Web services is increasing rapidly in Web-based business scenarios. Because of this, several platforms including Java and .NET offer you tools that you can use to create XML Web services.

This chapter introduces you to Java Web services and how they fit into the Java platform. It also teaches you about the role of XML in Java Web services and the Java Web services architecture. Next, it examines the Java service model and its components. From there, it delves into the life cycle of Web services and the roles and standards that are defined in the Java service model. Finally, it introduces you to the various components of Java Web services that include Java servlets, JSP, JAXP, JAXB, JAXM, JAX-RPC, and JAXR.

Overview of Java Web Services

Java Web services, implemented on the Java platform, are similar to Web services that you create by using Visual Studio .NET. The need for Java Web services is a result of the growing popularity of e-business. This increasing popularity has forced all the big players in the IT industry to provide their own means of creating Web services.

Toward this end, IBM has come up with a toolkit to create Web services. You have already learned to create Web services on the .NET platform. Similarly, Sun Microsystems, Inc. has introduced the Sun Open Net Environment (Sun One) and Java 2 Enterprise Edition (J2EE) as two significant solutions to develop and deploy Web services created on the Java platform.

Web Services and the Java Platform

As you know, Web services use the XML technology to enable isolated and different systems to communicate with each other. In addition, XML Web services allow sharing of data and functionality across different systems and are, therefore, interoperable. On the other hand, Java has evolved as a complete and robust platform because of its code portability and platform interoperability. These features of Java make it an ideal solution for business houses to develop and deploy Java Web services.

In addition, Java Web services integrate with XML to provide a solution for creating robust, secure, and scalable Web services. This solution is in the form of Web services that are created by using the Java APIs or the J2EE platform. You will learn about the Java APIs in the later section titled "Components of Java Web Services."

Java, which is integrated with XML, forms the Java service model. This model uses XML as a format for exchanging data and Java as a platform for developing Web services. Web services that are based on the Java service model can be deployed on a wide range of Web servers, such as WebLogic, Tomcat, and so on. In addition, these Web services can be called from any client application that is built on any platform, such as Java or the .NET platform. The following section describes the Java service model in detail.

Java Service Model

The Java service model forms the basis of the Java Web services architecture, which is similar to any other Web services architecture. The Java service model is based on the Service-Oriented Architecture (SOA). The SOA considers a Web service a process or a group of processes that are made up of components. These components are objects that form the building blocks of Web services.

The Java service model is similar to the Java Service Framework (JSF), which is a framework for creating interoperable applications on the Java platform. The JSF is a means of creating cost-effective applications easily and quickly. Also, the applications that the JSF creates are reusable components that several applications on the Java platform can use. In addition, the JSF defines a relationship between an application and its management.

The JSF uses J2EE to develop Web services. As a result, the programmers benefit from the components that J2EE provides for easy deployment of the Web services.

Features of the Java Service Model

The Java service model has the following features:

- Abstraction
- Encapsulation
- Modularity
- Polymorphism

These features are found in Object-Oriented Programming (OOP)-based languages. This implies that the SOA is similar to the Object-Oriented Architecture (OOA). Therefore, as objects are the building blocks in the OOA, similarly, components are the building blocks of services, which are the basic elements in the SOA. At this point, we will discuss the features of the SOA in detail.

Abstraction

Consider a simple example in which a user tries to log on to an authorized site by specifying a username and password. In this case, the user is given access permissions only if the username and password are validated.

This entire process of validating the user data is internally divided into several subprocesses, as discussed in the following list:

1. A user provides the user data, username, and password.
2. Validation tests are performed on the username and password. For example, the password should be at least four characters long; the password should consist of special characters, such as @, #, &, *, and so on in addition to letters and numerals; and the username should begin with a letter.
3. If the validation tests are verified, the username and password are matched against the data in the database that stores the authorized usernames and passwords. To validate a username and password, a query is used.
4. If the username and password are invalid, an exception is raised and the user is denied access to the site.
5. If the username and password are valid, the user is allowed to access the site.

All processes mentioned in the preceding list comprise a single process: verification of the user data. However, to the end user, the entire process seems simple. This method of hiding the complex functionality from the end user is called *service abstraction*. In this method, the end user is cognitively familiarized with the functionality that the Web service performs.

Encapsulation

As in OOPs, encapsulation is a method of implementing abstraction. Similarly, service encapsulation is used to implement service abstraction.

In the previous example, we briefly described each of the subprocesses that is performed within the main process of validating user data. To implement the subprocesses and the main process, the programmer needs to write the business logic or the code for the Web service. However, the business logic is separated from the user interface. This implies that the end user does not have access to the code of the Web service. This method of separating the business code from the user interface and, therefore, hiding the business logic from the end user, is called *service encapsulation*.

In addition to implementing service abstraction, service encapsulation provides several other benefits for the end user and the programmer. For example, the end user or the client application can implement the functionality of the Web service in different ways. This mechanism of implementing functionality in different ways is explained in detail in the later section titled "Polymorphism."

The process of encapsulation benefits both the programmer and the client application. The programmer benefits by having the freedom to modify earlier versions of existing code without affecting any of the client applications. The client application in this case has access to the new and improved version of the Web service without making changes to the framework.

Modularity

Service modularity is a mechanism of creating modules of services that are closely related to each other. For example, the user validation service that we discussed in the previous example is closely related to the credit card validation service. As a result, the user validation service can be placed in the same module as the credit card validation service. The modules of services, in turn, are grouped together to form the *service library*. A service library allows you to categorize various services based on their functionality or any other criterion.

As you know, a Web service is a reusable piece of code. Therefore, the concept of a service library allows several users to reuse existing services by customizing an available piece of code according to their needs. Categorizing services into modules enables a user to easily locate a required service, and therefore, provide reusability of Web services.

To understand the concept of service modularity, consider an example of a module of services called the Travel service module. This module consists of a travel Web service, which in turn consists of several other Web services, such as a ticketing Web service that allows you to book your tickets online. Then, it might consist of a tourism Web service that acts as a guide for places you will visit. The travel Web service might also contain hotel reservation and cab booking Web services. All these Web services work together to create a package called the Travel and Tourism package.

It is important to note, however, that the services included in the same module only complement each other. In the absence of any service, the working of other services is not affected. For example, if the Travel and Tourism package does not include the hotel reservation or cab booking Web service, then the functionality of the ticket reservation Web service is unaffected. However, the presence of these services does extend the functionality of the module as a whole. As a result, to implement reusability of the Web services, the user can benefit from the entire module rather than individual Web services.

Polymorphism

Polymorphism enables an entity to exist in multiple forms. As in OOP, an object can exist in multiple forms to implement polymorphism. Similarly, in SOA, a service can be implemented in several ways. Polymorphism extends the features of abstraction and encapsulation to enable a client application to differently implement the same Web service. This implies that a generic Web service interface is created, which you can customize according to your needs.

Consider an example of the Travel and Tourism package that we discussed in the previous section. In this case, the package can include a generic code for the ticketing and tourism Web service. The user can then modify the existing code to provide different implementations. For example, he can use the ticketing Web service to book tickets for railways or airplanes. Similarly, the tourism Web service can be tailored to guide you about any place that you specify.

Polymorphism is a result of encapsulation. This is because the business logic of the service is hidden from the end user; therefore, the programmer can modify the existing code to implement a new functionality. As a result, the user can benefit from multiple implementations.

Components of the Java Service Model

The Java service model consists of various components that include the roles in the Web service architecture and the standards or the technologies used in the Java service model. These components are shown in Figure 13-1.

The following sections discuss these components in detail.

Roles in the Java Service Model

The roles that are defined in the Java Web service architecture are similar to the roles in any other Web service architecture. These roles are defined in the following list:

- Service requestor
- Service broker
- Service provider

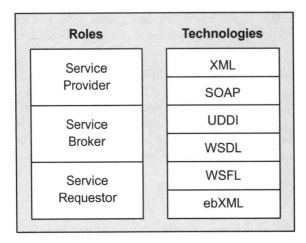

FIGURE 13-1 *Components in the Java service model.*

We will discuss these roles in detail in the following sections.

Service Requestor

A service requestor is a client application that sends in a request for a Web service. A Web service that is created is registered in the service registry. Therefore, whenever it's required, the service requestor application looks for a Web service in the service registry and then binds to the required Web service.

For example, several Web services already exist that perform the same functionality as the Web services in the Travel and Tourism package. These Web services are registered with the service registry. Therefore, a user can reuse an existing Web service by locating it on the service registry.

To access the desired Web service, a client application sends a request for the Web service to the service provider application. You will learn about service providers and service registries in the following sections.

 NOTE

It is important to note that a service requestor application can be any application that is created on any platform and by using any programming language. It is not necessary that a Java Web service be accessible only from a Java client application. In addition, a Web service can act as a client application when a Web service requests another Web service.

To summarize, the service requestor application performs the following activities:

- Identifies the need for a Web service
- Looks for the Web service in the service registry
- Discovers the Web service
- Obtains the proxy address of the provider application that hosts the Web service
- Binds to the required Web service
- Accesses the Web service

Service Broker

A service broker is a service registry that provides a list of all existing Web services. When a user creates a Web service, he needs to register it with the service registry. This helps a client look for desired Web services. A UDDI is an example of a service registry. You learned about UDDIs in Chapter 4, "Introduction to UDDI."

A service broker provides a mechanism for registering a Web service. The information about the Web service is made accessible to the service clients. In addition, the service broker application manages the request for the Web service. Similarly, when a service provider processes the request and sends in the response, the service broker application manages the response.

After a service requestor application binds to a Web service, a contract is signed between the service requestor application and service provider. The contract can be for a lifetime or for a definite lease period. The service broker application manages this contract. When a lease period of a contract is over, the service broker can renew or terminate the contract, as required. Therefore, as you can see, the service broker application acts as an interface between the service requestor and the service provider application that I will discuss in the following section.

Service Provider

The service provider application hosts a Web service. In other words, it provides the Web service to any application that requests it. A service provider application operates in the following stages:

- **Developing the Web service.** This stage includes creating the design of the Web service, creating the Web service, and testing and deploying the Web service.
- **Publishing the Web service.** In this stage, the business organization that hosts the Web service publishes the Web service with the service registry.
- **Managing the access of the Web service.** In this stage, the service provider application provides the Web service to the requesting application so that the client application can access it.

Figure 13-2 shows the roles in the Java Web services architecture.

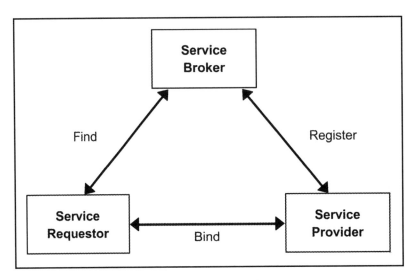

FIGURE 13-2 *Roles in the Java Web services architecture.*

Standards Used in the Java Service Model

Similar to the standards used in any Web services architecture, the Java service model uses the following standards:

◆ **SOAP.** As in any other Web services scenario, SOAP is used to communicate between applications that are a part of the Java service model. SOAP generally uses HTTP to transfer data between these applications. All the communication that takes place between the applications is packaged as a SOAP message. For example, the request and response are packaged as SOAP messages to be transferred across the applications.

◆ **UDDI.** UDDI is a standard that is used to register a Web service. It allows a client application to access the registered information about a Web service.

◆ **WSDL.** WSDL provides a standard format for publishing and describing a Web service.

◆ **WSFL.** Web Services Flow Language (WSFL) is an XML-based language that describes the composition of a Web service. WSFL consists of two types of compositions: flow models and global models. The flow model defines a composition of a business process, whereas the global model describes the interactions of the business partners who are involved in a business interaction.

◆ **ebXML.** Electronic Business XML Initiative (ebXML) is an international initiative developed by the United Nations Center for Trade Facilitation and Electronic Business (UN/CEFACT) and the Organization for the Advancement of Structured Information Standards (OASIS). ebXML aims to standardize XML business specifications. ebXML defines a standard that worldwide business organizations can use to exchange data in an XML format.

Figure 13-3 shows how the standards fit into the Java service model.

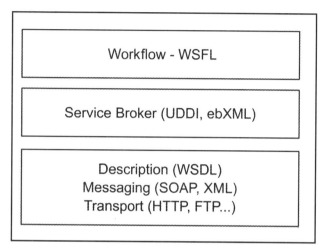

FIGURE 13-3 *Standards that the Java service model uses.*

Life Cycle of Web Services in the Java Service Model

The life cycle of Java Web services is the same as that of .NET Web services. Therefore, we will just summarize the stages in the life cycle of Java Web services.

Following is the life cycle of Java Web services in relation to the roles in the Java service model:

1. Develop the Web service by using the J2EE framework or various Java APIs for XML. Developing the Web services involves creating the interface for the Web service and writing the business logic of the application. This step is performed at the service endpoint.

2. Describe the Web service by using WSDL. This step involves creating the WSDL document that contains a description of the Web service. This step is also performed at the service endpoint.

3. Register the Web service with the service registry.

4. Discover the Web service by looking for the required application in the service registry. The service requestor role performs this step.

5. Send a request for the required Web service to the service provider role. The request is in the form of a SOAP message.

6. Process the request and send a response in the form of a SOAP message back to the client application.

Figure 13-4 shows the life cycle of Java Web services.

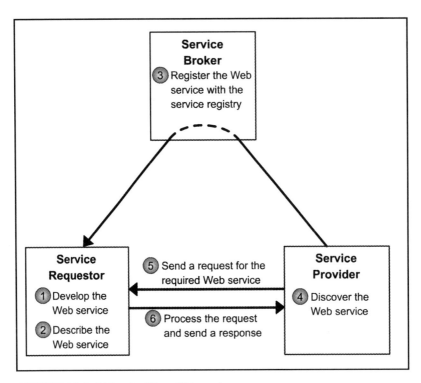

FIGURE 13-4 *Life cycle of Java Web services.*

Working of the Java Service Model

To understand the role of the Web service standards in the Java service model, you need to understand the working of the Java service model. In this model, a client application, usually a Java application, sends a request for a Web service. The data that is transferred between the applications is in the XML format. As a result, you use the APIs provided in the Java service model to work with this XML data. The APIs allow you to access any Web method that a Web service exposes. This request that a client application sends is then converted to a SOAP message by using a SOAP serializer.

As discussed, SOAP generally uses HTTP as the transfer protocol. Therefore, the SOAP message needs to be converted in the form of an HTTP request. This is performed by an HTTP encoder. Then, the HTTP request is sent over the network to the Web server that hosts the Java Web service.

At the Web server end, a servlet receives the request and then forwards it to the HTTP decoder, which decodes the request back to the XML format. Then the XML request is read by an Enterprise Java Bean (EJB) component, which performs the required processing of the request. Then, again at the server end, a SOAP encoder creates the response of the request and converts it back to the SOAP message.

Next, to transfer the response, the EJB component sends the response over the HTTP protocol. Finally, at the client end, the HTTP decoders decode the HTTP response to the SOAP message, which is further deserialized to an XML message. The entire working of a Java service model is shown in Figure 13-5.

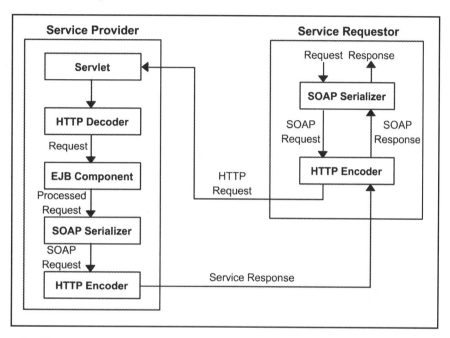

FIGURE 13-5 *Working of the Java service model.*

Value Chain of the Java Service Model

Based on the service roles and the steps in the life cycle of the Java Web services, the Java service model defines a value chain for the Java Web services. This value chain is described in the following bulleted list:

◆ **Standards body.** A standards body is a group of organizations that defines the standards of Web services, such as SOAP, UDDI, and WSDL. The standards body includes the consortium, such as W3C, RosettaNet, and so on.

◆ **Framework.** Frameworks comprise the organizations that provide a framework for developing the Web services based on the Web service standards. These organizations involve Sun Microsystems, Inc., Microsoft, Inc., IBM, and so on.

◆ **Vendors.** Due to the increase in popularity of Web services, several small and large vendors in the IT industry provide tools or products that you can use to automate stages in the creation of Web services. The common vendors such as Sun Microsystems, Inc., Microsoft, Inc., and IBM provide toolkits for this purpose.

◆ **Web Services Developers (WSDs).** WSDs are the programmers who create the Web services, their interface, and their business logic.

◆ **Web Services Marketers (WSMs).** As the name suggests, WSMs are the individuals or the business organizations that promote or market a Web service. With the increasing participation of Web services in the e-business, the WSMs contribute by bringing in money for the WSD organizations. To do this, they create a demand for Web services in the market.

 NOTE

For a Web service, a WSD and a WSM can be the same person or the same organization.

◆ **Web Services Providers (WSPs).** WSPs host the Web services. They help any client access a required Web service.

◆ **Web Services Consumers (WSCs).** WSCs are the ultimate users of a Web service. They are the beneficiaries who profit from the functionality of a Web service. They form the most important component of the value chain because they bring in the economy for a Web service.

The value chain for a Web service in the Java service model is illustrated in Figure 13-6.

Components of Java Web Services

A Java Web service uses one or more of the following components:

◆ Java servlets
◆ Java Server Pages
◆ JAXP
◆ JAXB
◆ JAXM
◆ JAX-RPC
◆ JAXR

The following sections discuss these components in brief.

Java Servlets

Servlets are special Java programs that enhance the existing functionality of a Web site. These programs are deployed on the Web server that supports Java. You can include servlets in your Web site to make it dynamic. For example, you can include a Java servlet to display a welcome message to a user who logs on to a Web service.

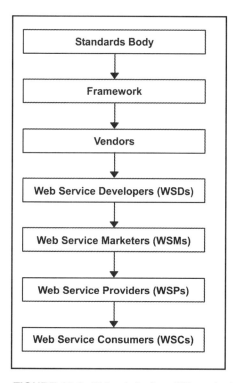

FIGURE 13-6 *Value chain for a Web service in the Java service model.*

Servlets created by using Java offer several benefits:

◆ Servlets use the features of Java, such as multithreading, accessing a database, networking, Remote Method Invocation (RMI), and so on. These features make servlets widely used programs.

◆ Similar to Java programs, servlets are robust and portable. Servlets benefit from the exception handling and garbage collection features of Java.

◆ Applications that use servlets are highly efficient. This is because the code that initializes a servlet is executed only the first time. Therefore, unnecessary processes are avoided, resulting in a higher efficiency of the Web servers that host servlets.

◆ Servlets increase the performance of an application by storing the frequently used data in a temporary memory location. This saves the time taken to frequently access a disk.

To invoke a servlet, a client application needs to send in a request by using the HTTP GET or the HTTP POST methods. Then, the Web server processes the request and sends the result to the Web browser or the client application.

Java Server Pages

Java Server Pages (JSP) is another technology that is used to create dynamic Web pages. JSP provides encapsulation of the code of the Web page by separating the code written using Java from the interface of the Web page.

A JSP page contains HTML and JSP constructs. When a request is sent for a JSP page for the first time, the HTML and the JSP constructs in a JSP source file are compiled and converted into a servlet. After that, the servlets are loaded to handle any further request. Therefore, whenever a request for a JSP file is made, the Web server executes the respective servlet.

As discussed, a JSP source file contains JSP constructs. These constructs enable you to include code written in Java in a JSP page and provide the business logic or the programming code for the JSP page. The following list discusses the categories of JSP constructs:

◆ **JSP directives.** These constructs provide additional information about a JSP page. They also allow you to import or include packages in your JSP page. The following code is an example of JSP directives:

```
<%@include file="/sample.jsp">
```

The JSP directives contain several attributes that store the information about a JSP page. These attributes are defined in Table 13-1.

◆ **JSP declarations.** These constructs declare methods and variables that are used in the JSP page. The following code is an example of the JSP declarations:

```
<%!
    int num1=0;
    int num2=0;
    String str1="";
%>
```

◆ **JSP expressions.** These constructs store references to variables and methods that are used in a JSP page. The JSP expressions allow you to insert Java values directly to an output. However, before doing this, the Java values are converted into string values. An example of the JSP expressions is shown in the following code:

```
<%= num1 %>
<%= num2 %>
<%= str1 %>
```

◆ **JSP scriptlet.** These constructs are used to include Java code in JSP pages. They allow you to benefit from the features of the Java programming language in a JSP page. The features include decision-making and iteration loops, making the content in a JSP page dynamic. For example, a user tries to log on to the home page of a Web site. To do so, he needs to enter a username and a password. However, the programmer has applied a validation that a password must be at least eight characters long. If the password is eight characters or more, a welcome message is displayed;

otherwise, an error message is displayed. The code for the JSP scriptlets is shown in the following example:

```
<%@ page import="java.util.*" %>
      <%@ page import="java.lang.*" %>


      <%
            String usrName=request.getParameter("txtUsrName");
            String usrPassword=request.getParameter("txtUsrPwd");
            int len=usrPassword.length();
            if(len<10)
            out.println("Password should be minimum of 10 characters");
      %>
```

◆ **JSP comments.** These constructs are used to include comments in your JSP page. The JSP comments can be of different types, as explained in Table 13-2.

◆ **JSP actions.** These constructs are used to extend the functionality of JSP pages. To do this, you can use the Java objects or include files or other JSP pages in your JSP page. The JSP actions are of several types, as explained in Table 13-3.

Table 13-1 Attributes of JSP Directives

Attribute	Description
language= "language"	This attribute specifies the language that is used to write the code for the JSP pages. For Java Web services, Java is the language that is supported.
contentType="text/html"	This attribute defines the type of request and response.
extends=" packagename.classname"	This attribute declares the parent class that you can inherit in a `servlet` class.
import="file"	This attribute specifies the file that you can import in the JSP page. This `import` directive is the same as the import statements in Java or C++ languages.
session="true¦false"	This attribute specifies whether session data is available for a JSP page.
errorPage="page_url"	This attribute specifies a URL of an error page that will handle the exceptions that the JSP page generates.
isErrorPage="true¦false"	This attribute specifies whether the current JSP page can be used as an error page. By default, the value for the `isErrorPage` attribute is `False`.

Table 13-2 Types of JSP Comments

Type	Description
HTML comments	These comments are added to the HTML code for the response that is sent to a browser. To display the content that is specified in the HTML code for the response, the browser ignores the comment tags. The HTML comment tags are enclosed within the <! - - and - - > tags. The following code is an example of HTML comment tags: ```\n<!-- Sample HTML comment -->\n<!--- This is a sample JSP response page. -->\n```
JSP comments	These comments are used to document the JSP code. They do not appear in the HTML code for the response that is sent to the browser. Unlike HTML comment tags, JSP comment tags are included in the <%-- and --%> tags. Following is an example of the JSP comment tag: ```\n<%-- Sample JSP comment --%>\n```
Java comments	These comments are used to comment the Java code that is embedded in a JSP page. To comment a single Java code statement, you can precede the statement with //. However, to comment multiple lines of code, you need to use the /* and */ tags. The Java comment tags are enclosed between script-let tags, as shown in the following example: ```\n/* Sample Java comment\nUsed to comment Java code in a JSP page*/\n```

Table 13-3 Types of JSP Actions

Type	Description
jsp:include	This action tag is used to include a file when a request for a page is received. The following code statement is an example of the jsp:include action tag: ```\n<jsp:include page="sample.jsp" />\n```
jsp:useBean	This action tag is used to handle Java beans. For example, you can use the jsp:useBean action tag to load a Java bean for use in a JSP page. To load a Java bean class, you need to create a reference to an instance of the Java bean class. To do so, you can use the id attributes of the class. In addition, you can include the scope attribute with the jsp:useBean action tag to specify a scope for the Java bean class object. The scope attribute takes the value as page, request, session, or scope. The syntax for the jsp:useBean action tag is as follows:

Type	Description
	`<jsp:useBean id="object name" class="package.class" scope="any value" />.`
`jsp:forward`	This action tag is used to forward a request that is sent by a user from one JSP page to another. The syntax for the `jsp:forward` action tag is as follows: `< page="JSP_path" />`
`jsp:setProperty`	Similar to the `jsp:useBean` action tag, the `jsp:setProperty` tag is used to handle Java beans. It sets a property of a Java bean that a JSP page references. The syntax for the `jsp:setProperty` tag is as follows: `<jsp:setProperty name="name" property="property name" value="any value"/>`
`jsp:getProperty`	This action tag retrieves the property name of the Java bean that the JSP page references. The syntax of the `jsp:getProperty` tag is as follows: `<jsp:getProperty name="name"  property="property name" value="any value"/>`

JAXP

As already discussed, the Java platform provides you with several APIs that you can use to create Web services and Web applications with the Java programming language. Java API for XML Processing (JAXP) is one such API that is used to process and transform XML documents.

JAXP, developed by JavaSoft and the JCP community, is a Java API that is used to easily and efficiently process XML documents. To do this, JAXP uses several parsers and applications that are created using the Java programming language. JAXP is a standard available in the Java XML Pack (JAX-Pack) and Java WSDP.

JAXP supports the industry standards, such as SOAP, UDDI, and WSDL. As you know, these industry standards are based on XML; therefore, it becomes important to have an API that processes an XML document. As a result, JAXP specifications were developed that allow you to access, convert, and process XML documents.

The latest version of JAXP specifications is version 1.2. You can download this version from the official Web site of JCP (http://java.sun.com/aboutJava/communityprocess/jsr/jsr_063_ jaxp.html) as a JSR 63 document.

This version of JAXP includes support for XSLT and XML schema. The following list discusses the versions of specifications that are included in JAXP 1.2:

◆ W3C XML 1.0 Recommendation (Second edition)
◆ SAX 2.0

- DOM Level 2
- W3C XML Namespaces 1.0 Recommendation
- XSLT 1.0

As discussed, Java APIs are flexible. This flexibility of JAXP is achieved because of the pluggability layer, which allows you to use XML parsers from your Web application. In addition, this layer allows you to plug an XSLT processor so that you can serialize XML data into various formats.

However, it is important to note that JAXP does not parse the XML documents. To do so, JAXP uses already-existing industry specifications. These specifications include Simple API for XML Parsing (SAX) and Document Object Model (DOM), as explained in the following sections.

SAX

The SAX specifications provide means to serially access an XML document. To do so, SAX uses a data stream; therefore, it's an event-based parser. The data stream serially reads data from top to bottom in an XML document and notifies the application about syntax construction. To notify the running application, the SAX API uses the `ContentHandler` interface. This interface contains several methods that are called whenever the SAX parser comes across a tag.

For example, the `startElement()` method is called for the < (start of element) tag, and the `endElement()` method is called for the /> (end of element tag). To understand the working of a SAX parser, consider the following example of an XML document:

```
<Books>
    <Technical>
```

JAVA APIS FOR XML

Java APIs for XML enables developers to work easily and efficiently with XML documents in the Java Web services framework. These Java APIs support industry standards, such as SOAP, XML, and so on. As a result, the Web services and applications that are created by using these Java APIs are interoperable across languages and platforms.

In addition to interoperability, Java APIs offer flexibility to the programmers. Java programmers have flexibility in the way they use various Java APIs. For example, the JAXP API provides you with the SAX and DOM APIs that you can use to process XML documents.

The following are the Java APIs for XML:

- JAXP
- JAXB
- JAXM
- JAX-RPC
- JAXR
- JWSDL

You will learn about JAXP, JAXB, JAXM, JAX-RPC, and JAXR in this chapter. However, because the Java API for Web Service Description Language (JWSDL) API is under construction and is not released, we will not discuss it.

```
              <Software/>
              <Operating_Systems/>
              <Programming_Languages/>
          </Technical>
          <Non_Technical>
              <Literature/>
              <Fiction/>
              <Autobiographies/>
          </Non_Technical>
  </Books>
```

To parse the previous XML document, the XML parser performs the following steps:

1. The parser calls the startElement() method for the <Books> element.
2. Similarly, the parser calls the startElement() method for the <Technical> element.
3. The parser calls the characters() and endElement() methods for the <Software>, <Operating_Systems>, and <Programming_Languages> elements.

 NOTE

The characters() method parses character data. This method also lies in the ContentHandler interface.

---

4. Next, the endElement() method is called for the <Technical> element.
5. Steps 2–4 are repeated for the <Non_Technical> element.
6. Finally, the endElement() method is called for the <Books> element.

The previous steps are used to parse the XML document according to the SAX specifications. However, it is important to note that the SAX parsers do not explicitly parse an XML document. To do so, you need to perform the following steps:

1. Create a class that extends DefaultHandler, which is the default implementation of the ContentHandler interface.
2. Write implementations for the methods of the ContentHandler interface.
3. Create an instance of the SAXParserFactory class.
4. Create an object of the SAXParser class.
5. Call the parse() method from this instance.
6. Pass the instance of the class that extends DefaultHandler to the parse() method.

DOM

The W3C DOM Working Group developed the DOM API to access an XML document in the form of an object tree. The DOM API contains several interfaces that contain methods, such as `insert()` and `remove()`. These methods allow you to modify an object tree by adding or deleting elements, respectively.

As a result of the tree-like structure, a user can randomly access data by using the DOM API. In addition, by using a SAX parser, you can only read data from an XML document. However, in contrast, a DOM API allows you to add or delete elements from the XML document. Therefore, a DOM parser is used when a user needs to modify the existing XML document. On the other hand, the SAX parser is used when you need to access small pieces of data. This is because a DOM parser requires the tree object of the whole XML document to be placed in the memory. As a result, if the document is large enough, the search for a small piece of data will be time consuming and, therefore, less efficient.

NOTE

The steps to access a DOM parser are the same as for that of the SAX parser, as explained in the previous section.

Java API for XML Binding

Java API for XML Binding (JAXB) is another Java API. In fact, it is an architecture that maps a Java object to an XML document. To do this, a Java object is created that is bound to the XML document. This process is called *data binding*. It is essential to incorporate data binding of Java objects with XML documents because the industry standards for transferring data over the Web are mainly XML based.

In the process of data binding, a class hierarchy is created that is similar to the structure of an XML document that allows you to access or modify data in this class hierarchy without actually considering the structure of the XML document. To do this, a DTD and an XML schema are required as inputs. From there, the elements of the XML document are mapped to the values or Java classes. For example, an XML element that contains subelements is mapped to Java classes, and the XML elements that do not contain subelements are mapped to the Java values.

Then a Java source file is created by using the schema compiler. Finally, the Java compiler compiles these Java source files to Java classes. JAXB uses the process of unmarshalling and marshalling. *Unmarshalling* is the process of creating applications that contain classes required to convert an XML document to a tree object. *Marshalling* is the process of converting a tree object back to an XML document.

Components of the JAXB API

The following list discusses the components of the Java API:

- **Binding language.** This is an XML-based language that defines the data binding of a DTD to the Java classes.
- **Schema compiler.** This is used to generate the Java source files based on the DTD and the schema.
- **Binding framework.** This is a set of Java classes and interfaces that help in the process of marshalling and unmarshalling. In addition, JAXB performs validation of the XML documents. The classes required for the validation are also included in the binding framework.

These components work together to bind an XML document to the corresponding Java classes. The following section discusses the working of these components.

Working of the JAXB API

To work with the JAXB API, you need to perform the following steps:

1. Create a DTD document for the corresponding XML document.
2. Define a binding schema to generate the Java-derived classes.
3. Run the command to enable the schema compiler to generate the derived classes.
4. Convert the XML document to an object tree by using the `unmarshall()` method. You can then work with the Java object tree.
5. Perform validation on the object tree.
6. Convert the object tree back to the XML document.

Advantages of the JAXB API

The JAXB API has several advantages, as discussed in the following list:

- JAXB is faster than the other XML parsers, such as SAX and DOM, because JAXB uses compiled Java classes. These classes already have a schema defined for them, which saves time. In addition, JAXB does not require you to create complex code that is required to process an XML document.
- JAXB uses both Java and XML. As a result, JAXB benefits from the advantages of both.
- Before binding an XML document to the corresponding Java classes, JAXB verifies whether the document is valid according to a schema. Only after the verification is complete is the XML document bound to the corresponding Java classes.
- As already discussed, JAXB converts an XML document to a Java class. Therefore, JAXB supports data conversion.

Limitations of the JAXB API

In addition to the previously listed advantages, JAXB has certain limitations:

◆ The schema compiler that is used with JAXB does not fully support all specifications defined in JAXB.

◆ JAXB supports only the DTD that is specified in the XML 1.0 recommendation.

◆ The code that the compiler generates is not very efficient.

Java API for XML Messaging

As you know, the data that is transferred over the network is in XML format. The Java API for XML Messaging (JAXM) is an API used to transfer these XML messages. JAXM is based on industry standards, such as SOAP 1.1. Therefore, it is a standard used to exchange SOAP messages between the service provider and the service requestor applications.

In the e-business scenario, messages are exchanged between various applications or members of the value chain. To allow a smooth exchange of messages over the network, JAXM defines a framework that consists of the following types of messages:

◆ **Asynchronous message.** These messages are one-way operations, such as a request from a service requestor application. In this case, the service provider application does not expect a prompt response. The concept of an asynchronous message is explained in Figure 13-7.

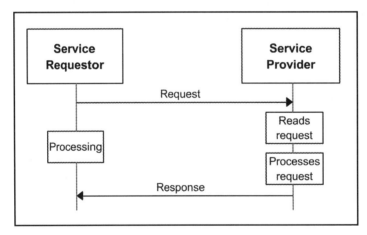

FIGURE 13-7 *The asynchronous message.*

◆ **Asynchronous message with acknowledgement.** This is also a one-way operation, but in this case, the service provider sends an acknowledgement to the service requestor application. An asynchronous message with acknowledgement is explained in Figure 13-8.

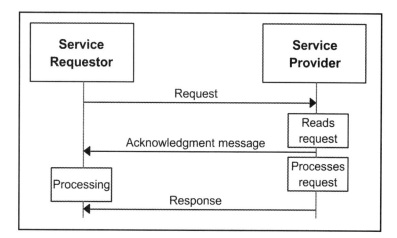

FIGURE 13-8 *The asynchronous message with acknowledgement.*

◆ **Synchronous message.** This is a two-way message in which a service requestor application sends a request to a service provider application and then waits for the response from the service provider application. In this case, the service requestor application is blocked until the time it receives a response from the service provider application. Figure 13-9 shows a synchronous message.

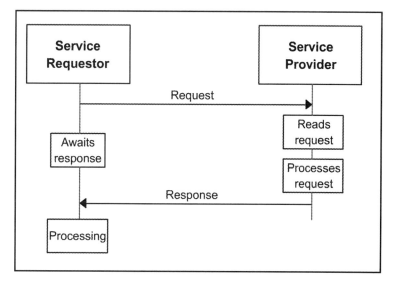

FIGURE 13-9 *The synchronous message.*

◆ **Synchronous message with acknowledgement.** This is a synchronous message in which the service provider application waits for an acknowledgement from the service requestor application. The synchronous message with acknowledgement is shown in Figure 13-10.

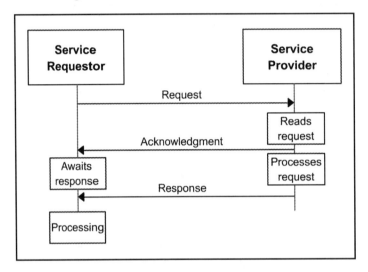

FIGURE 13-10 *The synchronous message with acknowledgement.*

◆ **One-way with no reply.** As the name suggests, this is a one-way operation in which a requestor application sends a request to the provider application, but it does not expect a response or an acknowledgement from the provider application. Figure 13-11 shows a one-way with no reply message.

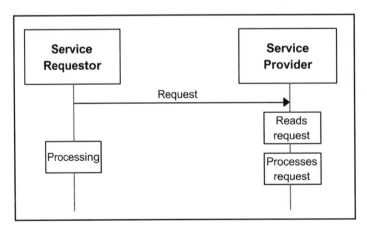

FIGURE 13-11 *The one-way with no reply message.*

JAXM might use a messaging provider service to exchange or transfer messages between applications. This service routes the messages from one application to another. Therefore, when a message is sent from a client application (a service provider application in the case of Web services), the message goes to the messaging provider of the client application. The messaging provider then routes the message to the messaging provider of the receiving application, or the service provider application in the case of Web services. Finally, the messaging provider of the receiving application forwards the request to the receiving application—the ultimate destination of the request.

 NOTE

It is important to note that JAXM can be used in all business scenarios that require transfer of data. This implies that JAXM is not limited to the Web services scenario.

Figure 13-12 shows the transfer of messages by using the JAXM API.

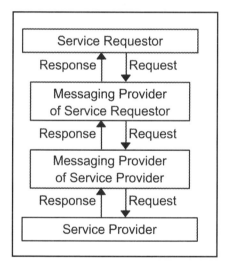

FIGURE 13-12 *Transfer of messages by using the JAXM API.*

JAX-RPC

In today's business world, RPC-based Web services are used extensively. An RPC-based Web service contains Web methods that can be called remotely over the network. For example, a weather forecast Web service is an example of an RPC-based Web service that accepts the name of a place as a parameter and uses the SOAP message to return the temperature for the specified place.

Java API for XML-based RPC (JAX-RPC) is a set of APIs that allow you to develop a Web service that you can call remotely from a Java client application. The packages contained within the JAX-RPC are client-side API packages, as shown in the following list:

- javax.xml.namespace
- javax.xml.rpc
- javax.xml.rpc.encoding
- javax.xml.rpc.handler
- javax.xml.rpc.handler.soap
- javax.xml.rpc.holders
- javax.xml.rpc.servers
- javax.xml.rpc.soap

JAX-RPC hides the complexities of making calls to remote Web services from client applications. To do this, JAX-RPC uses the concepts of stubs, ties, and configuration files. In fact, JAX-RPC uses the SOAP-based XML messaging framework to invoke Web methods remotely. This framework is built on the concepts of SOAP, XML RPC, RMI, CORBA, and Messaging.

 NOTE

You can install the latest version, JAX-RPC 0.8, from the official site of JCP. The URL for this site is http://jcp.org/jsr/detail/101.jsp.

JAX-RPC Framework

The JAX-RPC framework includes the Java initiative, which you can use to create Web services that can be accessed remotely from a client application. The creation of Web services by using the Java initiative includes the following stages:

- **Service definition.** The service definition stage defines an interface for the Web service that is similar to the RMI interface. In addition, it defines the endpoints of a remote service.
- **Service implementation.** The services created by using the JAX-RPC framework are implemented by using the Java platform. To do this, several tools are available that allow you to implement a Web service as a container that manages the Web service.
- **Service deployment.** The JAX-RPC framework allows you to deploy a Web service both on the client side and the server side. The framework provides you with a deployment tool, such as xrpcc, that allows you to deploy a Web service within a container. This tool is used for protocol bindings, to create a configuration for the binding, and to provide a service description in the form of a WSDL document.

◆ **Service description.** This stage involves creating a WSDL document for the Web service. For simplicity, you can use the deployment tool to describe a Web service in the form of a WSDL document.

◆ **Service invocation.** In this stage, a client application remotely invokes a Web service. To do this, the deployment tool obtains a service definition in the form of WSDL-to-Java-stubs. These stubs are the proxy definitions of a Web service at the client end. The client application then uses the stubs to invoke a Web service.

Figure 13-13 shows the JAX-RPC framework.

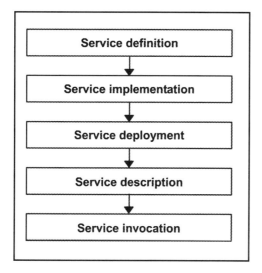

FIGURE 13-13 *The JAX-RPC framework.*

Advantages of JAX-RPC

As discussed earlier, JAX-RPC allows you to remotely invoke the Web methods that a Web service exposes. To do this, JAX-RPC allows you to create client applications in Java and other platforms that can remotely access a Web service. In addition, JAX-RPC offers several advantages, as discussed in the following list:

◆ The most important feature of a Web service is its interoperability. This feature is extended by using JAX-RPC because it allows you to create client applications in all platforms that can access the Java Web services. In addition, any Java client application can access any Web service created on any platform. This feature of interoperability is the result of JAX-RPC support for industry standards, such as SOAP, UDDI, and WSDL.

◆ JAX-RPC is a user-friendly API. Programmers who have worked with RPC will definitely appreciate the ease that JAX-RPC provides to its users. JAX-RPC hides the implementation of the RPC-based Web services from the client and the server applications.

NOTE

JAX-RPC is based on the standards defined in the SOAP specifications 1.1. These standards act as guidelines or rules for remotely accessing a Web service.

◆ JAX-RPC provides an architecture that supports all protocols used for binding SOAP services. In addition, this architecture, called the *Java initiative,* is built such that it can be extended to support binding protocols that will be developed in the future. The Java initiative remotely implements a Web service from a Java client application. You learned about the Java initiative earlier in the section "JAX-RPC Framework."

◆ JAX-RPC provides several advantages over RPC. For example, JAX-RPC allows you to exchange complete documents or parts of documents, as required. In addition, JAX-RPC can be used to transfer asynchronous and one-way messages.

◆ JAX-RPC supports advanced SOAP message handlers that allow you to transfer SOAP messages in various formats over the network.

Java APIs for XML Registries

Java APIs for XML Registries (JAXR) provide APIs that allow you to conveniently and quickly access a business registry. As you know, a Web service needs to be registered with the business registries where the users can search for the required Web service. This search is facilitated by the JAXR APIs. To do this, JAXR supports a pluggable architecture, which allows you to connect to various business registries, such as the registries based on ebXML or UDDI registries. These registries are collectively called *XML registries.* We discussed the components of Java Web services that included a layer called the service broker in the section titled "Roles in the Java Service Model." These XML registries perform the role of a service broker in the Web services scenario.

NOTE

Registries that ebXML or OASIS develop are open standards registries that derive from existing registry standards. In contrast, a consortium of industry leaders develop and maintain UDDI registries. As a result, UDDI registries are more widely used.

APIs in JAXR

JAXR, developed by the JCP organization, is currently in version 1.0. You can download this version from http://jcp.org/jsr/detail/93.jsp, where the jsr of the JAXR API is 93. The 0.9 version of JAXR contains several interfaces, which are further contained within APIs. The

APIs in the JAXR API package are broadly categorized into two categories, as discussed in the following list:

◆ **javax.xml.registry.infomodel.** This API includes interfaces that define the objects in a service registry. For example, the javax.xml.registry.infomodel API includes interfaces such as `Association`, `Concept`, `EmailAddress`, `Key`, `User`, `Service`, `Slot`, `Organization`, and so on.

◆ **javax.xml.registry.** This API includes interfaces that allow a JAXR client to access the service registry. The interfaces that are included in the JAXR API package include `BulkResponse`, `CapabilityProfile`, `Query`, `Federation`, `RegistryService`, `Connection`, and so on.

JAXR is an API that allows a Java client application to access various registry standards. This is the limitation of JAXR; only Java client applications can access the registries. This feature is illustrated in Figure 13-14.

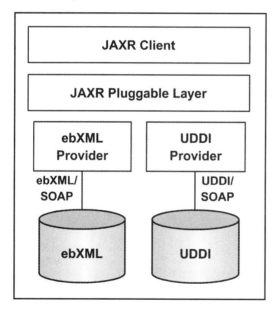

FIGURE 13-14 *The interoperability feature of JAXR.*

As you know, JAXR allows a client application to access registries that are based on XML. This implies that JAXR supports the feature of interoperability. In fact, XML-based registries aim to integrate various Web services developed on different standards, enabling these Web services to interoperate using a common standard, XML. Therefore, any communication that takes place between the components of a Web service uses XML messaging technology.

Due to support for interoperability of Web services, JAXR API is extensively used in a B2B scenario. To understand the feature of interoperability that JAXR supports, it is important for you to understand the working of the JAXR API. The following section discusses this.

Working of JAXR API

The following steps show the working of JAXR in the B2B scenario:

1. The client application sends a request by using JAXR to the service registry.
2. The XML-based registry sends an XML specification document to the client application. This specification defines the process of information exchange in the B2B scenario.
3. The client application implements the business process, as defined in the XML specifications.
4. The provider application registers its service with the service registry by using JAXR.
5. The client application searches for this information about the service in the service registry.
6. A list of Web services that matches the search criteria is displayed.
7. The client application can access the detailed information about any desired Web service in the available list. To do this, the client application uses JAXR.
8. If the available Web service is appropriate for the client, the client negotiates with the provider of the service and signs a contract with service provider.
9. The client binds to the contracted Web service and implements it.

The working of the JAXR API is illustrated in Figure 13-15.

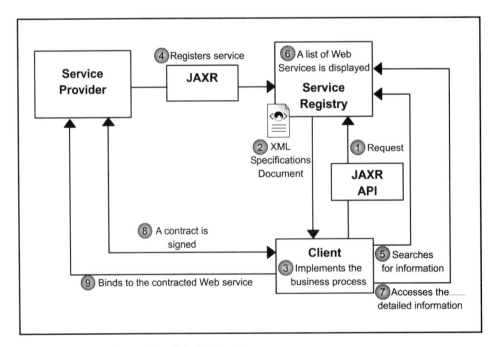

FIGURE 13-15 *The working of the JAXR API.*

Summary

This chapter introduced the important concepts that you need to understand before you create a Java Web service, which runs on the Java platform. The Java service model forms the basis of the architecture of the Java Web services, which is similar to any other Web services architecture. The Java service model is based on SOA.

You looked at the features, components, roles, and standards used in the Java service model. Finally, you looked at the components of Java Web services that include Java servlets, JSP, JAXP, JAXB, JAXM, JAX-RPC, and JAXR.

Chapter 14

In Chapter 13, "Introduction to Java XML Technologies," you learned about the Java Web services and the role of XML in Java Web services. You also learned about the role of Java servlets—such as JSP, JAXP, JAXB, JAXM, JAX-RPC, and JAXR—in Java Web services.

This chapter discusses how to develop Java Web services on two platforms: Java Web Services Developers Pack and Sun ONE Studio. You will learn how to develop Java Web services on each of these platforms.

The first section discusses Java Web Services Developer Pack (JWSDP), which is a set of tools that integrates all components of a Web service. JWSDP allows you to develop and deploy XML applications, Web services, and Web applications. You will learn how to install and configure JWSDP and the API implementations provided in the Java XML Pack of JWSDP.

This chapter also discusses the Registry server, which acts as a test registry in JWSDP, and how to use the Ant Build tool to build Java applications. Finally, it discusses the method to deploy Web applications in the Tomcat container by using the JWSDP Application Deployment tool.

Overview of JWSDP

JWSDP consists of software, tools, and a set of APIs that Sun Microsystems, Inc. provides. You can use these components of JWSDP to develop, deploy, and test Java Web services.

NOTE

JWSDP is available as a free downloadable file at http://java.sun.com/webservices/downloads/webservicespack.html.

While you're unpacking and installing the JWSDP package, you are prompted for a username and a password. You need to provide this username and password (see Figure 14-1) while you deploy the application in the Tomcat container.

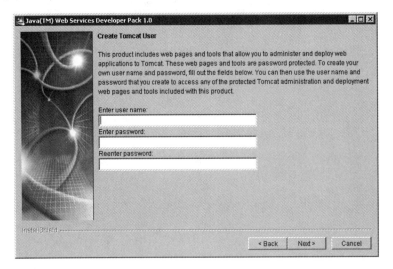

FIGURE 14-1 *The interface for accepting the username and password.*

However, if you forget your username and password, you can look up the tomcat-users.xml file to find them. You will learn more about the tomcat-users.xml file in the later section "Authenticating Users to Access Web Services."

You need to install Java2SDK Standard Edition version 1.3.1_03 or later to be able to use JWSDP. After you have installed the JWSDP toolkit, you need to set the following paths:

♦ Create and set the environment variable JWSDP_HOME to the directory where the JWSDP is installed.

♦ Set the Path variable of the system to the Bin folder of the JWSDP parent directory.

JWSDP consists of the following components:

- ◆ JAXM
- ◆ JAXP
- ◆ JAXR
- ◆ JAX-RPC
- ◆ Java Server Pages Standard Tag Library (JSTL)
- ◆ JWSDP Registry Server
- ◆ Apache Tomcat
- ◆ Web Application Deployment tool
- ◆ Ant Build tool

You learned about JAXM, JAXP, JAXR, and JAX-RPC in Chapter 13. Therefore, at this point, we will discuss only the remaining components.

JSTL

JSPs are dynamic Web pages that are executed at a server. A JSP page contains Java code scriptlets that are executed during runtime. The output of execution of Java scriptlets is displayed on the client Web browser. You can write the code for scriptlets to perform numerous tasks, such as accessing databases, performing numerical calculations, and so on.

Many tasks are common across JSP applications. To perform such common tasks, you are provided with a set of standard tags that work the same way everywhere. These tags are packaged in Java Server Pages Standard Tag Library (JSTL).

JSTL contains tags for performing tasks that include editing XML documents, querying databases, performing iteration, performing conditional operations, and so on. JSTL also enables you to integrate existing tag libraries with JSTL.

JSTL uses multiple Tag Library Descriptors (TLDs) to specify a namespace and its functionality. You can categorize the tags in JSTL into the following divisions:

- ◆ **Core.** Some of the tags in this category are `catch`, `out`, `choose`, `forEach`, `forTokens`, `import`, and `url`.
- ◆ **XML.** Some of the tags in this category are `out`, `parse`, `forEach`, `if`, and `transform`.
- ◆ **Internationalization.** Some of the tags in this category are `setLocale`, `bundle`, `formatNumber`, and `parseDate`.
- ◆ **Database.** Some of the tags in this category are `setDatasource`, `query`, and `transaction`.

You can use a JSTL core tag in a JSP page by using the `taglib` directive, as shown in the following example:

```
<%@ taglib uri="/jstl-core" prefix="c" %>
```

In a web.xml file, TLDs are referenced by using the following code snippet:

```
<taglib>
<taglib-uri>/jstl-c</taglib-uri>
<taglib-location>/WEB-INF/c.tld</taglib-location>
</taglib>
```

You can also reference TLDs in a `taglib` directive with an absolute URI. Some of these URIs are shown in the following list:

- **Core tags.** http://java.sun.com/jstl/core
- **XML tags.** http://java.sun.com/jstl/xml
- **Internationalization tags.** http://java.sun.com/jstl/fmt
- **SQL tags.** http://java.sun.com/jstl/sql

JSTL tag libraries are available in two versions:

- JSTL-RT tag library
- JSTL-ET tag library

These libraries differ in the way they support the use of runtime expressions. Expressions are specified in a scripting language by the tags in the JSTL-RT tag library. In contrast, for the tags in the JSTL-EL tag library, expressions are specified in the JSTL expression language. The naming conventions of the TLDs in both the libraries are as follows:

```
JSTL-RT library   -  <name>-rt.tld
JSTL-EL library   -  <name>.tld
```

You can find the JSTL TLDs in JWSDP in the directory <JWSDP_HOME>/tools/jstl/tlds.

NOTE

To enable a Web application to use the tag libraries, you need to ensure that the JSTL API is available to the application. In addition, you must ensure that the application can implement the API.

JWSDP provides you with JSTL API and its implementation in the form of the archives jstl.jar and standard.jar. The jstl.jar archive is available in the <JWSDP_HOME>/tools/jstl directory. You can access the standard.jar archive from the <JWSDP_HOME>/tools/jstl/standard directory.

The JSTL API defines some implicit objects for JSP. These implicit objects are as listed:

- pageContext
- pageScope

- requestScope
- sessionScope
- applicationScope
- param
- paramValues
- header
- headerValues
- cookie
- initParam

You can refer to these implicit objects by using the following syntax:

```
${implicit_object_nam}
```

For example:

```
<c:If test="{sessionScope.numberOfItems > 1"}
----------------
</c:if>
```

In the preceding example, the number of items in the current session is being evaluated.

JWSDP Registry Server

Another important component of JWSDP is the JWSDP registry server. You need to register the Web services that you create and deploy so that a client is able to access them. To enable registration of Web services, JWSDP provides you with the JWSDP registry server. The registry server provides UDDI registry for Web services in a private environment.

You can use the registry server to test the applications that you develop by using the JAXR API. The registry server includes the following components:

- A database based on the Xindice database, which is part of the Apache XML project. This database is a repository of registry data.
- A tool named Indri that allows you to create and inspect database data by using a graphical user interface.

Starting the Registry Server

Before you use the registry server, you need to start both Tomcat and the Xindice database. To start Tomcat, execute the following command at the command prompt:

```
C:\> startup
```

TIP

You can execute this command from any directory if you have set the environment variable PATH to <JWSDP_HOME>/bin.

To verify that the Tomcat server has started, type the following address in the address bar of the Web browser:

`http://localhost:8080`

To start the Xindice database, execute the following command:

`Xindice-start`

To stop the Xindice database, execute the following command:

`Xindice-stop`

The registry server provides a shell script to perform the following tasks:

◆ Obtain authentication from the registry server.
◆ Add a business to the registry server.
◆ Search for a business.
◆ Obtain business details.
◆ Delete a business.
◆ Validate UDDI messages.
◆ Retrieve the business that belongs to a specific user.
◆ Send UDDI request messages.

The Indri tool provides a GUI interface to access the registry server database. To start the Indri tool, execute the following command at the command prompt:

`<JWSDP_HOME>/samples/registry-server> registry-server-test run-indri`

The output is displayed in Figure 14-2.

The GUI interface of Indri is displayed in Figure 14-3.

Working with Service Registries by Using JAXR

Service registries allow you to publish, access, and use Web services. Service brokers host Service registries that can implement different registry standards, such as UDDI, OASIS, and ebXML.

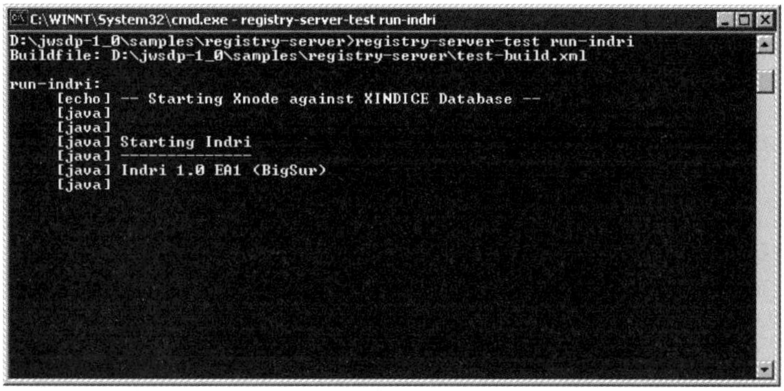

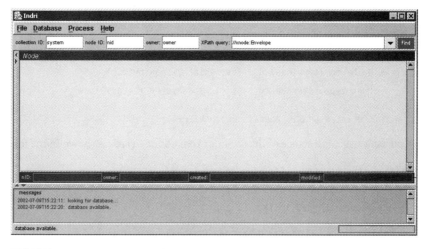

FIGURE 14-2 *The output of the command to run Indri.*

FIGURE 14-3 *The GUI interface of Indri.*

Microsoft and IBM provide registries that implement UDDI Version 2. You can use these test registries to publish your service by accessing the following links:

- http://uddi.rte.microsoft.com/
- http://www3.ibm.com/services/uddi/v2beta/protect/
- registry.html

In Java, you can use different applications to publish or access registered services. These registered services can implement different registry standards. JAXR helps you work with disparate registries. For example, you can use JAXR in your application to search for services in the IBM registry. Similarly, you can use JAXR to publish your service and manage your service data in some registries that might implement other registry standards.

The following two packages are used to encapsulate the complexities of working with registries in the Java service model:

◆ javax.xml.registry

◆ javax.xml.registry.infomodel

 TIP

To use JAXR in your application, you need to import these packages.

We will now discuss the code sample that uses JAXR. When you create an application, you need to create an instance of the `Properties` class, which specifies the URL of the UDDI registry. Instead of the UDDI registry, you can specify the URL of the IBM test query registry:

```
Properties properties = new Properties();
            properties.setProperty("javax.xml.registry.queryManagerURL",
"http://www-3.ibm.com/services/uddi/testregistry/inquiryapi");
            properties.setProperty("javax.xml.registry.factoryClass",
"com.sun.xml.registry.uddi.ConnectionFactoryImpl");
```

Next, you can create an instance of the `ConnectionFactory` class, as shown in the following code:

```
ConnectionFactory factory = ConnectionFactory.newInstance();
factory.setProperties(properties);
con = factory.createConnection();
```

You need to obtain a `BusinessQueryManager` object for performing simple queries. To obtain the `BusinessQueryManager` object, you first need to obtain the `RegistryService` object. The following code discusses how to obtain the `RegistryService` object and use it to create an object of the `BusinessQueryManager` type:

```
RegistryService rs = con.getRegistryService();
        BusinessQueryManager bqm = rs.getBusinessQueryManager();
```

To query an UDDI registry for an organization, you can use the `findOrganization()` method. The usage of the `findOrganization()` method is shown in the following code:

```
Collection fq = new ArrayList();
        fq.add(col.SORT_BY_NAME_ASC);
            Collection np = new ArrayList();
            np.add("%OrganizationName%");
        BulkResponse resp = busQryMgr.findOrganizations(fq, np, null,
null, null, null);
```

Observe in the code that the findOrganization() method returns a BulkResponse object. The BulkResponse object is used to obtain the Collection objects. After you obtain the Collection objects, you can iterate through these objects to locate the Organization object.

In the preceding code, notice the add() method. You can hard-code the organization name you want to query in the add() method. Alternatively, you can use a command-line argument that represents an organization name.

The following code shows how to locate the Organization object:

```
Collection org = response.getCollection();
          Iterator itr = org.iterator();
          while (itr.hasNext())
          {
                Organization orgs = (Organization) itr.next();
          }
```

After you locate the Organization object, you can use it to obtain a collection of the services that the organization offers. The following code prints the service information and shows how you can obtain the service information:

```
Collection servcoll = orgs.getServices();
  Iterator servitr = servcoll.iterator();
      while (servitr.hasNext())
      {
            Service serviceinfo = (Service) servitr.next();
            System.out.println(" SERVICE NAME:" + serviceinfo.getName().getValue());
            System.out.println("SERVICE DESCRIPTION:" +
serviceinfo.getDescription().getValue());
      }
```

In addition to querying registries, you can perform simple queries on registries and use JAXR in your application to register your service in a registry. You can also delete your service from a registry by using JAXR.

Processing XML Documents by Using JAXP

In the Java service model, information is exchanged in the form of XML documents. Therefore, developers for the Java service model often need to process XML documents from within Java applications. JAXP enables developers to easily access, process, and transform XML documents.

As you know, JAXP parses the XML documents by using the SAX or DOM parsers. JAXP encapsulates the complexities of using SAX and DOM APIs from Java applications to parse XML documents.

JAXP also enables you to switch effortlessly between different vendor-specific parsers. You can switch between parsers without needing to recompile your Java application. JAXP also supports the format transformation of XML documents by using XSLT.

 NOTE

You can download the Java API for XML Processing Specification 1.1 from http://java.sun.com/Download5.

To process XML documents by using JAXP, you need to perform the following steps:

◆ Start the JWSDP and include xercesImpl.jar in the classpath.

◆ Create an XML document called organization.xml that provides information about organizations.

◆ Create a DTD with the name organization.dtd to which your XML document should conform.

We will now discuss the content of these files.

organization.dtd File

The code of the organization.dtd file is as follows:

```
<?xml encoding="UTF-8"?>
<!ELEMENT organization (organizationinfo*)>
<!ELEMENT stockinfo (name, address,services)>
<!ELEMENT name (#PCDATA)>
<!ELEMENT address (#PCDATA)>
```

organization.xml File

The code of the organization.xml file is as shown:

```
<?xml version="1.0" encoding="UTF-8"?>
<!DOCTYPE organization SYSTEM "organization.dtd">
    <organization>
        <organizationinfo>
            <name>ABC Services</name>
            <address>New York</address>
            <services>Currency converter service</services>
        </organizationinfo>
        <organizationinfo>
```

```
        <name>Infotech Systems Inc</name>
        <address>Washington</address>
        <services>Weather report service</services>
    </organizationinfo>
</organization>
```

OrganizationInfo *Class*

To parse the XML document and display the result, create a Java class with the name `OrganizationInfo`. The packages that you need to import are as listed:

```
import java.io.*;
import org.xml.sax.*;
import org.xml.sax.helpers.*;
import javax.xml.parsers.*;
```

The `OrganizationInfo` class extends the `DefaultHandler` class. In the `OrganizationInfo` class, you need to implement the required callback methods that the parser calls. The following code illustrates the implementations of the required callback methods:

```
public void startDocument() throws SAXException
{
    System.out.println("\nOrganization Information");
}
  public void endDocument() throws SAXException
{
    System.out.println("\nInformation Display Completed");
}
    public void characters(char[] ch, int start, int length) throws SAXException
{
    System.out.println(new String(ch, start, length));
}
```

Next, create an object of the `OrganizationInfo` class in the `main()` method of the `OrganizationInfo` class. Then create an instance of the `SAXParser` class. Using this instance, parse the XML document, organization.xml. The following code illustrates the `main()` method of the `OrganizationInfo` class:

```
public static void main(String[] args) {
    try
    {
        OrganizationInfo orginfo = new OrganizationInfo();
```

```
        SAXParserFactory fact = SAXParserFactory.newInstance();
        SAXParser parser = fact.newSAXParser();
        parser.parse(new File("organization.xml"), orginfo);
    }
    catch (Exception e)
    {
        e.printStackTrace();
    }
}
```

Compile and run the `OrganizationInfo` class.

Performing Service Message Transactions by Using JAXM

As discussed in Chapter 13, JAXM enables you to create, send, and receive SOAP messages. JAXM conforms to SOAP version 1.1 and SOAP with Attachment specifications.

A JAXM client can use a messaging provider, which is a service that transmits messages. JAXM provides the following packages to perform messaging in the Java service model:

- ◆ javax.xml.messaging
- ◆ javax.xml.SOAP

In the applications used, you provide the URL of the receiver of a message. The `SoapConnection` object obtains a connection directly to the receiver. The `SoapConnection` object is obtained from the factory class `SoapConnectionFactory`. The code for specifying the URL of the receiver and obtaining a connection is shown in the following snippet:

```
URLEndpoint endpoint = new
URLEndpoint("http://www.receiverurl.com/message");
SOAPConnectionFactory soapConnectionFact =
SOAPConnectionFactory.newInstance();
SOAPConnection connection = soapConnectionFact.createConnection();
```

After you obtain a connection, you need to create a SOAP message. You then obtain the various parts of the SOAP message to add your message content. The following code illustrates how to add contents to a SOAP message:

```
MessageFactory messageFact = MessageFactory.newInstance();
    SOAPMessage soapMessage = messageFact.createMessage();
    SOAPPart soapPart=message.getSOAPPart();
    SOAPEnvelope soapEnvelope - soapPart.getEnvelope();
        SOAPHeader soapHeader = envelope.getHeader();
        SOAPBody soapBody = envelope.getBody();
            Name name = soapEnvelope.createName("messaging", "message",
```

```
"http://www.myreceiver.com/message/");
            SOAPBodyElement soapBodyElement =
soapBody.addBodyElement(soapBodyElement);
```

After you add contents to the SOAP message, save the message and send it to the receiver. The following code illustrates how to send the SOAP message to a receiver:

```
soapMessage.saveChanges();
SOAPMessage response = connection.call(message, endpoint);
```

You can use the **SOAPMessage** object to print the receiver's response.

Tomcat Administration Tool

The Tomcat Administration tool, also known as admintool, configures the behavior of the Tomcat JSP container. You can save the changes persistently that you made to the Tomcat container by using the admintool. This ensures that the changes are in effect when the Tomcat server restarts. Otherwise, the changes remain effective during the current session only.

Running the Admintool

To run the admintool, you need to start Tomcat by executing the following command at the command prompt:

```
C:\> startup
```

After you start Tomcat, type the following address in the address bar of your Web browser:

```
http://localhost:8080\admin
```

The login interface to the admintool is displayed in Figure 14-4.

As you can see, you need to provide your username and password. A user can be assigned the role of admin, manager, and provider. By default, the user is assigned to all three roles. The username and password are specified in the tomcat-users.xml file. The tomcat-users.xml can be found at the <JWSDP_HOME>/conf directory. A sample tomcat-users.xml is shown here:

```
<?xml version='1.0'?>
<tomcat-users>
  <role rolename="admin"/>
  <role rolename="manager"/>
  <role rolename="provider"/>
  <user username="username" password="password" roles="admin,manager,provider"/>
</tomcat-users>
```

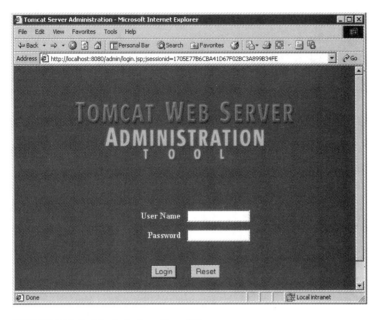

FIGURE 14-4 *The login interface of Tomcat.*

After successful logon, the interface, as shown in Figure 14-5, is displayed.

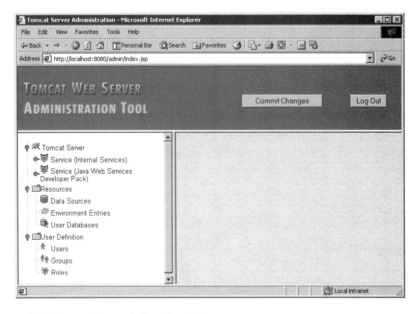

FIGURE 14-5 *The main interface of Tomcat.*

Notice that in Figure 14-5, the admintool provides you with access to various elements that can be configured. These elements are listed in the left pane of the interface. These elements are one of three main categories:

◆ Tomcat server elements

◆ Resource elements

◆ Elements for user definitions

The interface to configure Tomcat server properties is displayed in Figure 14-6.

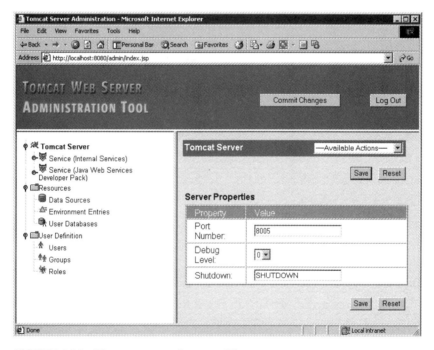

FIGURE 14-6 *The server properties page of Tomcat.*

In the interface, as shown in Figure 14-5, you can perform and save the changes. You have the option of saving the changes either for the current session or persistently. To save the changes for the current session, you need to click the Save button. To save the changes persistently, you need to click the Commit Changes button. When you click the Commit Changes button, the changes are saved to the <JWSDP_HOME>/conf/server.xml file.

The elements in the Resources group represent global JNDI resources. You can configure the following resources by using the admintool:

◆ Data sources

◆ Environment entries

◆ User databases

The interface to configure environment entries is displayed in Figure 14-7.

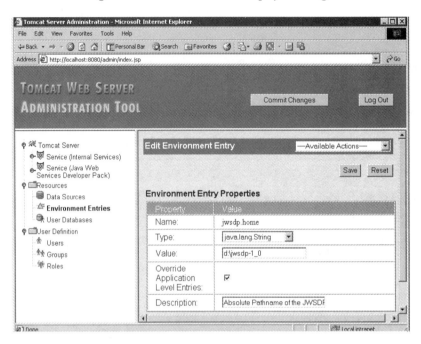

FIGURE 14-7 *The Environment Properties page.*

Authenticating Users to Access Web Services

When you're designing Web services, you need to decide the types of users who will access them. Not all users should be given the right to access all services. The Tomcat user authentication service includes the following:

♦ **Role.** Role is used to identify the set of resources you are allowed to access.

♦ **User.** User is authenticated individually.

♦ **Group.** Group is a set of users.

♦ **Realm.** Realm is a set of roles, users, and groups that identifies the valid users of a Web service.

The User page of the Tomcat server is displayed in Figure 14-8.

You can use this interface to create new users or delete existing ones. You can do this by selecting the appropriate option from the Edit Existing User Properties list box, shown in Figure 14-9.

If you select the Create New User option from the drop-down list, the User Properties interface is displayed in the right pane of the admintool interface, as shown in Figure 14-10.

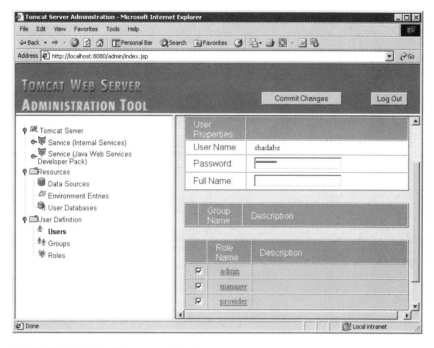

FIGURE 14-8 *The User page of the Tomcat server.*

FIGURE 14-9 *The Edit Existing User Properties list box.*

You can specify user details in the screen displayed in Figure 14-9. When you save the changes, the tomcat-users.xml file is modified, as shown in the following code:

```xml
<?xml version='1.0'?>
<tomcat-users>
    <role rolename="admin"/>
    <role rolename="user"/>
    <role rolename="manager"/>
    <role rolename="provider"/>
    <user username="user1" password="password1" roles="admin,manager,provider"/>
    <user username="user2" password="password2" roles="user"/>
</tomcat-users>
```

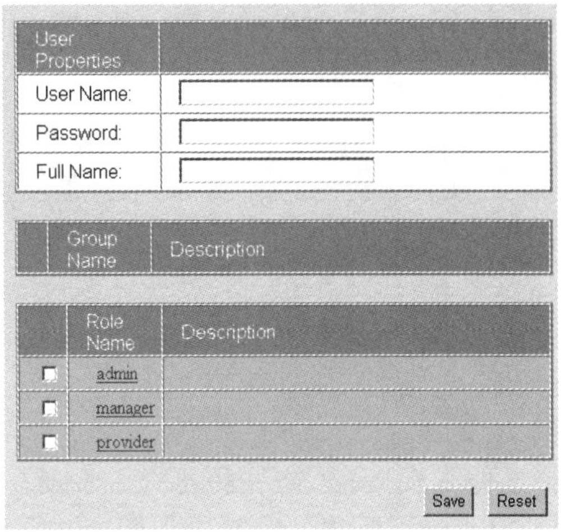

FIGURE 14-10 *The interface for creating new users.*

After saving the changes, you can log out of the admintool by clicking on the Log Out button.

Web Application Deployment Tool

JWSDP provides a tool for deploying Web applications. This tool enables you to create, modify, and delete Web applications. You can start the Application Deployment tool by executing the following command at the command prompt:

```
C:/> deploytool
```

Before allowing you to access the Application Deployment tool, JWSDP prompts you for the administrator's username and password, as shown in Figure 14-11.

You are allowed access to the Application Deployment tool only after authentication. The interface of the Application Deployment tool is displayed in Figure 14-12.

As you can see, Figure 14-12 displays some Web applications that are already deployed in the left pane of the Application Deployment tool.

Creating a Sample Application by Using the Application Deployment Tool

We will now discuss how to develop a sample interest calculator application by using the Application Deployment tool of JWSDP. This will help you understand the procedure for creating an

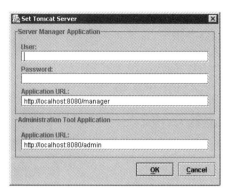

FIGURE 14-11 *The username and password screen.*

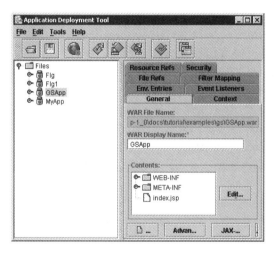

FIGURE 14-12 *The Application Deployment tool.*

application by using the tool; therefore, it will be useful when you create the actual application for your project.

The interest calculator application calculates the interest payable on a specified amount for a specified period and rate of interest. The application consists of two files as listed:

◆ Interest_calc.htm

◆ Interest_calc.jsp

Interest_calc.htm File

The Interest_calc.htm file displays a form to the user. In this form, the user enters the following information into the appropriate text boxes:

◆ Principal amount

◆ Period

◆ Rate of interest

When the user submits the form after providing the values, the values are passed to a JSP page, which calculates and displays the result to the user.

The code for the Interest_calc.htm is as follows:

```
<html>
    <head>
        <title>Interest Calculator</title>
    </head>
    <body bgproperties="fixed" bgcolor="#CCCCFF">
        <p></p>
        <p align="center"><b><font size="4">Interest Calculator</font></b></p>
        <form method="POST" action="Interest_calc.jsp">
         <p><font size="4">Enter Principal Amount:</font><font
size="4" color="#FF0000">    
        </font><input type="text" name="amount" size="20"></p>
        <p ><font size="4">Enter Period in Months:</font><font
size="4" color="#FF0000">    
        </font><input type="text" name="period" size="20"></p>
        <p ><font size="4">Enter Rate of Interest:</font><font
size="4" color="#FF0000">      
        </font><input type="text" name="int_rate" size="20"></p>
        <p><font size="4">Interest
        Payable:</font><font size="4"
color="#FF0000">         &n
bsp;  
          </font><input type="text" name="int_pay" size="20"></p>
        <p align="center"><input type="submit" value="Submit"
name="Submit"><input type="reset" value="Reset" name="Reset"></p>
        </form>
    </body>
</html>
```

Interest_calc.jsp File

The Interest_calc.jsp file accesses the values that the user enters into the HTML page. The JSP page performs calculation on these values and displays the calculated interest to the user.

The code for the Interest_calc.jsp file is as follows:

```
<title>Interest Calculator</title>
<%@ page language = "java" %>
    <body bgproperties="fixed" bgcolor="#CCCCFF">
    <p></p>
    <p align="center"><b><font size="4">Interest Calculator</font></b></p>
    <p><font size="4">Enter Principal Amount: 
    </font>  <%= (String)request.getParameter("amount") %>
    <%! double amnt=0; %>
    <%
        String str1;
        str1=request.getParameter("amount");
        str1=str1.trim();
        amnt=Double.parseDouble(str1);
      %>
    </p>
    <p ><font size="4">Enter Period in Months: </font>
    <%= (String)request.getParameter("period") %>
    <%
        double prd=0;
        String str2=request.getParameter("period");
        str2=str2.trim();
        prd=Double.parseDouble(str2);
    %>
    </p>
    <p ><font size="4">Enter Rate of Interest: </font>
        <%= (String)request.getParameter("int_rate") %>
        <%
            double rate=0;
             String str3=request.getParameter("int_rate");
            str3=str3.trim();
            rate=Double.parseDouble(str3);
        %>
    </p>
    <p><font size="4">Interest
    Payable: </font>
    <% double tot_int=(rate*prd*amnt)/100;
```

```
        out.println(tot_int);
%>
</p>
    <form method="POST" action="Interest_calc.htm">
        <p align="center"><input type="submit" value="OK" name="OK" ></p>
    </form>
</body>
</html>
```

Deploying the Interest Calculator Application

Now that you have created the files for the Interest Calculator application, you need to deploy the application. You can use the Application Deployment tool of the JWSDP to deploy the application. To deploy the interest calculator application, you need to perform the following steps:

1. Open the Application Deployment tool by executing the following command at the command prompt:

   ```
   C:/> deploytool
   ```

2. The Application Deployment tool is displayed in Figure 14-13.

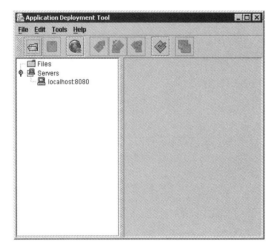

FIGURE 14-13 *The Application Deployment tool of the JWSDP.*

3. Go to File, New Web Application. The Introduction page of the New Web Application Wizard is displayed.

4. Click the Next button. The WAR File page of the wizard is displayed, as shown in Figure 14-14.

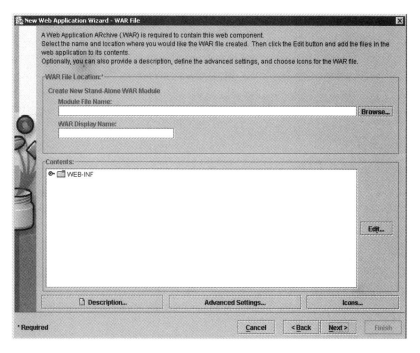

FIGURE 14-14 *The WAR File page of the wizard.*

5. On this page, specify the name and location of the WAR file by clicking on the Browse button. The Choose Module File dialog box is displayed.

6. Select the path and name of the WAR file, as shown in Figure 14-15, and then click on the Choose Module File button.

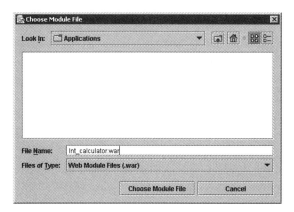

FIGURE 14-15 *The dialog box to specify the WAR file.*

7. The WAR File page of the wizard is displayed again. Specify WAR Display Name as Int_calculator.

8. To specify the contents of the WAR file, click on the Edit button. The Edit Contents of Int_calculator dialog box is displayed, as shown in Figure 14-16.

FIGURE 14-16 *The Edit Contents of Int_calculator dialog box.*

9. Select the Interest_calc.htm and Interest_calc.jsp files and click on the Add button. The files are displayed in the Contents of Int_calculator box, as displayed in Figure 14-17.

10. Click the OK button to close the Edit Contents of Int_calculator dialog box.

11. The WAR File page of the wizard is displayed again. Notice that the two selected files are displayed in the Contents box, as shown in Figure 14-18.

12. Click on the Next button.

13. The Choose Component Type page of the New Application Wizard is displayed, as shown in Figure 14-19. You need to select the JSP option button and then click the Next button.

14. The Component General Properties page is displayed. Select the Interest_calc.jsp file from the JSP Filename drop-down list, as shown in Figure 14-20.

15. Click the Next button. The Review Settings dialog box displays the deployment descriptor of the WAR file. This dialog box is shown in Figure 14-21.

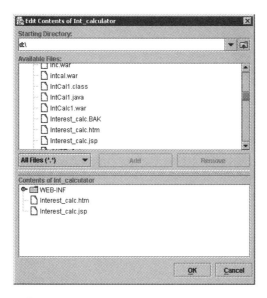

FIGURE 14-17 *The dialog box used to specify the content of the WAR files.*

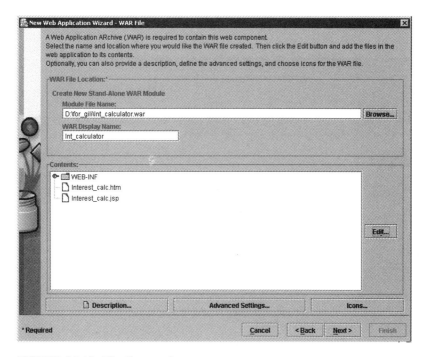

FIGURE 14-18 *The Contents box.*

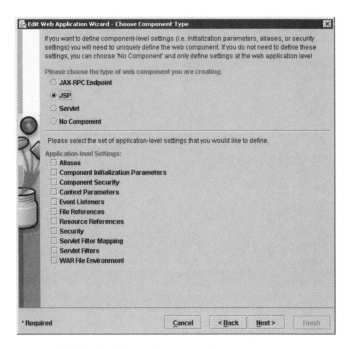

FIGURE 14-19 *The Choose Component Type page.*

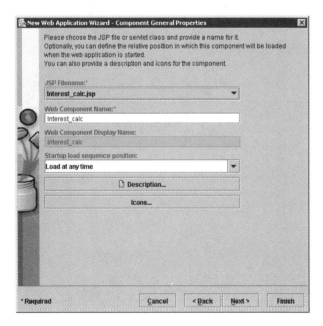

FIGURE 14-20 *The Component General Properties page.*

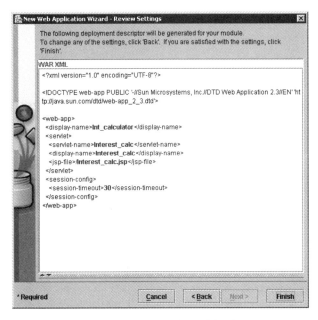

FIGURE 14-21 *The Review Settings dialog box.*

16. Click on the Finish button. The Application Deployment tool is displayed again. The WAR file that you created is displayed in the left pane, as shown in Figure 14-22.

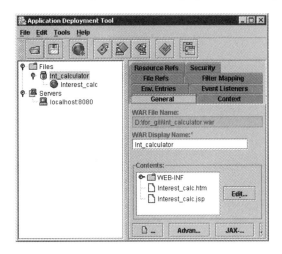

FIGURE 14-22 *The Application Deployment tool with the WAR file.*

17. You have created the WAR file. To deploy it, go to the Tools menu and select Deploy.

18. In the Text Input Dialog dialog box, specify the Web context of the WAR file, as shown in Figure 14-23.

FIGURE 14-23 *The Text Input Dialog dialog box.*

19. The Deployment Console dialog box displays the status of the deployment. Click on the Close button when the deployment is complete.

Running the Interest Calculator Application

You have now deployed the interest calculator application. The application is ready to be executed. To run the interest calculator application, type the following command in the address bar of the Web browser:

```
http://localhost:8080/Int_calculator/Interest_calc.htm
```

The interest calculator is displayed. You need to enter a principal amount, interest rate, and period values, as displayed in Figure 14-24.

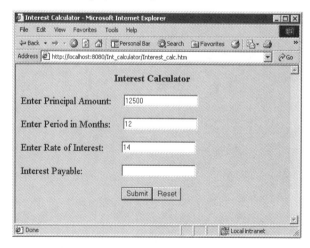

FIGURE 14-24 *The form for entering the values.*

When you click the Submit button, the values are passed to the JSP page, Interest_calc.jsp, which calculates and displays the result, shown in Figure 14-25.

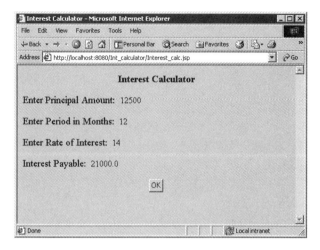

FIGURE 14-25 *The calculated interest.*

Ant Build Tool

JWSDP includes a Java-based Ant tool, which is portable across different platforms. You can use the Ant tool, developed by the Apache Software Foundation, to deploy the Web services. The configuration files of the Ant tool are XML based. An object that implements the particular task interface runs each task in the object tree of XML. Because the Ant tool is Java based, you can execute it on any platform.

The Ant tool is installed as part of the JWSDP. You can use it to manage the compilation of Java code and determine the hierarchy of the deployed application. A build file, called build.xml, controls the tasks that the Ant tool performs.

A sample build.xml is shown in the following code:

```
<!DOCTYPE project>
<project name="JAX-RPC: message" default="setdir" basedir=".">
  <property environment="env" />
  <property file="build.properties"/>
  <target name="setdir"
    description="Creates build directory" >
    <message message="Creating the directories..." />
    <mkdir dir="${build.dir}/${example-dir}" />
  </target>
  <target name="compile-server" depends="setdir"
      description="Compiles server-side code">
```

```xml
            <message message="Compiling server-side code..."/>
            <javac
                srcdir="."
                destdir="${build.dir}"
                includes="*.java"
                excludes="*Client.java"
            />
    </target>
    <target name="xrpcc" depends="setdir"
        description="Runs the xrpcc tool for the example.">
        <message message="Running xrpcc:"/>
        <message message="${xrpcc} -classpath ${build.dir} -both -keep -d
${build.dir} config.xml"/>
        <message message="xrpcc is running..."/>
        <exec executable="${xrpcc}">
            <arg line="-classpath ${build.dir}" />
            <arg line="-both" />
            <arg line="-keep" />
            <arg line="-d ${build.dir}" />
            <arg line="config.xml" />
        </exec>
    </target>
    <target name="compile-client" depends="setdir"
        description="Compiles client-side code">
        <message message="Compiling client code"/>
    <javac
            srcdir="."
            destdir="${build.dir}"
            classpath="${cpath}"
            includes="*Client.java"
        />
    </target>
    <target name="packagewar" depends="setdir"
        description="Builds WAR file">
        <message message="Building war file"/>
        <war warfile="${war-file}" webxml="web.xml">
            <classes dir="${build.dir}"
```

```
                        includes="${example-dir}/**" />
            <webinf dir="${build.dir}"
                        includes="${webinf-config}" />
        </war>
    </target>
    <target name="deploy"
        description="Copies WAR file to Catalina">
        <message message="Copying war file to webapps..."/>
        <copy
            file="${war-file}"
            todir="${CATALINA_HOME}/webapps"
            overwrite="yes"
        />
    </target>
    <target name="run"
        description="Runs client">
        <message message="Running the client..." />
<message message=" " />
        <java
            fork="on"
            classpath="${cpath}"
            classname="${client-class}" >
            <arg value="${endpoint}" />
            <!-- <classpath  refid="jaxpack-classpath" /> -->
        </java>
    </target>
</project>
```

As you can see from the preceding code, you can use the build.xml file to perform the following tasks:

- Create a build directory.
- Compile server-side code.
- Run the xrpcc tool.
- Compile client-side code.
- Build the WAR file.
- Copy the WAR file to Catalina.
- Run the client.

Some of the built-in tasks that the Ant tool performs are as follows:

♦ Copy a file or a set of files to a new file or a directory.

♦ Delete a file or a directory along with the files and subdirectories it encloses.

♦ Create a directory.

♦ Create a JAR file.

♦ Compile Java files.

♦ Execute Java files.

♦ Create a zip file.

 NOTE

You can view the complete list of the Ant built-in tasks at the http://jakarta.apache.org/ant/manual/coretasklist.html site.

To run the Ant tool, type the following command at the command prompt:

```
C:/> ant
```

This is the syntax of the `ant` command:

```
ant [options] [target [ target2 [target 3] ..]…]
```

If no parameter is passed with the command, the Ant tool looks for a build.xml file in the current directory. To search for a build.xml file, you can use the `-find` option with the `ant` command. When you use the `-find` option, the Ant tool searches for a build.xml file in the parent directory. The Ant tool searches until the root directory of the file system is reached. The other command-line options used with the Ant tool are discussed in Table 14-1.

Table 14-1 Command-Line Options Used with the Ant Tool

Option	Description
-help	This option prints the usage statement of the `ant` command.
-Projecthelp	This option prints project help information.
-version	This option prints version information.
-quiet	This option suppresses the output that is displayed during the compilation of a build.xml file.
-verbose	This option works differently from the `-quiet` option. It enables the display of output during the compilation of the build.xml file.

Option	Description
-debug	This option prints debugging information.
-logfile file	This option specifies a file for log output.
-logger classname	This option specifies the class that performs the logon operation.
-listener classname	This option specifies a class used as a project listener.
-buildfile file	This option instructs the Ant tool to use the specified build.xml file.
-Dproperty=value	This option sets the specified property to a specified value.

We will now discuss how to create a simple Web service and deploy it by using the Ant tool.

Sample Message Web Service

In this section, you will learn how to implement a simple Web service that sends a message. This message is sent to the service endpoint and then back to the client. The service definition code for the Message service is as follows:

```
package Message;
import java.rmi.Remote;
import java.rmi.RemoteException;
public interface MessageIF extends Remote
{
    public String Message(String str) throws RemoteException;
}
```

In the preceding code, you first need to import the rmi package because the JAX-RPC messaging model is based on Java's RMI method invocation. The methods declared in the MessageIF interface throw a RemoteException exception to ensure compliance with the JAX-RPC specifications.

 NOTE

The specifications state that all mappings of wsdl:operation to the Java type should throw the RemoteException exception and any other application-specific exceptions.

The code uses the MessageIF interface that extends the Remote interface. The MessageImpl class, provided by the MessageIF interface, implements the service definitions. The code for the MessageImpl class is as follows:

```
package Message;

public class MessageImpl implements MessageIF
{
    public String Message(String msg)
    {
        System.out.println("Messaging" + msg+ " back to the client...");
        return new String("Messaging... " + msg);
    }
}
```

You should compile these files using the Ant Build tool, which is packaged with the JWSDP. You should place the files in a single directory.

build.xml File

To run the Ant tool on the files, you first need to create a build script. The build script controls the tasks that the Ant tool performs. The build script is shown in the following code:

```
<!DOCTYPE project>
<project name="JAX-RPC: Message" default="setdir" basedir=".">
  <property environment="env" />
  <property file="build.properties"/>
  <target name="setdir"
     description="Creates build directory" >
     <message message="Creating the directories..." />
     <mkdir dir="${build.dir}/${example-dir}" />
  </target>
  <target name="compile-server" depends="setdir"
      description="Compiles server-side code">
      <message message="Compiling server-side code..."/>
      <javac
         srcdir="."
         destdir="${build.dir}"
         includes="*.java"
         excludes="*Client.java"
      />
  </target>
  <target name="xrpcc" depends="setdir"
      description="Runs the xrpcc tool for the example.">
```

```xml
        <message message="Running xrpcc:"/>
        <message message="${xrpcc} -classpath ${build.dir} -both -keep -d
${build.dir} config.xml"/>
        <message message="xrpcc is running..."/>
        <exec executable="${xrpcc}">
            <arg line="-classpath ${build.dir}" />
            <arg line="-both" />
            <arg line="-keep" />
            <arg line="-d ${build.dir}" />
            <arg line="config.xml" />
        </exec>
    </target>
    <target name="compile-client" depends="setdir"
        description="Compiles client-side code"  >
        <message message="Compiling client code..."/>
 <javac
        srcdir="."
        destdir="${build.dir}"
        classpath="${cpath}"
        includes="*Client.java"
    />
    </target>
    <target name="packagewar" depends="setdir"
        description="Builds WAR file">
        <message message="Building war file..."/>
        <war warfile="${war-file}" webxml="web.xml">
            <classes dir="${build.dir}"
                    includes="${example-dir}/**" />
            <webinf dir="${build.dir}"
                    includes="${webinf-config}" />
        </war>
    </target>
    <target name="deploy"
        description="Copies WAR file to Catalina">
        <message message="Copying war file to webapps"/>
        <copy
           file="${war-file}"
           todir="${CATALINA_HOME}/webapps"
```

```
              overwrite="yes"
          />
    </target>
    <target name="run"
        description="Runs client">
        <message message="Running the client" />
<message message=" " />
        <java
            fork="on"
            classpath="${cpath}"
            classname="${client-class}" >
          <arg value="${endpoint}" />
          <!-- <classpath  refid="jaxpack-classpath" /> -->
        </java>
    </target>
</project>
```

Save the preceding code as the build.xml file. Place the Java files and the build.xml files in the same directory.

build.properties File

In addition to the build.xml and Java files, you need to create a build.properties file in the same directory. The build.properties file contains the username and password. This username and password is set up at installation time. The content of the build.properties file is shown in the following code:

```
# This file is referenced by the build.xml file.

release-version=Java(tm) Web Services Developer Pack EA1


script-suffix=bat
PACK_HOME=${env.JWSDP_HOME}
CATALINA_HOME=${env.JWSDP_HOME}
build.dir=build
webinf-config=MyMessage_Config.properties
xrpcc=${PACK_HOME}/bin/xrpcc.${script-suffix}
clib=${PACK_HOME}/common/lib
jwsdp-jars=${clib}/jaxrpc-ri.jar:${clib}/jaxrpc-api.jar:${clib}/
activation.jar:${clib}/dom4j.jar:${clib}/jaxm-api.jar:${clib}/jaxm-
client.jar:${clib}/log4j.jar:${clib}/mail.jar:${clib}/xalan.jar:${clib}/xerces.jar
```

```
cpath=${jwsdp-jars}:${build.dir}

example-dir=message
client-class=MessageClient
endpoint=http://localhost:8080/jaxrpc-message/jaxrpc/MessageIF
webapps-subdir=jaxrpc-message
war-file=${webapps-subdir}.war
```

TIP

Ensure that the environment variable, JWSDP_HOME, is set properly. The JWSDP_HOME variable should point to the home directory of the JWSDP. In addition, the PATH variable should be set to the <JWSDP_HOME>\bin directory.

You need to compile the Java files by using the Ant tool. Type the following command at the command prompt:

```
ant compile-server
```

TIP

While you're executing the preceding command, ensure that you are in the same directory where you have stored the Java file, the build.properties file, and the build.xml file.

The output that is displayed when you execute the command is shown in Figure 14-26.

FIGURE 14-26 *The output of the* ant *COMPILE-SERVER COMMAND.*

After successful execution of the ant compile-server command, two class files—MessageIF.class and MessageImpl.class—are created under the \build\message directory.

Configuration File

Next, you need to create a configuration file that allows you to create a WSDL definition of your class file. The structure of the configuration file is as follows:

```xml
<?xml version="1.0" encoding="UTF-8"?>
 <configuration
 xmlns="http://java.sun.com/jax-rpc-ri/xrpcc-config">
   <rmi name="Name"
        targetNamespace="Target Namespace for WSDL"
        typeNamespace="Target Namespace for the schema">
     <service name="Service Name"
        packageName="package name">
    <interface name=" Fully qualified name of the interface"
                servantName="Fully qualified name of the Impl"
                soapAction="Optional SoapAction string"
                soapActionBase="Optional prefix for SoapAction"/>
     </service>
    <typeMappingRegistry>
    Optional type mapping information
    </typeMappingRegistry>
    </rmi>
 </configuration>
```

The code for the configuration file, config.xml, is as follows:

```xml
<?xml version="1.0" encoding="UTF-8"?>
<configuration
    xmlns="http://java.sun.com/jax-rpc-ri/xrpcc-config">
    <rmi name="MessageService"
        targetNamespace="http://messageuri.com/wsdl"
        typeNamespace="http://messageuri.com/types">
        <service name="MyMessage" packageName="message">
        <interface name="message.MessageIF"
            servantName="message.MessageImpl"/>
        </service>
    </rmi>
</configuration>
```

```
    <types/>
    <message name="message">
      <part name="String_1" type="xsd:string"/>
    </message>
    <message name="messageResponse">
      <part name="result" type="xsd:string"/>
    </message>
    <portType name="MessageIFPortType">
      <operation name="message">
        <input message="tns:message"/>
        <output message="tns:messageResponse"/>
      </operation>
    </portType>
    <binding name="MessageIFBinding" type="tns:MessageIFPortType">
      <operation name="message">
        <input>
          <soap:body encodingStyle="http://schemas.xmlsoap.org/soap/encoding/"
use="encoded" namespace="http://someuri.com/wsdl"/>
        </input>
        <output>
          <soap:body encodingStyle="http://schemas.xmlsoap.org/soap/encoding/"
use="encoded" namespace="http://someuri.com/wsdl"/>
        </output>
        <soap:operation soapAction=""/></operation>
      <soap:binding transport="http://schemas.xmlsoap.org/soap/http" style="rpc"/>
      </binding>
    <service name="MyMessage">
      <port name="MessageIFPort" binding="tns:MessageIFBinding">
        <soap:address location="REPLACE_WITH_ACTUAL_URL"/>
      </port>
    </service>
</definitions>
```

After you finish generating the appropriate stubs, ties, and configuration files, the next step is to prepare a deployment descriptor for the Apache Tomcat server that is bundled with the JWSDP. Creating the deployment descriptor for the Apache Tomcat server is explained in the following section.

Creating the Deployment Descriptor for the Apache Tomcat Server

The web.xml file contains the deployment descriptor. The deployment descriptor contains various deployment details. The deployment descriptor is shown in the following code:

```xml
<?xml version="1.0" encoding="UTF-8"?>

<!DOCTYPE web-app
    PUBLIC "-//Sun Microsystems, Inc.//DTD Web Application 2.3//EN"
    "http://java.sun.com/j2ee/dtds/web-app_2_3.dtd">

<web-app>
    <display-name>
MessageApplication
    </display-name>
    <description>
Message Application
    </description>
    <servlet>
        <servlet-name>
JAXRPCEndpoint
 </servlet-name>
        <display-name>
JAXRPCEndpoint
 </display-name>
        <description>
Endpoint for Message Application
 </description>
        <servlet-class>
com.sun.xml.rpc.server.http.JAXRPCServlet
</servlet-class>
        <init-param>
            <param-name>
configuration.file
    </param-name>
            <param-value>
/WEB-INF/MyMessage_Config.properties
    </param-value>
```

```
        </init-param>
        <load-on-startup>
0
        </load-on-startup>
    </servlet>
    <servlet-mapping>
        <servlet-name>
JAXRPCEndpoint
 </servlet-name>
        <url-pattern>
/jaxrpc/*
 </url-pattern>
    </servlet-mapping>
    <session-config>
        <session-timeout>
60
 </session-timeout>
    </session-config>
</web-app>
```

In the preceding deployment descriptor, the servlet mappings are specified to the servlet, `com.sun.xml.rpc.server.http.JAXRPCServlet`. This servlet obtains the configuration details from the Message_Config.properties file. You should copy this file under the /WEB-INF directory of the webapps\root directory of the Tomcat container.

Similar to the Message_Config.properties file, the web.xml file is also saved under the WEB-INF directory. If you do not want to manually move these files to the appropriate directories, you can package the contents into a WAR file and deploy it on the server using the Ant tool.

Packaging Service in a WAR File

Next, you need to pack the service in the WAR file. To package the service definition into a WAR file, execute the following command at the command prompt:

```
ant packagewar
```

When you execute the preceding command successfully, you should be able to locate a jaxrpc-message.war file under the current directory.

The following files are packaged in the jaxrpc-message.war file:

◆ Service definition interfaces
◆ Service definition classes

◆ xrpcc-generated files

◆ Classes for pluggable serializers and deserializers

◆ Other files required by the service implementation classes

◆ A file containing the deployment descriptor

◆ A WSDL file that describes the service (optional)

Deploying the Packaged File

The next step after creating the WAR package is to deploy the package in the Tomcat container. To deploy the package, execute the following command at the command prompt:

```
ant deploy
```

The output of the preceding command is displayed in Figure 14-27.

FIGURE 14-27 *The output of the* ant deploy *COMMAND.*

> **NOTE**
>
> When you execute the ant deploy command, a WAR file is created and placed in the <JWSDP_HOME> \webapps directory. Therefore, in this example, the jaxrpc-message.war file is created in the <JWSDP_HOME> \webapps directory.

Testing the Deployment

You have almost deployed the service to the Web server. To verify the deployment, proceed with the following steps:

1. Start the Tomcat server by executing the following command:

```
startup
```

2. Open a browser window and then type the following URL in the address bar of the browser:

```
http://localhost:8080/jaxrpc-message/jaxrpc
```

After you execute the preceding step, you should be able to view the contents in the Web browser. The output is displayed in Figure 14-28.

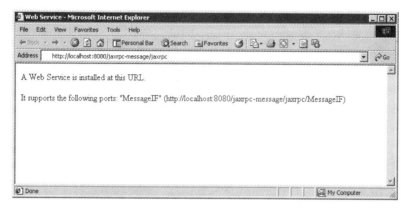

FIGURE 14-28 *The deployment of the Message service.*

Creating a Client Application

Now that you have successfully implemented a service at the endpoint, it is time to create a client to execute the service. The following is the code for the MessageClient program:

```java
package message;
public class MessageClient
{
    public static void main(String[] args)
    {
        try
        {
            MessageIF_Stub stub = (MessageIF_Stub)(new
MyMessageImpl().getMessageIF());
            System.out.println("Obtained the stub object...");
            System.out.println("Setting the target endpoint to " + args[0]);
            stub._setTargetEndpoint(args[0]);
            System.out.println("Invoking the message method on the stub...");
            System.out.println(stub.message("Enter a message..."));
```

```
        }
        catch (Exception ex)
        {
            ex.printStackTrace();
        }
    }
}
```

MessageClient is a standalone program that calls the message operation from the service provider endpoint. You need to compile the service before executing it.

To compile the service, you need to execute the following command:

```
ant compile-client
```

The output of the preceding command is shown in Figure 14-29.

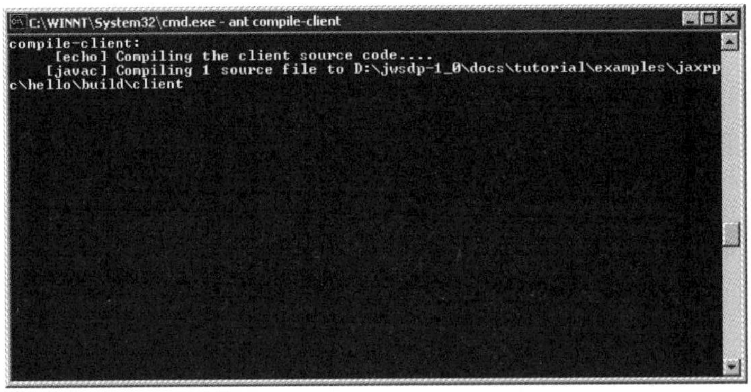

FIGURE 14-29 *The output of the* ant compile *CLIENT COMMAND.*

To execute the program, you need to execute the following command:

```
ant run
```

The Hello Web Service

In the previous section, we gave an example of a message service. This section discusses another example, the Hello Web service. You will create and deploy the Hello Web service by using JWSDP.

The `HelloIF` Interface

You need to create an interface `HelloIF`, which exposes the service method in a hello directory. The `HelloIF` interface needs to extend the `Remote` interface. The `HelloIF` interface exposes a single method that clients can invoke. The following code listing illustrates the `HelloIF` interface:

```
package hello;
import java.rmi.Remote;
import java.rmi.RemoteException;
public interface HelloIF extends Remote
{
    public String Hello(String str) throws RemoteException;
}
```

Next, you need to implement the `HelloIF` interface in a Java class, `HelloImpl`. The following code listing illustrates the `HelloImpl.java` class:

```
package hello;
public class HelloImpl implements HelloInf
{
    public String hello(String username)
    {
                return new String("Hello " + username +"Welcome to the Hello Web
service!!!");
    }
}
```

build.xml File

You can compile, package, and deploy the Hello service by using the Ant Build tool. To do this, create the build.xml file that the Ant tool uses as the build file. Place the build.xml file in the hello directory. The following code listing illustrates the build.xml file:

```
<!DOCTYPE project>
<project name="My First Service" default="setdir" basedir=".">
  <property environment="env" />
  <property file="build.properties"/>
  <target name="setdir" >
    <mkdir dir="${build.dir}/${example-dir}" />
  </target>
  <target name="compile " depends="setdir"
      >
```

```xml
    <javac
        srcdir="."
        destdir="${build.dir}"
        includes="*.java"
        excludes="*Client.java"
    />
  </target>
  <target name="xrpcc" depends="setdir"
      description="Runs the xrpcc tool for the example.">
      <message message="Running xrpcc:"/>
      <message message="${xrpcc} -classpath ${build.dir} -both -keep -d
${build.dir} config.xml"/>
      <message message="xrpcc is running..."/>
      <exec executable="${xrpcc}">
        <arg line="-classpath ${build.dir}" />
        <arg line="-both" />
        <arg line="-keep" />
        <arg line="-d ${build.dir}" />
        <arg line="config.xml" />
      </exec>
  </target>
  <target name="package" depends="setdir">        <war warfile="${war-
file}" webxml="web.xml">
        <classes dir="${build.dir}"
                    includes="${example-dir}/**" />
        <webinf dir="${build.dir}"
                    includes="${webinf-config}" />
      </war>
  </target>
  <target name="deployservice" >
   <copy
        file="${war-file}"
        todir="${CATALINA_HOME}/webapps"
        overwrite="yes"
      />
  </target>
</project>
```

build.properties File

Create a build.properties file in your hello directory. The build.xml file uses the build.properties file to build your service. The following code listing displays the content of the build.properties file:

```
script-suffix=bat
PACK_HOME=${env.JWSDP_HOME}
CATALINA_HOME=${env.JWSDP_HOME}
build.dir=build
webinf-config=MyHello_Config.properties
xrpcc=${PACK_HOME}/bin/xrpcc.${script-suffix}
clib=${PACK_HOME}/common/lib
jwsdp-jars=${clib}/jaxrpc-ri.jar:${clib}/jaxrpc-api.jar:${clib}/
activation.jar:${clib}/dom4j.jar:${clib}/jaxm-api.jar:${clib}/jaxm-client.jar:${clib}/
log4j.jar:${clib}/mail.jar:${clib}/xalan.jar:${clib}/xerces.jar
cpath=${jwsdp-jars}:${build.dir}
example-dir=hello
client-class=HelloClient
endpoint=http://localhost:8080/jaxrpc-hello/jaxrpc/HelloIF
webapps-subdir=jaxrpc-hello
war-file=${webapps-subdir}.war
```

Compiling the Interface

Next, you need to compile the interface and the implementation files by using the Ant tool. You can do so by executing the following command:

```
ant compile
```

After the successful execution of this command, verify the presence of two class files in the \build\hello directory.

 TIP

You should run the preceding command from the directory where the build.xml file for the Hello Web service is stored.

Configuration File

The next step is to create the config.xml file. The xrpcc tool uses the config.xml file to generate stubs and ties of your implementation class. The xrpcc tool also generates a WSDL file corresponding to the interface.

The code of the config.xml file is as displayed:

```
<?xml version="1.0" encoding="UTF-8"?>
<configuration
    xmlns="http://java.sun.com/jax-rpc-ri/xrpcc-config">
    <rmi name="HelloService"
        targetNamespace="http://Hellouri.com/wsdl"
        typeNamespace="http://Hellouri.com/types">
        <service name="MyHello" packageName="hello">
        <interface name="hello.HelloInf"
            servantName="hello.HelloImpl"/>
        </service>
    </rmi>
</configuration>
```

Now you should run the following command:

```
xrpcc.bat -classpath build -both -d build config.xml
```

The following classes are generated in the ./build/hello directory:

- Hello_RequestStruct.class
- Hello_RequestStruct_SOAPSerializer.class
- Hello_ResponseStruct.class
- Hello_ResponseStruct_SOAPSerializer.class
- HelloInf_Stub.class
- HelloInf_Tie.class
- MyHello.class
- MyHello_Impl.class
- MyHello_SerializerRegistry.class

In addition, the WSDL file, HelloService, is generated in the ./build directory. The build directory also contains a MyHello_Config.properties file.

Packaging the Service

After you generate the required files, you need to package the service as a WAR file and deploy it in the Tomcat container of the JWSDP pack. To package your service, run the following command:

```
ant package
```

Notice the jaxrpc-hello.war file in your hello directory. Run the following command to deploy your service in the Tomcat container:

```
ant deployservice
```

The jaxrpc-hello.war file is copied in the webapps directory of your JWSDP installation.

Run the following command to start the Tomcat container:

```
startup
```

Open your browser and type the following address in the address bar:

```
http://localhost:8080/jaxrpc-hello/jaxrpc
```

A page appears indicating that your service is deployed, as shown in Figure 14-30.

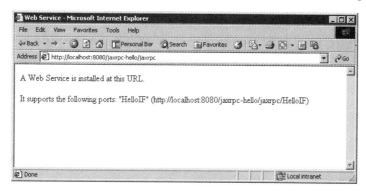

FIGURE 14-30 *The Web service has been deployed.*

Developing a Java Web Service by Using Sun ONE Studio

Sun ONE Studio, known earlier as Forte Tools for Java, is an IDE. You can use Sun ONE Studio to develop and deploy enterprise applications, Web applications, and Web services. Sun ONE Studio currently provides the following editions:

- ◆ Enterprise Edition
- ◆ Community Edition
- ◆ Mobile Edition

To use Sun ONE Studio, you need to install the following software:

- ◆ **Java 2 Platform, Standard Edition (J2SE).** You can download this software from http://java.sun.com/j2se/1.4/download.html.

◆ **Sun ONE Studio.** You can download this software from http://wwws.sun.com/ software/sundev/jde/buy/index.html. However, the available version is a 60-day trial version.

 NOTE

You need to specify the Java HOME and PATH environment variables for J2SE. For Sun ONE Studio, you need to configure the FORTE4J_HOME environment variable. This variable should point to the directory where Sun ONE Studio is installed.

We will now develop a Currency Converter Web service by using Sun ONE Studio Enterprise Edition.

The Currency Converter Web Service

The Currency Converter Web service is used to convert one currency into another. This Web service accepts units of a particular currency and then converts them to another currency. This currency is then displayed as a result. The steps involved in the creation of the Currency Converter Web service are listed next:

◆ Create the directory that will contain the files for the service.

◆ Create a Web service.

◆ Create and implement a class for performing the conversion to the Web service.

◆ Add XML operations.

◆ Add a reference of the implementation method and the XML operator to the service.

◆ Compile the Java files.

◆ Add a client to the Web service.

◆ Run the Web service.

We will now explain how to perform each of these steps.

Creating the Directory

You need to create a directory that will store the files of the Web service. To create a directory, perform the following steps:

1. Start Sun ONE Studio. The main interface that is displayed is shown in Figure 14-31.

2. Open the Explorer window by selecting the Explorer command on the View menu. The Explorer window is displayed as in Figure 14-32.

FIGURE 14-31 *The main interface of Sun ONE Studio.*

FIGURE 14-32 *The Explorer window.*

3. Create a new folder from the Explorer by right-clicking and selecting the `Folder` command on the New menu, as displayed in Figure 14-33.

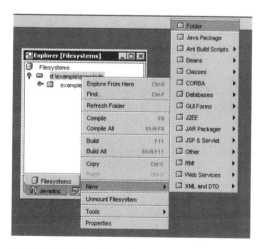

FIGURE 14-33 *The selection of the* `Folder` *COMMAND.*

4. The New Wizard—Folder dialog box is displayed, as shown in Figure 14-34. Specify the folder name and then click on the Finish button. In this example, we have specified the folder name as Currency_Converter.

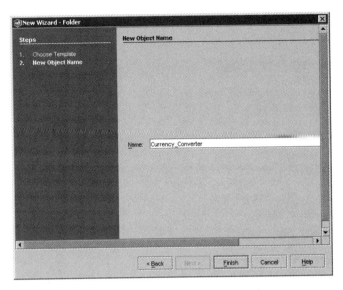

FIGURE 14-34 *The New Wizard—Folder dialog box.*

5. Click on the Finish button. Notice that the Currency_Converter node is added to the Explorer window, as shown in Figure 14-35.

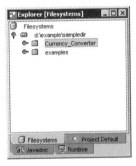

FIGURE 14-35 *The Explorer window.*

Creating the Web Service

As discussed, the next step is to create the Web service. To do this, perform the following steps:

1. Right-click the Currency_Converter folder and select the New, Web Services, Web Service command from the shortcut menu, as shown in Figure 14-36.
2. The New Wizard—Web Service dialog box is displayed. In this dialog box, specify the Web service name as well as other details, as shown in Figure 14-37.

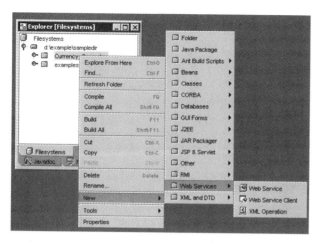

FIGURE 14-36 *The* Web Services *COMMAND ON THE NEW SUBMENU.*

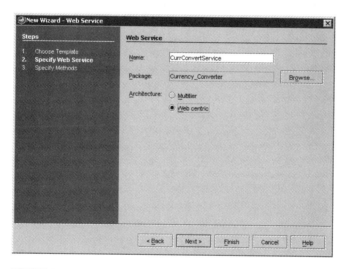

FIGURE 14-37 *The New Wizard—Web Service dialog box.*

3. Click on the Finish button to complete the process. When you click the Finish button, the Explorer window is again displayed, as shown in Figure 14-38.

Creating and Implementing the Class

The next step is to add the implementation class to the service. The class contains methods that will implement the logic of the tasks that the Web service will perform. Carry out the following steps to add the implementation method:

FIGURE 14-38 *The Explorer window.*

1. Select the File, New command. In the New Wizard dialog box that is displayed, select Empty under the Classes folder, as shown in Figure 14-39.

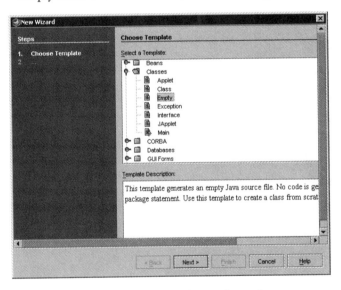

FIGURE 14-39 *The selection of the Empty class option.*

2. Click the Next button. The Target Location page of the New Wizard—Empty dialog box is displayed.

3. Specify the class name as CurrConverter in the Name text box, and then select the package as Currency_Converter, as shown in Figure 14-40.

4. Click the Finish button to close the dialog box. The Explorer window is displayed again with the class name added to it.

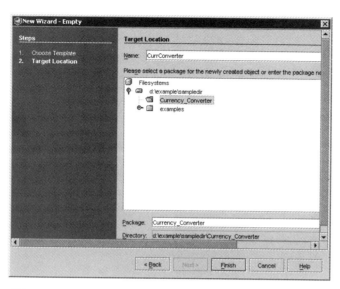

FIGURE 14-40 *The Target Location page.*

FIGURE 14-41 *The Explorer window displays the class that you created.*

5. Add the code to the implementation class. You can do this by adding the code in the Source Editor dialog box, as shown in Figure 14-42.

6. To save the code, right-click and select the Save command from the shortcut menu. Notice in Figure 14-43 that the class name is added to the Explorer window.

7. To compile the class, right-click the class name and select the Compile command from the shortcut menu. The output of the compilation process is displayed in the Output window, as shown in Figure 14-44.

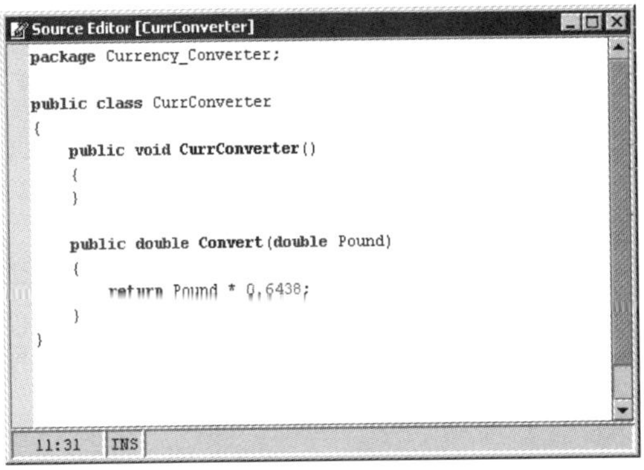

FIGURE 14-42 *The Source Editor window.*

FIGURE 14-43 *The class name in the Explorer window.*

FIGURE 14-44 *The Output window shows the compilation result.*

Adding the XML Operation

Next, you need to add the XML operations to the Web service. The XML operation encapsulated the business method. It specifies how a request to the Web service will be processed.

1. Right-click the Currency_Converter node and then select the New, Web Services, XML Operation command from the shortcut menu that is displayed, as shown in Figure 14-45.

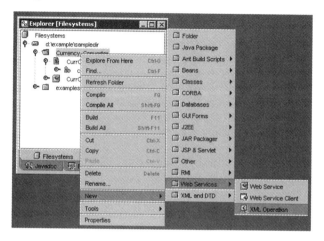

FIGURE 14-45 *The selection of the XML Operation command.*

2. The New Wizard—XML Operation dialog box is displayed. Specify the operation name as CurrencyOperation in the Name text box, as shown in Figure 14-46.

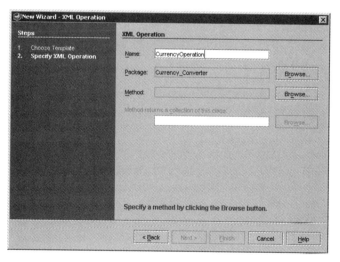

FIGURE 14-46 *The New Wizard—XML Operation dialog box.*

3. Click the Browse button next to the Method text box. Select the method name, as shown in Figure 14-47.

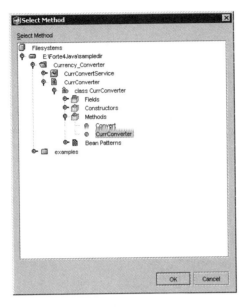

FIGURE 14-47 *The Select Method dialog box.*

4. Click the OK button to close the Select Method dialog box. The New Wizard—
   XML Operation dialog box is displayed again.

5. Click on the Finish button to close the dialog box. In the Explorer window, as shown
   in Figure 14-48, notice that the CurrencyOperation node is added.

FIGURE 14-48 *The Explorer window displays the XML operation that you added.*

Adding a Reference to the Web Service

The next step is to add a reference to the method and XML operations that you created for
the Web service. To add the reference, you need to perform the following steps:

1. Right-click CurrConvertService and select the Add Reference command from the shortcut menu.

2. In the Add Reference dialog box, select the method name and the XML operation name. The Add Reference dialog box is displayed, as shown in Figure 14-49.

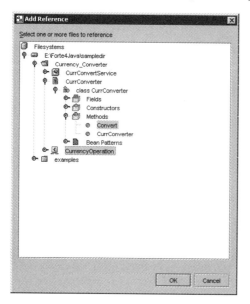

FIGURE 14-49 *The Add Reference dialog box.*

3. Click the OK button to close the Add Reference dialog box.

Compiling the Java Files

You need to compile the Java files. You create some of these files, whereas Sun ONE Studio creates others. To compile the files, right-click CurrConvertService and then select Generate/Compile Java File from the shortcut menu. The output window shows the result, as shown in Figure 14-50.

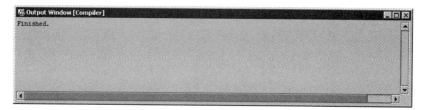

FIGURE 14-50 *The output window.*

Adding a Client to the Web Service

The last step in developing the Web service is to create the client that will access the service. To create the client, perform the following steps:

1. Right-click CurrConvertService and then select the New Client command from the shortcut menu. The New Client dialog box is shown, as displayed in Figure 14-51.

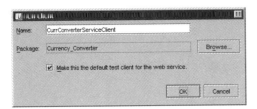

FIGURE 14-51 *The New Client dialog box.*

2. Click on the OK button to close the New Client dialog box.

Executing the Web Service

Now that you have created the client, you're ready to execute the Web service. To execute the Web service, right-click CurrConvertService and then click the Execute command. The progress bar displays the progress, as shown in Figure 14-52.

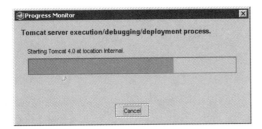

FIGURE 14-52 *The Progress Monitor.*

Running the Web Service

Sun ONE Studio automatically opens the browser and displays the client to you. You can now enter a value to convert and click the Invoke button to view the result, as shown in Figure 14-53.

For example, if you enter 100 in the Pound text box and then click the Invoke button, the result is displayed in Figure 14-54.

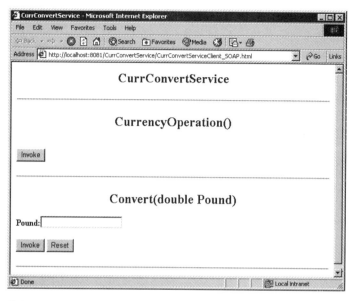

FIGURE 14-53 *The Web browser.*

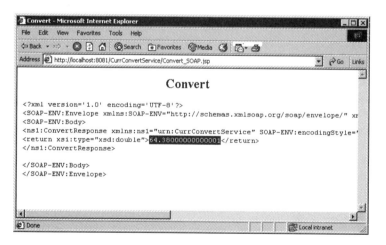

FIGURE 14-54 *The result of the currency conversion.*

You have now learned how to create the Java Web service in the Sun ONE Studio IDE.

Summary

In this chapter, you learned to create the Java Web services by using JWSDP and Sun ONE Studio. You learned about various components of JWSDP, such as JAXM, JAXP, JAXR, the registry server, the Application Deployment tool, and the Ant Build tool. In addition, you learned about the role played by each in the creation, development, and working of the Java Web services. Next, you learned to create some sample Web services, such as an interest calculator.

You also learned about the creation and development of the Java Web service on the Sun ONE Studio IDE. Sun ONE Studio provides a GUI for developing Web services. Finally, you looked at the steps to create, deploy, and execute a Currency Calculator Web service by using the Sun ONE Studio IDE.

PART X

**Professional
Project 7**

Project 7

Design and Creation of a Web Service Using the IBM Toolkit

Project 7 Overview

IBM, along with Microsoft, has played an important role in shaping the Web service standards. Toward this end, IBM has provided many tools that allow you to create Web services.

In this project, you will look at creating a Web service that checks a given number for compliance with the Luhn algorithm. Most credit card companies use the Luhn algorithm to generate credit card numbers, and most online stores use the algorithm to validate credit card numbers that users specify. This validation prevents spurious or incorrect entries. Validation of credit card numbers by using the Luhn algorithm happens before the credit card details are verified with a validation service provider.

In this project, you will use IBM's Web Services ToolKit and Websphere Studio Application Developer to create Web services that contain Web methods so that you can verify the credit card number by using the Luhn algorithm.

Chapter 15

Design and Creation of a Web Service Using the IBM Toolkit

IBM has played a critical role in the evolution of Web services. As a result, several useful tools, tutorials, and informative articles are present on IBM's Web site. Two of the most important toolsets provided by IBM are the Web Services ToolKit and the Websphere Studio Application Developer.

This chapter explores how Web services can be built using IBM tools, such as the Web Services Toolkit and the Websphere Studio Application Developer. It also covers the interoperability of these Web services with client applications developed using Microsoft tools.

The chapter begins by introducing you to a case study and the design of an application for which you will construct a Web service.

Case Study of the Credit Card Validation Web Service

LifeStyle, Inc. is a big department store in California that sells a wide range of household products. In addition to selling the products at the department store, LifeStyle, Inc. now has a Web site (http://www.lifestyledepartment.com) to sell its products online. In addition to ordering products online, users can use the kiosks at the store, which act as client applications, to order products. This will enable the store to increase its clientele and its revenues.

The Web site of LifeStyle, Inc. accepts orders from online customers and then prompts them to enter their credit card details. This is because payments for products that are bought online are made through credit cards. Therefore, the major task in a purchase transaction is validating the details of the credit card that the user enters. After the credit card number is validated, the order and customer details are stored in the database of LifeStyle, Inc. Finally, the product is delivered to the client. However, if the credit card details are not validated, an error message is displayed and the product is not delivered to the client.

The credit card validation involves using the services of a credit card validation service provider. The service provider charges per transaction. However, the site owner noticed that visitors enter junk numbers or make a mistake in entering the numbers, and the validation provider charges LifeStyle, Inc. for these, too. The programmers at LifeStyle, Inc. who created the Web site, plan to create a Web service to validate the credit card details to ensure that spurious or inaccurate numbers are detected locally and rejected. The Web site for LifeStyle, Inc. is created using J2EE; therefore, the programmers plan to use the IBM toolkit to create the Web service. To create the Web service, the management has appointed John Billing, an efficient Java programmer who created the Web site for the organization. In addition, Michael Burton, a project manager, is assigned to handle the project.

We will now discuss the project life cycle for the credit card validation Web service created using the IBM toolkit.

Project Life Cycle

While the development team is creating the project, they implement the following phases:

◆ Project initiation
◆ Project execution
◆ Project deployment

You learned about these phases in earlier projects. Therefore, we will discuss only the project execution phase, which is different for each project.

The Project Execution Phase

In the project execution phase, the development team creates the design of an application. After creating the design, they develop the application. The project execution phase consists of the following stages:

◆ Analyzing requirements

◆ Creating the design of an application

◆ Constructing the application

Analyzing the Requirements

During the requirements analysis phase, the development team at Lifestyle, Inc. analyzes the need for creating a Web service. This need for a Web service is based on the problem stated by Lucy Snyder, the sales manager of Lifestyle, Inc.

Says Snyder, "We want to validate the credit card details of a customer who places an order for a product on our Web site."

After analyzing the requirements of the organization, the development team feels a need for a Web service. Credit card validation is a common scenario and Web services are a reusable piece of code. Therefore, the Web service that the development team creates can be used across multiple applications.

The Web service that the team creates should perform the following functions:

◆ The Web service should accept the credit card details of a user, including the credit card number and the name of the customer.

◆ The Web service should validate the credit card number based on the Luhn algorithm.

◆ The result of the validation should be returned to the Web site of LifeStyle, Inc.

Creating the Design of the Application

During the design phase of the application, the development team decides upon the functionality to be implemented and the technology to be used. The development team plans to create a Web service. In addition, because the Web site is created using J2EE, the development team plans to use the IBM toolkit, which, in turn, uses the Java technology.

Construction

During the construction phase, the development team constructs the application. The following are the primary tasks that the team performs in the construction phase:

1. Create the Web service.
2. Deploy the Web service on a client computer.
3. Test the Web service.

Having learned about the Development Life Cycle (DLC) of the project, you will now learn about the software that you need to install to run the IBM toolkit.

Software Required for the Web Service

Before starting the development of the Web service, ensure that the following software programs are installed on the machine:

- ◆ **Tomcat application server.** You will be using Tomcat as the application server for most examples in this chapter. Tomcat is available for free download at http://jakarta.apache.org/tomcat.
- ◆ **IBM's Web Services ToolKit (WSTK).** WSTK is not a commercial product; rather it's a collection of tools from IBM. You can download the free version of the toolkit from http://www.alphaworks.ibm.com/tech/webservicestoolkit.
- ◆ **Websphere Studio Application Developer.** Provided by IBM, this is a complete Java application environment for building, testing, and developing Java applications. You can download a trial version of Websphere Studio Application Developer from http://www-3.ibm.com/software/ad/studioappdev.
- ◆ **Axis SOAP kit.** This is the latest SOAP toolkit from Apache. You can download the latest version from http://xml.apache.org/axis/. The latest version of the Axis SOAP kit is also bundled with WSTK.
- ◆ **Latest Java Development Kit (JDK).** Most IBM tools, such as Tomcat and the WSTK, require JDK version 1.3 or above to be installed on your computer.

After you have downloaded the software from the specified Web sites, you can install them on your computer. The installation process is discussed in the following sections.

Installing Tomcat

Because you have already used Tomcat in the Java project, we will not discuss the installation of Tomcat in detail here. The installation of Tomcat is simple and straight-forward.

To install and run Tomcat, perform the following steps:

1. Download the installation file from the specified URL.
2. Run the executable file.
3. Install Tomcat in the desired folder.
4. Run the server by executing the batch file, startup.bat, from the Bin folder of your Tomcat installation.

Installing the WSTK

Installing the WSTK simply requires you to run the InstallShield Setup Wizard. To run it, perform the following steps:

1. Run the InstallShield Setup Wizard. Figure 15-1 shows the first page of the InstallShield Setup Wizard. Click on the Next button to proceed.

FIGURE 15-1 *The first page of the InstallShield Setup Wizard.*

2. Click on the Accept button in the License Agreement window to proceed with the installation, and click Next.

3. The installation continues by specifying the install variables and options that you can set. In most cases, you need to accept the default settings for these variables.

4. Set the path to the folder where you have installed JDK, as shown in Figure 15-2, and click Next.

5. Specify the location, as shown in Figure 15-3, where you want to install the WSTK. Then click Next.

6. Select the type of installation, as shown in Figure 15-4, and click Next.

7. Click on the Next button on all the following screens.

8. The screen confirming the installation of the toolkit is displayed, as shown in Figure 15-5.

Configuring the WSTK

The WSTK is designed to run as a plug-in within any standard Java application server that supports Java Servlet and JSP specifications. Before you use the WSTK, you need to configure

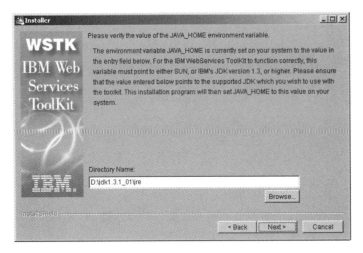

FIGURE 15-2 *Set the JAVA_HOME path.*

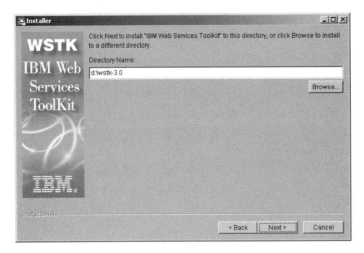

FIGURE 15-3 *Specifying the location for installing the Web Services ToolKit.*

your application server to use the toolkit. To do this, IBM provides you with a utility called the Web Services ToolKit Configuration Tool. This utility ships along with the WSTK.

The Web Services ToolKit Configuration Tool automates the configuration process for building services in the WebSphere, WebSphere MicroEdition, or Jakarta-Tomcat 4.0 environments. In addition, the tool allows you to specify the default UDDI registry that the WSTK will use to publish and locate the Web service.

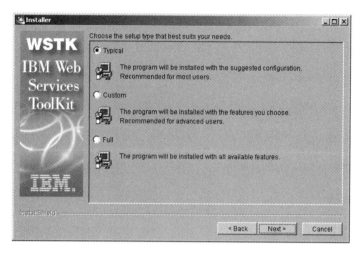

FIGURE 15-4 *Select the installation type.*

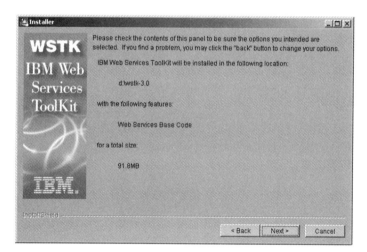

FIGURE 15-5 *The end of installation.*

To run the Web Services ToolKit Configuration Tool, perform the following steps:

1. Use the following command to launch the Web Services ToolKit Configuration Tool:

   ```
   %WSTK_HOME%\bin\wstkconfig.bat
   ```

   Running the toolkit presents a wizard-style GUI interface, as shown in Figure 15-6.

   As you can see, the wizard prompts you to specify the Web server that you need to use with the WSTK.

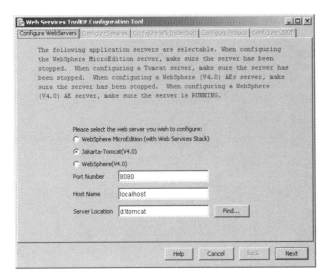

FIGURE 15-6 *Running the Web Services ToolKit Configuration Tool.*

2. Select the host name, port number, and location of the Web server.

 NOTE

In this case, you would be using a Tomcat server. Therefore, specify the port number as 8080, the host name as localhost, and the location of the folder where you have installed Tomcat.

3. Click on the Configure Services tab, as shown in Figure 15-7. The displayed window contains a list of all Web services files under the Services folder of the WSTK installation.

4. Select the Web services you want to activate and click on the Next button.

5. The third page of the tool allows you to configure options for the Web Service Inspection Language (WSIL) implementation, as shown in Figure 15-8.

 NOTE

WSIL is a new language that helps you discover Web services. You can use WSIL as an alternative to UDDI.

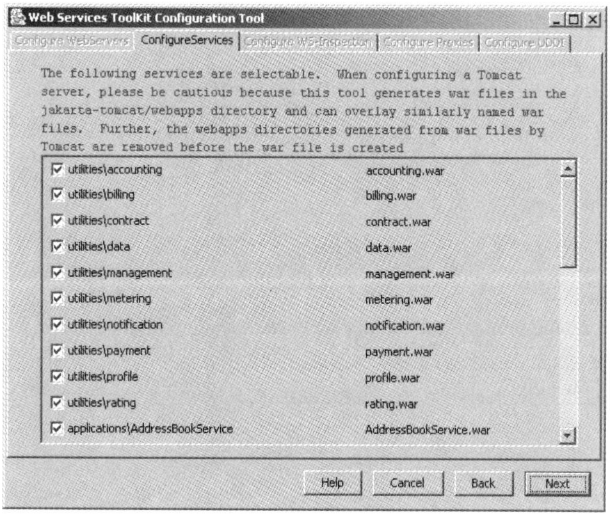

FIGURE 15-7 *The Configure Services tab.*

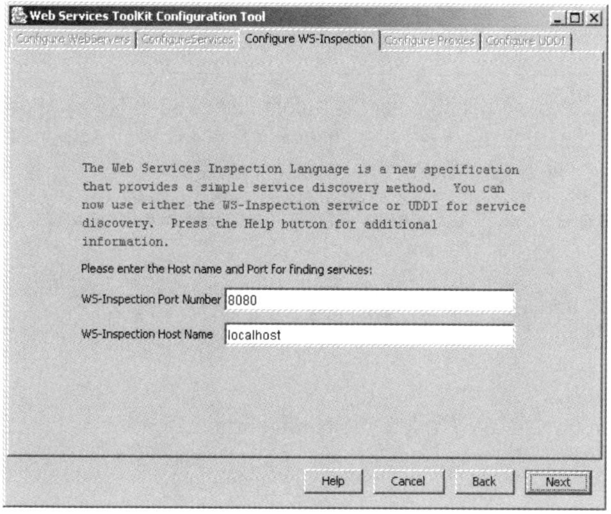

FIGURE 15-8 *Configuring WSIL.*

6. Click on the Next button. The last page of the tool is displayed. This page allows you to select the UDDI registry that you want to use as a default registry for the Web Services ToolKit, as shown in Figure 15-9.

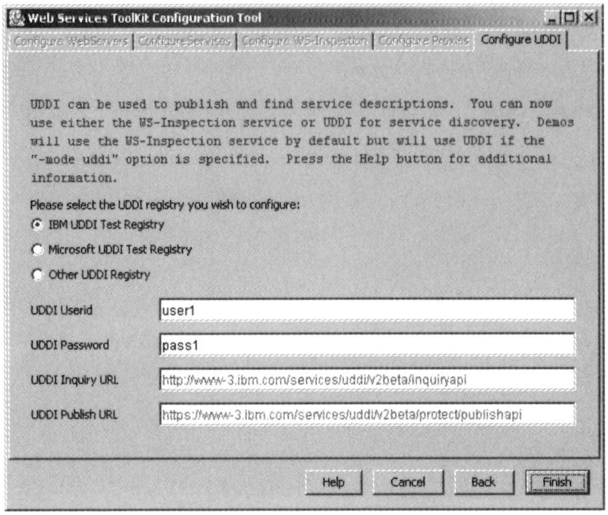

FIGURE 15-9 *Selecting the UDDI registry.*

 NOTE

The registry that you choose will be selected automatically each time you perform an UDDI-related operation within the WSTK. However, to select any other UDDI, you need to explicitly specify in the toolkit.

To change the settings of the UDDI directory in the Configuration tool, use the following command:

```
%WSTK_HOME%\lib\wstkproperties.xml file
```

7. Click on the Finish button to complete the configuration.

The WSTK is now ready to use.

Installing the Axis SOAP Toolkit

You use the toolkits provided by various vendors for various products to reduce the time required to create the application. Similarly, to reduce the time taken to create the applications that involve SOAP messages, several toolkits, such as Microsoft SOAP Toolkit, the Apache SOAP toolkit, and the PocketSOAP toolkit, are available. Without the use of such toolkits, coding for SOAP messages would be tedious.

Apache SOAP toolkit, also called the Axis SOAP toolkit, was originally based on an IBM implementation. Apache rearchitectured the SOAP toolkit to allow easier usage and configuration. As a result, a new toolkit called Axis was created.

 NOTE

You can download the beta of the latest version of the Apache SOAP toolkit from http://xml.apache.org/axis.

Features of the Axis SOAP Toolkit

The latest version of the Apache SOAP toolkit has the following features:

◆ It supports SOAP 1.1, similar to its earlier version, Apache SOAP 2.2. The final release of Axis supports a few features of SOAP 1.2 and provides partial support for pluggable XML protocols.

◆ It provides a simple and convenient method of transporting SOAP messages between requestor and provider applications over protocols, such as FTP, SMTP, and so on.

◆ The toolkit aims to automatically generate the WSDL documents for creating the Web services. To do this, the latest version of the Axis toolkit provides a tool called the wsdl2java tool. You will learn about this tool in the section titled "Creating a Client Application by Using Axis Tools."

You can use the wsdl2java tool to create stubs and skeletons from WSDL documents and proxies for Java classes. You can further use these stubs and skeletons to easily and conveniently code for the client applications that access the corresponding Web service.

◆ The latest version of the Apache SOAP toolkit is more efficient that its previous versions. This is mainly because Apache SOAP toolkit uses SAX instead of DOM.

◆ The toolkit also provides support for deploying EJB as services.

◆ In addition to the support for creating a Web service and a client application, the toolkit extends support for deploying a Web service. The toolkit also helps expose the Java classes in the form of services.

◆ The toolkit provides interoperability with the SOAP implementations provided by Microsoft and its .NET services.

We will now continue the discussion on installing the Axis SOAP toolkit. To install the toolkit, perform the following steps:

1. Unzip the contents of the Axis distribution that you have downloaded into a folder.

 TIP

Ensure that the Tomcat server is up and running.

2. Copy the Axis folder from AXIS_HOME\webapps to TOMCAT_HOME\webapps.

3. Copy xerces.jar to the TOCMAT_HOME\webapps\axis\WEB-INF\lib directory.

 NOTE

Xerces is the XML parser from Apache that is part of the WSTK distribution. You can download Xerces from http://xml.apache.org/xerces2-j/index.html.

4. Make the modification to the server.xml file in the TOMCAT_HOME\conf directory, as highlighted in the following code:

```
<!-- Define properties for each web application. This is only needed if you
want to set non-default properties, or have web application document roots
in places other than the virtual host's appBase directory.-->
        <!-- Tomcat Root Context -->
        <Context debug="0" docBase="axis" path="/axis" reloadable="true"/>
        <!-- Tomcat Manager Context -->
        <Context debug="0" docBase="manager" path="/manager" privileged="true"/>
```

5. Shut down Tomcat and then restart it. To shut down the server, you need to run the shutdown.bat file in the Bin folder under TOMCAT_HOME.

As discussed, you will use the Axis SOAP toolkit to create the Credit Card Web service. This Web service uses the Luhn algorithm to verify the credit card number. The Luhn algorithm is discussed in the following section.

The Luhn Algorithm

The Luhn formula, created in the late 1960s, is a standard algorithm used to validate the details of a credit card number. It is popularly called the mod 10 or modulus 10 algorithm. To validate a credit card number, the Luhn algorithm uses a check digit, which is the last digit in the credit card number. The check digit is generated by applying the Luhn formula to the credit card number. Therefore, to validate the credit card number, the check digit is passed to the Luhn algorithm.

To help you understand the Luhn formula, the following list discusses how it works:

1. Moving left and starting from the second to the last digit, multiply the values of all alternate digits by 2. If the resulting digits are two-digit numbers, add the two resulting digits to form a one-digit number.

2. Starting from the left, add the digits that are not multiplied by 2 in step 1 to the results of the individual digits of step 1.

3. Multiply the result by 10.

4. The result of step 2 should end with a 0. The result must be 0 for the credit card number to be valid.

 NOTE

It is important to note that the Luhn algorithm does not actually validate a credit card number. Instead, it just validates that the number, entered by a user, conforms to the algorithm. The actual credit card validation can happen only through the bank that issues the credit card.

You can use the Luhn algorithm to validate the credit card number prior to validating the number against the bank records. This ensures that the user does not enter junk data and avoids typos.

Creating the Web Service by Using Axis

To implement the Luhn algorithm, you first need to create a Java class that implements the algorithm. The code for the class is shown in the following example:

```java
import java.io.StringReader;
import java.io.InputStream;

public class CCheck
{
        public static String isValid (String CCNo)
        {
                String strnumbers = converToDigits (CCNo);
                int sum = 0;
                int no = 0;
                int addend = 0;
                boolean timesTwo = false;

                for (int i = strnumbers.length () - 1; i >= 0; i—)
                {
                        no = Integer.parseInt (strnumbers.substring (i, i + 1));
                        if (timesTwo)
                        {
                                addend = no * 2;
                                if (addend > 9)
```

```
                        {
                            addend -= 9;
                        }
                }
                else
                {
                        addend = no;
                }
                sum += addend;
                timesTwo = !timesTwo;
            }
            if(sum % 10==0)
                return "Valid";
            else
                return "Invalid";
        }

    private static String converToDigits (String s)
    {
            StringBuffer strnumbers = new StringBuffer ();
            char c;
            for (int i = 0; i < s.length (); i++) {
                    c = s.charAt (i);
                    if (Character.isDigit (c))
                    {
                            strnumbers.append (c);
                    }
            }
            return strnumbers.toString ();
    }
}
```

Deploying a Java Class as a Web Service

Next, you need to deploy a Java class as an Axis-based Web service.

To deploy this credit card validation Web service, just copy the CCheck.java file to the TOMCAT_HOME\webapps\axis directory and change its extension from .java to .jws. Doing this deploys the Web service so that it is ready for use. As you can see, deploying a Web service does not require a change in the code.

When a client application invokes a service as deployed in the preceding manner, the Axis SOAP toolkit automatically locates the file, compiles the class, and converts SOAP calls to your Java service class.

It is important to note that the service name corresponds to the name of the .jws file. Therefore, when the .jws file is requested, the Web server invokes the Axis engine, a servlet that is located in the TOMCAT_HOME\webapps\axis\WEB-INF directory.

Whenever Tomcat or any J2EE-compliant Web server encounters a .jws file in the Axis context, it invokes the AxisServlet. The AxisServlet then invokes the corresponding .jws file.

Testing the Web Service by Using a Client Application

The following code calls the Web service:

```
import org.apache.axis.client.Call;
import org.apache.axis.client.Service;
import javax.xml.rpc.namespace.QName;
public class Client1{

public static void main(String args[])
{
try{
String endpoint="http://localhost:8080/axis/CCheck.jws";
Service service=new Service();
Call call=(Call)service.createCall();
call.setTargetEndpointAddress(new java.net.URL(endpoint));
call.setOperationName(new QName(" ","isValid"));

String ret=(String) call.invoke(new Object[]{"4111111111111111"});
System.out.println(ret);
}
catch(Exception e)
{
System.out.println(e);
}
}
}
```

The preceding code creates new `Service` and `Call` objects, which are JAX-RPC objects. These objects store metadata about the Web service that you need to invoke.

If you have worked with the earlier versions of the Apache SOAP toolkit, you will appreciate the simplicity of the code used in the latest version.

You need to define the URL of the receiver application that receives a SOAP message. In addition, you need to specify the Web service to be invoked by passing parameters to it. The parameters are passed as an array.

The following code sample shows the SOAP message generated when the client application sends a request:

```
<?xml version="1.0" encoding="UTF-8" ?>
<SOAP-ENV:Envelope SOAP-ENV:encodingStyle="http://schemas.xmlsoap.org/soap/encoding/"
xmlns:SOAP-ENV="http://schemas.xmlsoap.org/soap/envelope/"
xmlns:xsd="http://www.w3.org/2001/XMLSchema" xmlns:xsi="http://www.w3.org/2001/
XMLSchema-instance">
      <SOAP-ENV:Body>
      <isValid>
      <arg0 xsi:type="xsd:string">1111111111111</arg0>
      </isValid>
      </SOAP-ENV:Body>
      </SOAP-ENV:Envelope>
```

As you see in the preceding code, the value passed as a parameter to the Java client application is serialized into XML. The following code shows the corresponding response for the request. The response is sent from the Web service to the client application:

```
<?xml version="1.0" encoding="UTF-8" ?>
      <SOAP-ENV:Envelope SOAP-ENV:encodingStyle="http://schemas.xmlsoap.org/soap/
encoding/" xmlns:SOAP-ENV="http://schemas.xmlsoap.org/soap/envelope/"
xmlns:xsd="http://www.w3.org/2001/XMLSchema" xmlns:xsi="http://www.w3.org/
2001/XMLSchema-instance">
      <SOAP-ENV:Body>
      <isValidResponse>
      <isValidResult xsi:type="xsd:string">Invalid</isValidResult>
      </isValidResponse>
      </SOAP-ENV:Body>
      </SOAP-ENV:Envelope>
```

The Web service validates the number 1111111111111, which you passed for testing, and sends a response. In the preceding response, the Web service finds the number to be invalid.

TIP

Remember to shut down and restart the Tomcat server when you copy the .jws file for the first time to the Axis folder or make changes to the .jws file.

As you can see, using .jws files is one of the simplest ways to create Web services. However, in some cases, you might face problems while working with the .jws file. For example, you might experience problems while trying to fit the entire functionality of a Web service into a single .jws file. Similarly, you can run into problems when the code to be deployed is in the form of a class file. In such a case, the deployment can be done using a .wsdd file.

Creating a Web Service from a Class File

In most real-life situations, deploying a Web service as a .jws file is insufficient. This implies that these Web services are not able to meet the requirements of a real-life Web service, such as the ability to specify custom type mappings or create handler chains. Therefore, in such complicated cases, a deployment file, as shown in the following code, is used:

```
<deployment xmlns="http://xml.apache.org/axis/wsdd/" xmlns:java="http://xml.apache.org/
axis/wsdd/providers/java">
        <service name="CCheck" provider="java:RPC">
        <parameter name="className" value="CCheck"/>
        <parameter name="methodName" value="isValid"/>
        </service>
</deployment>
```

Save the file as deploy.wsdd.

In the preceding code, we created a new Web service that uses the Java class: CCheck. Then, the code exposes the isValid() method.

NOTE

You can expose several methods in the preceding code. To do so, you need to separate the names of methods with spaces.

The next step is to deploy the Web service. The steps to do so are as shown:

1. Start the Tomcat server if it is not working.

2. Compile the CCheckServer.Java file.

3. Copy the resulting CCheckServer class to the TOMCAT_HOME\webapps\axis\ WEB-INF\classes folder.

4. Execute the following command:

```
java org.apache.axis.client.AdminClient deploy.wsdd
```

In this case, the requestor and provider applications (endpoints in a Web services scenario) are AxisServlet instead of .jws files. Now, the servlet locates and creates an instance of the class that corresponds to the service name CCheckServer. Next, the servlet converts the SOAP messages into Java calls and invokes the Java calls on the instantiated service class.

Testing the Web Service

Now you can test the Web service created in the previous section by using a client application. The client application used in this case is similar to the client application used to test the Web service in which the endpoints were .jws files. However, please note the change in the endpoint.

```
import org.apache.axis.client.Call;

import org.apache.axis.client.Service;

import javax.xml.rpc.namespace.QName;

public class Client2{


public static void main(String args[])

{

try{

String endpoint="http://localhost:8080/axis/services/CCheck";

Service service=new Service();

Call call=(Call)service.createCall();

call.setTargetEndpointAddress(new java.net.URL(endpoint));

call.setOperationName(new QName(" ","isValid"));


String ret=(String) call.invoke(new Object[]{"4111111111111111"});

System.out.println(ret);

}

catch(Exception e)

{

System.out.println(e);

}

}

}
```

NOTE

The differences in the preceding code and the code used to call a Web service with endpoints as .jws files are in bold type.

Creating a Client Application by Using Axis Tools

In addition to the client application discussed in the previous section, you can create a client application by using the tools that the Axis toolkit provides. You can then use this client application to test the Web service.

To create a client application by using the tools in the Axis toolkit, you first need to create a proxy class for the Web service. To do this, use the following command:

```
java org.apache.axis.wsdl.WSDL2Java -p proxy
http://localhost:8080/axis/services/CCheck?wsdl
```

The preceding code uses the Wsdl2java command. Some of the commonly used options with the Wsdl2java command are discussed in Table 15-1.

Table 15-1 Options Used with the Wsdl2java Command

Option	Function	Description
-h	help	This option prints the syntax of the command and the list of options.
-v	verbose	This option prints messages that indicate the current status of the process.
-s	skeleton	This option emits a `skeleton` class for the Web service.
-m	messageContext	This option emits a `MessageContext` parameter to `skeleton` methods.
-N	NStoPkg <argument>=<value>	This option maps the namespace to a package.
-p	package <argument>	This option overrides all namespaces to package mappings.
-o	output <argument>	This option specifies the output directory for emitted files.

(continues...)

Table 15-1 Options Used with the Wsdl2java Command

Option	Function	Description
-d	deployScope <argument>	This option specifies the scope of the deploy.XML file. For example, the scope that the −d option can add includes Application, Request, and Session.
-t	testCase	This option emits the testcase class for the Web service.
-n	noImports	This option generates code for the immediate WSDL document.

When you execute the Wsdl2java command, a folder named proxy, which contains three files, is created. The files in the proxy folder represent the SOAP bindings, the port type, and the Web service proxy class. In addition, the Wsdl2java command creates the following:

◆ A Java class for each type
◆ A Java interface for each port type
◆ A stub class for each binding
◆ A service interface and implementation for the service interfaces, also called the locator class

The following section discusses the contents of these files in detail.

File That Contains Port Types

As discussed, the Wsdl2java command creates a file that contains a Java class, CCheckServerPortType.Java. The code for this file is as follows:

```
/**
 * CCheckPortType.java
 *
 * This file was auto-generated from WSDL
 * by the Apache Axis Wsdl2java emitter.
 */

package Proxy;

    public interface CCheckPortType extends java.rmi.Remote
    {
        public java.lang.String isValid(java.lang.String arg0) throws
java.rmi.RemoteException;
    }
```

File That Contains Bindings

In addition, a file that contains stubs is created. The content of the CCheckServerSoapBinding Stub.java file is as follows:

```
/**
 * CCheckSoapBindingStub.java
 *
 * This file was auto-generated from WSDL
 * by the Apache Axis Wsdl2java emitter.
 */

package Proxy;

public class CCheckSoapBindingStub extends javax.xml.rpc.Stub implements
Proxy.CCheckPortType {
    private org.apache.axis.client.Service service = null ;
    private org.apache.axis.client.Call call = null ;
    private java.util.Hashtable properties = new java.util.Hashtable();

    public CCheckSoapBindingStub(java.net.URL endpointURL) throws
org.apache.axis.AxisFault
    {
        this();
        call.setTargetEndpointAddress( endpointURL );
        call.setProperty(org.apache.axis.transport.http.HTTPTransport.URL,
endpointURL.toString());
    }

    public CCheckSoapBindingStub() throws org.apache.axis.AxisFault
    {
        try
        {
            service = new org.apache.axis.client.Service();
            call = (org.apache.axis.client.Call) service.createCall();
        }
        catch(Exception t)
        {
            throw org.apache.axis.AxisFault.makeFault(t);
        }
```

```
}

    public void _setProperty(String name, Object value)
    {
        properties.put(name, value);
    }


// From javax.xml.rpc.Stub
    public Object _getProperty(String name)
    {
        return properties.get(name);
    }


// From javax.xml.rpc.Stub
    public void _setTargetEndpoint(java.net.URL address)
    {
        call.setProperty(org.apache.axis.transport.http.HTTPTransport.URL,
address.toString());
    }


// From javax.xml.rpc.Stub
    public java.net.URL _getTargetEndpoint()
    {
        try
        {
            return new java.net.URL((String)
call.getProperty(org.apache.axis.transport.http.HTTPTransport.URL));
        }
        catch (java.net.MalformedURLException mue)
        {
            return null;        }
    }


// From javax.xml.rpc.Stub
    public synchronized void setMaintainSession(boolean session)
    {
        call.setMaintainSession(session);
    }
```

```
// From javax.naming.Referenceable
    public javax.naming.Reference getReference()
    {
        return null;
    }


    public java.lang.String isValid(java.lang.String arg0) throws
java.rmi.RemoteException{
        if (call.getProperty(org.apache.axis.transport.http.HTTPTransport.URL)
== null)
        {
            throw new org.apache.axis.NoEndPointException();
        }

        call.removeAllParameters();
        call.addParameter("arg0", new org.apache.axis.encoding.XMLType( new
javax.xml.rpc.namespace.QName("http://www.w3.org/2001/XMLSchema", "string")),
org.apache.axis.client.Call.PARAM_MODE_IN);
        call.setReturnType(new org.apache.axis.encoding.XMLType(new
javax.xml.rpc.namespace.QName("http://www.w3.org/2001/XMLSchema", "string")));

        call.setProperty(org.apache.axis.transport.http.HTTPTransport.ACTION, "");
        call.setProperty(call.NAMESPACE, "CCheckServer");
        call.setOperationName( "isValid");
        Object resp = call.invoke(new Object[] {arg0});

        if (resp instanceof java.rmi.RemoteException)
        {
            throw (java.rmi.RemoteException)resp;
        }
        else
        {
            return (java.lang.String) resp;
        }
    }
```

File That Contains the Web Service Proxy Interface Class

The Wsdl2java command creates a file that contains the code for the Web service proxy class. The content of the CCheckServer.Java file is shown in the following code:

```
/**
 * CCheck.java
 *
 * This file was auto-generated from WSDL
 * by the Apache Axis Wsdl2java emitter.
 */


package Proxy;


public interface CCheck2 extends javax.xml.rpc.Service {
    public String getCCheck2PortAddress();

    public Prxy.CCheck2PortType getCCheck2Port() throws
javax.xml.rpc.ServiceException;

    public Prxy.CCheck2PortType getCCheck2Port(java.net.URL portAddress) throws
javax.xml.rpc.ServiceException;
}
```

File That Contains the Web Service Proxy Implementation

A client program does not instantiate a stub; it would rather instantiate a service locator class, which exposes a method that would return a stub. This locator class implements the service interface class shown earlier. Following is the code for a service locator class for the CCheck Web service:

```
/**
 * CCheckLocator.java
 *
 * This file was auto-generated from WSDL
 * by the Apache Axis Wsdl2java emitter.
 */

package Proxy;

public class CCheckLocator extends org.apache.axis.client.Service implements
Proxy.CCheck {
```

```
        // Use to get a proxy class for CCheck2Port
        private final java.lang.String CCheck2Port_address =
    "http://localhost:8080/axis/services/CCheck2";

        public String getCCheckPortAddress() {
            return CCheckPort_address;
        }


        public Proxy.CCheck2PortType getCCheckPort() throws
    javax.xml.rpc.ServiceException {
            java.net.URL endpoint;
            try {
                endpoint = new java.net.URL(CCheckPort_address);
            }
            catch (java.net.MalformedURLException e) {
                return null; // unlikely as URL was validated in WSDL2Java
            }
            return getCCheckPort(endpoint);
        }


        public Proxy.CCheckPortType getCCheckPort(java.net.URL portAddress) throws
    javax.xml.rpc.ServiceException {
            try {
                return new Proxy.CCheckSoapBindingStub(portAddress, this);
            }
            catch (org.apache.axis.AxisFault e) {
                return null; // ???
            }
        }
    }
}
```

Compiling the Files That the Wsdl2java Command Created

When these files are created, you need to compile them in the following order:

1. java proxy/CCheckrPortType.java
2. java proxy/CCheckSoapBindingStub.java
3. javac proxy/CCheckLocator.java

Create a Client Application That Uses the Files

Next, you need to create a client application that calls the Web service by using the classes that are contained within the three files discussed in the previous sections. The code for the client application is as follows:

```
import Proxy.*;
public class Client
{

public static void main(String args[])
{
Proxy.CCheck service=new CCheckLocator();
try{
Proxy.CCheckPortType port=service.getCCheckPort();

String ret=port.isValid("411111111111111");

System.out.println(ret);
}
catch(Exception e)
{
}
}
}
```

Creating a Web Service by Using the WSTK

Before creating a Web service by using the WSTK, we will discuss the toolkit in general.

The WSTK contains several tools that help you to create, discover, and invoke a Web service. These tools are explained in the following list:

◆ **Runtime API for the client side.** This API implements the discovery and proxy functionality for the implementation of IBM's open source. IBM's open sources include the SOAP implementations, WSDL for Java (WSDL4J), and UDDI for Java (UDDI4J).

◆ **Runtime API for the server side.** This API deploys and exposes Axis-based Web services.

◆ **Sample code.** This helps you understand the creation of Web services by using the WSTK.

◆ **HTTPr.** This is an extension of the standard HTTP protocol. HTTPr adds messaging capabilities to your Web service and is present in the %WSTK_HOME%\HTTPR directory. The WSTK contains both the reference and demo version of HTTPr.

◆ **Apache Axis.** This is the latest version of open source SOAP implementation from the Apache Software Foundation. The Axis toolkit offers better performance and flexibility than its earlier versions.

◆ **SOAP digital signatures and encryption.** These specifications define the methods in which encrypted data within a SOAP message can be included within the SOAP header.

◆ **XKMS.** This is an emerging standard for accessing and managing public key infrastructure services. These services are based on the Web services architecture. The WSTK implements two components of XKMS: XML Key Information Service Specification (X-KISS) and XML Key Registration Service Specification (X-KRSS).

◆ **Utility services.** These are pluggable service interfaces that you can use to plug additional functionalities into the WSTK.

Creating the Web Service

To create a Web service, you first create a Java class file. In this case, because you are creating a credit card validation Web service, you need to use the CCheck.java file. Compile the .java file to create the .class file.

The next step is to create a WSDL file from the class file that you created. To do this, you use the java2wsdl.bat file present in the WSTK_HOME\bin folder. Create a folder Ccheck in the <WSTK_HOME>\services\applications folder. The command to create a WSDL file is shown in the following example:

```
java org.apache.axis.wsdl.Java2WSDL -N "http://CCheck" -n"http://CCheck-Interface" -o
  "<drive>:\wstk-3.1\services\applications\CCheck\CCheck_Interface.wsdl" -O
"<drive>:\wstk-3.1\services\applications\CCheck\CCheck_Impl.wsdl" -L
 "http://localhost:8080/CCheck/CCheck_Interface.wsdl" -m "isValid" -l
 "http://localhost:8080/CCheck/services/CCheck" CCheck
```

As you can see, the preceding code uses the java2wsdl command, which has several options, as explained in Table 15-2.

Table 15-2 Options Used with the java2wsdl Command

Option	Function	Description
-h	help	This option prints a message and exits the application.
-n	namespace <argument>	This option specifies the target namespace.

(continues...)

Table 15-2 Options Used with the java2wsdl Command

Option	Function	Description
-N	namespaceImpl <argument>	This option specifies the target namespace for the implementation of the WSDL file.
-p	PkgtoNS <argument>=<value>	This option replaces package references with appropriate namespace references.
-l	location <argument>	This option specifies the service location.
-s	service name <argument>	This option specifies the service name.
-L	locationImport <argument>	This option specifies the location of the WSDL file.
-m	methods <argument>	This option specifies a list of methods to be exported. A space separates this list of methods.
-a	methods	This option looks for allowed methods in the inherited class.
-w	outputWsdlMode <argument>	This option specifies the output WSDL mode, which can be All, Interface, or Implementation.
-o	output <argument>	This option specifies the name of the output WSDL file.
-O	outputImpl <argument>	This option specifies the output implementation of the WSDL file.

The java2wsdl command creates a WSDL file. The content of this file is as shown:

```
<?xml version="1.0" encoding="UTF-8"?>
<wsdl:definitions xmlns:wsdl="http://schemas.xmlsoap.org/wsdl/"
xmlns="http://schemas.xmlsoap.org/wsdl/" xmlns:impl="urn:CCheckServerImpl"
xmlns:intf="urn:CCheckServer" xmlns:soap="http://schemas.xmlsoap.org/wsdl/soap/"
xmlns:soapenc="http://schemas.xmlsoap.org/soap/encoding/"
xmlns:xsd="http://www.w3.org/2001/XMLSchema" targetNamespace="urn:CCheckServer">
    <wsdl:message name="isValidResponse">
        <wsdl:part name="isValidResult" type="xsd:string"/>
    </wsdl:message>
```

```
        <wsdl:message name="isValidRequest">
           <wsdl:part name="arg0" type="xsd:string"/>
        </wsdl:message>


        <wsdl:portType name="CCheckServerPortType">
           <wsdl:operation name="isValid">
              <wsdl:input message="intf:isValidRequest"/>
              <wsdl:output message="intf:isValidResponse"/>
           </wsdl:operation>
        </wsdl:portType>


        <wsdl:binding name="CCheckrSoapBinding" type="intf:CCheckServerPortType">
           <soap:binding style="rpc" transport="http://schemas.xmlsoap.org/soap/http"/>
           <wsdl:operation name="isValid">
              <soap:operation soapAction="" style="rpc"/>
              <wsdl:input>
                 <soap:body encodingStyle="http://schemas.xmlsoap.org/soap/encoding/"
namespace="urn:CCheck" use="encoded"/>
              </wsdl:input>
              <wsdl:output>
                 <soap:body encodingStyle="http://schemas.xmlsoap.org/soap/encoding/"
namespace="urn:CCheck" use="encoded"/>
              </wsdl:output>
           </wsdl:operation>
        </wsdl:binding>


        <wsdl:service name="CCheck">
           <wsdl:port binding="intf:CCheckSoapBinding" name="CCheckPort">
              <soap:address location="http://localhost:8080/axis/services/CCheck"/>
           </wsdl:port>
        </wsdl:service>
</wsdl:definitions>
```

Creating the Deployment Descriptor

The deployment descriptor is a file, usually in the XML format, which stores the data used to deploy a Java application. Version 3.0 of the WSTK uses the old version of the deployment descriptor instead of the WSDD version. Therefore, you need to create the deployment descriptor. You can do this by using the following code:

```
<deployment xmlns="http://xml.apache.org/axis/wsdd/"
 xmlns:java="http://xml.apache.org/axis/wsdd/providers/java" name="test">
  <service name="CCheck" provider="java:RPC">
    <parameter value="CCheck" name="className"/>
    <parameter value="isValid" name="allowedMethods"/>
  </service>
  <beanMapping xmlns:nq="urn:CCheck-types" languageSpecificType="java:CCheck"
qname="nq:CCheck"/>
</deployment>
```

Creating a Folder Structure for the WSTK

A folder structure for the WSTK includes a root folder containing all Web service files that are deployed by using the WSTK.

 TIP

You need to create the exact folder structure for each Web service that you deploy using the WSTK. Therefore, it is advisable that you replicate the folder structure for the sample Web services created by using the toolkit to create the folder structure for your Web service.

Whenever you want to deploy a new service, create a new folder under the Applications directory. This folder should contain at least three subdirectories, as discussed in the following list:

◆ **client.** This subdirectory contains the client files that are associated with the Web service.

◆ **deployment.** This subdirectory contains the deployment files that are associated with the Web service.

◆ **webapp.** The contents of this subdirectory must conform to the standard WAR file structure. However, an exception to the standard WAR file structure is the import.XML file located in the META-INF directory. The import.xml file contains a list of all JAR files and other files that the service requires to run.

The contents of the import.xml file are as shown:

```
<import>
  <copy name="axis.jar" fromdir="axis/lib" todir="lib"/>
  <copy name="clutil.jar" fromdir="axis/lib" todir="lib"/>
  <copy name="log4j-core.jar" fromdir="axis/lib" todir="lib"/>
  <copy name="wsdl4j.jar" fromdir="wsdl4j/lib" todir="lib"/>
  <copy name="xerces.jar" fromdir="lib" todir="lib"/>
```

```
<copy name="wstk.jar" fromdir="lib" todir="lib"/>
<copy name="logEnglish.jar" fromdir="lib" todir="lib"/>
<copy name="wstkProperties.xml" fromdir="lib" todir="classes"/>

<copy name="ldapjdk.jar" fromdir="lib" todir="lib"/>
<copy name="local_policy.jar" fromdir="lib" todir="lib"/>
<copy name="soapenc.jar" fromdir="lib" todir="lib"/>
<copy name="sse.jar" fromdir="lib" todir="lib"/>
<copy name="US_export_policy.jar" fromdir="lib" todir="lib"/>
<copy name="xalan.jar" fromdir="lib" todir="lib"/>
<copy name="xenc.jar" fromdir="lib" todir="lib"/>
<copy name="xss4j.jar" fromdir="lib" todir="lib"/>

<copy name="server-config.wsdd" fromdir="axis" todir="."/>
</import>
```

The preceding code uses the `fromdir` attribute to indicate a path to the source file relative to %WSTK_HOME%. The files identified by the `fromdir` attribute are copied into the directory indicated by the `todir` attribute. However, you need to copy the actual class file for the `CCheckServer` class to the WEB-INF\classes folder.

The WEB-INF folder contains a web.xml file, which is a standard Java Web application deployment descriptor. This file deploys the AxisServlet that is used as the entry point for the service. The contents of the web.xml file are shown in the following code:

```
<?xml version="1.0" encoding="UTF-8"?>
  <!DOCTYPE web-app PUBLIC "-//Sun Microsystems, Inc.//DTD Web Application
2.3//EN"  "http://java.sun.com/j2ee/dtds/web-app_2.2.dtd">
  <web-app>
  <display-name>StockQuoteService</display-name>

  <servlet>
    <servlet-name>Axis</servlet-name>
    <servlet-class>org.apache.axis.transport.http.AxisServlet</servlet-class>
  </servlet>

  <servlet-mapping>
    <servlet-name>Axis</servlet-name>
    <url-pattern>/services/*</url-pattern>
  </servlet-mapping>
```

```
<mime-mapping>
   <extension>wsdl</extension>
   <mime-type>text/xml</mime-type>
</mime-mapping>

<mime-mapping>
   <extension>xsd</extension>
   <mime-type>text/xml</mime-type>
</mime-mapping>
</web-app>
```

Deploying the Web Service

After you create the directory structure, you need to deploy the Web service on the Tomcat server. To do this, perform the following steps:

1. Execute the wstkconfig.bat file from the WSTK_HOME\bin folder. The tool launches and displays a dialog box, as shown in Figure 15-10.

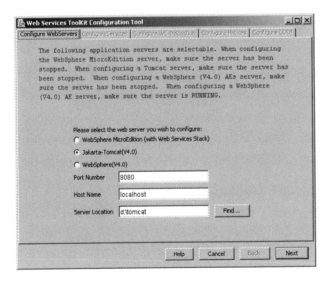

FIGURE 15-10 *Running WstkConfig.*

2. Click on the Configure Services tab and select your Web service, as shown in Figure 15-11, and click Next.
3. Click on the Configure UDDI tab, and then click on the Finish button.

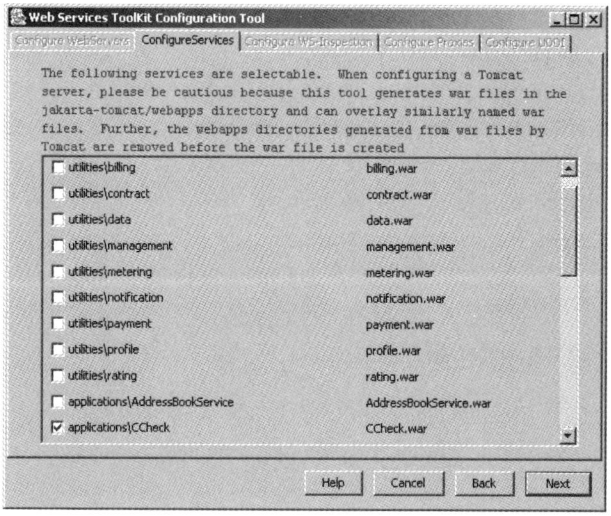

FIGURE 15-11 *Selecting the Web service to be deployed.*

Performing these steps deploys the WAR files. Next, you need to perform an additional task: registering the Web service with the Axis toolkit. The following section discusses this.

Registering the Web Service with the Axis Toolkit

Copy the file deploy.bat from one of the sample applications in the <WSTK_HOME>\ services\applications folder and use it to deploy your Web service.

The command used to register a Web service with the Axis toolkit is as follows:

```
deploy admin_servelet_url [deployment descriptor]
```

In the case of the CCheck Web service, the command would be as follows:

```
deploy http://localhost:8080/CCheck/services/AdminService deploy.wsdd
```

After you execute the previous command, your Web service is ready to be used. You can use the following client code to test the Web service:

```
import org.apache.axis.client.Call;
import org.apache.axis.client.Service;
import javax.xml.rpc.namespace.QName;
public class TestClient2 {
    public static void main(String [] args) {
try {
  String endpoint =
```

```
        "http://localhost:8080/CCheck/services/CCheck";
        Service  service = new Service();
        Call call    = (Call) service.createCall();
        call.setTargetEndpointAddress( new java.net.URL(endpoint) );
        call.setOperationName(new QName("http://CCheck", "isValid"));
        String ret = (String) call.invoke( new Object[] { "411111111111111" } );
        System.out.println("Credit card is " + ret);
    }
 catch (Exception e) {
        System.err.println(e.toString());
    }
  }
}
```

However, the steps followed in the previous sections to create and deploy a Web service can be tedious and time consuming, especially when you need to deploy large-scale Web services. Therefore, IBM provides you with a complete commercial IDE, which simplifies greatly the task of building all kinds of J2EE applications, including Web services t, the Websphere Studio Application Developer.

Using the Websphere Studio Application Developer

As discussed, the Websphere Studio Application Developer makes the task of developing Web services simple. In this section, you will create the credit card validation Web service by using the studio. In addition, you will learn to develop a sample client application by using the studio.

To create a Web service, you first need to create a Web project.

Creating a Web Project

Follow these steps to create a Web project:

1. Start the Websphere Studio Application Developer.
2. Create a new Web project by selecting the File, New, Web Project options. The Define the Web Project page opens, as shown in Figure 15-12.
3. Specify the name of the project and the EAR container for the project.
4. Click on the Next button. The Define Java Build Settings page is displayed, as shown in Figure 15-13.

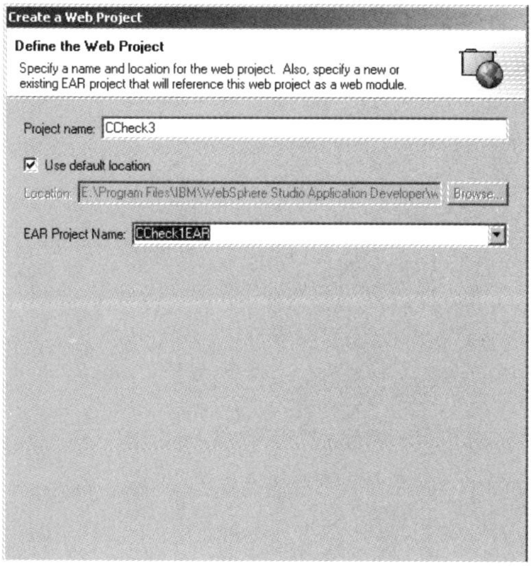

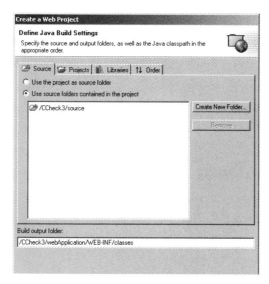

FIGURE 15-12 *Creating a Web project.*

FIGURE 15-13 *Defining Java Build Settings.*

5. The first tabbed window allows you to specify the source folder for the project. Accept the default values.

6. The next tabbed window, Projects, allows you to include any other projects while building the project (see Figure 15-14).

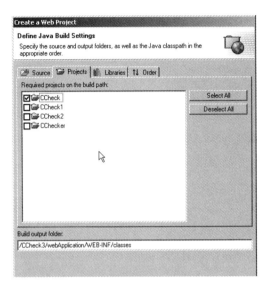

FIGURE 15-14 *The Projects tab.*

7. Click on the Libraries tab. The window is displayed, as shown in Figure 15-15. Because XML is used, you need to specify the build path to the JAR file with the parser.

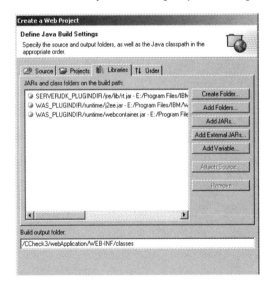

FIGURE 15-15 *The Libraries tab.*

8. Click on the Add External JARs button.

9. Browse to the plugins/com.ibm.etools.websphere.runtime/runtime folder and select xerces.jar.

10. Click on the Finish button to complete the creation of the Web project.

Importing the Java File

Next, you need to import the Java file that contains the credit card validation code. To import the Ccheck.java file, perform the following steps:

1. Select Import from the File menu. The Import Wizard starts, as shown in Figure 15-16.

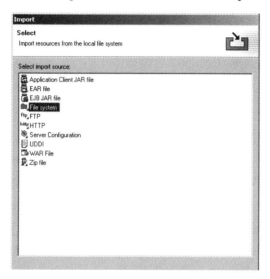

FIGURE 15-16 *The Import Wizard.*

2. In the wizard, select File System and click on the Next button. The File System pane of the wizard is displayed, as shown in Figure 15-17.

3. Click on the Browse button next to the Directory text box and select the folder containing the Ccheck.java file.

4. Next, select the directory name check box.

5. Click on the Select Types button. The Select Types dialog box is displayed, as shown in Figure 15-18.

6. Select the check box next to *.java and click on the OK button to close the window.

7. Double-click on the folder name. A list of all files of the types you selected appears on the right side.

8. Select the Ccheck.Java file, as shown in Figure 15-19.

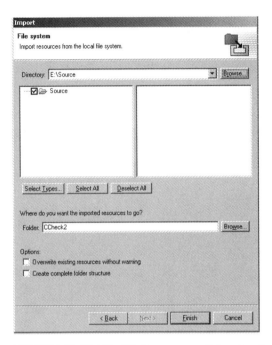

FIGURE 15-17 *The File System pane of the wizard.*

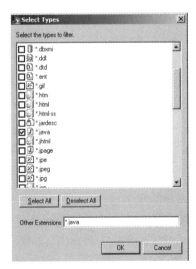

FIGURE 15-18 *The Select Types dialog box.*

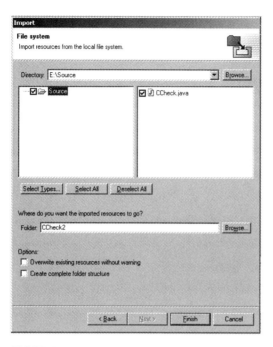

FIGURE 15-19 *Importing the Java source file.*

9. Specify the folder where you need to copy the files that you have selected.

10. Click on the Browse button next to the Folder text box and select the folder where you want to import these files.

11. Click on the Finish button to close the Import Wizard.

Creating the Web Service

To create the Web service, perform the following steps:

1. Select the New, Web Services option from the File menu. The Select page appears, as shown in Figure 15-20.

2. Click on the Next button. The Web Service Wizard starts.

3. Select the Web project to which you want to add the Web service.

4. Click on the Next button. The Web Service Type selection pane is displayed, as shown in Figure 15-21.

5. From the available files, select Ccheck.Java.

FIGURE 15-20 *Creating a Web service.*

FIGURE 15-21 *The Web Service Type Selection pane.*

6. Click on the Next button. The Web Service Java Bean Identity pane is displayed, as shown in Figure 15-22.

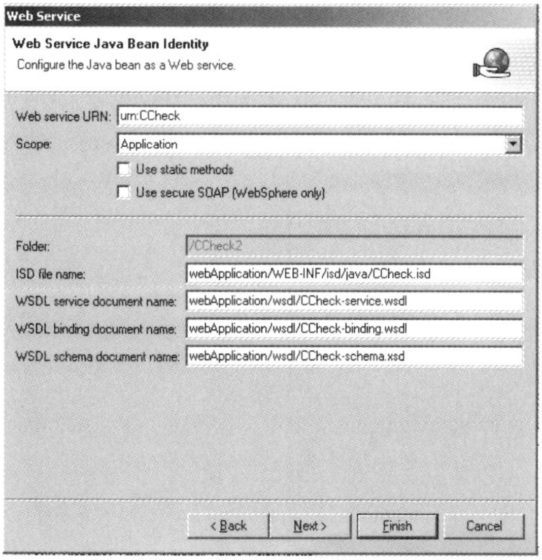

FIGURE 15-22 *The Web Service Java Bean Identity pane.*

7. Change the scope from Application to Session. This ensures that a new object for each user is created so that caching of the service works properly for each user.

8. Click on the Next button. The Web Service Java Bean Methods pane is displayed, as shown in Figure 15-23.

FIGURE 15-23 *The Web Service Java Bean Methods pane.*

9. Select the `isValid()` method. You can decide whether to use the encoding style by the Web service.

10. Click on the Next button. The Web Service Java to XML Mappings pane is displayed, as shown in Figure 15-24.

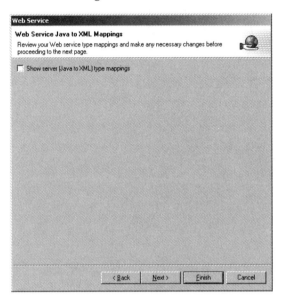

FIGURE 15-24 *The Web Service Java to XML Mappings pane.*

11. Click on the Next button. The Web Service Proxy Generation pane is displayed, as shown in Figure 15-25.

12. Select the Generate a Proxy check box to create a proxy for the Web service, which you can further use to build Web service clients.

13. Click on the Next button. The Web Service Client XML to Java Mappings pane is displayed, as shown in Figure 15-26.

14. Click on the Next button. The Web Service Sample Generation pane is displayed, as shown in Figure 15-27.

 NOTE

Note that the Web Services Sample Generation pane is only active if you chose to create the proxy previously.

FIGURE 15-25 *The Web Service Proxy Generation pane.*

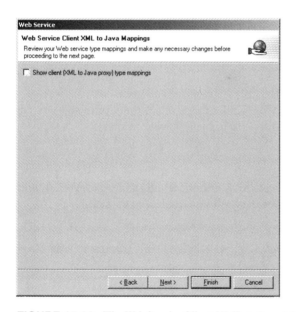

FIGURE 15-26 *The Web Service Client XML to Java Mappings pane.*

FIGURE 15-27 *The Web Service Sample Generation pane.*

15. Select the Generate a Sample check box. The other controls are then activated.

16. Check the Launch the Sample check box and click on the Finish button to create the Web service, create a client application for the Web service, and launch the client application.

The preceding steps create two WSDL files that contain the service and interface details of the Web service. These files are discussed in the following sections.

WSDL Service File

The IDE creates a implementation WSDL document and an interface WSDL document. The content of the interface WSDL for the Web service file is as shown:

```
<?xml version="1.0" encoding="UTF-8"?>
<definitions name="CCheckService" targetNamespace="http://localhost:8080/CCheck1/
wsdl/CCheck-service.wsdl" xmlns="http://schemas.xmlsoap.org/wsdl/"
xmlns:tns="http://localhost:8080/CCheck1/wsdl/CCheck-service.wsdl"
xmlns:binding="http://www.ccheck.com/definitions/CCheckRemoteInterface"
xmlns:soap="http://schemas.xmlsoap.org/wsdl/soap/">
    <import namespace="http://www.ccheck.com/definitions/CCheckRemoteInterface"
location="http://localhost:8080/CCheck1/wsdl/CCheck-binding.wsdl"/>
    <service name="CCheckService">
```

```
        <port name="CCheckPort" binding="binding:CCheckBinding">
            <soap:address
location="http://localhost:8080/CCheck1/servlet/rpcrouter"/>
        </port>
    </service>
</definitions>
```

WSDL Interface File

The following code is the content of the WSDL document, which defines the interface of the
Web service:

```
<?xml version="1.0" encoding="UTF-8"?>
<definitions name="CCheckRemoteInterface" targetNamespace="http://www.ccheck.com/
definitions/CCheckRemoteInterface" xmlns="http://schemas.xmlsoap.org/wsdl/"
xmlns:tns="http://www.ccheck.com/definitions/CCheckRemoteInterface"
xmlns:xsd="http://www.w3.org/2001/XMLSchema" xmlns:soap="http://
schemas.xmlsoap.org/wsdl/soap/">
  <message name="isValidRequest">
    <part name="CCNo" type="xsd:string"/>
  </message>
  <message name="isValidResponse">
    <part name="result" type="xsd:string"/>
  </message>
  <portType name="CCheck">
    <operation name="isValid">
      <input name="isValidRequest" message="tns:isValidRequest"/>
      <output name="isValidResponse" message="tns:isValidResponse"/>
    </operation>
  </portType>
  <binding name="CCheckBinding" type="tns:CCheck">
    <soap:binding style="rpc" transport="http://schemas.xmlsoap.org/soap/http"/>
    <operation name="isValid">
      <soap:operation soapAction="urn:CCheck" style="rpc"/>
      <input>
        <soap:body use="encoded"
encodingStyle="http://schemas.xmlsoap.org/soap/encoding/"/>
      </input>
      <output>
        <soap:body use="encoded"
```

```
encodingStyle="http://schemas.xmlsoap.org/soap/encoding/"/>
        </output>
    </operation>
  </binding>
</definitions>
```

Apache SOAP Deployment Descriptor

In addition to the WSDL service and interface files, the studio creates an earlier version of the Apache SOAP deployment descriptor. The descriptor is stored in the CCheck.isd file. The following code shows the content of this file:

```
<isd:service id="urn:CCheck" xmlns:isd="http://xml.apache.org/xml-soap/deployment">
  <isd:provider type="java" scope="Session" methods="isValid">
        <isd:java class="CCheck" static="false"/>
  </isd:provider>
  <isd:mappings>
  </isd:mappings>
</isd:service>
```

The IDE creates and uses an earlier version of the deployment descriptor. Compare this with the newer deployment descriptors we have already discussed. The preceding code uses the `id` attribute of the `service` element, which identifies the Web service requestors. Next, the `scope` attribute controls how the SOAP server handles the requests for the service. As you can see, the value of the `scope` attribute is set to `Session`. This implies that a separate service instance is created for each user session.

The value for the `scope` attribute also can be `Application`. In such a situation, one service instance handles all requests. Another alternative for the value of the `scope` attribute is `Request`. In such a situation, a new service instance handles each new request. The `class` attribute of the `Java` element identifies the class that implements the Web service.

Interoperability Between Java and .NET Web Services

You have created Web services by using the .NET platform and Java. However, it is essential that the Web services you created using the two platforms are interoperable with each other.

In this section, you will test the interoperability between Web services created using Java and .NET. To do this, you will create a client application in .NET by using Visual Studio .NET. Then you will access the Java Web services that you have created in this chapter by using the .NET client application.

Creating a Visual Basic .NET Client Application

To create a .NET client application, perform the following steps:

1. Create a Visual Basic .NET Windows application in Visual Studio .NET.

2. In the Solution Explorer window, right-click on the project name and select Add Web Reference from the displayed menu. The Add Web Reference dialog box is displayed, as shown in Figure 15-28.

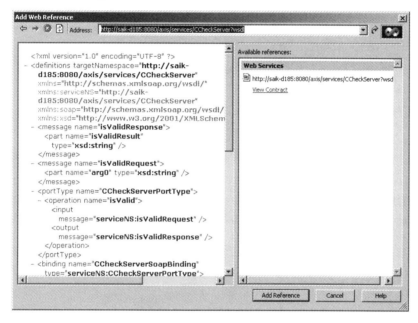

FIGURE 15-28 *The Add Web Reference dialog box.*

3. Enter the URL for the WSDL of the Web service that you created.

 NOTE

Note that the Websphere Studio does not come with a full-fledged application server. Instead, it comes with a micro version of the Websphere application server, which you can use only within the Studio IDE. As a result, you cannot connect to it from Visual Studio .NET.

The Web service that you built using Websphere Studio Application Developer is deployed on an internal version of Websphere; therefore, it uses one of the other Web services that you have deployed on Tomcat. Tomcat is a complete application server that can be accessed from external applications.

4. After the WSDL file is displayed, click on the Add Reference button. The IDE will locally create a WSDL file and proxy.

The following code shows the content of the WSDL file for the Web service that you created and deployed on Tomcat:

```xml
<?xml version="1.0" encoding="utf-8"?>
<definitions xmlns:soap="http://schemas.xmlsoap.org/wsdl/soap/"
xmlns:tns="http://saik-d185:80/axis/services/CCheckServer"
xmlns:s="http://www.w3.org/2001/XMLSchema"
xmlns:http="http://schemas.xmlsoap.org/wsdl/http/"
xmlns:tm="http://microsoft.com/wsdl/mime/textMatching/"
xmlns:mime="http://schemas.xmlsoap.org/wsdl/mime/"
xmlns:soapenc="http://schemas.xmlsoap.org/soap/encoding/"
targetNamespace="http://saik-d185:80/axis/services/CCheckServer"
xmlns="http://schemas.xmlsoap.org/wsdl/">

  <types/>
  <message name="isValidRequest">
    <part name="arg0" type="s:string"/>
  </message>
  <message name="isValidResponse">
    <part name="isValidResult" type="s:string"/>
  </message>

  <portType name="CCheckServerPortType">
    <operation name="isValid">
      <input message="tns:isValidRequest" />
      <output message="tns:isValidResponse" />
    </operation>
  </portType>

  <binding name="CCheckServerSoapBinding" type="tns:CCheckServerPortType">
    <soap:binding transport="http://schemas.xmlsoap.org/soap/http" style="rpc" />
    <operation name="isValid">
      <soap:operation soapAction="" style="rpc" />
      <input>
        <soap:body use="encoded" namespace="CCheckServer"
encodingStyle="http://schemas.xmlsoap.org/soap/encoding/" />
```

```
    </input>
    <output>
       <soap:body use="encoded" namespace="CCheckServer"
encodingStyle="http://schemas.xmlsoap.org/soap/encoding/" />
    </output>
  </operation>
</binding>

<service name="CCheckServer">
  <port name="CCheckServerPort" binding="tns:CCheckServerSoapBinding">
    <soap:address location="http://saik-d185:80/axis/services/CCheckServer"/>
  </port>
</service>
</definitions>
```

As you can see, the preceding WSDL file is not very different from the WSDL file that you could have created using the Java2Wsdl tool.

The following code shows the content of the proxy class created in Visual Basic .NET, which represents the remote Web service:

```
'------------------------------------------------------------------------------
' <autogenerated>
'       This code was generated by a tool.
'       Runtime Version: 1.0.3705.0
'
'       Changes to this file may cause incorrect behavior and will be lost if
'       the code is regenerated.
' </autogenerated>
'------------------------------------------------------------------------------


Option Strict Off
Option Explicit On

Imports System
Imports System.ComponentModel
Imports System.Diagnostics
Imports System.Web.Services
Imports System.Web.Services.Protocols
Imports System.Xml.Serialization
```

```vb
'
'This source code was auto-generated by Microsoft.VSDesigner, Version 1.0.3705.0.
'
Namespace saik_d185

    '<remarks/>
    <System.Diagnostics.DebuggerStepThroughAttribute(),  _
     System.ComponentModel.DesignerCategoryAttribute("code"),  _
     System.Web.Services.WebServiceBindingAttribute(Name:="CCheckServerSoapBinding",
[Namespace]:="http://saik-d185:80/axis/services/CCheckServer")>  _
    Public Class CCheckServer
        Inherits System.Web.Services.Protocols.SoapHttpClientProtocol

        '<remarks/>
        Public Sub New()
            MyBase.New
            Me.Url = "http://saik-d185:80/axis/services/CCheckServer"
        End Sub

        '<remarks/>
        <System.Web.Services.Protocols.SoapRpcMethodAttribute("",
RequestNamespace:="CCheckServer", ResponseNamespace:="CCheckServer")>  _
        Public Function isValid(ByVal arg0 As String) As String
            Dim results() As Object = Me.Invoke("isValid", New Object() {arg0})
            Return CType(results(0),String)
        End Function

        '<remarks/>
        Public Function BeginisValid(ByVal arg0 As String, ByVal callback As
System.AsyncCallback, ByVal asyncState As Object) As System.IAsyncResult
            Return Me.BeginInvoke("isValid", New Object() {arg0}, callback,
asyncState)
        End Function

        '<remarks/>
        Public Function EndisValid(ByVal asyncResult As System.IAsyncResult) As String
            Dim results() As Object = Me.EndInvoke(asyncResult)
            Return CType(results(0),String)
```

```
            End Function
        End Class
End Namespace
```

The bold part of the preceding code shows the isValid() method and how neatly it encapsulates the isValid() method of the Web service.

Adding Code to the Button Control

Add a Button control to the Visual Basic .NET Windows application. To add functionality to the Button control, add the following code to the Click event of the button:

```
Private Sub Button1_Click(ByVal sender As System.Object, ByVal e As
System.EventArgs) Handles Button1.Click
    Dim ws As New WindowsApplication1.saik_d185.CCheckServer()
        MsgBox(ws.isValid("111111111111111"))
End Sub
```

Now run the application and verify the functioning of the Web service by passing appropriate values to the isValid() method.

Summary

In this chapter, you created a Web service project by using the IBM toolkit, which is similar to creating Web services by using Java and the .NET technologies. Two of the most important toolkits that IBM provides are the Web Services ToolKit and the Websphere Studio Application Developer.

Next, you looked at the software required to develop a Web service by using the IBM toolkits. The software includes the Tomcat application server, WSTK, Websphere Studio Application Developer, the Axis SOAP kit, and JDK. You also looked at the installation of all this software.

From there, you created, deployed, and tested a Web service by using the Axis toolkit. In addition to creating a Web service by using Axis, you learned to create a Web service from a class file. You also tested the Web service by a client application created by using the Axis tools. Finally, you tested the Web service from a client application created on the .NET platform. This enabled you to appreciate the interoperability of Web services created using the IBM toolkit and the .NET platform.

PART XI

Professional Project 8

Project 8

Creating the Rent-a-Car Web Service and Mobile Application

Project 8 Overview

Until now, you have learned to develop Web services that you can access from client applications that are built on various platforms. Similarly, you can access Web services from different devices that include PC and mobile devices, such as mobile phone, PDA, and so on.

In this project, you will create a Web service that the customers of a car rental company can use to book a car. Then you will create a mobile application that accesses this Web service. This mobile application provides a front end that mobile phone users can use to book cars with the car rental company. This project uses Visual Studio .NET to create the Web service and Visual Studio .NET with the Microsoft Mobile Internet Toolkit to create the mobile Web application. This project also discusses the advantages and limitations of accessing Web services from mobile applications.

Chapter 16

Introduction to Mobile Applications

In this book, you have already learned how to create Windows applications, Web applications, and Web services in Visual Studio .NET. In this chapter, you will learn how to create a mobile Web application. To begin, you will read a brief introduction to mobile Web applications and the need to develop them.

In addition, you will be introduced to the technologies used to create, transfer, and deploy mobile Web applications. These technologies include Transmission Control Protocol (TCP/IP) and Wireless Application Protocol (WAP). Finally, we will discuss how to create a simple mobile Web application.

Introducing Mobile Web Applications

Mobile Web applications, as the name suggests, are applications that you can access from a mobile device, such as a mobile phone or a Pocket PC. In today's dynamic business scenario, it is essential that users not be limited to accessing their data or the Internet only from their personal computers at home or at the office. Instead, it has become a necessity to be able to access their personal or business data and Internet from anywhere at any time. Users should have the capability to access their data or an Internet site from their mobile devices. This can be achieved through the use of mobile Web applications.

Until recently, mobile Web applications were not widely used, mainly because of certain limitations of mobile Web applications, as discussed in the following list:

◆ Due to the small size of a mobile device's screen, it's difficult for users to access and navigate a Web page from their mobile devices.

◆ Accessing a mobile Web application from a mobile device requires higher bandwidth than is available. For example, mobile phones offer a bandwidth of 9.6 kbps, which is not sufficient to transfer large data. This increases the overall cost of running the application from a mobile device.

◆ You cannot access a mobile Web application from a mobile device for an extended time because of the mobile device's short battery life and limited memory capacity. Therefore, mobile devices cannot be a primary mode of accessing applications; however, you can use mobile devices to access applications whenever required.

To enable users to benefit from a mobile Web application, the .NET Framework allows you to create mobile Web applications that you can access from a mobile device without much problem. In addition, you can optimize these mobile applications for the capabilities of the targeted device.

You can create mobile Web applications that you can access in the same way that you access a Web page from a browser window. In addition, a mobile Web application that you create by using the .NET technologies allows you to access a Web application from a mobile device. This caters to a user's requirement of accessing an application or a Web site from a mobile device. We will discuss the technologies that have made this possible in the later section "The Transfer Protocols for Accessing Mobile Web Applications."

However, Visual Studio .NET does not allow you to create mobile Web applications by default. To be able to create a mobile Web application in Visual Studio .NET, you first need to install the Microsoft Mobile Internet Toolkit. The following section discusses the Microsoft Mobile Internet Toolkit in detail.

The Microsoft Mobile Internet Toolkit

The Microsoft Mobile Internet Toolkit is an easy-to-use toolkit based on the .NET Framework that you install on your machine to create mobile Web applications. You learned to create ASP.NET Web applications by using Visual Studio .NET. The Mobile Internet Toolkit makes creating mobile Web applications as simple as creating ASP.NET applications in Visual

Studio .NET. This is because the Mobile Internet Toolkit provides you with the tools that you can use to create, test, and deploy a mobile Web application. Using the tools provided by the Mobile Internet Toolkit, such as controls and components, you can create the mobile Web forms that are the building blocks of a mobile Web application.

Following are the features of the Mobile Internet Toolkit that make it easy to create mobile Web applications in Visual Studio .NET:

◆ To create the mobile Web forms, the Mobile Internet Toolkit provides a toolbox that contains several controls. To add these controls to the form, you can drag the controls onto the form. You will learn about various mobile Web controls in the section "Mobile Web Form Controls." Figure 16-1 shows the toolbox provided by Visual Studio .NET to add controls in a mobile Web form.

FIGURE 16-1 *The toolbox containing mobile Web controls.*

◆ The Mobile Internet Toolkit contains a visual tool for creating mobile Web applications called the mobile Internet designer. You can integrate this tool easily with the Visual Studio .NET IDE. Figure 16-2 shows the mobile Internet designer.

◆ The Mobile Internet Toolkit converts the code written for a mobile Web application in any of the .NET languages, such as Visual Basic .NET or Visual C#, to the managed code that is used to debug and deploy applications that are created in Visual Studio .NET.

◆ The major advantage of using the Mobile Internet Toolkit is that it allows you to create a common code for mobile Web applications that you can access from various mobile devices. This implies that if you create a mobile Web application for a mobile phone, you can access the same application from any other mobile device, such as a PDA or a pager.

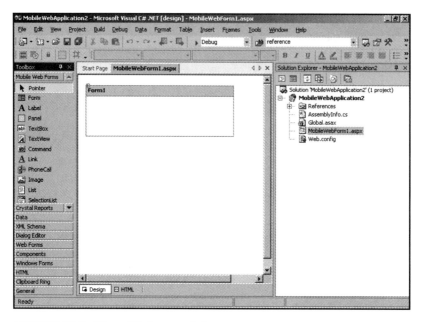

FIGURE 16-2 *The mobile Internet designer.*

After you write a code for a mobile Web application, the code adapts to the features of the mobile device from which the application is accessed. These features of the mobile device include the bandwidth, screen size, memory, and processor capacity.

Although the code of a mobile Web application that you access from various mobile devices is the same, the Internet protocols used to transfer mobile Web applications are different for different devices. For example, the transfer protocol for a mobile phone is WAP and for a PDA it's TCP/IP.

◆ As discussed earlier, the Mobile Internet Toolkit allows you to create mobile Web applications that can display Web pages on a mobile device. You create these mobile Web pages in the form of mobile Web forms that contain mobile Web controls. After you create a mobile Web form, the controls in the Web form are broken down into smaller units called *screens*. You can then display the content of the Web site in these screens. The mobile device from which you access the application determines the size of the screens that are created. Figure 16-3 shows a mobile Web form with a control added.

◆ You can access easily the Mobile Internet Toolkit by using an emulator that can test a mobile Web application. You can test the mobile Web applications that you create in the Internet Explorer window and an emulator.

An *emulator* is a device that simulates the mobile Web application environment on your personal computer. To do this, you first need to install an emulator and emulator software on your machine. Figure 16-4 shows an emulator for a mobile phone.

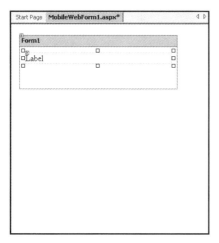

FIGURE 16-3 *The mobile Web form with a control added.*

FIGURE 16-4 *A mobile Web form emulator.*

You've probably noticed the ease that the Mobile Internet Toolkit provides you for creating mobile Web applications. However, as discussed earlier, Visual Studio .NET does not allow you to create mobile Web applications by default. This is because the Mobile Internet Toolkit does not come as part of Visual Studio .NET. You need to install the Mobile Internet Toolkit, which is available as a free download on Microsoft's Web site (http://www.microsoft.com). You can install the Mobile Internet Toolkit on any machine that runs Windows NT or higher and has the .NET Framework or Visual Studio .NET installed on it. The Mobile Internet Toolkit is available at http://msdn.microsoft.com/downloads/default.asp?url=/downloads/sample.asp?url=/msdn-files/027/001/817/msdncompositedoc.xml.

After you install the Mobile Internet Toolkit, several project types are added to the New Project dialog box. These project types include Pocket PC Application, Pocket PC Class Library, Pocket PC Control Library, Mobile Web Application, and Mobile Phone Application. Figure 16-5 shows the New Project dialog box with new project types added.

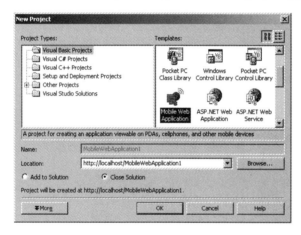

FIGURE 16-5 *The New Project dialog box with new project types added.*

The Transfer Protocols for Accessing Mobile Web Applications

As discussed earlier, different protocols are used to transfer mobile Web applications on different mobile devices. These protocols include TCP/IP, WAP, HTTP, and so on. This section discusses some of these protocols.

TCP/IP

As the name suggests, TCP/IP is a set of protocols that transfers data over the network. This implies that TCP/IP defines the set of rules to follow while you're transferring data across computers over the network. In addition to transferring data over a network, TCP/IP allows you to share resources and enable communication across computers over the same network or different networks. Therefore, TCP/IP is a platform-independent protocol that can transfer data over networks in the form of data packets. For example, you can use TCP/IP to transfer data from a computer that is running Windows to another computer that is running DOS, Unix, or NetWare.

When you need to transfer data across a network, TCP/IP breaks the data into smaller data packets that you can transfer over the network easily. Then, at the receiver end, the data packets are reassembled to produce the original data. The IP address of the destination location defines the address of the location to which the data packets need to be transferred.

As discussed earlier, TCP/IP is the transfer protocol that accesses a mobile Web application from a PDA or other device that supports TCP/IP-based network communication.

WAP

WAP is the transfer protocol that accesses a mobile Web application from a wireless device, such as a mobile phone. In addition, WAP allows you to access an Internet site from a wireless device. However, to be able to access a mobile Web application or an Internet site from a wireless device, you need to have a WAP-enabled mobile device.

In earlier sections, we discussed the problems that the users face while accessing traditional mobile Web applications from a mobile device. These problems include higher bandwidth requirements, higher processor and memory capacities, and smaller screen sizes. As a solution to these problems, the WAP Forum developed an industry standard that defines the set of rules for communication between wireless devices and the application developed to be accessed from a wireless device. A WAP-enabled device has features that are appropriate for accessing mobile applications. These features include limited memory, a battery, and the ability to utilize maximum processor capacity. As a result, it has become significantly easier to access an application or an Internet site from a WAP-enabled device.

Having introduced you to the WAP technology, we will now discuss the WAP architecture that makes it possible to transfer a mobile Web application to a wireless device.

The WAP Architecture

The WAP architecture is a three-layered structure that includes a client, a server, and an intermediate layer. This intermediate layer includes a WAP gateway, which is an interface between the client and the server. A WAP gateway is software that comprises encoders and decoders used to transmit data in the format that the receiving device understands. This is made possible because of the support that the WAP gateway extends to technologies such as WML (Wireless Markup Language) and XML (Extensible Markup Language). These markup languages define the format for displaying data and describe the data to be displayed in a text format.

When a client—a wireless device in our case—sends a request to the server, a connection is made to the WAP gateway. The encoders that are present in the WAP gateway then encode the request as per the transfer protocols. The request is then transferred to the server, and the server sends a response to the client in the form of a site that the client requested. However, the server can process only the request made for a WAP-enabled Web site. See Figure 16-6 so that you can more easily understand this architecture.

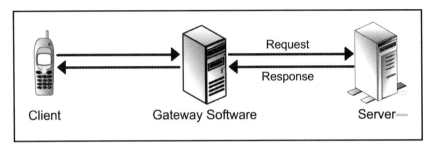

FIGURE 16-6 *The WAP architecture.*

A discussion of the Web architecture will enhance your understanding about the WAP architecture, so we will discuss it next. Learning about the Web architecture will also help you appreciate its similarities to the WAP architecture.

The Web Architecture

The WAP architecture is similar to the Web architecture. However, the Web architecture does not include the intermediate layer, which is the WAP gateway software in the WAP architecture.

In the Web architecture, the client sends a request to the Web server in the form of the Internet address of the requested Web site. The server processes the request and sends the response in the HTML format to the client. Figure 16-7 shows the Web architecture in detail.

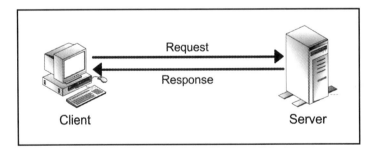

FIGURE 16-7 *The Web architecture.*

Components of a Mobile Web Application

The mobile Web application consists of mobile Web forms that are the building blocks of a mobile Web application. In addition, the mobile Web application consists of mobile Form controls that you can add to the mobile Web forms. The mobile Web controls are used to display text and images, accept input from users, and display the output to the user. The following section discusses these components in detail.

The Mobile Web Forms

When you create a mobile Web application in Visual Studio .NET, the application contains a mobile Web form by default. A mobile Web form is a container control in the toolbox that you can use to hold other controls. The mobile Web form is similar to an ASP.NET Web form except for the size of the mobile Web form, which is far smaller than the ASP.NET Web form. In addition, the mobile Web form comes as a control in the Mobile Web Forms toolbox. Figure 16-8 shows the Mobile Web Forms toolbox with a Form control selected.

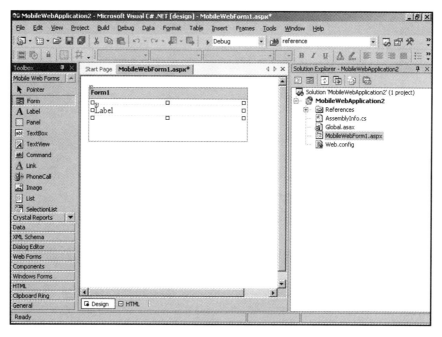

FIGURE 16-8 *The Mobile Web Forms toolbox with a Form control selected.*

To add a mobile Web form to your application, drag the Web Form control to the MobilePage control. The MobilePage control is another container control that contains all mobile Web forms included in the application. You can include as many mobile Web Form controls to a MobilePage control as you need. Figure 16-9 shows the MobilePage control with a mobile Web Form control.

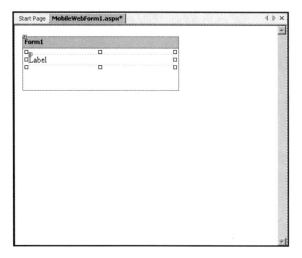

FIGURE 16-9 *The MobilePage control with a mobile Web Form control.*

 NOTE

A mobile Web form that you create in your application has a default extension of .aspx.

As you can see in Figure 16-8, the Mobile Web Forms toolbox contains several controls that you can add to the mobile Web forms. The following section discusses these controls in detail.

Mobile Web Form Controls

Similar to providing controls for developing Windows applications or Web applications, Visual Studio .NET also provides you with controls for creating mobile Web forms. Table 16-1 lists some of these controls in detail.

Table 16-1 The Mobile Web Form Controls

Mobile Web Form Control	Description
MobilePage control	A MobilePage control is a container control that holds Form controls created for a mobile Web application.
Form control	A Form control is a container control that holds Panel controls or any other control present in the Mobile Web Forms toolbox.
Panel control	A Panel control is a container control that groups related controls or other Panel controls.

Mobile Web Form Control	Description
Label control	A Label control displays text in a mobile Web form.
TextBox control	A TextBox control allows users to enter text in a mobile Web form. However, a TextBox control is used to display only single-line text.
TextView control	A TextView control displays text in more than one line. You can use a TextView control to display multiple lines of text.
Command control	A Command control posts the values that a user inputs to the server.
Link control	A Link control creates text as a hyperlink to another Web form.
Image control	An Image control adds an image to the mobile Web form.
List control	A List control groups a list of items in a mobile Web form.
SelectionList control	A SelectionList control displays a list of items in the form of a drop-down list, check boxes, option buttons, or combo boxes.
Calendar control	A Calendar control adds a calendar to the mobile Web forms.
StyleSheet control	A StyleSheet control defines the styles that you want to apply to the Web forms controls. A StyleSheet control can be directly added to the MobilePage control.
Validation controls	The validation controls perform validations on the text that the user enters. These validation controls include RequiredFieldValidator, CompareValidator, RangeValidator, RegularExpressionValidator, and CustomValidator.

Creating a Sample Mobile Web Application

After learning the basics of a mobile Web application, you can now create a sample mobile Web application. To create a mobile Web application, perform the following steps:

1. Launch Visual Studio .NET from the Programs menu.
2. Select File, New, Project.
3. In the New Project dialog box, create a C# project.

 NOTE

You can also create a mobile Web application in Visual Basic .NET; however, in this chapter, you will create the application in C#.

4. Select the Mobile Web Application option in the Templates pane.

5. In the Location text box, specify the name and location of the mobile Web application, and click on the OK button. Visual Studio .NET creates a framework for the mobile Web application, as shown in Figure 16-10.

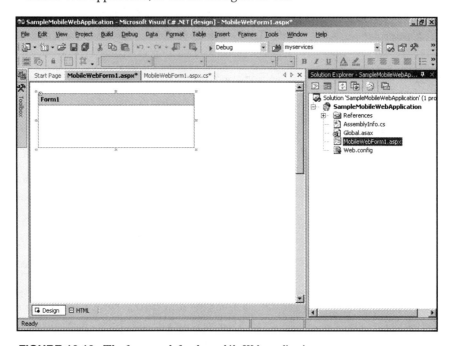

FIGURE 16-10 *The framework for the mobile Web application.*

As you can see, Visual Studio .NET creates a blank form for your application. When you double-click on the blank form, the code window appears, which contains a default code for a mobile Web application as shown:

```
using System;
using System.Collections;
using System.ComponentModel;
using System.Data;
using System.Drawing;
using System.Web;
using System.Web.Mobile;
using System.Web.SessionState;
using System.Web.UI;
using System.Web.UI.MobileControls;
using System.Web.UI.WebControls;
```

```
using System.Web.UI.HtmlControls;

namespace SampleMobileWebApplication
{
                public class MobileWebForm1 : System.Web.UI.MobileControls.MobilePage
                {
                                protected System.Web.UI.MobileControls.Form Form1;
                                private void Page_Load(object sender, System.EventArgs e)
                                {

                                }
                }
}
```

The preceding code uses the using statements to include namespaces in your application. In addition to the default namespaces, Visual Studio .NET creates a namespace with the same name as that of your application, SampleMobileWebApplication. Inside this namespace, Visual Studio .NET creates a public class with the name MobileWebForm1. This class is derived from the System.Web.UI.MobileControls.MobilePage class.

The MobileWebForm1 class declares an instance, Form1, of the Form class. Form1 represents the blank form that is included in the mobile Web application by default. In addition, the MobileWebForm1 class contains the Page_Load() method. You can include the statements required for initializing the mobile page in the Page_Load() method.

You can now add controls to the mobile Web form. At this point, though, it's important to discuss the functioning of the mobile Web application so that you can code the application more easily.

Working of the Mobile Web Application

The working of the mobile Web application is as follows:

1. The user selects a song in the SelectItem form.
2. The user clicks on the Show Review button.
3. Form1 is displayed, which shows the review of the selected song. The review is stored in an XML file.
4. The user clicks on the Back button.
5. The SelectItem form is displayed.

Creating the XML File

In the text file, add the following code:

```
<?xml version='1.0'?>
<!--Songs Review -->
<Songs_Review>
    <Song name="Blue" singer="Eiffel 65">
        <Review>As Mambo No. 5 has finally fallen down the charts, Blue is the
latest big novelty hit. In its low budget sound and quirkiness, Blue brings to
mind some of the fun, silly disco of the late 70's. Blue begins with the surreal
tale of living in a world where everything, and he means everything, is blue.
Then it just drifts along with lots of da da dees, not totally unlike Crystal
Waters' homeless song. You might enjoy it for a while until hearing it
repeatedly drives you crazy.</Review>
    </Song>
    <Song name="The Real Slim Shady" singer="Eminem">
        <Review>On the first single from the Marshall Mathers Lp, Eminem is, as
usual, obnoxious, self pitying but also pretty funny. Real Slim Shady is getting
played on alternative radio while Forgot About Dre, also produced by Dr. Dre
with a similar light but sinister nursery rhyme type backing track, isn't. Is it
because of Eminem's color? Regardless, Real Slim Shady is fun. Despite his dopey
demeanor and accent, Eminem is a pretty fluid rapper and Real Slim Shady is fast
with good momentum. Eminem is conflicted, excited about the prospect of lots of
Eminem wannabes "who could be workin' at Burger King, spittin' on your onion
rings" yet so insecure about the possibility of a white rap usurper that he
needs to repeatedly tell us that he's the real thing. He rightly says he doesn't
care about those who say that Will Smith has hits without swearing but whines
about an unfair world where Tom Green can be dirty and he can't. He disses and
distances himself from Britney and Christina, refusing to admit that he, like
them, owes much of their career to image and MTV. Eminem's a fascinating
character, bursting with ideas, some foolish, some insightful.</Review>
    </Song>
    <Song name="Stan" singer="Eminem">
        <Review>Stan, the latest single from Eminem's Marshall Mathers LP, is
one of most interesting singles to hit mainstream radio this year. Dido's easy
vocals and the unhurried groove, with Mike Elizondo's smooth bass line, provide
a great contrast with Eminem's fast, fluid rap that becomes increasingly
agitated along with his character's troubled mind. As usual, the lyrics
alternate between fascinating and irritating. Eminem concedes he has an effect
```

on his fans. He raises legitimate issues about a society where people are encouraged to believe celebrities are just like them. Stan is a frightening, obsessive character, "a biggest fan" who bases his life on Eminem, menacingly suggests "we should be together" and is infuriated when his idol doesn't respond to his letters. Stan is undoubtedly based on real people who want to connect with Eminem, sometimes in scary ways. I'd prefer Stan without its self-serving final verse. Eminem suddenly becomes caring, writing Stan that he shouldn't take his self-destructive lyrics seriously and should get counseling and treat his girl better. The end is silly. Eminem warns Stan not to end up like a guy he saw on TV who killed himself and his pregnant girlfriend and then realizes, "his name was . . . it was you. Damn."</Review>

    </Song>

    <Song name="Bailamos" singer="Enrique Igleias">

       <Review>With every hit the mainstream success of Latin music is looking more like a trend than a fluke. The first pop hit from Julio's kid is on the soundtrack of Wild, Wild West. Iglesias' call to dance is a weird mix of traditional Spanish flamenco and sleek, cheesy pop.</Review>

    </Song>

    <Song name="Be With You" singer="Enrique Igleias">

       <Review>Be With You is pretty generic, if effective, dance music. Iglesias' voice rides fairly effectively with the cold, steady beat, though he sounds a little uncomfortable when his singing is rushed (perhaps electronically) to keep up with the beat. Iglesias is generally presented as a macho guy. I don't get why the lyrics make him seem like such a pathetic loser. Iglesias sings about his tears, how his life is meaningless without her, and how the sound of her voice could save his soul.</Review>

    </Song>

    <Song name="Escape" singer="Enrique Igleias">

       <Review>Enrique Iglesias follows the big, empty soaring ballad Hero with an empty, generic dance pop song. Iglesias' American success is apparently attributable to his genial, unchallenging music and exotic hunkiness. The video for the title track and second single from Iglesias' Escape CD emphasizes Iglesias' looks by pairing him with exotic babe Anna Kournikova. Escape is pleasant enough, but it basically has no personality. Escape has a decent if familiar guitar riff but also has an uninteresting, very programmed beat and innocuous synth sounds. Like on most of his English language work, Iglesias doesn't sound completely comfortable. He seems handcuffed by the tight, synthetic production and tentative in some of his English pronunciations. I do like the end of Escape when Iglesias gets a rare chance to let loose with a

falsetto repeating "you can run." Iglesias predicts on Escape that, even if she leaves now, his partner will want to come back to a relationship that "was good, it was bad but it was real."</Review>

    </Song>

    <Song name="Hero" singer="Enrique Igleias">

        <Review>Hero, from Iglesias' Escape CD, is another song that's found a September 11 connection. Some TV stations used it with footage of World Trade Center rescuers, and Iglesias sang it at one of the benefit shows. Hero is actually a sappy love song with Iglesias selflessly offering to be a romantic savior. Iglesias slowly and seriously intones the lyrics, sounding a little like he's pronouncing them phonetically. The music starts fairly minimally but builds to an unsubtle conclusion with big, sweeping strings. That said, Hero isn't as cheesy and synthetic sounding as much of Iglesias' English language work. It does what it's supposed to with emotional romance novel imagery of an exotic Latin lover that's bound to appeal to millions of women.</Review>

    </Song>

    <Song name="Only Time" singer="Enva">

        <Review>Besides providing vaguely mystical sounding background music for commercials, soothing is what Enya's ultra-lite music does best. So it's not surprising that some have found that in a troubled time, Only Time, from Enya's A Day Without Rain CD, has therapeutic qualities. Rather than being about time healing, Only Time's message is that the future is unpredictable so there's no point worrying about it. Only Time is potentially sleep inducing elevator music, but it's also a striking, delicately gauzy example of Enya's usual ethereal formula of filtered voices, layered keyboards, and polite, programmed beat.</Review>

    </Song>

    <Song name="Superman Inside" singer="Eric Clapton">

        <Review>I'm indifferent to Clapton's new age lyric about "gettin' closer to peace of mind" and finding the Superman inside, but his "need to let it out" is matched in the music's buoyant mood. The new Reptile CD has good musicians including Billy Preston and Paul Carrack on keyboards. Superman Inside has the kind of loose, rollicking piano Preston did for the Rolling Stones. Clapton's recent singles have been so mellow and serious that it's good he's doing the kind of fun song he hasn't done much since Forever Man. Superman Inside has a big sound with slide guitar, backing vocals, and Clapton's confident lead.</Review>

    </Song>

    <Song name="Here's To The Night" singer="Eve 6">

<Review>It's a cliche of contemporary rock for an otherwise tough band to include a slow song or two on their CD in an attempt at pop success. Here's To The Night stands out jarringly among the otherwise tough, somewhat unpleasant rock songs on Eve 6's Horrorscope CD. With its strings and pleasant but empty pop sound, Here's To The Night probably fits more comfortably on pop or easy listening radio. It resembles an 80's rock ballad like John Waite's Missing You. Max Collins tries to sound like a sensitive male, but the lyrics, like many of Horrorscope, are pretty backward about women. Collins tells the woman he lied to, "don't let me let you go."</Review>

   </Song>

</Songs_Review>

 NOTE

Please note that we took these reviews from the URL http://www.all-reviews.com/song-lists/song-artist-E.htm.

After adding the code, save the file as Songs.xml in the C drive. To view the file, open the file in a Web browser. The Songs.xml file looks like Figure 16-11.

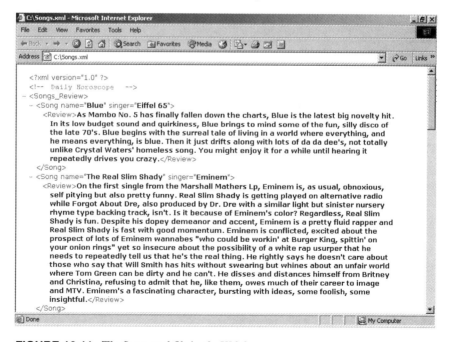

FIGURE 16-11 *The Songs.xml file in the Web browser.*

Adding Controls to the Mobile Web Form

As you have seen, Visual Studio .NET creates a blank form for the application. To this form, add a Label, SelectionList, and Command control. After adding the controls to the form, the form looks like Figure 16-12.

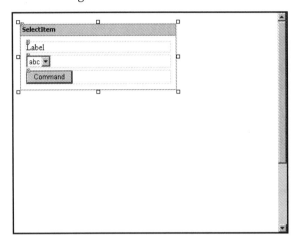

FIGURE 16-12 *The SelectItem form in Design view.*

Now change the properties of the control, as discussed in Table 16-2.

Table 16-2 Controls in the Mobile Web Form

Control Type	Control ID	Properties Changed
Label	Label1	Text: `Select the required song:`
SelectionList	SelectionList1	`Items`
Command	Command1	Text: `Show Review`

A SelectionList control allows you to display multiple items in the form of a list. To add items to a SelectionList control, perform the following steps:

1. Click on the SelectionList control to display its properties.

TIP

If the Properties window is not displayed, press the F4 key.

2. In the Properties window, select the Items property by clicking on the Ellipsis button. The SelectionList1 Properties window is displayed.

3. Click on the Create New Item button to add an item to the list.

4. In the Item Text pane, specify the item as Eiffel 65, "Blue".

5. In the Value text box, specify the value as Blue.

6. Check the Selected check box.

7. Repeat steps 4 and 5 to add more items to the SelectionList control.

 NOTE

You can add the Eminem, "The Real Slim Shady," Eminem, "Stan," Enrique Iglesias, "Bailamos," Enrique Iglesias, "Be With You," Enrique Iglesias, "Escape," Enrique Iglesias, "Hero," Enya, "Only Time," Eric Clapton, "Superman Inside," and Eve 6, "Here's to the Night" items to the SelectionList control.

---

8. Click on the OK button to add items to the SelectionList control.

After you add items to the SelectionList control, the form looks like Figure 16-13.

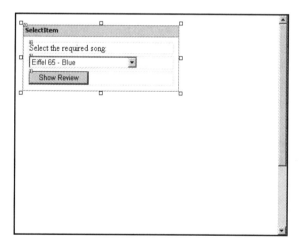

FIGURE 16-13 *The SelectItem form in Design view.*

Adding Controls to Form1

When a user selects an item from the SelectionList control and clicks on the Show Review button, the review of the form is displayed in another form. To do this, you need to add another form to the mobile Web page from the Mobile Web Forms toolbox. Now, add a Label, TextView, and Command control to the Web form, and change the properties of the control, as specified in Table 16-3.

Table 16-3 Controls in the Mobile Web Form

Control Type	Control ID	Properties Changed
Label	Label2	Text: `Label`
TextView	TextView1	`TextView`
Command	Command2	Text: `Back`

After you change the properties of the controls, the mobile Web form looks like Figure 16-14.

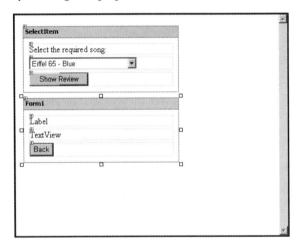

FIGURE 16-14 *The Form1 form in Design view.*

Adding Code to the Controls

The controls that you have added to the form do not perform an operation. To specify the functionality to a control, you need to add code to the control, as discussed in the following sections.

Adding Code to the Command1 Control

When a user selects the song and clicks on the Show Review button, the application reads the review of the selected song from the Songs.xml file and displays the result in Form1. To perform this functionality, add the following code to the `Click` event of the Command1 control:

```
private void Command1_Click(object sender, System.EventArgs e)
{
    XmlTextReader reader = new XmlTextReader("C:\\Songs.xml");
    reader.MoveToContent();
    while (reader.Read())
    {
```

```
        if (reader.HasAttributes)
        {
                reader.MoveToNextAttribute();
                        if(reader.Value==SelectionList1.Selection.Value)
                        {
                                Label2.Text=reader.Value + " (";
                                reader.MoveToNextAttribute();
                                Label2.Text=Label2.Text + reader.Value + ")";
                                reader.MoveToElement();
                                TextView1.Text=reader.ReadInnerXml();
                        }
                }
        }


        reader.Close();
        ActiveForm=Form1;
}
```

The preceding code creates an object, reader, of the XMLTextReader class and initializes it to the Songs.xml file in the C drive. Next, the MoveToContent() method of the XmlReader class is used to check whether the current node in the XML document is a content node. Then the content in the nodes of the XML document are read by using the Read() method.

Next, the HasAttributes property of the XmlReader class is used to check whether the current node has attributes associated with it. The HasAttributes property returns a Boolean type value. If the current node has an associated attribute, the HasAttributes property returns a true value.

If the HasAttributes property returns a true value, the reader object is moved to the first attribute in the current node. Then, an if loop is used to match the value in the attribute of the current node to the value that the user selects. If the values match, the value is displayed in the Label control in Form1. Similarly, the review, which is the next element in the Songs.xml file, is displayed in the TextView control. Finally, the reader object is closed and the control is passed to Form1 by using the ActiveForm property.

 NOTE

Because the preceding code uses the classes in the System.XML namespace, you need to include this namespace in the beginning of the application by using the following statement:

```
using System.Xml;
```

Adding Code to the Command2 Control

When the Command2 control is clicked, the user is returned to the SelectItem form. To do this, add the following code to the Click event of the Command2 control:

```
private void Command2_Click(object sender, System.EventArgs e)
{
        ActiveForm=SelectItem;
}
```

When you add code to the Command controls, the entire code for the application is as follows:

```csharp
using System;
using System.Collections;
using System.ComponentModel;
using System.Data;
using System.Drawing;
using System.Web;
using System.Web.Mobile;
using System.Web.SessionState;
using System.Web.UI;
using System.Web.UI.MobileControls;
using System.Web.UI.WebControls;
using System.Web.UI.HtmlControls;
using System.Xml;


namespace SampleMobileWebApplication
{
        /// <summary>
        /// Summary description for MobileWebForm1.
        /// </summary>
        public class MobileWebForm1 : System.Web.UI.MobileControls.MobilePage
        {
                protected System.Web.UI.MobileControls.Form SelectItem;
                protected System.Web.UI.MobileControls.Label Label1;
                protected System.Web.UI.MobileControls.SelectionList SelectionList1;
                protected System.Web.UI.MobileControls.Form ViewDescription;
                protected System.Web.UI.MobileControls.Label Label2;
                protected System.Web.UI.MobileControls.TextView TextView1;
                protected System.Web.UI.MobileControls.Command Command2;
```

```
        protected System.Web.UI.MobileControls.Form Form1;
        protected System.Web.UI.MobileControls.Command Command1;


        private void Page_Load(object sender, System.EventArgs e)
        {
                // Put user code to initialize the page here
        }

#region Web Form Designer generated code
override protected void OnInit(EventArgs e)
{
        //
        // CODEGEN: This call is required by the ASP.NET Web Form Designer.
        //
        InitializeComponent();
        base.OnInit(e);
}


/// <summary>
/// Required method for Designer support - do not modify
/// the contents of this method with the code editor.
/// </summary>
        private void InitializeComponent()
        {
                this.Command1.Click += new System.EventHandler(this.Command1_Click);
                this.Command2.Click += new System.EventHandler(this.Command2_Click);
                this.Load += new System.EventHandler(this.Page_Load);
        }
#endregion

private void Command1_Click(object sender, System.EventArgs e)
{
        XmlTextReader reader = new XmlTextReader("C:\\Songs.xml");
        reader.MoveToContent();
        while (reader.Read())
        {
                if (reader.HasAttributes)
                {
```

```
                        reader.MoveToNextAttribute();
                        if(reader.Value==SelectionList1.Selection.Value)
                        {
                                Label2.Text=reader.Value + " (";
                                reader.MoveToNextAttribute();
                                Label2.Text=Label2.Text + reader.Value + ")";
                                reader.MoveToElement();
                                TextView1.Text=reader.ReadInnerXml();
                        }
                }
            }
            reader.Close();
            ActiveForm=Form1;
        }


        private void Command2_Click(object sender, System.EventArgs e)
        {
                ActiveForm=SelectItem;
        }
    }
}
```

Testing the Application

Your application is now ready to be tested. To test your application, select the Start option on the Debug menu. The SelectItem form is displayed in the browser window, as shown in Figure 16-15.

Now select an item from the SelectionList control and click on the Show Review button. The review of the selected song is displayed in Figure 16-16.

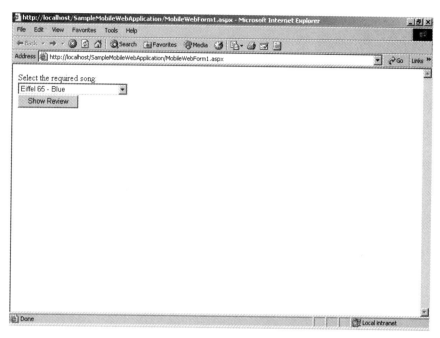

FIGURE 16-15 *The SelectItem form at runtime.*

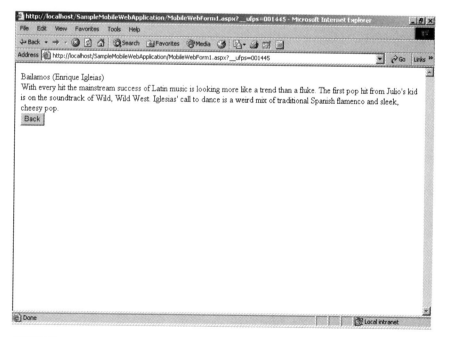

FIGURE 16-16 *The Form1 form at runtime.*

Summary

This chapter introduced you to mobile Web applications. Mobile Web applications, as the name suggests, are applications that you can access from a mobile device, such as a mobile phone or a Pocket PC. To create mobile Web applications in Visual Studio .NET, Microsoft provides you with the Microsoft Mobile Internet Toolkit. This toolkit is easy to use and is based on the .NET Framework.

You learned about the technologies used to create, transfer, and deploy mobile Web applications. These technologies include TCP/IP and WAP. In addition, you were introduced to the mobile Web forms and various mobile Web forms controls. Finally, you created a sample mobile Web application by using these forms and controls.

Chapter 17

You learned about XML Web services and some of its components in the preceding chapter. Chapter 16, "Introduction to Mobile Applications," introduced you to creating mobile applications by using Visual Studio .NET and the Mobile Internet Toolkit. This chapter explores how the functionality of Web services can be supplied with a mobile application.

This chapter introduces you to a case study and design of a mobile Web application that accesses a Web service. Then it teaches you how to create the application.

Case Study for the Rent-a-Car Internet Services

Rent-a-Car is a car rental company. The cars are available in a wide range of styles and prices that extend from the economy range to the expensive luxury range. Until now, the interaction with the business clients has been primarily on the telephone. Now the owners of the company have decided to be more accessible to the customers by having an Internet presence.

To do this, the organization created a Web site with the http://www.RentACar.net URL. The site was created using ASP.NET and uses the .NET Framework and SQL Server as a back-end. The site also makes its car reservation and tracking features accessible to other Web sites, which can allow their visitors to rent a car. This facility is available to a number of general-purpose Web portals that provide their own visitors with the facility of making car reservations. To make the features of the site available to third-party sites, the Web site uses Web services.

To further increase its business, Rent-a-Car decided to provide its customers with access to the reservation facilities through mobile devices. To provide the services of the organization on mobile devices, the company decided to create an alternative site for mobile applications. Further, it will create the application by using the Microsoft Mobile Internet Toolkit and power the application by the Web services that are used by the HTML-based site. To create this application, Rent-a-Car decided on a team of two people: John Carson, the project manager, and Bill Donnovan, the developer. The development team follows the project life cycle as discussed in the following section.

Project Life Cycle

The development life cycle of a mobile application project involves the following three phases:

- Project initiation
- Project execution
- Project deployment

We will only discuss the project execution phase because this phase is different from the earlier projects discussed in this book.

The Project Execution Phase

As you know, you create the design of the application in the project execution phase. After you create the design, you develop the application. The project execution phase consists of the following stages:

- Requirements analysis
- Design

◆ Construction

◆ Testing

In the subsequent sections, we will detail the tasks that the team members perform in each of these stages.

Requirements Analysis

During the requirements analysis phase, the development team at Rent-a-Car analyzed the need to create a Web service. The analysis was done on the basis of the problem stated by Raymond Sutton, the company's marketing manager.

Sutton commented, "We need to increase our visibility and reach; therefore, we need to make our services easily accessible. In addition, our services should be made accessible at all times and from various devices including a mobile phone."

Based on the previous problem statement, the development team analyzed the following requirements:

◆ The Web service will provide data to both an HTML-based site and a mobile application.

◆ The Web service should expose operations that allow a user to make reservations, view reservation details for a specified customer, and modify and delete reservations.

◆ Therefore, the customer should be able to make reservations, view reservation details, and modify and delete reservations from a mobile phone.

Design

During the design phase of the application, the development team decides on the functionality to be implemented and the technology to be used. To create a Web service for Rent-a-Car, the development team decides to use Visual Studio .NET primarily for the following reasons:

◆ The original Web site for the organization is already built by using ASP.NET.

◆ Visual Studio .NET provides a complete set of tools for building both Web services and mobile applications.

As a result, the team decides to develop both applications—the Web service and the mobile application that consumes it—by using Visual Studio .NET and the Mobile Internet Toolkit.

Construction

During this phase, the team constructs the application. The primary tasks that the team needs to perform in this phase are discussed in the following list:

◆ Create a Web service to expose the functionality required to allow a client application to reserve a car, find the rental cost, and modify and delete a reservation.

◆ Create a mobile application that will consume the Web service.

Testing

In the testing phase, various tests and validations are carried out on the application, and the functionality is checked. The Web service is tested by running the mobile application in a browser window, such as Internet Explorer.

Web Services and Mobile Applications

The same Web service can be accessed from any application that includes both a desktop application and a mobile application. In addition, these applications can run on various devices, including a mobile phone, a Pocket PC, a regular PC, and so on. This implies that regardless of the devices that the end users use, your applications can connect to the same Web service and access the Web methods and other features of the service.

Web services provide a standard SOAP-based communication protocol for devices of different kinds and applications built on different platforms. Because the Web services are also language independent, you can build the clients by using languages that are most suited to a particular device or platform. This flexibility of creating applications in any language allows you to leverage your services to any mobile device. In addition, it extends tremendous benefit to the end user.

Consider an example of how you can use a variety of Web services in a single application for a mobile traveler. This imaginary application is a travel manager that provides basic information about an upcoming trip. It keeps track of hotel reservations, car rental, and flight reservations, and it also provides the user with the status of reservations data.

The users could simply store this static information in a data file on their PDAs. However, if you want to offer updated data or allow users to access the same information from their mobile phone, you need to take advantage of Web services. The application that uses Web services in this scenario should work as explained in the following paragraph.

When a user executes the application, it uses a Web service to display the itinerary that the travel agent provides. Then the user downloads the required information to a device. Next, to see the flight details, the user selects the flight, and a Web service contacts the airline. The user can also use a Web service to access the weather conditions at the destination location and accordingly pack the luggage for the trip. Finally, using a separate Web service, the user can arrange for car rental and update the itinerary back to the travel agent.

Although this scenario seems complicated, the end user only needs to access a single application. However, at the back end, the application uses six Web services from five Web service providers. The significant aspect of using Web services is that the back-end Web services are unaffected by the type of device they are interacting with.

You could have easily accessed the same functionality from a mobile phone application that is based on Wireless Application Protocol (WAP), a Java client, or a C# application. Various platform vendors have created new toolkits to ease the development process of consuming Web services on their particular platform. You will learn about the toolkits used to create mobile applications that consume a Web service in the section "Devices and the .NET Framework."

Issues with Web Services

The whole scenario of accessing Web services looks great, but it has certain limitations, especially when a Web service is used in a wireless environment:

◆ Web services might be verbose when required to transfer large documents to a device. The typical bandwidth of current and emerging Wireless LAN services, including the latest 2.5-generation networks, is measured in tens of kilobits per second (Kbps). At times, this bandwidth can be above 100Kbps, which can be compared to a fast desktop dial-up connection but not a LAN connection.

◆ Web services can be slow because SOAP transfers XML over HTTP, which is a rather slow protocol. The system of transferring a message over HTTP can take time to make its way over the wire, process it, and send a response. The situation can be worse if a wireless device is accessing the Web service.

◆ Another important issue while you're using Web services is obtaining up-to-date information about Web services and their availability. Consider a situation in which a Web service published by an organization is registered in the UDDI directory. Perhaps the organization changes the URL to access a Web service or stops publishing the Web service, but it does not update the directory. As a result, the directory has an incorrect entry. This is a common scenario that results in several inaccurate or inaccessible Web services registered with the UDDI.

 NOTE

A recent survey shows that more than 48 percent of UDDI entries are invalid. This means that almost one out of every two Web services published in the UDDI directory is no longer available.

Mobile applications must be designed to compensate for devices' limited size and power. Web services can then be a perfect fit for mobile users who allow them to identify and use highly specific services as and when required. However, Web services have a number of limitations that limit its potential for mobile users. These limitations are discussed in the following list:

◆ When you access an application from a mobile device, the negotiation and discovery of the application requires multiple network round trips. In such a case, if the wireless networks on which mobile users rely have high latency, the overall performance of the application is affected.

◆ Large documents might be unsuitable for processing on a mobile device. They might require greater working memory to store than is available in a mobile device. Large documents might also require more processing power to parse than is currently available. If a service is accessed from a mobile device with limited memory and processing power, the application will send inappropriate responses that a mobile application might use.

◆ Web services depend on the availability of the network. Although they are a wonderful mechanism for separating a specific functionality from the software, they are located across a network. Users want to use their software while on the road or in low bandwidth conditions. Software designers should ensure that their applications that use Web services function accurately even if the network is unavailable. Because mobile devices are typically on the edge of the network and are constantly losing network connections, providing a good user experience will be extremely difficult. Therefore, software designers should make special efforts to provide an offline experience that is equally seamless to the online connection.

◆ Device limitations are a major challenge. The highest-end PDAs in today's world run at hundreds of megahertz (MHz) and offer 64 megabytes (MB) of memory. However, it is hopeful that according to Moore's Law, the next generation of devices will be able to cope with large and complex documents. As a result, Web services will be a mainstream of mobile communications.

Devices and the .NET Framework

In the new programming world of .NET, devices are becoming first-rate players in total solutions that involve Web access, wireless connectivity, mobility, and access to server and the Internet information through Web services. As a result, several toolkits are available for creating applications that are targeted at various devices. The following list discusses some of the commonly used toolkits available to create applications for various devices.

◆ .NET Compact Framework (CF)

◆ Smart Device Extensions (SDE) for Visual Studio .NET

◆ Microsoft Mobile Internet Toolkit

We will now discuss these toolkits in detail.

.NET CF

The .NET CF is the most important announcement for developers who are focusing on devices. The .NET CF brings to device developers the ability to program in C# and VB.NET using the same toolset, Visual Studio .NET, as their desktop counterparts and establishes managed code as an important and viable device platform.

The .NET CF is used to deliver the information at any time, at any place, and on any device. The .NET CF is similar to the Windows CE operating system because .NET CF supports only a subset of the .NET Framework functionality.

 NOTE

The Windows CE operating system includes a subset of features of desktop Windows.

The .NET CF does not include portions of the .NET Framework that do not involve devices or are too resource intensive. Instead, it introduces new classes that are exclusive to devices. The .NET CF is positioned as a hardware-independent program execution environment for devices, such as PDAs, set-top boxes, Web pads, and other embedded devices.

NOTE

The .NET CF is currently available in its Beta phase.

Comparing the design of Windows CE to desktop Windows and .NET CF to the .NET Framework reveals similar constraints. The main difference in Windows CE and desktop Windows lies in the area of COM support. Windows CE supports only a small subset of COM with no real support for DCOM. .NET CF follows this same tradition by supporting neither COM interoperability nor remoting/serialization. The decision was based on the thought that most device-to-server communication would be done through XML and Web services. As a result, direct COM interop with managed code needs to be done explicitly on the .NET CF.

SDE for Visual Studio .NET

The SDE for Visual Studio .NET extends the unified programming environment of .NET to devices powered by the .NET CF. The SDE provides the ability to create additional project types for Pocket PC and Windows CE-based devices and allows you to program and debug these projects by using a single development environment. In addition to the same IDE features, SDE enables device developers to use the same visual forms designers as on the desktop, build applications that operate with XML-based Web services, and leverage the same ADO.NET data access components.

The SDE is an open environment, which means that manufacturers of custom CE devices that support .NET CF can integrate the capabilities of their devices into the Visual Studio IDE seamlessly. A stronger emulation environment allows device developers to program and test their code completely on the desktop prior to deploying it on real devices.

NOTE

The SDE for Visual Studio .NET is a Technology Preview that will be released around the same time as .NET CF.

Visual Studio .NET will use the SDE to develop managed code applications for devices. However, native applications for Pocket PC and Windows CE will still be developed using eMbedded Visual C++ (eVC) support. However, support for eMbedded Visual Basic (eVB) will not be required because the SDE supports both C# and VB.NET.

It is interesting to note how the development environments for Windows CE evolved over time. Originally, the Windows CE tools were add-ons to the Visual Studio IDE. However, as Visual Studio evolved and expanded in subsequent versions, the compatibility of the CE add-on broke, forcing CE developers to use an older version of Visual Studio. In response to this, Microsoft released the eMbedded Visual Tools (eVT) suite, which consisted of both eVC and eVB environments. These environments replicate their VC++ and Visual Basic desktop counterparts.

Microsoft Mobile Internet Toolkit

Microsoft has two distinct views of how devices will play in the .NET arena. The first view centers around the .NET CF. This view primarily sees devices as rich and capable clients that can both interact with Web services and operate in a disconnected mode. The other view has a large set of disparate wireless devices, each with its own distinct set of capabilities and protocol support that are required to get access to corporate and the Internet information. This second view of devices is addressed by the Microsoft Mobile Internet Toolkit (MMIT).

The MMIT is a set of server side .NET components that is able to handle and hide the complexities of developing applications for a variety of wireless devices. Primarily aimed at digital cell phones, MMIT allows Web developers to concentrate on the content information to be delivered to these devices. This is done by handling all differences of various wireless device protocols, such as WAP, iMode, cHTML, and RIM Blackberry. MMIT provides a suite of smart mobile forms and device detection and abstraction classes, which automatically refactors a display suitable for different device characteristics.

Key to MMIT is its expandability. As more wireless devices come to market, resulting in changing protocols, MMIT adapts by supporting a pluggable architecture in which new device components can be integrated without changing the content information. MMIT truly supports encapsulation of the logic of a wireless application from its device-specific presentation.

Creating the Web Service for Rent-a-Car

In this section, you will create the Web service, which a mobile application will consume. Before moving on to the actual creation of a Web service, we will discuss the database tables that the Web service will use.

Database of Rent-a-Car

The tables in the database of Rent-a-Car are discussed in the following list:

♦ **Reservation table.** This table contains entries for all reservations that are made at Rent-a-Car. To store this information, the table contains fields, such as the pickup location as specified by a client who makes the reservation, the date and time of the pickup, the type of car the client wants, and so on. The type of car can include economy, compact, intermediate, premium, and luxury in the increasing order of the rental cost per day. Also, the client needs to specify the number of days for which the car is required. In addition, the name, the customer password, and the customer phone number are stored in the Reservation table. The customer uses the password to modify or delete the reservations that are made. The structure of the Reservation table is shown in Figure 17-1.

Column Name	Data Type	Length	Allow Nulls
RID	int	4	
Location	varchar	25	
PDate	datetime	8	
PTime	char	10	
Duration	int	4	✓
VehicleType	varchar	25	✓
CustName	varchar	25	✓
CustKey	varchar	25	✓
CustPhone	varchar	25	✓

FIGURE 17-1 *The Reservation table.*

◆ **VehicleTypes table.** This table contains a list of the different vehicles available at Rent-a-Car and their rental cost per day. The structure of the VehicleTypes table is shown in Figure 17-2.

Column Name	Data Type	Length	Allow Nulls
VID	int	4	
VType	varchar	25	
Description	varchar	100	✓
Rate	float	8	✓

FIGURE 17-2 *The VehicleTypes table.*

To access data from these tables, the Web service uses stored procedures. These stored procedures are discussed in the following list:

◆ **GetRate stored procedure.** This stored procedure accepts a vehicle type and returns the fare per day for it from the VehicleTypes table.

◆ **Reserve stored procedure.** This stored procedure is used to enter a record into the Reservation table.

◆ **GetVType stored procedure.** This stored procedure returns a list of all vehicle types.

◆ **UpdateReservation stored procedure.** This stored procedure updates the reservation details for a particular customer.

◆ **ViewReservation stored procedure.** This stored procedure views the reservation details for a particular customer.

 NOTE

You can use the SQL Server Enterprise Manager to create the stored procedures.

You will now write the code to create the preceding stored procedures. The code for the `GetRate` stored procedure is as follows:

```
CREATE PROCEDURE dbo.GetRate(@vType varchar(25))
AS
Select rate from VehicleType where vType=@vType
GO
```

Now add the code for the `Reserve` stored procedure as follows:

```
CREATE PROCEDURE dbo.Reserve (@Location varchar(25), @PDate datetime, @PTime
varchar(10),@Duration int,@VType varchar(25),@CustName varchar(25),@CustKey
varchar(25),@CustPhone varchar(25))
AS
insert into
Reservation(Location,PDate,PTime,Duration,VehicleType,CustName,CustKey,CustPhone)
values(@Location , @PDate ,
@PTime ,@Duration ,@VType ,@CustName ,@CustKey,@CustPhone )
Return @@Identity
```

Then add the code for the `GetVType` stored procedure:

```
CREATE PROCEDURE dbo.GetVType
AS
Select Vtype from VehicleType
GO
```

 NOTE

You can use the `GetVType` stored procedure when you want to populate a user-interface element, such as a list box with the values of all possible vehicle types.

Next, add the code for the `UpdateReservation` stored procedure:

```
CREATE PROCEDURE dbo.UpdateReservation (@Location varchar(25),@PDate datetime,@pTime
char(10),@Duration integer,@VType varchar(10),@CustName varchar(10),
@CustKey varchar(10))
AS
update reservation
set Location=@Location, PDate=@PDate,PTime=@pTime,
Duration=@Duration,VehicleType=@VType
```

```
where CustName=@CustName and CustKey=@CustKey
GO
```

Finally, add the code for the `ViewReservation` stored procedure. The code for the `ViewReservation` stored procedure is as follows:

```
CREATE PROCEDURE dbo.ViewReservation(@CustName varchar(25), @CustKey varchar(25))
AS
select Location,PDate,PTime,Duration,VehicleType from Reservation where
CustName=@CustName and CustKey=@CustKey
GO
```

Creating the ASP.NET Web Service

After the stored procedures are created, the next step in creating the Web service is creating an ASP.NET Web service by using Visual Studio .NET. To create an ASP.NET Web service, perform the following steps:

1. Launch Visual Studio .NET from the Programs menu.
2. Select the File, New, Project option.
3. In the New Projects dialog box that is displayed, create a Visual Basic .NET project.
4. Select the ASP.NET Web Service option in the Templates pane.
5. Click on the OK button.

The preceding steps create a framework for a Web service application. Now you can modify the Web service code. In the Service1.asmx file for the Web service, add the declarations for various methods as shown in the following code:

```
<WebMethod()> Public Function MakeReservation(ByVal strLocation As String, ByVal
strDate As String, ByVal strTime As String, ByVal nDuration As Integer, ByVal
strVType As String, ByVal strCustName As String, ByVal strCustKey As String,
ByVal strCustPhone As String) As Integer
End Function


<WebMethod()> Public Function GetRate(ByVal strType As String, ByVal nDuration
As Integer) As Single
End Function


<WebMethod()> Public Function GetVehicleTypes() As String()
End Function


<WebMethod()> Public Function CancelReservation(ByVal strCustName As String,
```

```
ByVal strCustKey As String, ByVal strPDate As String)
End Function


<WebMethod()> Public Function ViewReservation(ByVal strCustName As String, ByVal
strCustKey As String, ByRef strLocation As String, ByRef strPDate As String,
ByRef strPTime As String, ByRef nDuration As Integer, ByRef strVType As String)
End Function


<WebMethod()> Public Function ModifyReservation(ByVal strLocation As String,
ByVal strDate As String, ByVal strTime As String, ByVal nDuration As Integer,
ByVal strVType As String, ByVal strCustName As String, ByVal strCustKey As
String)
End Function
```

The preceding code adds the declarations for the following methods:

◆ **MakeReservation() method.** This Web method accepts the data the client enters to make a reservation and stores it in the Reservation table.

◆ **GetRate() method.** This Web method calculates and returns the total fare for the selected vehicle type for a given number of days. To do this, the method accesses the rent per day from the VehicleType table and multiplies it by the number of days for which the customer wants to rent the car.

◆ **GetVehicleTypes() method.** This Web method returns an array of strings that contain the different vehicle types applicable to the company.

◆ **CancelReservation() method.** This Web method allows a client application to cancel a reservation after specifying the customer name and password.

◆ **ViewReservation() method.** This Web method returns the details of the reservation that a customer made.

◆ **ModifyReservation() method.** This Web method allows a client application to modify the details of a reservation that a customer made.

Now you will learn to implement these Web methods.

Implementing the MakeReservation() *Method*

The MakeReservation() method accepts the data required to make a reservation. To do this, the Web method calls the Reserve stored procedure as shown in the following code snippet:

```
<WebMethod()> Public Function MakeReservation(ByVal strLocation As String, ByVal
strDate As String, ByVal strTime As String, ByVal nDuration As Integer, ByVal
strVType As String, ByVal strCustName As String, ByVal strCustKey As String,
ByVal strCustPhone As String) As Integer
```

```
        Dim conn As New SqlConnection("Data Source=server1;initial
catalog=CarRental;Integrated Security=SSPI")
        conn.Open()
        Dim cmd As New SqlCommand("", conn)
        cmd.CommandText = "Reserve"
        cmd.CommandType = CommandType.StoredProcedure
        cmd.Parameters.Add("@Location", strLocation)
        cmd.Parameters.Add("@pDate", strDate)
        cmd.Parameters.Add("@pTime", strTime)
        cmd.Parameters.Add("@Duration", nDuration)
        cmd.Parameters.Add("@VType", strVType)
        cmd.Parameters.Add("@CustName", strCustName)
        cmd.Parameters.Add("@CustKey", strCustKey)
        cmd.Parameters.Add("@CustPhone", strCustPhone)

        MakeReservation = cmd.ExecuteScalar()
End Function
```

NOTE

Please note that most of these Web methods access a database by using ADO.NET; therefore, you need to include the following statement in the file:

```
Imports System.Data.SqlClient
```

Implementing the GetRate() Method

The GetRate() method accepts a vehicle type, connects to the database, and retrieves the fare per day for the specified car type. Then the code multiplies the given fare with the number of days for which the reservation is made and returns the total fare. The code for the GetRate() method is shown in the following example:

```
<WebMethod()> Public Function GetRate(ByVal strType As String, ByVal nDuration
As Integer) As Single
        Dim rate As Single
        Dim conn As New SqlConnection("Data Source=server1;initial
catalog=CarRental;Integrated Security=SSPI")
        conn.Open()
        Dim cmd As New SqlCommand("", conn)
        cmd.CommandText = "GetRate"
```

```
        cmd.CommandType = CommandType.StoredProcedure
        cmd.Parameters.Add("@vType", strType)
        rate = cmd.ExecuteScalar()
        GetRate = rate * nDuration
End Function
```

The preceding code uses the `ExecuteScalar()` method of the `SqlCommand` object that returns the value in the first column of the first row of the result set.

 NOTE

In some of the previous chapters, we used the `ExecuteReader()` method to retrieve data from the database. The `ExecuteReader()` method returns the result as an object of the `SqlDataReader` class. However, if you need to retrieve only one value, as in this case, the `ExecuteScalar()` method is preferred.

Implementing the `GetVehicleTypes()` Method

The `GetVehicleTypes()` method returns an array of strings to the client application as shown in the following code:

```
<WebMethod()> Public Function GetVehicleTypes() As String()
Dim conn As New SqlConnection("Data Source=server1;initial
catalog=CarRental;Integrated Security=SSPI")
        conn.Open()
        Dim cmd As New SqlCommand("", conn)
        Dim NoOfRecords As Integer
        Dim reader As SqlDataReader
        Dim i As Integer = 0
        cmd.CommandText = "Select count(*) from vehicleType"
        NoOfRecords = cmd.ExecuteScalar()
        Dim strArray(NoOfRecords) As String

        cmd.CommandText = "GetVType"
        cmd.CommandType = CommandType.StoredProcedure
        reader = cmd.ExecuteReader()
        While (reader.Read())
        strArray(i) ¬ reader(0)
        End While
        GetVehicleTypes = strArray
End Function
```

Implementing the `CancelReservation()` Method

The `CancelReservation()` method accepts the name, key (password), and pickup date for a user and deletes the reservation by calling the `CancelReservation` stored procedure. The code for the `CancelReservation()` method is as shown:

```
<WebMethod()> Public Function CancelReservation(ByVal strCustName As String,
ByVal strCustKey As String, ByVal strPDate As String) as Integer
     Dim conn As New SqlConnection("Data Source=server1;initial
catalog=CarRental;Integrated Security=SSPI")


     conn.Open()
     Dim cmd As New SqlCommand("", conn)
     cmd.CommandText = "CancelReservation"
     cmd.CommandType = CommandType.StoredProcedure
     cmd.Parameters.Add("@CustName", strCustName)
     cmd.Parameters.Add("@CustKey", strCustKey)
     cmd.Parameters.Add("@pDate", strPDate)
     CancelReservation =  cmd.ExecuteNonQuery()
End Function
```

Implementing the `ViewReservation()` Method

The `ViewReservation()` method returns the details of a reservation. To do this, the user needs to specify the customer name and the customer key. The code for the `ViewReservation()` method is as shown:

```
<WebMethod()> Public Function ViewReservation(ByVal strCustName As String, ByVal
strCustKey As String, ByRef strLocation As String, ByRef strPDate As String,
ByRef strPTime As String, ByRef nDuration As Integer, ByRef strVType As String)

        Dim conn As New SqlConnection("Data Source=saik-d185;initial
catalog=CarRental;Integrated Security=SSPI")

        conn.Open()
        Dim reader As SqlDataReader
        Dim cmd As New SqlCommand("", conn)

        cmd.CommandText = "ViewReservation"
        cmd.CommandType = CommandType.StoredProcedure
        cmd.Parameters.Add("@CustName", strCustName)
        cmd.Parameters.Add("@CustKey", strCustKey)
```

```
    reader = cmd.ExecuteReader()
    reader.Read()
    strLocation = reader(0)
    strPDate = reader(1)
    strPTime = reader(2)
    nDuration = reader(3)
    strVType = reader(4)
End Function
```

Implementing the `ModifyReservation()` Method

After a reservation is made, you can make changes to it by using the `ModifyReservation()` method. The code for the `ModifyReservation()` method is as shown:

```
<WebMethod()> Public Function ModifyReservation(ByVal strLocation As String,
ByVal strDate As String, ByVal strTime As String, ByVal nDuration As Integer,
ByVal strVType As String, ByVal strCustName As String, ByVal strCustKey As
String) as Integer

        Dim conn As New SqlConnection("Data Source=saik-d185;initial
catalog=CarRental;Integrated Security=SSPI")
        conn.Open()
        Dim cmd As New SqlCommand("", conn)

        cmd.CommandText = "UpdateReservation"
        cmd.CommandType = CommandType.StoredProcedure
        cmd.Parameters.Add("@Location", strLocation)
        cmd.Parameters.Add("@pDate", strDate)
        cmd.Parameters.Add("@pTime", strTime)
        cmd.Parameters.Add("@Duration", nDuration)
        cmd.Parameters.Add("@VType", strVType)
        cmd.Parameters.Add("@CustName", strCustName)
        cmd.Parameters.Add("@CustKey", strCustKey)
        ModifyReservation =   cmd.ExecuteNonQuery()
End Function
```

Building the Web Service

The final step in the creation of the Web service is to build the project and deploy the Web service. To build the project, either run the application or start Internet Explorer and connect to http://localhost/rental/service1.asmx. A list of operations that the Web service supports is displayed, as shown in Figure 17-3.

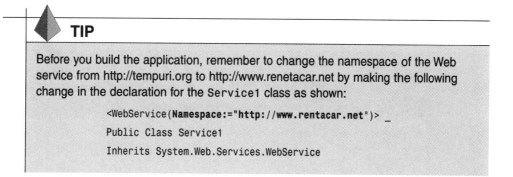

Service1

The following operations are supported. For a formal definition, please review the <u>Service Description</u>.

- <u>ViewReservation</u>
- <u>MakeReservation</u>
- <u>ModifyReservation</u>
- <u>CancelReservation</u>
- <u>GetRate</u>
- <u>GetVehicleTypes</u>

FIGURE 17-3 *The operations that the Web service supports.*

TIP

Before you build the application, remember to change the namespace of the Web service from http://tempuri.org to http://www.renetacar.net by making the following change in the declaration for the `Service1` class as shown:

```
<WebService(Namespace:="http://www.rentacar.net")> _
Public Class Service1
Inherits System.Web.Services.WebService
```

Now click on the `GetRate()` method, and in the resulting screen, as shown in Figure 17-4, specify the vehicle type as Premium and click on the Invoke button. Verify that the Web service returns the correct value.

Service1

Click <u>here</u> for a complete list of operations.

GetRate

Test

To test the operation using the HTTP GET protocol, click the 'Invoke' button.

Parameter	Value
strType:	
nDuration:	

Invoke

FIGURE 17-4 *Invoking a Web method.*

After you have verified that the Web service is working, you will create the mobile application that consumes this Web service.

Creating the Mobile Application That Consumes the Web Service

To create a mobile application that consumes the Web service, add a new Mobile ASP.NET application project to the solution. The opening screen of the application will contain links that redirect a user to the Reservation.aspx, ViewReservation.aspx, ModifyReservation.aspx, and CancelReservation.aspx pages. You will learn to create these pages in the following sections.

Because this application will consume the Web services that you have created, add a Web reference to the Web service. After you have created links to the preceding pages, the MobileWebform1.aspx page should look like Figure 17-5. The figure shows the MobileWebform1.aspx page in the Internet Explorer window.

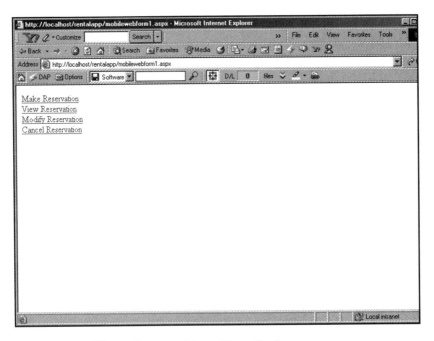

FIGURE 17-5 *The opening page of the mobile application.*

NOTE

In this chapter, you will be using Internet Explorer to view and debug the mobile application. However, you can also use a mobile phone emulator.

You can download and install the mobile SDK from http://www.openwave.com, which contains many emulators. Figure 17-6 shows the view of the opening page in one of the emulators available with the SDK.

FIGURE 17-6 *The opening page of the mobile application in a mobile emulator.*

The code for the ASP.NET application in the mobileWebform1.aspx file is as shown:

```
<%@ Register TagPrefix="mobile" Namespace="System.Web.UI.MobileControls"
Assembly="System.Web.Mobile, Version=1.0.3300.0, Culture=neutral,
PublicKeyToken=b03f5f7f11d50a3a" %>
<%@ Page Language="vb" AutoEventWireup="false"
Codebehind="MobileWebForm1.aspx.vb" Inherits="RentalApp.MobileWebForm1" %>
<meta name="GENERATOR" content="Microsoft Visual Studio.NET 7.0">
<meta name="CODE_LANGUAGE" content="Visual Basic 7.0">
<meta name="vs_targetSchema" content="http://schemas.microsoft.com/Mobile/Page">
<body Xmlns:mobile="http://schemas.microsoft.com/Mobile/WebForm">
        <mobile:Form id="Form1" runat="server">
                <mobile:Link id="Link1" runat="server"
NavigateUrl="Reservation.aspx">Make Reservation </mobile:Link>
```

```
                    <mobile:Link id="Link2" runat="server"
NavigateUrl="ViewReservation.aspx">View Reservation</mobile:Link>
                    <mobile:Link id="Link3" runat="server">Modify
Reservation</mobile:Link>
                    <mobile:Link id="Link4" runat="server"
NavigateUrl="CancelReservation.aspx">Cancel Reservation</mobile:Link>
            </mobile:Form>
    </body>
```

The MakeReservations Page

The mobile application contains a MakeReservations page that allows a user to make reservations. In addition, this page allows the user to specify the data required to make a reservation. The data that the user needs to enter in the MakeReservations page is shown in the following list:

- ◆ Pickup location
- ◆ Pickup date
- ◆ Pickup time
- ◆ Duration of rental
- ◆ Vehicle type
- ◆ Customer name
- ◆ Customer key
- ◆ Customer phone

 TIP

In a mobile application, the user should type as little as possible because it is difficult to enter lengthy pieces of text into a mobile phone. Therefore, instead of using text boxes, try to use other user-interface controls, such as option buttons, list boxes, and so on.

Adding Controls to the MakeReservations Page

The MakeReservations page contains three Panel controls. Initially, only Panel1 is visible. The first panel contains all user-interface elements, which allows the user to specify the data as discussed in the previous list. In addition, Panel1 contains a Button control, which the user needs to click after specifying the required data. Clicking on the Button control invokes the GetRate() Web method. The Panel1 control is displayed in Figure 17-7.

FIGURE 17-7 *Panel1 of the reservation.aspx page in Design view.*

When the GetRate() method returns a value, Panel1 becomes invisible and the control is passed to Panel2. The Panel2 control displays the fare that is charged to the customer. Figure 17-8 shows the Panel2 control in Design view.

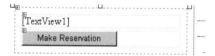

FIGURE 17-8 *Panel2 of the reservation.aspx page in Design view.*

The Panel2 control allows a user to either return to Panel1 or click on the Make Reservation button to make a reservation. Clicking on this button invokes the MakeReservation() Web method. This method displays the third panel control, Panel3, which allows the user to return to the opening screen. The Panel3 control is displayed in Figure 17-9.

FIGURE 17-9 *Panel3 of the reservation.aspx page in Design view.*

Adding Code to the MakeReservations Page

After you add controls to the form, you need to add the code to the MakeReservations page. The code for the MakeReservations page follows:

```
<%@ Page Language="vb" AutoEventWireup="false" Codebehind="Reservation.aspx.vb"
Inherits="RentalApp.Reservation" %>
```

```
<%@ Register TagPrefix="mobile" Namespace="System.Web.UI.MobileControls"
Assembly="System.Web.Mobile, Version=1.0.3300.0, Culture=neutral,
PublicKeyToken=b03f5f7f11d50a3a" %>
<META content="Microsoft Visual Studio.NET 7.0" name="GENERATOR">
<META content="Visual Basic 7.0" name="CODE_LANGUAGE">
<META content="http://schemas.microsoft.com/Mobile/Page" name="vs_targetSchema">
<BODY Xmlns:mobile="http://schemas.microsoft.com/Mobile/WebForm">
        <mobile:Form id="Form1" runat="server">
        <mobile:Panel id="Panel1" runat="server">
                <mobile:Label id="Label1" runat="server">Pickup Location</mobile:Label>
                <mobile:TextBox id="txtLocation" runat="server"></mobile:TextBox>
                <mobile:Label id="Label2" runat="server">Pickup Date</mobile:Label>
                <mobile:TextBox id="txtPDate" runat="server"></mobile:TextBox>
                <mobile:Label id="Label3" runat="server">Pickup Time</mobile:Label>
                <mobile:TextBox id="txtPTime" runat="server"></mobile:TextBox>
                <mobile:Label id="Label4" runat="server">Rental Duration</mobile:Label>
                <mobile:TextBox id="txtDuration" runat="server"></mobile:TextBox>
                <mobile:Label id="Label5" runat="server">Vehicle Type</mobile:Label>
                <mobile:SelectionList id="VTypeList"
runat="server"></mobile:SelectionList>
                <mobile:Label id="Label6" runat="server">Customer Name</mobile:Label>
                <mobile:TextBox id="txtCustName" runat="server"></mobile:TextBox>
                <mobile:Label id="Label7" runat="server">Customer Key</mobile:Label>
                <mobile:TextBox id="txtCustKey" runat="server"
Password="True"></mobile:TextBox>
                <mobile:Label id="Label8" runat="server">Customer Phone</mobile:Label>
                <mobile:TextBox id="txtCustPhone" runat="server"></mobile:TextBox>
                <mobile:Command id="cmdGetRate" runat="server">Calcuate
Rental</mobile:Command>
        </mobile:Panel>

        <mobile:Panel id="Panel2" runat="server" Visible="False">
                <mobile:TextView id="TextView1" runat="server"
Wrapping="Wrap"></mobile:TextView>
                <mobile:Command id="cmdReserve" runat="server">Make
Reservation</mobile:Command>
        </mobile:Panel>
```

```
<mobile:Panel id="Panel3" runat="server" Visible="False">
        <mobile:Label id="Label9" runat="server">Your Car has been reserved.
Click on the link below to return.</mobile:Label>
        <mobile:Link id="Link1" runat="server"
NavigateUrl="MobileWebForm1.aspx">Back</mobile:Link>
    </mobile:Panel>


    </mobile:Form>
</BODY>
```

The preceding code snippets from the Reservation.aspx.vb file specify the action that takes place whenever an event occurs on the page. For example, when the page loads, the page makes a call to the `GetVehicleTypes()` Web method and populates the list box with the values that the method returns. To do this, you need to create an instance of the Web service proxy class, which would have been created when you added a Web reference to the Web service. This is done by declaring an instance in the class as shown in the following code snippet:

```
Imports RentalApp.localhost
Dim ws As Service1
```

Next, initialize the ws object in the `Page_Load` event handler and call the `GetVehicleTypes()` Web method as shown in the following code:

```
Dim strArr() As String
Dim i As Integer
ws = New Service1()
strArr = ws.GetVehicleTypes()
```

After you add the code to the `Page_Load` event handler, the entire code for the Reservation.aspx.vb file is as shown:

```
imports RentalApp.localhost
Public Class Reservation
        Inherits System.Web.UI.MobileControls.MobilePage
        Protected WithEvents Panel1 As System.Web.UI.MobileControls.Panel
        Protected WithEvents Label1 As System.Web.UI.MobileControls.Label
        Protected WithEvents txtLocation As System.Web.UI.MobileControls.TextBox
        Protected WithEvents Label2 As System.Web.UI.MobileControls.Label
        Protected WithEvents txtPDate As System.Web.UI.MobileControls.TextBox
        Protected WithEvents Label3 As System.Web.UI.MobileControls.Label
        Protected WithEvents txtPTime As System.Web.UI.MobileControls.TextBox
        Protected WithEvents Label4 As System.Web.UI.MobileControls.Label
        Protected WithEvents txtDuration As System.Web.UI.MobileControls.TextBox
```

```vbnet
Protected WithEvents Label5 As System.Web.UI.MobileControls.Label
Protected WithEvents Label6 As System.Web.UI.MobileControls.Label
Protected WithEvents txtCustName As System.Web.UI.MobileControls.TextBox
Protected WithEvents Label7 As System.Web.UI.MobileControls.Label
Protected WithEvents txtCustKey As System.Web.UI.MobileControls.TextBox
Protected WithEvents Label8 As System.Web.UI.MobileControls.Label
Protected WithEvents txtCustPhone As System.Web.UI.MobileControls.TextBox
Protected WithEvents Form1 As System.Web.UI.MobileControls.Form
Protected WithEvents VTypeList As System.Web.UI.MobileControls.SelectionList
Protected WithEvents cmdGetRate As System.Web.UI.MobileControls.Command
Protected WithEvents Panel2 As System.Web.UI.MobileControls.Panel
Protected WithEvents TextView1 As System.Web.UI.MobileControls.TextView
Protected WithEvents cmdReserve As System.Web.UI.MobileControls.Command
Protected WithEvents Panel3 As System.Web.UI.MobileControls.Panel
Protected WithEvents Label9 As System.Web.UI.MobileControls.Label
Protected WithEvents Link1 As System.Web.UI.MobileControls.Link

Dim ws As Service1

Private Sub Page_Init(ByVal sender As System.Object, ByVal e As
System.EventArgs) Handles MyBase.Init
        'CODEGEN: This method call is required by the Web Form Designer
        'Do not modify it using the code editor.
        InitializeComponent()
End Sub

Private Sub Page_Load(ByVal sender As System.Object, ByVal e As
System.EventArgs) Handles MyBase.Load
        'Put user code to initialize the page here
        Dim strArr() As String
        Dim i As Integer

        ws = New Service1()
        strArr = ws.GetVehicleTypes()
        i = 0
        While (i < strArr.Length)
            VTypeList.Items.Add(strArr(i))
            i = i + 1
        End While
```

```
        End Sub


        Private Sub cmdGetRate_Click(ByVal sender As System.Object, ByVal e As
System.EventArgs) Handles cmdGetRate.Click
                Dim sRate As Single
                sRate = ws.GetRate(VTypeList.Selection.Text, txtDuration.Text)
                Panel1.Visible = False
                Panel2.Visible = True
                TextView1.Text = " The rental charge for the choices you have made
is " & sRate & " Dollars. To confirm the reservation, click on the button below"
        End Sub


        Private Sub cmdReserve_Click(ByVal sender As System.Object, ByVal e As
  System.EventArgs) Handles cmdReserve.Click
                Dim nId As Integer


                nId = ws.MakeReservation(txtLocation.Text, txtPDate.Text,
txtPTime.Text, txtDuration.Text, VTypeList.Selection.Text, txtCustName.Text,
txtCustKey.Text, txtCustPhone.Text)
                Panel1.Visible = False
                Panel2.Visible = False
                panel3.visible = True
        End Sub
End Class
```

The CancelReservation Page

A user can cancel a reservation in the CancelReservation page. To do this, the user needs to specify the name and the key value. The CancelReservation page looks like Figure 17-10.

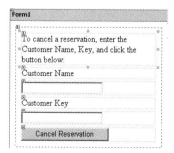

FIGURE 17-10 *The CancelReservation page.*

The code listing of the CancelReservation.aspx page is as shown:

```
<%@ Register TagPrefix="mobile" Namespace="System.Web.UI.MobileControls"
Assembly="System.Web.Mobile, Version=1.0.3300.0, Culture=neutral,
PublicKeyToken=b03f5f7f11d50a3a" %>
<%@ Page Language="vb" AutoEventWireup="false"
Codebehind="CancelReservation.aspx.vb" Inherits="RentalApp.CancelReservation" %>
<meta content="Microsoft Visual Studio.NET 7.0" name="GENERATOR">
<meta content="Visual Basic 7.0" name="CODE_LANGUAGE">
<meta content="http://schemas.microsoft.com/Mobile/Page" name="vs_targetSchema">
<body Xmlns:mobile="http://schemas.microsoft.com/Mobile/WebForm">
        <mobile:form id="Form1" runat="server">
                <mobile:Panel id="Panel1" runat="server">
                        <mobile:Label id="Label1" runat="server">To cancel a
reservation, enter the Customer Name, Key, and click the button below:</mobile:Label>
                        <mobile:Label id="Label2" runat="server">Customer
Name</mobile:Label>
                        <mobile:TextBox id="txtCustName"
runat="server"></mobile:TextBox>
                        <mobile:Label id="Label3" runat="server">Customer
Key</mobile:Label>
                        <mobile:TextBox id="txtCustKey"
runat="server"></mobile:TextBox>
                        <mobile:Command id="cmdCancel" runat="server">Cancel
Reservation</mobile:Command>
                </mobile:Panel>
                <mobile:Panel id="Panel2" runat="server" Visible="False">
                        <mobile:TextView id="TextView1" runat="server"
Wrapping="Wrap">Your reservation has been cancelled. Click on the link below to
return to the main page.</mobile:TextView>
                        <mobile:Link id="Link1" runat="server"
NavigateUrl="MobileWebForm1.aspx">Back</mobile:Link>
                </mobile:Panel>
                <mobile:Panel id="Panel3" runat="server" Visible="False">
                        <P>Could not find any matching records. Click on the link
below to return to the main page.</P>
                        <P>
                                <mobile:Link id="Link2" runat="server"
```

```
                    NavigateUrl="MobileWebForm1.aspx">Back</mobile:Link>
                                        </P>
                            </mobile:Panel>
                </mobile:form>
        </body>
```

The CancelReservation page contains a Cancel Reservation button. When a user clicks on this button, the `CancelReservation()` Web method is called. The code for the CancelReservati on.aspx.vb page is as shown:

```
Public Class CancelReservation
    Inherits System.Web.UI.MobileControls.MobilePage
    Protected WithEvents Panel1 As System.Web.UI.MobileControls.Panel
    Protected WithEvents Label1 As System.Web.UI.MobileControls.Label
    Protected WithEvents txtCustName As System.Web.UI.MobileControls.TextBox
    Protected WithEvents Label2 As System.Web.UI.MobileControls.Label
    Protected WithEvents Label3 As System.Web.UI.MobileControls.Label
    Protected WithEvents txtCustKey As System.Web.UI.MobileControls.TextBox
    Protected WithEvents cmdCancel As System.Web.UI.MobileControls.Command
    Protected WithEvents Form1 As System.Web.UI.MobileControls.Form
    Protected WithEvents Panel2 As System.Web.UI.MobileControls.Panel
    Protected WithEvents TextView1 As System.Web.UI.MobileControls.TextView
    Protected WithEvents Link1 As System.Web.UI.MobileControls.Link
    Protected WithEvents Panel3 As System.Web.UI.MobileControls.Panel
    Protected WithEvents Link2 As System.Web.UI.MobileControls.Link
    Dim ws As RentalApp.localhost.Service1


#Region " Web Form Designer Generated Code "


    'This call is required by the Web Form Designer.
    <System.Diagnostics.DebuggerStepThrough()> Private Sub InitializeComponent()


    End Sub


    Private Sub Page_Init(ByVal sender As System.Object, ByVal e As
System.EventArgs) Handles MyBase.Init
            'CODEGEN: This method call is required by the Web Form Designer
            'Do not modify it using the code editor.
            InitializeComponent()
```

```vb
        End Sub

#End Region

    Private Sub Page_Load(ByVal sender As System.Object, ByVal e As
System.EventArgs) Handles MyBase.Load
        'Put user code to initialize the page here
        Try
            ws = New RentalApp.localhost.Service1()
        Catch
        End Try
    End Sub

    Private Sub cmdCancel_Click(ByVal sender As System.Object, ByVal e As
System.EventArgs) Handles cmdCancel.Click
        Dim n As String
        Try


            n = ws.CancelReservation(txtCustName.Text, txtCustKey.Text)


        Catch
        End Try

        If Trim(n) = "0" Then
            Panel3.Visible = True
            Panel1.Visible = False
            Panel2.Visible = False
            Exit Sub
        End If


        txtCustName.Text = n
        'Panel1.Visible = False
        Panel2.Visible = True
    End Sub
```

```
      Private Sub Form1_Activate(ByVal sender As System.Object, ByVal e As
  System.EventArgs) Handles Form1.Activate


      End Sub
  End Class
```

The ModifyReservation Page

In the ModifyReservation page, you can modify the details of a reservation. However, before you modify the details of a reservation, you first need to retrieve a specified record. To do this, add two TextBox controls that accept the name of a customer and the customer key. In addition, add a Button control that retrieves the record from the database.

After you add the controls, modify the code for the ModifyReservation page as shown in the following code sample:

```
<%@ Register TagPrefix="mobile" Namespace="System.Web.UI.MobileControls"
Assembly="System.Web.Mobile, Version=1.0.3300.0, Culture=neutral
PublicKeyToken=b03f5f7f11d50a3a" %>
<%@ Page Language="vb" AutoEventWireup="false"
Codebehind="ModifyReservation.aspx.vb" Inherits="RentalApp.ModifyReservation" %>
<meta content="Microsoft Visual Studio.NET 7.0" name="GENERATOR">
<meta content="Visual Basic 7.0" name="CODE_LANGUAGE">
<meta content="http://schemas.microsoft.com/Mobile/Page" name="vs_targetSchema">
<body Xmlns:mobile="http://schemas.microsoft.com/Mobile/WebForm">
        <mobile:form id="Form1" runat="server">
                <mobile:Panel id="Panel1" runat="server">
                        <mobile:Label id="Label1" runat="server">To modify a
reservation, enter the Customer Name and Key</mobile:Label>
                        <mobile:Label id="Label2" runat="server">Customer
Name</mobile:Label>
                        <mobile:TextBox id="txtCustName" runat="server"></mobile:TextBox>
                        <mobile:Label id="Label3" runat="server">Customer
Key</mobile:Label>
                        <mobile:TextBox id="txtCustKey" runat="server"
Password="True"></mobile:TextBox>
                        <mobile:Command id="cmdGetData" runat="server">Get
Data</mobile:Command>
                </mobile:Panel>
                <mobile:Panel id="Panel2" runat="server" Visible="False">
```

```
                    <mobile:Label id="Label4" runat="server">Location</mobile:Label>
                    <mobile:TextBox id="txtLocation" runat="server"></mobile:TextBox>
                    <mobile:Label id="Label5" runat="server">Pickup
Date</mobile:Label>
                    <mobile:TextBox id="txtDate" runat="server"></mobile:TextBox>
                    <mobile:Calendar id="Calendar1" runat="server"></mobile:Calendar>
                    <mobile:Label id="Label7" runat="server">Pickup
Time</mobile:Label>
                    <mobile:TextBox id="txtPTime" runat="server"></mobile:TextBox>
                    <mobile:Command id="cmdSave" runat="server">Save
Data</mobile:Command>
                </mobile:Panel>
                <mobile:Panel id="Panel3" runat="server" Visible="False">
                    <mobile:TextView id="TextView1" runat="server">Your
reservation data has been updated.</mobile:TextView>
                    <mobile:Link id="Link1" runat="server" Visible="False"
NavigateUrl="MobileWebForm1.aspx">Back</mobile:Link>
                </mobile:Panel>
        </mobile:form>
</body>
```

When a user clicks on the Button control in the ModifyReservation page, the details of the reservation are displayed. You can make the desired changes to the data and click on the Save Data button. The modifications that you make are saved to the database. The code for the ModifyReservation.aspx.vb page is as shown:

```
Imports RentalApp.localhost


Public Class ModifyReservation
    Inherits System.Web.UI.MobileControls.MobilePage
    Protected WithEvents Panel1 As System.Web.UI.MobileControls.Panel
    Protected WithEvents Label1 As System.Web.UI.MobileControls.Label
    Protected WithEvents Label2 As System.Web.UI.MobileControls.Label
    Protected WithEvents txtCustName As System.Web.UI.MobileControls.TextBox
    Protected WithEvents Label3 As System.Web.UI.MobileControls.Label
    Protected WithEvents txtCustKey As System.Web.UI.MobileControls.TextBox
    Protected WithEvents cmdGetData As System.Web.UI.MobileControls.Command
    Protected WithEvents Panel2 As System.Web.UI.MobileControls.Panel
    Protected WithEvents Label4 As System.Web.UI.MobileControls.Label
    Protected WithEvents txtLocation As System.Web.UI.MobileControls.TextBox
```

```
    Protected WithEvents Label5 As System.Web.UI.MobileControls.Label
    Protected WithEvents txtDate As System.Web.UI.MobileControls.TextBox
    Protected WithEvents Calendar1 As System.Web.UI.MobileControls.Calendar
    Protected WithEvents cmdSave As System.Web.UI.MobileControls.Command
    Protected WithEvents Form1 As System.Web.UI.MobileControls.Form

    Dim ws As Service1
    Dim strVType As String
    Protected WithEvents Label7 As System.Web.UI.MobileControls.Label
    Protected WithEvents txtPTime As System.Web.UI.MobileControls.TextBox
    Protected WithEvents Panel3 As System.Web.UI.MobileControls.Panel
    Protected WithEvents TextView1 As System.Web.UI.MobileControls.TextView
    Protected WithEvents Link1 As System.Web.UI.MobileControls.Link
    Dim nDuration As Integer

#Region " Web Form Designer Generated Code "

    'This call is required by the Web Form Designer.
    <System.Diagnostics.DebuggerStepThrough()> Private Sub InitializeComponent()

    End Sub

    Private Sub Page_Init(ByVal sender As System.Object, ByVal e As
System.EventArgs) Handles MyBase.Init
        'CODEGEN: This method call is required by the Web Form Designer
        'Do not modify it using the code editor.
        InitializeComponent()
    End Sub

#End Region

    Private Sub Page_Load(ByVal sender As System.Object, ByVal e As
System.EventArgs) Handles MyBase.Load
        'Put user code to initialize the page here
        txtDate.Text = " "
        ws = New Service1()

    End Sub
```

```
    Private Sub Calendar1_SelectionChanged(ByVal sender As System.Object, ByVal
e As System.EventArgs) Handles Calendar1.SelectionChanged
        txtDate.Text = Calendar1.SelectedDate.ToShortDateString()
        End Sub


    Private Sub cmdGetData_Click(ByVal sender As System.Object, ByVal e As
System.EventArgs) Handles cmdGetData.Click

        Try
            ws.ViewReservation(txtCustName.Text, txtCustKey.Text,
txtLocation.Text, txtDate.Text, txtPTime.Text, nDuration, strVType)


        Catch

        End Try
        Panel1.Visible = False
        Panel2.Visible = True
    End Sub


    Private Sub cmdSave_Click(ByVal sender As System.Object, ByVal e As
System.EventArgs) Handles cmdSave.Click
        Try
            ws.ModifyReservation(txtLocation.Text, txtDate.Text, txtPTime.Text,
nDuration, strVType, txtCustName.Text, txtCustKey.Text)
        Catch
        End Try
        PAnel3.visible = True


    End Sub
End Class
```

The ViewReservation Page

The ViewReservation page allows you to view the details of a specified reservation. For this, you need to specify the customer name and customer key. The code for the ViewReservation page is as follows:

```
<%@ Register TagPrefix="mobile" Namespace="System.Web.UI.MobileControls"
Assembly="System.Web.Mobile, Version=1.0.3300.0, Culture=neutral,
```

```
PublicKeyToken=b03f5f7f11d50a3a" %>
<%@ Page Language="vb" AutoEventWireup="false" Codebehind="ViewReservation.aspx.vb"
Inherits="RentalApp.ViewReservation" %>
<meta name="GENERATOR" content="Microsoft Visual Studio.NET 7.0">
<meta name="CODE_LANGUAGE" content="Visual Basic 7.0">
<meta name="vs_targetSchema" content="http://schemas.microsoft.com/Mobile/Page">
<body Xmlns:mobile="http://schemas.microsoft.com/Mobile/WebForm">
        <mobile:Form id="Form1" runat="server">
                <mobile:Panel id="Panel1" runat="server">
                        <mobile:Label id="Label1" runat="server">Please enter the
Customer Name, Key  to view the details.</mobile:Label>
                        <mobile:Label id="Label2" runat="server">Customer
Name</mobile:Label>
                        <mobile:TextBox id="txtCustName"
runat="server"></mobile:TextBox>
                        <mobile:Label id="Label3" runat="server">Customer
Key</mobile:Label>
                        <mobile:TextBox id="txtCustKey" runat="server"
Password="True"></mobile:TextBox>
                        <mobile:Command id="cmdViewRes" runat="server">Get
Reservation Details</mobile:Command>
                </mobile:Panel>
                <mobile:Panel id="Panel2" runat="server" Visible="False">
                        <mobile:Label id="Label4"
runat="server">Location</mobile:Label>
                        <mobile:TextView id="txtLocation"
runat="server"></mobile:TextView>
                        <mobile:Label id="Label5"
runat="server">Date</mobile:Label>
                        <mobile:TextView id="txtPDate"
runat="server"></mobile:TextView>
                        <mobile:Label id="Label6"
runat="server">Duration</mobile:Label>
                        <mobile:TextView id="txtDuration"
runat="server"></mobile:TextView>
                        <mobile:Label id="Label7" runat="server">Vehicle
Type</mobile:Label>
                        <mobile:TextView id="txtVType"
```

```
runat="server"></mobile:TextView>
                            <mobile:Link id="Link1" runat="server"
NavigateUrl="MobileWebForm1.aspx">Back</mobile:Link>
            </mobile:Panel>
            <mobile:Panel id="Panel3" runat="server">
                <P>Reservation not found. Please click on the link below to
return to the main page.</P>
                <P>
                        <mobile:Link id="Link2" runat="server"
NavigateUrl="MobileWebForm1.aspx">Back</mobile:Link>
                </P>
            </mobile:Panel>
        </mobile:Form>
</body>
```

When the user specifies the required information and clicks on the Get Reservations Details button, the reservation details are shown in the Panel2 control of the ViewReservation page. The code for the ViewReservation.aspx.vb page is as follows:

```
Imports RentalApp.localhost
Public Class ViewReservation
    Inherits System.Web.UI.MobileControls.MobilePage
    Protected WithEvents Form1 As System.Web.UI.MobileControls.Form
    Protected WithEvents Panel1 As System.Web.UI.MobileControls.Panel
    Protected WithEvents Label1 As System.Web.UI.MobileControls.Label
    Protected WithEvents Label2 As System.Web.UI.MobileControls.Label
    Protected WithEvents txtCustName As System.Web.UI.MobileControls.TextBox
    Protected WithEvents Label3 As System.Web.UI.MobileControls.Label
    Protected WithEvents txtCustKey As System.Web.UI.MobileControls.TextBox
    Protected WithEvents cmdViewRes As System.Web.UI.MobileControls.Command
    Protected WithEvents Panel2 As System.Web.UI.MobileControls.Panel
    Protected WithEvents Label4 As System.Web.UI.MobileControls.Label
    Protected WithEvents txtLocation As System.Web.UI.MobileControls.TextView
    Protected WithEvents Label5 As System.Web.UI.MobileControls.Label
    Protected WithEvents txtPDate As System.Web.UI.MobileControls.TextView
    Protected WithEvents Label6 As System.Web.UI.MobileControls.Label
    Protected WithEvents txtDuration As System.Web.UI.MobileControls.TextView
    Protected WithEvents Label7 As System.Web.UI.MobileControls.Label
```

```vbnet
    Protected WithEvents txtVType As System.Web.UI.MobileControls.TextView
    Protected WithEvents Link1 As System.Web.UI.MobileControls.Link
    Protected WithEvents Panel3 As System.Web.UI.MobileControls.Panel
    Protected WithEvents Link2 As System.Web.UI.MobileControls.Link
    Dim ws As Service1

#Region " Web Form Designer Generated Code "

    'This call is required by the Web Form Designer.
    <System.Diagnostics.DebuggerStepThrough()> Private Sub InitializeComponent()

    End Sub


    Private Sub Page_Init(ByVal sender As System.Object, ByVal e As
System.EventArgs) Handles MyBase.Init
        'CODEGEN: This method call is required by the Web Form Designer
        'Do not modify it using the code editor.
        InitializeComponent()
    End Sub

#End Region

    Private Sub Page_Load(ByVal sender As System.Object, ByVal e As
System.EventArgs) Handles MyBase.Load
        'Put user code to initialize the page here
        ws = New Service1()
        Panel3.Visible = False

    End Sub


    Private Sub Form1_Activate(ByVal sender As System.Object, ByVal e As
System.EventArgs) Handles Form1.Activate

    End Sub


    Private Sub cmdViewRes_Click(ByVal sender As System.Object, ByVal e As
System.EventArgs) Handles cmdViewRes.Click
        Dim strLocation As String
```

```
            Dim nDuration As Integer
            Dim strVType As String
            Dim strPDate As String
            Dim strPTime As String

            nDuration = 0
            Try
                ws.ViewReservation(txtCustName.Text, txtCustKey.Text, strLocation,
    strPDate, strPTime, nDuration, strVType)
            Catch
            End Try
            Panel1.Visible = False
            If nDuration > 0 Then
                Panel2.Visible = True
                txtLocation.Text = strLocation
                txtPDate.Text = strPDate
                txtDuration.Text = nDuration
                txtVType.Text = strVType
            Else
                Panel2.Visible = False
                Panel3.Visible = True
            End If
        End Sub
End Class
```

With this, the mobile application is ready.

Testing the Mobile Application

You can now build and run the application to test it. When you run the application, the opening screen, MobileWebform1.aspx page, is displayed, as shown in Figure 17-11.

As you can see, the opening page contains links to the MakeReservations, ViewReservations, ModifyReservations, and CancelReservations pages. You can click on all these links to test the respective pages. To test these pages, perform the following steps:

1. Click on the Make Reservation link. Clicking on this link takes you to the Panel1 control of the MakeReservations page, as shown in Figure 17-12.

FIGURE 17-11   *The MobileWebform1.aspx page at runtime.*

FIGURE 17-12   *The Panel1 control of the MakeReservations page at runtime.*

2. Specify the required information and click on the Calculate Rental button. The Panel2 control of the MakeReservations page is displayed, as shown in Figure 17-13.

   The Panel2 control shows the rental charges for the information specified in the Panel1 control. In addition, the Panel2 control contains a Make Reservation button that allows you to make a reservation.

FIGURE 17-13 *The Panel2 control of the MakeReservations page at runtime.*

3. Click on the Make Reservation button. The Panel3 control, as shown in Figure 17-14, is displayed.

FIGURE 17-14 *The Panel3 control of the MakeReservations page at runtime.*

As you can see, this control shows a confirmation message for your reservation. It also contains a Back button that takes you back to the opening screen.

4. Click on the Back button.
5. Click on the View Reservation link. The ViewReservations page is displayed, as shown in Figure 17-15.

FIGURE 17-15 *The ViewReservations page at runtime.*

6. In the ViewReservations page, specify values in the Customer Name and Customer Key text boxes, and click on the Get Reservations Details button.

7. The Panel2 control of the ViewReservations page is displayed. This page shows the details of the reservation, such as Location, Date, Duration, and Vehicle Type. Access this information and click on the Back button, as shown in Figure 17-16. Clicking on the Back button takes you to the opening screen.

FIGURE 17-16 *The Panel2 control of the ViewReservations page at runtime.*

8. In the opening screen, click on the Modify Reservation link. The ModifyReservations page is displayed, as shown in Figure 17-17.

FIGURE 17-17 *The ModifyReservations page at runtime.*

9. Specify the Customer Name and Customer Key, and click on the Get Details button. The Panel2 control of the ModifyReservations page is displayed, as shown in Figure 17-18.

FIGURE 17-18 *The Panel2 control of the ModifyReservations page at runtime.*

10. Modify the data as required, and click on the Save Data button.

11. The Panel3 control of the ModifyReservations page that contains a confirmation message is displayed. The Panel3 control is shown in Figure 17-19. Click on the Back button to return to the opening screen.

FIGURE 17-19 *The Panel3 control of the ModifyReservations page at runtime.*

12. Click on the Cancel Reservation link. The CancelReservations page is displayed. This page is shown in Figure 17-20.

FIGURE 17-20 *The CancelReservations page at runtime.*

13. This page prompts you to specify the information required to cancel a reservation. The information includes the name of the customer, the customer key, and the pickup date. Specify the required information, and click on the Cancel Reservation button. A message confirming the cancellation is displayed, as shown in Figure 17-21.

FIGURE 17-21 *The message confirming the cancellation.*

14. Click on the Back button. The Back button takes you to the opening screen.

Summary

In this chapter, you learned about the case study and design of the Rent-a-Car Web service. Next, you looked at the different phases in the execution of this project. You also learned about the limitations of accessing Web services from a mobile application. Finally, you created and tested a mobile application that uses an XML Web service.

PART XII

Professional Project 9

Project 9

Web Service Development with JDeveloper

Project 9 Overview

This project introduces you to Oracle's JDeveloper. JDeveloper is a feature-rich IDE that allows you to create different types of J2EE applications, including Web services.

In this project, you will look at creating a Web service that allows people to register with a reminder service for an online store that sells gift items. You also will learn how the IDE makes it easy to deploy the Web services to different application servers. You will use JDeveloper to create the Web service and the Oracle9*i* Containers for J2EE for hosting the Web service.

Chapter 18

Web Services Development with JDeveloper

In previous projects, you learned to create Web services by using the SOAP toolkit and ASP.NET. However, you have several other options for creating Web services, such as using the ATL Server library.

Before you create a Web service by using the ATL Server, you need to learn about the ATL Server library. This chapter provides a brief introduction of the ATL Server library. In addition, you will create a simple Web application by using the ATL Server.

Most of the major J2EE application servers now provide support for implementing Web services. A number of Web services products integrate with more than one application server to provide a set of tools for developing and deploying Web services. Some of these products include the following:

- JDeveloper from Oracle
- Websphere Studio Application Developer from IBM
- JBuilder from Borland
- Glue from Mind Electric
- CapeConnect and CapeStudio from Cape Clear
- Axis from Apache

However, most of these tools don't follow any specifications to provide support for Web services because no such specification existed before Java 1.4. Most of these tools implement deployment support that works only with certain application servers. Therefore, even if a stateless session EJB is used to implement a Web service on different application servers, there might be differences in the packaging format used or the deployment descriptor format and its location. A Web service application that is packaged for a particular application server is not directly reusable with any other application server that supports Web services. In this way, the J2EE Web services application is bound to the J2EE application server on which the application is meant to be deployed.

This chapter explores the features of JDeveloper for Oracle9*i* that help you to create and deploy Web services for the Oracle 9*i* application server. It also explores CapeStudio from Cape Clear, which is one of the simplest applications to create and deploy J2EE Web services and Web service clients.

The Case Study

Choco-Bar is a chocolate retailing company with stores all over the U.S. and Canada and an online store at http://www.chocobar.net. The company conducts a major portion of its online business through portals that are its affiliates.

Choco-Bar wants to add a feature called the Reminder Service to its Web site. After a user registers for this feature, he will be able to store dates of special occasions at this site. Choco-Bar will then send the user a reminder two days before the occasion along with suggestions of chocolate-related gifts suitable for the occasion and available from Choco-Bar. The company intends to make this feature available on its site and at the sites of its affiliates.

We will now discuss the project life cycle for the Reminder Service Web service that is created by using JDeveloper.

Project Life Cycle

The life cycle of the project involves the following three stages:

- Project initiation
- Project execution
- Project deployment

You learned about these phases in the earlier projects. Therefore, we will discuss only the project execution phase, which is different for each project.

The Project Execution Phase

In the project execution phase, the development team creates the design of an application. After they create the design, they develop the application. The project execution phase consists of the following stages:

- Analyzing the requirements
- Creating the design of the application
- Constructing and testing the application

Analyzing the Requirements

During the requirements analysis phase, the development team at Choco-Bar analyzed the stated requirements for the new feature. They decided to create a Web service to address this because the Reminder service needs to be accessible to all the affiliates of the company. Using Web services was the best option because each of these affiliates would host their sites by using different technologies.

Based on the requirement analysis, the development team arrived at the following specifications for the Web service:

- The Web service should accept registration details—including username, password, and e-mail address—from the client application.
- The Web service should allow the user to enter dates and details of various occasions.

Creating the Design of the Application

During the design phase of the application, the development team decides upon the functionality to be implemented and the technology to be used.

In this project, the development team decided to create the Web service by using Oracle JDeveloper because the Web site is created by using J2EE.

Construction

During the construction phase, the development team constructs the application. The primary tasks that the team does in the construction phase are as follows:

◆ Create the Web service.

◆ Deploy the Web service.

◆ Test the Web service.

Having learned about the Development Life Cycle (DLC) of the project, you will now learn about the software that you need to install to run the IBM toolkit.

Oracle9iAS Containers for J2EE

The Oracle9iAS Containers for J2EE (OC4J) Developer Preview provides a complete J2EE environment, which you can use to develop and deploy J2EE applications. In this chapter, you will learn how to publish Java classes as Web services using OC4J and JDeveloper.

Installing OC4J and JDeveloper

Both OC4J and JDeveloper products are downloadable from Oracle's Web site (http://www.oracle.com). After you have downloaded them, follow these steps to install them:

1. Create a folder to contain the OC4J files.

2. Unzip the contents of the OC4J zip file into this folder. You can use any standard unzip tool or the following Java command from within the installation folder:

   ```
   jar xvf oc4j.zip
   ```

3. Move to the J2EE\Home folder under the installation folder and run the following command:

   ```
   java -jar oc4j.jar -install
   ```

 TIP

Before running the preceding command, ensure that the system PATH includes the <Java_HOME>\bin folder.

The installation of the product starts.

4. Enter a password for the admin login. After the installation is complete, OC4J is ready to use.

To start OC4J from the J2EE\Home folder, execute the following command:

```
java -jar oc4j.jar
```

To stop OC4J, use this command:

```
java -jar admin.jar ormi://localhost admin <password> -shutdown [force]
```

To set up JDeveloper, just unzip the downloaded zip file into a folder. For example, assume this folder to be Jdev9i.

To run JDeveloper, run the file JdevW.exe from the folder Jdev9i\jdev\bin.

Oracle9*i* JDeveloper and Web Services

The Oracle9*i* JDeveloper IDE supports Oracle9*i*AS Web services. The IDE has the following features:

- ◆ It allows the creation of Java stubs to be used in client applications from WSDL documents of existing Web services.
- ◆ It allows the creation of Web services from existing Java classes, EJB classes, and PL/SQL stored procedures.
- ◆ It allows schema-driven WSDL file editing.
- ◆ It allows easy Web service deployment to supported application servers.

Oracle9*i*AS Web Services Architecture

The Oracle9*i*AS Containers for J2EE (OC4J) provide support for building Web services from existing code.

To use Oracle9*i*AS Web services, you need to deploy a J2EE .ear file to Oracle9*i*AS. The J2EE .ear file contains a Web Services Servlet configuration, and it includes an implementation of the Web service. Oracle9*i*AS Web services supplies the servlet classes, one for each supported implementation type. At runtime, Oracle9*i*AS uses the servlet classes to access the user-supplied Web service implementation.

The Oracle9*i*AS Web Services Servlet classes support the following Web services implementation types:

- ◆ Java Class (Stateless)
- ◆ Java Class (Stateful)
- ◆ Stateless Session EJBs
- ◆ PL/SQL Stored Procedure or Function

The OC4J Web services support the following data types:

- ◆ `byte`

- ◆ `boolean`
- ◆ `double`
- ◆ `float`
- ◆ `int`
- ◆ `long`
- ◆ `short`
- ◆ `string`
- ◆ `java.util.date`
- ◆ `org.w3c.dom.element`
- ◆ `org.w3c.dom.document`
- ◆ `org.w3c.dom.documentFragment`

Developing and Deploying Java Class Web Services

Creating Web services from Java classes is a straightforward process. The class must have one or more methods that a servlet running under Oracle9*i*AS Web services can invoke. This invocation happens when a client of that Web service calls the corresponding Web service method. This section discusses the theory and issues involved in creating Web services out of Java classes for Oracle9*i*AS.

Oracle9*i*AS Web services support two types of implementations for Java classes running as Web services:

- ◆ **Stateful Java implementation.** For this type, Oracle9*i*AS Web services allow a single Java instance to serve the Web service requests from an individual client.
- ◆ **Stateless Java implementation.** For this type, Oracle9*i*AS Web services create multiple instances of the Java class in a pool. You can use any one of the instances from the pool to service a request. After servicing the request, the object is returned to the pool for use by a subsequent request.

To deploy a Java class Web service, you need to package a J2EE .ear file that includes the required files and deployment descriptors. You also need to make some modifications in the web.xml file and package the Java class file into a .war file.

To use a Java class as a Web service, you need to add a `<servlet>` entry and a corresponding `<servlet-mapping>` entry into web.xml. The resulting web.xml file is assembled as part of a J2EE .war file that is included in the .ear file, which defines the Web service. Following is the syntax for these tags:

```
<servlet-name>ReminderService</servlet-name>
<servlet-class>oracle.j2ee.ws.StatelessJavaRpcWebService</servlet-class>
```

Adding these tags allows the Oracle9*i*AS Web services servlet to access the Java class for the Web service.

The following list presents the servlet tags and the tags under them:

◆ **<INIT-PARAM>.** This tag contains a name value pair in `<param-name>` and `<param-value>`. The Web services servlet definition requires at least one `<param-name>` with the value `class-name` and a corresponding `<param-value>` set to the fully qualified name of the Java class used for the Web service implementation.

An optional `<param-name>` with the value `session-timeout` and a corresponding `<param-value>` set to an `integer` value in seconds specify the timeout for the session. This optional parameter only applies for stateful Java Web services. The default value for the session timeout for stateful Java sessions, in which no session timeout is specified, is 60 seconds.

An optional `<param-name>` with the value `interface-name` and a corresponding `<param-value>` set to the fully qualified name of the Java interface specify the methods to include in the Web service. This `init` parameter tells the Web service servlet generation code which methods the Web service should expose. If the parameter `interface-name` is not included in the `<servlet>` definition, then all public methods in the class are included in the Web service.

◆ **<SERVLET-CLASS>.** This tag takes the value `oracle.j2ee.ws.StatelessJavaRpc WebService` for all stateless Java Web services and `oracle.j2ee.ws.JavaRpcWeb Service` for all stateful Java Web services.

◆ **<SERVLET-NAME>.** This tag specifies the name for the servlet that runs the Web service.

Here is an example of a sample web.xml file:

```
<?xml version = '1.0' encoding = 'windows-1252'?>
<!DOCTYPE web-app PUBLIC "-//Sun Microsystems, Inc.//DTD Web Application 2.2//EN"
"http://java.sun.com/j2ee/dtds/web-app_2_2.dtd">
<web-app>
   <description>Generated by the Oracle9i JDeveloper Web Services WebXML
Generator</description>
   <servlet>
      <servlet-name>ReminderService</servlet-name>
      <servlet-class>oracle.j2ee.ws.StatelessJavaRpcWebService</servlet-class>
      <init-param>
         <param-name>class-name</param-name>
         <param-value>ReminderService</param-value>
      </init-param>
```

```
    <init-param>
        <param-name>interface-name</param-name>
        <param-value>IReminderService</param-value>
    </init-param>
  </servlet>
  <servlet-mapping>
    <servlet-name>ReminderService</servlet-name>
    <url-pattern>/ReminderService</url-pattern>
  </servlet-mapping>
</web-app>
```

After the web.xml file is modified, add the Java class, which provides the functionality of the Web service, and any other support files to a .jar file either under WEB-INF/classes or WEB-INF/lib.

To add Web services based on Java classes, you need to include an application.xml file and package the application.xml and .war file containing the Java classes into a J2EE .ear file. Here is the code of a sample application.xml file:

```
<?xml version = '1.0' encoding = 'windows-1252'?>
<!DOCTYPE application PUBLIC "-//Sun Microsystems, Inc.//DTD J2EE Application 1.2//EN"
"http://java.sun.com/j2ee/dtds/application_1_2.dtd">
<application>
    <display-name>WS1-P1-WS</display-name>
    <module>
        <web>
            <web-uri>WebServices.war</web-uri>
            <context-root>WS1-P1-context-root</context-root>
        </web>
    </module>
</application>
```

After you have created the .ear file, your Web service is ready for deployment and use. From there, you can deploy the Web service as you would deploy any standard J2EE application that is stored in an .ear file (to run under OC4J).

Notice that we haven't really spoken of what tools to use for various tasks, such as creating the .ear file. That is because JDeveloper automates the whole process.

Creating the Reminder Web Service

In this section, you will create the Reminder Web service as explained in the case study. The Web service requires use of a database. The following sections discuss the SQL Server database structure. However, because we are developing the application in Java and will be using the JDBC-ODBC bridge to access the database, you can also use any other type of database.

The ReminderService Database

The ReminderService database contains the following tables:

◆ **Users.** This table has a list of users who have signed up with the service. This table contains the user's login name, password, and e-mail ID. The structure of the table is shown in Figure 18-1.

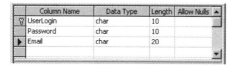

	Column Name	Data Type	Length	Allow Nulls	
🔑	UserLogin	char	10		
	Password	char	10		
▶	Email	char	20		

FIGURE 18-1 *Structure of the Users table.*

◆ **Occasions.** This table contains a list of occasions for which the service can send a reminder. The fields in the table include Occasion ID, details, and suggestions for a gift for that occasion. The structure of the table is given in Figure 18-2.

	Column Name	Data Type	Length	Allow Nulls	
🔑	OccasionID	int	4		
	OccasionName	char	10		
	Suggestion	varchar	50		

FIGURE 18-2 *Structure of the Occasions table.*

◆ **Reminders.** This table contains the reminders stored by various users. The structure of the table is shown in Figure 18-3.

Column Name	Data Type	Length	Allow Nulls
ReminderID	int	4	
RemDate	datetime	8	
UserLogin	char	10	
OccasionID	int	4	
Details	varchar	50	

FIGURE 18-3 *Structure of the Reminders table.*

Next, you will look at the stored procedures created for the database.

Here is the code for the AddNewUser stored procedure:

```
CREATE PROCEDURE dbo.AddNewUser(@UserName varchar(10),@Pass varchar(10), @email
varchar(20))
 AS
insert into users(UserLogin,Password,email) values(@UserName,@Pass,@email)
GO
```

Next, create the AddReminder stored procedure that allows a user to store the reminder for any occasion:

```
CREATE PROCEDURE dbo.AddReminder(@user varchar(10),@pass varchar(10),@RDate datetime,
@occasionID int,@details varchar(50))
 AS
if exists(select count(*) from users where userlogin=@user and password=@pass)
Begin
insert into Reminders(RemDate,UserLogin, OccasionID,Details) values(@RDate,@user,
@occasionID,@details)
return 1
```

```
End
else
return -1
GO
```

Last, the `GetReminders` stored procedure that allows a user to view his reminders is created, as shown in the following code:

```
CREATE PROCEDURE dbo.GetReminders(@User varchar(10))
 AS
select RemDate,Details from Reminders where UserLogin=@User
GO
```

Next, you will create the Java class that forms the basis of the Reminder Web service.

Creating the Java Class

The Java class, whose functionality will be exposed as a Web service, will call the stored procedures to access the data in the ReminderService database. Before you construct the Java classes, you need to configure the ODBC data source to establish backend connectivity in the class.

Configuring the ODBC Data Source

The Java class will make use of the JDBC-ODBC bridge to connect to the database. This implies that you have to configure an ODBC database, which you can accomplish as follows:

1. From the Control Panel, select Administrative Tools, and double-click Data Sources (ODBC) application. This brings up the dialog box shown in Figure 18-4.

   The dialog box shows a list of data sources that are already configured. To create a new data source, click on the Add button. This brings up the Create New Data Source dialog box, which is shown in Figure 18-5.

2. Select the driver for the database you are using. In this project, we are using the SQL Server 2000 database; therefore, we will select the SQL Server driver. Click on the Finish button. This closes the window and opens the Create a New Data Source to SQL Server dialog box shown in Figure 18-6.

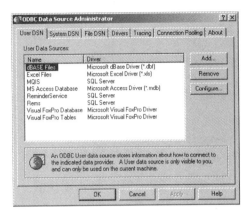

FIGURE 18-4 *ODBC Data Source Administrator window.*

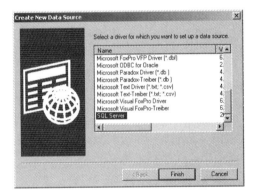

FIGURE 18-5 *Create New Data Source dialog box.*

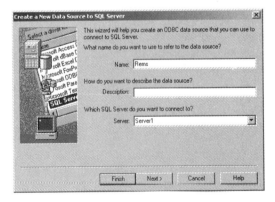

FIGURE 18-6 *Create a New Data source to SQL Server dialog box.*

3. Enter the name and a description for the data source, and select the local SQL Server installation from the drop-down list. Click on the Next button to bring up the page of the dialog box shown in Figure 18-7.

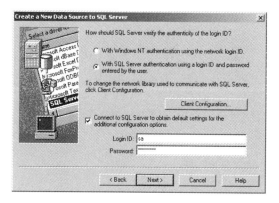

FIGURE 18-7 *Configuring the authentication options.*

This page allows you to select the appropriate authentication type. Select the SQL Server authentication, provide the username and password, and click on the Next button. This brings up the page shown in Figure 18-8.

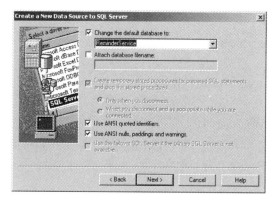

FIGURE 18-8 *Selecting the default database.*

4. Select the default database, which is the ReminderService database. Click on the Next button. This brings up a page with some additional configuration details, such as language. Click on the Finish button to open the Test page of the wizard, as shown in Figure 18-9.

5. Click on the Test Data Source button to check the connection to the database.

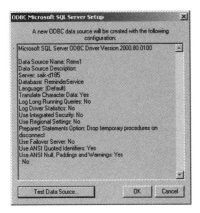

FIGURE 18-9 *Testing the data source connection.*

Creating the `ReminderService` *Class*

You will now create the `ReminderService` class. This class will contain three public methods:

- ◆ `addUser()`. This method registers a new user for the reminder service.
- ◆ `addReminder()`. This method adds a new reminder for the user for a particular date.
- ◆ `GetReminders()`. This method retrieves a list of all the reminders for a user.

 NOTE

As you can see, this list is not conclusive. You will need more methods, for example, to modify or delete reminders, which you can develop later.

Each of the preceding methods reads or writes from the database. We will now introduce you to using JDBC to connect to a data source, which further connects to the database, and then reads and writes data from it.

First, you will have to connect to the ODBC data source that is configured and make use of it from within your Java class. To do so, you first have to load the required driver by using the following code:

```
Class.forName("sun.jdbc.odbc.JdbcOdbcDriver");
```

Next, you must retrieve the connection with the database. To do so, use the following code:

```
Connection con=DriverManager.getConnection("jdbc:odbc:Rems","user1","pass1");
```

You will be using `Callable` and `Prepared` statements in this class to access the database. `Callable` statements allow you to call stored procedures from JDBC applications.

A `CallableStatement` object is created using the `prepareCall()` method in the `Connection` class, and the general syntax of the method is as shown next:

```
{[?=] call <Stored procedure name> (<?>,<?>)}
```

In the preceding syntax, ? represents the parameters and the return values to be passed and retrieved from the method.

The following is a section of the `ReminderService` Java class that shows the `AddReminder` stored procedure being called using a `CallableStatement`:

```
CallableStatement stmt;
stmt=con.prepareCall("{call AddReminder(?,?,?,?,?)}");
stmt.setString(1,sUserName);
stmt.setString(2,sPass);
stmt.setString(3, sDate);
stmt.setInt(4,nOccasionID);
stmt.setString(5,sDetails); int Retval=stmt.executeUpdate();
```

To create a `PreparedStatement`, you would use the `prepareStatement()` method of the `Connection` class. The `PreparedStatement()` method takes an SQL string and passes it to the underlying database. The database verifies the syntax and does the query plan optimization but does not run the command. Instead, it returns a handle to the JDBC driver, which is then stored in a `PreparedStatement` object. You can use this object to execute the SQL command. Prepared statements are efficient. The `PreparedStatement` class has three methods: `executeQuery()`, `executeUpdate()`, and `execute()`, none of which take parameters.

Here is an example of a prepared statement being used in the Java class that is created for the Reminder service:

```
PreparedStatement prep;


//Check for a user named "JohnK" in the database
prep=con.prepareStatement("Select count(*) from reminders where UserLogin=?");
prep.setString(1,"JohnK");
ResultSet rs=prep.executeQuery();
rs.next();
nRows=rs.getInt(1);
```

Here is the code for the complete Java class:

```
import java.lang.*;
import java.sql.*;
public class ReminderService{
```

```java
public void addUser(String sUserName,String sPass, String sEmail)
//method to add a new user
{
CallableStatement stmt;
try
{
Class.forName("sun.jdbc.odbc.JdbcOdbcDriver");
Connection con=DriverManager.getConnection("jdbc:odbc:Rems","user1","pass1");

stmt=con.prepareCall("{call AddNewUser(?,?,?)}");
stmt.setString(1,sUserName);
stmt.setString(2,sPass);
stmt.setString(3,sEmail);
int Retval=stmt.executeUpdate();
}

catch(Exception e)
{
}
}

public void addReminder(String sUserName,String sPass, String sDate, int nOccasionID,
String sDetails)
//method to add a reminder
{
CallableStatement stmt;
try
{
Class.forName("sun.jdbc.odbc.JdbcOdbcDriver");
Connection con=DriverManager.getConnection("jdbc:odbc:Rems","user1","pass1");
stmt=con.prepareCall("{call AddReminder(?,?,?,?,?)}");
stmt.setString(1,sUserName);
stmt.setString(2,sPass);
stmt.setString(3, sDate);
stmt.setInt(4,nOccasionID);
stmt.setString(5,sDetails);
int Retval=stmt.executeUpdate();
}
```

```
catch(Exception e)
{
}
}


public String[] getReminders(String sUserName)
//method to retrieve reminders based on the given username
{
CallableStatement stmt;
PreparedStatement prep;
int nRows;
int i=0;
String results[];


try
{
Class.forName("sun.jdbc.odbc.JdbcOdbcDriver");
Connection con=DriverManager.getConnection("jdbc:odbc:Rems","user1","pass1");
prep=con.prepareStatement("Select count(*) from reminders where UserLogin=?");
prep.setString(1,"user1");
ResultSet s=prep.executeQuery();
s.next();
nRows=s.getInt(1);


results=new String[nRows];


stmt=con.prepareCall("{call getReminders(?)}");
stmt.setString(1,sUserName);
ResultSet Retval=stmt.executeQuery();


while(Retval.next())
{
String strTemp;
strTemp=Retval.getString(1);
strTemp=strTemp + Retval.getString(2);
results[i]=strTemp;
i=i+1;
}
```

```
return results;
}
catch(Exception e)
{
}
return new String[1];
}
/*public static void main(String args[])
{
        try{
        ReminderService s=new ReminderService();
        String str[]=s.getReminders("user1");
        System.out.println(str[0]);
}
catch(Exception e)
{
        System.out.println(e);
}
}
*/
}
```

In the preceding code, notice that the main() method is marked as a comment block. You can use this method to test the functionality of the class before you create the Web service from it.

Creating and Deploying the Web Service

You are going to use the JDeveloper's Web Service Publishing Wizard to create a J2EE Web service from the Java class you created earlier. To run the JDeveloper for Oracle9i, run <JDeveloper_ Home>\Jdev\Bin\jdevw.exe. The user interface of JDeveloper is shown in Figure 18-10.

Connecting to Oracle9i Containers for J2EE

You need to run the Oracle Containers for J2EE server. To do this, from your <OC4J_Home\J2EE\ Home> folder, where you have installed it, execute the following command from the command line:

```
java -jar oc4j.jar
```

Next, you need to set up a connection to the Oracle9i containers, which enables you to deploy your Web service to the application server. To do this, perform the following steps:

1. Expand the Connections node in the Navigator, and choose New Connection from the Application Server context menu, as shown in Figure 18-11.

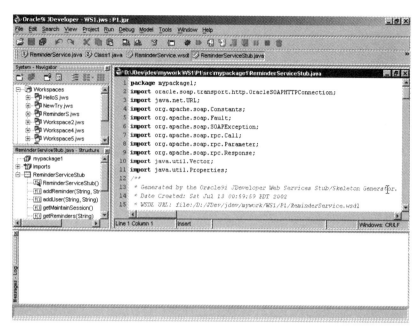

FIGURE 18-10 *The JDeveloper IDE.*

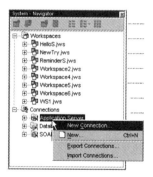

FIGURE 18-11 *Creating a new Application Server connection.*

The Connection Wizard is shown in Figure 18-12.

2. Click on the Next button on the Welcome page, and in the resulting page, shown in Figure 18-13, enter the name of the connection or `Connection1`.

3. Click on the Next button to display the authentication page shown in Figure 18-14.

   This requires the authentication information to connect to OC4J. Enter the username as `Admin` and the password you would have given while setting up OC4J.

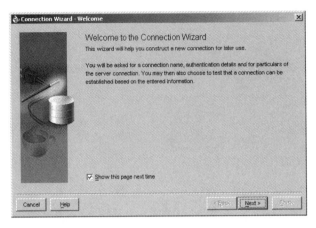

FIGURE 18-12 *The Connection Wizard.*

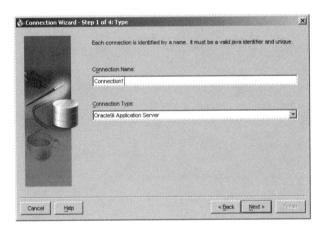

FIGURE 18-13 *Naming the connection.*

4. Click on the Next button. This brings up the Connection page shown in Figure 18-15.

   Enter the data for the local machine name, the target Web site, and the path for the local directory where the admin.jar file is located.

5. Click on the Next button to display the Test page shown in Figure 18-16.

6. Click on the Test Connection button. If the test succeeds, then click on the Finish button to establish a connection to the OC4J server.

Now that you have an OC4J connection, you can use the JDeveloper's Web Service Publishing Wizard to create your J2EE Web service.

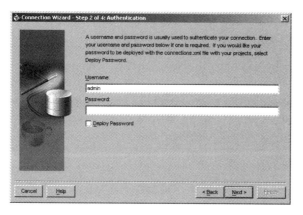

FIGURE 18-14 *Authentication information page.*

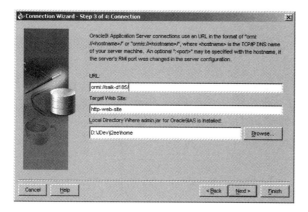

FIGURE 18-15 *Connection page in the Connection Wizard.*

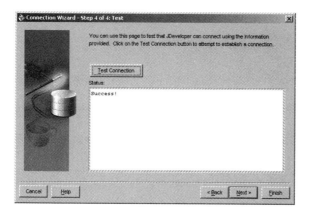

FIGURE 18-16 *Testing the connection.*

Using JDeveloper to Create a J2EE Web Service

Perform the following steps to create a J2EE Web service:

1. Create a new workspace by selecting File, New, Workspace in the menu. Name the workspace and the project appropriately.

2. From the Project menu, select Add to Project and add the Java file, which you created in the preceding step, to the project. In the resulting dialog box, select Yes.

NOTE

Just to keep all files together, you might want to copy the Java file to the workspace\ project folder that will be created under the <Jdev_Home>\jdev\mywork folder.

3. Right-click on the Java file name in the Explorer and select Build to compile and build your class.

4. Select File, New from the project menu, and in the resulting dialog box shown in Figure 18-17, select Project to create a new project.

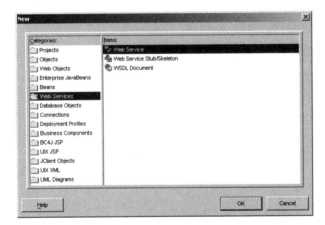

FIGURE 18-17 *New Project dialog box.*

5. Select Web Services in the Categories pane and Web service in the Items page. This will display the Web Service Publishing Wizard shown in Figure 18-18.

6. Click on the Next button on the Welcome page to display the page shown in Figure 18-19.

7. Click on the Browse button to open the Class Browser dialog box, shown in Figure 18-20.

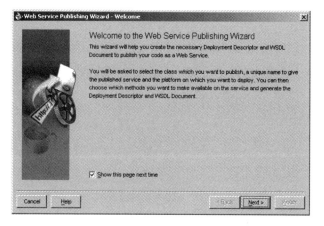

FIGURE 18-18 *Web Service Publishing Wizard.*

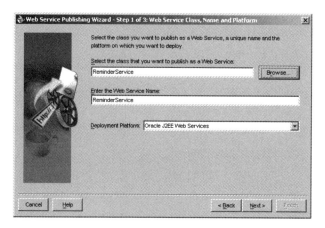

FIGURE 18-19 *Step 1 page of the Web Service Publishing Wizard.*

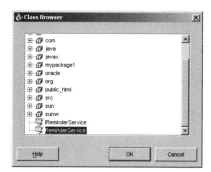

FIGURE 18-20 *The Class Browser dialog box.*

8. Select the `ReminderService` class and click on the OK button to close the window. The Web service will have the same name as the class. You can change the name of the Web service if you want. Let the Deployment platform be Oracle J2EE Web server.

9. Click on the Next button to display the Exposed Methods page shown in Figure 18-21.

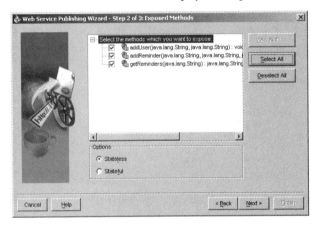

FIGURE 18-21 *Step 2 page of the Web Service Publishing Wizard.*

10. Click on the Select All button to select all methods that are available in the original Java class.

11. Click on the Next button to display the File Locations page displayed in Figure 18-22.

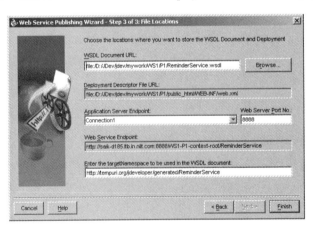

FIGURE 18-22 *Step 3 page of the Web Service Publishing Wizard.*

12. On this page, select the `Connection1` connection, which you created earlier, as the Application server endpoint. The target namespace will contain a namespace http://tempuri.org. You can change it if you want to.

13. Click on the OK button. If you haven't changed the target namespace, this displays a warning message. Ignore the message. The following files are generated:

◆ A WSDL document

◆ WebService.deploy

◆ Web.xml

◆ A ReminderService interface file

The WSDL document contains a description of the Web service. Various tools use the WSDL document to create Web service clients. The content of the WSDL document created by the wizard is explained next:

```
<?xml version = '1.0' encoding = 'windows-1252'?>

<!--Generated by the Oracle9i JDeveloper Web Services WSDL Generator-->

<!--Date Created: Fri Jul 12 22:57:18 PDT 2002-->

<definitions

    name="ReminderService"

    targetNamespace="http://tempuri.org/jdeveloper/generated/ReminderService"

    xmlns="http://schemas.xmlsoap.org/wsdl/"

    xmlns:xsd="http://www.w3.org/2001/XMLSchema"

    xmlns:soap="http://schemas.xmlsoap.org/wsdl/soap/"

    xmlns:tns="http://tempuri.org/jdeveloper/generated/ReminderService"

    xmlns:ns1="http://tempuri.org/jdeveloper/generated/ReminderService/schema">

    <types>
```

Because the target namespace was not changed, the namespace remains as http://tempuri.org:

```
  <schema targetNamespace="http://tempuri.org/jdeveloper/generated/ReminderService/
schema"

        xmlns="http://www.w3.org/2001/XMLSchema"

        xmlns:SOAP-ENC="http://schemas.xmlsoap.org/soap/encoding/">
```

One of the methods exposed by the Web service, getReminders(), returns an array of strings. Here is the complexType declaration for that:

```
<complexType name="ArrayOfstring" xmlns:wsdl="http://schemas.xmlsoap.org/wsdl/">

            <complexContent>

                <restriction base="SOAP-ENC:Array">

                    <attribute ref="SOAP-ENC:arrayType" wsdl:arrayType="xsd:string[]"/>

                </restriction>

            </complexContent>

        </complexType>

    </schema>

  </types>
```

The Web service defines three operations: addUser, addReminder, and getReminder. Each of these operations uses two messages. For example, the addUser operation has the corresponding Request and Response message declarations shown next:

```
<message name="addUser0Request">
    <part name="sUserName" type="xsd:string"/>
    <part name="sPass" type="xsd:string"/>
</message>
<message name="addUser0Response"/>


<message name="addReminder1Request">
    <part name="sUserName" type="xsd:string"/>
    <part name="sPass" type="xsd:string"/>
    <part name="sDate" type="xsd:string"/>
    <part name="nOccasionID" type="xsd:int"/>
    <part name="sDetails" type="xsd:string"/>
</message>
<message name="addReminder1Response"/>


<message name="getReminders2Request">
    <part name="sUserName" type="xsd:string"/>
</message>
<message name="getReminders2Response">
    <part name="return" type="ns1:ArrayOfstring"/>
</message>
```

The port type and the operation declarations are shown next. As mentioned earlier, each of the operations uses a Request and a Response message defined earlier:

```
<portType name="ReminderServicePortType">
    <operation name="addUser">
        <input name="addUser0Request" message="tns:addUser0Request"/>
        <output name="addUser0Response" message="tns:addUser0Response"/>
    </operation>
    <operation name="addReminder">
        <input name="addReminder1Request" message="tns:addReminder1Request"/>
        <output name="addReminder1Response" message="tns:addReminder1Response"/>
    </operation>
    <operation name="getReminders">
        <input name="getReminders2Request" message="tns:getReminders2Request"/>
```

```
            <output name="getReminders2Response" message="tns:getReminders2Response"/>
        </operation>
    </portType>


    <binding name="ReminderServiceBinding" type="tns:ReminderServicePortType">
        <soap:binding style="rpc" transport="http://schemas.xmlsoap.org/soap/http"/>
        <operation name="addUser">
            <soap:operation soapAction="" style="rpc"/>
            <input name="addUser0Request">
                <soap:body use="encoded" namespace="ReminderService" encodingStyle=
"http://schemas.xmlsoap.org/soap/encoding/"/>
            </input>
            <output name="addUser0Response">
                <soap:body use="encoded" namespace="ReminderService" encodingStyle=
"http://schemas.xmlsoap.org/soap/encoding/"/>
            </output>
        </operation>
        <operation name="addReminder">
            <soap:operation soapAction="" style="rpc"/>
            <input name="addReminder1Request">
                <soap:body use="encoded" namespace="ReminderService"
encodingStyle="http://schemas.xmlsoap.org/soap/encoding/"/>
            </input>
            <output name="addReminder1Response">
                <soap:body use="encoded" namespace="ReminderService"
encodingStyle="http://schemas.xmlsoap.org/soap/encoding/"/>
            </output>
        </operation>
        <operation name="getReminders">
            <soap:operation soapAction="" style="rpc"/>
            <input name="getReminders2Request">
                <soap:body use="encoded" namespace="ReminderService"
encodingStyle="http://schemas.xmlsoap.org/soap/encoding/"/>
            </input>
            <output name="getReminders2Response">
                <soap:body use="encoded" namespace="ReminderService"
encodingStyle="http://schemas.xmlsoap.org/soap/encoding/"/>
            </output>
```

```
      </operation>
   </binding>

   <service name="ReminderService">
      <port name="ReminderServicePort" binding="tns:ReminderServiceBinding">
         <soap:address location="http://saik:8888/
WS1-P1-context-root/ReminderService"/>
      </port>
   </service>
</definitions>
```

 NOTE

Notice the value of the location attribute of the soap:address tag. This tells you the
URL where the Web service can be accessed.

Next, look at the deployment file. This file contains a list of the files to be deployed, the connection to which the Web service will be deployed, and the name of the WAR file that will
be generated.

```
<?xml version = '1.0' encoding = 'windows-1252'?>
<web-app-deployment xmlns="http://xmlns.oracle.com/jdeveloper/902/deploy/
j2ee-war" nselem="web-app-deployment" class="oracle.jdeveloper.deploy.war.WarProfile">
<appletArchiveName/>
 <appletArchives>
      <archives/>
      <selectionMode>0</selectionMode>
 </appletArchives>

  <appletDeployedAsArchive>false</appletDeployedAsArchive>


  <appletDeployment>false</appletDeployment>


  <appletFiles>
     <autoInclude>true</autoInclude>
     <deploySourceAs>0</deploySourceAs>
   <files/>
   <selectionFilters>
        <Item id="0">oracle.jdevimpl.deploy.common.JavaSelectionFilter</Item>
```

```xml
        </selectionFilters>
    </appletFiles>


    <appletLocation/>
    <cdaSettings>
        <additionalArchives/>
        <afterFilters/>
        <beforeFilters/>
        <duringFilters/>
        <selectedArchives>
            <archives/>
            <selectionMode>0</selectionMode>
        </selectedArchives>
    </cdaSettings>


    <contextRoot/>
    <defaultConnection>Connection1</defaultConnection>
    <deployClientMaxHeapSize/>
    <earURL path="WS1-P1-WS.ear"/>
    <enterpriseAppName>WS1-P1-WS</enterpriseAppName>
    <htmlRootRules>
        <filters/>
    </htmlRootRules>
    <javaFiles>
        <autoInclude>false</autoInclude>
        <deploySourceAs>0</deploySourceAs>
        <files>
            <Item path="IReminderService.java"/>
            <Item path="ReminderService.wsdl"/>
            <Item path="ReminderService.java"/>
        </files>
        <selectionFilters>
            <Item idref="0"/>
        </selectionFilters>
    </javaFiles>
    <profileDeps/>
    <warURL path="WebServices.war"/>
</web-app-deployment>
```

The web.xml file, shown next, contains information on the Web service and the servlet deployment:

```xml
<?xml version = '1.0' encoding = 'windows-1252'?>
<!DOCTYPE web-app PUBLIC "-//Sun Microsystems, Inc.//DTD Web Application 2.2//EN"
 "http://java.sun.com/j2ee/dtds/web-app_2_2.dtd">
<web-app>
    <description>Generated by the Oracle9i JDeveloper Web Services WebXML Generator</description>
    <servlet>
        <servlet-name>ReminderService</servlet-name>
        <servlet-class>oracle.j2ee.ws.StatelessJavaRpcWebService</servlet-class>
        <init-param>
            <param-name>class-name</param-name>
            <param-value>ReminderService</param-value>
        </init-param>
        <init-param>
            <param-name>interface-name</param-name>
            <param-value>IReminderService</param-value>
        </init-param>
    </servlet>

    <servlet-mapping>
        <servlet-name>ReminderService</servlet-name>
        <url-pattern>/ReminderService</url-pattern>
    </servlet-mapping>
</web-app>
```

Last, look at the interface file that defines the interface of the Web service:

```java
/**
 * Generated by the Oracle9i JDeveloper Web Services Interface Generator
 * Date Created: Fri Jul 12 22:57:18 PDT 2002
 *
 * This interface lists the subset of public methods that you
 * selected for inclusion in your web service's public interface.
 * It is referenced in the web.xml deployment descriptor for this service.
 *
 * Please do not edit this file!
 */
```

```
public interface IReminderService
{
  public void addUser(String sUserName, String sPass);
  public void addReminder(String sUserName, String sPass, String sDate,
int nOccasionID, String sDetails);
  public String[] getReminders(String sUserName);
}
```

Now that you have used the Web Service Publishing Wizard to create the files needed for your Web service, you need to deploy the Web service.

To deploy the Web service, perform the following steps:

1. Select the Webservices.deploy file from the Navigator and right-click to display the context menu.

2. From the menu, select the Deploy To option and select Connection1. It will take a moment, but when it is done, you will have created and deployed a J2EE Web service.

Next, you will create a Java application that will test this Web service.

Testing the Web Service

This section shows you how to test your new J2EE Web service by creating an application that invokes one of the methods exposed by the Web service. The first client application will be created by using the JDeveloper for Oracle9*i*. Next, we will use Cape Clear's CapeStudio 3.0 to create test client applications in Visual Basic 6.0 and Java.

Creating the Client Application by Using JDeveloper

First, you need to create a Web service stub. You can then add this stub to a new project or to the existing project.

To do so, perform the following steps:

1. Add a new empty project to the workspace. Then invoke the ReminderClient project. With the ReminderClient project selected, select New from the File menu.

2. In the resulting gallery window, select Web Services in the Categories pane. Select the Web service Stub/Skeleton option in the Items pane, as shown in Figure 18-23.

   The Web Service Stub/Skeleton Wizard is displayed, as shown in Figure 18-24.

3. If the welcome message is showing, click on the Next button to display the page shown in Figure 18-25.

4. Browse to the WSDL file that you created and click on the Open button. In Generation Options, make sure that Generate Client-Side Stubs is selected and that other options are not selected.

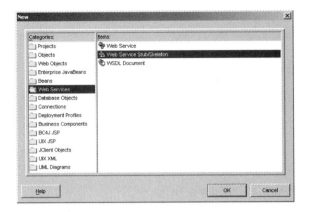

FIGURE 18-23 *Creating a Stub/Skeleton for a Web service.*

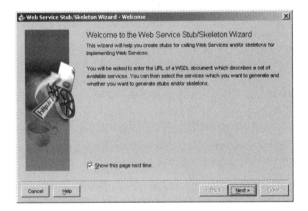

FIGURE 18-24 *The Web Service Stub/Skeleton Wizard.*

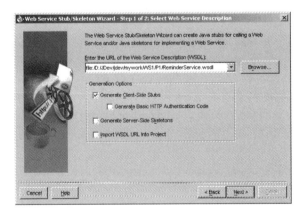

FIGURE 18-25 *The Select Web Service Description page of the Stub/Skeleton Wizard.*

5. Click on the Next button to display the Select Stubs/Skeletons to Generate page, shown in Figure 18-26.

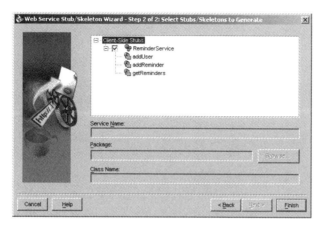

FIGURE 18-26 *The Select Stubs/Skeletons to Generate page of the Stub/Skeleton Wizard.*

6. In the resulting page, ensure that all methods are selected. You can change the name of the package and the class. After you make the required selection and changes, click on the Finish button to generate the stub.

   Here is the content of the ReminderServiceStub.java file:

```
package mypackage1;
import oracle.soap.transport.http.OracleSOAPHTTPConnection;
import java.net.URL;
import org.apache.soap.Constants;
import org.apache.soap.Fault;
import org.apache.soap.SOAPException;
import org.apache.soap.rpc.Call;
import org.apache.soap.rpc.Parameter;
import org.apache.soap.rpc.Response;
import java.util.Vector;
import java.util.Properties;
/**
 * Generated by the Oracle9i JDeveloper Web Services Stub/Skeleton Generator.
 * Date Created: Sat Jul 13 03:02:41 IST 2002
 * WSDL URL: file:/D:/jdev/jdev/mywork/WS1/P1/ReminderService.wsdl
 */


public class ReminderServiceStub
```

```
{
  public String endpoint = "http://saik:8888/WS1-P1-context-root/ReminderService";
  private OracleSOAPHTTPConnection m_httpConnection = null;

  public ReminderServiceStub()
  {
    m_httpConnection = new OracleSOAPHTTPConnection();
  }

  public void addUser(String sUserName, String sPass) throws Exception
  {
    URL endpointURL = new URL(endpoint);
    Call call = new Call();
    call.setSOAPTransport(m_httpConnection);
    call.setTargetObjectURI("ReminderService");
    call.setMethodName("addUser");
    call.setEncodingStyleURI(Constants.NS_URI_SOAP_ENC);
    Vector params = new Vector();
    params.addElement(new Parameter("sUserName", String.class, sUserName, null));
    params.addElement(new Parameter("sPass", String.class, sPass, null));
    call.setParams(params);

    Response response = call.invoke(endpointURL, "");

    if (!response.generatedFault())
    {
      Parameter result = response.getReturnValue();
    }
      else
      {
        Fault fault = response.getFault();
        throw new SOAPException(fault.getFaultCode(), fault.getFaultString());
      }

  }
public void addReminder(String sUserName, String sPass, String sDate, Integer
nOccasionID, String sDetails) throws Exception
  {
```

```
      URL endpointURL = new URL(endpoint);
      Call call = new Call();
      call.setSOAPTransport(m_httpConnection);
      call.setTargetObjectURI("ReminderService");
      call.setMethodName("addReminder");
      call.setEncodingStyleURI(Constants.NS_URI_SOAP_ENC);
      Vector params = new Vector();
      params.addElement(new Parameter("sUserName", String.class, sUserName, null));
      params.addElement(new Parameter("sPass", String.class, sPass, null));
      params.addElement(new Parameter("sDate", String.class, sDate, null));
      params.addElement(new Parameter("nOccasionID", Integer.class, nOccasionID, null));
      params.addElement(new Parameter("sDetails", String.class, sDetails, null));
      call.setParams(params);

      Response response = call.invoke(endpointURL, "");

      if (!response.generatedFault())
      {
        Parameter result = response.getReturnValue();
      }
        else
        {
          Fault fault = response.getFault();
          throw new SOAPException(fault.getFaultCode(),fault.getFaultString());
        }

  }

public String[] getReminders(String sUserName) throws Exception
{
    String[] returnVal = null;

    URL endpointURL = new URL(endpoint);
    Call call = new Call();
    call.setSOAPTransport(m_httpConnection);
    call.setTargetObjectURI("ReminderService");
    call.setMethodName("getReminders");
    call.setEncodingStyleURI(Constants.NS_URI_SOAP_ENC);
```

```java
        Vector params = new Vector();
        params.addElement(new Parameter("sUserName", String.class, sUserName, null));
        call.setParams(params);

        Response response = call.invoke(endpointURL, "");

        if (!response.generatedFault())
        {
          Parameter result = response.getReturnValue();
          returnVal = (String[])result.getValue();
        }
          else
          {
            Fault fault = response.getFault();
            throw new SOAPException(fault.getFaultCode(),fault.getFaultString());
          }


        return returnVal;
      }


      public void setMaintainSession(boolean maintainSession)
      {
        m_httpConnection.setMaintainSession(maintainSession);
      }


      public boolean getMaintainSession()
      {
        return m_httpConnection.getMaintainSession();
      }


      public void setTransportProperties(Properties props)
      {
        m_httpConnection.setProperties(props);
      }
      public Properties getTransportProperties()
      {
        return m_httpConnection.getProperties();
      }
    }
```

Note how neatly the methods in the stub encapsulate those in the Web service. Each method accepts the parameters from a client application and then makes a call to the Web service by using HTTP. Next, the method passes the parameters to the appropriate methods of the Web service.

7. Right-click on the ReminderServiceStub.java file in the Navigator and select Build to build the class.

Finally, you will create an application that will invoke the Web service. To do so, perform the following steps:

1. Right-click on the project ReminderServiceClient and select New Class from the context menu. This brings up the New dialog box, shown in Figure 18-27. Click on the OK button.

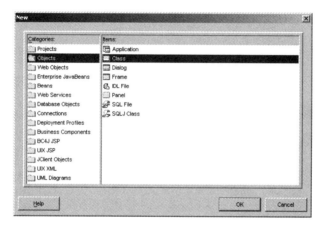

FIGURE 18-27 *The New dialog box.*

2. In the resulting New Class dialog box, enter the name of the class as Client1. The package name should be the same as that of the stub created earlier.

3. Select the Generate Main Method check box. This ensures that a main() method is added to the generated code.

4. Click on the OK button. The generated code is displayed in the code editor. Add the following code to call the Web service method:

```
package mypackage1;
public class Class2
{
  public Class2()
  {
  }
```

```
public static void main(String[] args)
{
  Class2 class2 = new Class2();
  ReminderServiceStub s=new ReminderServiceStub();
  try
  {
    String str[]= s.getReminders("JohnK");
    System.out.println(str[0]);
  }
  catch(Exception e)
  {
    System.out.println(e);}
  }
}
```

Run the application and check the returned values.

Creating Client Applications by Using CapeStudio

Cape Clear offers an easy-to-use set of tools called CapeStudio for creating and deploying Web services. You also can use CapeStudio to create client applications for Web services created using other tools.

In this section, you will use a tool called WSDL Assistant, which is part of CapeStudio, to create client applications for the Java Web service you created earlier. You can download the software for a 30-day trial from http://www.capeclear.com.

 NOTE

You will find a host of live Web services, articles, and tutorials on Web services in general and Cape Clear's products at http://capescience.capeclear.com.

Creating a Visual Basic 6.0 Client

To generate a Visual Basic 6.0 client for the Web service you created earlier, you will use the WSDL Assistant tool that is part of the CapeStudio software. Figure 18-28 shows the interface of the WSDL Assistant.

In the text box labeled WSDL File, enter the path for the WSDL file of the ReminderService Web service. Specify an output directory where the files for the client can be generated.

In the Generate section of the page, select the Client option button. Then, select the VB option button and enter the Project name. Click on the Generate button.

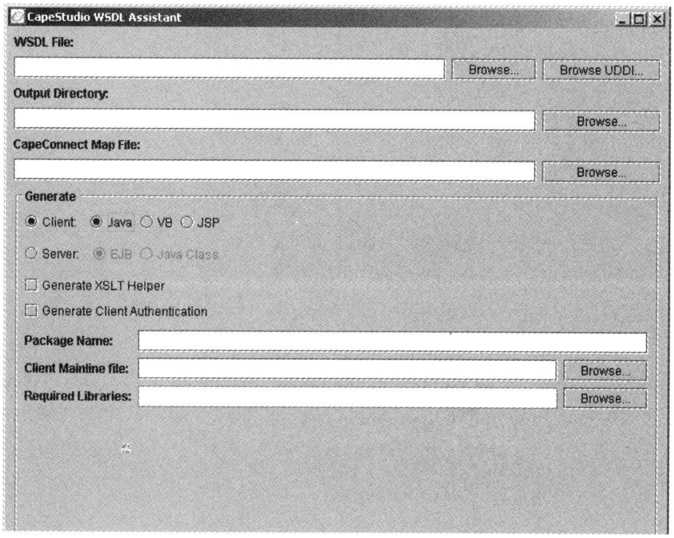

FIGURE 18-28 *WSDL client tool.*

The assistant will create a Visual Basic 6.0, Standard EXE type project in the folder you specified. Open the project, and you will find the definition for a class that is a proxy of the Web service.

A class called `ReminderServicePortTypeClient` is created. This class has a property called endpoint that is used to set and get the value for the Web service endpoint. The property is initialized to the endpoint in the WSDL:

```
' SOAP Encoding Namespace URI
Private Const SOAP_ENCODING_NS_URI = "http://schemas.xmlsoap.org/soap/encoding/"


' property for the SOAP endpoint
Private mvarEndpoint As String
' global declarations
Dim Serializer As SoapSerializer
Dim Reader As SoapReader
Dim Connector As SoapConnector


Private Sub Class_Initialize()


    mvarEndpoint = "http://saik:8888/WS1-P1-context-root/ReminderService"


End Sub
```

```
' Let endpoint
Public Property Let endpoint(ByVal vData As String)
    mvarEndpoint = vData
End Property


' Get endpoint
Public Property Get endpoint() As String
    endpoint = mvarEndpoint
End Property
```

The following is the implementation for the `addUser()` method in the class, which, in turn, calls the `addUser()` method of the ReminderService Web service. The generated code uses the Soap Toolkit methods to serialize the method call into a SOAP message and then calls the Web service.

 NOTE

You need to download the Microsoft SOAP Toolkit ver2.0 SP 2.0 and install it because the code generated for the Visual Basic client uses it.

```
' addUser
Function addUser(ByVal sUserName As String, ByVal sPass As String)
    ' create a new HttpConnector
    Set Connector = New HttpConnector

    ' set the "EndPointURL"
    Connector.Property("EndPointURL") = mvarEndpoint

    ' initialize the SoapConnector object and prepare the connection
    Connector.Connect


    ' set the "SoapAction"
    Connector.Property("SoapAction") = """"
    ' signal the start of a SOAP message being sent to the server
    Connector.BeginMessage

    ' create a SoapSerializer
    Set Serializer = New SoapSerializer
```

```
' set the destination to which the SoapSerializer object writes its text
' i.e. the soap endpoint
Serializer.Init Connector.InputStream

' start request envelope
Serializer.startEnvelope

' add the following attributes to the SOAP-Envelope
Serializer.SoapAttribute "xmlns:SOAP-ENC", , SOAP_ENCODING_NS_URI
Serializer.SoapAttribute "targetNamespace", , "http://tempuri.org/jdeveloper/
generated/ReminderService/schema"
Serializer.SoapAttribute "xmlns:xsi", , "http://www.w3.org/2001/XMLSchema-instance"
Serializer.SoapAttribute "xmlns:xsd", , "http://www.w3.org/2001/XMLSchema"


' start request body
Serializer.startBody

' serialize request for addUser
Serializer.startElement "addUser", "ReminderService", SOAP_ENCODING_NS_URI, "ns1"

    ' Start element "sUserName"
    Serializer.startElement "sUserName"
        Serializer.SoapAttribute "xsi:type", , "xsd:string"
        Serializer.writeString sUserName
    Serializer.endElement
' Start element "sPass"
    Serializer.startElement "sPass"
        Serializer.SoapAttribute "xsi:type", , "xsd:string"
        Serializer.writeString sPass
    Serializer.endElement

Serializer.endElement

' close SOAP-Body
Serializer.endBody

' close SOAP-Envelope
```

```
     Serializer.endEnvelope

     ' signal the end of the SOAP message being sent to the server
     Connector.EndMessage

     ' create a new SoapReader
     Set Reader = New SoapReader

     ' load the XML from the Stream
     Reader.Load Connector.OutputStream

         ' if there is a fault, use a message box to report it
     If Not Reader.Fault Is Nothing Then
  MsgBox "addUser" & " failed:- " & Reader.faultstring.Text, vbExclamation, "Error"
  Else
     End If
End Function
```

This is a Standard EXE project. Therefore, to execute this application, you need to add a form or a main procedure.

Add a form to the project and set it as the startup object in the Project Properties dialog box. Add a button to the form and the code to invoke a Web service method, as shown next:

```
Dim ws As New ReminderServicePortTypeClient
 Str1 = ws.getReminders("Johnk")
MsgBox Str1(0)
```

Here, the code invokes the `getReminders()` method and displays the first reminder it returns. Run the application and check the functioning of both the client and the Web service.

Creating a Java Client

Run the WSDL Assistant and follow the same steps as before. Select Java as the client type and generate the Web service client.

The assistant creates the following files for you in the folder that you specified:

◆ **ReminderServiceBindingClient.java.** This file has the `ReminderServiceBinding Client` class that has the interface, which defines the methods exposed by the Web service.

◆ **ReminderServiceBindingClientImpl.java.** This file has the `ReminderService BindingClientImpl` class, which implements the above interface at the client end.

◆ **ReminderServiceBindingClientFactory.java.** This file has the `ReminderService BindingClientFactory` classs, which creates the client proxy object. The class has a `create()` method that is used to create the proxy object.

◆ **ReminderServiceBindingClientMainline.java.** This file has a simple client application implementation, which you can compile and execute to test the working of the Web service.

Following is the definition of the `ReminderServiceBindingClient` class:

```
/**

    Generated by Cape Studio WSDL Assistant

    WSDL Assistant Copyright (c) 2001,2002 Cape Clear Software Ltd.

    http://www.capeclear.com/products/capestudio


    File: ReminderServiceBindingClient.java

    Creation Date: Sat, Jul 13, 2002 at 03:47:47 IST
 */
/**

 ClientInterface - ReminderServiceBindingClient
 */
public interface ReminderServiceBindingClient
{
    public void addUser(java.lang.String sUserName, java.lang.String sPass)
        throws java.rmi.RemoteException;
    public void addReminder(java.lang.String sUserName, java.lang.String sPass,
java.lang.String sDate, int nOccasionID, java.lang.String sDetails)
        throws java.rmi.RemoteException;
    public java.lang.String[] getReminders(java.lang.String sUserName)
        throws java.rmi.RemoteException;
}
```

Following is the definition of the `ReminderServiceBindingClientImpl` class:

```
/**

    Generated by Cape Studio WSDL Assistant

    WSDL Assistant Copyright (c) 2001,2002 Cape Clear Software Ltd.

    http://www.capeclear.com/products/capestudio


    File: ReminderServiceBindingClientImpl.java

    Creation Date: Sat, Jul 13, 2002 at 03:47:47 IST
 */
```

```java
/**

 Client Implementation - ReminderServiceBindingClientImpl
 */
public class ReminderServiceBindingClientImpl
    extends com.capeclear.capeconnect.soap.proxy.BaseSoapProxy
    implements ReminderServiceBindingClient
{

    /**
     * Constructor
     *
     * @param endpointURI the URI of the SOAP Message Router
     */
    public ReminderServiceBindingClientImpl(java.lang.String endpointURI)
        throws java.net.MalformedURLException
    {
        super(endpointURI);
    }

    public void addUser(java.lang.String sUserName, java.lang.String sPass)
        throws java.rmi.RemoteException
    {
        java.util.Map options = ReminderServiceBindingClientFactory.getDefaultOptions();

        $_setStyleAndUse( options, "rpc", "encoded" );

        java.lang.Object $__result = $_invokeRequest(
            "",
            "ReminderService",
            "addUser",
            new java.lang.String[]
            {
                "sUserName",
                "sPass",
                "sEmail"
            },
            new java.lang.Object[]
```

```
                {       sUserName,
                        sPass,
                        sEmail
                },
                null,
                options
        );


    }


public void addReminder(java.lang.String sUserName, java.lang.String sPass,
java.lang.String sDate, int nOccasionID, java.lang.String sDetails)
        throws java.rmi.RemoteException
    {
        java.util.Map options =
ReminderServiceBindingClientFactory.getDefaultOptions();


        $_setStyleAndUse( options, "rpc", "encoded" );


        java.lang.Object $__result = $_invokeRequest(
            "",
            "ReminderService",
            "addReminder",
            new java.lang.String[]
            {
                "sUserName",
                "sPass",
                "sDate",
                "nOccasionID",
                "sDetails"
            },
            new java.lang.Object[]
            {
                sUserName,
                sPass,
                sDate,
                new java.lang.Integer(nOccasionID),
                sDetails
```

```
            },
            null,
            options
        );


    }


    public java.lang.String[] getReminders(java.lang.String sUserName)
        throws java.rmi.RemoteException
    {
        java.util.Map options = ReminderServiceBindingClientFactory.getDefaultOptions();

        $_setStyleAndUse( options, "rpc", "encoded" );

        java.lang.Object $__result = $_invokeRequest(
            "",
            "ReminderService",
            "getReminders",
            new java.lang.String[]
            {
                "sUserName"
            },
            new java.lang.Object[]
            {
                sUserName
            },
            java.lang.String[].class,
            options
        );
        return ( java.lang.String[] )$__result;


    }
}
```

Following is the definition of the `ReminderServiceBindingClientFactory` class:

```
/**
    Generated by Cape Studio WSDL Assistant
    WSDL Assistant Copyright (c) 2001,2002 Cape Clear Software Ltd.
```

```
    http://www.capeclear.com/products/capestudio


    File: ReminderServiceBindingClientFactory.java
    Creation Date: Sat, Jul 13, 2002 at 03:47:47 IST
 */
/**
 * Client Factory
 */
public class ReminderServiceBindingClientFactory
    extends com.capeclear.capeconnect.soap.proxy.SoapProxyFactory
{

    static private final java.util.HashMap options = new java.util.HashMap();


    // retrieved from WSDL document
    static private java.lang.String ENDPOINT="http://saik:8888/WS1-P1-context-root/
ReminderService";


    static public java.lang.String getDefaultEndpoint ( )
    {
        return ENDPOINT;
    }
 static
    {
options.put(com.capeclear.capeconnect.soap.proxy.SoapProxy.KEY_TARGETSCHEMA,
            "http://tempuri.org/jdeveloper/generated/ReminderService/schema");
options.put(com.capeclear.capeconnect.soap.proxy.SoapProxy.KEY_SCHEMA_VERSION,
                  "http://www.w3.org/2001/XMLSchema");
$_mapTypeList("http://tempuri.org/jdeveloper/generated/ReminderService/schema",
        new java.lang.String[][]              {
              { "ArrayOfstring", java.lang.String[].class.getName()}
            }
        );
    }
/**
 * create
 */
    static public ReminderServiceBindingClient create( )
        throws java.net.MalformedURLException
```

```
    {
        return new ReminderServiceBindingClientImpl( ENDPOINT );
    }


    /**
     * create
     *
     * @param endpoint the URI to the SOAP message router
     */
    static public ReminderServiceBindingClient create( java.lang.String endpoint )
        throws java.net.MalformedURLException
    {
        return new ReminderServiceBindingClientImpl( endpoint );
    }


    /**
     * @return default options
     */
    static public java.util.Map getDefaultOptions()
    {
        return (java.util.Map)options.clone();
    }
}
```

Following is the client application. The client application calls the exposed methods of the Web service one after the other by passing dummy parameters and checks for an error:

```
/**
 Client Impl - ReminderServiceBindingClientMainline.java
 */
public class ReminderServiceBindingClientMainline
{
    public static void main( String[] args )
    {
        System.out.println( "CapeStudio Generated Mainline" );
        System.out.println( "Endpoint = " +
ReminderServiceBindingClientFactory.getDefaultEndpoint( ) );
        try
        {
```

```
              ReminderServiceBindingClient client =
ReminderServiceBindingClientFactory.create(  );
          {
              System.out.println( "invoke getReminders" );
              java.lang.String[] result = client.getReminders( "" );
              System.out.println( "getReminders result = " + result );
          }
          System.out.println( "Run Successful" );
      }
      catch( Throwable t )
      {
          System.out.println( "Run UnSuccessful" );
          t.printStackTrace( System.err );
      }
    }
}
```

You will also find two more folders created: classes and lib. The Classes folder will contain the compiled classes for all generated Java files. The Lib folder has all the compiled classes along with the required support files packaged into a .jar file.

Set the class path to include the xerces.jar, xalan.jar, common.jar, capeconnect.jar, soapdirect.jar, and wsdl4j.jar files in the Capeclear\capestudio3.0\lib folder.

Execute the `ReminderServiceBindingClientMainline` class to run the test Java client application and verify the functioning of the Web service.

Summary

In this chapter, you learned about developing and deploying Web services for Oracle9*i*AS by using JDeveloper Oracle 9*i*. You also learned to use the tools that are part of CapeStudio to easily create client applications, both in Visual Basic 6.0 and Java, for Web services created using any language and deployed on any application server.

PART XIII

Beyond the Labs

Chapter 19

Previous projects looked at how to create Web services using various programming languages, such as Visual Basic .NET, Visual C# .NET, Visual C++, and Java. This chapter explores building Web services using Perl, which is one of the most widely used scripting languages. First, the chapter introduces the scenario for which you will be building the Web service. Then it proceeds to give you a quick overview of the Perl language and details of the project.

Case Study

InSysPeripherals.com is an online store that sells computers and related peripherals. Visitors can buy products from their online site and through affiliate partners who display the wares of InSysPeripherals.com on their sites. Because the company does not advertise much, it has mostly repeat customers who are aware of the site and the products. First-time customers normally purchase through their affiliate partners, some of whom are horizontal portals, including other online stores, magazine sites, and search engines.

The data about the goods of InSysPeripherals is provided to the affiliates each month in the form of databases and in a format preferred by the partners because different sites use different databases as backends. InSysPeripherals has to sell items whose prices rise after the last update at the affiliate sites at the old lower prices to gain customers and also to keep its and the affiliate partner's credibility. Timely updates of data on the affiliate partner's site are also a problem because the information is updated only once a month. InSysPeripherals now intends to use the new Web service technology to share its catalog with its partners from a single source, which will be InSysPeripheral's Web site. The Web site is being built using Perl with the data stored in a flat text database.

Project Life Cycle

The Development Life Cycle (DLC) of a project involves the following three phases:

- ◆ Project initiation
- ◆ Project execution
- ◆ Project deployment

You learned about these phases in earlier projects. In this chapter, we will discuss only the project execution phase, which is different from the earlier projects.

The Project Execution Phase

In the project execution phase, the development team creates the design of an application. After creating the design, they develop the application. The project execution phase consists of the following stages:

- ◆ Analyzing the requirements
- ◆ Creating the design of the application
- ◆ Constructing the application

Analyzing the Requirements

During the requirements analysis phase, the development team at InSysPeripherals concluded that sharing the catalog from a central location would solve the problem of not having updated data accessible from the affiliate sites. To achieve this purpose, the team decided to create a Web service that allows the sites of the affiliates to access the data from http://www.InSysPeripherals.com. This Web service should contain Web methods that allow a user to retrieve price, description, and other such information of various products on sale.

Creating the Design of the Application

During the design phase of the application, the development team decides upon the functionality to be implemented and the technology to be used.

As discussed earlier, the solution to the organization's requirements is a Web service. Because the Web site is based primarily on Perl, and Perl with SOAP::Lite provides good support for creating Web services, it was decided to implement the Web services by using Perl.

Construction

During the construction phase, the development team constructs the application. The primary tasks that the team performs in the construction phase are as follows:

◆ Create the Web service
◆ Test the Web service

First, we will discuss the software required to work with Perl.

Required Software

For trying the examples in this chapter, you will need the following software:

◆ **Apache Web server.** You can download the latest version of the Apache Web server free of charge from http://httpd.apache.org/.
◆ **Active Perl.** You can download the latest version of Perl from http://www.Activestate.com.
◆ **SOAP::Lite kit.** You can download the latest version of this kit from http://www.soaplite.com.

 NOTE

Note that you need to install the Web server, Active Perl, and SOAP::Lite in the preceding order because the Perl installation needs to configure the Web server, and to configure SOAP:Lite, you execute a Perl script.

The installation of the Apache Web server and the Active Perl software is like any other Windows installation. The installation for the SOAP::Lite package is shown next.

You install SOAP::Lite as you install any Perl module. If you have the CPAN.pm module installed and you're connected to the Internet, use either of the following commands:

```
perl -MCPAN -e shell
install SOAP::Lite
```

or

```
perl -MCPAN -e 'install SOAP::Lite'
```

If you don't have the CPAN module, follow the given process:

```
perl Makefile.PL
make
make test
make install
```

 NOTE

Use nmake instead of make on Windows.

Before we delve into the process of creating Web services using Perl, it's important to provide you with a brief overview of Perl.

A Brief Introduction to Perl

Perl is a general-purpose scripting language ideally suited to handle words and text. Perl is admired for staying simple when you need to do simple things, but also having the power to do nearly every chore that a system administrator might require. To quote the Perl gurus: "It makes the easy things easy, and the difficult things possible."

Perl is a great language because after you get to know it, you can express yourself quickly and easily. Perl has a way of allowing you to do a lot by writing very little. It dispenses with a lot of programming "clutter" that accompanies many other programming languages. This ability allows you to write scripts in a natural and concise manner.

Another of Perl's strengths is that it offers many ways of accomplishing any particular bit of programming. This strength inspires Perl programmers to quote the motto "TIMTOWTDI" (pronounced *timtoady*), which is the acronym for "There Is More Than One Way To Do It." This variety leads to different personal styles and preferences, as well as a great deal of fun, comfort, and joyful discovery as you learn the ins and outs of the language.

Writing a Simple Program in Perl

After you install Active Perl, you can try out the first Perl program.

Create the following file in the cgi-bin folder of your Apache installation. Name the file try.pl.

```perl
#!perl -w
# This program reads some input and displays it with a Hello
$inputline = <STDIN>;
print("Hello ",  $inputline );
```

Examine the program. This is similar to a typical "Hello World" program. It waits for user input and then displays a message.

> **NOTE**
>
> Note that any line that starts with a # is a comment.

The first line with a # and a ! indicates the language used by this script, which is Perl. `<STDIN>` represents the standard input device, which is usually the keyboard.

Execute the file from the command line by using the following syntax:

```perl
perl try.pl
```

If you have installed the Active Perl package, then this program should execute without a problem.

In the preceding program, you stored the input from the keyboard into a variable. Variables in Perl should consist of the character $ followed by at least one letter, which can be further followed by any number of letters, digits, or underscore characters.

Operators in Perl

In addition, similar to any other scripting language, Perl allows you to use most of the basic arithmetic operators.

Here is a sample program that illustrates the use of variables and a basic multiplication operator:

```perl
#!/usr/local/bin/perl


print ("Enter the Weight in Kgs:");
$KGrms = <STDIN>;
chop ($KGrms);
$Grms = $KGrms * 1000 ;
print ($KGrms, " kilograms = ", $Grms," grams\n");
```

The input value stored in the variable, $KGrms, includes the number you entered and a new line character (from the Enter you pressed after the number). The chop function chops off the last character, which is a space.

Programming Constructs in Perl

Perl supports most of the programming constructs that other programming languages support. Let's look at some of the basic decision-making and looping constructs.

The If-Else statement is probably the most widely used decision-making statement. The following example shows the syntax of the If-Else statement::

```
$Name = "user1";
if ( $Name eq "user1" )
{
    print "Welcome user1";
}
else
{
    print "Unknown user.\n";
}
```

Here are examples of the while loop and the for loop.

```
$n = 0;
while ( $n < 4 )
{
#keep looping
$n = $nx + 1;
}
print "Out of the loop";


for ( 1 .. 8)
{
print "This loop will run 8 times;
}
```

Another use for the for loop is working with an array, as shown here:

```
@cat = ( "lion","tiger");
for $cat ( @cat )
{
```

```
print $cat;
print " belongs to the cat family";
print "\n";
}
```

The preceding code will work through the array, assigning the values to the variable `$cat`.

Receiving Keyboard Input

The following code accepts keyboard input and displays the characters entered:

```
#!/usr/local/bin/perl
$line = <STDIN>;
print ($line);
```

The script accepts a line of input from the standard input device—usually the keyboard—stores it in a variable, and then displays the contents of the variable.

Reading and Writing to Files

To open a file on the local system, you will need to use the `open` library function. The syntax for the `open` function is as follows:

```
open (var, filename);
```

where:

- ◆ `var` represents the name you want to use in your Perl program to refer to the file. A file-variable name can be any sequence of letters, digits, and underscores, as long as the first character is a letter.
- ◆ `filename` represents the location of the file on your machine.

You must decide how you want to open the file. Three different file access modes are available in Perl:

- ◆ **Read mode.** Allows the script to read the contents of a file but not make modifications to it.
- ◆ **Write mode.** Allows the script to overwrite the current contents of the file.
- ◆ **Append mode.** Allows the script to retain the existing content and add new content to it, if required.

You can use the following syntax to check whether a file has been opened successfully:

```
if (open(MYFILE, /dev/file1.dat"))
{
```

```
        # What should be done if the file opens
}
```

After the file is open, you can read its contents and store them in a variable as shown next:

```
if (open(FILEID, /dev/file1.dat"))
{
#The following command reads a line of input from the file and stores it in a variable
$Content=<FILEID>
}
```

Here is a short script that reads the contents of a file and displays it:

```
#!perl -w
use CGI;
 $input = new CGI;
 print $input->header;
  if (open(FILEID, "file.dat"))
{
    $val = <FILEID>;
    while ($val ne "")
    {
       print ($val);
       $val = <FILEID>;
    }
 }
```

Terminating a Program

If an error occurs, you can use the die command to terminate the script with an error message, as shown in the following code:

```
open(FILE,"$filename")|¦ die "cannot open: $filename\n";
```

Matching a Pattern

A *pattern* is a sequence of characters to be searched for in another string that is normally specified within two slashes (/pattern/). Consider the following syntax:

```
$line =~ /somepattern/;
```

In the preceding line of code, the =~ operator checks whether the pattern is within the string stored in the variable $line. The operator returns a non-zero value if a pattern is found, and 0 if the pattern is not found.

Some characters have special meanings as part of a pattern.

- ◆ The special character + means "one or more of the preceding characters." For example, the pattern /co+l/ matches col, column, cooler, cool, and so on.
- ◆ The [ ] special character enables you to define patterns that match one of a group of alternatives. For example, /p[ea]t/ matches pet or pat but not peat.
- ◆ The * special character matches zero or more occurrences of the preceding character. For example, /re*f/ matches ref and reef but not reaf.
- ◆ The ? character matches zero or one occurrence of the preceding character. For example, the pattern /spo?t/ matches spt and spot but not spoot.
- ◆ The backslash \ special character is used to include a special character as a normal character in a pattern. You need to precede the special character with a \ to treat it as a normal character. For example, to check for one or more occurrences of * in a string, use the pattern /*+/.
- ◆ The pattern anchors ^ and $ ensure that the pattern is matched only at the beginning or the end of a string. For example, the pattern /^cla/ matches only if c, l, and a are the first three characters in the string. Similarly, the pattern /cla$/ matches only if these are the last three characters in the string.

Following is a sample script that searches for a word in any number of sentences entered:

```
#!perl -w
use CGI;
$input = new CGI;
print $input->header;

$perlcount = 0;
print ("Enter the sentences:\n");
$line = <STDIN>;
while ($line ne "") {
if ($line =~ /\bperl\b/) {
$thecount += 1;
}
$line = <STDIN>;
}
print ("The number of lines having an instance of the word perl: $perlcount\n");
```

Subroutines

In Perl, a *subroutine* is a separate body of code designed to perform a particular task, much like a function of any programming language. Also similar to functions, you need to invoke the subroutine to execute it. This process is called a *subroutine invocation*.

Here is the code for a sample subroutine, which simply adds two numbers and returns the value:

```perl
#!perl -w
use CGI;
$input = new CGI;
print $input->header;

print "Enter the first number";
$a=<STDIN>;
print "Enter the second number";
$b=<STDIN>;
$c= &add;
print "Sum is :$c";

# add is the subroutine
sub add
{
return $a+$b;
}
```

Formatting the Output of a Script

To display output using a print format, you need to set the system variable $~ to the format you want to use and call the built-in function `write`. Here is a code sample that illustrates this:

```perl
#!perl -w
use CGI;
$input = new CGI;
print $input->header;

    $~ = "FORMAT1";


    write;
```

```
    format FORMAT1 =
***************
Some text
***************
    .
```

CAUTION

Don't miss the period in the preceding line, which indicates the end of the format statement.

An Introduction to Packages

A *package* is a collection of subroutines. Perl has two types of packages: modules and classes. *Modules* are collections of simple subroutines, whereas *classes* are based on object-oriented features. Although you can invoke a subroutine of a module directly, you can invoke subroutines (or methods) of a class only by using instances or objects of the respective class. Classes can have special subroutines, which act as constructors and destructors.

We will next introduce you to the general syntax for creating a module. First, create a text file called Demo.pm. The .pm extension, which is the default extension for packages, stands for Perl module.

```
package Demo;
#
#
#
# Just add code here
#
1;   # terminate the package with the required 1;
```

Note that all Perl packages end with a "1;". This statement is required for all packages in Perl. If you forget this statement, Perl won't process your package.

The CGI.pm Module

The CGI.pm module contains many functions that are helpful when you are writing CGI applications and have to output a lot of stuff in HTML. You can access this module as a set of functions or as objects. The following two code samples illustrate this.

The first code snippet accesses the module using the functional method:

```
#!/usr/bin/Perl
```

```
use CGI qw/:standard/;
print header(),
start_html(-title=>'Some title for the html page',
-BGCOLOR=>'blue'),
h1('Some Heading'),
end_html();
```

The next code snippet invokes the module using objects:

```
#!perl -w
use CGI;
$input = new CGI;
print $input->header;
$input->start_html(-title=>'Some title for the html page',
-BGCOLOR=>'blue'),
$input->h1('Some Heading'),
$input->end_html();
```

This concludes a brief discussion of Perl. You now know the basics that are required to understand the examples given in the rest of the chapter.

Introduction to SOAP::Lite

To program Web services in any language, you need a SOAP tool that serializes and deserializes SOAP messages. For Perl, SOAP::Lite is the tool. In this section, you'll learn about the SOAP::Lite tool, created by Paul Kulchenko. As you use it, you'll find that this tool makes programming Web services in Perl quite easy. The SOAP::Lite package is available at http://www.soaplite.com.

The latest SOAP::Lite version is freely available for download from http://www.soaplite.com and CPAN.org, for both Unix and Win32 platforms. This version of SOAP::Lite supports most of the SOAP 1.1, SOAP 1.2, and SOAP Messages with Attachments specifications.

Perl is one of the most popularly used scripting languages for creating CGI scripts. Therefore, the Web service design involves creating a CGI script to accept requests from a SOAP client and, in turn, pass on the request to a class, which will service the request.

Sample Web Service

You can create a simple Hello World service. The process involves creating three files:

◆ The CGI script
◆ The CGI class
◆ The client

Here is the CGI script and the class code. Note that you can install the class in a separate Perl module (.pm) file:

```perl
#!perl -w
  use SOAP::Transport::HTTP;
  SOAP::Transport::HTTP::CGI
    -> dispatch_to('Class1')
    -> handle;
    package Class1;
  sub greet
{
    return "Hello World";
  }
```

The preceding code consists of a CGI script that simply passes the HTTP calls, which it receives, to the class **Class1**.

Following is the Perl client that calls the SOAP service:

```perl
#!perl -w
use CGI;
use SOAP::Lite;
 $input = new CGI;
 print $input->header;
 print SOAP::Lite->uri('http://localhost/Class1')
 ->proxy('http://localhost/cgi-bin/h.cgi')->greet()
 ->result;
```

In the client code, the uri() refers to the class on the server, and the proxy() identifies the CGI script that provides access to the class.proxy(). proxy is the address of the server that is hosting the Web service. Each server can offer many different services through one proxy() URL. Each service has a unique URI-like identifier, which you specify to SOAP::Lite through the uri() method.

When you run your application, you should see the familiar Hello World message.

Debugging SOAP Scripts

If you need to debug a SOAP::Lite script, you have the option of viewing the client-server transactions in detail. The details displayed include how the request is processed, which is handy for tracking down errors. Most errors result from a mismatched URI or proxy address and are visible in the text of the SOAP packet. Add +trace => all after use SOAP::Lite to send all debugging output to the STDERR output stream:

```
use SOAP::Lite +trace=> all;
use SOAP::Lite+trace=>all;
 $input = new CGI;
 print $input->header;
   print SOAP::Lite->uri('http://localhost/Demo')
     ->proxy('http://localhost/cgi-bin/h.cgi')->greet()
     ->result;
```

SOAP Autodispatch

SOAP::Lite also has a feature called Autodispatch that allows you to bind remote methods to the execution of your program. When Autodispatch is enabled, methods that aren't available locally are automatically sent to a remote server for execution. Autodispatch using SOAP is a transparent process. In this process, after you establish the remote server, you can call the remote methods without referring to the remote server.

Enable Autodispatch with the +autodispatch flag:

```
use SOAP::Lite +autodispatch =>
 uri=>"World",
 proxy=>'http://somesite.com/soap/someserver.cgi';
print RemoteMethod();
print greet();
```

Because they aren't locally defined, the greet and RemoteMethod functions are sent automatically to the remote server named in proxy for execution.

Using Autodispatch is like inheriting from another class; therefore, be sure to define a function with the same name as the one you're trying to call on the remote server.

Creating Clients for Web Services Using SOAP::Lite

SOAP::Lite is a great tool for creating client application for Web services. In this section, you will look at creating Web service clients for live services.

First, we will look at an Apache-based Web service that you can find at http://www.Xmethods.net. This Web service accepts an ISBN number for a book and returns the price of the book from Amazon. Here is the code for the client script.

```
#!perl -w
   use SOAP::Lite;


   $data = SOAP::Lite
     -> uri('urn:xmethods-BNPriceCheck')
```

```
    -> proxy('http://services.xmethods.net/soap/servlet/rpcrouter');

  my $isbn = '1-931841-31-4';
  print $data->getPrice(SOAP::Data->type(string => $isbn))->result;
```

Notice that the implementation does not use the WSDL of the Web service to access the Web service.

Following is one more example that actually uses the WSDL of a Web service to access the Web service:

```
#!perl -w
  use SOAP::Lite;
  print SOAP::Lite
    -> service('http://www.xmethods.net/sd/StockQuoteService.wsdl')
    -> getQuote('MSFT');
```

As you can see, SOAP::Lite does indeed simplify the task of creating Web service clients.

Constructing the InSys Catalog Web Service

You will now start constructing the InSys Web service. You will need to create the following three files:

◆ The CGI script that redirects Web method calls to a package
◆ The package file
◆ The client to test the service

The CGI script is given next. Name the file `productinfo.cgi` and store it in the cgi-bin folder of your Apache installation.

```
#!perl -w
#productInfo.cgi
use SOAP::Transport::HTTP;

SOAP::Transport::HTTP::CGI
->dispatch_to('ProductInfo')
->handle
;
```

The CGI script, as you can see, simply redirects all calls to the package `ProductInfo`. Next, you need to create the package, which will handle all queries from the client. The package will support the following methods:

- ◆ **getProductInfo().** This method is exposed to the client and is called by all Web service clients. It accepts two parameters: the name of the product on which information is required and the kind of information that is requested.
- ◆ **getProductPrice().** The `getProductInfo()` method calls this method internally when the information requested is the price of a product.
- ◆ **getProductData().** The `getProductInfo()` method calls this method when the information requested is details about a particular product.
- ◆ **getProductID().** This method returns the ID of a product.
- ◆ **getProductVendor().** This method returns the name of the vendor of the product.
- ◆ **getCompanyURL().** This method returns the product manufacturer's URL.

The code chooses its data from a file databaseschema.conf, so the database file must be in the same folder as the script. First, the text file that contains the data is opened. If the file is not opened, the script exits.

```
open(FILE,"$filename")|| die "cannot open: $!\n";
#print $filename;
while(<FILE>)
{
        $conf .= $_;
}
#print $conf;
close(FILE);
```

In the preceding script, the file is opened first. If it's successful, its contents are read into a variable and the file is closed. The `getProductInfo()` method accepts two parameters. We will look at the SOAP message that the client sends when asking for the price of a product, such as Handspring Treo. The bold portions of the following code give the input values from the client application.

```
  <?xml version="1.0" encoding="UTF-8" ?>
<SOAP-ENV:Envelope xmlns:SOAP-ENC=http://schemas.xmlsoap.org/soap/encoding/
SOAP-ENV:encodingStyle=http://schemas.xmlsoap.org/soap/encoding/
xmlns:SOAP-ENV=http://schemas.xmlsoap.org/soap/envelope/
xmlns:xsi=http://www.w3.org/1999/XMLSchema-instance
xmlns:xsd="http://www.w3.org/1999/XMLSchema">
<SOAP-ENV:Body>
<namesp1:getProductInfo xmlns:namesp1="http://localhost:8080/ProductInfo">
```

```
<c-gensym3 xsi:type="xsd:string">product1</c-gensym3>
<c-gensym5 xsi:type="xsd:string">price</c-gensym5>
</namesp1:getProductInfo>
</SOAP-ENV:Body>
</SOAP-ENV:Envelope>
```

When the `getProductInfo()` method receives this data, the method checks the value of the second parameter. The values that are sent are accessible through a perl-define array $_.

```
sub getProductInfo
{
        my $self = shift;
```

Because the first value in the array contains the name of the script, it is shifted out. The first value in the array is the product name as passed by the client and the second value is the information that is required.

```
$second=$_[0];
```

The product name is stored in a variable, and the second value is checked against possible values to determine the method to be called. For example, if the value is `price`, then the method `getProductPrice()` is called.

```
if($_[1] eq "price")
{
        &getProductPrice;
```

If the value sent in by the client does not match any of the possible values, then an error message is returned.

```
else
{
        return "try other search";
}
```

Next, you will look at the `getProductPrice()` method. Each of these methods creates a search pattern depending on the information required, and a pattern search is made in the text database file. Perl is the best language to use for pattern matching because it has a lot of built-in commands and syntaxes specifically for this task, which is normally not available in other programming languages.

Before you continue, you need to look at the data source text file to learn how the data is stored in it and what pattern you can use to search for a particular piece of information. The following is a segment of the data in a flat text file. Save the file as databaseschema.conf.

```
company.product1.url="http://www.insysperipherals.com/products/treo.html"
company.product1.name="Handspring Treo"
company.product1.id="product1_id1"
company.product1.price="$300USD"
company.product1.vendor="vendor1_ABC,london"
company.product1.info="Handspring Treo models are favorites of reviewers for their
expansion slots. By plugging various modules (sold separately) into this unit's
"Springboard," you can turn it into a cell phone, digital camera, or MP3 player,
among other applications. The Prism has a color screen in addition to 8MB of memory
on the Palm OS. Experts say you'll get more battery life out of this color PDA than
a comparable Pocket PC color unit—over 12 hours. Keep in mind, however, that
monochrome models like the CLIE, above, can run for weeks without a recharge."
```

We have reproduced only the data for Product1.

As is evident from the content of the preceding file, the pattern to search when you want to look up the price is `company.product1.price`. The method `getProductPrice()` should search for this pattern. However, it cannot be specific to a product. Therefore, you need to use the variable `$second`, which stores the product name. The search pattern then becomes `company.$second.price`. Here is the code for searching for the pattern:

```
my $querystring="company.$second.price";


#retrieving the value from the $conf string
        if ($conf=~/$querystring=(.*?)\n/ ){
                $queryvalue=$1;

        }else{

                $queryvalue = "";

        }

        return $queryvalue;

}
```

SOAP::Lite serializes the reply into a SOAP message, and this message is sent back to the client. Following is the message:

```
<?xml version="1.0" encoding="UTF-8" ?>
<SOAP-ENV:Envelope xmlns:SOAP-ENC="http://schemas.xmlsoap.org/soap/encoding/" SOAP-
ENV:encodingStyle=http://schemas.xmlsoap.org/soap/encoding/xmlns:SOAP-
ENV=http://schemas.xmlsoap.org/soap/envelope/
xmlns:xsi=http://www.w3.org/1999/XMLSchema-instance
xmlns:xsd="http://www.w3.org/1999/XMLSchema">
```

```
<SOAP-ENV:Body>
<namesp1:getProductInfoResponse xmlns:namesp1="http://localhost:8080/ProductInfo">
<s-gensym3 xsi:type="xsd:string">"$300USD"</s-gensym3>
</namesp1:getProductInfoResponse>
</SOAP-ENV:Body>
</SOAP-ENV:Envelope>
```

All other methods use a similar pattern search and return appropriate values. Save the package file as ProductInfo.pm. Following is the complete code for the package:

```
package ProductInfo;


$filename = "databaseschema.conf";


open(FILE,"$filename")¦¦ die "cannot open: $!\n";
#print $filename;
    while(<FILE>){
        $conf .= $_;
    }
#print $conf;
close(FILE);


$second="";


#.........................................


sub getProductInfo
{
my $self = shift;


$second=$_[0];
if($_[1] eq "price"){
    &getProductPrice;
    }
elsif($_[1] eq "info")
{
    &getProductInformation;
}
elsif($_[1] eq "vendor")
```

```perl
        {
            &getProductVendor;
        }
        elsif($_[1] eq "id")
        {
            &getProductId;
        }
        elsif($_[1] eq "url")
        {
            &getCompanyUrl;
        }
        else
        {
        return "try other search";
        }
        }
        #..................................................

        sub getProductPrice
        {
        my $self = shift;
        my $querystring="company.$second.price";
        print
        $querystring;
        #retrieving the value from the $conf string
        if ($conf=~/$querystring=(.*?)\n/ )
        {
            $queryvalue=$1;
        }
        else
        {
            $queryvalue = "";
        }
        return $queryvalue;

        }

        #..........................................................
```

```perl
sub getProductInformation
{
my $self = shift;

my $querystring="company.$second.info";

print  $querystring;

#retrieving the value from the $conf string
if ($conf=~/$querystring=(.*?)\n/ )
{
    $queryvalue=$1;
}
else
{
    $queryvalue = "";
}
return $queryvalue;
}


#..........................................................
sub getProductId
{
my $self = shift;

my $querystring="company.$second.id";

#retrieving the value from the $conf string
if ($conf=~/$querystring=(.*?)\n/ )
{
    $queryvalue=$1;
}
else
{
    $queryvalue = "";
}
return $queryvalue;
}
```

```
#.......................................................

sub getCompanyUrl
{
    my $self = shift;

my $querystring="company.$second.url";

#retrieving the value from the $conf string
if ($conf=~/$querystring=(.*?)\n/ )
{
    $queryvalue=$1;
}
else
{
    $queryvalue = "";
}
return $queryvalue;
}

#.......................................................

sub getProductVendor
{
    my $self = shift;

my $querystring="company.$second.vendor";

#retrieving the value from the $conf string
if ($conf=~/$querystring=(.*?)\n/ )
{
    $queryvalue=$1;
}
else
{
    $queryvalue = "";
}
return $queryvalue;
```

```
}
1;
```

Now that the Web service is ready, we will turn our attention to creating a client for this Web service.

The client application consists of two parts:

◆ Taking input from the user by using an HTML form
◆ Processing and displaying the results retrieved from the client

The script decides which part of the form to display depending on the variable flag that is used. When the input form is to be displayed, the default value of the variable is 0. However, when the form is submitted, a hidden field sets the value to 1 and the script retrieves the data from the server and displays it.

```
#!perl -w
use CGI;
use SOAP::Lite;
 $input = new CGI;
 $flag=$input->param("flag");
$first=$input->param("first");
$second=$input->param("second");
 print $input->header;
print '<body bgcolor="#CCCCCC">';
#print "first".$first.".................."."second".$second;
 if($flag)
{
}
else
{
<Form  method= "post" action="webservice.pl">
<input type=hidden name=flag value="1">
}
```

When you click the Submit button, the input form posts two values: the product and the information required on the product. Here is the code in the script that does that:

```
<Form  method= "post" action="webservice.pl">
   <input type=hidden name=flag value="1">
    <select name="first" size="1">
    <option value="product1">HandHeld Trio</option>
    <option value="product2">Palm Computing m100</option>
```

```
<option value="product3">Color Paq 3835</option>
</select>
<input type="radio" name="second" value="info" CHECKED>
<input type="radio" name="second" value="price">
<input type="radio" name="second" value="id">
<input type="radio" name="second" value="vendor">
<input type="radio" name="second" value="url">
<input type="submit" name="Submit" value="Search">
</Form>
```

If you notice, the Select control has the name `first` and the set of radio buttons `second`. These are the names for the values that are sent to the script after the form has been posted. Here is the code that extracts the name-value pairs:

```
#!perl -w
use CGI;
use SOAP::Lite;
 $input = new CGI;
 $flag=$input->param("flag");
$first=$input->param("first");
$second=$input->param("second");
```

These values are passed to the Web service's `getProductInfo()` method. The code for doing this is shown next:

```
SOAP::Lite->uri("http://localhost/ProductInfo")
->proxy("http://localhost/cgi-bin/ProductInfo.cgi") -> getProductInfo($first,$second)
 ->result."\n\n";
```

The returned values are then displayed within a table. Save the client application as Webservice.pl. Here is the complete code for the client application:

```
#!perl -w
use CGI;
use SOAP::Lite;
 $input = new CGI;
 $flag=$input->param("flag");
$first=$input->param("first");
$second=$input->param("second");
 print $input->header;
print '<body bgcolor="#CCCCCC">';
```

```
#print "first".$first.".................."."second".$second;
 if($flag)
{
print '
<table width="100%" border="1">
  <tr>
    <td>
      <p align="center">
      <font size="5" face="Verdana, Arial, Helvetica, sans-serif">Search
      Results
      </font>
      </p>
    </td>
  </tr>
  <tr>
    <td >
     <center>
      <font size="2" face="Georgia, Times New Roman, Times, serif">';

        print SOAP::Lite->uri("http://localhost:8080/ProductInfo")
       ->proxy("http://localhost:8080/cgi-bin/ProductInfo.cgi")
       ->getProductInfo($first,$second)
       ->result."\n\n";
        print '
      </font>
     </center>
    </td>
 </tr>
 <tr>
 <td>
 <div align="center">
<a href="webservice.pl">
 <font face="Georgia, Times New Roman, Times, serif">Back </font>
</a>
 </div>
 </td>
 </tr>
 </table>';
```

```
    }
  else
  {
    print ' <h3>  </h3>
    <table width="100%" border="0" align="center">
    <tr>
    <td>
    <div align="center">
     <font size="4" face="Verdana, Arial, Helvetica, sans-serif">
     Product Search as Web Service Using Perl</font></div>
    </td>
    </tr>
    </table>
    <h3> </h3>   ';
  print '
  <Form  method= "post" action="webservice.pl">
    <table width="100%" border="0">
    <tr>
    <td>
    <div align="center">
    <table width="75%" border="1" height="206">
    <tr>
    <td colspan="2">
     <font face="Verdana, Arial, Helvetica, sans-serif" size="1">
     <b>To<i>    Search</i> Product Database,
     <i>Select</i> the product and choose  the field to
     <i>Search</i> on.</b>
     </font>
    </td>
    </tr>
    <input type=hidden name=flag value="1">
     <tr>
     <td><font size="1" face="Verdana, Arial, Helvetica, sans-serif">
     <b>Product List</b>
     </font>
     </td>
     <td>
     <div align="center">
```

```
<select name="first" size="1">
<option value="product1">HandHeld Trio</option>
<option value="product2">Palm Computing m100</option>
<option value="product3">Color Paq 3835</option>
</select>
</div>
</td>
</tr>
<tr>
<td><font size="1" face="Verdana, Arial, Helvetica, sans-serif"><b>Search
on any Product Field</b></font></td>
<td>
<table width="100%" border="1">
<tr>
<td width="16%">
<input type="radio" name="second" value="info" CHECKED>
</td>
<td width="84%">
 <font face="Verdana, Arial, Helvetica, sans-serif" size="1">
 Product Description
 </font></td>
</tr>
<tr>
<td width="16%">
<input type="radio" name="second" value="price">
</td>
<td width="84%">
<font face="Verdana, Arial, Helvetica, sans-serif" size="1">
Product Price
</font></td>
</tr>
<tr>
<td width="16%">
<input type="radio" name="second" value="id">
</td>
<td width="84%">
<font face="Verdana, Arial, Helvetica, sans-serif" size="1">
 Product  Id
```

```
  </font></td>
</tr>
<tr>
<td width="16%">
<input type="radio" name="second" value="vendor">
</td>
<td width="84%">
 <font face="Verdana, Arial, Helvetica, sans-serif" size="1">
 Product  Vendors
 </font> </td>
</tr>
<tr>
<td width="16%">
<input type="radio" name="second" value="url">
</td>
<td width="84%"> <font face="Verdana, Arial, Helvetica, sans-serif" size="1">
Company Url </font></td>
</tr>
</table>
</td>
</tr>
<tr>
<td colspan="2">
<div align="center">
<input type="submit" name="Submit" value="Search">
</div>
</td>
</tr>
</table>
</div>
</td>
</tr>
</table>
</Form>
';
}
```

Ensure that all three files you created are in the <Apache Web Server_Home>\cgi-bin folder. Try the application by connecting to the client using http://localhost/cgi-bin/webservice.pl. The client interface before the Web service is invoked is shown in Figure 19-1.

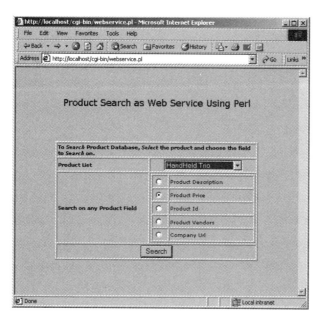

FIGURE 19-1 *The Web service client.*

The reply from the Web service is shown in Figure 19-2.

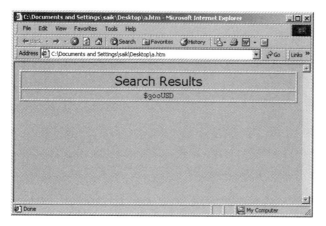

FIGURE 19-2 *Result of querying the Web service.*

Summary

In this chapter, you learned how to create Web services by using Perl. You also learned about the SOAP::Lite package that is used to SOAP-enable Perl. Finally, you learned to create a client for the Web service by using Perl.

Chapter 20

Web services have become an important part of distributed application development. As a result, various software vendors have released new tools that allow Web service development. For example, you looked at the tools that Microsoft and Sun Microsystems provide in previous projects.

In addition, software vendors have started adding support to their existing projects for creating and consuming Web services. Microsoft, as a pioneer in this field, has done the same by adding Web services support to Office XP and SQL Server 2000.

This chapter shows you how to use the SQLXML 3.0 package to expose stored procedures on an SQL Server database as Web services. It also examines how Office XP allows its applications to easily consume Web services.

The chapter begins with the case study for which you will construct an application.

The Case Study for JB Book Sellers

JB Book Sellers is a famous chain of bookstores in the U.S. The process of accepting orders at all bookstores of JB Book Sellers is automated. The bookstores use the Office XP platform and Microsoft Access to create the databases for the business.

The head office of JB Book Sellers is located in New York. The data related to the books they have published and sold is stored at the New York office. The books that JB Book Sellers sells are acquired at the New York office from various publishers and distributors and then distributed to the stores that are part of the chain. Sometimes a customer might want a particular book that is not available at the store, but might be available as part of the stock to be distributed at the New York office. Sometimes a customer might need several copies of the same book that are unavailable locally but might be available at the head office.

In such cases, an order for the required books is placed immediately after consulting the inventory details. The stores get a weekly update of the inventory available at the New York office. This inventory is somewhat inaccurate because the number of books in stock changes daily. Therefore, the company decided to allow online access to the inventory details so that the retail stores could have accurate data while accepting orders.

When a customer visits the bookstore, the salesperson uses a desktop application to accept orders for books. The details of the order are then stored in a Microsoft Access database. The desktop application that is used to enter the details of an order received or a sale made is a Microsoft Access form. The form includes details such as the credit card details, e-mail address, and Zip code of the person who is placing the order. This data needs to be validated before being stored in the database.

Integrating Web Services and SQL Server 2000

As you know, XML is no longer a simple markup language that programmers use to unclutter data on the Web. Instead, XML has become the basis for standards, such as SOAP and Web services. These standards will soon become the basis for the architecture used to develop the next generation of distributed applications.

To integrate XML with the application that uses SQL Server 2000, you can use SQLXML 3.0. This toolkit allows SQL Server 2000 to provide a more robust and varied support for XML than its built-in tools and commands. We will now discuss the SQLXML 3.0 package and its features in detail.

Introduction to SQLXML 3.0

As discussed earlier, SQLXML 3.0 uses SQL Server 2000 to expose Web services that use the SOAP messaging techniques. SOAP enables your applications to act as a client of the Web services that SQL Server exposes. Web services that are created by using SQLXML 3.0 extend support for the execution of stored procedures, user-defined functions, and templates.

Another key feature of SQLXML 3.0 is the managed classes that are exposed within the .NET Framework. These classes extend the ability to access XML data from Microsoft SQL Server from within the .NET environment.

In this project, you will learn how to expose a stored procedure as a Web service and how to access the Web service. You also will learn how to use the SQMLXML managed classes to execute SQL queries from the .NET applications.

Accessing SQL Server Data Through the Web

Before proceeding to work with the SQLXML 3.0 toolkit, you will need the following software:

◆ SQL Server 2000

◆ Microsoft SOAP Toolkit 2.0

◆ SQLXML 3.0

◆ MSXML Parser 4.0 (comes with SQLXML 3.0)

In this section, you will learn how to access data in an SQL Server database by using XML and Internet Explorer.

Querying the Database by Using XML Templates

To access the data in a SQL Server database, you first need to create a virtual directory and a few support files. You can do this in two ways, as mentioned in the following list:

◆ Using the Internet Services Manager from the Administrative tools

◆ Using the IIS Virtual Directory Management for SQLXML 3.0 Microsoft Management Console (MMC) snap-in

Because the IIS Virtual Directory Management for SQLXML 3.0 is designed for creating virtual directories for hosting XML templates and stored procedure-based Web services, in this section, we will discuss the second way of creating a virtual directory. These utilities install automatically with SQLXML 3.0 from the SQLXML 3.0 program group.

To run the MMC snap-in utilities, perform the following steps:

1. Create a folder on the local hard disk and name it `SqlXmlProj1`.

2. In the SqlXmlProj1folder, create a subfolder called `templates` that contains the XML templates.

3. Select Configure IIS Support from the program group. The IIS Virtual Directory Manager for SQLXML 3.0 starts, as shown in Figure 20-1.

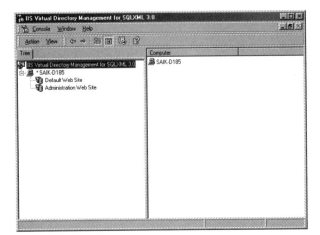

FIGURE 20-1 *The IIS Virtual Directory Manager.*

4. Click on the machine name in the tree view to expand the tree structure.

5. Right-click on Default Web Site and select New, Virtual Directory in the resulting menus. The New Virtual Directory Properties window is displayed, as shown in Figure 20-2.

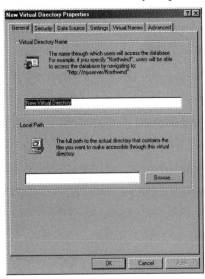

FIGURE 20-2 *The New Virtual Directory Properties window.*

6. In the dialog box that appears under the General tab, enter the name of the virtual directory. In this case, enter the name for the virtual directory as SqlXmlProj1.

7. In the text box for the local path, enter the path of the folder that you created in step 1.

8. Click on the Security tab to display the dialog box, as shown in Figure 20-3.

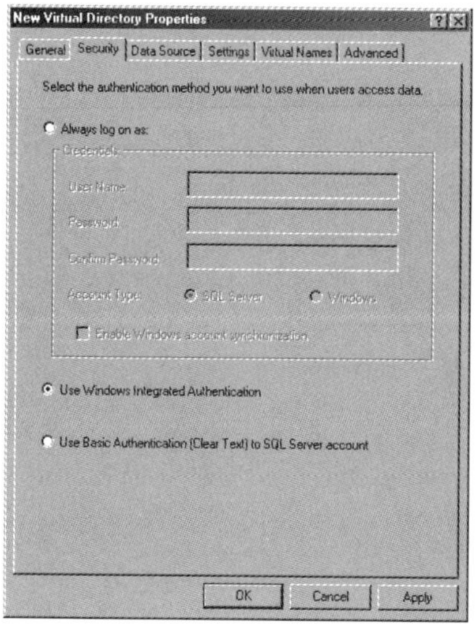

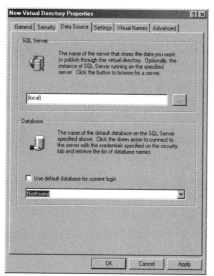

FIGURE 20-3 *The Security tab.*

9. In this dialog box, enter the login credentials for connecting to the SQL Server. Depending on the configuration of the server, you can use an SQL Server account, the Windows integrated security, or both to access the data in SQL Server.

10. Click on the Data Source tab. The dialog box that appears is shown in Figure 20-4.

FIGURE 20-4 *The Data Source tab.*

11. Specify the name of the SQL Server you need to use or select the name of the server from the drop-down list.

12. Uncheck the Use Default Database for Current Login check box.

13. Select the name of the database you will connect to. For this example, select the Northwind database, which is a sample SQL Server database.

14. Click on the Settings tab to display the dialog box shown in Figure 20-5.

15. In this dialog box, select the Allow Sql, Allow Template Queries, and Allow POST check boxes.

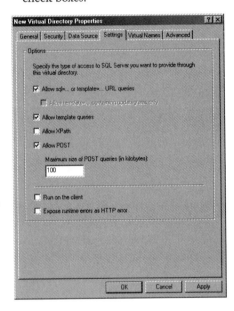

FIGURE 20-5 *The Settings tab.*

16. Click on the Virtual Names tab. The dialog box that appears is shown in Figure 20-6.

17. In the Name text box, type `templates` and select the templates folder that you created in step 1.

18. Click on the Save button.

19. Click on the Advanced tab to display the dialog box shown in Figure 20-7.

20. In this dialog box, ensure that the path of the ISAPI DLL that is required for processing your query is specified in the text box. If the path is not specified by default, enter the path of the ISAPI DLL that you plan to use.

 NOTE

If the ISAPI extension DLL that you plan to use is correctly installed and registered, the path in the dialog box will appear correctly.

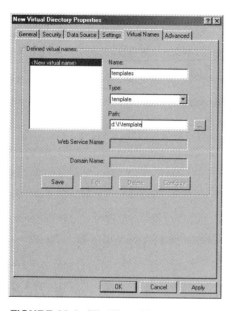

FIGURE 20-6 *The Virtual Names tab.*

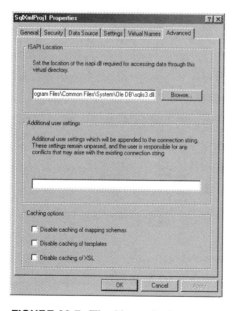

FIGURE 20-7 *The Advanced tab.*

21. Click on the OK button to close the window.

After performing the preceding steps, you can access the virtual directory that you created and configured by using the Internet protocols. The next step in accessing the data from an SQL Server database is to create an XML template, which you can access by using a browser.

The content of the template file is shown in the following code:

```
<ROOT xmlns:sql="urn:schemas-microsoft-com:xml-sql">
  <sql:query client-side-xml="0">
        SELECT *
        FROM Employees
        FOR XML AUTO
    </sql:query>
</ROOT>
```

The preceding code displays the contents of the Employees table in the Northwind database. Save the file as emp.xml in the templates folder.

The next step is to test the SQLXML installation by connecting to the virtual directory that you have created. To do this, you can use the http://localhost/SqlXmlProj1/templates/emp.xml URL. The emp.xml file, as shown in Figure 20-8, is displayed.

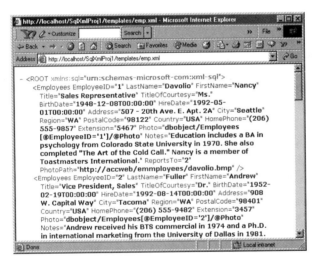

FIGURE 20-8 *Querying through a template.*

Creating a Web Service

Next, you will create a Web service that accesses data from a database and returns some values. In this case, you will create a Web service that exposes the functionality of a stored procedure called Ten Most Expensive Products from the Northwind sample database.

To create a Web service, perform the following steps:

1. In the SqlXmlProj1 folder that contains the templates subfolder, create another folder, Soap. You will use this folder to store the files that the Web service requires.
2. On the Start menu, in the SQLXML group, click on the Configure IIS Support option.
3. Select the name of the virtual directory that you have created from the list view on the right.
4. Right-click the name of the virtual directory and select Properties to open the Virtual Directory Properties window.
5. Click on the Settings tab and ensure that the Allow POST check box is selected.
6. Click on the Virtual Names tab. Enter the name as Soap.
7. Select the type as SOAP.
8. The Web Service Name and the Domain Name text boxes are activated. Enter the name for the Web service and the domain.
9. Click on Save. The Configure button is activated.
10. Click on the Configure button. The Soap Virtual Name Configuration dialog box is displayed, as shown in Figure 20-9.

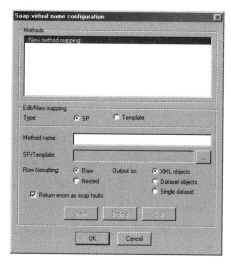

FIGURE 20-9 *The Soap Virtual Name Configuration dialog box.*

11. Select SP as the type that specifies the stored procedures.
12. Click on the Ellipsis button (…) to the right of the SP/Template text box. The SOAP Stored Procedure Mapping dialog box is displayed, as shown in Figure 20-10.

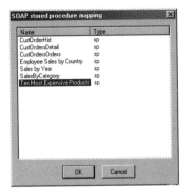

FIGURE 20-10 *The SOAP Stored Procedure Mapping dialog box.*

13. Select the Ten Most Expensive Products stored procedure and click on the OK button.

14. Click on the OK button to close the Virtual Directory Properties window.

15. Check the contents of the Soap folder. It contains two files, as discussed in Table 20-1.

Table 20-1 Files in the Soap Folder

File	Description
.wsdl file	This file describes the Web service.
.ssc file	This file connects the Web service to the stored procedure.

The following code displays the contents of the .wsdl file for the Web service:

```
<?xml version="1.0"?><wsdl:definitions name="ss" targetNamespace="http://SAIK-
D185/SqlXmlProj1/ss" xmlns:tns="http://SAIK-D185/SqlXmlProj1/ss"
xmlns:xsd="http://www.w3.org/2001/XMLSchema"
xmlns:wsdl="http://schemas.xmlsoap.org/wsdl/"
xmlns:soap="http://schemas.xmlsoap.org/wsdl/soap/"
xmlns:sql="http://schemas.microsoft.com/SQLServer/2001/12/SOAP"
xmlns:sqltypes="http://schemas.microsoft.com/SQLServer/2001/12/SOAP/types"
xmlns:sqlmessage="http://schemas.microsoft.com/SQLServer/2001/12/SOAP/types/
SqlMessage" xmlns:sqlresultstream="http://schemas.microsoft.com/SQLServer/2001/
12/SOAP/types/SqlResultStream">
        <wsdl:types><xsd:schema
targetNamespace='http://schemas.microsoft.com/SQLServer/2001/12/SOAP/types'
            elementFormDefault='qualified' attributeFormDefault='qualified'>
                <xsd:import namespace='http://www.w3.org/2001/XMLSchema'/>
                <xsd:simpleType name='nonNegativeInteger'>
```

```
                                <xsd:restriction base='xsd:int'>
                                        <xsd:minInclusive value='0'/>
                                </xsd:restriction>
                        </xsd:simpleType>
                        <xsd:attribute name='IsNested' type='xsd:boolean'/>
                        <xsd:complexType name='SqlRowSet'>
                                <xsd:sequence>
                                        <xsd:element ref='xsd:schema'/>
                                        <xsd:any/>
                                </xsd:sequence>
                                <xsd:attribute ref='sqltypes:IsNested'/>
                        </xsd:complexType>
                        <xsd:complexType name='SqlXml' mixed='true'>
                                <xsd:sequence>
                                        <xsd:any/>
                                </xsd:sequence>
                        </xsd:complexType>
                        <xsd:simpleType name='SqlResultCode'>
                                <xsd:restriction base='xsd:int'>
                                        <xsd:minInclusive value='0'/>
                                </xsd:restriction>
                        </xsd:simpleType>
        </xsd:schema>


        <xsd:schema targetNamespace='http://schemas.microsoft.com/SQLServer/2001/12/
SOAP/types/SqlMessage'
                elementFormDefault='qualified' attributeFormDefault='qualified'>
                <xsd:import namespace='http://www.w3.org/2001/XMLSchema'/>
                <xsd:import namespace='http://schemas.microsoft.com/SQLServer/2001/12/
SOAP/types'/>
                        <xsd:complexType name='SqlMessage'>
                        <xsd:sequence minOccurs='1' maxOccurs='1'>
                                <xsd:element name='Class' type='sqltypes:nonNegativeInteger'/>
                                <xsd:element name='LineNumber'
type='sqltypes:nonNegativeInteger'/>
                                <xsd:element name='Message' type='xsd:string'/>
                                <xsd:element name='Number'
type='sqltypes:nonNegativeInteger'/>
                                <xsd:element name='Procedure' type='xsd:string'/>
```

```
                          <xsd:element name='Server' type='xsd:string'/>
                          <xsd:element name='Source' type='xsd:string'/>
                          <xsd:element name='State' type='sqltypes:nonNegativeInteger'/>
                    </xsd:sequence>
                    <xsd:attribute ref='sqltypes:IsNested'/>
                    </xsd:complexType>
        </xsd:schema>


        <xsd:schema targetNamespace='http://schemas.microsoft.com/SQLServer/2001/12/
SOAP/types/SqlResultStream'   elementFormDefault='qualified'
attributeFormDefault='qualified'>
                <xsd:import namespace='http://www.w3.org/2001/XMLSchema'/>
                <xsd:import namespace='http://schemas.microsoft.com/SQLServer/2001/
12/SOAP/types'/>
                <xsd:import namespace='http://schemas.microsoft.com/SQLServer/2001/
12/SOAP/types/SqlMessage'/>
                    <xsd:complexType name='SqlResultStream'>
                        <xsd:choice minOccurs='1' maxOccurs='unbounded'>
                        <xsd:element name='SqlRowSet' type='sqltypes:SqlRowSet'/>
                        <xsd:element name='SqlXml' type='sqltypes:SqlXml'/>
                        <xsd:element name='SqlMessage' type='sqlmessage:SqlMessage'/>
                        <xsd:element name='SqlResultCode'
type='sqltypes:SqlResultCode'/>
                        </xsd:choice>
                    </xsd:complexType>
        </xsd:schema>


        <xsd:schema targetNamespace="http://SAIK-D185/SqlXmlProj1/ss"
elementFormDefault="qualified" attributeFormDefault="qualified">
                <xsd:import namespace="http://www.w3.org/2001/XMLSchema"/>
                <xsd:import namespace="http://schemas.microsoft.com/SQLServer/2001/12/
SOAP/types"/>
                <xsd:import namespace=http://schemas.microsoft.com/SQLServer/2001/12/
SOAP/types/SqlMessage/>
                <xsd:import namespace="http://schemas.microsoft.com/SQLServer/2001/
12/SOAP/types/SqlResultStream"/>
                    <xsd:element name="Ten_Most_Expensive_Products">
                    <xsd:complexType>
```

```
                        <xsd:sequence/>
                    </xsd:complexType>
                    </xsd:element>
               <xsd:element name="Ten_Most_Expensive_ProductsResponse">
                    <xsd:complexType>
                         <xsd:sequence>
                               <xsd:element minOccurs="1" maxOccurs="1"
  name="Ten_Most_Expensive_ProductsResult" type="sqlresultstream:SqlResultStream"/>
                         </xsd:sequence>
                    </xsd:complexType>
               </xsd:element>
          </xsd:schema>
  </wsdl:types>


  <wsdl:message name="Ten_Most_Expensive_ProductsIn">
         <wsdl:part name="parameters" element="tns:Ten_Most_Expensive_Products"/>
  </wsdl:message>


  <wsdl:message name="Ten_Most_Expensive_ProductsOut">
         <wsdl:part name="parameters" element="tns:Ten_Most_Expensive_ProductsResponse"/>
  </wsdl:message>


  <wsdl:portType name="SXSPort">
         <wsdl:operation name="Ten_Most_Expensive_Products">
               <wsdl:input message="tns:Ten_Most_Expensive_ProductsIn"/>
               <wsdl:output message="tns:Ten_Most_Expensive_ProductsOut"/>
         </wsdl:operation>
  </wsdl:portType>


  <wsdl:binding name="SXSBinding" type="tns:SXSPort">
         <soap:binding style="document" transport="http://schemas.xmlsoap.org/soap/
  http"/>
         <wsdl:operation name="Ten_Most_Expensive_Products">
               <soap:operation soapAction="http://SAIK-D185/SqlXmlProj1/ss/
  Ten_Most_Expensive_Products" style="document"/>
               <wsdl:input>
                    <soap:body use="literal"/>
               </wsdl:input>
```

```
        <wsdl:output>
                <soap:body use="literal"/>
        </wsdl:output>
    </wsdl:operation>
</wsdl:binding>

    <wsdl:service name="ss">
        <wsdl:port name="SXSPort" binding="tns:SXSBinding">
            <soap:address location="http://localhost//MyWebsercie"/>
        </wsdl:port>
    </wsdl:service>
</wsdl:definitions>
```

The Web service that the preceding .wsdl file supports contains only a single Web method called `Ten_Most_Expensive_Products()`. The .wsdl file also specifies the location where you can connect to the Web service.

After looking at the .wsdl file, consider the contents of the .ssc file, as shown in the following code snippet:

```
<?xml version="1.0"?>
    <sxs:methods name="GetTenMostExpProds" domain="SAIK-D185"
url=http://SAIK-D185/SqlXmlProj1/TenMost
        xmlns:sxs="http://schemas.microsoft.com/SQLServer/2001/12/SOAPxml">
            <sxs:method name="Ten_Most_Expensive_Products" type="storedproc"
spname="[Ten Most Expensive Products]" format="raw" output="xmlobject"
faults="true">
                <parameter name="@RETURN_VALUE" type="3" paramSize="4"
precision="10" input="false" output="true" is-="false"/>
            </sxs:method>
    </sxs:methods>
```

Notice that the preceding file connects the Web service method to the stored procedure.

Testing the Web Service

To test a Web service, create a client application that accesses the Web service. In this case, you will create a Visual Basic 6.0 client application that makes use of the SOAP Toolkit to connect to the Web service.

The client application contains a Button control. When you click on the Button control, the application connects to a Web service and returns the required data. The returned data is in the form of an XML node list. You then need to parse the XML node list, which is displayed in a message box.

To create a client application in Visual Basic 6.0, perform the following steps:

1. Create a desktop application in Visual basic 6.0.
2. From the Reference dialog box, add a reference to the MS SOAP type library and MSXML 4.0 type library.
3. Add a button to the form.
4. In the Click event handler of the Button control, add the following code:

```
private Sub Connect_Click()
    On Error GoTo fail
    Set soapclient = New soapclient
    soapclient.mssoapinit "http://localhost/ SqlXmlProj1/YourWebServiceName?wsdl"
    soapclient.ConnectorProperty("EndPointURL") = "http://localhost/WsTry2/WS"

    Dim retList As IXMLDOMNodeList
    Dim node As IXMLDOMNode

    Set retList = soapclient.CustOrderHist("ALFKI")

    For Each node In retList
        MsgBox node.xml
    Next
        fail:
        Debug.Print soapclient.Detail
        Debug.Print Err.Description
End Sub
```

Creating the Inventory Web Service

You will create the Inventory Web service that allows online access to up-to-date inventory information of the stock at the headquarters of JB Book Sellers. This Web service simply needs to retrieve some data from an SQL Server 2000 database and make it accessible online. You will construct the Web service by using the tools available with the SQL XML 3.0 pack.

Creating the Database

The database at the head office of JB Book Sellers contains the InventoryData table, as shown in Figure 20-11.

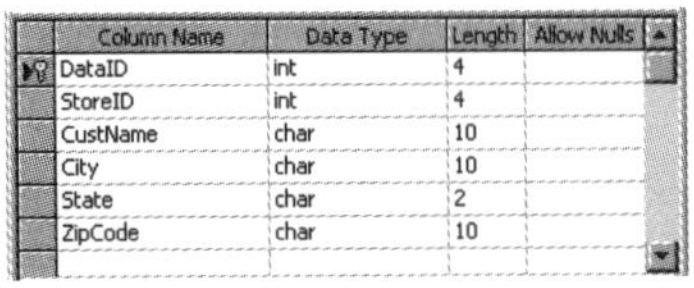

Column Name	Data Type	Length	Allow Nulls
DataID	int	4	
StoreID	int	4	
CustName	char	10	
City	char	10	
State	char	2	
ZipCode	char	10	

FIGURE 20-11 *The InventoryData table.*

The InventoryData table maintains an inventory of the available stock. After creating the database, the next step is to create a stored procedure, `GetInventory`, which retrieves the inventory information from the table.

You use the SQL Server 2000 Enterprise Manager to create the following stored procedure:

```
CREATE PROCEDURE DBO.GetInventory AS
Select Title,Category,Author,Price,Stock from InventoryDataGO
```

Creating the Web Service for JB Book Sellers

After you create the database and the stored procedure, create a Web service to expose the stored procedure. You learned the steps to create a Web service in the earlier section "Creating a Web Service."

After you have finished the steps, you will find that the following files have been created:

- Inventory.wsdl
- InVentory.ssc

The WSDL file contains the description of the Web service required by client applications and maps the methods exposed by the Web service to the corresponding stored procedures. To do this, an .ssc file is generated. The following code is a sample .ssc file that connects the Web service to the stored procedure:

```
<?xml version="1.0"?>
<sxs:methods name="Inventory" domain="server1"
url="http://server1/InventoryWS/Inventory"
xmlns:sxs="http://schemas.microsoft.com/SQLServer/2001/12/SOAPxml">
<sxs:method name="GetInventory" type="storedproc" spname="[GetInventory]" format="raw"
output="xmlobject" faults="true">
<parameter name="@RETURN_VALUE" type="3" paramSize="4" precision="10"
input="false" output="true" is-="false"/>
</sxs:method>
</sxs:methods>
```

This creates the Web service. You can test it by creating a client application in Visual Basic 6.0, as discussed in the section, "Testing the Web Service."

Integrating Web Services and Office XP

You are aware of several benefits of XML Web Services. In this section, we will discuss the benefits that are in context to Office XP. These benefits are discussed in the following list:

- ◆ XML Web Services enable traditional challenging requests that query enterprise data to be exposed as simple HTTP requests.
- ◆ Complex business logic is hidden from the developer and surfaced as an HTTP request.

It is believed that Microsoft will use XML Web Services to solve the enterprise-data-integration challenge. In addition, Microsoft aims to soon migrate to XML Web Services as the replacement for technologies, such as Distributed Component Object Model (DCOM) and Remote Procedure Call (RPC).

However, not much work has been done in the area that deals with the interaction of end users with XML Web Services. Ultimately, as with all custom solutions, a user who is working on a PC will be able to invoke that piece of business logic or launch that enterprise-data query.

Microsoft has positioned Office XP as the front end, exposing XML Web Services to end users. This is mainly because Office XP is easy to use and is already integrated into your daily routines.

To help developers incorporate XML Web Services into their Office XP-based applications, Microsoft recently released the Office XP Web Services Toolkit. The next section discusses the Office XP Web Services Toolkit in detail.

Introduction to the Office XP Web Services Toolkit

The Office XP Web Services Toolkit provides developers with an easy way to incorporate XML Web Services into their Office XP-based applications. Specifically, the toolkit enables you to search for XML Web services and incorporate them into your Office XP-based solutions. The toolkit provides an add-in to the Visual Basic for Applications (VBA) development environment that replicates the XML Web service find-and-reference capabilities found in Visual Studio .NET.

The Office XP Web Services Toolkit provides a Web Service References Tool that allows you to create and reference a Web service. The following section discusses the Web Service References Tool.

To create a Web service by using the Office XP Web Services Toolkit, you first need to install the following software on the development computer:

- ◆ Microsoft Windows XP
- ◆ Microsoft Office XP
- ◆ The Web Service References Tool
- ◆ The SOAP Toolkit 2.0 SP2

After you have installed the Web Service References Tool on the development server, open the Office Visual Basic Editor in any application that supports VBA. These applications include Office applications. You will learn to do this while creating the Web service for JB Book Sellers. Creation of the Web service is discussed in the following section.

Constructing the JB Book Seller's Application

As discussed in the case study, the individual bookstores use the Office XP-based solution to maintain their daily transactions. The following steps discuss the transactions that take place at the bookstores of JB Book Sellers.

1. When a user places an order for a book, the bookstore receives the order and saves the details of the order in the database.

2. The bookstores also accept orders through mail, e-mail messages, or phone calls. Therefore, the details of the customer, such as the name and address, are stored in the Microsoft Access database by using the Microsoft Access forms-based interface.

3. The details of the order, such as order number and credit card details, are also stored in the Microsoft Access database.

4. To validate the data that the customer entered, certain validation tests are done. These tests include validating the ZIP Code against the given city and state, verifying the e-mail address, and checking the credit card number for Mod 10 compatibility. You learned about the Mod 10 formula in Chapter 15, "Design and Creation of a Web Service Using the IBM Toolkit."

Calling Web Services from an Office XP Application

Before you call Web services from an Office XP application, you need to create a Microsoft Access application. Therefore, it's necessary to add the support for the Web service.

The Microsoft Access application contains an OrderDetails form. The form is shown in Figure 20-12.

As you can see, the OrderDetails form contains text boxes that accept user input for ZIP Code, E-mail, Credit Card, and Card Type. The ZIP Code needs to be validated against the state and the city, as specified by the user. The e-mail address needs to be verified and, finally, the credit card number needs to be checked for Mod 10 compliance. When the credit card number is validated, the card type is detected and filled in the text box.

You can use the existing Web services to perform the preceding tasks. You can search for information about these Web services in the UDDI directory. As you know, however, UDDI is too cluttered with false and junk data. Therefore, you can search for information about the Web services in Web sites, such as at http://www.SalCentral.com or http://www.XMethods.com.

FIGURE 20-12 *The OrderDetails form.*

 NOTE

Web sites such as SalCentral and XMethods are commonly used sites for searching information about Web services and their features.

Adding Reference to a Web Service

To call a Web service from an Office XP application, perform the following steps:

1. Open the OrderDetails form in the Design view and add a button next to the Credit Card text box.

2. Label the button Validate Credit Card.

3. Right-click on the button and select Build Event.

4. In the resulting menu, select Code Builder. The internal VBA editor is displayed, as shown in Figure 20-13.

   Notice that installing the Web services toolkit has resulted in a change in the Add Web Services References option in the Tools menu.

5. Click on the Add Web Services References option. A window, as shown in Figure 20-14, is displayed.

   This window is similar to the Add Web Reference dialog box in Visual Studio .NET that is used to add a Web reference to a Web service from a .NET application.

6. Browse the http://www.xmethods.com site to locate a Web service that can perform the required validations.

 NOTE

We have used a Web service present at the http://www.richsolutions.com/ RichPayments/RichCardValidator.asmx?WSDL URL.

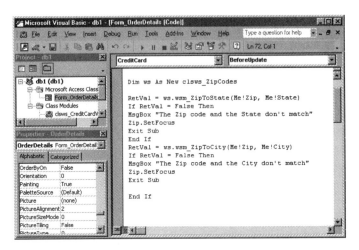

FIGURE 20-13 *The Office's internal VBA editor.*

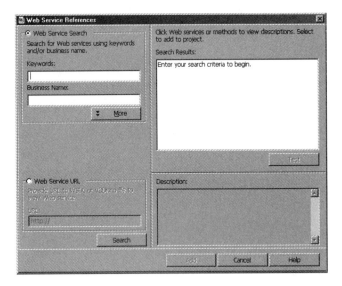

FIGURE 20-14 *The Add Web Services References option.*

7. In Office XP, click on Web Services Reference in the Tools menu.

8. In the resulting dialog box, click on the Web Service URL option button. A text box is activated.

9. Enter the path to the .wsdl file of the Web service you have chosen.

NOTE

This dialog box allows you to search for various UDDIs of a service by using business or service types or keywords.

10. Click on the Search button. The Web service and the Web methods are displayed in the dialog box.

 NOTE

If the Web service that is found is grayed out, it implies that a Web method of the Web service returns a complex type variable, which Office XP doesn't support.

11. Select one or more XML Web services for which you want the tool to create proxy classes, and click on the Add to Project button.

Selecting the Add to Project button enables the Web Service References Tool to perform several activities, as discussed in the following list:

◆ Create a class module file, which is a .cls file, for each Web service. The name of the class module file contains a prefix clsws_ followed by the name of the Web service. For example, if the name of the Web service is CreditCardValidator, the name of the .cls file would be clsws_ CreditCardValidator.

◆ Create a private constant, c_WSDL_URL, in the .cls file that corresponds to the .wsdl file of the Web service.

◆ Create public functions that correspond to the Web methods in the Web service. The name of the function is prefixed with wsm_ followed by the name of the Web method.

The Web Service References Tool in this case creates a class module with the name clsws_ CreditCardValidator. The code for the clsws_ CreditCardValidator file contains two sections. The first part contains comments that describe the details of the class module. The next section discusses the instructions to declare and instantiate this class in the code. The code for the class module is shown in the following example:

```
Option Compare Database
'*****************************************************************
' This class was created by the Web Service References Tool.
'
' Created: 7/3/2002 05:48:21 AM
'
```

```
' Description:
' This class is a Visual Basic for Applications class representation of
' the Web service
' CreditCardValidator
' as defined by http://www.richsolutions.com/RichPayments/RichCardValidator.asmx?WSDL,
'
' This class only contains methods that use simple data types,
' as defined in the WSDL.
'
' To Use:
' Dimension a variable as new clsws_CreditCardValidator, and then write
' code to use the methods provided by the class.
'
' Example:
'      Dim ExampVar as New clsws_CreditCardValidator
'      Debug.Print ExampVar.wsm_GetCardType("Sample Input")
'
' Changes to the code in this class may result in incorrect behavior.
'
'*****************************************************************
```

Next, two internal class variables are initialized to the SoapClient proxy object and the URL of the .wsdl file, respectively. This SoapClient proxy object is used to exchange XML Web service calls between the client application and the Web server.

 NOTE

The SoapClient proxy class variable is prefixed with sc_, whereas the name of the variable initialized to the URL is always c_WSDL_URL.

The code for the class variables is as follows:

```
'Dimensioning private class variables.
Private sc_CreditCardValidator As SoapClient
Private Const c_WSDL_URL As String = http://www.richsolutions.com/RichPayments/
RichCardValidator.asmx?WSDL
```

Next, you need to create an instance of the SoapClient proxy object. To do this, use the Class_Intialize event. The code for the Class_Intialize event is as follows:

```
Private Sub Class_Initialize()
```

```
'*****************************************************************
' Subroutine will be called each time the class is instantiated.
' Creates sc_CreditCardValidator as new SoapClient, and then
' initializes sc_CreditCardValidator.mssoapinit with WSDL file found in
' http://www.richsolutions.com/RichPayments/RichCardValidator.asmx?WSDL.
'*****************************************************************

        Set sc_CreditCardValidator = New SoapClient
        sc_CreditCardValidator.mssoapinit c_WSDL_URL
```

The preceding code creates a SoapClient object and initializes it with the URL of the Web service represented by the proxy class. However, if your application accesses the Web through a proxy server, you need to add the following code that provides the credentials for authentication by the proxy server or the corporate firewall:

```
        sc_CreditCardValidator.ConnectorProperty("ProxyServer") = "del-d190okh-ps1"
        sc_CreditCardValidator.ConnectorProperty("ProxyPort") = 80
        sc_CreditCardValidator.ConnectorProperty("ProxyUser") = "user1"
        sc_CreditCardValidator.ConnectorProperty("ProxyPassword") = "pass1"
End Sub
```

Next, the `Class_Terminate` event is used to deallocate memory to resources that are no longer used. For example, when the SoapClient proxy object is no longer used, its memory is deallocated by using the `Class_Terminate` event, as shown in the following code:

```
Private Sub Class_Terminate()
'*****************************************************************
' Subroutine will be called each time the class is destructed.
' Sets sc_CreditCardValidator to Nothing.
'*****************************************************************

        'Error Trap
        On Error GoTo Class_TerminateTrap

        Set sc_CreditCardValidator = Nothing
Exit Sub

        Class_TerminateTrap:
                CreditCardValidatorErrorHandler "Class_terminate"
End Sub
```

In the preceding code, the `CreditCardValidatorErrorHandler` subroutine is used to handle the errors generated by the Web server hosting the Web service. As you can see, the name of the subroutine contains the keyword `ErrorHandler` preceded by the name of the Web service, CreditCardValidator.

```
Private Sub CreditCardValidatorErrorHandler(str_Function As String)
'****************************************************************
' This subroutine is the class error handler. It can be called from any class
subroutine or function
' when that subroutine or function encounters an error. Then it will raise the error
 along with the name of the calling subroutine or function


'****************************************************************


     ' SOAP Error
    If sc_CreditCardValidator.faultcode <> "" Then
         Err.Raise vbObjectError, str_Function,
sc_CreditCardValidator.faultstring
          ' Non SOAP Error
    Else
         Err.Raise Err.Number, str_Function, Err.Description
    End If
End Sub
```

Finally, declare the methods in the Web service. It is important to note that Web methods created by the Web Service References Tool are always public, prefixed with wsm_ followed by the Web method name, and list input parameters with a data type prefix followed by the Web method parameter.

The code that the Web Service References Tool generates for the Web methods is as follows:

```
Public Function wsm_GetCardType(ByVal str_CardNumber As String) As String
'****************************************************************
' Proxy function created from http://www.richsolutions.com/RichPayments/
RichCardValidator.asmx?WSDL
'****************************************************************


     'Set error trap
    On Error GoTo wsm_GetCardTypeTrap
    wsm_GetCardType = sc_CreditCardValidator.GetCardType(str_CardNumber)
Exit Function
```

```
        wsm_GetCardTypeTrap:
            CreditCardValidatorErrorHandler "wsm_GetCardType"
End Function


Public Function wsm_IsCommercialCard(ByVal str_CardNumber As String) As Boolean
'*************************************************************
' Proxy function created from http://www.richsolutions.com/RichPayments/
RichCardValidator.asmx?WSDL
'*************************************************************


        'Set error trap
        On Error GoTo wsm_IsCommercialCardTrap


        wsm_IsCommercialCard = sc_CreditCardValidator.IsCommercialCard(str_CardNumber)
Exit Function


        wsm_IsCommercialCardTrap:
        CreditCardValidatorErrorHandler "wsm_IsCommercialCard"
End Function


Public Function wsm_ValidCard(ByVal str_CardNumber As String, ByVal str_ExpDate
As String) As Long
'*************************************************************
' Proxy function created from http://www.richsolutions.com/RichPayments/
RichCardValidator.asmx?WSDL
'*************************************************************


        'Set error trap
        On Error GoTo wsm_ValidCardTrap


        wsm_ValidCard = sc_CreditCardValidator.ValidCard(str_CardNumber, str_ExpDate)

Exit Function


        wsm_ValidCardTrap:
        CreditCardValidatorErrorHandler "wsm_ValidCard"
End Function
```

```
Public Function wsm_ValidCardLength(ByVal str_CardNumber As String) As Boolean
'**************************************************************
' Proxy function created from http://www.richsolutions.com/RichPayments/
RichCardValidator.asmx?WSDL
'**************************************************************

    'Set error trap
    On Error GoTo wsm_ValidCardLengthTrap

    wsm_ValidCardLength = sc_CreditCardValidator.ValidCardLength(str_CardNumber)

Exit Function

    wsm_ValidCardLengthTrap:
    CreditCardValidatorErrorHandler "wsm_ValidCardLength"
End Function

Public Function wsm_ValidExpDate(ByVal str_ExpDate As String) As Boolean
'**************************************************************
' Proxy function created from http://www.richsolutions.com/RichPayments/
RichCardValidator.asmx?WSDL
'**************************************************************

    'Set error trap
    On Error GoTo wsm_ValidExpDateTrap

    wsm_ValidExpDate = sc_CreditCardValidator.ValidExpDate(str_ExpDate)
Exit Function

    wsm_ValidExpDateTrap:
    CreditCardValidatorErrorHandler "wsm_ValidExpDate"
End Function

Public Function wsm_ValidMod10(ByVal str_CardNumber As String) As Boolean
'**************************************************************
' Proxy function created from http://www.richsolutions.com/RichPayments/
RichCardValidator.asmx?WSDL
'**************************************************************
```

```
'Set error trap
On Error GoTo wsm_ValidMod10Trap


wsm_ValidMod10 = sc_CreditCardValidator.ValidMod10(str_CardNumber)
Exit Function


wsm_ValidMod10Trap:
CreditCardValidatorErrorHandler "wsm_ValidMod10"
End Function
```

Adding Code to the Validate Credit Card Button

After you add a reference to the Credit Card validation Web service, add the following code for the Validate Credit Card button:

```
Private Sub CCValidate_Click()
    On Error GoTo Err
    //Check if valid
    Dim ws As New clsws_CreditCardValidator
    ResVal = ws.wsm_ValidMod10(Me!CreditCard)
    If ResVal = False Then
        MsgBox "Credit Card number fails Luhn check!"
        CreditCard.SetFocus
        Exit Sub
    End If


        //Get the card type
        CCType = ws.wsm_GetCardType(Me!CreditCard)
        CardType.SetFocus
        CardType.Text = CCType
    Exit Sub


        Err:
        MsgBox Err.Description
        Exit Sub
End Sub
```

The preceding code creates an instance of the proxy class. First, the code checks whether the credit card number is a valid number and retrieves the card type. Then it displays the card type in the Card Type text box.

Adding a Web Service to Validate the E-Mail

Similarly, you can add references to the Web services that validate the e-mail address.

 NOTE

To validate the e-mail address, we have used the Web service with WSDL at http://www.dev1.eraserver.net/WebServices/mxchecker/mxchecker.asmx?WSDL.

After you have created the proxy for the mxchecker Web service, you can call its methods, as shown in the following code:

```
Private Sub EmailValidate_Click()
    Dim ws As New clsws_MXChecker
    If ws.wsm_bCheckEmail(9999, Me!Email) Then
        MsgBox "Valid Email"
    Else
        MsgBox "Email ID not found."
    End If
End Sub
```

Adding a Web Service to Validate the ZIP Code

To enable validation of the ZIP Code, a Web service at http://services.pagedownweb.com/ZipCodes.asmx?WSDL offers methods that accept a ZIP Code and state or a ZIP Code and city as parameters. This Web service returns True or False after validation. The code for invoking the Web service at the click of a button is shown in the following sample:

```
Private Sub ZipCodeValidate_Click()
    On Error GoTo Err_Command15_Click
    Dim ws As New clsws_ZipCodes

    RetVal = ws.wsm_ZipToState(Me!Zip, Me!State)
    If RetVal = False Then
        MsgBox "The Zip code and the State don't match"
        Zip.SetFocus
        Exit Sub
    End If

    RetVal = ws.wsm_ZipToCity(Me!Zip, Me!City)
    If RetVal = False Then
```

```
            MsgBox "The Zip code and the City don't match"
            Zip.SetFocus
            Exit Sub
      End If


Exit_Command15_Click:
      Exit Sub


Err_Command15_Click:
      MsgBox Err.Description
      Resume Exit_Command15_Click
End Sub
```

Summary

In this chapter, you learned to integrate a Web service in an SQL Server 2000 and Office XP application. You also learned how to use XML templates to query SQL Server 2000 databases and how stored procedures can be exposed as Web services. Finally, you discovered how to use existing Web services to implement specific functionality.

PART XIV

Appendixes

Appendix A

In Chapter 6, "Creating a Web Service Using the Microsoft SOAP Toolkit," you learned to expose the functionality of a COM component over the Web by creating a Web service. The Web service was created using the Microsoft SOAP Toolkit. In Chapter 6, we had assumed that the COM component already existed. This chapter discusses how to create the component that was used in Chapter 6.

You will use Visual Basic 6.0 to create the COM component. In addition, you will learn how to access a database by using ADO.

Overview of the COM Component

The COM component in Chapter 6 is used on a Web site called CompareNShop.Net. This Web site allows visitors to check the prices of various commercial goods and compare their prices and features. Various components work together to bring about the functionality that the Web site requires. You will create a simple component that retrieves data from the CompareNShop.Net database and other applications, such as other Web sites and portals, used to integrate and display the data on their sites.

The component that you will create uses stored procedures created on an SQL database. These stored procedures query data from the database. In addition, the component contains a class called `ExecSP`, which exposes two methods: `GetAll()` and `GetByCategory()`.

The `GetAll()` method returns the details of all products whose information is stored in the database. The `GetByCategory()` method returns information about all products of a specified category.

Creating the COM Component

The creation of the COM component depends on the database design of CompareNShop. Therefore, before creating the component, first look at the design of the database at Compare-NShop.

The Database Design

A partial display of the CompareNShop database with the relevant tables is shown in Figure A-1. You looked at the database design in detail in Chapter 6.

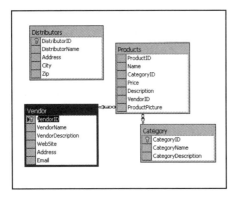

FIGURE A-1 *The CompareNShop database.*

Creating a COM Component by Using Visual Basic 6.0

To create the COM component, perform the following steps:

1. Launch Visual Basic 6.0 from the Programs menu.
2. Select New, Project. The New Project dialog box is displayed, as shown in Figure A-2.

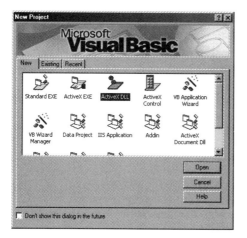

FIGURE A-2 *The New Project dialog box.*

3. In the New Project dialog box, select ActiveX DLL as the project type. The ActiveX DLL project opens.
4. Change the default names of the project and the component.
5. Right-click on the project name and select Properties from the pop-up menu, as shown in Figure A-3. The Project1 Properties dialog box is displayed, as shown in Figure A-4.
6. Change the Project Name to CNSComponent1, and click on the OK button to close the dialog box.

FIGURE A-3 *The pop-up menu.*

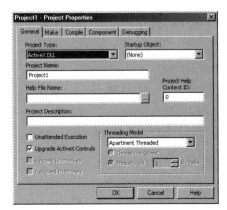

FIGURE A-4 *The Project1 properties dialog box.*

 NOTE

As you can see in Figure A-4, the default Project type is ActiveX DLL. The other project types are ActiveX EXE, ActiveX Control, and Standard EXE.

Because you are creating a COM-based component, retain the selection of ActiveX DLL as the project type.

Similarly, change the name of the class from `class1` to `ExecSP`. In the class, add the following function definitions:

```
Function getAll() As ADODB.Recordset
        'This method retrieves the details of all the products in the CNS database
End Function
Function getByCategory(category As String) As ADODB.Recordset
        'This method retrieves details of products of a particular category.
End Function
```

To make these methods functional, connect them to the database. You can then retrieve data from the tables in the database.

 NOTE

In this example, you will use ADO to connect to the database and retrieve data from it.

To use ADO, add a reference to its type library to the current project. To do this, perform the following steps:

1. Select References from the Project menu. The References dialog box is displayed, as shown in Figure A-5.

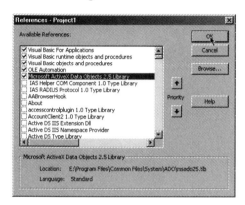

FIGURE A-5 *The References dialog box.*

2. Select Microsoft ActiveX Data Objects 2.5 Library.

3. Add the code to the empty methods, which you created, to access the database, execute the stored procedure, and return the data that the stored procedures return. After adding the code, the methods are as follows:

```
Function getAll() As ADODB.Recordset '
        Dim cnn As New ADODB.Connection
        Dim rs As New ADODB.Recordset
        cnn.Open "Provider=SQLOLEDB;DData Source=Server1;Initial
Catalog=CompareNShop;Integrated Security=SSPI"
        rs.Open "exec sp_getAll", cnn
        Set getAll = rs
End Function


Function getByCategory(category As String) As ADODB.Recordset
        Dim cnn As New ADODB.Connection
        Dim rs As New ADODB.Recordset
        cnn.Open "Provider=SQLOLEDB;DData Source=Server1;Initial
Catalog=CompareNShop;Integrated Security=SSPI"
        rs.Open "exec sp_getByCategory '" & category & "'", cnn
        Set getByCategory = rs
End Function
```

In the preceding code, the ADO Connection and Recordset objects are used to access a database. The ADO connection object is used to create an open connection to a data source. You can use this connection to access and manipulate a database.

You can use the Recordset object to store a set of records from a database. In this case, the Recordset object executes a stored procedure, stores the set of records that the stored procedures returns, and makes the stored procedure accessible to the application.

To create the Active DLL file, select Make CNSComponent1.dll from the File menu. The IDE will compile the project, build the DLL, and register it. Your component is ready to be used.

Summary

In this Appendix, you learned to create a COM component that can be used in the sample program of Chapter 6. You also learned how to build a COM component by using Visual Basic 6.0. Finally, you learned how to connect to a database by using ADO.

Appendix B

Visual Basic .NET (VB.NET) is the latest version of Visual Basic that is based on the .NET Framework. Similar to any other .NET language, such as C#, you can create Windows applications, Web applications, and Web services by using VB.NET. To enable you to create applications easily and efficiently, Visual Studio .NET provides you with various templates. In addition, you can benefit from other features of the .NET Framework while you're working with VB.NET. You will learn about these features in the later section titled "Features of the .NET Framework."

In Project 2 (found in Chapters 7, "Building Web Applications on the .NET Platform," and 8, "Creating an ASP.NET Web Service"), you created a Web service in Visual Studio .NET by using VB.NET. This Appendix introduces you to the .NET Framework and the VB.NET language. It also teaches you about the features of an object-oriented language and identifies the components that make VB.NET an object-oriented language. Finally, it shows you how to create a small application in VB.NET.

Overview of the .NET Framework

The .NET Framework is a new platform that Microsoft developed to provide complete support for creating applications. These applications include standalone applications—such as Console applications and Windows applications—and applications for the distributed environment—such as Web applications and Web services. In the .NET Framework, you also can create mobile applications that you can access from a mobile device.

To help you create applications, the .NET Framework provides you with a development tool called Visual Studio .NET (VS.NET). In addition to creating different kinds of applications, Visual Studio .NET provides compilers and debuggers for various programming languages. The programming languages that Visual Studio .NET supports include Visual C# .NET, VB.NET, Visual C++ .NET, Visual FoxPro, and so on. All these languages use a common Integrated Development Environment (IDE), which provides a common set of tools and facilities for creating applications in any of the .NET languages.

Features of the .NET Framework

The .NET Framework has the following features:

◆ **Support for creating interoperable applications.** Prior to .NET, it was not easy to create applications that were interoperable across platforms. The .NET Framework makes your work easier by allowing you to create applications that you can access through the Internet. These applications are called Web services. You can access a Web service from any computer running on any platform.

The .NET Framework allows you to create these applications in a .NET-based language. In addition, Visual Studio .NET provides full support for creating Web services by providing you with a template, as shown in Figure B-1.

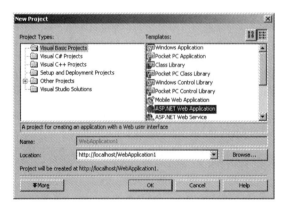

FIGURE B-1 *VS.NET templates for creating Web services.*

◆ **Support for creating applications that are independent of the language.** The .NET Framework provides a set of base classes for creating applications in any .NET-based language. These classes are independent of the language used because they are compiled by using a common runtime environment for the .NET Framework called the Common Language Runtime (CLR).

For example, the Thread class is a base class in the .NET base class library that you use to create threads. This class can be used in a VB.NET application as well as a C# application.

◆ **Support for Microsoft Intermediate Language (MSIL).** All code for the .NET applications are converted to managed code. Managed code, which the CLR executes, contains information about the code. This information includes the classes, methods, variables, and so on that are used in the code. When you compile a .NET application, the managed code is MSIL. MSIL is a set of CPU-independent instructions and is, therefore, independent of the operating environment of the computer on which it is run.

◆ **The basic functionality to create different applications.** As you know, in the .NET Framework, you can use VS.NET to create applications easily and efficiently. VS.NET, in turn, provides you with templates to create different applications. When you create an application by using these templates, Visual Studio .NET creates a framework for these applications. The framework includes a default form. It's a Windows form for a Windows application and a Web form for Web applications. Also included is default code that contains the namespaces and classes to be used in the application.

Visual Studio .NET provides a toolbox that contains various controls, such as Windows controls and Web controls, which you can add to your application. After you add the controls, you simply need to add methods to implement the functionality into the application. The framework for a VB.NET application is shown in Figure B-2.

◆ **Use of assemblies.** Assemblies are self-describing structures that contain the compiled code for a .NET application. These assemblies contain the classes, namespaces, and other resources used in the application and the information about the assembly, called the *metadata*. Therefore, when you create an application, you can use the resources contained in the assembly. This makes developing the applications easier, and when an application is deployed at the client side, the resources are added to the client's computer.

Working with a .NET assembly is easy because you do not need to register the assembly with the client registry. This is in contrast to the COM .dll files that you need to explicitly register with the registry of your computer. To use the assembly with the client application, you simply need to copy the assembly files to the application directory. Assemblies solve the version problem by maintaining information about the versions in the metadata.

◆ **Support for object-oriented (OO) language.** The .NET Framework contains a library of base classes called the *.NET base class library*. You can use these classes to create applications in several .NET- based languages. You can also derive a class from the base class to use it in the application.

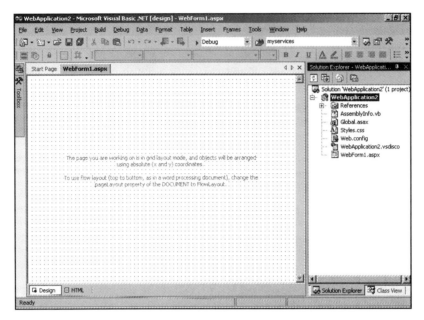

FIGURE B-2 *The framework for a VB.NET application.*

◆ **An integrated debugger.** Code that is created in any of the .NET languages can be debugged using an integrated debugger that Visual Studio .NET provides. You can use the same debugger to debug applications created in VB.NET or C#. By using the integrated debugger, you can debug your application while it is running.

◆ **Effective management of memory.** The .NET Framework contains a garbage collection feature that is used for effective management of memory. The garbage collection feature searches for the resources that are not referenced by any application for a long period of time. If a garbage collector finds such a resource, it automatically releases the memory of the resource, thereby providing effective management of resources.

◆ **A security mechanism for applications.** The .NET Framework provides security to applications through role-based security and Code Access Security (CAS). By applying role-based security to applications, .NET ensures that no unauthorized user can access the application. To implement role-based security, you assign rights to a user. These rights are called *principals*. As a result, whenever a user tries to access an application, the .NET Framework validates the user's principal and provides access to the application based on the results of the validation.

Unlike role-based security, CAS applies permissions to the application's code. CAS determines the actions that the code can perform.

Languages of the .NET Framework

As discussed, the .NET Framework includes the following languages:

- Visual Basic .NET
- Visual C# .NET
- Visual C++ .NET

VB.NET

VB.NET is the latest version of Visual Basic (VB), which allows developers to create applications for the Windows platform. With the evolution of the Web, Microsoft developed the VB.NET language, which facilitates you to create Web applications and Web services in addition to Windows-based applications. Although VB.NET evolved from earlier versions of VB, it has many features that are different from the earlier versions. You will learn about these features in the section "Differences Between VB.NET and VB 6.0."

Visual C# .NET

Visual C# .NET, commonly called C# (C sharp), is a new object-oriented language included in Visual Studio .NET. C# includes the features of several programming languages, such as C, C++, VB, and Java. In addition, C# contains many new features that you will learn about in Appendix C, "Introduction to Visual C# .NET."

Visual C++ .NET

Visual C++ .NET (VC++ .NET) is the latest version of Visual C++ (VC++). VC++ .NET is used to create several applications in Visual Studio .NET, including ATL Project, ATL Server project, ATL Web services, Managed C++ applications, and so on. These applications are shown in Figure B-3.

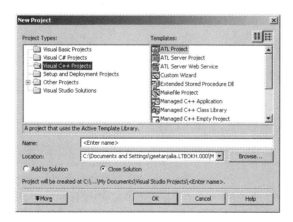

FIGURE B-3 *The applications that you can create using VC++ .NET.*

Although, VC++ .NET is included in the .NET Framework, it is different from other .NET languages, such as VB.NET and C#. This is because code in VB.NET and C# complies to MSIL by using the corresponding compiler. However, VC++ .NET is the only language in the .NET family that also can be used to create native code applications.

VC++ .NET supports features such as managed extensions. You can use managed extensions to create .NET Framework applications. In addition, you can convert the existing components of C++ to .NET components. Therefore, managed extensions enable reusability of existing components to create new components.

You have looked at the languages in the .NET Framework. In this Appendix, we will discuss VB.NET in detail.

Overview of VB.NET

VB.NET is a programming language available in the .NET Framework. Similar to any other .NET language, VB.NET is used to create Windows applications, Web applications, ASP.NET Web services, and so on.

VB.NET is an object-oriented language in contrast to its predecessor VB 6.0. In addition, there are several other differences between VB.NET and VB 6.0. We will now discuss the differences between VB.NET and VB 6.0.

Differences Between VB.NET and VB 6.0

As discussed, VB.NET is different from its immediate predecessor VB 6.0. The main difference between VB.NET and VB 6.0 is that VB.NET is an object-oriented language and VB 6.0 is not. An object-oriented language uses objects that are the building blocks of an application.

Another major difference between VB.NET and VB 6.0 is that VB.NET supports implementation inheritance, whereas VB 6.0 supports interface inheritance. This implies that VB 6.0 allows you to implement only interfaces, whereas VB.NET allows you to inherit classes. You can derive a class from a base class. VB.NET supports single-inheritance, which implies that a class in VB.NET can be inherited from only one class.

When a class is derived from a base class, the derived class also inherits the properties and methods of the base class. You can implement the methods in the derived class with the same functionality as that in the base class. In addition, you can override the methods of the base class in the derived class. This is called *method overriding*.

In addition to overriding a method, you can overload a method, which is known as *method overloading*. Method overloading enables you to create two or more methods with the same name but a different signature. For example, you can overload two methods with the name Add() by passing parameters with different data types to them. Alternatively, you can overload the Add() method by passing a different number of parameters to them. VB 6.0 does not support method overloading.

In addition to these differences, there are several differences between VB.NET and VB 6.0, as shown in Table B-1.

Table B-1 Differences Between VB.NET and VB 6.0

Feature	VB 6.0	VB.NET
Declaring structures	Type-End Type	Structure-End Structure
Remote Data Objects (RDO) data binding	Supported	Not supported
OLE Container control	Available	Not available
Shape controls	Available	Not available
Option base statement	Available	Not available
Line control	Available	Not available
Dynamic Data Exchange (DDE) support	Available	Not available
Data Access Objects (DAO) data binding	Supported	Not supported
Fixed-length strings	Supported	Not supported
Fixed-size arrays	Supported	Not supported
Data type to store date values	Double	DateTime
`DefType` statements	Supported	Not supported
Use of the `ReDim` statement	Array declaration	Array resizing
Universal data	Variant	Object
Currency data type	Supported	Not supported
`Eqv` operator	Supported	Not supported
`Imp` operator	Supported	Not supported
Default properties for objects	Supported	Not supported
Syntax of `while` loop	While-Wend	While-End While
Declaring procedures as static	Supported	Not supported
Declaring scope of a variable in a block of code within a procedure	Procedure scope	Block scope
Providing values for optional arguments	Not required	Required
`Class_Initialize` event	Supported	Not supported

(continues...)

Feature	VB 6.0	VB.NET
Class_Terminate event	Supported	Not supported
Empty keyword	Supported	Not supported
GoSub statement	Available	Not available
Default mechanism for passing arguments	ByRef	ByVal
Null keyword	Supported	Not supported
IsEmpty function	Supported	Not supported
Option Private Module statement	Supported	Not supported

Overview of an Object-Oriented Language

The concept of object-oriented programming was introduced in VB.NET. In an object-oriented programming language, objects are used as the building blocks of programming. As already discussed, while you're programming with VB.NET, you can use the classes that are present in the .NET base classes. In addition, you can create custom classes to be used in the application. However, to use a class in your application, you first need to create an instance of a class. This instance of a class is called an *object*.

After you have created an object, you can use it to perform a specific function. An object's function is defined in its method. An object has attributes and properties that store additional information about the object. All these components form a complete object-oriented programming language.

Features of an Object-Oriented Language

The following list discusses the features of an object-oriented language:

◆ **Abstraction.** An object contains methods, properties, and attributes. Some of the components of an object are not of any use to the user. Therefore, as a developer, you need to hide these components from the user. The method of hiding the non-essential information from a user is called *abstraction*.

For example, you can create a class with the name Employees. This class is used to store information about the employees, such as name, address, phone number, designation, and so on. Any employee of the organization can access this information. In addition, the Employees class stores information about the employee's salary. This information is not to be shared with all employees. You can hide this information by using abstraction.

◆ **Encapsulation.** Encapsulation is the method of implementing abstraction in an object-oriented language. Encapsulation enables you to expose only the properties and methods of a class to the user, while hiding their implementation. This helps you to have different implementations of the same object, while hiding the complexities from the users.

For example, consider a situation in which an organization decides to give a bonus to the employees. This bonus is calculated on the basis of the basic salary and other allowances given to the employee. Therefore, you can create a `protected` method that accepts the `private` information, such as basic pay and allowances, and calculates a bonus on that. The method is shown in the following code:

```
protected float Bonus (float Basic, float Allowances)
{
----------
}
```

A user can only see the result returned by the `Bonus()` method. The implementation of the method is hidden from the user.

◆ **Inheritance.** Inheritance is the most important feature of an object-oriented language. It enables you to derive a class from a base class, such as a .NET base class. When a class is derived from another class, the derived class automatically inherits the properties and methods of the class.

For example, you can create a base class, `ClassA`, and declare a method, `Method1()`, in it. You can then derive `ClassB` from it. `ClassB` automatically inherits `Method1()`. In addition, you can declare another method, `Method2()`, in `ClassB`.

◆ **Polymorphism.** Polymorphism allows an object to exist in more than one form. Therefore, when you derive a class from a base class, the base class methods are implemented in the derived class. You can either retain the same functionality of the method or change the functionality of the method in the derived class. The name of the method in both classes is the same.

For example, you can create a method with the name `Add()` in the base class to add two `integer` numbers. You can then implement the same method in the derive class to add two `string` values.

Components of VB.NET

To implement object-oriented features in VB.NET, you use classes. A *class* is a data structure that is used to create objects. Classes contain class members, which include data and methods to perform actions on the data. The following section discusses classes in VB.NET.

Classes in VB.NET

Visual Studio .NET contains several base classes, such as `Thread`, `Forms`, and `Exceptions`, in the .NET class library. You also can create custom classes by either deriving classes from existing classes or creating new ones.

Declaring Classes

The syntax for declaring a class in VB.NET is as follows:

```
<access modifier> Class <name>
            <data and methods>
End Class
```

In the preceding syntax, the access modifier specifies the scope of the class. The access modifiers that VB.NET supports are discussed in Table B-2.

Table B-2 Access Modifiers in VB.NET

Access Modifier	Means of Access
Public	You can access a class with a Public access modifier from anywhere.
Friend	You can access a class with a Friend access modifier from within the project.
Protected Friend	You can access a class with a Protected Friend access modifier from within the project and its derived classes.
Private	You can access a class with a Private access modifier from the same module or class.
Protected	You can access a class with a Protected access modifier from within the containing class or its derived classes.

The syntax for the class declaration contains a Class keyword, which is used to declare a class. When you create a class, you need to provide a name for the class and include the data and methods in the class. A declaration of a class is marked with the keyword End Class.

Creating Derived Classes

To derive a class from a base class, you use the Inherits keyword. The syntax for using the Inherits keyword is as follows:

```
<access modifiers> Class DerivedClass
            Inherits BaseClass
                <data and methods>
End Class
```

Namespaces

Namespaces are containers used to organize similar classes in a hierarchical manner. You can group classes with related functionality in a namespace. It is mandatory to include all classes in a namespace. If you do not explicitly declare a class in a namespace, Visual Studio .NET automatically includes the class in the default namespace.

To declare a namespace, use the following syntax:

```
Namespace <name>
        <class declarations>
```

The preceding syntax uses the `Namespace` keyword to declare a namespace. Inside the namespace declaration statement, you can declare classes. For example, consider the following code:

```
Public Class Form1
    Inherits System.Windows.Forms.Form

    Private Sub Form1_Load(ByVal sender As System.Object, ByVal
e As System.EventArgs) Handles MyBase.Load
        MessageBox.Show("This is a sample namesapce")
    End Sub
End Class
```

The preceding code contains a default class, `Form1`, which is derived from the `Form` class. The `Form` class is present in the `System.Windows.Forms` namespace. The `Inherits` keyword is used to derive the `Form1` class from the `Form` class.

The `Form1` class contains a `private` method `Form1_Load()`, which is used to handle the `Load` event of the form. Inside the `Load` event, the `Show()` method of the `MessageBox` class is called to display a message box when a form is loaded. The `Show()` method takes the text to be displayed in the message box as the parameter. The output of the preceding code is shown in Figure B-4.

FIGURE B-4 *The output of the preceding code.*

While you're working with namespaces, consider the following points:

◆ All classes need to be included in namespaces.

◆ Namespaces are `public` by default.

◆ Namespaces can be nested. Consider the following example:

```
Namespace Nampspace1
    Namespace Nampspace2
        <class declarations
```

The preceding code creates a namespace, `Namespace2`, within another namespace, `Namespace1`.

◆ In addition to namespaces and classes, namespaces can include structs, enumerations, and interfaces.

◆ When you declare a class in a namespace, the fully qualified name of the class contains the name of a class preceded by the name of the namespace, as shown in the following example:

```
System.Windows.Forms.Form
```

The preceding code snippet defines the fully qualified name of the `Form` class, which is contained in the `Forms` namespace. The `Forms` namespace is included in the `Systems.Windows` namespace.

◆ No two classes in a namespace can have the same name. However, you can create classes with the same name in different namespaces.

◆ When you create a project in Visual Studio .NET, it, by default, creates a namespace for your project. The namespace that is created has the same name as that of the project. If you declare a class in the application, the class is included in the default namespace of the application.

Interfaces

An *interface* is a template that contains the declarations of methods and properties. Methods that are declared in an interface are never implemented. However, you can include an interface in a class to implement the data members of the interface. You cannot create an instance of an interface.

To create an interface, use the following syntax:

```
Interface <name>
          <method declarations>
```

Interfaces are used to implement polymorphism. You can implement the methods of an interface differently in different classes. Consider the following example:

```
Interface Calculations
          Public Sub Area()
          Public Sub Perimeter()
```

The preceding code declares an interface, `Calculations`, which contains declarations for two methods, `Area()` and `Perimeter()`. These methods can be implemented by different classes. For example, you can create three classes—`Square`, `Rectangle`, and `Circle`—to implement these methods. You can implement the `Area()` and `Perimeter()` methods to calculate the area and perimeter of a square, rectangle, and circle, respectively.

As discussed earlier, VB.NET supports only single inheritance. This implies that a class can inherit from only one class. However, to enable a class to inherit multiple functionalities, you can include these functionalities in interfaces. Then, the class can include multiple interfaces that contain the required functionality.

 NOTE

When a class includes an interface, it needs to implement all the functions of the interface.

Variables

A class contains data that is stored in storage locations called *variables*. You can use variables to store the details of a customer, such as name, address, and phone number. A variable has a name and a data type. You can create a `string` type variable called `Name` that stores the name of a customer. In this case, the name of the variable is `Name` and the data type of the variable is `string`.

Declaring Variables

To use a variable in a class, you first need to declare it. To declare a variable, use the following syntax:

```
<access modifier> Dim <name> As <data type>
```

In the preceding syntax, the access modifier specifies the accessibility of the variable. The access modifiers that VB.NET supports are `internal`, `private`, `protected`, `public`, `read-only`, and `static`.

The `Dim` keyword declares a variable, and the `As` keyword specifies the data type of the variable. For example, to declare variables that store information about the name, address, and phone number, use the following code snippet:

```
Dim Name As String
Dim Address As String
Dim Phone As Integer
```

Variable Data Types

A variable data type defines the type of data that you can store in a variable. The variable data types that VB.NET supports are described in Table B-3.

Table B-3 Variable Data Types Supported by VB.NET

Variable Data Types	Description
Char	A char type variable is used to store a single character.
String	A string type variable is used to store alphanumeric characters.
Short	A short type variable is used to store 16-bit signed integer numbers.
Integer	An integer type variable is used to store 32-bit signed integer numbers.
Long	A long type variable is used to store 64-bit signed integer numbers.
Byte	A byte type variable is used to store 8-bit unsigned integer numbers.
Single	A single type variable is used to store 32-bit floating-point numbers.
Double	A double type variable is used to store 64-bit floating-point numbers.
Decimal	A decimal type variable is used to store 128-bit floating-point numbers.
DateTime	A DateTime type variable is used to store the date and time.
Object	An Object type variable is the base type of all types.
Boolean	A Boolean type variable is used to store the Boolean values true or false.

Initializing Variables

When you declare a variable, by default, it stores some initial value. Initializing a variable means overwriting this initial value. You can initialize a variable as shown in the following code:

```
Dim Name As String = "John"
```

 NOTE

Earlier versions of VB do not allow you to declare and initialize a variable in the same line. Therefore, to declare a variable in an earlier version of VB, use the following statements:

```
Dim Name As String
Name = "John"
```

As you can see, the variable is actually created when you initialize it. However, if required, you can create a variable when it is declared by using the new keyword.

```
Dim Name As String
Name = New String()
```

Constants

Similar to variables, constants also store data. Constants are used to store data whose value does not change after it's created. To declare a constant, use the `Const` keyword, as shown in the following code:

```
Const constant1 = 50
```

Operators

Operators are used to perform operations on variables and constants. These variables and constants are called *operands*. The operators that are used in VB.NET can be classified as follows:

- **Assignment operator.** The assignment operators are used to assign a value to a variable. The assignment operators used with VB.NET are =, +=, -=, *=, /=, and so on. The following syntax shows an example of an assignment operator:

```
Dim Num1 As Integer = 10
Dim Num2 As Integer
Num2 += Num1
```

- **Arithmetic operator.** The arithmetic operators are used to perform arithmetic calculations. The arithmetic operators used with VB.NET are +, -, *, /, ^, and `Mod`. An example of an arithmetic operator follows:

```
Dim Num1 As Integer = 10
Dim Num2 As Integer = 20
Dim Num3 As Integer
Num3 = Num1 + Num3
```

- **Concatenation operators.** The concatenation operators are used to combine two strings. The concatenation operator used with VB.NET is +, as shown in the following example:

```
Dim String1 As String = "John"
Dim String2 As String = "Floyd"
Dim String3 As String
String3 = String1 + String2
```

- **Comparison operators.** The comparison operators are used to compare values stored in variables. The comparison operators used with VB.NET are <, >, =, <>, <=, >=, `is`, and `like`. An example of a comparison operator is shown in the following code:

```
Dim Num1 As Integer = 10
Dim Num2 As Integer = 20
Num2 > Num1
```

◆ **Logical operators.** The logical operators are used to perform logical operations. The logical operators are And, Or, Xor, Not, AndAlso, and OrElse. An example of an And operator is as follows:

```
Dim Exp1 As Boolean
Dim Exp2 As Boolean
Dim Result As Boolean
Result = Exp2 And Exp1
```

Arrays

Arrays are also used to store values. An array stores multiple values of the same data type, and all values in an array are referenced by the same name. The values in an array are called *array elements*. Each element of an array has an index value associated with it. The index of an array starts from 0. Therefore, the fourth value in an array has an index value of 3.

 NOTE

Unlike earlier versions of VB, you cannot change the starting index of an array. Arrays in VB.NET always start from 0.

VB.NET contains a class Array in the System namespace. All arrays that you declare are derived from the Array class. To declare an array, use the following syntax:

```
Dim <name> As <data type> = New <data type> (number of elements) {}
```

To declare an integer type array Array1 with 10 elements, use the following code:

```
Dim Array1 As Integer = New Integer (9) {}
```

After declaring an array, you can initialize it as follows:

```
Dim Array1(4) As Integer
Array1(0) = 1
Array1(1) = 2
Array1(2) = 3
Array1(3) = 4
Array1(4) = 5
```

You can also initialize an array in a single line by using the following code snippet:

```
Dim Array1() As Integer = {1,2,3,4,5}
```

Procedures

A procedure is a set of statements that performs a specific functionality. For example, consider a scenario in which you need to calculate the bonus given to the employees of an organization. Because this functionality is to be performed several times, you can group the statements used to calculate the bonus in a procedure. This enables you to reuse a piece of code in your application.

To create a procedure, use the Sub keyword. The syntax for creating a Sub procedure is as follows:

```
<access modifiers> Sub <name> [<parameter1>, <parameter2>,·······]
            <statements>
End Sub
```

> **NOTE**
>
> A Sub procedure is a special procedure that does not return a value.

We will create a simple procedure that calculates the area of a rectangle. The code for the procedure is as follows:

```
Public Sub Area (Length As Integer, Breadth As Integer)
      Dim Result = Length * Breadth
      MessageBox (Result)
End Sub
```

That procedure calculates the area of a rectangle from its length and breadth, which are sent to the procedure as parameters. The statement that calls the procedure provides the values to these parameters. This statement is called the *calling statement*. The calling statement includes the Call keyword followed by the name of the procedure, as shown in the following example:

```
Call Area (30, 32)
```

The preceding statement calls the Area() method and passes the value to the Length and Breadth parameters.

You will now learn to create a sample application in VB.NET that uses these components.

Creating a Sample Application in VB.NET

VB.NET provides you with templates to create several applications, such as Windows applications, Web applications, Web Services, Console applications, and so on. In this section, you will learn to create a sample Web application in VB.NET. To create a Web application in VB.NET, perform the following steps:

1. Launch Visual Studio .NET from the Programs menu.
2. Select the File, New, Project option. The New Project dialog box is displayed.
3. In the Project Types pane of the New Project dialog box, select the Visual Basic Projects option.
4. In the Templates pane, select the ASP.NET Web Application option.
5. In the Locations text box, select the name of the development server where you want to create the application. Specify the name of the application as SampleWebApplication1. The New Project dialog box is shown in Figure B-5.

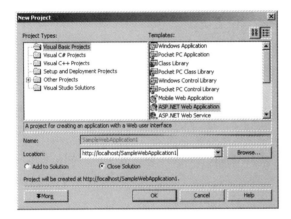

FIGURE B-5 *The New Project dialog box.*

6. Click on the OK button.

When you click on the OK button, Visual Studio .NET creates a framework of the application, as shown in Figure B-6.

Notice that the Web application contains a blank Web form. You can now add controls to this form. Visual Studio .NET provides you with a toolbox that contains several tabs, such as Data, Web Forms, Components, General, and so on. The Web form controls that you can add to a Web application are present in the Web Forms tab of the toolbox.

TIP

If the toolbox is not visible, select the Toolbox option on the View menu.

Adding Controls to the Web Form

The Web form for the sample Web application is shown in Figure B-7.

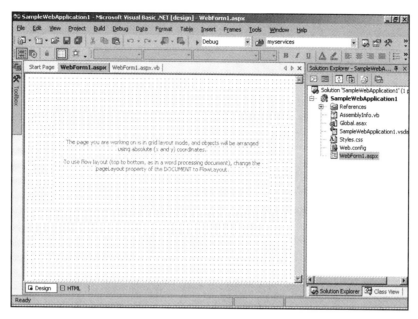

FIGURE B-6 *The framework for SampleWebApplication1.*

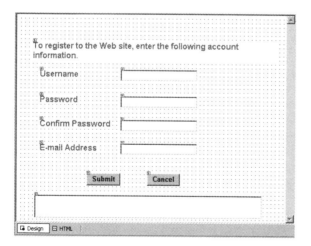

FIGURE B-7 *The Web form for SampleWebApplication1.*

To create the Web form, as shown in the preceding figure, you need to add five label controls, five text box controls, and two button controls to the blank form. To add these controls, drag them from the Web Forms toolbox to the form, and arrange the controls, as shown in Figure B-7.

Next, change the properties of the controls. You can change the properties of the control in the Properties window.

To change the properties of a control, select the control to display its Properties window. The Properties window is shown in Figure B-8.

FIGURE B-8 *The Properties window.*

 NOTE

To view the Properties window, select the Properties window option on the View menu. Alternatively, you can press the F4 key.

Table B-4 discusses the changes that you need to make to the properties of the controls.

Table B-4 Controls in the Web Form

Control Type	Control ID	Properties Changed
Label	Label1	Text: To register to the Web site, enter the following account information:
		ForeColor: `DarkCyan`
		Font: Name: `Arial`
		Font: Bold: `True`
Label	Label2	Text: `Username`
		ForeColor: `DarkCyan`
		Font: Name: `Arial`
		Font: Bold: `True`

Control Type	Control ID	Properties Changed
Label	Label3	Text: `Password`
		ForeColor: `DarkCyan`
		Font: Name: `Arial`
		Font: Bold: `True`
Label	Label4	Text: `Confirm Password`
		ForeColor: `DarkCyan`
		Font: Name: `Arial`
		Font: Bold: `True`
Label	Label5	Text: `E-mail Address`
		ForeColor: `DarkCyan`
		Font: Name: `Arial`
		Font: Bold: `True`
TextBox	TextBox1	None
TextBox	TextBox2	TextMode: `Password`
TextBox	TextBox3	TextMode: `Password`
TextBox	TextBox4	None
TextBox	TextBox5	None
Button	Button1	Text: `Submit`
Button	Button2	Text: `Cancel`

After you add controls to the form, you need to modify the code in the form. Modifying the code involves specifying the functionality that the controls will perform. The following section discusses adding code to the form.

Adding Code to the Web Form

You can modify or add code to the form in the Code window. To access the Code window, double-click on the form or press the F7 key.

When you add controls to the Web form, Visual Studio .NET adds the declarations of the controls to the form, as shown in Figure B-9.

The code that Visual Studio .NET generated contains only the declaration of the controls. You need to explicitly define the functionality for the controls.

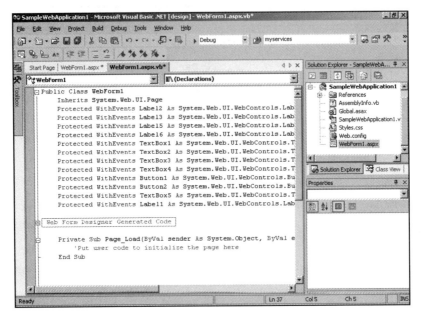

FIGURE B-9 *The code for the Web form.*

Adding Functionality to the Submit Button

When the Web form is run, the user needs to provide the account information. After the user provides the required information, he needs to click on the Submit button. This displays a message to the user in the TextBox control that the information that the user submitted is saved.

To display a message in the TextBox control when the user clicks on the Submit button, add the following control to the `Click` event of the Button control, as shown in the following code snippet:

```
Private Sub Button1_Click(ByVal sender As System.Object, ByVal e As
 System.EventArgs) Handles Button1.Click
        TextBox5.Text = "Your account information has been stored."
End Sub
```

The preceding code contains an event handler, `Button1_Click`, for the `Click` event of the Button control. The `Text` property of the TextBox control is used to dynamically set the text in the TextBox control.

 NOTE

In addition to specifying the text for the TextBox control at design time, you can specify the text at runtime.

Adding Functionality to the Cancel Button

If a user clicks on the Cancel button without submitting the required information, he is given a warning to fill the required information. If the user has specified some information in the TextBox controls but has not submitted the information, the information is lost. To specify this functionality, add the following code to the `Click` event of the Button control:

```
Private Sub Button2_Click(ByVal sender As System.Object, ByVal e As
  System.EventArgs) Handles Button2.Click
        TextBox1.Text = ""
        TextBox2.Text = ""
        TextBox3.Text = ""
        TextBox4.Text = ""
        TextBox5.Text = "To register to the site, you need to provide the
  account information."
End Sub
```

The Code for the Sample Web Application

After you add the code for the Button controls, the complete code for the application is as follows:

```
Public Class WebForm1
    Inherits System.Web.UI.Page
    Protected WithEvents Label2 As System.Web.UI.WebControls.Label
    Protected WithEvents Label3 As System.Web.UI.WebControls.Label
    Protected WithEvents Label5 As System.Web.UI.WebControls.Label
    Protected WithEvents Label6 As System.Web.UI.WebControls.Label
    Protected WithEvents TextBox1 As System.Web.UI.WebControls.TextBox
    Protected WithEvents TextBox2 As System.Web.UI.WebControls.TextBox
    Protected WithEvents TextBox3 As System.Web.UI.WebControls.TextBox
    Protected WithEvents TextBox4 As System.Web.UI.WebControls.TextBox
    Protected WithEvents Button1 As System.Web.UI.WebControls.Button
    Protected WithEvents Button2 As System.Web.UI.WebControls.Button
    Protected WithEvents TextBox5 As System.Web.UI.WebControls.TextBox
    Protected WithEvents Label1 As System.Web.UI.WebControls.Label


#Region " Web Form Designer Generated Code "
    'This call is required by the Web Form Designer.
    <System.Diagnostics.DebuggerStepThrough()> Private Sub InitializeComponent()
    End Sub
```

```
    Private Sub Page_Init(ByVal sender As System.Object, ByVal
e As System.EventArgs) Handles MyBase.Init
        'CODEGEN: This method call is required by the Web Form Designer
        'Do not modify it using the code editor.
        InitializeComponent()
    End Sub
#End Region

    Private Sub Page_Load(ByVal sender As System.Object, ByVal
e As System.EventArgs) Handles MyBase.Load
        'Put user code to initialize the page here
    End Sub

    Private Sub Button1_Click(ByVal sender As System.Object, ByVal
e As System.EventArgs) Handles Button1.Click
        TextBox5.Text = "Your account information has been stored."
    End Sub

    Private Sub Button2_Click(ByVal sender As System.Object, ByVal
e As System.EventArgs) Handles Button2.Click
        TextBox1.Text = ""
        TextBox2.Text = ""
        TextBox3.Text = ""
        TextBox4.Text = ""
        TextBox5.Text = "To register to the site, you need to provide the account
information."
    End Sub
End Class
```

Testing the Web Application

After you create the application, you can test it. To test the application, perform the following steps:

1. Select the Start option on the Debug menu. Alternatively, you can press the F5 key. The Web form opens in the Explorer window, as shown in Figure B-10.

2. Fill in the data in the text boxes and click on the Submit button. A message is displayed in the text box, as shown in Figure B-11.

3. Click on the Cancel button to test it. A warning is displayed, as shown in Figure B-12.

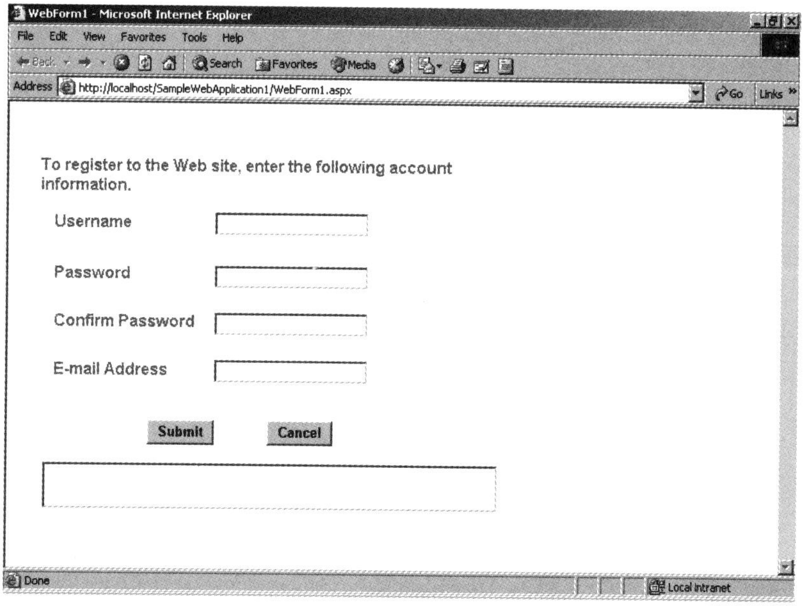

FIGURE B-10 *The Web form in the Explorer window.*

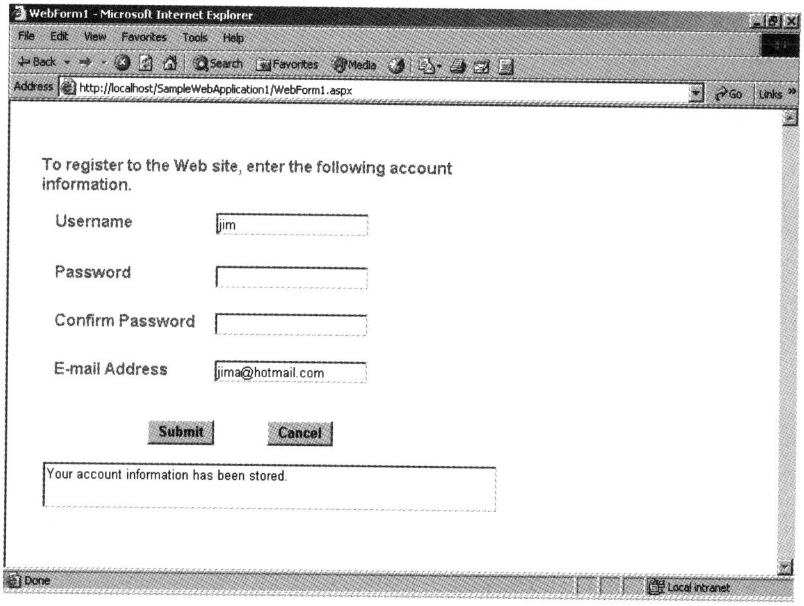

FIGURE B-11 *The message in the text box.*

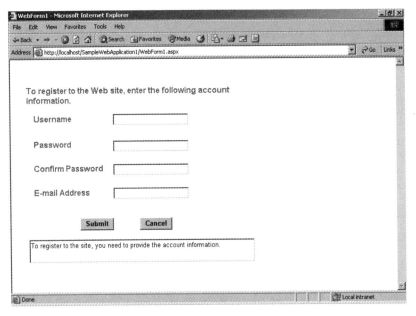

FIGURE B-12 *The warning in the text box.*

Summary

This Appendix introduced you to the .NET Framework and Visual Studio .NET. The .NET Framework is a new platform that Microsoft developed to provide complete support for creating applications. To help you create applications in the .NET Framework, Microsoft has provided a development environment called Visual Studio .NET. This Appendix also taught you about the features and languages of the .NET Framework, which include VB.NET, Visual C# .NET, and Visual C++ .NET.

Finally, you learned about VB.NET in detail. You will learn about Visual C# .NET in Appendix C.

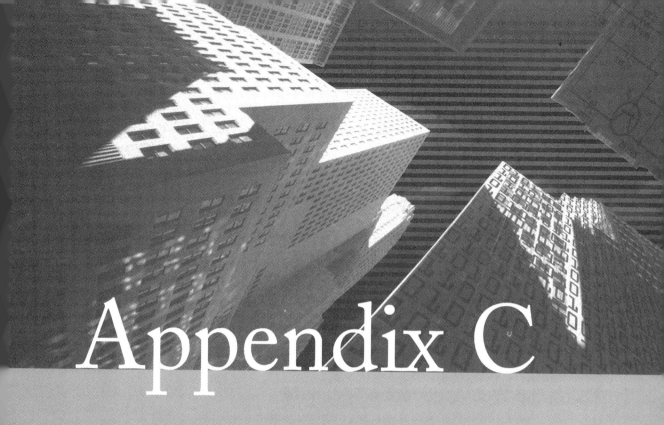

Appendix C

The Visual Studio .NET suite consists of a new object-oriented language called Visual C# .NET, commonly called C#. C# is pronounced as *C sharp* and is based on the .NET platform. Similar to any other programming language of the .NET Framework, C# also benefits from the features of the .NET Framework. You learned about the features of the .NET Framework in Appendix B, "Introduction to Visual Basic .NET."

C# is derived from C and C++. Therefore, learning C# for C or C++ programmers should not be a problem. Although C# is derived from these languages, it is simpler and more productive than its parent languages. This is mainly because the programming concepts that were a problem for the C++ programmers, such as pointers, global functions, and so on, are omitted from C#. In addition, C# includes advanced programming features of programming languages, such as Java and Visual Basic. C# combines the features of several programming languages that programmers can use to create high-level advanced business solutions.

In addition to programming for standalone applications, C# provides you with the convenience of creating applications for a distributed environment. These applications include Web applications and Web services, which run from the Internet. As a result, users worldwide can access information over the network.

In this Appendix, you will learn to create a simple Web application in C#. Then you will look at the components that are used to create an application in C#. Finally, you will compare a C# application with a VB.NET application.

Create a Web Application in C#

In Appendix B, you created a simple VB.NET Web application that included controls to accept user input. You will now create the same application in C#. Doing this enables you to appreciate the similarities between creating an application in the two .NET languages: C# and VB.NET.

Visual Studio .NET provides you with tools to create different applications in C#. Using these tools, you can create an application easily and efficiently. The most important tools are the templates that Visual Studio .NET provides to create various applications. You will learn about these project templates in the section "Templates That C# Provides."

Creating a Web Application by Using the Web Application Template

To access the ASP.NET Web application template, perform the following steps:

1. Launch Visual Studio .NET from the Programs menu.
2. Select the File, New, Project option. The New Projects dialog box is displayed.
3. In the Projects pane, select the Visual C# .NET option. Visual Studio .NET displays a list of projects that you can create in C#. These projects are shown in Figure C-1.

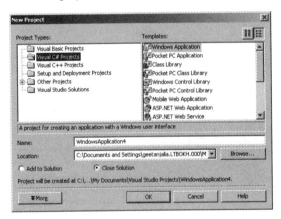

FIGURE C-1 *The projects in C#.*

4. In the Templates pane, select the ASP.NET Web Application project option.
5. In the Location text box, specify the location of the Web development server.
6. Click on the OK button.

Templates That C# Provides

When you use a template to create an application in C#, Visual Studio .NET creates a framework for the application. This framework includes a blank form, default files, and default code. In addition, Visual Studio .NET provides the controls that you can add to the form.

The following list discusses the templates that Visual Studio .NET provides:

◆ **Console Applications.** These are standalone applications that do not have a graphical interface. The output of the console application is sent to the console window.

◆ **Windows Applications.** These are standalone applications that run locally on a user's computer. A Windows application contains a Windows form to which you can add Windows Form controls. These controls are used to display text and images, accept user inputs, and so on.

◆ **Windows Control Library.** This is a project template that is used to create custom controls. You can use these custom controls in a Windows application.

◆ **Windows Service.** These applications are the executable applications that are installed as a service. Similar to console applications, Windows services do not have an interface and can be programmed to start when you start your computer.

◆ **ASP.NET Web Applications and ASP.NET Web Services.** Visual Studio .NET provides you with the ASP.NET technology that you can use to create Web services and Web applications that run on the Web. You can use the ASP.NET technology to create Web forms, which are an interface of a Web application. A Web service does not have an interface.

◆ **Mobile applications.** These applications are accessible from a mobile device, such as a mobile phone, a Pocket PC, and so on. These applications allow you to access a Web site from your mobile device. To create a mobile application in Visual Studio .NET, you need to install the Microsoft Mobile Internet Toolkit. By using this toolkit, you can create, test, and deploy a mobile application.

◆ **Class Library.** In addition to the .NET base class library, you can create a class library for your application. This class library would include all the classes, interfaces, structs, and value types that the application requires.

Default Code That Visual Studio .NET Creates

When you create an application by using the Visual Studio .NET templates, Visual Studio .NET creates some code for the application. You can then modify the code as required.

When Visual Studio .NET creates a framework for the application, the application opens in the Design view. The code for the application is contained in the Code window. To view the Code window, double-click on the form. Alternatively, press the F7 key.

The default code for the Web application is as follows:

```
using System.Web;
using System.Web.SessionState;
```

```csharp
using System.Web.UI;
using System.Web.UI.WebControls;
using System.Web.UI.HtmlControls;

namespace SampleWebApplication2
{
/// <summary>
/// Summary description for WebForm1.
/// </summary>
    public class WebForm1 : System.Web.UI.Page
    {
        private void Page_Load(object sender, System.EventArgs e)
        {
            // Put user code to initialize the page here
        }

        #region Web Form Designer generated code
        override protected void OnInit(EventArgs e)
        {
            // CODEGEN: This call is required by the ASP.NET Web Form Designer.

            InitializeComponent();
            base.OnInit(e);
        }

        /// <summary>
        /// Required method for Designer support - do not modify
        /// the contents of this method with the code editor.
        /// </summary>
        private void InitializeComponent()
        {
            this.Load += new System.EventHandler(this.Page_Load);
        }
        #endregion
    }
}
```

We will now discuss the components that are used in the preceding code.

Namespaces

The code for the application starts with the `using` statement. The `using` statement allows you to include a namespace in your application. A namespace is a collection of related classes, structs, interfaces, enumerations, value types, and so on. Namespaces in Visual Studio .NET can also be nested. This implies that a namespace can include other namespaces.

All applications in Visual Studio .NET include the `System` namespace by default. In addition, Visual Studio .NET includes other namespaces, such as `System.Collections`, `System.Data`, `System.Web`, and so on. All these namespaces are included in the `System` namespace and contain related classes.

The concept of including classes in a namespace was developed because the .NET base class library includes several thousand classes. In addition, because C# is an object-oriented language, users can create custom classes. While creating a class, users can assign any name to the class. It is likely that two or more users will create classes with the same name, which might cause confusion for the compiler. To avoid this confusion, classes are included within namespaces.

Aliases

Consider a situation in which you need to call a method that is contained within a nested class, which is contained within a nested namespace, as shown in the following example:

```
NamespaceA
{
        NamespaceB
        {
            ClassA
            {
                    ClassB
                {
                            Method1
                            {
                                 - - - - - - - - - - -
                            }
                    }
                }
            }
        }
}
```

In this case, to access `Method1()`, you need to use the fully qualified name of the method, as shown in the following code snippet:

```
NamespaceA.NamespaceB.ClassA.ClassB.Method1();
```

Writing the fully qualified name in your application repeatedly can be tiring. One way to avoid doing this is by using the using keyword in the beginning of the application, as follows:

```
using NamespaceA;
```

Another solution is to create an alias for the namespace, as follows:

```
using alias1 = NamespaceA;
```

In addition to creating an alias for a namespace, you can create an alias for the class, as shown in the following statement:

```
using alias1 = NamespaceA.NamespaceB.ClassA.ClassB;
```

Therefore, to refer to Method1(), you can use alias1, as shown in the following statement:

```
alias1.Method1();
```

Creating Namespaces

In the preceding examples, we used a namespace called NamespaceA, which is not an existing namespace. This implies that you can create a namespace in C#. To create a namespace, use the following statement:

```
Namocpace NamespaceA
{
        . . . . . . . . . . .
}
```

The preceding syntax uses the namespace keyword to create a namespace in C#. Within the declaration for the namespace, you can include other namespaces, classes, and so on.

As you have seen, when you create an application in C#, Visual Studio .NET includes several default namespaces in the application. In addition, it creates a custom namespace in the application with the same name as that of the application. For example, the sample Web application that you have created contains a namespace like this:

```
namespace SampleWebApplication2
{
        . . . . . . . . . . .
}
```

All the classes and methods that are used with the Web application are contained within this namespace.

Classes

Inside the `SampleWebApplication2` namespace, Visual Studio .NET creates a default class `WebForm1`, which is derived from the `System.Web.UI.Page` class.

```
public class WebForm1 : System.Web.UI.Page
{
        . . . . . . . . . .
}
```

A class is a data structure that contains class members, such as data and methods. Data is the information that is contained in the class, and methods define the functionality that is performed on the data.

Creating Classes

You can create classes in C# by using the following syntax:

```
<modifier> class <name>
{
        . . . . . . . . . .
}
```

Consider the following example:

```
Public class WebForm1
{
        . . . . . . . . . .
}
```

In the preceding code, `public` is the access modifier, `class` is the keyword that is used to create classes, and `WebForm1` is the name of the class.

 NOTE

The access modifiers that C# supports are `public`, `protected`, `private`, `internal`, `abstract`, and `sealed`.

Inheriting Classes

As discussed earlier, the .NET Framework contains a .NET base class library that contains several thousand classes. You can use these classes in your application. In addition, you can derive classes from these classes. The class that is derived from a base class is called a *derived class*. The syntax for deriving a class from a base class is as follows:

```
class <derived class> : <base class>
```

For example, consider the WebForm1 class, which is derived from the Page class as follows:

```
public class WebForm1 : System.Web.UI.Page
{
        . . . . . . . . . .
}
```

Deriving WebForm1 from the Page class enables the WebForm1 class to reuse the data and methods of the Page class. By default, all methods of the base class are accessible to the derived class. However, to access the methods of the base class in the derived class, you need to create an instance of the base class in the derived class, as shown in the following statement:

```
<class name> <object name> = new <class name>();
```

An instance of a class is called an object. An object is the building block of all applications in any object-oriented language, such as C# and VB.NET.

For example, to create an instance of the WebForm1 class, you can use the following syntax:

```
WebForm1 object1 = new WebForm1();
```

You can now use object1 to access any method of the Page class.

The new Keyword

A derived class implicitly inherits all methods of the base class. However, if required, you can hide a method of the base class from its derived class. For example, consider a base class, ClassA, which contains a method, Method1(), as shown:

```
class ClassA
{
        public void Method1
        {
                . . . . . . . . . .
        }
}
```

Now derive a class, ClassB, from ClassA and declare another method with the same name, Method1(), in ClassB, as shown in the following code:

```
class ClassB : ClassA
{
        public void Method1
        {
                . . . . . . . . . .
```

```
        }
}
```

The preceding code creates a method, Method1(), with the same signature as that of the base class method. When a compiler finds such a method, it generates a warning. To suppress the warning, you can use the new keyword. To hide the base class method from the derived class, create the derived class method, as shown in the following code snippet:

```
class ClassB : ClassA
{
        new public void Method1
        {
                - - - - - - - - - -
        }
}
```

In addition to methods, a class contains a constructor. The following section discusses constructors in detail.

Constructors

A class contains a default constructor with the same name as that of the class. A constructor is a public method that does not return a value and contains declarations of the objects used in a class. The syntax for a constructor is as follows:

```
public <constructor name>
{
        - - - - - - - - - -
}
```

NOTE

In addition to the default constructor, you can create a custom constructor for a class in C#.

When you create an instance of a class, the default constructor of the class is implicitly invoked. In addition, a constructor of a base class is not implicitly inherited by its derived classes.

Methods

The WebForm1 class in a Web application contains a private void method Page_Load(). This method contains code for initializing the form when the application is run. For example, you need to display a welcome message to a user who visits the Web page. You can include the code to display the welcome message in the Page_Load() method, as shown:

```
private void Page_Load(object sender, System.EventArgs e)
{
        TextBox1.Text = "Welcome to the Web Page.";
        // Put user code to initialize the page here
}
```

A method is an important component of a class that includes statements to perform an operation on the data contained in the class. A method is a set of statements that is referred by a common name, called the *method name*.

Creating Methods

To declare a method in C#, you use the following statement:

```
<modifier> <return type> <method name> (<parameter list>)
{
        . . . . . . . . . .
}
```

In the preceding syntax, the `<modifier>` is the access modifier that defines the scope of the method. For example, if you declare a method as `public`, you can access the method from anywhere. However, a method declared as `private` can only be accessed from within the class in which it is created. Access modifiers for a method are similar to that of the class.

The `<return type>` of the method defines the data type of the value that the method returns.

NOTE

A method with the return type of `void` does not return a value.

Next, a method declaration statement includes a name of the method followed by a list of parameters that are passed to the method. Parameters are passed to a method to supply values to a method. For example, consider the following method that calculates the interest:

```
public float CalculateInterest (float initialAmount, float finalAmount)
{
        float Interest;
        interest = finalAmount - initialAmount;
        return Interest;
}
```

The preceding code creates a `public` method called `CalculateInterest()` that returns a `float` type value called `Interest`. As you can see, the `CalculateInterest()` method takes two `float` type parameters: `initialAmount` and `finalAmount`. These parameters are passed as values to the method. The following section discusses passing parameters to a method.

Passing Parameters

C# allows you to pass parameters to a method in four ways, as discussed in the following list:

◆ **By value.** When a parameter is passed by value to a method, a copy of the variable is made. As a result, the method does not have access to the original copy of the variable. If the value of the variable is changed in the method, the change is made only to the copy of the variable. However, the original variable remains unaffected. This is the default method of passing parameters to a method, as shown in the following example:

```
object1.Method1(paramter1, parameter2);
```

In the preceding syntax, `object1` is the instance of the class that calls the method.

NOTE

All methods except the `static` methods can be called only by using the instance of a class. However, the `static` methods are called by the actual class.

◆ **By reference.** When a parameter is passed by reference to a method, the method contains a reference to the original variable. Therefore, if the value of the variable changes during the execution of the program, the change is made to the original value. To pass a parameter by reference to a method, use the `ref` keyword, as shown in the following syntax:

```
object1.Method1(parameter1, ref parameter2);
```

In the preceding syntax, `parameter1` is passed by value, and `parameter2` is passed by reference.

◆ **By parameter arrays.** You can pass an array as a parameter to a method. To do so, use `parameter` arrays, as shown in the following syntax:

```
object1.Method1(params <data type>[] paramater1);
```

The preceding syntax uses the `params` keyword to pass `parameter1` as an array to `Method1()`. The data type defines the type of the array.

TIP

You can only pass a one-dimensional array as a parameter to a method. If you pass multiple parameters to a method, one of which is a `parameter` array, the parameter array should be the last in the parameter list, as shown in the following statement:

```
object1.Method1(parameter1, params <data type>[] paramater2);
```

◆ **By output parameters.** You need to initialize all variables that are declared in C# before you use them. However, parameters that are passed with an `out` keyword are an exception because when a method returns a value, this value overwrites the initial value of the variable. Therefore, initializing variables that are returned by a method is a waste of memory. To avoid this, you can declare a variable returned by a method as an output parameter, as shown in the following statement:

```
object1.Method1(out paramter1);
```

Variables

Variables in a programming language store data. A data type defines the type of data that is stored in a variable. A variable in C# is declared by using the following syntax:

```
<access modifiers> <data type> <variable name>;
```

After declaring a variable, you need to initialize it. When a variable is declared, it stores a value by default. For example, an `integer` type variable stores the value `0`, and a `Boolean` type variable stores the value `False`. When you initialize a variable, the default value in the variable is overwritten. To initialize a variable, use the following syntax:

```
public string Variable1;
Variable1 = "Sample string";
```

You can also declare and initialize a variable in one statement, as shown in the following statement:

```
public string Variable1 = "Sample string";
```

In addition, you can declare multiple variables of the same data type in a single statement as follows:

```
public string Variable1, Variable2;
```

NOTE

Some of the data types that C# supports include `integer`, `character`, `string`, `Boolean`, `byte`, `sbyte`, `float`, `double`, `object`, `short`, and `long`.

The access modifiers that you can use with variables in C# are `public`, `private`, `protected`, `internal`, `static`, and `read-only`.

After you understand the default code, you can proceed with the creation of the sample Web application.

Adding Controls to a Web Form

The procedure to add controls to the Web form is similar in both C# and VB.NET. Therefore, as discussed in Appendix B, add five text boxes, five labels, and two Button controls to the form. When you add controls to the form, Visual Studio .NET automatically adds the declarations of the controls to the code, as shown in Figure C-2.

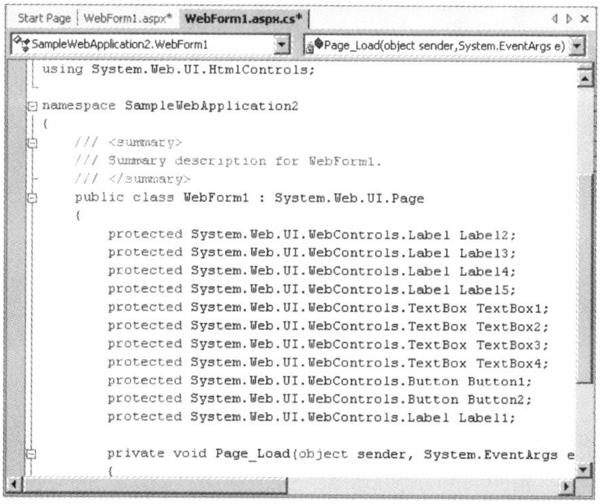

FIGURE C-2 *The declaration of the controls in a C# application.*

Changing Properties of Controls in a Web Form

You can change the properties of the controls, as discussed in Table C-1. The procedure for changing the properties of the controls in C# is similar to that in VB.NET.

Table B-4 Controls in the Web Form

Control Type	Control ID	Properties Changed
Label	Label1	Text: `To register to the Web site, enter the following account information:`
		ForeColor: `DarkCyan`
		Font: Name: `Arial`
		Font: Bold: `True`
Label	Label2	Text: `Username`
		ForeColor: `DarkCyan`
		Font: Name: `Arial`
		Font: Bold: `True`

(continues...)

Control Type	Control ID	Properties Changed
Label	Label3	Text: Password
		ForeColor: DarkCyan
		Font: Name: Arial
		Font: Bold: True
Label	Label4	Text: Confirm Password
		ForeColor: DarkCyan
		Font: Name: Arial
		Font: Bold: True
Label	Label5	Text: E-mail Address
		ForeColor: DarkCyan
		Font: Name: Arial
		Font: Bold: True
TextBox	TextBox1	None
TextBox	TextBox2	TextMode: Password
TextBox	TextBox3	TextMode: Password
TextBox	TextBox4	None
TextBox	TextBox5	None
Button	Button1	Text: Submit
Button	Button2	Text: Cancel

After you change the properties of the controls, the Web form should look like Figure C-3.

Adding Code to a Web Form

The final step to creating an application is to add code to the Button controls.

Adding Code to the Submit Button

To enable the application to perform a specified action when a user clicks on the Submit button, you need to add code to the Click event of the Button control, as shown in the following code:

```
private void Button1_Click(object sender, System.EventArgs e)
{
```

```
        TextBox5.Text = "Your account information has been stored.";
}
```

As you can see, there is no difference in writing a code in VB.NET and C#. The Click event in both languages takes the same parameters. However, the syntax is different. In addition, all statements in C# end with a semi-colon (;), which is in contrast to the statements in VB.NET, which do not.

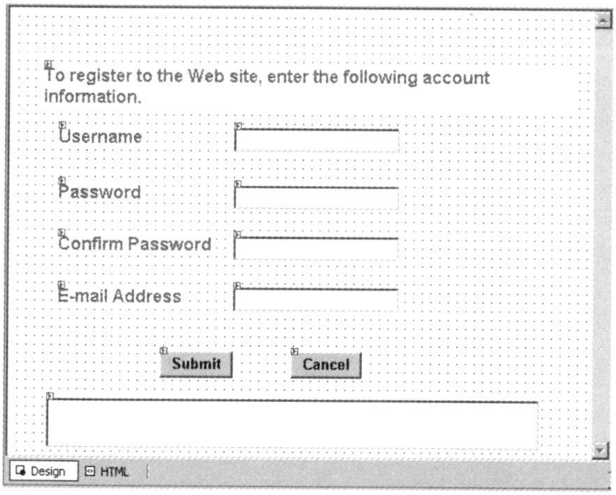

FIGURE C-3 *The Web form in a C# application.*

Adding Code to the Cancel Button

Similar to adding code to the Cancel button in VB.NET, you can add code in C#. The code for the Cancel button in C# is as follows:

```
private void Button2_Click(object sender, System.EventArgs e)
{
        TextBox1.Text = "";
        TextBox2.Text = "";
        TextBox3.Text = "";
        TextBox4.Text = "";
        TextBox5.Text = "To register to the site, you need to provide the
 account information.";
}
```

Testing the Web Application

You can test the sample Web application in C# by following the same steps as in VB.NET. When you run the application, the application looks like Figure C-4.

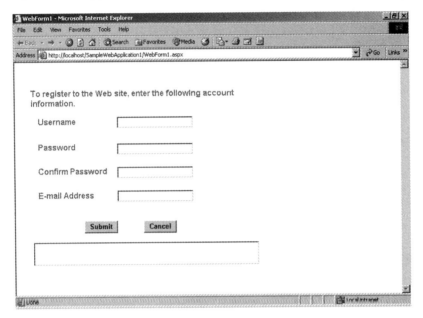

FIGURE C-4 *The Web form in an Explorer window.*

Summary

In this appendix, you were introduced to another .NET language: C#. C# is a new object-oriented language that is present in the Visual Studio .NET suite. You also created a sample Web application in C# and learned about the components of the C# language. These components include namespaces, classes, methods, and variables.

Finally, you looked at the similarities and the differences between creating an application in VB.NET and C#. The procedure for creating an application in C# and VB.NET is the same, but the syntax for the code is different. Therefore, you can easily convert an application in C# to an application in VB.NET, and vice versa.

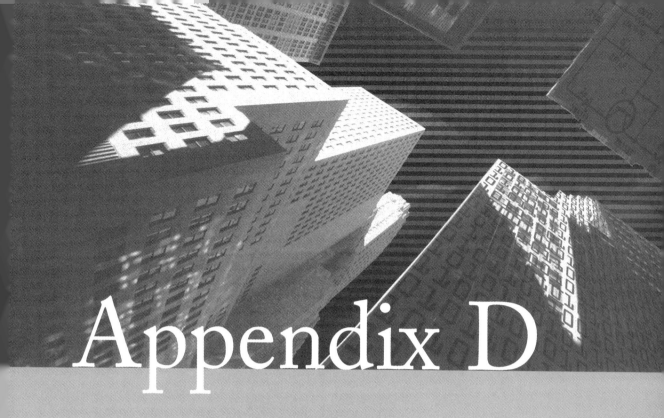

Appendix D

The Internet is a huge reservoir of data. Unfortunately, users can't get the optimal benefits from the data, technology, and other resources that are available on the Internet mainly because the available technologies are not able to communicate with each other, thereby making it difficult for the technologies to work together. To allow the technologies, data, and other resources to integrate with each other, Microsoft has introduced a set of XML Web services called .NET My Services.

This chapter introduces you to .NET My Services. You will learn about the advantages and the scenarios in which you can use .NET My Services. You also will learn about the .NET My Services architecture and how to implement security in the Web services present in .NET My Services.

Overview of .NET My Services

.NET My Services is part of the .NET initiative that consists of 15 (at present) XML Web services. These Web services are created to enable you to benefit from the resources and information that are available on the Internet. To make this data readily available to you, .NET My Services stores this data at a central location.

.NET My Services is the latest Web-based technology that is oriented toward the users. .NET My Services enables users to manage and control the tasks that they perform in everyday life. For example, consider a situation in which you want to maintain a list of your contacts. You can easily do this by using an XML Web service provided in the .NET My Services collection.

Consider another situation in which you want to set appointments with your contacts based on your daily schedule. To do this, you need a calendar, which is also one of the Web services that are available in the .NET My Services suite. Let's say that you want to prepare a list of your favorite Web sites and forward the list to some of your contacts. You can do all this by integrating various Web services that come as part of .NET My Services. You will learn about these XML Web services in detail in the later section titled "The Web Services Present in .NET My Services."

In addition to allowing you to perform everyday tasks, .NET My Services enables you to manage and control your personal data by providing a level of personalization and security of your data. The Web services that allow you to save a list of your personal contacts and favorite Web sites are examples of services that allow you to maintain your personal data safely.

As you know, with the increasing popularity of the Internet, it has become necessary to access data from anywhere, anytime, and from any device. Microsoft developed .NET My Services with this vision in mind. Therefore, .NET My Services are built on the .NET platform by using the .NET technologies. This makes the Web services in .NET My Services interoperable across applications and platforms.

In addition, you can access the .NET My Services Web services from any device ranging from mobile devices to regular PCs. This enables you to conveniently perform your everyday activities from any device, such as a mobile phone, smart phone, PDA, Pocket PC, and so on. For example, you can book your air tickets, access any kind of list, and access your personal mail and documents from any device.

Advantages That .NET My Services Offers

There are several scenarios in which you can benefit from the advantages of the Web services in .NET My Services. We will first discuss the advantages of .NET My Services and then discuss the scenarios in which you can use these services. The following list discusses the advantages of .NET My Services:

- ◆ The first and foremost advantage of .NET My Services is that it was developed with a user-centric approach. .NET My Services contains a set of XML Web services that you can use to perform your everyday activities. In addition, .NET My Services allows you to maintain your data on the Internet. You can then securely access this data from several devices or applications by using the .NET My Services secure subscriptions.

◆ NET My Services allows you to control and integrate several technologies and data at a central location. For example, you can maintain all data on the Internet, thereby preventing you from manually copying data from one device to another. In addition, you can securely maintain your personal data and control it by specifying the users with whom you want to share your personal data. To do this, .NET My Services works on an affirmative consent model. This means that when a user hosts some data, the user is the owner of the data. Therefore, any modifications to the data, the users who can access the data, and so on cannot happen without the consent of the owner. The owner has full control of the data.

◆ Despite operating on the affirmative consent model, the consent of the owner has a limited scope because the permissions that the owner assigns to the data have a short lifetime, after which they expire. As a solution to this, .NET My Services uses security mechanisms to prevent unauthorized users from accessing the legal data (the data that a user owns).

◆ .NET My Services allows you to access various Web sites, Web applications, and other applications by using a single signon service called the .NET Passport service. You will learn about the .NET Passport service in the later section titled "Interaction of the Components of the .NET My Services Architecture."

◆ The .NET Passport login service allows you to receive important notification messages that any Web service present in the .NET My Services sends. For example, you have added a reminder for an important meeting or subscribed to a news service. You can receive messages from these services on any device based on your preferences. The instant messaging service of .NET My Services is more flexible than any other chat application that is available today.

◆ .NET My Services allows you to save your preferences with a specific identity, which is not restricted to individuals but is assigned for groups and organizations who access the .NET My Services Web services. Every group or organization is assigned a unique identification number called the Personal Unique Identifier (PUID). The PUID that is assigned to a member is based on an e-mail address and forms the global Internet identity for the member. The information about the PUID of a user is saved in the .NET Profile service.

 TIP

Any member can have multiple PUIDs based on the number of e-mail addresses. For example, you might have different e-mail addresses for your personal and official mails. Therefore, you will have different PUIDs for saving your personal and official preferences.

◆ .NET My Services uses XML and SOAP messages to deliver the services to a user. As you know, both XML and SOAP are open Internet standards; therefore, Web services in the .NET My Services are interoperable services that you can access from any device or application that is running on any platform that supports SOAP and XML.

Scenarios in Which .NET My Services Web Services Are Used

Based on the previously discussed advantages, you can use .NET My Services Web services in several scenarios. The following list discusses some of these common scenarios:

◆ Consider a scenario in which you shop on multiple e-commerce sites and have your profile made on all these sites. Now consider that you change your current job and join a new office. In this case, you need to update your new office information on all sites, which is time-consuming. To avoid this, you can save your profile information that includes your office address, telephone, and e-mail address in a central location, such as the Web services that .NET My Services provides. Now all Web sites on which you want to shop can access the data from this central location and retrieve updated data.

◆ Consider another scenario in which you are traveling all across the U.S. and need to carry some important data with you. One way to do this is to carry the data in a storage medium, such as floppy or compact discs. You make some changes to the data, and you need to replicate the changes in the storage medium and in all other places that have accessed your data from the storage medium. To prevent this, you can make your data available on the Internet. In addition, when you update the data on the Internet site, the updated data is readily accessible to all users who have the rights to access the site.

◆ Consider another scenario in which you need to reserve your air tickets based on your appointments made in the calendar. In addition, you have some personal preferences of air flights, timings, and so on. Then a .NET My Services Web service, called the .NET travel service, displays the available options based on your individual preferences, itinerary, and preferred schedule and books the tickets for you. You can also share all this information with the people with whom you plan to visit during your trip.

◆ Some users store their data in several locations or on multiple devices. The .NET My Services Web services can be used to link the isolated data or store the data at a central location that any device can access at any time.

The .NET My Services Architecture

The architecture of .NET My Services is similar to any other Web services architecture, and it involves the following two components:

◆ .NET My Services endpoints
◆ .NET My Services Web services

You can better understand the architecture of the Web service by looking at Figure D-1.

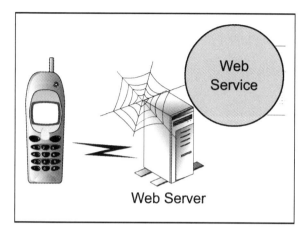

FIGURE D-1 *The .NET My Services architecture.*

We will now discuss these components in detail.

The .NET My Services Endpoints

As already discussed, you can access a .NET My Services Web service from any application, platform, service, or device. All these are collectively called .NET My Services endpoints. The .NET My Services endpoints include the .NET My Services-enabled devices or applications, such as mobile phones, Pocket PCs, PDAs, and Palm Pilots. These endpoints can use an application to directly connect to a .NET My Services Web service; therefore, you can easily access a .NET My Services Web service by using these endpoints.

To access the .NET My Services Web service, you need to develop applications that run on these endpoints. The following sections discuss some of the commonly used endpoints in detail.

Mobile Phones

Mobile phones are the most commonly used wireless devices that are lightweight, easy to use, and affordable. You can develop mobile phone applications that allow you to directly connect to the .NET My Services Web services. You learned to create a mobile application in Chapter 17, "Creating a Mobile Application That Consumes a Web Service." In that chapter, you used the Microsoft Mobile Internet toolkit to create a mobile application.

However, to access a .NET My Services Web service from your mobile phone, the phone should be .NET My Services-enabled. Figure D-2 shows a .NET My Services-enabled mobile phone.

FIGURE D-2 *The .NET My Services-enabled mobile phone.*

 NOTE

It is essential to note that you can access the same service from various devices without changing the basic platform of the service. However, when the service is accessed, the compiler converts the service to a code that the device can understand.

Personal Digital Assistants (PDAs)

The term *PDA* refers to any hand-held device that allows you to store and retrieve personal and business information, such as schedules and address book information. PDAs are standalone, wireless devices that either do not have a keyboard or use a small keyboard. Some PDAs that do not have a keyboard use a pen-based entry and navigation system. These PDAs contain an electronically sensitive pad, which can receive and interpret handwriting. PDAs are expensive, large, heavy devices that you can integrate with other handheld devices, such as mobile phones, pagers, and laptops. Figure D-3 shows a sample PDA.

FIGURE D-3 *A sample PDA.*

Pocket PCs

A Pocket PC is software that PDAs use to function. PDAs use the Pocket PC OS application components that are created to target PDAs. These components include a set of system components from the Windows CE OS and various applications, such as Microsoft Pocket Internet Explorer, Microsoft Pocket Word, Microsoft Pocket Excel, and Microsoft Pocket Outlook.

Pocket PCs run on the Windows CE operating system, which consists of a set of components used to create an OS. You can use the Smart Device Extensions SDK, which is part of Visual Studio .NET, to create a Pocket PC application. The Smart Device Extensions SDK includes the project templates that target PDAs. Figure D-4 shows an example of a Pocket PC.

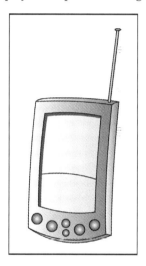

FIGURE D-4 *A sample Pocket PC.*

The Web Services Present in .NET My Services

The .NET My Services Web services are XML Web services that are based on industry standards, such as SOAP and XML. Therefore, these services are interoperable and do not require a runtime to be accessed. To simplify the access of these Web services, Microsoft Visual Studio .NET, Microsoft .NET Enterprise Servers, and Microsoft .NET Framework are used. In addition, these tools provide support for creating applications that can access the .NET My Services Web services.

As already discussed, .NET My Services is a collection of 15 Web services. Therefore, it forms a platform, called the .NET My Services platform, for reusing Web services. Similar to any other XML Web service, you can either reuse these Web services or modify them to adapt to your requirements. Therefore, the .NET My Services platform can be compared to any other operating system because an operating system is a platform on which you can create applications. Similarly, .NET My Services is a platform on which you can create, reuse, or modify existing Web services.

The .NET My Services platform provides an infrastructure on which you can easily create Web services. The following list discusses the features of the .NET My Services platform:

◆ Authenticates users who try to log on to a Web service

◆ Provides security to a Web service

◆ Processes the SOAP messages that are transferred between the Web service and the calling application

◆ Sends notification messages to the users and applications

◆ Monitors users and applications

◆ Creates log files

The XML Web services that are available in the first release of the .NET My Services platform are shown in the following list:

◆ .NET Services

◆ .NET Contacts

◆ .NET Calendar

◆ .NET FavoriteWebSites

◆ .NET Categories

◆ .NET Lists

◆ .NET Alerts

◆ .NET Documents

◆ .NET Inbox

◆ .NET ApplicationSettings

◆ .NET Presence

◆ .NET Devices

◆ .NET Locations

◆ .NET Profile

◆ .NET Wallet

We will now discuss these services in detail.

.NET Services

You might subscribe to several Web services. You can store the information about all these services in the .NET Services Web service. For example, you are part of the organization and have subscribed to a Web service. Similarly, your colleagues might have subscribed to the same or other Web services. Therefore, you can maintain a list of all Web services to which you and other members of your organization have subscribed. This would help you and your colleagues benefit from the subscribed Web services whenever required.

.NET Contacts

You might want to store a list of your personal and business contacts. You can store this list by using the .NET Contacts service. This service is similar to the buddy list that you create in MSN Messenger or the Calendar feature of Microsoft Outlook. In addition to saving a list of contacts, you can store personal and business information about these contacts.

A user who has subscribed to .NET My Services has one Contacts document that contains multiple contact records. The .NET Contacts service reflects these contact records. In addition, the .NET Contacts service allows you to categorize contacts, such as personal, business, and so on.

The .NET Contacts service also allows you to share your contact information with other users. For this, you can grant rights to other users to access your contact information. For example, if you are going on leave, you can make the business contacts accessible to your colleagues in your absence. However, if you want, you can prevent another user from modifying your contact information.

.NET Calendar

The .NET Calendar service allows you to plan your day or create a schedule on a daily basis. You can also do this by using Microsoft Outlook. With Microsoft Outlook, you can access the information only from your PC. With .NET Calendar service, you can create and store your schedule at a central location from which you and others can access the information. In addition, you can access this information from any device, such as your mobile phone.

You can integrate the .NET Calendar service with other .NET My Services Web services. For example, you can integrate the .NET Calendar service with the .NET Contacts service to set appointments with the members of the contact list. You also can use the .NET Alerts service to remind you of your appointments. You will learn about the .NET Alerts service in the later section titled ".NET Alerts."

.NET FavoriteWebSites

While you're surfing on the Internet, you can visit several sites and save the sites that you like as Favorites in the Web browser. You can also do this by using the .NET FavoriteWebSites service. Using the .NET FavoriteWebSites service enables you to access your list of favorite sites from any device. In addition, you can organize the list of favorite sites according to their usage.

Consider a situation in which a marketing manager of a department store has performed an online survey by accessing the Web sites of different department stores and stored these sites as favorites with the Favorites feature of Internet Explorer. The manager needs to share this data with their suppliers in various locations, but he can't because the addresses of the favorite sites are maintained on the manager's PC. If the manager would have used the .NET FavoriteWebSites service to maintain a list of favorite sites, he would have been able to access the information from any device, such as a mobile phone or the supplier's PC.

.NET Categories

The .NET Categories service allows you to group related documents in the form of categories. It stores a standard list of categories that is available across all .NET services. You can integrate the .NET Categories service with other .NET services. For example, you can group various contacts, lists, or profile information as required.

.NET Lists

In your everyday life, you prepare several lists, such as a list of tasks you want to accomplish on the weekend, a birthday list for the current month, a weekly grocery list, and so on. All these lists can be stored in the .NET Lists service.

.NET Alerts

.NET My Services can send instant messages to its users by using the .NET Alerts service. In addition to the .NET My Services Web services, several applications, XML Web services, and Web sites can use the .NET Alerts service to send notification messages to the users. You can specify the device and the time at which the service should send the message. You also can integrate this service with other services to customize the usage.

For example, you can use the .NET Calendar service to decide on a time when you and your colleagues are free for a birthday celebration. Next, you can use the .NET Alerts service to send a message about the birthday celebration to the members who are specified in your contact list, which is created using the .NET Contacts service.

.NET Documents

As the name suggests, the .NET Documents service is used to store and group several documents that you can access from several devices. You can store all personal and business documents safely by using the .NET Documents service. In addition, you can give rights to users to access your documents, which ensures safety of your documents because only authorized users can access the documents.

.NET Inbox

With the development of the .NET Inbox service, you are no longer limited to accessing your e-mails from your PC or laptop. Now you can access your e-mails from any device from which you can log on to the .NET My Services Web services.

.NET ApplicationSettings

You can use the .NET ApplicationSettings service to store the preferred system settings, such as the desktop settings, screensavers, menu bars, button colors, and so on. Therefore, whenever you log in with your login information, the system is automatically updated according to the settings that are defined in the .NET ApplicationSettings service.

.NET Presence

As discussed earlier, you can receive notification messages from the .NET services. For this, you need to specify the address at which you want to receive the messages. This address is specified in the .NET Presence service.

.NET Devices

You might use several devices, such as a mobile phone, pager, PDA, laptop, and so on in your everyday life. The information about the settings, configuration, and functionalities of these devices is stored in the .NET Devices service.

.NET Locations

The .NET Locations service is used to specify your present physical location. For example, when you are at home, you can specify your location as At Home, and when you are in the office, you can specify the location as At Work. This will enable authorized users to contact you. You also can integrate this service with the .NET Contacts service to enable the members in the contacts list to know your present location.

.NET Profile

Your personal information is stored in the .NET Profile service. This information includes your name, age, address, phone numbers, birthday, e-mail address, and so on. When you access any of the .NET services, your profile is created in a document called the .NET Profile service document. You can access this document by using the .NET Profile service. You can maintain and protect your profile information by specifying the users who can access this information. You can also specify Web sites and applications that can access this information.

We discussed a scenario in which a user changed the organization and needed to update the new address of the organization for all sites for which he had registered. Instead of going to all this trouble, the user can simply update the information in the .NET Profile service, and all sites can automatically pick the updated information from the .NET Profile service.

.NET Wallet

Consider a user who frequently shops on various sites on the Internet. The profile information of the user can be accessed from the .NET Profile service. However, the user still needs to provide certain information (credit card information, shipping details, and so on) each time he buys a product on any of the Web sites. He can solve this problem by storing the information in the .NET Wallet service. This service allows a person to store information that he uses for online shopping.

When you shop on the Internet, you can use two methods that the .NET Wallet Service supports to make online payments. These methods are as follows:

- ◆ **Account-based payment methods.** In this method, you can make payments by check or a savings account.
- ◆ **Card-based payment methods.** In this method, you make the payments by using a credit card.

You learned about the different Web services that are available in the .NET My Services suite of services. These services are small and are used to perform simple tasks. However, you can combine one or more of these services to create a service according to your needs. Consider an example of an Invoice service. This service stores and maintains information about the hardware stock of an organization.

To create the Invoice service, you can integrate several .NET My Services Web services. For example, you can store a list of the hardware products that the organization manufactures by using the .NET Lists service. Next, you can use the .NET Calendar service to keep track of the stock that is available in the warehouse on a daily basis. If stock of a particular product is limited or is depleted, you can use the .NET Alerts service to send a notification message to the purchase manager of the organization. You can find the purchase manager by using the .NET Locations service.

The purchase manager can further send a notification message by using the .NET Alerts service or e-mail by using the .NET Inbox service to the supplier of the product. The information about the supplier is available in the purchase manager's .NET Contacts service. Therefore, after the supplier learns of the shortage of the product, he can supply the product, and the Accounts department can make payments to the supplier by using the .NET Wallet service. Finally, when the stock is available, its information can be updated in the .NET Lists service. This process of integrating several services to form a complete business service is called *orchestration*. The process of orchestration is shown in Figure D-5.

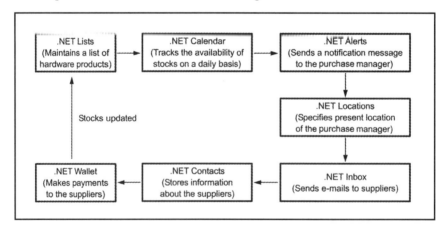

FIGURE D-5 *The process of orchestration.*

As you can see, by using the services that are available in the .NET My Services suite of services, creating a complex service such as the one explained in the previous example can be easy. .NET My Services provides you with all relevant information that makes functionality available as a standard building block for all services.

As a result of the integration of .NET My Services Web services, several real-life applications are being built. Some of these applications are discussed in the following list:

♦ Groove Networks, founded by Ray Ozzie, uses various .NET My Services Web services to provide security of the business data, support the infrastructure, and maintain a contacts list.

♦ ebay is planning to use the .NET Alerts service to send notification messages to the bidders who bid on its auction services.

♦ American Express Blue Card is currently using its .NET Alerts service to send messages to its clients regarding the orders they place.

Interaction of the Components of the .NET My Services Architecture

You saw the components of the .NET My Services architecture. Now we will discuss how these components interact within the .NET My Services architecture.

An application that is created on any of the endpoints accesses a .NET My Services Web service. When an application tries to access a .NET My Services service, the .NET My Services architecture uses the .NET Passport Web Service to authenticate the system that tries to access the service. To do this, the .NET Passport Web Service defines the identity, security, and data models that are common to all services in the .NET My Services suite. Therefore, the method of applying security to a system that accesses the .NET ApplicationSettings service or any other service is the same.

The development procedure is the same for all services in .NET My Services. For example, all services in the .NET My Services suite are XML Web services that are accessed by any system by using XML message interfaces (XMIs).

The .NET Passport service maintains information about the users who access the .NET My Services Web services in databases that are maintained on Microsoft servers all over the world. To access the user data, you need to create a database and specify PUID as the primary key. Then you need to pass the PUID number as a parameter to the service, which then returns the data for the specified PUID.

End users cannot access the .NET My Services Web services directly. This implies that an end user cannot directly call a .NET My Services Web service. Instead,

.NET Passport Web Service

The .NET Passport Web Service is an online authentication service that allows you to log on to a Web site or a service by using your e-mail address and a password. This prevents you from remembering different passwords to log on to different sites. However, it is important to note that the Web site or the service to which you want to log on should be a .NET Passport-enabled Web site or service.

The .NET Passport Web service contains a service called the .NET Passport express purchase that makes it convenient for you to shop online. In addition, the .NET Passport Web service contains a .NET Kids Passport service that allows you to specify your kid's profile that the Kids Passport-participating sites can access.

only a listener application or device can access a .NET My Services Web service. The listener application and the device are collectively called the *endpoints*.

As already discussed, the calling or the listener application uses SOAP to exchange data with the .NET My Services Web services. Therefore, to access a .NET My Services Web service, you need to create a SOAP message that contains headers and body elements. These elements contain information about the .NET My Services Web service that you need to access. To create the header and body elements of such a message, you can use the HailStorm Data Manipulation Language (HSDL).

The data that is exchanged between a listener application and the Web service is in XML format, which makes it easier for the calling application to implement and understand the Web services present in the .NET My Services suite of services. Consider the following code that shows the sample XML implementation of a few of the .NET My Services Web services:

XML Message Interfaces (XMIs)

XMIs are SOAP messages that expose service interfaces as standard SOAP messages. In addition, in XMIs, the arguments and return values are in the XML format, and the services are transferred by using the HTTP POST transfer protocol.

HSDL

HSDL is the manipulation language for .NET My Services. HSDL uses commands to interact with the services available in the .NET My Services suite of services. For example, you can use HSDL to access or modify the information in a .NET My Services service.

HSDL transfers data between the .NET My Services service and the accessing application. In addition, HSDL provides security and defines the data structure.

```
<Services>
        <webService name = "..........">
                <webURL>..........</webURL>
                <webMethods>..........</webMethods>
        </webService>
</Services>


<Contacts>
        <Category name = "..........">
                <contactName>..........</contactName>
                <contactAddress>..........</contactAddress>
                <contactEmail>..........</contactEmail>
                <contactPhone>..........</contactPhone>
        </Category>
```

```
</Contacts>

<Calendar>
        <Date value = "............">
                <Schedule>............</Schedule>
        </Date>
</Calendar>
```

You can implement the rest of the Web services in a similar way.

Security of .NET My Services Web Services

.NET My Services, as you know, is developed with an aim to provide centralized information. However, this does not imply that a user has access to resources or data. Instead, the owner of the data has control over the data. This means that to access any data that another user owns, you first need to seek the owner's permission. To do this, .NET My Services operates in the affirmative consent model. According to this model, no data or information is shared until the owner of the data explicitly specifies the .NET My Services Web service to share the data.

To specify the .NET My Services Web service to share your data or information, you need to define certain parameters, as discussed in the following list:

- ◆ **Who.** A .NET My Services Web service can be accessed from a calling application that is running on any device. The information about the calling application or the user who requests a service is specified in the Who part of the request.
- ◆ **What.** This part of the request defines the data that is made available to the requesting application or the user.
- ◆ **How.** This part of the request specifies the methods that the requesting application or user is able to request from the .NET My Services Web services.

By specifying the information, as discussed in the previous list, you can authenticate users or applications to access your data or prevent them from accessing the data.

Summary

This chapter introduced you to Microsoft .NET My Services. .NET My Services is part of the .NET initiative that consists of 15 XML Web services. These Web services were created to enable users to benefit from the resources and information that are available on the Internet.

You learned about the advantages and the scenarios in which you can use the .NET My Services Web services. Then, you learned about the .NET My Services architecture that includes the .NET My Services endpoints and the .NET My Services Web services. .NET My Services endpoints are the applications, platforms, services, or devices that allow you to access a .NET My Services Web service.

You learned about the 15 .NET My Services Web services that include .NET Services, .NET Contacts, .NET Calendar, .NET FavoriteWebSites, .NET Categories, .NET Lists, .NET Alerts, .NET Documents, .NET Inbox, .NET ApplicationSettings, .NET Presence, .NET Devices, .NET Locations, .NET Profile, and .NET Wallet. You also learned how the different components of the .NET My Services architecture interact with each other. Finally, you learned how to implement security in .NET My Services.

Appendix E

In this book, you have explored some of the tools available today for Web service creation and deployment. This is one technology that seems to have caught everybody's attention. Consequently, Web service technologies and tools are in a state of constant change. This Appendix gives you an overview of some of these future developments and takes a brief look at some of the areas in which Web services might be the right solution. This Appendix explores the following areas:

- ◆ Direct Internet Message Encapsulation (DIME)
- ◆ Securing Web services
- ◆ Coordinating Web services
- ◆ Using Web services

DIME

DIME is a specification for defining a mechanism for encapsulating binary data with Simple Object Access Protocol (SOAP) messages. SOAP provides text-based XML data to be encapsulated within a SOAP message. The SOAP messages can contain data from any XML schema. The drawback to using SOAP is that, while working with legacy systems or custom developed systems, data is not available in the XML format. For example, most of the legacy applications don't provide support for the XML-centric data access; instead, they make their data available in their own proprietary format.

DIME overcomes this disadvantage of SOAP. It enables Web services to interact with the data in any form—not just the XML format. In addition to this benefit, DIME provides all the features of SOAP. Therefore, it is becoming popular among Web services developers.

When you're using SOAP to encapsulate XML data, SOAP has three major limitations:

◆ The legacy systems don't support it.

◆ Serializing data into XML might not be recommended if the data is too large.

◆ If the data is digitally signed, you should not apply SOAP encapsulation over it. Doing so invalidates the signature.

DIME helps to overcome these problems. DIME specifies the standards for encapsulating multiple binary data within a single package. The binary data can be of any type, such as SOAP messages, images, and Multipurpose Internet Mail Extension (MIME) messages. The amount of data you can send using DIME is unlimited

DIME and MIME

MIME is a specification that defines how messages are formatted and sent between e-mail systems over the Internet. It enables you to include almost any type of file in an e-mail message, and it can support files such as audio, video, images, and so on.

The functionality of the SOAP Messages with Attachments specification is similar to MIME. This specification enables you to package SOAP requests with data in a MIME message. In addition, it defines a mechanism for referencing the related data from within the encapsulated SOAP request.

A unique string, which is defined at the beginning of the MIME message, separates the data records in MIME. The data in the message is scanned for the instance of the string. The problem with this approach is that all data needs to be scanned to find the data records. If the data in the message happens to contain the same string as the data record separator string, the search for the data records might produce incorrect results. On the other hand, in DIME, you don't have to scan through all the data to find a particular data record. The length of the data record is easily calculated.

The flexibility of MIME might be a problem when you're using it with Web services. For example, you can add any MIME header field to the messages. Because the header length is unknown, you need to parse through the header fields to determine their impact on data processing. This renders a much more complicated MIME-based solution because the focus is on XML rather than MIME. In contrast to MIME, the headers in DIME are of a specified size. These headers provide the functionality that a SOAP message requires, which makes processing of DIME messages fast and efficient.

MIME is more flexible than DIME. However, the content type of MIME is restricted to the text/html type of syntax. The new content type needs to be registered with the Internet Assigned Numbers Authority (IANA). This is done because IANA is responsible for industry standardization of various services, such as IP address and Protocol number assignment. In contrast to MIME, DIME supports the following:

◆ The MIME content type mechanism

◆ Content types specified with the URI mechanism

The DIME specification addresses the requirements for including binary data with SOAP messages. It is an efficient mechanism for including data objects of various types in a message. Following are the advantages offered by DIME:

◆ Specifies the data type with more flexibility

◆ Cross-references data objects within a DIME message

◆ Provides benefits of data chunking, such as improved input and output performance

Web Services Security

Security is a critical aspect of Web services. Besides cost and reliability, security is one of the most significant determining factors behind the success of Web services. Web services, like any other applications over the networks, are prone to network attacks. The prevention of such attacks gains more importance especially if it is a commercial Web service. Various groups and organizations are working toward making Web services more secure. The next section discusses some of the methods to secure your Web services:

◆ SSL

◆ XML Signature

SSL

Secure Socket Layer (SSL) is an industry standard that aims to provide privacy and reliability between two communicating applications. The SSL protocol runs between the TCP/IP and other higher-level protocols, such as Telnet, FTP, and HTTP. SSL provides security features, such as encryption, server and client authentication, and message authentication.

SSL secures the channel over which the communicating entities exchange information and encrypts the data that is sent. Therefore, the intermediate devices—such as computers, routers, switches, and so on—that route the information can neither understand nor corrupt the secured information. SSL does have a couple of drawbacks, as listed:

- The SSL secures communication only at the Transport level. Therefore, messages are protected only during transmission.
- The SSL design doesn't support point-to-point security. Each resource in the SSL network should be capable of verifying the information in the message.

XML Signature

The XML Signature specification defines an XML-based language for representing digital signatures. You can generate XML Signatures for any type of digital content. You can even generate the XML Signatures for XML documents. When XML Signatures are generated for XML documents, they can be attached to the XML document that is being signed. In addition to signature information, an XML Signature can contain other information, such as the key that was used to sign the content.

XML Signatures provide the following components of security:

- Authentication
- Message integrity

Digital signatures are generated based on the content of the document. In contrast, XML Signatures are generated based on a specific portion of an XML document. Therefore, XML Signatures can be used to protect some information in an XML document while ignoring others.

One of the features that the XML language provides is a searching ability. You can use the information that the Document Type Definition (DTD) or schema provides during the search. However, if you encrypt a section of a document, your ability to search for the data within that section is lost. Therefore, if you need to search on a section of the document, you should not apply the XML Signature over it.

A signed XML document consists of many sections. Some of these sections are listed here:

- The first important section is the SignedInfo section, which classifies the resource that is being signed. This section contains details of all operations that are performed on the information before the signature is generated. In addition, this section identifies the signature algorithm that is used. One of the common operations that is performed is *canonicalization*, or the process by which a hierarchical representation of an XML document is generated. This canonical representation can be compared with another XML document.
- The SignatureValue section specifies the actual signature value.
- The KeyInfo section stores details regarding the key used to sign the XML document. This section eases the validation process for the receiving entity.
- The Object section, which is the last section, stores the XML document.

The information that is contained in these sections enables a recipient to authenticate the signer of the document.

Other Security Methods

Several technologies are emerging for securing XML documents. Each of these technologies addresses a different aspect of security. We will briefly discuss some of these technologies in the following sections.

XML Encryption

XML encryption supplements the XML Signature. It takes care of the encryption and decryption of XML documents. It also enables you to encrypt specific portions of a document.

XML Key Management Specification

XML Key Management Specification (XKMS) defines protocols for distributing and registering public keys. XKMS is composed of two parts:

- XML Key Information Service Specification (X-KISS)
- XML Key Registration Service Specification (X-KRSS)

 NOTE

XML Key Management Specification (XKMS) is suitable for use with the proposed standard for XML Signature (XML-SIG). XKMS specifies the protocols for registration and distribution of public keys. The W3C and the IETF are developing this standard.

The X-KISS specification defines a protocol for a trust service. This protocol resolves public key information in XML-SIG elements. A protocol that conforms to the X-KISS specification allows a client of a trust service to delegate part or all of the tasks required to process KeyInfo elements.

The X-KRSS specification defines a protocol for a Web service. The Web service that is defined accepts registration of public key information. You can use the public key with other Web services after you register the Web service.

Both the X-KISS and X-KRSS protocols are defined as per the structures expressed in the XML Schema Language and conform to the SOAP 1.1 specification. In addition, WDSL 1.0 defines relationships among messages in the two protocols.

Security Assertion Markup Language

Security Assertion Markup Language (SAML) enables the components of distributed business applications to share authentication and authorization information. It addresses the security needs of the distributed applications.

Extensible Access Control Markup Language

Extensible Access Control Markup Language (XACML) is an XML specification that helps to define policies for accessing information over a network.

Coordinating Web Services

In the past, business transactions were managed using proprietary technologies. Traditional approaches were used for automation because these methods were most suited for automation of high-volume production processes. These projects were typically associated with huge costs.

The emergence of XML Web services standards has provided an opportunity to extend the benefits of process management to a wider scope of problems. Using Web services, enterprise developers can coordinate component services from dissimilar sources into complex and readily implementable applications and processes.

This new model based on Web services operates on a business logic that sequences, coordinates, and manages conversations among Web services. This process is referred to as *orchestration*.

The specifications that form the basis of orchestration are as follows:

◆ SOAP
◆ WSDL
◆ UDDI
◆ XSD
◆ XSLT

A key capability of an orchestration system is its ability to handle message sequencing among distributed systems. To ensure this, the processes should be able to communicate asynchronously. The modification in one component should not affect the other components. Another aspect of orchestration is its requirement for sophisticated development tools to integrate business solutions. This enables business users as well as developers to directly participate in the design, implementation, and deployment of Web services.

Using Web Services

Development of real-time business Web services is in an early stage. In this section, we explore some of the business areas in which Web services will be useful. Two of the main areas in which Web services will play a prime role are business-to-business (B2B) integration and ERP.

B2B Integration

B2B integration, or B2Bi, refers to the secured coordination of information among businesses and other business entities. B2Bi holds the key to revolutionizing the way business is conducted among partners, suppliers, and customers or buyers. Following are some of the advantages of B2Bi:

- Faster time to market
- Reduced cycle time
- Increased customer service

The benefits that the company obtains by integrating the business and technical processes are as follows:

- Strong relationships between partners and customers
- Smooth and efficient integration
- Real-time views of customer accounts
- Efficiency in the operations
- Cost reduction

B2Bi is a big challenge, especially for larger corporations that have a worldwide presence. Such large corporations usually have hundreds to thousands of trading partners, and integrating them is an overwhelming task.

In recent years, XML has been emerging as the common dialect in the e-business sector. It has devised a common mechanism based on open standards to publish, share, and exchange data over the Internet. As a result, in the future, XML will undoubtedly be used in any B2B scenario.

However, XML is not an integration solution in itself. It is just a data definition language. For an effective and seamless implementation of businesses globally, the companies who are participating in B2Bi need to agree to a common XML-based B2B standard. This will define a common standard that will provide information, including document formats and process descriptions. Several organizations, including OASIS, have been working to define these standards.

Web services that are based on XML standards will definitely play a critical role in achieving dynamic B2B.

Enterprise Resource Planning and Web Services

Enterprise Resource Planning (ERP) is application software that defines a set of activities that helps any business to manage vital transactions. Typically, an ERP constitutes multiple modules that take care of these different activities. RDBMS is used at the back end.

In the context of ERP, Web services offer these advantages:

- **Ease of integration.** In the current scenario, enterprises are spending heavily on systems integrations. ERP is complex and is intended for big businesses—not for public consumption. Therefore, you might need to devise ways to protect the critical information of your business. In such scenarios, Web services come in handy because they enable you to provide public access only to data that is noncritical and hide the rest.

◆ **Reduction in costs.** Web services enable the proprietary applications to communicate over the Web. The main intent of the developers is to make use of efficient tools that can turn any other proprietary application program into a Web service. These tools might include HP's E-Speak toolsets and IBM's Dynamic e-business.

Summary

This appendix introduced you to various new technologies in the field of XML Web services. These technologies include DIME. In addition, you learned about securing, coordinating, and using Web services.

In this book, you have looked at the basics of XML Web services and various ways of creating, testing, and deploying Web services. XML Web service is a huge and upcoming field where extensive research is being done and new inventions are added to the XML Web services community each day.

What we have covered in this book forms a small part of this vast subject. After reading this book, you have gained insight into XML Web services and are equipped to work with it. However, you still have a lot to explore.

Index

Symbols

A